SPECIAL NEEDS IN MAINSTREAM SCHOOLS

Series Editor: Keith Postlethwaite

ORGANISING **T**HE **S**CHOOL'S **R**ESPONSE

Keith Postlethwaite and Ann Hackney

First published 1988 by Macmillan Education Ltd
Reprinted 1989

Reprinted 1992
by Routledge
11 New Fetter Lane, London EC4P 4EE

Simultaneously published in the USA and Canada
by Routledge
a division of Routledge, Chapman and Hall, Inc.
29 West 35th Street, New York, NY 10001

Printed and bound in Hong Kong by
Dah Hau Printing Press

British Library Cataloguing in Publication Data

A catalogue record for this book is available from the British Library.

ISBN 0-415-09076-8

Contents

1

2

Preface

This book, and its companion volumes, are intended for teachers and student teachers interested in mainstream secondary education. This volume deals with responses which a school can make to support that fifth of its pupils who have special educational needs. The other volumes deal with the responses which individual teachers can make to learning difficulties and to disruptive behaviour within their own classrooms.

The approach taken in the series is based on the idea that special needs can only be adequately met in schools if all teachers recognise that they have a role to play, and if all are able to develop some appropriate skills. However, this starting point does not negate the importance of specialist provision from special needs departments and from professionals who are based outside the school. Indeed the task of managing a school's special needs response involves enabling individual teachers to extend their own expertise, organising the special needs department so that it can help these teachers and the individual pupils who need more support than mainstream staff can provide, and co-ordinating the whole enterprise so that all teachers are aware of their own role and of the other services on which they and their pupils can draw.

The other books in this series concentrate on the classroom skills of the mainstream teacher. In this book we aim to do two main things which complement this emphasis on classroom skills. First, we hope to raise mainstream teachers' awareness of some of the broader issues which surround provision for pupils with special educational needs so that they are better able to relate to the special needs system of their own school, and to engage in discussion about how it should be organised. Secondly we hope to help special needs staff and senior management in designing, co-ordinating and operating the overall special needs response in the school – including the specific response to staff and pupils that can be made by the special needs department. At key points in the text we suggest activities which might help to extend thinking about these organisational and managerial issues. To draw attention to these activities we have used a tinted background with an **A** in the margin. Information and summaries of major points are highlighted between heavy horizontal lines, with an **i** in the margin.

We hope the book will be useful to individual teachers or students working on their own, to senior staff faced with decisions on special needs issues, to groups of teachers following formal pre-service and in-service training courses and, perhaps especially, to ad hoc groups that might come together in individual schools to explore some of the most fascinating and demanding tasks which we have to undertake as teachers.

K.C.P.
Oxford 1987

Acknowledgements

In preparing this book we have been given a great deal of help by a wide range of people, all of whom were busy with their own work but gave extensively of their time to answer our questions and discuss our ideas.

From time to time throughout the book we refer to the findings of our survey of practice in Oxfordshire schools (in 11–16 and 11–18 schools, in middle and upper schools, and in special schools) and to the more detailed research we were able to conduct in four case study schools in the county. We would like to thank the headteachers of all the schools involved in the survey, and especially the headteachers, staff and pupils of the four case study schools, for their co-operation and for the time and energy they gave to us despite the other, more pressing calls on their time.

We would also like to thank the wide range of 'other professionals' in Oxfordshire who responded to our request for information about their work with schools. It was from the data which they supplied that we were able to construct Chapter 8.

Another important source of ideas, of constructive criticism and of support, has been the group of teachers with expertise in the special needs field who have been seconded to the Oxford Department of Educational Studies over the past four years. The close association which we have enjoyed with this group of teachers, and with the Oxfordshire special needs advisers, has been of great help to us. Furthermore, we have drawn directly on the research work undertaken by some members of this group – and, of course, have acknowledged this at appropriate points in the text.

We would particularly like to thank Bridie Raban, Mike Deans and Elizabeth Hitchfield for many hours of discussion which helped us to formulate some ideas and clarify others.

Finally, we would like to thank Elizabeth Paren, our editor at Macmillan, for applying just enough pressure to keep us to the task, and for her helpful comments on the text itself.

The authors and publishers would like to thank NFER-Nelson for permission to reproduce the table in Chapter 7.

x

This book was produced by the Special Needs Research Team within the Oxford Educational Research Group. Team members were Beverley Davies, James Gray, Ann Hackney, Keith Postlethwaite and Bridie Raban. This book was prepared for the research team by Keith Postlethwaite and Ann Hackney. The book, which is one of a series of three, is one product of a research project which was funded by the Rayne Foundation and based at the University of Oxford, Department of Educational Studies.

Introduction

1.1 Outline

This book is one of three in a series dealing with responses to the issue of special educational needs in mainstream secondary schools. These books are one of the products of a three year study that was conducted by the Oxford Educational Research Group following a grant from the Rayne Foundation. The research involved two quite tightly focussed investigations: one on disruptive behaviour in classrooms, and one on the early educational implications of medical disorders at or near the time of birth. It also involved two broader studies: one on provision for special needs children of secondary age in Oxfordshire, and one on the nature and effect of special needs input to initial teacher training courses in universities in England and Wales. While the books are not formal research reports, the results of the four aspects of our research programme have been a major influence on what is presented here. The research is also relevant to the books in another way. During the project, the research team came to agree on some general principles relating to special needs. These are reflected in this series of books and play a particularly important role in the approach taken in this volume.

In this introductory chapter we will briefly discuss these principles so that the reader is clear about our own starting points. We will then describe the intended purpose of this book and its relationship to the other two.

1.2 Some general principles

a) The interactive nature of special needs

Our research has led us to regard as crucial the view that special needs arise out of an interaction between the characteristics of the pupil and the nature of the learning environment which the school and the individual teacher construct. A wide range of individual characteristics can make a pupil particularly vulnerable to less than ideal learning environments. (Discussion of such characteristics is provided in Chapter 4.) Pupils with these characteristics will have special educational needs if, for example, schools fail to match the time available for a subject to the scale of the syllabus, if their timetabling is insensitive, or if they resource their courses inappropriately. Also, individual teachers can create special needs for these pupils by their attitudes towards them and by specific aspects of the way in which they work in their classrooms. For example, a teacher who uses a history text written in complex language may create learning problems for a poor reader who could cope perfectly well with the historical concepts being considered, and a teacher who lectures with his or her back to a window can create learning difficulties for a partially hearing child who can normally supplement limited hearing by lip-reading. The notion of interaction clearly influences the way in which we should conceptualise 'pupils with special needs' and is a major factor in determining the way in which we should plan our responses to them.

b) The scale of the problem

Despite regional variations (Rutter *et al.*, 1975) and variations from school to school within a broad geographical region, and despite the somewhat arbitrary nature of some of the underpinning research (Gipps and Goldstein, 1984) the best estimate of the proportion of pupils who will have special educational needs in schools as they are currently organised remains that of the Warnock Committee: namely that some 20 per cent of pupils will have special educational needs at some point in their educational career and that one pupil in six will have such needs at any one time. To this group we would wish to add a group explicitly excluded from Warnock's terms of reference. This is the group of pupils who have need of additional or alternative provision as a result of their high ability. Denton and Postlethwaite (1985) have argued (on the basis of HMI reports) that this additional group might be as large as 10 per cent in any one area of the curriculum. The special needs group as a whole therefore makes up at least a third of the total school population.

Special educational needs lie on a continuum. There is no clear-cut distinction between pupils who have special needs and those who do not.

Most of these pupils who have special needs are in mainstream schools, and always have been in mainstream schools. Our own school-based research suggests that they are often, and perhaps increasingly, in ordinary classes within those schools.

c) Special educational needs and general ability

Pupil characteristics which may give rise to special educational needs include low or high general ability, specific cognitive difficulties, high ability of a specific kind, behavioural and emotional difficulties, physical handicaps and medical conditions. Although pupils with low general ability are, of course, a part of this group, the range of general ability within the group as a whole will clearly be very large. Even if we exclude the pupils with special needs arising out of high ability, we would be wrong to assume that the remaining special needs pupils will necessarily have low general ability. Many physical handicaps and behaviour problems, and even some specific learning difficulties, are unrelated – or only loosely related – to low general ability. (Some relevant evidence is presented in Chapter 3.) Pupils with special needs can therefore appear in every class. They will be there in a first year mixed ability group, where we might find a child with less than average general ability having difficulty with a wide range of tasks; they will be there in a third year middle ability set, where there may be a physically handicapped child experiencing difficulty with practical work in science; they will be there in an

A-level history group, where there may be a very able pupil who is unable to spell.

Although some special needs persist throughout school, and beyond into adult life, others may be quite short-lived giving little time for response from adults outside the group of class teachers and form teacher with whom the pupil has regular contact.

d) The individual nature of special needs

The needs of individual pupils cannot be inferred simply from the category of their main disability even where this can be clearly distinguished. For example, two children with partial hearing may have very different needs. One may need nothing more than a good hearing aid, the other may have suffered such a loss of confidence in earlier stages of schooling that it is this loss of confidence, rather than the present hearing problem, which is the major need. The implication is, of course, that the needs of each pupil must be carefully assessed on an individual basis.

e) The response of the mainstream teacher

These starting points (individually perhaps, but certainly when taken together) suggest that response to special needs cannot be exclusively the responsibility of a small number of specialist teachers. Further support for this statement is provided in Chapter 3. They imply that all teachers will work with special needs pupils. All teachers therefore need an awareness of the main issues. What is more, for most special needs pupils, ordinary mainstream teachers will be an important source of day to day practical support. Indeed, for some of these pupils, mainstream teachers will be the *only* source of such support. It follows that all teachers need more than awareness. They also need practical skills – skills of identification and assessment, and strategies for provision that they can call upon in their normal teaching. These skills are discussed in the other two books of this series.

f) The severity of some special needs

There is an enormous range in the severity of the problems which pupils with special needs have. Some problems are relatively minor, others are severe or even profound.

g) The thrust of integration

Some children with quite severe difficulties always have been in ordinary schools, either as a result of a specific decision or as a result of the inadequacy of screening techniques. The Warnock Report and the Education Act 1981 have provided some support for an increase in the trend to educate pupils with quite severe difficulties in mainstream schools. We certainly found evidence of such integration in our own research in Oxfordshire, some of which is summarised in Chapter 7.

h) Specialist involvement

The last two points suggest that although individual teacher's responses to special needs in their own classrooms are of enormous importance, mainstream teachers should not be expected to be sufficiently expert in all aspects of special needs to handle all of them without specialist help.

4

Sometimes this will be help for the mainstream teacher, sometimes it will be direct help for the pupils themselves. Such help can be provided by senior staff in subject departments, by senior pastoral staff, by teachers in special needs departments, by teachers in special schools, by LEA services such as educational psychology and the advisory service and by other local services such as social services and the health service. However, if this help is to be effectively deployed, mainstream teachers must be able to relate to it. They need an awareness of the nature of the help available from different sources, they need skills of assessment and referral, they need the skills of working alongside the support services when it is deemed appropriate that the help should be delivered to the pupil in their own classroom (e.g. when a support teacher works with a child in a mainstream class), and they need the skills of co-ordinating their own teaching with other forms of provision when it is deemed necessary to remove a pupil for specialist help for part of a lesson each week, for one of a number of lessons each week or for all lessons for a short period of time.

i) The significance of the issues to education generally

The whole list of starting points outlined above, places formidable demands upon mainstream teachers both in their individual work in classrooms, and in their more general professional activities as members of the school staff. It is inevitable that some readers will wonder whether these are appropriate demands, given all the other aspects of the teacher's job and the needs of all of the other pupils in the school. Surely what is implied above, though perhaps desirable in theory, is unrealistic in practice.

We base our response to this comment on an extremely interesting analysis of the problem put forward by Fish (1985). He argues that the search for higher standards in schools can lead in two directions. The first results in 'a narrower common curriculum, a less flexible approach to individual needs and the stigmatisation of pupils as not up to standard'. In this context special provision is held to be 'charitable provision for failures'. If this is the view, then we would agree that teachers would be unwise to devote as much of their energy to special needs as we have been suggesting in the paragraphs above. However, Fish outlines a second route to improved standards which involves 'better matching of tasks, objectives and materials to individuals'. In this approach, special needs work can be seen as the most refined application of the philosophy of the school as a whole. As such it provides a context in which one can obtain sophisticated and powerful insights into ways of achieving the most effective matching for all pupils. By accepting the demands which we have been outlining above, teachers would, on this model, be making a major contribution to the improvement of the education system as a whole.

1.3 Ideas for the use of this book

The intention behind this series of books is to help the student teacher and the practising teacher to respond realistically to these demands. The books on learning difficulties and behavioural difficulties are focused particularly on extending the range of the 'strategies for identification, assessment and provision' that are available to the individual teacher in his or her own teaching.

The intention of the present volume is to address some of the broader issues. We hope that this book will help to raise awareness of the legal context, of some of the arguments about the nature of the curriculum for special needs pupils, of the nature and scope of the special needs field, of the organisation of school-based identification procedures, of the organisation of special needs departments, of the arguments surrounding the integration of pupils with severe needs into mainstream schools and of the issue of liaison with support services outside school. We hope, by raising these issues, to help student teachers and beginning teachers to be better prepared to take part in discussions about their own school's response to special needs and to understand their own role in the overall structure. We hope also that the book may be of some help to more senior staff who bear the major responsibility for decisions on the organisation of the special needs response of their schools.

This book, like the other two, can be used by individual teachers who wish to explore this area of education. However it can also be used by *groups* of students or practising teachers. In the pre-service context we hope that it might be used by groups made up of students with different subject backgrounds. Many of the curriculum and organisational issues will be rather differently perceived by teachers of different subjects and in defining a whole-school response, compromise will be inevitable. Mixed groups of students would be well placed to explore the range of perspectives and to examine the problems and possibilities while working towards a compromise. In the INSET context the book might be used by a group of teachers meeting together on a course or by a school staff seeking to develop the special needs structure of their own school. The book might be used as a whole, defining the agenda of a series of meetings and providing some starting points for the work, or an individual chapter might be taken to initiate discussion of a particular point. With this 'group use' of the book in mind, we have often provided simulation exercises or lists of key questions at the end of chapters.

The legal context in England and Wales

2

2.1 Documentation

Because this chapter can present only the briefest outline of the relevant legislation, it is important to begin by indicating other, more detailed sources of reference.

The official documents which apply most directly to mainstream secondary schools are the Education Act 1981 (the key piece of legislation specifically concerned with pupils with special educational needs), the Education (Special Educational Needs) Regulations 1983 (detailed guidelines on parts of the 1981 Act which are legally binding), and various circulars from the DES and the DHSS. These circulars are not legally binding but give advice on the Act and might well be referred to by courts in appropriate cases. Key circulars from the DES are Circular 8/81 which discusses the 1981 Act in general, and Circular 1/83 which is particularly concerned with assessments and 'statementing'. There are also three DHSS circulars which discuss the relationship between the education and health services with respect to children with special educational needs. These are Circulars HRC (74)5, HC(80)8/LAC(80)3 and HN(82)9/LASSL(82)3.

Parts of other Education Acts (especially the 1944 and 1980 Acts) continue to apply to children with special needs. Two useful documents which cover the whole range of relevant legislation and therefore point out the implications of these earlier pieces of legislation are the *ACE Special Education Handbook* and the book by Cox (1985) entitled *The Law of Special Educational Needs – A Guide to the Education Act 1981*.

2.2 Focus of this chapter

In this chapter we shall concentrate on the law as it relates to children of school age and to local authority schools.

The duties of an LEA that are described below do, however, apply to pupils for whom the LEA has arranged placement at an independent school. Under some circumstances they also apply to children in the LEA area who are not attending schools, and to other pupils in the LEA area (e.g. pupils whose parents have placed them in an independent school in the area). For such children the duties apply when individuals have been 'brought to the attention of the LEA' as having (or probably having) special needs.

The law is rather different for children under the age of 2.

2.3 Definitions

The Education Act 1981 states that a child has 'special needs' if s/he 'has a learning difficulty which calls for special educational provision to be made'. It explains that the term 'learning difficulty' should be taken to mean a 'significantly greater difficulty in learning than the majority of children of his (or her) age' *or* 'a disability which either prevents or hinders (the child) from making use of educational facilities of a kind generally provided in schools, within the area of the local authority concerned, for children of his (or her) age'. It also explains that the term 'special educational provision' should be taken to mean 'educational provision which is additional to, or otherwise different from, the educational provision made generally for children of his (or her) age in schools maintained by the local education authority concerned'.

In the terms of the 1981 Act pupils have **special educational needs** if:

They have a learning difficulty

i.e. *either* they have a 'significantly greater' difficulty in learning than their peers
or they have a disability that prevents or hinders their use of normal resources provided in schools in their area.

AND

This learning difficulty calls for special provision to be made

i.e. it calls for 'additional and otherwise different provision' to be made

---

It is interesting that, in the Act, the term 'learning difficulty' is used in a far broader sense than is normal. Normally it carries the implication of low general ability (e.g. low IQ), or low specific ability (e.g. difficulty with reading, or spatial reasoning). Indeed it is used in this way elsewhere in this series of books. However, in the Act, being in a wheelchair or being disruptive, could bring even an able pupil into the group with 'learning difficulties' if these characteristics were such as to 'prevent or hinder' use of normal resources. It is also interesting that the term 'learning difficulty' is defined by norm-referencing: i.e. by comparison with the difficulties in learning faced by the majority of children of the same age. Furthermore, the definition provides no clear-cut dividing line between pupils who have learning difficulties and those who do not. This is consistent with the idea of a continuum of need.

Similarly, the definitions of the terms 'learning difficulty', and 'special provision' involve the notion of the resources which are 'normal' or 'generally available' in the schools of a given LEA. Since special educational needs are defined with reference to both these terms, one should certainly expect variation, from area to area, in the population which has special needs under the terms of the Act. The variation can arise in two ways. First, a child with a given disability may be regarded as having 'learning difficulties' in one LEA but not another because schools in the two areas are resourced differently. Secondly, children acknowledged to have the same 'significantly greater' difficulty in learning in the two geographical areas might be regarded as having special needs in one area but not in the other, because, in the second area, the provision needed to overcome this difficulty is regarded as part of the provision 'made generally for children' in schools and no 'additional or otherwise different provision' is therefore required. This is consistent with the notion that special needs arise out of an interaction between pupil and school characteristics.

Section 1.4 of the 1981 Act makes it clear that a child should not be regarded as having learning difficulties *solely* because the language in which s/he is taught is not the language of his or her home. This does not, of course, imply that no special provision is needed – simply that this would not be made under the terms of the 1981 Act. Also, Section 1.4 does not prevent a pupil for whom English is a second language from qualifying as a pupil with a learning difficulty (and thus perhaps as a pupil with special needs) if there is some additional problem such as generally low ability and/or a physical handicap. Section 1.4 does, however, run the risk of fragmenting provision for pupils of this kind. At the level of service to the pupil, this possible fragmentation is something that schools should clearly try to avoid.

As we have already mentioned, children with physical handicaps or medical problems clearly come within the terms of the Act and children with behavioural difficulties could also be included if it were argued that they too had a difficulty that 'prevents or hinders . . .' their use of normal resources. Very able pupils, who are in practice regarded as having special needs in some schools, do not seem to be covered by the legal definition. In terms of the 1981 Act, the legal duties of LEAs and others towards special needs pupils would not, therefore, seem to extend to this group.

2.4 General requirements of the 1981 Act

The 1981 Act makes some general points which apply to all special needs children who fall within its definition and these are listed below.

a) The duties of LEAs, school governors and teachers

Section 2.1 reformulates a section of the 1944 Act so that it effectively requires LEAs to secure that special educational provision *is* made for pupils who have special educational needs. There is, then, a duty to provide. Section 2.4 requires LEAs to keep this provision under review.

To this requirement for the LEA is added a duty for school governors. Section 2.5 states that they must 'use their best endeavours' to ensure that appropriate special provision is made for each individual and to ensure that the teachers of special needs pupils are informed about the nature of each pupil's needs. They must also try to see that, in general terms, 'teachers in the school are aware of the importance of identifying, and providing for, those registered pupils who have special needs'.

There is also a general duty which will, at least in part, rest on teachers. Section 2.7 requires that, *where a pupil with special needs in education in an ordinary school,* those who are concerned with making special provision for that pupil should ensure that s/he 'engages in the activities of the school together with children who do not have special needs'. This requirement for what is effectively functional integration of the child into the school (see Chapter 7) is subject to the conditions that:

a) the pupil receives the special educational provision that s/he requires;
b) an efficient education is provided for the other pupils;

c) there is efficient use of resources; and

d) the functional integration is 'reasonably practicable'.

As long as these conditions are met, the Act does not exclude from this expectation any pupils with severe needs who might be in mainstream schools. Very different pastoral, extra-curricular and even academic arrangements for pupils with special needs would seem (subject, of course, to the conditions) to be contrary to the requirements of the Act. This part of the Act could therefore be seen as providing pressure towards the 'normalisation' of the special needs child which is a theme which recurs from time to time in this book.

Circular 1/83 expands on these general requirements – though its recommendations do not, of course, have the status of law. For example, it suggests that LEAs should encourage in-service training to improve teachers' abilities to identify, assess and provide for pupils with special needs, and it draws attention to the central role of mainstream teachers in 'recognising the child who is experiencing difficulties in learning', in assessing his or her needs and in trying out different ways of providing support.

b) Integration into mainstream schools

Another general point is that *the Act requires that children with special needs are educated in mainstream schools*, though this is, again, subject to the conditions a) to d) above, and to the requirement that account has been taken of the views of the child's parents (Section 2.2 and 2.3).

LEAs and schools who clearly wish to integrate pupils with more severe problems into mainstream schools might be expected to find ways of ensuring that conditions a) to d) were met wherever possible. The 1981 Act can therefore be seen as enabling integration to take place. However there is no duty on LEAs to try to fulfil these conditions, and since they are very broad, it is by no means clear that the Act will push less willing Authorities to integrate – even though its general spirit provides encouragement to do so. Swann (1985) discusses this point in some detail and concludes that 'there will be no national trend towards the integration of pupils with special needs' as a consequence of the Act. However, under the influence of similar legislation in the United States integration has increased, the crucial factor being pressure for mainstreaming from parents when they first discover that their child has special needs. Discussing this point, Biklen (1982) argues that parents whose children were already in special schools tended not to seek integration, whereas parents with a child newly identified as having special needs, who had no existing link with special schools, tended to press for a mainstream education for their child. As we shall explain later in this chapter, the 1981 Act does give some powers to parents to question LEA decisions about school placement and so, perhaps over quite a long period of time, the mechanism outlined here could result in increased integration.

c) The importance of assessment

Much of Circular 1/83 concentrates on the question of the assessment of pupils' needs. This, it emphasises, is not an end in itself but an essential step in making the right sort of support available to each pupil. It suggests that assessments should focus on pupils' strengths as well as weaknesses, and that they should take account of the nature of the support that the pupil has from home and from school. Thus assessment is related to the specific environment of the child, with the implication that features in this environment, as well as the characteristics of the child, may contribute to the child's special needs.

The circular expands on the central role of teachers in assessment by saying that teachers should be encouraged to keep full records of their pupils' progress, including records of any professional consultations and assessments and points out that assessment is not a single event but a continuous process.

Although it puts great weight on the role of the teacher, the circular points out that assessment may also call for input from others. It argues that parental involvement in assessment is always essential and that the child's point of view should also be taken into account. It goes on to recommend that the assessment system should allow for the 'progressive involvement' of other professionals so that as much information as is needed to adequately understand the child's problem is available. It suggests that LEAs should draw up guidelines for schools to help them to develop appropriate systems of assessment and referral to external professionals.

An example of LEA guidelines

A better sense of the implications of the circular might be gained from the guidelines of one LEA which set out a five stage process.

At Stage 1 the head and school-based teachers, with parents where possible, are to be the only people involved. Observation of the pupil, results of normal school tests and of classwork and so on, parental information and data from medical and other records should be used to decide upon relevant action which would be classroom-based. On review, the intervention may be found to be successful, or teachers may wish to go on to Stages 2 or 3.

At Stage 2 visiting teachers such as teachers for the hearing impaired or visually handicapped or 'Special Needs Advisory and Support Teachers' might be involved with the school staff. Through a similar range of investigations as at Stage 1, but with the inclusion of more detailed school-based tests, decisions may be made about further classroom-based action, about the use of aids or special materials, and about the possible need for some curriculum modification.

At Stage 3 special needs advisers, educational psychologists, school medical officers and the social services might be added to the assessment team. Only appropriate professionals would be approached and there need not be multiple referrals. This could lead to more substantial intervention in the pupil's education but the aim would still be to maintain the pupil in the mainstream school. At this stage parents' involvement would be essential.

If the information about the pupil's difficulties are still inadequate, Stage 4 would follow. This would be a full multi-professional assessment (MPA) under the terms of the 1981 Act. If the MPA was to indicate that the child's problems were so severe that the LEA, rather than the school itself, needed to make provision (for example, if the LEA had to provide a service to the child that is not normally available in its mainstream schools, or if it had to place the child in a special school) then a 'statement' would be produced. This statement would constitute Stage 5 of the assessment procedure. The details of MPAs and of statements will be discussed in the next section.

2.5 Formal procedures

The duties of LEAs, governors and teachers that have been discussed in the preceding sections of this chapter apply to all children who, in the Act's definition, have special educational needs. However the Act also lays down additional, detailed procedures which have to be followed in cases of severe or complex need – cases which call for the *authority,* rather than the individual school, to determine the special provision that should be made. These procedures consist of making an assessment of need and then, if necessary in the light of that assessment, making a statement about the provision which will be made.

Section 5 of the Act states that in cases where the LEA is of the opinion that a child has special needs which call for *it* (not the school) to determine the necessary provision, or in cases where it thinks a child probably has such needs, then it shall make an assessment. LEAs could, of course, come to such opinions about children as a result of earlier stages of the kind of informal assessment procedure that we discussed in the previous section.

If they intend to make such an assessment they must inform the parents, provide them with the name of LEA an officer of the LEA from whom they can get information and tell them of their right to make representations and submit evidence (Section 5.3).

After a prescribed time the LEA will consider any representations made and any evidence submitted by the parents and decide whether or not to proceed. In the case of children over two years of age, parents cannot actually stop the LEA from making an assessment if the LEA considers that it is necessary to do so – though parents could appeal under the 1944 Act on the grounds that the LEA was acting unreasonably.

If the LEA decides *not* to proceed it must notify the parents of its decision (Secion 5.10).

If the LEA decides that it *will* proceed it must notify the parents and explain its reasons for wishing to do so; it must take educational, medical and psychological advice on the child; and it may take other advice (Regulations, 1983). We will discuss the details of these formal assessment procedures later in this chapter.

On the basis of this advice the LEA must decide whether it does indeed need to determine the special provision that is to be made for the child. If it decides that it does need to do so, then the LEA must produce a 'statement' setting out what must be done for the child (Section 7). We will discuss the nature and effect of these statements later in this chapter.

If the LEA decides that it does *not* need to determine the provision it must inform the parents and explain its reasons. The parent can then appeal to the Secretary of State in an attempt to get a statement made (Section 5.6). A recent survey reported by Sharron (1985) showed that by January 1985 twenty-six appeals had been made to the Secretary of State: fourteen had been resolved in favour of the LEAs, in three cases LEAs had been asked to prepare a statement and in nine cases the result was not known at the time of the study.

The whole procedure can also be initiated by the parents who can ask the LEA to carry out an assessment. This it must do unless it regards the request as 'unreasonable' (Section 9.1). By reference to the Education Act 1944, parents can appeal against an Authority's decision not to carry out an assessment when asked to do so. To defend its view that the request was unreasonable the LEA would have to be able to make a case that no sensible LEA would accede to it.

a) Assessment

We have mentioned that an LEA intending to undertake a formal assessment of a child must obtain educational, medical and psychological advice and may seek other advice. Details of the required procedures are given in the Regulations (1983) and in Circular 1/83.

These documents make it clear that the educational advice must be obtained from the headteacher of a school the child has attended in the preceding eighteen months. If the head has not taught the child s/he must consult a teacher who has. Specialist teachers of the hearing impaired or visually handicapped can also contribute to the educational advice. The medical advice must be sought from a designated medical officer who will consult other doctors (including psychiatrists) and co-ordinate their comments. Advice from speech and physiotherapists can be incorporated into medical advice. Psychological advice must be sought from an educational psychologist who will consult other psychologists, including clinical and occupational psychologists if appropriate. The 'other advice' might include input from, say, an officer of the social services. The social services and a designated nursing officer must be informed of the intention to assess a child. The LEA can ask for advice from these services if it is not volunteered following such a notification.

Circular 1/83 gives some fairly detailed guidance on the kind of advice that should be given. It suggests that there should be:

1. a description of the child's strengths and weaknesses (including physical health and development, emotional state, cognitive functioning, communication skills, perceptual and motor skills, adaptive skills, social skills, approaches and attitudes to learning, educational attainments, self image, interests and behaviour);

2. comments about the child's home and school environment, and about his or her personal, medical and educational history;

3. descriptions of the aims of any special provision to be made, e.g. general aims such as the aim that provision should encourage physical development and self-care skills, or cognitive development such as the ability to classify, or language, social or motor development, and more specific comments about approaches to be used or specific gaps in the child's development that need to be attended to;

4. comments about the resources that the child will need if these aims are to be met. This might include comment about special equipment (e.g. visual aids), special facilities (e.g. use of a private place for the administration of medication), specialist teaching materials, specialist services (e.g. physiotherapy), modifications to the physical environment (ramps etc.) or special arrangements for school attendance and transport.

Circular 1/83 recognises that this is a detailed list and says that each professional should concentrate on things which lie within his or her area of expertise. Also each person giving advice should highlight the particularly important points in their replies. The circular gives other general guidelines such as the idea that advice could be given separately or through case conferences, and that the final decision on placement should be made by the LEA so should not be pre-empted by the comments of the advisers. Similarly advisers' comments should not be restricted by knowledge of limitations in the resources available in the LEA but should reflect their professional assessment of the problems and needs of the child. However Sharron (1985) reports that there have been occasions when advice has been returned to professionals by LEAs with instructions to revise it. The system does not always seem to work as was originally intended!

The circular reminds professionals that, if the LEA decides to make a 'statement' on the child, copies of all advice will be made available to parents. Parents have no legal right to receive copies of the advice if the LEA decides not to make a statement. However, they could take the view that they were handicapped in challenging this decision by having no access to the advice and could, therefore, complain to the Secretary of State under the 1944 Act on the grounds that the LEA was acting unreasonably. It seems sensible, therefore, to assume that parents will see all advice submitted as part of a formal assessment.

Finally, the emphasis in the assessment is placed on co-operation between the professionals with the parents being kept 'informed and involved'. There is, therefore, a concept of partnership which, Circular 1/83 argues, should be extended to include the child or young person where appropriate.

b) Statements

We have already outlined the consequences of an LEA decision not to make a statement after carrying out an assessment. If the LEA *does* decide to make a statement then it will produce a document along the lines of the model annexed to the Regulations 1983. This will state the nature of the pupil's needs, the educational provision it deems appropriate to enable it to meet those needs, the school placement that it considers appropriate, and any non-educational provision that will be made available by the LEA, the health authority or social services to enable the child to benefit from the special educational provision. It will also contain copies of the advice and representations made by parents and of the professional advice collected by the LEA.

A copy of the statement in draft form will be sent to the parents who can make representations upon it and ask for meetings with an officer of the LEA or with any of the professional advisers (Section 7).

After these representations the LEA has three options. It can decide not to make a statement after all, and must inform parents of that decision. It can make a modified statement. It can make a statement in the original form (Section 7.8). Parents must have a copy of this final version and must be informed by the LEA of their rights to appeal.

If parents wish to appeal against the final version of the statement, they can do so to a local appeals committee which is empowered to confirm the statement or to ask the LEA to review it. If still unsatisfied, parents can appeal to the Secretary of State who can confirm the statement, ask for a review or instruct the LEA to cease to maintain a statement on the child (Section 8).

At the time of the survey reported by Sharron (1985), nineteen statements had been referred to the Secretary of State. In six cases the LEA statement was upheld; in six cases it was amended; seven cases were still to be decided at the time of the study.

If parents do not appeal against the final version of the statement it comes into force and is then legally binding on the LEA which has a duty to make the provision described in the statement unless the child's parents have made 'suitable arrangements' (Section 7.2). Such arrangements might, for example, include placement of the child in an independent school.

Statements are reviewed annually, on the basis of reports from school, and comments from parents and other professionals if appropriate. The review, or a request from the parents, can initiate a re-assessment of the pupil's needs. In any case a re-assessment is mandatory within a year of the child reaching the age of 13 years 6 months if the original assessment was done before the child was 12 years 6 months (Regulations 1983).

The LEA can change a statement, or decide that it no longer needs to maintain one, on the basis of a review or re-assessment. It must tell parents of its intentions, invite their views, consider them and inform parents of its final decision. Parents have rights of appeal against such changes.

LEAs differ in their interpretation of the Act. For example, at least one authority regards the provision, in some mainstream schools, of 'units' for children with moderate learning difficulties as part of the normal arrangements made for education in the county. It therefore argues that children who attend these units, who would have been regarded as ESN(M) under previous legislation, do so as a result of the normal procedures of the system and are not children for whom the *Authority* has to determine provision. The implication is that it does not need to go through the formal assessment and statementing procedures for these children. Other authorities do make statements for children in mainstream schools. In so far as statements can protect any special provision that a child might require they could be seen as useful for the children. However statementing can be seen to imply the proliferation of bureaucratic procedures and, above all, the creation of a new category of pupils distinct from those 'ordinary' pupils who do not have statements. This could deflect teachers' and other professionals' attention away from co-operation in active support of pupils and into a complex paperchase, could over-emphasise differences between statemented and non-statemented pupils and under-emphasise similarities and common aims and needs, and could deflect attention away from the very real needs of many pupils who do not have statements but who still need support in order to achieve what they are capable of achieving in school. This issue has been discussed at some length by Sayer (1983, 1985). There do not seem to be easy answers, but teachers should perhaps try to find ways of minimising the problems which tend to follow from either extensive or minimal use of the statementing procedure.

2.6 Study suggestions

a) As discussed in this chapter, the general requirements of the 1981 Act include:

- that governors try to ensure that special provision is made for each pupil with special needs and that teachers are informed about the special needs of any pupil they teach;

- that governors try to ensure that teachers are aware of the importance of identifying and providing for pupils with special needs;

- that there is functional integration of pupils, subject to certain conditions;

- that assessment procedures begin with teacher-based assessment based on 'full records' of pupils' progress and move on to a progressive involvement of other professionals, with parents informed and involved.

Use this information to carry out Activity 2.6a.

b) In this chapter we have listed some of the areas which should be assessed when formal procedures are under way (pp 13–14). Using this list carry out Activity 2.6b.

Activity 2.6a

Consider the following questions:

1. How do the procedures in your school match the requirements of the 1981 Act?
2. What developments would be needed to achieve a better match?

Activity 2.6b

Consult the list and make a note of the areas which are reasonably the *teacher's* responsibility. Then:

1. For each of these decide what should be assessed. (E.g. What are the components of 'communication skills'?)
2. For each thing to be assessed, decide how you could collect relevant information. (E.g. How would you collect information on pupils' behaviour?)
3. How could these detailed assessments be related to the normal record keeping that teachers do?

It might be interesting to consider these questions again after reading Chapter 5.

Aims, expectations and curriculum

3.1 Aims and special needs support systems

In all aspects of the school's life it is important that the organisational systems which we set up reflect the aims which we are trying to achieve. For instance, if we are trying to promote the skills of co-operating with others, we would clearly be foolish to adopt teaching styles and to organise extra-curricular activities which place emphasis solely on competition between individual pupils. Again, if we are trying to encourage independent study in Year Six we would be unwise to arrange for the sixth form timetable to be one hundred per cent teacher-contact-time. This line of reasoning is no less relevant when we are considering the organisation of support systems for pupils with special educational needs. In developing organisational structures, setting up identification and provision procedures and planning pupils' activities, we should be clear about the aims which we intend the special needs pupils to achieve and should check back from time to time to ensure that the steps we take are consistent with these intentions.

What, then, are the appropriate aims for pupils with special educational needs? Since aims are necessarily broad statements of the school's intentions one can argue that aims for special needs pupils should be the same as the aims which are established for all other pupils. This principle is clearly articulated in the Warnock Report (DES, 1978) which states that 'the purpose of education for all children is the same; the goals are the same' (Para 1.4). It is confirmed in recent DES curriculum statements, notably 'The Organisation and Content of the Curriculum: Special Schools' (DES/WO, 1984a). This paper states that the curriculum principles which are developed for most pupils in mainstream schools should also apply to the children with special educational needs who are educated in these schools. Furthermore it argues that the general aims of education, and the overall range of the curriculum, should still be essentially the same even when pupils 'have special needs on a scale that makes it necessary for them to attend either special schools or designated classes or units in ordinary schools'.

A good indication of the kinds of general aims that should, on this basis, be taken to apply to children with special needs can be found in the results of the curriculum enquiry which DES undertook in partnership with five LEAs and teachers from forty-one schools, beginning in 1977. Twelve aims regularly emerged in the course of this enquiry. These are set out in Figure 3.1.

Figure 3.1

Twelve general aims

1. To give children the experience of school as a caring, supportive community where life is enjoyable and where there is equal provision regardless of sex, race or culture.

2. To enable all children to develop as fully as possible their abilities, interests and aptitudes and to make additional provision necessary for those who are in any way disadvantaged.

3. To allow children to develop lively enquiring minds, to be capable of independent thought and to experience enjoyment in learning so that they may be encouraged to take advantage of educational opportunities in later life.

4. To develop appropriate skills in, for example, literacy and numeracy.

5. To develop a curriculum which ensures contact with those major areas of knowledge and experience which will help children to know more about themselves and the society in which they live.

6. To work in ways which will enhance the self-respect and confidence of young people and encourage them to take responsibility for themselves and their activities.

7. To establish a partnership between the school and the community it serves and to develop understanding of a wider community and of the ways in which individuals and groups relate.

8. To give children the skills necessary to respond effectively to social, economic and political changes and to changing patterns of work.

9. To develop the social skills necessary to work successfully with other people.

10. To equip children for their adult roles in society and to help them to understand the responsibilities of being parents, citizens and consumers.

11. To encourage appreciation and concern for the environment.

12. To develop interests and skills which will continue to give personal satisfaction in the use of leisure time.

(DES, 1984)

If we decide that the aims shown in Figure 3.1, or similar aims of education are appropriate for most pupils, then we clearly have a duty to ensure that the mainstream academic and pastoral organisation of the school provides the opportunities that will enable the pupils to attain all of them. (This could clearly imply significant shifts from present practice, at least in some schools.) More importantly in the context of this book, if we also accept such aims for pupils with special educational needs, and if, like Warnock and the DES, we accept that these pupils will need additional help to attain them, then we must ensure that this additional help also matches the full range of the aims.

Some practical implications

Some of the implications of this position can be seen by considering three of the above aims. First, if we want special needs pupils to experience a curriculum which ensures contact with the major areas of knowledge and experience, we might wonder at the adequacy of a special needs support system that offers help only in the area of literacy. This is undoubtedly an important area, but can we be sure that this support alone is enough to help pupils to experience success in their learning in, for example, science? If we are relying on the science teachers to provide the support in areas other than literacy, is this an explicit expectation, are they aware of it, and do they have access to appropriate materials and in-service training? Secondly, if we want children to work in ways that will enhance their self-respect, are we wise to withdraw pupils for small group teaching and then to use the time to work mainly on content such as literacy or numeracy in which they have a history of failure? Indeed, are we wise to withdraw pupils at all? Thirdly, if we want to encourage the development of social skills, are systems of support which emphasise the academic aspects of school sufficient?

These are not rhetorical questions. Successful support with numeracy might well enhance self-respect even if other opportunities to develop this are neglected. However it is worth considering that more success might be achieved through other approaches. One may, for example, use the special needs support structure to help a pupil to do some serious work in the context of an area of interest which s/he might have. In this area s/he might be capable of creating something impressive which other, generally more able pupils, would not easily be able to produce. Achievement of this kind might greatly enhance self-respect and confidence as a learner. Again, the development of social skills *may* take place in the close adult/pupil or pupil/pupil interactions that can go on in small group teaching, even if that teaching is focused on academic aims. However, social skills might be more fully developed if more systematic attention were to be paid to them in their own right.

What matters, therefore, is not that we automatically discard existing practice, but that we re-examine this practice in the light of the full range of aims which we have set. One likely consequence of such a re-examination is that there will be some changes in what 'special needs teachers' actually do with pupils, or at least changes in the emphasis on different aspects of their work. Another likely consequence is that we will be forced to conceive of special needs support as something which permeates the academic, pastoral, administrative and interpersonal procedures of the whole school. This follows from the fact that the aims are very broad. Because of this, pupils with special needs (like all other pupils) will require input from adults with a wide range of expertise if they are to begin to achieve the aims. What is more, this widely ranging expertise will have to be exercised in a variety of situations, for example, in teaching and tutoring situations, in the context of extra-curricular activities, and in the hidden curriculum of how teachers and pupils relate to one another, how they respond to disability or difference, how decisions are taken, how rewards and punishments are handled. It is logically as well as practically impossible for the 'special needs staff' alone to have responsibility for providing this range of expertise in this range of contexts to all pupils with special needs. Inevitably every member of staff will be involved, with 'special needs staff' providing particular sorts of expertise, sometimes in direct support of pupils, but also in support of their colleagues.

3.2 Other curriculum issues

As we have seen, the argument that the *aims* of education should be the same for all does, in itself, have significant practical implications. However, these aims are very general and cannot be directly translated into a fully detailed specification of what should happen in school. To achieve such a specification we must determine, for each aim, a number of more detailed objectives. In the light of the aims and objectives we must then select specific areas of content and set up appropriate teaching and learning situations. We must also choose teaching methods and obtain resources. Finally we must adopt appropriate methods of assessment so that pupils' progress towards the original aims can be monitored. Through such a process we determine the overall school curriculum; if the original aims are broad, this curriculum will cover academic and pastoral goals, and also the goals usually served by the so-called hidden curriculum.

There is much to discuss about each stage of this process when we are considering curriculum development in general terms. However, in the context of pupils with special educational needs, the essential question is at what point in this sequence should planning for 'normal' and 'special needs' pupils diverge?

a) Defining objectives for pupils with special needs

The Warnock Report (DES, 1978) suggests that there *may* be divergence at the stage of defining detailed objectives which, it argues, should be 'related to the particular children to whom they apply' (Para 11.7). However, the report goes on to say that, even where children have quite extensive needs, 'every attempt should be made to see that the chosen objectives are as near in scope and quality to those of other children of the same age as is practicable'. It also stresses that children with special educational needs in mainstream schools need 'access to the whole range of the curriculum, not just a limited part of it'. The report therefore argues that the major point at which diversity is to be expected and welcomed is not at the level of different objectives, but at the level of choosing 'materials, experiences and teaching and learning methods' that will enable pupils to strive for the same objectives (Para 11.8). Similar points are implicit in the DES paper on the 'entitlement curriculum' (DES, 1984) which also provides useful guidelines on the kinds of objectives that might be considered in such areas as skills, attitudes, concepts and knowledge.

This emphasis on finding ways of helping all pupils towards the same aims and objectives is an extremely important one. It is not impracticable idealism. It does not imply that all pupils will be able to achieve the same curriculum objectives at the same pace. It does, however, mean that these objectives remain as the basis for structuring every pupil's programme. Some pupils with special needs will achieve the objectives far more slowly than their peers –

indeed, some may still not have achieved them by the end of their schooling – but a full range of learning experiences appropriate to the full set of objectives *will* have been presented to every pupil, including every special needs pupil, throughout that period of schooling.

b) Defining objectives for the profoundly handicapped

However desirable it is that most pupils with special needs should strive towards the common objectives set for pupils generally, the needs of the small group of profoundly handicapped pupils are so special that no amount of support could make these normal secondary school objectives the most appropriate ones for them. This leads to the conclusion that their special need is for a curriculum focused on different objectives. This curriculum would provide explicit teaching on things which were on the 'curriculum' for all other pupils, but which most will have mastered at earlier stages in life, e.g. before entry to primary schools. The curriculum for such pupils is not, therefore, arcane, even though it is very different from what secondary schools usually provide.

c) The range of curriculum options

The range of options discussed above is also recognised in the note produced by the Department of Education and Science and the Welsh Office (DES/WO, 1984a). The authors suggest that most special needs children will continue to receive their education in mainstream classes of ordinary schools and that the curriculum principles expressed in general curriculum documents (e.g. DES/WO, 1984b) apply to them. They need a *mainstream curriculum* even though they may need help to pursue it successfully.

The authors then point out that some pupils have more severe needs. (It is clear that the kinds of pupils they refer to at this point are those who, in the past, might have been placed in a special school or in a special unit or designated class in an ordinary school.) Some of these pupils may still need a *mainstream curriculum but with considerable support* from the use of special aids, or from ancillary helpers or through specially skilled teaching. They may also need adjustments to the balance or detailed content of the curriculum, and may need to spend longer in school to achieve the standards normally expected of sixteen year olds.

Other pupils with complex difficulties may need a *modified curriculum* which is similar to that provided in ordinary schools but is a curriculum which, 'while not restricted in its expectations, has objectives more appropriate to (these) children'. For this group, subjects may be taught in less depth and there 'should be a strong emphasis on personal and social development'.

Still other pupils may need a *developmental curriculum* 'covering selected and sharply focused educational, social and other experiences with precisely defined objectives . . . designed to encourage a measure of personal autonomy'. It is suggested that this be achieved through emphasis on the 'acquisition of communication, self help, mobility and social skills, very basic literacy and numeracy and an understanding of the world about them including simple science and its application to everyday life.'

This DES paper therefore outlines interesting options in planning for pupils with special educational needs. At one end of the continuum, this planning has much in common with that undertaken for all other pupils. Decisions on aims and objectives, on content and on the nature of the appropriate teaching and learning situations are essentially the same as the decisions made for mainstream pupils. Modifications lie mainly in the area of teaching methods and materials. At the other end of the continuum is planning for a developmental curriculum in which only the broadest general goals are held in common with the plans for mainstream pupils. Planned objectives, content, teaching and learning situations (even to the extent of school placement), teaching methods and materials, while sometimes influenced by choices made for mainstream pupils, are all special.

d) Designing a curriculum

In designing an overall curriculum for a given mainstream school, decisions have to be taken about how far along this continuum the range of special needs planning should extend. The most important points, in our view, are:

a) that these decisions should be taken quite explicitly;
b) that the special needs support structures in the school should be consistent with these decisions; and
c) that whatever general decisions are taken, the possibility of a specific and different response to the needs of an individual pupil should always be open.

In connection with the first point we would argue that special needs pupils should not have to follow courses with different aims and objectives just because no attempts have been made to find teaching methods that can enable them to be successful in attaining the general objectives of the school; equally, pupils with severe problems should not be forced to strive for these general objectives just because insufficient attention has been given to the possibility that their needs might be better met in other ways. The decision about the appropriate objectives for the pupils with special needs should be made explicitly, the implications should be worked through and ideas (e.g. for alternative teaching styles) tried out. Such developments should be evaluated at agreed intervals and the original decisions should be reconsidered in the light of these trials. The issues are complex; they are affected by the range of need that the school's pupils have, by the facilities and resources available, by the range of expertise amongst the staff. Therefore, there can be no ready-made answers, but a procedure such as that outlined could enable a school to find the answers that suit it and its pupils best.

In connection with the second point we would suggest that some special needs support structures are more appropriate to some curriculum decisions than to others. For example, if it had been decided that a modified or developmental curriculum was needed it would not seem appropriate to design the special needs support system entirely upon the principle of support from a second teacher in mainstream classes, for the mainstream class environment would place too many constraints on the content of the alternative curriculum. Similarly, if a 'mainstream plus support' curriculum was chosen, it would not seem appropriate to support pupils entirely through work in special classes with limited access to mainstream facilities and the full range of subject teacher expertise.

The final point is self-evident. However carefully considered a school's overall plan for special needs pupils is, the particular problems of an individual pupil may render that plan inappropriate for that child. The system should always be flexible enough to respond so that children are not forced to fit a system which does not suit them.

e) Some practical implications

We suggest that staff should discuss whether the needs of their pupils can be served by the mainstream curriculum alone, or whether, for some pupils, it is also necessary to consider the incorporation of 'mainstream plus considerable support' or even 'modified' curricula. The need to consider a developmental curriculum in mainstream secondary schools is unlikely to arise at present, but examples of the integration of children with severe learning difficulties into mainstream schools (Hackney, 1985) demonstrate that it is by no means inevitable that it should always be dismissed.

Since we have argued that all staff will be involved in the support of children with special needs (see Chapter 1 and earlier discussion in the present chapter), we suggest that all staff should have a clearly defined role in these discussions.

In these discussions, staff should clearly go on to consider the nature of the school's special needs support system that is implied by the curriculum choices which they have made. Attention should also be given to the nature of the responsibility of mainstream staff for the development of alternative materials or teaching styles for use in their own teaching, and for helping to develop ways of working with special needs staff in their classes, and ways of supporting special needs staff who are involved in teaching their subject to 'special classes'.

Finally, we suggest that decisions should be made on a clear procedure for responding to the situation of individual children for whom the general system adopted by the school does not seem appropriate.

Clearly, the range of problems faced by the pupils who are members of the school will be a major influence on these discussions. Nevertheless, general points can be made and in the rest of this chapter we will discuss some of these.

3.3 Some points on appropriate curricula

a) Richness

Brennan (1979) provides clear evidence that the curriculum offered to special needs pupils (especially in mainstream schools) was less rich than that made available to other pupils. They were less often involved in educational and recreational visits, and their lessons less often involved the use of audio-visual aids. In our own case studies of schools, we have examples of special needs pupils doing 'science' without access to a laboratory and with no emphasis on practical work, and of emphasis on literacy and numeracy to the exclusion of other enriching activities. This seems to be tragic, partly because research evidence quoted by Brennan suggests that special needs pupils make less 'use' of their environment than their normal peers and that schools are therefore missing an opportunity to provide some compensation, and partly because the provision of rich experiences might enable teachers to identify activities or topics that especially interest individual children with special needs – activities and topics which might be then used to stimulate their thinking and learning. It would seem, therefore, to be particularly important to consider whether any planned curriculum does provide sufficient richness for all pupils, however severe their needs.

b) Special needs and ability

Many children with special educational needs do not have low general ability. There is for example no evidence that behavioural or emotional problems are always associated with low IQ. Indeed even the title of Kellmer-Pringle's book *Able Misfits* suggests that the opposite can be true (1970).

Where special needs arise as a result of physical handicap or of a chronic medical disorder the link with low ability, though it can be present, as in the case of children with cerebral palsy, is by no means inevitable. For example, Rutter and colleagues (1970) demonstrated that the IQs of pupils with 'uncomplicated epilepsy' were normally distributed across the range of intelligence. Presumably, Rutter was excluding from this group pupils whose epilepsy was 'complicated' by cerebral palsy. Roughly a third of children with cerebral palsy do have epilepsy and the inclusion of this group skews the IQ distribution of pupils with epilepsy towards the lower end of the IQ range.

Similar results have been found by Kubany and colleagues who discovered that the intelligence of diabetic children was comparable to that of non-diabetics, and in a further study by the New York City Board of Education which showed that that IQs of children with heart disorders were even somewhat above average. (For accounts of the last two studies see Cruickshank, 1980.) Also, a number of researchers have shown that the IQ of partially hearing children followed the same distribution as that of their hearing peers and that partially sighted children also had IQs in the normal range although they seemed to bunch somewhat below average (Mittler, 1970).

The overall implication of these studies would appear to be that it is sensible to think in terms of curriculum aims and objectives for such pupils that are the same as those for mainstream pupils. Indeed it would be hard to justify offering them a very different curriculum if their potential to cope with a curriculum which leads to qualifications that are regarded as 'saleable' by society, is comparable to that of their non-handicapped peers. The tendency noted by all of the above authors for the school performance of such pupils to be below average does not weaken this case though it does, of course, emphasise the importance of greater understanding of the educational implications of such handicaps and of commitment to the development of appropriate teaching styles to help the pupils achieve these goals.

c) The potential of children with learning problems

Even where special needs do arise directly from a learning difficulty, it is easy to underestimate the potential of pupils to succeed.

In his excellent book *Yes They Can!* Weber (1978) makes this point very clearly and gives an interesting account of the achievements of a group of slow learners in areas such as writing, reading, and creative, logical and critical thinking. He also discusses how such achievements can be encouraged.

Similarly Malecka (1985) has described an experiment in which children in an ESN(M) school were taught some French and reported that this led to 'enhanced self esteem and peer group esteem in and out of school' which was 'ample motive and reward for the children . . .'

Again, when HMI discussed their visits to a number of secondary schools to inspect the arrangements made for slow learners they commented that pupils 'though handicapped by their considerable language difficulties, showed good understanding and an ability to arrive at well considered conclusions' (DES, 1984). They went on to say that 'ideas which are in themselves complex can be handled by less able pupils if they are introduced in the right context and through appropriate methods'.

These points stress again that although there may be good reasons for changing the basic aims and objectives of the curriculum for some children with special needs, we must be very sure of our ground before we make these alterations simply on the assumption that they would not be able to succeed with mainstream aims and objectives. With appropriate teaching many of them can.

d) What mainstream curriculum?

The emphasis in the previous paragraphs on mainstream aims and objectives should not be taken to imply that the *present* mainstream curriculum is necessarily ideal for special needs pupils, any more than it is ideal for pupils in general. The thrust is rather that the basic educational needs of almost all pupils are essentially the same and therefore that as we develop the mainstream curriculum, perhaps along the lines suggested by the list of aims suggested in the DES enquiry and quoted in Figure 3.1 (page 18), we should take account of insights from the special needs world in order to produce a curriculum which better serves (almost) everyone. Having done so, we should then consider the special needs group again to determine what special forms of teaching, what special resources, what special support – in general what special delivery systems – are necessary to enable them to succeed with this new curriculum.

An example of this process can be drawn from Fish (1985) who argues that we easily underestimate the employment potential of young people with learning difficulties. He suggests that, however difficult the labour market, people with special needs have a right to a reasonable share of that market. He then shows that this is realistic by citing experience in the USA of 'mentally retarded girls who in other countries might go from schools to day centres, (who) are able to carry out laboratory testing techniques in an oil company laboratory'. He argues that the specialist vocational training that is needed to bring about such outcomes is relatively straightforward, but that the difficulty is in giving the young people help to develop adequate social skills to sustain a role in open employment. Recognising this need within this group of pupils may encourage us to place more emphasis on the basic aim 'to develop the social skills necessary to work successfully with other people' when we are designing the curriculum for all pupils. However, we might still think about special ways of emphasising this aim in the educational programme of the special group.

3.4 Study suggestions

The overall thrust of this chapter can be summarised in these statements:
1. That mainstream curriculum development should be carried out in the expectation that the general aims and objectives of the curriculum will be appropriate for most of the school's pupils with special needs.
2. That explicit decisions have to be taken about the need to provide alternative curricula, with different objectives for some pupils with the most severe problems.
3. That the school's special needs support system should be set up in ways that are consistent with the curriculum decisions which have been taken.
4. That great attention should be paid to the development and trial of alternative teaching styles and of special resources so that the option of the

mainstream curriculum can be kept open for as many pupils as possible, for as long as possible.

5. That all teachers should be aware of their own responsibilities in relation to special needs pupils in their teaching and their tutoring and of their role in relation to the formal special needs support system.

6. That the system should always be flexible to the particular needs of an individual pupil and that there should be clearly understood ways of initiating discussions about such a case.

Activity 3.4

Consider the statements made at the end of this chapter in the context of your own school.

1. How far do they apply to its present practice?
2. What practical changes would be involved in implementing them?
3. How desirable are these changes in your own situation?

The range of special educational needs

4

4.1 The Warnock Report

When the Warnock Committee in 1978 reported upon the education of handicapped children and young people the concept of 'special educational needs' was central to its thinking. This concept was to replace the previous categorisation of handicapped pupils enshrined in the 1944 Act and subsequent Regulations. The intention of the statutory categories had been to ensure that local authorities made provision, in special or ordinary schools, for a wide range of disabilities. By 1959 the categories were as follows:

Blind pupils
Partially sighted pupils
Deaf pupils
Partially hearing pupils
Educationally subnormal pupils*
Epileptic pupils
Maladjusted pupils
Physically handicapped pupils
Pupils suffering from speech defect
Delicate pupils

The Warnock Committee acknowledged the value of the categories in focusing upon the existence and needs of different groups of handicapped pupils but came to the conclusion that the categorisation was nevertheless unsatisfactory. Many children had more than one disability and a single label concealed additional needs. The essentially medical nature of most of the categories did not necessarily have any bearing upon educational need. The use of such categories also unhelpfully implied that children who shared a disability would be suited by similar educational provision. In many instances the category label could be stigmatising and remain with the child beyond the school period. This particular categorisation might also be an obstacle to special provision for many children whose needs were acknowledged but who failed to fall neatly into any statutory category. However, the perpetuation in

---

* In 1970 when mentally handicapped children became the responsibility of local education authorities the ESN category was extended to include those children but was subdivided into ESN(M) – moderate educational subnormality to cover the existing pupils and ESN(S) – severe educational subnormality – to categorise the new clients.

categories of 'the sharp distinction between two groups of children – the handicapped and the non-handicapped' – was the most compelling argument for the Committee in recommending their abolition.

The Committee advocated the use of a detailed description of special educational need in place of a category of handicap. It was acknowledged that notions of disability might still be needed, especially for children with sensory and physical disorders, but only in so far as they contributed to the child's educational need. The 'educationally subnormal' label, which was regarded as both offensive and imprecise, should be replaced by the idea of a learning difficulty of different degrees of severity and of certain 'specific learning difficulties' – such as in reading. By employing such an all-embracing notion as a 'learning difficulty' it was possible to acknowledge the needs of the child in a remedial class or group as well as the child with a severe mental handicap. It is interesting to note that the Committee advocated the retention of the term 'maladjusted' despite its possible stigma because it implied that 'behaviour can sometimes be meaningfully considered only in relation to the circumstances in which it occurs'. The importance of considering the context as well as the child will be taken up later.

In addition to loosening up the definition of special educational needs the Committee suggested, on the evidence of surveys, that up to one in five children might have such needs at some stage in their school careers with one in six in need of special provision at any one time. In this way too, the static feel of the categories was abolished. Some children would need support throughout their school careers, but for many that support would be needed only occasionally or intermittently.

4.2 Special educational needs and the 1981 Act

In the wake of the Warnock Report came the 1981 Education Act, implemented in 1983, under which special educational provision is now made. Many Warnock ideas are incorporated and the idea of 'special educational needs' is central. As we discussed in detail in Chapter 2, a child is deemed to have a special educational need under the terms of the Act, if s/he has a 'learning difficulty' calling for special educational provision to be made. A child is defined as having a learning difficulty if

a) s/he has a significantly greater difficulty in learning than the majority of children of his/her age, or

b) s/he has a disability which either prevents or hinders him/her from making use of educational facilities of a kind generally provided in schools, within the area of the local authority concerned, for children of his/her age.

These definitions although somewhat evasive certainly suggest something of the range of needs which teachers might encounter.

a) Children with a 'significantly greater difficulty in learning'

Mild

It is difficult to know what 'significantly greater' means in relation to a learning difficulty but we should perhaps mention first the pupils who are in remedial groups. Although they may not be severely educationally handicapped nevertheless it seems important that there is some extra help given to their needs. As, however, schools usually make provision of this kind perhaps this group does not strictly come under the terms of the Act but, as we remark elsewhere, their needs could become very special if existing resources were eroded or re-allocated under pressure from other educational initiatives.

Moderate

The 'greater difficulty in learning' phrase seems to encompass many of the children encountered in the old ESN(M) schools, units, or classes, children who might also be labelled slow learners. When assessed for special provision, particularly on verbal tests, these children have often been allocated low IQ scores, usually within the range 50–70. Their limited intellectual skills have often been associated with social and emotional immaturity, and at times, physical or behavioural disorders. Academic progress has usually been slow but discernible and in more prosperous times these children have gained employment and ceased to be 'special' when free of educational demands. That picture is of course a massive generalisation which has to encompass many individual variations. In educational terms these children need considerable support, modification to the curriculum to match their slower learning pace and immaturity and teachers who appreciate their needs and can foster a growing sense of confidence and competence.

Severe

Another group of children in this 'greater difficulty in learning' category are the more severely handicapped pupils who even now may be found in the special schools which were labelled ESN(S). At one time teachers in mainstream schools had no need to be concerned at a professional level for the provision for these children, but that is no longer the case. In many areas some of these children are now being integrated full or part-time into their local schools with varying degrees of support and their needs have to be considered with the rest of the children. (For examples see Chapter 7.)

Among such children are the majority of children with Down's syndrome and other handicapping syndromes and conditions, either congenital or acquired early in life, which leave them with limited intellectual functioning. Again this may be associated with physical or behavioural disorders. The experience of the last fifteen years in the special schools has demonstrated quite clearly the educability of these children and the various teaching strategies and curriculum adaptations which meet their very special needs.

There is such diversity among this group in terms of ability and disability that it is impossible to spell out in any general way what their educational needs are. Each child has to be assessed and managed on an individual basis. What can be said, however, is that they need a good deal of individual help and teachers with particular skills of diagnosis, assessment and management suited to very slow, uneven and/or deviant learning styles. Their curricular needs may include help in passing through the early developmental stages usually reached in the pre-school years and a detailed analysis of any programme to allow for small step learning.

Specific learning difficulties

The 'greater difficulty' in learning must also cover children with specific learning difficulties whose overall functioning is within the normal range.

(This is not to imply that children with moderate or severe learning difficulties cannot also have specific learning difficulties.) Frequently the weakness is in the area of literacy – particularly reading or writing – but one may also cite children with severe numeracy problems, those with specific expressive or receptive language disorders and those with weaknesses in specific cognitive functions such as comparing and categorising, sequencing and reasoning. Those unfortunate children who find it difficult to master the basic literacy skills which are so crucial in later academic success certainly need very specific help. This need not necessarily occur in withdrawal classes but must be geared to their particular weakness. For some the problem may be remediable, but experience has shown that others need to be restored to self confidence and to learn strategies that will help them to develop and progress despite a persistent disability.

Undoubtedly there are many other specific learning difficulties but in our society we are not so concerned with aesthetic, creative, practical or physical aspects of development so that children who fail utterly in music making, art, woodwork or P.E. do not acquire a 'special needs' label. Perhaps they should. That would certainly change our concept of special needs. Further discussion of our limited views on special needs may be found in Wilson and Cowell (1984).

b) Disabilities that hinder progress

Physical and sensory handicaps

The second part of the definition refers to a disability which prevents or hinders a child in making use of ordinary educational facilities. This immediately suggests a physical disability which may hinder access to school buildings or specialist rooms or to areas of the curriculum which necessitate physical co-ordination, mobility or manual dexterity. We are also reminded of children with sensory disabilities which cut them off in part or entirely from the visual or verbal signals which are a key feature of the teaching and learning processes.

Some of the needs of these children can be met in very obvious and practical ways through physical adaptations to buildings, availability and use of disability aids and, in some cases, the support of welfare assistants (see Hodgson (1985)). It is, however, important to remember that their disabilities may have generated secondary handicaps such as emotional or social problems, learning difficulties, restricted experience and missed schooling. In the effort to compensate for their disability in an able-bodied world they may tire easily and be unable to compete in pace with their peers. Although therefore a disability should not be a bar to a mainstream education it needs to be understood and allowed for if the child is to benefit. There are circumstances where pupils have taken a slightly reduced range of subjects to allow extra time for writing or typing. This sort of experience is reported in the account of the integration of physically disabled pupils into a secondary comprehensive (C.S.I.E. undated). It may be necessary too for mainstream teaching staff to be supported by visiting specialists who can advise on appropriate teaching strategies and on the most effective use of mechanical or electronic aids.

Chronic medical disorders

Similar needs for understanding and awareness may be met in children with chronic medical disorders such as epilepsy or diabetes. The actual disability may be managed by others and the child may appear quite unremarkable in the school context except for occasional physical manifestations but the chronic disorders do carry educational implications. The children may have missed vital steps in schooling, they may suffer in psychological or social ways because of their disability, their general well being and awareness may be inconsistent in a way which is fairly unobtrusive but potentially damaging for academic success. In such cases part of the understanding and awareness needs to be an adequate system of monitoring progress and the facility to offer appropriate support after a period of learning disruption. A more detailed discussion of the implications of a chronic medical disorder may be found in Hackney (1985a).

Emotional disorders

Children with emotional or psychological disorders must also be regarded as having special educational needs. Behavioural disturbances are often associated with established learning difficulties although the direction of any causal connection may not be easy to unravel. Behavioural difficulties arising from some traumatic experience, though not associated with learning difficulties in the past, almost certainly prevent or hinder satisfactory learning. The children's needs are various but the experience of success in terms of academic or other school work as well as some kind of satisfactory relationship with at least one authority figure may be beneficial. Outside help may be sought and used but solutions also need to be found within the school. Although it would be a mistake to have low expectations for such pupils, a certain flexibility may avert potential crisis and breakdown points. Support for staff under stress, however, may be as important as support for the disturbed children. Wilson and Evans (1980) provide a comprehensive account of this special educational need.

c) Other aspects of special need

The needs of the most able

There are some categories of need which are either omitted from the Act or specifically excluded. Children who are very able or 'gifted' hardly seem to qualify under the Act's definition but there is undoubtedly evidence that their special abilities may hinder them from making best use of a mainstream education either because they become social misfits and disturbed or because their talents are unrecognised or neglected. Such children may be content to drift through school with the minimum of effort or become frustrated and disillusioned with the mismatch between their abilities and the schools' demands. Either way their education cannot be counted a great success. The school has somehow to challenge their talents in a way which encourages development but remains acceptable to their need for social approval from their peer group. The recent development of enrichment programmes for more able children may help in this effort and demonstrate the appropriateness of a wide range of resources and materials for all groups. Such programmes may on occasions need to be supplemented by more intensive provision, for example withdrawal from timetabled work for a day to engage in special activities, tutorial work with teachers and visiting experts, attendance at a residential school and so on. Tannenbaum (1983) is an excellent source of discussion about all aspects of giftedness. There is no clear divide in general terms between the average and the more able and individual children may be endowed with very disparate abilities. In the end, therefore, all children gain if the needs of all ranges of ability can be met.

Social disadvantage

Social disadvantage too is not specifically mentioned in the Act although it may perhaps constitute a 'disability' which hinders some children. They may be deprived of common childhood experiences, forced to live in unsuitable conditions which endanger their physical and mental energies and compelled to face day-to-day difficulties in living which would tax the strongest adult. Mortimore and Blackstone's book *Disadvantage and Education* (1982) presents an overview of this aspect of special needs. Schools cannot change social conditions but can compensate to some extent and this is recognised in part by the extra staffing in Social Priority areas. This help, however, may not be available to individual children in a relatively advantaged school. Nevertheless children can be supported through counselling, through homework facilities at school and through the school's close liaison with social services and families where possible.

Children with English as a second language

The Act specifically excludes children from the special needs label if their difficulty stems from speaking a language other than English at home. This nod to the acceptability of cultural diversity in our schools cannot conceal the fact that a poor command of written and spoken English is a disadvantage in our current educational system and that children may need more than a short intensive language course to compensate. Moreover it makes for difficulties when children for whom English is a second language also have special educational needs as recognised by the Act. For the everyday working of a school it probably makes sense to regard these children as having a temporary special educational need until they can manage as well in English as in their first language. The ESL language teaching catered for by Section 11 funding (Local Government Act 1966) is often not enough to ensure that the children can express themselves or comprehend as competently as in their first language. There needs to be co-ordinated support from special needs and ESL teachers as advocated by Roaf (1985).

d) Severity and persistence

There is one aspect of special needs which has been mentioned only briefly but which ties in well with the idea of a school developing flexible systems of support. Just as special needs are defined to some extent by the context, and so have a measure of relativity, so too we have to consider them in the dimensions of severity and persistence. Factors bearing the same name – such as a reading problem, anxiety, epilepsy, inattention – need considerable examination before an appropriate response can be made otherwise we return to the criticisms made about the old handicapping categories when the label rather than the individual needs dictated provision.

There are some children whose special educational needs are likely to be both severe and chronic, such as children with a severe mental handicap or those with virtually no sight. Although with appropriate teaching they will gain increasingly in competence and independence it is unlikely that progress will be maintained without continuous support and provision of a special kind. Other children have severe needs of a much shorter duration. The child who is immobilised by an accident and unable to attend school needs educational support within the home or hospital to ensure continuity of progress and this support may well have to be closely tailored to immediate factors of health and mobility. Once a recovery is made, however, and essential learning checked, that support should no longer be needed. Similarly, a child whose psychological balance is upset by some trauma such as a bereavement may need very intense support for a period. This may involve counselling, social work participation, modified academic requirements, even access to a sanctuary or retreat within the school. Although the healing process in this case may be slower than in the case of a physical hurt, in time the support may be reduced and relaxed and the special provision no longer needed.

Other children have moderate or mild problems which require less support but perhaps for a long period. One example may be the child with a moderate hearing loss which is not remediable and so will always need to be taken into account. The support needed, however, may be relatively minor, such as care over seating arrangements and careful monitoring of progress in language comprehension and competence. Other moderate or mild needs may be of short duration, such as those arising from several short absences through illness or from a change of school. In both cases care has to be taken to ensure that key elements in the curriculum have been covered and that the child is not left at a permanent disadvantage through a temporary disturbance. This analysis can be summarised and the independence of the dimensions emphasised by Figure 4.2d.

Figure 4.2d

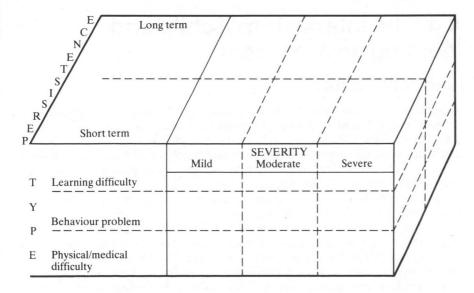

4.3 Relativity of need

A learning difficulty may be identified in a child who has a 'disability which either prevents or hinders him/her from making use of educational facilities of a kind generally provided by schools within the area of the local authority concerned, for children of his/her age.' The wording of the last part of this definition implies that the difficulty is not an absolute fixed entity but a condition that is relative to the provision made in schools in the area. It is important to be clear about the distinction between situations here. If a child has a disability of the kind listed above and the school or LEA is not yet in a position to accommodate that child with the minimum bar to learning, then that special educational need is unmet, and the school is not fulfilling its duty by the child. If, however, the school as part of its normal range of provision can accommodate the child the needs are being met. Except in strictly legal terms, that does not, of course, mean that the need is no longer there. A blind child in a school with specialist facilities for teaching the visually handicapped does not cease to have the special needs associated with blindness. Should the school cease to make that kind of provision the need will again become apparent as an unmet need. However, it is in cases of *unmet* needs that authorities and schools have a duty to make some special provision *over and above or different from* what is normally available. The extent of special needs, therefore, is defined not only by pupils but by the ability and willingness of a school to cater as a general rule for the diversity of ability and disability within its potential pupils.

This idea of relativity of needs leads on to the view that special educational needs arise from the interaction of the child with the learning environment, and factors which create problems may lie in the child or the environment or, most likely, in a combination of the two. When making some assessment, therefore, of the nature of an apparent special educational need with a view to meeting that need it is crucial not only to examine the educational implications of within-child factors but also those of situational factors in the school.

4.4 The interaction of child and learning environment

a) Within-child factors

In some ways it is easiest to appreciate the limitations imposed by physical or sensory disability and to make appropriate responses in teaching. Children with physical disabilities may need assistance to get to classes on time, may need lifts or ramps to obtain access to different areas of the school, may need work surfaces of different heights to take part in various practical activities, may need typewriters, computers or amanuenses to complete written work, or may need some satisfactory alternative to physical education lessons. The child with a hearing loss may need to use a hearing aid, the teacher may need to use a radio microphone; the position of the child and the teacher in oral presentations may be crucial for lip readers; group discussion time needs to be organised carefully if the child is not to be isolated and written hand-outs may be necessary to ensure that key information is available. The child with a visual handicap may need a variety of low vision aids to maximise the sight she or he has as well as specially developed materials in braille or large type; the lighting in classrooms and work surfaces also need to be suitable.

Children who are chronically ill or occasionally miss large periods of schooling for hospitalisation obviously need to receive work to enable them to keep up with their peers and their progress has to be carefully monitored to avoid key gaps in understanding.

In some ways the needs which have such an obvious profile and can be met in highly practical ways are the easiest to understand. Help may be needed from outside specialists because children are affected differently by seemingly similar disabilities. What is suitable provision for one child with cerebral palsy may be totally inappropriate for another. Nevertheless, teachers may feel that there is something tangible to tackle. It is, however, important to remember that such children's needs may also include teaching which takes account of delays in higher concept formation due to lack of the normal sensory and perceptual experiences. They may also need emotional support to cope with their own and others' response to chronic disability.

Other within-child factors are less easy to grasp because they are less obvious, less dramatic, less susceptible to practical solutions. The child with epilepsy may not always show the major symptoms. While the convulsion is disturbing it is obviously something to be dealt with as a short term emergency and it is easy to see that it effectively blocks learning for a while. The child with epilepsy may also, however, experience frequent and short periods of altered consciousness which may be almost unnoticable in a classroom but which may interfere much more radically with satisfactory learning over a long period. The child with diabetes will not often, if ever, enter a coma, another obvious medical emergency, but his or her alertness and responsiveness may vary with the fluctuations in blood sugar levels which are difficult to eradicate even with the most sophisticated medication.

Any child who is on regular drug therapy may suffer from unwanted side effects which may alter behaviour or attention. Children with any sort of physical or sensory disability may become tired more easily than their peers in their efforts to compete on equal terms in work and play.

The child who is worried or anxious or otherwise psychologically disturbed may draw attention to his or her needs in very obvious ways through tears or aggression or bizarre behaviour, but many may switch off from school in much more subtle ways which are liable to misinterpretation as some defect in attention or co-operation.

It would seem that the needs of children with intellectual handicaps should be easy to understand too and amenable to the psychologist's tests. However, the risk here seems to be that the child's difficulty is seen in global terms – an inability to read or write or spell – and the diagnosis which leads to useful remedial or supportive measures has still to be done. An IQ figure, even two figures, for verbal or performance tests, can only hint at how the child might function, at the level of conceptual thinking, at the disparities which have to be appreciated if the child is to be appropriately taught.

All these within-child factors suggest that the teacher cannot simply rely on the 'label' to know how a child is affected and how best to help. We are back with the 'categories' dilemma. The label is only the starting point for understanding and much more investigation has to be completed by the teacher and with the help of other agents, before appropriate strategies can be devised.

b) School factors

The idea of 'appropriate' teaching reminds us of the need to examine the school factors which may contribute to special educational needs. The Warnock Report put forward a figure of approximately 20 per cent for children who might at some time have special educational needs. The size of that figure, which is meeting with some agreement in local authorities (e.g. Burnham and Robbins 1980), emphasises the importance of the part which schools play in creating special educational needs. There will always be a few children whose needs are so special that in any context the school has to rethink its curriculum or style of teaching, but to do that for 20 per cent implies that the general educational offering is not shaped for the range and diversity of a normal comprehensive intake. To make 20 per cent special is to throw doubts on the suitability of the ordinary provision.

To cater well for the problems caused by disabilities may seem a tall order for the average school. Undoubtedly it would be unreasonable to expect any school to fulfil the individual needs of diversely handicapped children without some special effort but some of these needs are common in modified form to very many children. The need for good working conditions, the clear presentation of material in different modes, and the monitoring of progress, particularly at times of stress or ill health, is not confined to the obviously disabled and if these things were provided as routine the extra needs of a few children would not seem too onerous. Indeed, in meeting these needs teachers might well extend their own expertise to the benefit of many more pupils.

To cater well for intellectual needs seems perhaps an even more obvious obligation for schools. If the individual styles of learning and levels of ability are not taken into account when curricula are devised and implemented some children will inevitably be condemned to constant failure. This is not to suggest that meeting the intellectual needs of all children is easy. To offer alternative or modified curricula to children who appear to be struggling raises issues of equality of opportunity, internal segregation, labelling, under-expectation and mistaking a specific, remediable difficulty for a chronic general deficiency. The alternative solution, now being attempted by some schools, is to rethink radically the whole curriculum, teaching strategies and learning support systems so that all children can benefit from an integrated programme which takes account of diversity but does not consign any child to a rigidly limited educational programme.

4.5 Conclusion

We are almost in the position of saying that the needs of all children are special and that if we cater for the individual we shall eliminate unmet needs. That is appropriate if we are thinking in terms of individual tutorial work but is not attainable when we think in terms of groups of learners. It would be impossible, and perhaps unwise, to cater solely for the individual when we live in a society which requires us to live and work in groups. Within that constraint, however, we need to give every child a fair opportunity to make the most of whatever talents s/he has and that means making every effort to meet the special educational needs discussed earlier – needs which, whether arising from within the child or the environment or both are likely to block that opportunity. In meeting special educational needs, however, we have to work for a flexible and informed system of support which is open to constant re-appraisal and change, which can respond quickly to emergencies but also respond in a stimulating way to long term needs. For this reason any one style of provision or any static remedy is likely to be inadequate.

4.6 Study suggestions

This chapter acknowledges that the former categories of 'handicap' were a poor basis on which to plan for special educational provision. It does suggest, however, that the component parts of special educational needs do have to be understood in all their diversity if an appropriate response is to be made. It also raises issues of severity and persistence of need and proposes that most needs arise from a mismatch between the pupils' capabilities and the school environment.

Activity 4.6 may be undertaken by an individual teacher, a group of teachers (e.g. a year team) or by a whole staff.

Activity 4.6
Consider any group of pupils identified as having special educational needs and try to be explicit about the nature of each pupil's needs.

The following checklist taken from the chapter sections may provide guidelines:

- mild learning difficulties;
- moderate learning difficulties;
- severe learning difficulties;
- specific learning difficulties;
- physical or sensory handicaps;
- chronic medical disorders;
- emotional or psychological disorders;
- outstanding ability;
- social disadvantage;
- English as a second language.

For each pupil consider the following questions:

1. Does the 'label' explain the child's difficulty at school?
2. Does the 'label' immediately suggest a remedy?
3. What part does the school (curriculum, teaching styles, buildings etc.) play in the situation?
4. Is the 'need' mild, moderate or severe?
5. Is the 'need' likely to be short-lived or chronic?
6. Are there factors raised which require further investigation or training in order to answer the question fully (e.g. educational implications of a particular physical disability)?

When you have considered each pupil ask yourself whether you have used some 'labels' heavily or others not at all. If so, is this a true reflection of the population or is it a reflection of traditional patterns of thinking about special needs which may have more to do with existing provision and expertise than with the children?

Identification and diagnosis procedures

5.1 Introduction

Identification and diagnosis are components of the process which enables the school to make the right sort of special needs provision available to the right pupils. Identification is essentially a screening process through which pupils who have special educational needs are singled out from those of their peers who do not. Diagnosis is the process through which the nature of the needs of each identified child is explored. 'Identification' identifies the pupils, 'diagnosis' identifies the need.

5.2 Identification

a) The need for identification

In his introduction to 'TIPS' (the Teacher Information Pack), Dawson (1985) quotes teachers as saying 'We don't need to be shown which of our pupils have special needs. What we want help with is i) how to identify more precisely what those needs are and ii) how we, as class teachers, can meet those needs more efficiently.' The request for advice on diagnosis and provision stimulated the production of the TIPS material and is also reflected in much of the content of the books in the present series. However, are teachers right to be certain that they know which pupils have special needs?

It is certainly an understandable position, as many pupils with special needs do identify themselves by their behaviour or their difficulty with school work. However, there may be other pupils who deserve special attention but who do not make themselves known so easily. For example, an extremely able pupil may be sufficiently disenchanted with school that she does not demonstrate her high ability and goes unnoticed and unstimulated by appropriate teaching. A child with significant hearing problems may be sufficiently adept at lip reading that he can 'get by' in school. He might, nevertheless, be able to achieve a great deal more if his problem were recognised and steps were taken to reduce the need for him to devote a lot of his attention to overcoming his hearing loss. There may also be pupils who are using strategies to reduce their reading difficulties, or other specific learning difficulties, who are successful enough to avoid recognition as pupils with special needs but not successful enough to enable them to reach their potential.

There is, therefore, a need for a process of identification. Pupils do not always identify themselves.

b) The likelihood of errors

The end point of this identification process is a list of names of pupils thought to have special educational needs. If the process is completely effective the list will contain all the pupils who have special needs and none who do not. In practice, however, identification processes will make errors: some pupils with special needs will be overlooked and some who actually do not have special needs will be placed on the list. These two types of error will not necessarily be equally serious. Being identified when they do not have special needs may be a relatively unimportant error if the pupils are then involved in the subsequent stage of diagnosis and if this diagnostic investigation can reveal that no special provision is required. However, it can lead to serious problems if the diagnostic process is omitted and pupils are straight away placed in some distinct form of provision (e.g. a remedial set) from which they cannot easily 'escape', or if they suffer considerable loss of self-esteem as a result of insensitive treatment. The other sort of error in identification, that of pupils being overlooked when they do have real difficulties, can be relatively unimportant if there are later occasions when the pupils' needs are re-assessed. However, it can be serious if this does not happen and if pupils' needs thereafter go unsupported.

c) A diagnostic process for all?

Given that we cannot rely on children to identify themselves and that procedures designed to reveal the less obvious cases may still overlook some individuals, why not go through the diagnostic process with all children?

Some diagnostic information will arise from the normal record keeping procedures of the school, and opportunities should be taken to develop these procedures to improve the value of this information. However, if they are to produce findings which are sufficiently detailed to be useful in the more complex cases, diagnostic procedures are likely to be carried out by teachers and pupils working together on an individual basis, sometimes with formal or informal input from external professionals such as the educational psychologist or the school doctor. A full scale diagnosis will therefore be expensive, not least in terms of the time of pupils and teachers. Though it may provide vital clues to the best form of help for children with quite complex special needs, it may have little that is useful to offer to pupils who do not have any difficulties, so that for these pupils it is a waste of time. Diagnosis for all is therefore neither practicable nor desirable. An identification stage is needed so that diagnostic resources can be directed to where they will have greatest effect.

Unfortunately, the development of really precise identification procedures is itself time consuming, sophisticated procedures may take a considerable amount of teacher and pupil time to administer and to interpret and, anyway, totally error-free systems are probably impossible to achieve (at least in practical terms). Clearly, there has to be a compromise between the sophisticated and highly effective system and the simpler but more error-prone approach. It should be remembered that the diagnostic stage will provide an opportunity for teachers to pick out pupils who were identified in error but that pupils who are overlooked at the stage of identification are not put through the diagnostic process, which can therefore do nothing to compensate for this kind of identification error.

d) The need for repetition

A final point, in this general discussion of identification, is that the identification process should not be something which takes place on a single occasion. Repeated identification is important because it can minimise the effect of the error in the identification process and, more significantly, because changes in the demands of the curriculum, in teaching style, even (for pupils with physical handicaps or medical problems) changes in the timing of activities in the day can create problems for a pupil who had not previously been at risk. Also, as some special needs are short-lived, there may always be individuals who are beginning to experience a need for support for the first time even when there are not any obvious changes in what is being done by the school.

e) General recommendations

We therefore recommend that identification procedures should be fairly simple and should err on the side of over-inclusion so that there is less chance of pupils being overlooked. The process should be sensitive to the whole range of special needs and should not be exclusively concerned with the identification of, say, children with low general ability or poor reading. What is more, identification should either be a continuous process or it should be repeated at intervals so that changes in pupils' circumstances can be noted, and those who were originally overlooked can be picked up later.

5.3 Diagnosis

There is much that is appropriate in the use of the medical term 'diagnosis', and much to be lost by giving too little attention to this stage of the school's response to special needs pupils. However, the term 'diagnosis' does have the unfortunate connotation that the pupils' difficulties arise entirely out of problems within the pupils themselves. We would suggest that an important perspective on special needs, to which we have already drawn attention, is that special needs arise out of an interaction between pupils and their environment (see Chapter 1). Whilst continuing to use the term 'diagnosis' we would therefore want to make the point that both the pupils, and the environment – the general school environment and the precise nature of the lessons in which the pupil has difficulty – should be subject to investigation at the diagnostic stage.

The purpose of diagnosis is to reveal the nature of the problem which individual pupils are experiencing and bring to light any pupils who were included in the list of identified pupils in error. Diagnosis should not be restricted to the investigation of, say, reading problems but should be flexible enough to explore other learning difficulties, to explore the characteristics of a disruptive pupil (see *Classroom Responses to Disruptive Behaviour* in this series) and to explore the educational impact of a physical handicap or medical condition.

It is important that the information generated at the diagnostic stage is helpful in structuring provision. For example, the various sub-scores of the WISC IQ test, which is often administered to pupils with moderate to severe learning problems by educational psychologists, may be quite helpful in mapping some of the strengths and weaknesses in a pupil's cognitive functioning. However, if these results are not interpreted (either by or for the teacher) in ways that are related to that pupil's learning in science, modern languages and so on, then the information is not being put to best use. In designing the diagnostic stage of the special needs support system, those responsible should check that the information derived from the process is useful in guiding the mainstream and 'special needs' teachers who work with the pupils. Examples of procedures which fit this specification in the area of learning difficulties, can be found in *Classroom Responses to Learning Difficulties* in this series.

General recommendations

We recommend that diagnostic procedures should be designed on a two or more stage basis. The first stage should be quite straightforward so that any inappropriately identified pupils can readily be sorted out. The detailed information which is provided by the later stage(s) which are carried out with the pupils who do indeed have special needs must be relevant to the teachers who will have to make use of it, and should therefore be geared to the kinds of work which the pupils do in mainstream classes and in any special session which they might have with special needs staff. For this reason, and because diagnostic assessment should include assessment of the environment as well as the pupil, some part of the diagnostic process should involve observation of the pupil in the mainstream (and/or special) classroom. This might be the responsibility of the mainstream teacher, suitably briefed, or of a special needs teacher who might go into mainstream classes with a pupil to make the assessment. Where external professionals are involved in diagnosis someone on the school staff should have the responsibility of liaising with them to ensure that the *educational* implications of their advice are clear.

These two tasks of identification and diagnosis will now be discussed in greater detail.

5.4 Current identification procedures

In 1982/3, as part of the research programme in which we were engaged, we interviewed the headteachers of 31 of the 32 Oxfordshire secondary schools which dealt with pupils in the 11–16 or 11–18 age range. The purpose of the interview was to find out about the special needs support system in each school. This survey was followed up by a questionnaire in 1985 which enabled us to enquire about any changes in the approach of each school.

The 1982/3 survey revealed that in 77 per cent of the secondary schools teachers made use of primary school records as a means of identifying pupils with special needs. In just over half these schools they supplemented this information by making personal visits to the partner primary schools, and in one school they had arranged that primary teacher colleagues would fill in a detailed referral form on any pupil whom they felt might need support. There was little doubt that this information was highly valued by the secondary headteachers and one remarked specifically on its accuracy.

In 61 per cent of the schools teachers made use of a screening test which pupils took at the time of, or soon after, entry to the secondary school. A further 23 per cent had arranged with their colleagues in primary school that a screening test would be done before the pupils transferred to the secondary school. The timing of these tests was often regarded as problematic. There was a case for testing at primary school or in the very early days of the pupils' secondary career so that any support that was needed could be provided before the pupil began to experience difficulty in the new school. There was also a case for delaying the testing so that pupils would be spared the trauma of a test soon after arrival in their new school. Of the schools which did set a test after transfer, five used the Gapadol Test of Reading Comprehension, four the Daniels and Diack Test of Reading Experience, and others used verbal reasoning, non-verbal reasoning and numeracy tests from NFER. A third of the schools used a battery of tests.

Two headteachers specifically referred to the fact that the tests were useful sources of information but that they were not treated as infallible. One said that the staff could always override test results on the basis of their own judgement; the other said that the tests were useful in encouraging staff to take a second look at pupils with unexpected results.

In 19 per cent of the schools, parents were asked to contribute to the identification process.

In 62 per cent of the schools an important component of the identification process was the nomination of pupils by their secondary school teachers. One headteacher commented that this was crucial: as the system of provision gave a good deal of responsibility to the mainstream class teacher, that teacher *must* have the last word in referring a pupil to the special needs department. It also seemed to the interviewer that this reference to staff opinion was the main way in which any repeated identification took place. There did not appear to be repeated testing sessions for the purpose of updating (and possibly correcting) identification information.

In the follow-up survey, of the 20 schools responding, 12 reported no change in their process and 8 reported increased emphasis on one or more of these techniques. Only three of these eight schools reported any decrease in emphasis (two placed less emphasis on tests, one on secondary teachers' judgements) so one must assume that there was an overall increase in the effort expended on identification in at least five schools.

The overall picture was, therefore, that in recent years most schools were making use of different kinds of information which included information from primary schools, from screening tests of general ability, literacy and numeracy, and from the opinions of the subject teachers in the secondary school.

5.5 Developing an identification system

The survey which is summarised above indicated that it was not unusual for schools to combine test results and teachers' judgements to make up a special needs identification system. Such a combination could be a good starting point for a system that fits with the recommendations in Section 5.1, though hopefully schools would also take account of parents' views and of nominations made by other professionals (for example doctors, speech therapists and the like). The test-based element in such a system could provide sensitivity to pupils' difficulties which have not yet made an impact on teachers. The use of the views of parents and of other professionals, and especially the inclusion of a teacher-based element, could ensure that the system was sufficiently wide ranging and that there was an element of continuous monitoring built in. However, to make such a system as effective as it might be, some development work will be needed.

The problem of including parents' views in the process of identification is largely an organisational one. The school needs to let them know how it tries to identify and provide for pupils with special needs, and to tell them that, if they suspect that their child might have special needs, their comments would be welcomed, and to ensure that they know to whom to make their comments. The same sorts of points apply to the involvement, in the identification process, of professionals who are not school-based. (More will be said about the involvement of these groups in diagnosis in a later section.) However the matter of the use of tests and of teachers' judgements in identification calls for some quite basic development work within the school, and some suggestions for this are made below.

a) Tests

Where tests are used as part of an identification process, care must obviously be taken in their selection and interpretation. In selecting tests there has to be compromise between comprehensive testing and testing that is realistic in terms of the time and costs involved. A reasonable compromise giving good coverage of a range of cognitive abilities might be achieved by the use of a test of reading, a test of mathematics and a test of non-verbal reasoning.

Maths and non-verbal reasoning tests

The NFER tests that were often used in the schools we surveyed could certainly cover the maths and non-verbal areas of a screening programme for pupils at the time of transfer to secondary school. The NFER maths tests (for example *Basic Mathematics Test DE*) cover a range of mathematical abilities which will not only be challenged by secondary school maths teaching, but also by work in other curriculum areas. Pupils with low scores on such tests are therefore likely to have learning difficulties in secondary school that go well beyond any difficulties which they might have in mathematics classes. Some of the NFER maths tests can reveal diagnostic detail as well as serving as a screening tool.

Non-verbal reasoning tests (for example *Non-verbal Test DH*) test such things as how well pupils can reason with geometric shapes when words and written instructions have been deliberately excluded. This kind of test can be useful diagnostically, especially in revealing whether a pupil with reading difficulties (or with English as a second language) has general learning difficulties or whether other aspects of his or her thinking are more highly developed. As a screening tool they might reveal areas of potential difficulty for a pupil who gets by in reading and maths tests because of particularly good teaching or support with these basic skills from home.

These NFER maths and non-verbal tests each take under an hour to administer, and can be given to groups of pupils. A range of similar tests is available in each area. Each one is designed for a specific age range and tends to have slightly different emphasis in terms of content. Inspection of the catalogues of NFER or other test publishers should enable a school to select the non-verbal and maths tests which best suit its needs.

Reading tests

Both of the reading tests that we found to be in common use (the Gapadol and the Daniels and Diack *Standard Reading Tests*) are discussed by Vincent and colleagues (1983) in their critical review of reading tests. Gapadol is described as a 'quick general guide to reading ability' but the reviewers point out that it ignores the variety and specialisation of written material in secondary education. The *Standard Reading Tests* series is described as 'a useful approach for screening pupils entering the secondary stage' but its theoretical basis is criticised and its typography is described as 'among the least satisfactory of such tests'. In testing pupils' reading ability, it would therefore seem that some reassessment of appropriate instruments might be called for.

The *London Reading Test* (published by NFER) is designed specifically as a screening tool for use at the stage of secondary transfer. It aims to test pupils' ability to comprehend material of a kind that is used in secondary teaching, it uses cloze procedure as well as questions designed to test higher order comprehension skills that are often required of pupils in secondary teaching situations, it is particularly discriminating at the lower end of the ability range and it uses material that pays attention to the multicultural context of schools. Another interesting test series is the *Effective Reading Tests* written by Vincent and de la Mare (published in 1986, by Macmillan). This series asks questions based on specially written texts. Relatively quick 'Progress Tests' are designed for screening purposes. These are in an objective and multiple choice format and are easy to administer and mark. There are also related 'Skills Tests' which provide diagnostic information covering reading skills such as skimming and scanning, critical awareness of content and use of indexes. The 'London Reading Test' and the 'Effective Reading Tests' would seem to be well worth considering as alternatives to the older tests which still seem to be in use.

The interpretation of the test results requires some decisions to be taken. One must, for example, choose the cut-off scores below which pupils are considered to be in need of diagnostic investigation. Test manuals may give useful advice on this and initial decisions can be monitored and modified in the light of experience. Decisions have also to be taken about what to do if there is disagreement between the tests, or between teachers and tests, as to whether or not a child has difficulties. In the light of our recommendation that identification procedures should err on the side of over-inclusiveness we would suggest that a child who is regarded as in difficulty by any one test or by his or her teachers should be investigated. If this approach leads to the identification of too many pupils who later prove not to have special needs, it might be modified by saying that any two indications of difficulty would serve to identify the pupil as one who needs diagnostic assessment or that, where teachers and tests disagree teachers would carefully review their decision before making a final judgement about the need for assessment. Certainly there is no logic in saying, for example, that 'teachers automatically overrule tests'. In such a regime the tests are serving no purpose and the time devoted to them is being wasted.

As elsewhere in the special needs field there are few hard and fast rules about interpretation that can be provided and that will apply equally well in all situations. What is needed is a serious enquiring approach in which decisions are monitored and reconsidered in the light of experience.

b) Teachers

Teacher opinion is an important complement to the test-based screening that has been described above. As a headteacher in our survey pointed out, a mainstream teacher is, at least in part, responsible for helping pupils with special needs so that teacher must be able to refer pupils for diagnostic assessment when s/he is worried about their learning or behaviour. It would be ridiculous if this referral could only take place if the pupils happened to score below some cut-off point on one or more of the tests. Furthermore, a teacher will be well placed to identify emotional and behavioural difficulties and may be the first to notice the effects of some physical handicap or medical condition. These aspects of special needs are not directly screened by the sort of test battery outlined in the previous section. Teacher-based identification is also important as it can be a regular process. It can therefore complement the use of a test battery which might be feasible only at transfer and at perhaps one later stage in the pupils' secondary school career.

If a school seeks to develop this sort of role in the identification process for its teachers, it should be certain to provide opportunities for all staff to discuss the nature and purpose of their proposed role and to understand how it fits into the system of identification, diagnosis and (especially) provision. There should be opportunities to consider the importance of regular or continuous monitoring, and to clarify the range of difficulties which the teachers are being expected to identify. Finally, teachers should be clear that identification *will* be followed by a more detailed investigation of the pupils' difficulty before decisions are taken about provision, and that therefore the identification stage itself need not be highly sophisticated. All that is necessary at the identification stage is that teachers indicate that they are concerned about a pupil to the extent that they feel that a diagnostic investigation might be useful.

These points apply equally to primary school staff if they are involved in identifying pupils who may have special needs at the point of transfer. If it is intended to involve primary teachers in the identification process for new entrants to the secondary school then the staff of that secondary school might do well to involve their primary colleagues in discussions of this kind.

Although teacher-based identification need not be sophisticated, the gradual improvement of teachers' abilities to identify appropriate pupils is a worthwhile aim if pupils with special needs can then be identified earlier, thus being saved from the experience of repeated failure which might be a consequence of later identification. Also, the number of pupils who are put up for diagnostic assessment but who then prove not to have any significant difficulties will be reduced, with consequent savings of time and resources. One way in which teachers' abilities can be improved is to help each teacher to understand what it is that he or she tends to notice about the pupils s/he teaches, and thus to look for gaps that might be filled by more structured observation of pupils in class or more structured assessment of their written work. One way in which this increased awareness can be obtained is outlined in Activity 5.5b.

This exercise can be done by any individual teacher working alone, but is better done by a pair, one of whom acts as interviewer to encourage the other to describe the pupil characteristics in ways that are clear to others. Questions like 'What do you mean by "writes badly", do you mean it's a matter of handwriting or that sentence structure or prose structure is weak?' can do much to clarify thinking and to make the resulting list of dimensions more valuable to colleagues at the stage of comparing individual teachers' results.

In work on the identification of more able pupils in Year Three, one of the present authors used this sort of technique and discovered that physics teachers tended to produce lists that contained a high proportion of attitudinal, motivational and behavioural characteristics, whereas English teachers tended to produce lists with a higher proportion of characteristics that were related to specific abilities in English (Denton & Postlethwaite, 1985; Postlethwaite, 1984). The value of this finding is clear from the fact that English teachers were also more accurate than physics teachers in identifying pupils with high ability in their subject, and that physics teachers' abilities to do this task improved when they were encouraged to look for specific scientific abilities amongst their pupils. (This 'encouragement' consisted of asking them to complete, for each pupil, a checklist of science behaviours that

Activity 5.5b
What do you notice about pupils?

1. List the names of all the pupils in one or two classes that you teach in a particular age range.
2. By randomly selecting three pupils at a time from this list make up fifteen to twenty groups of three.
3. Take the first group of three pupils.
   Ask yourself to divide the group into a pair who are in some way alike and yet different from the other pupil.
4. Write down what it is about the pair that makes them alike.
5. Write down the contrasting characteristic of the single pupil.

   For example:
   The randomly chosen group of three is John, Sarah and Susan.
   Your view is that John and Susan are alike and different from Sarah.
   This distinction is based on your perception that John and Susan are lazy whereas Sarah is hardworking.

6. Check that this dimension (e.g. 'Lazy – Hardworking') can be applied to the other pupils in your class. That is, can you place most of the rest of the group somewhere on a scale from lazy to hardworking?

   If not, this dimension is something that you have noticed about these three pupils but which is rather idiosyncratic to these individuals and may not play an important part in your general thinking about pupils. If so, this is something that you tend to notice about the whole group of pupils in your class.

7. Go back to **3** and repeat the process with the other groups of three pupils until you can no longer find new ways of characterising the differences.

8. List all of the dimensions which you were able to apply to most of the pupils in your class. These are the things that you notice about pupils and within this range of things will be the pupil characteristics on which you are likely to be basing your judgements, e.g. about their likeability, their attitudes to school and whether or not they have special needs.

   Not all the dimensions you have listed will necessarily be involved in all the decisions you will make, but if 'Good orally – Bad orally' is *not* one of the dimensions you have listed then it is unlikely that you are responding to differences between pupils on this dimension however much you may, in theory, feel that it is an important characteristic of pupils.

9. List the dimensions which emerged which seemed to apply to only a small number of pupils in your list.

   These are pupil characteristics which you notice about some individuals and which could be influencing your judgement of some pupils.

10. Compare your lists with those of colleagues to see if there are general areas of which you are all aware or areas which most of you overlook.

This procedure is based on Personal Construct methodology. For more details see Fransella and Bannister (1977).

might be expected to be indicative of high ability in the subject.) Therefore, the technique described above provided information that was useful in explaining the limited accuracy of physics teachers' judgements and in indicating ways of making improvements.

In the present context we can expect such an exercise to alert teachers to the nature, and possible shortcomings, of their personal approach to identifying pupils who may have special needs of any kind, and to reveal for a school any common problems where joint in-service work might be helpful.

5.6 Current diagnostic procedures

In the survey of practice in Oxfordshire which has been referred to above, we found that 97 per cent of the schools recognised the importance of a diagnostic stage in the special needs identification and provision process. However, ten per cent of the schools regarded this as appropriate only in cases of severe or complex need and therefore regarded diagnosis as the exclusive domain of the educational psychologist.

In 13 per cent of the schools diagnosis was based on inspection of pupils' work in class, reports from teachers and, when these approaches gave no useful information, a psychologist's report.

However, in most schools diagnostic tests were used, with the educational psychologist as the 'back stop' if these gave no clues, or if the clues were contradictory. The range of tests which were in use was considerable, though most of them dealt with aspects of literacy. The Aston Index, the Neale Analysis of Reading Ability and the Schonell test were frequently mentioned but other tests were in use in individual schools. In seven schools (23 per cent) this test-based diagnostic information was supplemented by discussion with the usual teachers of each pupil being assessed.

5.7 Developing a system of diagnosis

As indicated above, schools (at least in one LEA) tended to base diagnosis on teachers' judgements, on test results and on the comments of educational psychologists. These are clearly important sources of data. If the child's needs are sufficiently severe as to call for a multi-professional assessment (an MPA) under the Education Act 1981, the views of medical practitioners, and on occasion those of other professionals such as social services staff, were also sought. However, one might expect there to be informal contact with these groups in less severe cases, just as there were some informal contacts with educational psychologists even in cases where an MPA was not in question. One might also involve parents in the diagnostic process both because they may have valuable insights into their child's difficulty and because their involvement should strengthen the concept of partnership between the home and the school without which support from the school can run into difficulty.

In this section we will therefore discuss aspects of diagnosis based on teachers' opinions, on test results, on parents' views and on the views of professionals outside school. In relation to this last category we will concentrate on the informal stages of assessment rather than the formal stages involved in a multi-professional assessment.

a) Teachers

Context-related assessments

It would seem that the unique contribution that each teacher can make to the diagnostic procedure is that s/he can assess the pupil's difficulties *in relation to his or her own teaching* – which is, of course, an extremely important context for at least one part of the pupil's learning. There are, perhaps, two important elements in this context-related assessment. First, the teacher can assess the pupil against the demands made by the content of the subject on which they work together. A science teacher, for example, can assess the pupil's strengths and difficulties in practical work, in using mathematical processes, in following detailed instructions, in learning and applying science concepts: all of which might give important clues to any general learning problem which the pupil might have, all of which will be areas in which the pupil may need support if s/he is to be successful in science, and some of which will be insights which are available only to the science teacher. Secondly, the teacher can assess the pupil's strengths and weaknesses in relation to the different teaching styles used by the teacher, the different learning activities required of the pupil and the different kinds of material to which the pupil is exposed.

Learning difficulties – the use of checklists and subject-specific profiles

If the teachers are clear that these are the kinds of assessment that they are expected to make, then their ability to do the job could be improved by use of a checklist to systematise the recording of information about pupils' responses to different teaching and learning styles, and to different materials. It could also be extremely valuable to develop criterion referenced, subject-specific profiles to help teachers to record their observations of what a pupil can and cannot do in their subject. To serve as diagnostic information such profiles would need to be interpreted in terms of a list of things which a pupil of that age needs to be able to do to cope with mainstream lessons in that subject. Ainscow and Tweddle (1979) discuss the general principle of criterion-referenced diagnosis at some length. Subject-specific guidelines in science and mathematics, as well as discussion of general principles and of the assessment of reading, can be found in the series *Guides to Assessment in Education*, edited by Wrigley.

Although no-one should underestimate the *time* that might be needed for the development of highly sophisticated versions of a subject-specific profile, the *expertise* needed to undertake such development is very much that of the subject teacher. Such teachers are therefore well placed to make a start on the production of criterion referenced assessment instruments, which can then be refined through use.

Detailed subject-specific, criterion referenced, diagnostic assessment can be based largely on observations of pupils in class and on the assessment of their normal written work. When called for in the case of a small number of pupils, it need not necessarily impose an enormous extra load on teachers. It is worth remembering, however, that although the costs in terms of teachers' time are not vast, they will exist. In particular, teachers may find that they need to spend a little time with the pupils on an individual basis to clarify some points about which they cannot be certain on the basis of routine observation. Some evidence on this point in relation to the assessment of able pupils has been provided by Postlethwaite and Denton (1985).

One further point about this style of diagnostic assessment is that, perhaps in a somewhat less detailed form, it is relevant to the question of record keeping for all pupils. It could provide teachers with far better assessment of all pupils than the more usual 'marks out of ten' approach which often provides nothing more than an indication of one pupil's overall performance in relation to that of his or her classmates. Certainly two pupils with 'six out of ten' could have had very different difficulties with the work concerned – differences which would be revealed by assessment of the kind we have been discussing. If a school is using a criterion referenced profile as part of its normal assessment routine, then the somewhat greater detail of the diagnostic assessment of special needs pupils would certainly not impose undue demands on teachers' time. This is an important consequence, but saved time is not the only advantage of this suggested match between routine and special needs assessment. The similarity would serve to emphasise that special needs pupils are indeed on a continuum with other pupils, that good practice for them is likely to be good practice for all, and that responsibility for them should not be shifted entirely on to the shoulders of a small number of special needs staff.

These comments apply to the assessment of all aspects of special need. The kind of teacher-based assessment outlined above would help to show up the educational implications of a medical condition and to reveal any learning difficulties that might be associated with behaviour problems, as well as providing details about any learning difficulty that was not apparently associated with problems of these kinds.

Behaviour problems

In considering teacher-based assessment of a pupil who was identified in the first instance as having behavioural problems some further points do apply. For example, it might be particularly important for teachers to note the kinds of teaching and learning situations in which undesirable behaviour occurred in their lessons. It might also be important to try to assess whether the pupil has poor social skills with adults and/or a poor academic self image. In the part of our research programme that was concerned with disruptive behaviour in classrooms, Gray found that these two characteristics were associated with disruptiveness and that pupils who had both characteristics tended to be very disruptive. These characteristics are therefore relevant to an understanding of disruption and of considerable importance as the implications for intervention of one or other problem could be rather different.

Initial assessment of pupils in these terms need not be complex, for Gray also found that pupils whom teachers regarded as 'malicious' or 'rude' were pupils who often had poor social skills with adults, whereas pupils whom teachers regarded as 'lazy' or as having 'short attention span' tended to have poor academic self-image (Gray, et al., in press). Re-interpretations of subjective assessments such as 'rudeness', could therefore be a way of making a simple assessment of the characteristics of a pupil. However, if one wanted to go further, there are more objective instruments that could be used to measure pupils' social skills functioning and their academic self-image. These instruments, and details of the technique of sociometry which might also be valuable in some cases, can be found in handbooks of educational research such as that compiled by Cohen (1976). The relationship between the characteristics of disruptive pupils that are mapped by these assessments and the response which can be made to the pupils in school is discussed at length in the book on disruptive behaviour in this present series.

Finally, it should be remembered that once some specialist support is in place for a pupil, the work that the pupil does with the special needs teacher, be it in ordinary lessons or in withdrawal situations, will give further clues to the nature of his or her problem. Thus diagnosis can continue after a start has been made on provision.

b) Tests

Much of the test-based diagnosis that was reported to us in our survey of schools in Oxfordshire was concerned with diagnostic testing in the area of literacy, and especially of reading skills. This is clearly a necessary area for exploration because difficulties in literacy can be the source of difficulties in all subject areas. One might, however, also hope that diagnosis of pupils' difficulties with numeracy and more general aspects of mathematics would be undertaken because of the possible influence of these skills on pupils' understanding of a wide range of subject content.

Before deciding upon the use of diagnostic tests of literacy and numeracy, teachers should note that diagnostic information can be obtained from some of the literacy and numeracy tests which are primarily used for identification purposes. A close look at the answer sheets of identified pupils (e.g. at sub-scores for different parts of the test) can yield information that reduces the need for further testing.

It should also be remembered that there are some subject-specific diagnostic tests (for example *Science Skills* published by Macmillan) and tests which can diagnose weaknesses in pupils' ways of working (for example the *Survey of Study Habits and Attitudes* published by NFER). Diagnostic testing need not, therefore, be limited to the areas of literacy and numeracy.

Perhaps the most important advice relating to the selection of diagnostic tests is that teachers should decide what is missing from other aspects of the diagnostic process and where they might need confirmation of information from other sources. They should then consult recent catalogues from the test publishers because many fairly new tests are intended for diagnostic use. Selection of diagnostic tests is also perhaps an area in which general advice from an educational psychologist might be very helpful.

c) External professionals

In our survey it was clear that schools made considerable use of educational psychologists (EPs) in diagnosing the difficulties faced by some special needs pupils. This often involved asking the EP to assess a pupil with severe or complex difficulties or to assess a pupil about whom the school's diagnostic process had produced little useful information. These will always be important aspects of an EP's work, but we feel that psychologists could also be asked to give general advice about the identification, diagnosis and support of pupils with special needs. This might be done through general INSET activities so that teachers' own procedures can become more effective. This use of EPs would be in line with advice given by Mittler (1985) who argued that psychologists should 'demystify what they do and "give psychology away" in a systematic and orderly fashion'.

Where a physical or sensory handicap, or chronic medical difficulties are involved in a pupil's problems, the school might ask for diagnostic advice from the school doctor. This would not be diagnosis in the normal medical sense, but a detailed assessment of the educational implications of the pupil's condition. Schools could help to make such an enquiry more profitable by providing the doctor with information about the contexts in which the pupil is expected to work in school. Thus one might remind the doctor that the pupil may be involved in the use of tape recorders and computers, in laboratory work, that both boys and girls will use workshop and domestic science equipment and that pupils will be involved in a number of sporting activities and educational field trips and excursions. Indeed, whatever the school usually organises for pupils of the appropriate age might be listed. A request for information about any of these situations in which the pupil's health problem may have significant repercussions might then generate specific and useful guidelines.

d) Parents

Parents may be able to provide crucial information about the problems which their child is experiencing at school. They may know that there are particular activities or kinds of work which are especially troublesome for the child, or special times of day when his or her difficulties have greatest impact. They may wish to tell the school about home circumstances which are relevant to the problem, or about aspects of the child's previous educational history which might help to explain present difficulties. It therefore seems wise to invite parents to contribute to any diagnostic process. This also prepares the ground, in what should be an informal and co-operative way, for their formal involvement in the assessment and statementing procedures of the Education Act 1981, should it prove necessary to go this far in order to meet the needs of their child.

Of course, what is true of parents is to a considerable extent true of the child too. At some stage in the diagnostic process (and in some sense at all stages throughout that process) the child should be encouraged to talk generally about the difficulties which s/he is experiencing.

5.8 Organising the system of identification and diagnosis

The most obvious organisational need is for someone to act as the co-ordinator of the identification and diagnosis process both at the stage of planning and developing the system in association with colleagues, and at the stage of running the system on a day to day basis. We suggest that this co-ordinator will often be the school's head of special needs, who, as in other aspects of his or her work, may need to be supported by an advisory group made up of a small number of staff representing both the senior management and classroom teachers.

Details of the work of this co-ordinating team will inevitably be very specific to individual schools. In this final section all that we will try to do is to raise some general questions which might be asked in order to ensure that a well organised and well co-ordinated system is put in place.

a) Decisions on details

Decisions will clearly have to be made by the co-ordinator and the advisory group about all kinds of detail, such as:

- Who will administer and mark tests? (the co-ordinator? special needs staff? form teachers?)

- When will screening tests be done, and when will teachers be asked to identify pupils?
- How can teachers refer pupils for assessment at other times?
- How will parents and external professionals be invited to identify a pupil as someone who might have special needs?
- How will written records from previous schools, or from external professionals be used to identify pupils with possible difficulties?
- Who will initiate the diagnostic process for those pupils who are identified as possibly having special needs?
- Who will be asked to contribute to the first stages of a diagnostic assessment? (just the teachers who referred the pupil?, these teachers and the parents?, this group plus teachers of English and maths?)
- In what circumstances will the decision be made to ask all teachers of a pupil to make a diagnostic assessment and to ask the pupil to do some diagnostic tests?
- Who will decide to draw in external professionals in any given case?
- Who will contact parents for diagnostic information?

b) Broader issues

The co-ordinator should also give attention to broader issues such as:

- How to ensure that the identification and diagnosis system is always closely linked to the system of special needs provision in the school, (a widely based identification system of the kind we have been discussing will be of no use if the only support available to pupils is, say, remedial reading).
- How to bring into line the normal assessment procedures used by the school and the special needs procedures that we have been discussing, so that there is a minimum of wasted effort, (for example, the teacher-based identification system might be as simple as the inclusion in any regular pupil reviews (half-termly reviews, internal reports, internal copies of reports for parents etc.) of a question such as 'Do you think this child has learning difficulties, behavioural problems or other characteristics which suggest that a more detailed special needs asessment might be useful?')
- How to provide feedback for teachers, parents and external professionals on the outcomes of an enquiry about a pupil (which, certainly for teachers, could lead to improvements in their ability to identify pupils and diagnose problems and for everyone could lead to increased confidence in the value of the system from the pupils' points of view).
- How to keep the identification and diagnosis system under review so that it continues to be sensitive to special needs of any kind, at whatever stage of the school year they should first arise.
- Who should have access to the information which is generated? (special needs staff, form teacher, subject teachers, parents, pupil?)

Even from these lists of examples it is clear that co-ordinating the system of identification and diagnosis is by no means a straightforward task. It calls for expertise and for the skills of management. The system itself calls for some active involvement from everyone in school and from people who are outside it – even though the extent of this involvement may sometimes be quite limited. Nevertheless, pupils can only be helped to achieve their best if those

who have difficulties are known and if their difficulties are sufficiently understood that appropriate intervention can be made by their class teachers and by specialist staff. The energy invested in a good identification and diagnosis system could therefore be repaid by increased standards of achievement by pupils who might otherwise get little out of their time in school.

Provision for pupils with special needs in mainstream schools

6

The focus of this chapter is on the ways in which mainstream schools can organise their responses to pupils who have special educational needs. The chapter is therefore complementary to the other two books in this series which discuss some of the practical techniques through which teachers may be able to help pupils who have learning problems, or behavioural difficulties in their own classrooms.

6.1 What is being done?

a) Reflecting on experience

In Chapter 4 we introduced the idea of a range of special needs which could be understood in terms of three largely independent dimensions – the nature of the pupil's difficulty; its severity; the temporary or long-term nature of the difficulty. It can be quite enlightening to look at the provision made by a school (a school you know well, the school to which you are attached for teaching practice, or the school in which you work) in the light of this model of special needs. Activity 6.1a on page 56 is designed to help you to do this.

We will return to the issues raised by this activity at various points in this chapter, but it might be useful at this stage to compare your notes on your school with some results from the survey of Oxfordshire secondary schools that we conducted in 1982/3. The results from this survey are discussed below.

b) Work of special needs departments

Thirty-one of the thirty-two Oxfordshire schools covering the 11–18 or 11–16 age range were involved in our survey. Not surprisingly, special needs departments in all 31 schools were described as being responsible for the special provision required by pupils with learning difficulties. In 14 schools the range of learning difficulty with which departments had to deal was extensive: some pupils had fairly minor problems, others were pupils who, in the past, would have been classified as ESN(M) and might well have been placed in a special school by some LEAs.

In 21 schools, pupils with behavioural problems were regarded as the responsibility of the special needs department, though sometimes only in a limited way. For example, some schools regarded pupils with long-term

56

A

Activity 6.1a
Provision for pupils with special needs

Fill in each cell of the table to show the ways in which your school generally responds to each type of need, e.g. what is the response to a severe, long-term behaviour problem, or the response to a mild short-term physical disability?

Type of difficulty	Long-term difficulties		Temporary difficulties	
	Mild	Severe	Mild	Severe
LEARNING				
BEHAVIOUR				
PHYSICAL/ MEDICAL				

Some points to consider

1. If there are cells which you were not able to complete, is this because you did not know what the school's system was?
   (Might it also be the case that other staff do not know the system?)

2. Is it because these are areas for which no agreed form of support exists in your school?
   (What could be done to fill the gaps?)

3. What do you think of these approaches? Are there alternative forms of support which might better serve the needs of pupils in each cell?

4. Is there one support strategy that could be expected to serve all special needs pupils properly?

behaviour problems as clients of the special needs department but did not expect that department to respond to 'emergency referrals'; some schools limited the responsibility of the special needs department to the provision of diagnostic information or advice to mainstream staff; some schools regarded the pupil with behaviour problems as the responsibility of the special needs department only if that pupil also had learning difficulties. Although ten schools did not regard behaviour problems as part of the work of the special needs department, most of them did make explicit reference to other support systems for these pupils. These usually involved the pastoral system of the school. In two cases there was also a separate unit for children with severe behavioural problems.

In ten schools, pupils with physical handicaps or chronic medical conditions were the responsibility of the special needs department. In the remaining schools, the headteacher's perception was often that very few pupils with this kind of difficulty attended the school, though three heads said that there was a separate system of support for such pupils based either on the services of a school nurse or on the pastoral system of the school.

In nine schools the special needs department had some role in relation to a wide spectrum of special needs including learning and behaviour difficulties, and physical/medical conditions of varying severity. Therefore, it would seem that, in these schools, some response was being made to pupils from many of the cells of the model of special needs that we have been discussing. In other schools, however, there was (in 1982/3) considerable emphasis on pupils with learning difficulties, to the exclusion of those who had other types of special need. In those schools a change in name, from remedial to special needs department, seemed not to be accompanied by a significant change in philosophy.

Of the twenty schools that replied to a follow-up survey in 1985, eight reported no change in the kinds of pupil that they tried to support through their special needs departments. Only one of these schools had responded to the full range of special needs in 1982/3 so, in seven schools, a rather narrow approach to special needs seems to have persisted, at least until 1985. However, the other twelve schools who replied to the survey revealed an increased tendency to include behavioural difficulties and/or physical handicaps in the brief of their special needs departments. Their approach seemed, therefore, to have moved at least some way towards the model which we have outlined. Schools also reported an increase in the severity of learning difficulty with which they had to deal. Perhaps there is some evidence here of increasing integration of pupils with learning difficulties into mainstream schools, or of a tendency to defer decisions to refer them out to special education.

c) How is provision organised?

In the Oxfordshire survey, we found that provision for pupils with special needs was made in a variety of ways. In one approach pupils were taught in mainstream classes for some lessons but, at other times, were withdrawn for individual or small group work with a special needs teacher. In another method pupils with special needs were supported in mainstream classes by arranging for a special needs teacher or non-teaching classroom assistant to accompany the pupil into the class to work alongside the pupil and the mainstream teacher. Another approach was to make indirect provision by giving advice to the mainstream teacher on the selection and design of materials, on teaching styles and on broader curriculum issues. In some schools, provision for pupils with learning difficulties (but not for pupils with behavioural or physical/medical problems) was also made by placing the pupils in small remedial sets or special classes.

In some schools only one of these strategies was used. However, in many schools several, or all of these strategies were used in support of pupils. For example fourteen schools used a three-tier system consisting of advice to the mainstream teacher, in-class support for some pupils and withdrawal of some pupils from mainstream classes.

The twenty schools who responded to the follow-up survey in 1985 provided useful information on the ways in which their system of provision for pupils with learning difficulties had changed in the intervening years. (In this follow-up, changes in their provision for pupils with behavioural or physical/medical problems were not explored.) Seven schools reported 'no change'. Eight reported less emphasis on the use of 'separate special classes or small remedial groups where some pupils receive most of their academic education'. Only one stated that there was increased emphasis on this style of provision. Five schools said that they were now placing less emphasis on 'long-term withdrawal for a part of the academic curriculum', though two were placing more emphasis on this approach. Five schools were making more use of 'short-term withdrawal for all or part of the academic curriculum', though one school was placing less emphasis on this approach. Eleven schools reported greater use of in-class support from a special needs teacher or classroom assistant, and nine mentioned increased use of the strategy of advice to mainstream teachers. No school reported decreased emphasis on in-class support or advice. Therefore, there would seem to be a general tendency to make greater use of these approaches and to reduce the extent to which pupils with learning difficulties were segregated into separate provision for most of their time each week, or for a long period of time.

This same range of provision has been described in other research such as that by Clunies-Ross and Wimshurst (1983) and by Kerry (1978). Kerry, for example, tabulates the extent to which the comprehensive schools in his sample made use of special classes and individual or small group withdrawal in support of pupils with learning difficulties, and comments in this text that 'one can also trace a trend for a specialist teacher to work with slow learners within the mixed ability class and alongside the class teacher'. Hyde (1984) also maps a similar range of provision with special classes and withdrawal being common forms of support, and in-class provision being used in four of his thirty-six schools. However, Hyde also comments that 'many respondents expressed surprise and shock at the idea of a remedial teacher being involved in the lesson of another teacher'.

6.2 Developing a system of provision

In discussing the development of a system of provision, the strategies which we have described above would seem to be the key things to consider. Clearly, these strategies are in use, and can therefore be regarded as sufficiently practicable to be worthy of discussion and development. However, they are not universally used and opinions about them differ. Things are not, therefore, so clear-cut that discussion is unnecessary.

We will therefore begin this section with some discussion of these individual strategies. We will then move on to the question of the development of a coherent system of provision and of the management of that system.

a) Advice to the mainstream teacher

In Chapter 1 we discussed the size of the special needs group, the fact that special needs can arise in any teaching group – be it a top or bottom set, a mixed ability class or a sixth form group – the temporary nature of some special needs and the concept of special needs being part of a continuum of learning ability with no objectively determined dividing lines to separate pupils with special needs from others without such needs. All these points imply that mainstream teachers will inevitably work with pupils who have special needs in many, if not all, of the classes they teach. They will be involved in the provision of support for almost all the pupils who have special needs; they will be the only source of support in some cases. Since this is inevitable, we would argue that it must be recognised by the system which the school establishes to support pupils with special needs. One way in which this recognition can be given is by making advice on special needs available to all teachers.

Pre-service courses

This advice should certainly begin at the stage of pre-service teacher training. The topic of special needs should be on the curriculum for all students following pre-service courses. This point is made in Circular 3/84 (DES/WO, 1984c) and in the report of the Advisory Committee on the Supply and Training of Teachers (ACSET, 1984), both of which provide some interesting guidelines on the nature of the required training. Our own view is that pre-service special needs training for all teachers should raise their awareness of general issues and help them to develop relevant, practical classroom skills. Certainly our experience of monitoring the opinions of PGCE students over three years in Oxford would suggest that students are not satisfied with an input which concentrates mainly on questions of awareness. We feel (like ACSET) that all teacher training staff have a role in this process, that it should not be the sole responsibility of special needs 'experts', that it should feature in all aspects of students' school experience during their training, that it should permeate many sessions on the course and not be a topic which is covered in a small number of special needs lectures or seminars. Indeed, one purpose of this series of books is to provide resources that might be useful in such a training context.

In-service training

We also feel that similar elements should be apparent in in-service courses of all kinds, not just those organised by special needs advisers. We have some recent experience of this taking place, for example through input on special needs to 4/84 and 3/85 in-service courses for heads of science departments and through liaison between subject-based INSET planning groups and a special needs INSET planning group in one LEA.

Continuous advice

As the two previous sections have indicated, in the area of advice to mainstream teachers, individual schools are not left entirely to their own devices. Nevertheless, mainstream teachers do need a system of 'consultant advice' within their individual school which should be organised as part of the special needs support system. This can be more situation-specific than advice

given in pre-service and in-service training. It can be more closely related to the circumstances of an individual pupil. Because it can take account of the detailed arrangements in the school for other sorts of special needs support, it can be more effective in helping a mainstream teacher to know how and when to seek more direct help for a pupil from these other forms of support. It can also be more continuous, so that effective suggestions can be further developed and ineffective suggestions can be followed up with advice on alternative approaches.

Several forms of advice should be available. In connection with learning difficulties, mainstream teachers may need practical, but generalised, 'tips' on how to help pupils over a given problem (such as spelling). It may also be possible to give more far-reaching advice on teaching methods which in effect extends the range of techniques available to the mainstream teacher and may therefore help in situations where it is general aspects of the classroom circumstances (rather than just a problem internal to the pupil) which generate the special need. Such advice could come from special needs staff, but heads of subject departments may also have an important contribution to make – especially if special needs topics have been included in INSET courses which they have attended. Another important form of advice is more specific to an individual pupil with learning difficulties. The mainstream teacher may find it of great value to be told of the details of that pupil's difficulties: for example, to be taken through the results of any diagnostic assessment of the pupil. This is clearly an area where special needs staff are likely to be the main agents in giving advice. The educational implications of physical and medical conditions is a further area in which advice is required. Special needs staff might again be particularly well-placed to give advice of this kind as they will not only have knowledge of the general condition (or have easy access to those with expert knowledge in the LEA) but they should also have specific information about the individual pupil. Finally, advice should be given on when and how to refer a pupil to the special needs staff, or to other agencies if the pupil's difficulties are sufficiently complex that they cannot be dealt with by the mainstream teacher alone. This is essential if the mainstream teacher is not to feel isolated in his or her work with pupils who have special needs, and if the needs of pupils with more complex difficulties are to be fully met.

It is worth noting that mainstream staff may need advice both in their roles as subject teachers, and their roles as form tutors. This might especially be the case if the form tutor is regarded as a key person in the management of pupils with behavioural difficulties, physical handicaps and medical conditions.

Teachers' reactions

In addition to our survey research to which we have referred before in this chapter, we conducted detailed case studies of four schools. In one part of these studies we interviewed a sample of fourteen mainstream teachers and asked their opinions of different forms of special needs support. The reaction to support via advice to the mainstream teacher was generally favourable. This is confirmed by a separate study of staff opinion in four other Oxfordshire schools where 47 out of 60 staff felt that it was important or essential that a head of special needs should give advice to mainstream teachers (Paton, 1984). Despite this generally positive reaction, some concerns were expressed during our case study interviews. For example, three teachers questioned the effectiveness of advice from special needs staff on subject-specific teaching problems. Here, perhaps, well-informed heads of subject departments may have an especially important part to play. A further very interesting point made by one teacher was that advice on teaching methods and materials should take the form of training for the mainstream teacher and not of special needs staff involvement in production of actual teaching schemes or worksheets. The teacher argued that training on the principles of worksheet design of pupils with learning difficulties would allow mainstream teachers to develop the advice they had been given, whereas joint development of specific worksheets could so easily result in a fossilised system lacking in regular review and improvement of what was being done. A more general concern expressed during the interviews was over the problem of finding time for effective conversations. This problem was alleviated in one school by making time available during staff meetings for the discussion of individual pupils. This provided a means whereby some of the aims of 'advice to mainstream staff' could be met without making further demands on the time of individual teachers.

In summary, we feel that advice to mainstream staff can be a powerful and all-pervasive element in the special needs support system of a school. It should certainly not be ignored, as mainstream teachers may be the only source of support for some special needs pupils, e.g. those with needs which are temporary and for which there is not time for other support services to be deployed, and will be the main form of support for others whose needs are sufficiently mild that any other support is available for only a small part of the week. It is an approach which seems to have general support from staff involved in the two studies which we have referred to above. However, there are possible drawbacks. Some were raised in the interviews which we have already discussed. There is the additional point that advice may be given and received, but not acted upon. There is a risk, therefore, that pupils will not be getting the help they require nor some system of monitoring, however informal. Another possible problem in some schools is that special needs staff may not have sufficiently high status or appropriate training to carry off this complex and demanding role. This has implications for the selection of teachers for special needs training, and for the content of that training. This is especially relevant in the case of teachers aspiring to become heads of special needs departments in schools.

b) In-class support

In-class support is provided by a second adult, often a special needs teacher, or a classroom assistant not trained as a teacher, who works alongside the normal teacher of a mainstream class in support of a special needs pupil in that class. The details of what goes on in such a system can obviously vary considerably. In-class support can be used as the general method of support for individual pupils with special needs, the expectation being that the second adult will attend the mainstream class on a regular long-term basis. Alternatively, the in-class support can be less regular, and can be designed to enable the second adult to keep in touch with the difficulties of a pupil in mainstream classes, so that more effective support for these difficulties can be offered elsewhere. Again, we have been told of situations in which the second adult has the specific aim of helping a pupil who has been withdrawn for special help to re-integrate into the mainstream class. The expectation in such a case would be that the in-class support would be offered on a fairly short-term basis and that it would be phased out as the pupil began to settle back into mainstream classes. Finally, in-class support from a special needs teacher (though not from a classroom assistant) could be seen as an extension of the system of giving advice to the mainstream teacher. In this case in-class support would represent a form of in-service training: the special needs teacher could identify the kinds of strategies that might be helpful to the pupil with special needs, could introduce the mainstream teacher to these strategies, could monitor their use and effectiveness in the early stages and could then gradually withdraw, leaving the mainstream teacher better able to meet the needs of the pupil.

One feature of the in-class system which has frequently been mentioned to us in our survey and case study interviews is that the second adult, though nominally attached to one or two pupils in a class, effectively offers help to a wider number of pupils who might need some assistance at a time when the mainstream teacher is otherwise engaged. Thus, support is more widely spread and the process of getting help from the extra adult becomes part of the normal routine of the classroom. This can be seen as normalising the experience of the special needs pupil without removing the support which he or she needs to succeed with the demands of the lesson.

In-class support can be used to help pupils with most kinds of special need. The second adult can take notes by dictation from a pupil who has difficulty in writing; s/he can read instructions to a pupil who has a reading difficulty; s/he can help a physically handicapped pupil deal with practical work; s/he can provide an immediate response to a medical difficulty; s/he can give one-to-one attention to a pupil with behaviour problems to avoid unacceptable incidents in the classroom. Though the approach may be of limited value for children with very severe difficulties and is clearly inappropriate where it has been decided that a pupil needs an alternative, rather than mainstream curriculum, it can be used for difficulties covering a wide range of severity. When a second adult is already assigned to a class, s/he may be able to respond to a new need as it arises, though generally the in-class approach is unlikely to be helpful in the case of temporary difficulties because of the length of time that would be needed to set up a response.

Teachers' reactions

Attitudes to in-class support amongst teachers appear to be mixed. Paton (1984) showed that a third of the sample of teachers in his four schools felt that it was important or essential for a head of special needs to be able to work as a second teacher in a mainstream classroom. Since it is possible that they saw value in this approach for the special needs department in general but they did not necessarily see it as one of the things in which the head of department must be active, one should perhaps interpret this as support for the system from *at least* one third of Paton's respondents. In our own case studies, two of the fourteen teachers interviewed gave whole-hearted support for the system, seeing benefits for the mainstream teacher, the pupil with special needs and the rest of the class. Other teachers generally felt that the system could work well if certain preconditions were satisfied. For example, they felt that there needed to be a match between the personalities of the mainstream teacher and the second adult, the roles of both needed to be carefully negotiated and the second adult needed to be present in all lessons with a given mainstream teacher. (This last point seems to presuppose certain aims for the system. It would seem to us that some aims listed above could be met without this full-time involvement of the second adult.) However, there was certainly no sense of unconditional rejection of the system on the part of any teacher, even though advantages and disadvantages were sometimes closely balanced in a teacher's responses. One teacher offered no opinion on the in-class system as he had no experience of working in this way.

Among the advantages which teachers saw for the system were that it gave opportunities for closely guided group work involving the special needs pupil;

it enabled a member of staff to provide immediate feedback to the pupil on his or her work; it allowed a wider range of activities to take place (e.g. oral assessment of course work); it helped to maintain a more relaxed atmosphere; it enabled the staff to diffuse disruptive incidents before a crisis point was reached; it kept lesson continuity going for a pupil who did not have to be held up over what was perhaps a minor stumbling block; it provided the second adult with a full understanding of what went on in the lesson so that s/he could be more helpful to the pupil with special needs in connection with homework; it could help to protect the pupil against any possible social 'nastiness'; it was less stigmatising than a system which withdraws the pupil from the classes attended by his or her peers.

Among the disadvantages of the in-class system teachers mentioned were that it could be more stigmatising of special needs pupils as it could emphasise the difference between them and the rest by making it easier, on a day-to-day basis, for pupils and teachers to compare the work and progress of the two groups; that it was too expensive of staffing so that the service could not be offered to all who needed it; that some teachers felt threatened by the presence of a second adult in their classroom; that it would be unfair to rely on this approach because some teachers were not prepared to have a second adult in their lessons and a pupil would then be denied the support s/he really needed; that the pupil with special needs could be confused about whether s/he should be listening to the mainstream teacher or to the second adult; that the mainstream teacher and the second adult may have different aims for the enterprise; that the mainstream teacher and the other adult, even where this other adult was a special needs teacher, often adopted hierarchical roles with little true sense of joint planning and team teaching; that the mainstream setting was inappropriate for some pupils who did not need help in coping with history, say, but who needed something quite different from history if they were to be prepared to play a part in society.

Perhaps the most revealing comment about the system was made by a head of special needs in one of our case study schools. She argued that the use of the in-class system of support challenged the appropriateness of the whole-class approach to teaching and was therefore revolutionary for some teachers. She also stated that, despite quite extensive experience of the approach, there was still much to be done in her school before colleagues were really clear about how to work together and that this was an area in which 'exciting developments' were possible.

This view of in-class support as a system which, at present, is by no means fully developed is consistent with the findings of Ferguson and Adams (1982) who discuss the team teaching role of the remedial teacher and raise many of the points which we have listed above. Their paper also makes a number of valuable general points about provision for pupils with special needs and we will return to it in more detail in the last sections of this chapter. Bines' (1986) in-depth study of the accounts given by special needs teachers and teachers of mainstream curriculum subjects of their differing and shared responsibilities for pupils with special educational needs is also very pertinent.

c) Withdrawal

Short-term

In this system pupils are withdrawn from all, or from some, lessons for a limited period of time after which the expectation is that they can be re-integrated into normal mainstream classes. Pupils may be withdrawn from a single lesson each week for a few weeks, from all lessons in a given subject for a short period, or even from all mainstream classes for the short time that support of this kind is being given. Some schools also operate a system of withdrawal for remedial reading which removes pupils from 10–15 minutes of a mainstream lesson on a regular basis. In any of these arrangements, work during the withdrawal sessions can be on an individual basis, or pupils can be taught in very small groups. Re-integration after short-term withdrawal can be without support or, as we have discussed above, it can be eased by in-class support. This subsequent in-class help may be organised on a long-term basis or as a short-term exercise to help the pupil over the transition back to mainstream classes.

Pupils may be withdrawn because of a learning difficulty which is handicapping their progress in a mainstream class. This could, for example, be a difficulty with reading or spelling or numeracy, a problem with some general cognitive process such as setting up or using categories, a problem of delayed intellectual development (perhaps a pupil is having difficulty with third form physics because he or she has not met the experiences which encourage the development of the various conservation rules that Piaget highlighted – conservation of volume, for example), or a difficulty arising simply out of a transfer from another school and another syllabus. The fact that, in our survey of provision in Oxfordshire in 1982/3, support during withdrawal sessions was shown to be focused mainly on literacy and, to a lesser extent, on numeracy should not close our eyes to the possibility that withdrawal could be used to help pupils over other learning dificulties of these kinds.

Short-term withdrawal can also be used to provide some specific help for pupils with behavioural difficulties (e.g. a series of social skills training sessions could take the place of some lessons for a short time). It can also allow a pupil with physical or medical conditions to overcome a 'bad patch' before continuing with normal lessons.

Teachers' reactions

In Paton's (1984) survey 40 out of a sample of 63 teachers in four schools favoured the inclusion of short-term withdrawal on a part-time basis in the overall system by which the school responded to pupils with special needs. 24 of the 63 teachers favoured short-term withdrawal on a full-time basis as at least a component of that system. Teachers' views, as expressed in our own case study interviews, were mixed. Some teachers saw an advantage in short-term withdrawal in that it allowed a specific response to be made to a specific difficulty. These teachers argued that, in the mainstream class situation, the general activities of the class and the requirement to keep the lesson going for the class as a whole, might make it impossible for this well-targeted help to be delivered even if a second adult was available to work with the pupil. One teacher argued that short-term withdrawal was appropriate when pupils' difficulties resulted from some gap in their previous learning. However, withdrawal was also seen negatively as it caused problems of re-entry, it was disruptive of the relationship between the pupil and the mainstream teacher, and it was potentially damaging to the pupil's social relationships with his or her peers.

A further view of withdrawal, which raises interesting issues, was offered by one headteacher who was interviewed in our 1982/3 survey. He was sceptical of its value and wary of the kinds of problems outlined above. However he argued that it was necessary to have a withdrawal system as a safety net if mainstream staff were to be encouraged to develop in-class support as a major component of the school's special needs system. He felt that mainstream teachers would be more comfortable with such developments if there was always the possibility of referring a pupil out of a mainstream class if his or her own needs, or those of the other pupils in the class, were being jeopardised. Without the safety net of withdrawal, confidence may be reduced and the in-class system rendered less effective. These comments would seem to apply equally well to withdrawal on a long-term basis that we discuss later in this chapter.

Effectiveness

The implication behind all forms of short-term withdrawal is, of course, that something can be done that will remedy the difficulty that the pupil has in the mainstream class. In some cases of special need this may well be possible, although one might be tempted to ask how many pupils have a specific difficulty which can be remedied in this way. For example, it is logically possible that a pupil may need special help to understand how to set up and use categories and that, having received specific help on this point, the pupil is better able to deal with normal lesson demands. However, one may speculate that the circumstances which place a pupil in this position, be they environmental circumstances at home or in previous schooling, or circumstances internal to the pupil, are likely, in many cases, to have an impact on other aspects of cognitive functioning and it may be naive to think that the pupil will benefit significantly from short-term withdrawal focused on this one problem. Certainly, research experience of remedial teaching via withdrawal does not reveal it to be a highly successful strategy, either in improving pupils' performance or their attitudes. (See Ferguson and Adams (1982) for a brief review of this work.) It may well be that, at least for pupils with learning difficulties, short-term withdrawal is a strategy with much narrower application than is usually imagined. It may help a pupil who needs to catch up with work after hospital treatment, or a pupil who has transferred from another syllabus, but it may be relatively rare to find pupils with other learning difficulties that can really be remedied by a short period of specific treatment.

Even where the pupil's learning difficulty or behavioural problem creates a situation which is susceptible to remedy by short-term withdrawal, the approach may be less successful than might be hoped. This may be because the withdrawal setting is so different from that of the mainstream class that what is learnt in one setting is irrelevant to the other, or it may be a result of the fact that, by concentrating on 'treatment' of the pupil, and doing nothing about the mainstream situation itself, only one side of the cause of the difficulty is being attended to. For example, a pupil may, in a short series of withdrawal sessions, be helped over some difficulty of reading to extract meaning from text and yet continue to have difficulty in a mainstream class because of the totally inappropriate selection of texts by the mainstream teacher, or because that teacher tends to use text in unhelpful ways. These two possible causes of the relative ineffectiveness of attempts to remedy difficulties through withdrawal are clearly related. Both may be rendered less damaging if in-class support is being used in connection with withdrawal. For example, the support teacher could attend the mainstream class before the pupil is withdrawn to get a clearer understanding of the difficulties that the pupil has in the particular circumstances of that class. Work in the withdrawal setting may then be more relevant to the mainstream situation. Also, the support teacher might attend the mainstream class before the withdrawn pupil is re-integrated so that some discussion of helpful developments in the mainstream situation can also take place. Finally, as mentioned earlier, a support teacher may accompany the pupil back into mainstream classes and thus help the pupil to make the links between what was done in the withdrawal setting and what is needed to thrive in the mainstream.

These issues of liaison between the teacher working in the withdrawal setting and the teacher of the mainstream class are equally applicable to the situation where short-term withdrawal is being used to provide sanctuary for a pupil, rather than remediation.

Long-term withdrawal

This approach can be used to provide a longer period of remedial support on the same model as short-term withdrawal – that is, with the expectation that the pupil will be reintegrated into the mainstream curriculum. Of course, if a pupil is withdrawn from a specific subject for a long period, the problems of re-entry that we discussed above are likely to be even more acute.

In another use of this approach, pupils are withdrawn from mainstream classes without there being any strong expectation that they will be re-integrated later. Long-term withdrawal of this kind might be organised on an individual basis, or a small group of pupils might be withdrawn together and be taught as a separate 'special class'. Such classes might exist throughout the school and the group of special classes may be regarded as a special needs unit.

Teachers' reactions

Long-term withdrawal from part of the mainstream curriculum was reasonably well regarded by Paton's sample of teachers, 27 out of 63 feeling that it had a place in the overall special needs system of a school. However, only 16 teachers in this sample favoured long-term withdrawal from all mainstream lessons. In our case study interviews opinions were very mixed. Some teachers were strongly opposed to the segregation and labelling problems seen to be associated with this approach; others felt that only by having special classes, or individual long-term withdrawal, could the needs of some pupils be met and the situation of their potential classmates be protected.

Curriculum implications

When long-term withdrawal is used with no expectation of re-entry to ordinary classes, this form of special needs provision takes on some unique characteristics. For example, there is no imperative to plan the work done in the withdrawal sessions with the details of the mainstream curriculum in mind. Long-term withdrawal can therefore be used to provide a mainstream curriculum at a much reduced pace or with very different teaching methods. It can also be used with, and is perhaps particularly well suited to, pupils who need an alternative curriculum, rather than support in attaining the objectives of the mainstream curriculum. Under these circumstances the arguments about long-term withdrawal revolve less around the effectiveness of the system in relieving pupils' difficulties, and more around the desirability of alternative curricula (see Chapter 3) and the social divisiveness of separating one group of pupils from the rest of the school.

Long-term withdrawal seems inevitable if a pupil needs some input which is not part of the normal curriculum: for example, if a pupil with quite severe learning difficulties needs a substantial programme of work on social and self-help skills in order to prepare for becoming an independent member of the adult community. This follows because opportunities for this sort of programme are very unlikely to arise in the contexts of the normal secondary school curriculum. Long-term withdrawal may also be essential in the interests of all concerned if a pupil is extremely disruptive of lessons over a substantial period of time – though hopefully the possibility of reintegration would always be kept in mind in such a case. Finally, this strategy may be desirable if, despite the best endeavours of all concerned, little success is being achieved in work related to the mainstream curriculum, for the pupil may benefit more from the experience of some success on a new curriculum than from repeated failure on the old.

Long-term withdrawal from all or some of the mainstream curriculum may therefore be an essential element in a school's special needs system. In the most extreme cases it may even involve withdrawal from the school to a separate special school. However, use of this strategy in a school, even though it may be necessary in some cases, should be regarded with caution for it carries one very significant risk. Once there is some long-term withdrawal system in a school or acceptance of the need for referral to special schooling, some teachers may regard it as an easy answer for pupils who could, in fact, have benefitted from further experience of mainstream work. In consequence, there is the risk that pressure to look critically at mainstream procedures will be reduced. This point does not magically reduce the need for long-term withdrawal, but it does suggest that its organisation and management must be carefully planned and monitored.

6.3 Organising a system of provision

It will be clear from all that has been said so far in this chapter that the task of organising a system of provision is not one of weighing the pros and cons of the various approaches and selecting the one which best suits the school, but rather it is the task of moulding together the various approaches into a multi-faceted system and of ensuring that the appropriate strategy is employed for each pupil.

Our own view is that advice to mainstream teachers and in-class support are essential components of any system for only in these ways will attention be given to both the pupil with special needs and the circumstances in which that pupil is taught. The strategy of advice to mainstream teachers also seems to be the way in which response can be sufficiently widespread to cover the whole special needs group and sufficiently flexible to make provision when it is needed for pupils who have a short-term difficulty. We feel that short-term withdrawal is a difficult strategy to use well, that it may generally be used too widely, but that it may, nevertheless, be appropriate for some pupils. We do feel, however, that where it is used it should be linked to in-class support either before or after withdrawal, or both. Long-term withdrawal, including withdrawal to special schools, would seem to be an option that must be considered for those whose difficulties are most severe, though we would hope that further development of the mainstream curriculum and of the methods and materials used to deliver it, would reduce the number of pupils for whom this option becomes a necessity. We suggest that the use of long-term withdrawal is particularly appropriate when it is thought necessary to provide an alternative curriculum.

In reflecting on the design of systems of provision, we have been much interested in one aspect of the comparisons we have made between two of our case study schools. In many respects (e.g. size and overall structure) these schools are similar but their approach to special needs is markedly different. One has no special unit, a considerable amount of in-class support for pupils, a system for liaison between subject departments and special needs staff, and a withdrawal system using some short-term withdrawal and some long-term, but part-time, withdrawal. The other school has a separate unit for pupils with quite extensive learning difficulties, some short-term withdrawal and long-term, part-time withdrawal, but very little in-class support. What is fascinating is that the IQ distribution of pupils in the two schools is not significantly different. Both have similar numbers of pupils who would have been classified as ESN(M) in the past. Clearly, what is regarded as impossible or undesirable in one school is being done in the other. The point of this is not to try to prove that one or other school is right, but to stress that the options really are open – that a school could consider the issues and make its choice without fearing that it was heading for a totally impracticable system.

a) Choosing a strategy

If you are charged with the planning of a school's support system you might begin by identifying the pros and cons of each approach to special needs provision. Next you might try to differentiate between different types of advantage and disadvantage. Ferguson and Adams (1982) draw attention to the fact that some features of an approach are fundamental characteristics of that way of doing things, whereas others are pros or cons which are likely (but not certain) to be present when that approach is used. For example, the fact that in-class support is limited by the normal curriculum of the class is inevitable. To do social skills training, say, in a normal geography lesson would be impossible, not only because of the geography teaching that would be going on, but also because of the social context of the mainstream classroom. However, there is nothing inevitable about the lack of relationship between work done in a short-term withdrawal session and the work of the class into which the pupil will be re-integrated. There is a risk that a problem of this kind will happen but it can be avoided, and indeed some ideas for doing so have already been discussed.

It seems to us that the proper response under such circumstances is to use the inevitable characteristics of each approach as a guide to the sorts of pupils who should be given support in that way. We have already given the example of the particular suitability of long-term withdrawal in circumstances where a pupil is thought to need an alternative curriculum. That decision exploits a basic characteristic of long-term withdrawal: namely that, if re-integration is not envisaged, the support does not have to be tied closely to mainstream curriculum objectives. On the other hand, the proper response to the things which are often associated with a given system of provision, but which are not inevitable characteristics of that approach, is to think about ways in which the likely advantages can be encouraged and the likely disadvantages overcome. Activity 6.3a is designed to focus some thinking of this kind. Ideally it would be done by a planning group involving mainstream and special needs staff.

This exercise might give some important clues as to what the component parts of your school's system of provision should be, what each part should be expected to do, and how the parts should be inter-related and related to mainstream planning and procedures in order to make the whole as effective as possible. It might be useful at this stage to go back to Activity 6.1a which began this chapter and to see how the proposed system caters for pupils of each kind. A combination of these two activities should help to refine the proposals.

Activity 6.3a
Designing a coordinated system

1. Go through the present text and, for each method of provision, underline advantages in blue and disadvantages in red.

2. Go through the text a second time and draw a blue box round any advantage that is an inevitable characteristic of the approach being discussed. Repeat the exercise drawing a red box round any disadvantage which is an inevitable characteristic.

3. For each approach, list the inevitable pros and cons (those now boxed).

4. Consider what these lists imply in terms of the suitability of each approach for pupils of different kinds. All kinds of pupil listed in the table that formed Activity 6.1a on page 56 should be considered.

5. For each approach, list the pros and cons that are likely to be associated with that response (those now underlined but not boxed).

6. Consider how the advantages can be exploited and the disadvantages minimised.

7. Consider how the system that you are beginning to map out in Steps 4 & 6 relates to the identification procedures you use. Should these be changed? Which ideas in Chapter 5 help?

Note
You may wish to do a similar exercise on other texts which discuss provision.

b) Implementing the strategy

In trying to put the proposed approach into practice, it is important to think about the likely reaction of colleagues to the ideas. This chapter will give some broad indications of what you might find. However, you might need to investigate these in more detail in your own school. One approach may be to charge someone on secondment to investigate the problems as their research project, for in-service courses often involve a research element for the secondee.

It may then be that you need to engage in some attitude change activities. Visits with key mainstream staff to other schools doing what you would like to do may be particularly effective. Certainly Deans (1983), surveying teacher opinion in twenty-five schools, found that visits were thought to be the most effective form of in-service training in raising awareness about the possibilities for provision. Other methods regarded as valuable by teachers as forms of INSET were workshops on materials and in-class support from specialist teachers. The method thought to be least effective was a series of weekly lectures.

Once you know what you want to do, and have generated support for the approach by activities of these kinds the problem becomes one of managing the system and monitoring it. A final suggestion – ask the pupils their

opinion. In our case studies we found that pupils with special needs had a considerable amount to say about what was done with them, and for them. Their ideas were perceptive and potentially of great help in checking on the system.

Integration

7

7.1 The context of integration

One necessary factor in the impetus to integrate handicapped children is the existence of segregated forms of special provision. Segregation can occur at very many different levels and it is important to remember that within any school there may be groupings and divisions which effectively bar some children from a full mainstream curriculum. This may be through rigid streaming which reduces options or through various forms of special needs provision which separate out some children for at least part of their education. Even in some special schools there may be groups – such as special care classes – whose educational diet may be very different from the rest. The attempts to reduce this kind of internal segregation through in-class support are discussed in Chapter 6. In this chapter our chief focus is the more widely acknowledged segregation which takes the form of completely separate schooling for some pupils and on the issues which need to be examined when these pupils become candidates for integration into ordinary schools.

Special schools have been in existence for well over a hundred years. In the nineteenth century the special schools were mainly for children with obvious sensory and physical handicaps. The motives for creating such schools were a typical Victorian mixture of benevolent humanitarianism and expediency. If children with disabilities could learn skills, not only would they be able to lead more satisfactory lives but they might cease to be a burden on society.

As universal education became established at the end of the century children with learning difficulties were increasingly identified by their failure to meet the demands of the payment by results system. Consequently other schools were opened which supposedly catered for their needs but also allowed the mainstream system to forge ahead unencumbered by 'slow' or 'difficult' children. The Open University Course E241 offers an interesting overview of the historical development and changing status of special education.

In recent years approximately 2 per cent of children have been educated in day or residential special schools. In the latter case fees will almost always be paid by the child's own local authority. These schools have tended to specialise in particular disabilities and although the 1981 Act has introduced the notion of 'special educational needs' instead of the old categories of handicap, nevertheless the special school populations still tend to a special bias. The table in Figure 7.1 gives the number of schools according to the old categories in the period 1972–1980.

Figure 7.1

	1972	1980	Change
Blind	17	16	−1
Partially sighted	19	17	−2
Blind and partially sighted	2	2	0
Deaf	20	24	4
Partially hearing	6	6	0
Deaf and partially hearing	22	21	−1
Deaf and partially sighted	1	1	0
Physically handicapped	77	102	25
Delicate	56	48	−8
Delicate and physically handicapped	71	60	−11
Delicate and maladjusted	4	6	2
Maladjusted	142	208	66
ESN	897	983	86
Epileptic	6	6	0
Speech defect	3	6	3
Autistic	0	10	10
Multiple handicaps	3	15	12
Hospital	155	141	−14
	1501	1672	171

Reproduced with permission from Hegarty, Pocklington and Lucas, (1981) *Educating Pupils with Special Needs in the Ordinary School* NFER-Nelson.

Several points should be made about Figure 7.1.

1. By no means all pupils with the named handicaps are in special schools. Many are in the mainstream schools as members of ordinary classes or in special classes or units in ordinary schools.

2. The ESN (Educationally Subnormal) category includes pupils with moderate learning difficulties (ESN[M]) and those with severe learning difficulties (ESN[S]). The latter group were deemed educable and became the responsibility of Education Authorities in 1970. In most cases there are separate schools for the old (M) and (S) groups but in some areas they share schools.

3. Within the same authority children with similar handicaps may be in different settings, e.g. in Oxfordshire children with moderate learning difficulties may be in segregated schools, in special classes or units in mainstream schools or in ordinary classes, largely according to accidents of local history and geography and policy differences from school to school in the mainstream sector.

4. The change figures demonstrate that the major increase in segregated provision in recent years has been for children with problems of learning or maladjustment. Later figures produced by Swann (1985) confirm this trend and show that the decrease in segregated provision lies mainly with children with physical and sensory disabilities.

a) How do children enter special schools?

If children are obviously severely handicapped they may be referred for admission to a special school from the beginning of their school career, others may be referred after some time in the mainstream sector. The assessment which precedes special placement has to include educational, psychological and medical input. Since the 1981 Act the assessment and placement procedures are much more clearly elaborated. The nature of the child's educational and associated needs has to be spelled out clearly and a statement of the appropriate provision made. Parents are consulted at each stage and asked to contribute their assessment. The period of assessment may be lengthy. It may not lead to a binding statement, but when a statement is made, it may, though not necessarily, state that the pupil should be placed in a special school, except in a few circumstances, e.g. for short periods of educational assessment. Pupils should not be placed in special schools without the formal assessment and statementing procedures of the 1981 Act.

b) What do special schools offer?

It may be fashionable to stress the main advantage of special schools as being a convenient receptacle for the rejects of the mainstream system but that would be too superficial. These costly establishments can maintain extremely favourable pupil-teacher ratios (e.g. 7:1 for maladjusted pupils). The teachers may have special qualifications (although this is mandatory only in the case of teachers for the visually handicapped or hearing impaired). In addition there is often further support from classroom assistants, special equipment and the advice or aid of outside agents such as educational psychologists, speech and physio-therapists. The external support, however, is patchy and thin on the ground even when concentrated in a relatively small number of schools.

As far as the curriculum is concerned, children may benefit from very specialist input – especially in the case of the sensorily impaired when all the school's resources are geared to making the most of their ability despite their particular limitations. In recent years too there have been considerable advances in developing modified or alternative curricula for children with learning difficulties.

When the Warnock Committee examined the educational provision for handicapped children they found many excellent special schools as well as many which were less satisfactory, a finding which could no doubt be made about any sector of education. The debate about integration or segregation, however, is not really about the quality of individual schools, just as the debate about the introduction of comprehensive schools was not about school quality. It began many years ago and incorporates many strands of thought. It became apparent that the categories of handicap under which children were assiged to special schools might have no bearing upon pupil' educational potential or needs. The clearest examples of the unsatisfactory nature of the arrangement were perhaps pupils with physical handicaps whose intellectual level was average or above but whose special school placement denied them access to a mainstream school curriculum and ordinary academic attainments. Their physical needs were probably very well met but their intellectual needs might be stifled.

The pressure for integration also has its roots in the growing criticism of the segregation of or discrimination against any groups because of factors like ethnic status, disability or gender. Equality of opportunity and human rights arguments are also invoked, as is clear from this statement by Peter Newell of the Children's Legal Centre:'We see ending segregation not first as a complex educational and professional issue, weighing up the advantages and disadvantages of two settings for meeting special needs, but first as a social and political issue, pursuing the human right not to be segregated outside the mainstream' (1985). This movement was particularly strong in the United States and their education law (PL94 142 The Education of All Handicapped Children Act) predated the British one by several years. In this same period most western countries also had an integration debate and tried varying ways to resolve what has proved to be a difficult problem. Sarason and Doris (1979) present a fascinating account of this experience in the United States.

It was in this context that the Warnock Committee reported on the educational provision for handicapped children and that the 1981 Education Act was introduced and later implemented. Although the Warnock Report was not about integration per se, that was how it was anticipated and received. In fact, although the Report made clear that many children were unnecessarily segregated it also claimed that some segregated provision would continue to be necessary. The Act too, while urging the education in ordinary schools of children with special educational needs, has a number of caveats that certainly allow for the continuation of separate special schools.

The continuing debate therefore is perhaps not about the wholesale closure of special schools, although that is certainly on the agenda for some (e.g. Booth 1985) but about which children with special needs should be in mainstream schools and how those mainstream schools are going to meet their needs. In some ways this is less threatening, but it also implies a long term uncertainty about the nature of a school's population as individual candidates are considered. It also implies considerable variation in the provision according to the wills and wishes of different schools and local authorities.

The rest of this chapter considers the arguments that are advanced for and against integration, the different meanings of integration in general terms and how one local authority has managed integration. It also gives some idea of the prerequisites for success. A role play exercise is included to enable teachers to identify their own reactions to the idea of integration and to rehearse with colleagues their contribution to the discussion.

7.2. Arguments for and against integration

The arguments for and against integration are very mixed and made from different stances and on behalf of different interest groups.

a) Arguments for

On behalf of the children to be integrated

- They have a basic right to education in the mainstream sector.
- They will have access to a wider curriculum or to the common curriculum deemed appropriate for all our children and to the publicly recognised qualifications which attend such curricula.

- They will have access to a wider range of teachers including subject specialists.
- They will have increased opportunities for social interaction with peers.
- They will be able to attend a neighbourhood school rather than be taken on special transport to a distant special school.
- They will remain members of their local community and will be accepted as such rather than viewed as outsiders.
- They will lose the stigma attached to special schooling.
- Their disability will be understood and accepted.
- They will learn at an early stage to live in the 'real' unprotective world and make a better adjustment than at the age of 16 or 19.

On behalf of other children in mainstream schools

- They will learn to understand and accept the diversity of human ability and disability without developing prejudice or fear of the unknown or misunderstood.
- They will have the opportunity to develop caring and sharing skills and attitudes at school that are not only worthwhile in themselves but may help to shape aptitudes for future work.

On behalf of special school teachers

Those that move with pupils into the mainstream sector will be able to extend their own skills in teaching a wide range of pupils and will be able to contribute their particular expertise to pupils and teachers in the ordinary sector.

On behalf of mainstream teachers

In meeting the challenge of children with difficulties they will not only gain in new skills in relation to those pupils but with adequate support will learn to offer more skilled and finely graded teaching to many more pupils.

On behalf of the parents of handicapped children

- They will have access, like their children, to a mainstream neighbourhood school. In this way they share the experience of local parents and are more likely to be able to make easy and regular contact.
- It is likely that all their children will be in the same group of schools as in most families.
- Becaue of the close contact they will meet with increased understanding and support from the community and lose any family stigma attached to the special school.

On behalf of other parents

They will gain directly, or indirectly through their children, in the understanding and acceptance of disability.

On behalf of other agents

Resources once concentrated in an exclusive and expensive way in a special school may be used for the benefit of a wider range of pupils in the mainstream schools.

On behalf of society

This would be the culmination of the comprehensive ideal – an opportunity to provide a good common education for all children.

b) Arguments against

On behalf of the children to be integrated

- They may lose out on specialist teaching and educational resources because of inadequate funding or personnel.
- They may suffer from too thin a spread of support therapies, like speech or physio-therapy, which are not likely in current circumstances to be increased to meet the needs of a more scattered population.
- They may be more isolated in a mainstream school than in a special school and their difficulties may be more obvious.
- They may be exposed at a vulnerable age to the harshness and prejudices and misunderstandings of society.

On behalf of other children in the mainstream schools

Their general progress might be slowed by the presence of children with difficulties who may need a disproportionate amount of teacher attention.

On behalf of other children in the special schools

- Their peer group would narrow and offer less stimulation.
- They might end up in a ghetto of the 'hard to place'.

On behalf of teachers in special schools

- Their experience and expertise would be either dissipated or underused by a move to a mainstream school.
- If they stayed in a special school the job satisfaction would decrease as their client population narrowed to the very 'hard to place'.

On behalf of teachers in mainstream schools

At a time when their resources are stretched very tight and increasing demands are made concerning different innovations they would be asked to manage more 'difficult' children with no guarantee of extra resources or training.

On behalf of parents of integrated children

They might need to fight constant battles to procure or retain for their children the kind of education appropriate to their special needs.

On behalf of other parents

They might resent the apparent erosion of resources to meet the needs of a minority of pupils and fear a deterioration in their own children's chances of progress.

On behalf of other agents

Visiting support agencies such as speech and physio-therapists would find it difficult to give the same support to a scattered population as was possible when children were concentrated in a few schools. Much of their time would be spent in travel rather than in working with teachers and children.

On behalf of society

The ideology of equality of opportunity might seem to be superseding the best interests of pupils with and without difficulties.

c) Can we reconcile the arguments?

If resources are scarce should they be concentrated for efficient use with the risk of segregating those who need the resources? Or are the arguments for integration so strong that we should not be deterred by lack of resources? We have to bear in mind that the 1981 Act, while encouraging integration, allows for no extra funding. Is 'integration on the cheap' either possible or desirable?

Education for personal development and education for life in society are as important for children with special needs as the rest. Is integration likely to improve education for them and their fellows? Is it a goal worth pursuing whatever the consequences?

Can one compare a broader curriculum available in the ordinary school with specialist individual teaching which may only be possible in a special school? Is membership of the local community school worth more than regular speech or physiotherapy? Can isolation in a small school be compared with possible isolation in a large ordinary school? Almost inevitably children will lose out on something but are the gains sufficient to compensate?

How do we take account of all the interests of the children with special needs and those without; of teachers in ordinary schools whose training, experience and expectations may have little to do with special needs and teachers working in segregated provision whose expertise and status may seem under threat; of parents of all children; of administrators who decide on placements and allocate resources? If their interests clash, who will arbitrate?

There is now considerable documentation of integration practices (e.g. Hegarty [1981], Hodgson [1984], Booth and Potts [1983]) and the Centre for Studies of Integration in Education was set up specifically to monitor progress nationwide. As yet, however, there is no clear cut picture of a solution to the questions raised here and each authority and school has to come to its own individual decision. According to a CSIE survey conducted as the 1981 Act was implemented, many authorities had been unable to decide on a coherent policy.

Obviously the most constructive action would be joint planning and policy making by all the parties whose interests are represented above, although no-one would suggest that that is an easy solution.

7.3. Are there limits to integration?

Pupils with every kind of disability have been integrated, at least on a locational basis, in some area of the country. Does this mean it could happen everywhere? How much depends on personal commitment? How much can be enforced? Are there particular problems with some groups of children?

Mention is made of the profoundly deaf, the blind, the severely mentally handicapped, the severely disturbed. Can a dividing line be drawn, and if so, who will draw it?

7.4. What is happening elsewhere?

Most western countries have been involved in the integration debate and many have legislation which urges integration. In the U.S.A. the system is probably the most elaborate and legally complex and has been well funded. Most segregated provision is closed but children may still receive much of their education separately from their peers according to individual programmes. In Italy segregated provision has also been largely abandoned but efforts are being made to educate most children in ordinary classes with support staff and reduced class size. In Scandinavia much of the integrated provision is locational only. In Britain at present it would be difficult to generalise.

7.5. Different models and levels of integration

When integration is debated it is important to distinguish the different models which may be implied. One is sometimes described as the 'limpet' model in which the host school, while itself remaining more or less unchanged, takes in children with problems as an addition to its normal population (Jones 1983). The onus for integrating seems to lie with the children with difficulties who will somehow adapt to the existing system. In another 'whole school' model the formerly disparate parts fuse to become a new whole in which all children are regarded as natural clients of the school and adaptation may need to be made on all sides (Sayer 1983).

In either model, but perhaps particularly the 'limpet' model, there may be different levels of integration. The Warnock Report described three levels of integration, often overlapping and representing progressive stages of association. At a 'locational' level the children with special needs share the same site as other children, but any other sharing will depend upon the wish and will of individual staff and pupils. If there is a 'social' level of integration the children will share recreational space and facilities, and usually dining arrangements. At a 'functional' level there is a sharing either full or part-time in educational, pastoral and extra-curricular programmes.

Another dimension to be considered, and in operation around the country, is the possibility of part-time integration or short-term integration, an example of which is discussed in the next section.

7.6. The example of one authority

This example is presented to demonstrate the diversity of practice that may be present even within a single authority. Oxfordshire still has special schools and still sends some pupils (although in smaller numbers than in earlier years) to residential schools outside the county. It also, however, has children with all kinds of difficulty integrated in ordinary schools.

Some are integrated as individuals and they may have support from specialist visiting teachers for the visually handicapped or hearing impaired. Some will be allocated welfare assistance support, particularly if they have physical disabilities. Others will be supported in class or in withdrawal sessions by the remedial or special needs arrangements used in that school. Their timetable may be completely normal or they may have considerable adjustments and adaptations. There is often extra support for two terms in the transitional period to allow the pupils to have individual attention either from the support teacher or the regular class teacher.

Children who have been segregated for reasons of maladjustment are being reintegraged on an individual basis into neighbourhood schools after an elaborate reintegration programme when their attendance at the ordinary school is carefully staged and supported by a liaison teacher from their special school until it is felt that the pupil and the school can cope. Children with autistic behaviours are also integrated on an individual basis from one of two autistic units and again there is a support system emanating from the special unit which may be gradually phased out as the pupil and the school gain in confidence but remains on 'emergency' stand-by if the pupil's behaviour should cause undue concern.

There are also other instances of integration in which groups of children are integrated into ordinary schools but remain technically on the roll of the special school. In these circumstances teaching staff are moved with the children. In the case of a group of physically handicapped children they are scattered among the ordinary classes of a county secondary school and the special school teacher and classroom assistant work with them as and when needed and provide specialist support and advice to the other teachers. In the case of children with severe learning difficulties the groups tend to stay for most of the time with the special school teacher but as the experience develops more and more opportunities are taken to enlarge the 'ordinary' experience of individual children and blur the divisions between groups.

Some of the instances of integration are full-time, others are part-time, including attendance at ordinary schools for particular courses which are unavailable in the special school. At the moment the experience of pupils with similar difficulties around the county may be very different because a good many examples of integration have sprung from the commitment of individual schools and teachers rather than an overall county policy.

7.7. Evaluation of integration

There remains a good deal of work to be done on the evaluation of integration initiatives and this will not be easy. Just as the arguments for and against integration are very mixed so are the aims and objectives and consequently the balance of outcomes is very difficult to assess. It is, however, possible to say that there are prerequisites for apparent success. One is adequate preparation before the integration takes place with a good exchange of information and visits; another is adequate resourcing so that the ordinary teacher does not feel overwhelmed by the new demands and the pupil is not immediately deprived of the benefits found in the special schools. Thirdly the good will of all concerned seems to be paramount. It is unlikely that everything will go smoothly in every respect and obstacles, however short-lived or minor, will fuel the fire of those who are not convinced of the wisdom of the exercise. Good will and optimism, however, can usually sustain people over these periods.

That is not to say, however, that ultimate success is always assured. There are times when the integration process breaks down and recourse is again made to the segregated system. While the two systems co-exist it is inevitable that some schools will be reluctant to change dramatically but the growing

body of successful experience may encourage many to accept the challenge and decide for themselves the merits or otherwise of integration.

Another implication of the, as yet, unclear effects of integration is that schools monitor carefully their own integration experience.

7.8. Role play exercise

For the purposes of the role play, you are members of staff of Mulchester Comprehensive attending a special staff meeting at which decisions are to be taken about the integration of three children at present in special schools. The following sections provide the necessary background information. Activity 7.8 then sets out some ideas for structuring the role play itself.

Background information
Mulchester Comprehensive

This is a school of 1500 pupils aged 11–18 situated on the edge of a Midlands industrial town. It is on a split site. The Upper School building is a three storey block. All pupils have to go to the Upper School for science. Its catchment area includes a large 1950s council housing development and a number of villages in the surrounding countryside which are popular with professional families. The school has a good academic record and a strong tradition in community service. It is firmly committed to mixed ability grouping for all pupils in years 1–3.

The school, which has a staff of 90, has a special needs department of 3 teachers which provides a remedial reading service on an extraction basis for 10 per cent of the pupils. A very small number of pupils (8) are withdrawn from most academic lessons and, on an ad-hoc basis, the special needs staff have developed an alternative curriculum for these pupils. This is not popular with many staff as it cuts across the mixed ability policy of the school.

As a response to the 1981 Act the LEA is asking the school, together with all other schools in the area, to accept pupils who, to date, have been educated in special schools. Cases to be considered at this meeting are given below. (It is likely that the LEA will be suggesting other names in the near future.)

The candidates for integration

Jane Wilson
Age 10.06
IQ (NFER group test) 105
Jane is wheel-chair bound and is presently attending a school for children with physical handicaps where she has been a pupil since the age of 3. She is of average ability and is making progress consistent with that ability. Although secondary age pupils attend this special school we feel that Jane is significantly limited by the lack of facilities here (particularly in science, where we have only rudimentary laboratories; and in modern languages, where we have no specialist staff). She is popular with her peers and has a mature attitude to her abilities and disabilities.

She may need help with her toileting and will need to return to the special school for physiotherapy for one afternoon a week for at least the next year.

John Williams
Age 13.00
IQ (group test) 68 IQ (Wisc) Verbal 60, Performance 90, Full score 75,
Reading age (at 12.06) 8.06
John is at present attending a day school for children with moderate learning
difficulties where he has been a pupil for four years. Reading has improved
considerably over the last six months with careful one to one teaching for two
twenty minute sessions each day. Once things have been explained to him
carefully his number work is good, but left to manage on his own he is
repeatedly let down by his lack of reading ability. He makes excellent use of
the very limited craft facilities in this school. John is shy about his reading
difficulties and tries to hide them from peers and teachers.

His parents are not particularly supportive of school.

Bill Johnstone
Age 14.00
NFER CE 115
Bill was referred to this school for maladjusted pupils after repeatedly
disrupting lessons. Referral was precipitated by an attack on another pupil
when he was 10.

In a tightly structured 'behaviour modification' setting, he has improved his
behaviour considerably, but has achieved little academically. Even now he
seems to have some difficulty in relating to male members of staff.

Activity 7.8
Role play activities

1. Ask colleagues to read the material in 7.8.

2. Hold the role play discussion. Shape the discussion of each candidate in
the form of a case conference. Ask colleagues to take on the role of
teachers at the comprehensive school, parents of the candidates,
representatives from the special schools, LEA officers or advisers, and the
candidates themselves. Put forward the possible views of the different
participants. Record the different arguments for and against integration
and any proposed action.

3. Encourage colleagues to reflect on what was said. After the discussion
decide what kinds of arguments have been used. Are they in direct
conflict? Are there obvious ways of resolving differences? Are there
critical elements in the discussion which suggest that there are insuperable
objections to integration or criteria which must be met before agreement is
reached?

Are the arguments the same for each candidate? If not what are the
distinguishing features?

Note
Of course colleagues in an individual school may prefer to consider the
candidates in the context of their own schools.

Liaison

As is clear from earlier chapters the primary responsibility for making provision to meet special educational needs has to rest with individual schools and the teachers within those schools. On a day to day basis it is the teacher's job to decide how best to help particular children within the educational setting. Giving that responsibility to another institution – the special school – is still possible but is likely to be less common as the move towards integration increases. Giving that responsibility totally to a small group of specialist teachers within a school is also possible but also less common if our research data are representative of current trends. It now seems far more likely that the responsibility will be shared between the ordinary class teacher and the specialist.

This increase in responsibility may seem oppressive, particularly at a time of scarce resources and a myriad other innovatory schemes. It is for this reason that we must emphasise the supportive network available to teachers in their enterprise. Information, advice and practical help are available, but teachers need to know how best to gain access to this support and how best to use it. In this chapter we shall examine support resources coming from outside the secondary school. Extra support within the school in the way of advice to mainstream teachers from special needs departments and direct support to pupils from welfare assistants and specialist teachers is discussed in Chapter 6.

The areas for discussion are primary/secondary transfer; parents and other community members; special schools acting as resource centres; and the professional external agents.

8.1. Primary/secondary transfer

The transition from primary to secondary school can be traumatic for any child but there are particular problems for children with special needs. Previous difficulties in the context of the primary school may have been alleviated to some extent by the security of being known by all staff and knowing all staff, by familiarity with the regime and by consistency of management. There will also have been advantages in interacting with a relatively small number of teachers on any day and in a relatively flexible timetable, maybe an integrated day, in which individual needs may be met unobtrusively. Most primary schools adopt mixed ability groupings so that even if a child has separate remedial sessions the regular base for work is an ordinary class or year base where diversity of ability and disability is the norm. This is not to suggest that children with special needs are automatically happy and secure in primary schools. All children recognise failure and difficulties and are unlikely to relish their special needs status but nevertheless there is usually sufficient relaxation and informality in the primary school to enable them to gain some satisfaction from school.

The average secondary school presents some marked contrasts. The establishment is much larger and children are not known to all teachers. In their turn they have to get to know and work with a considerable number of teachers in a week who will work in different styles and will inevitably need time to appreciate individual differences and needs because contact time with any class is relatively short. Although there may be a good deal of mixed ability teaching in the lower years of the secondary school almost inevitably there will soon be moves to band, set, or stream according to ability and the pupils with special needs are likely to gravitate to lower sets and streams and to encounter differences in curriculum and exam access in comparison with academically more successful peers.

The following suggestions are based on ideas adopted in a number of schools in our research area. Some arise from the main research study described in the introduction. Others were investigated in a separate Oxfordshire study of primary/secondary transfer in relation to children with special needs (Jones 1984).

a) Records

Although teachers are generally wary about the transfer of prejudice through written records and wish children who have been a cause for concern to have a fresh start there do seem to be some items of information which should be exchanged. These include:

- persistent learning difficulties, their nature and the way they have been managed at primary level;
- persistent behavioural difficulties and any record of serious home difficulties or involvement with psychiatric, psychological or social services;
- any physical handicaps, sensory handicaps or chronic medical disorders together with recommended management techniques;
- a note of lengthy or persistent absences from school which may have led to gaps in learning.

All this information is potentially valuable to all who teach the children and should be easily accessible – particularly to form tutors as the first line of referral when difficulties are identified. The issue of confidentiality is inevitably raised at times but the handling and management of such information should perhaps be seen as part of the professionalism of the teacher.

b) Visits

Exchange visits are usual – both by secondary pastoral staff to the primary schools and by the primary children to the secondary school. It is also helpful if special needs staff can visit primary schools and flesh out for themselves the profile of children who are most likely to need special support and also for all children on school visits to be introduced to any special needs base or resource area as an important part of the school's facilities. When parents too visit the secondary schools it may be sensible to introduce them from the outset to this part of the school's resources.

c) Curriculum continuity

The most usual point of contact in transfer arrangements is through the pastoral staff but there is now evidence that more schools feel the need to develop curriculum links so that some continuity is achieved between primary and secondary work. This seems appropriate for all children but has particular relevance for children with special needs who may have more difficulty in assimilating radical changes in content and style. In some cases teams of teachers between the schools work together to plan their work across the age sectors so that unnecessary and frustrating duplication is avoided and so that children may feel a sense of development rather than abrupt and unexplained change. In some schools the first year after transfer is organised in some ways on primary lines with pupils taught for up to half their timetable by one team of teachers who are usually first year tutors. In these circumstances the pupils gain in security from a more familiar routine and fewer teacher changes while beginning to come to terms with a more differentiated timetable.

d) Liaison teachers

In one of our research areas we were introduced to the idea of teachers who worked between sectors with particular responsibility for children with special needs. They were, therefore, familiar to the children long before transfer and could maintain that link when necessary in the secondary school – often working through consultation with the teachers rather than directly with the children. On a similar model some of the area support teams which are principally concerned in supporting teachers in the primary schools have now extended their role to the secondary schools. There is always a potential risk that such liaison work might confirm a child's reputation unnecessarily, because we know that some children who have caused concern at primary level thrive on the change. The risk, however, seems very slight, especially when the liaison teams are always pushed for time and under-resourced and unlikely to proffer support when it is no longer needed. And the risk is more than balanced by the benefits of a prompt and ready grasp of an obvious difficulty and knowledge of how it has been handled before.

e) Grouping policies

The final point is not at all new. All schools have policies for easing transfer when they group children in their basic tutor groups. Friendships and antagonisms are discussed and efforts made to make the children feel comfortable in those first anxious stages. The only point to be reinforced is that such considerations may be especially important for children with special needs who are less likely than others to be confident in their ability to adapt to new circumstances.

8.2. Help from parents

At primary level there tends to be fairly close contact between parents and teachers and information can easily be exchanged about difficulties, especially since for each child there is usually only one key teacher to consult at any time. Parents are also often to be seen in school in the role of volunteer helpers, preparing resources, escorting swimming groups, hearing children read, helping with cooking or sewing. In the relatively small community of the primary school the opportunities for consultation and co-operation are considerable. This in no way guarantees good collaboration over children with special needs but is helpful in promoting that collaboration.

At secondary level the complexities of most secondary schools militate against this ease of communication. Although pupils will have a form tutor as a key link person he or she may know the child in only a limited way compared with the primary teacher and the parent may not necessarily be able to ensure speedy contact with other key teachers or even know them at all except for very brief exchanges on parents' evenings.

There are, however, ways in which parents and teachers may establish a partnership over children with special needs to the benefit of all.

a) Parents as information givers

When children have special needs the parents often have information which is very important for the school in planning and evaluating its provision, e.g. details of physical or medical problems, drug therapies, family crises. Teachers need to understand these factors if the educational implications are to be grasped and tackled effectively. These may, however, be seen as sensitive areas and so a basis of trust has to be built up between school and home so that the parents recognise the value of their knowledge about their children and recognise the teachers' dependence upon their co-operation and that the teachers wish to use that information solely for the benefit of the children. The children's educational welfare has to be seen as a joint enterprise.

b) Parents as participants in assessment procedures

Parents were given more control over their children's special educational provision by the 1981 Act. They are to be consulted at every stage of a formal multi-professional assessment procedure and enabled to contribute their own views. There is also a clear expectation that parents will be involved in and consulted about earlier assessments of their child's educational difficulties. Consequently schools have an obligation to keep parents well informed of any steps taken to make special provision and to make them true partners in the decision making.

c) Parents as educators

There is a growing body of evidence that parents may be able to play a very important role in the education of their own children while at school. This emanates mainly from the primary sector and concentrates largely on experiments in shared or paired reading. Since many children with special needs are identified through their poor literacy skills it seems reasonable to suggest that even at secondary level parents might be invited to help their own children in this way so that the children may experience consistency of interest and support. Materials and approaches from the adult literacy movement may help to overcome the natural reluctance of young people to be seen as poor readers.

d) The need for good communication

In order to achieve these valuable links with parents it seems essential to have very clear lines of communication. Parents may get to know the key teachers in their child's school through planned initial visits and parents' evenings but there is also a need for visits, telephone calls and written communication at any crisis or stress points. This means, of course, that tutors must be given time to perform this valuable function and that a clear line of responsibility exists if there is to be a resolution of difficult circumstances. Further discussion of work with parents may be found in Wolfendale (1984) and Cunningham and Davis (1985).

8.3. Help from other members of the community

a) Adults as helpers

The advent of the community school era makes it easier to envisage an education system which has a give and take relationship with many sectors of the local population. The unemployed, part-employed and retired have much time to contribute to education and in turn can find a renewed purpose in their own lives. Children with special needs tend to flourish on a one to one basis with a sympathetic adult even though that adult may not be highly qualified as a teacher. It is possible to deploy such voluntary help in a number of ways:

- To work on resource materials, such as helping youngsters with literacy difficulties write and produce their own books, perhaps with the use of tape recorders or with computer programmes.
- To read to and with children, as well as oversee the children's own reading. At the teenage stage an outside helper may be more acceptable to some pupils than parents, and teachers will rarely have enough time to give to this task.
- To work with children who are integrated into ordinary schools, e.g. giving assistance with practical tasks, accompanying them on visits, supervising swimming or cooking. Although welfare assistants are sometimes available from the LEA their time allocation is often limited.

These examples are of community members acting as teachers' aides and assistants but there are examples of their being educators in their own right, bringing particular skills into the classroom which would otherwise be missing. Such extra expertise may be particularly valuable on short or modular courses. Examples could be first aid, child care, various crafts.

b) The pupils as helpers

Community schools often play host to groups such as the disabled and local pensioners, offering meals and hospitality. If children with special needs are

able to establish good relationships with these visitors and to learn to meet their needs it can be a source of confidence and enhanced self-image. For once they are not on the receiving end of extra support but can offer it to others.

c) How easy is a community programme?

The potential benefits of enlisting the support of parents and the community are immense for all pupils and have a particular significance for children with special needs. The potential hazards are not insignificant. At a superficial level schools may want to consider insurance and other financial implications of help from persons other than members of staff. More seriously, those who volunteer are not always suitable helpers; some will want to take over from the teacher, others may work against the prevailing style and ethos of the school, some may become unhealthily attached to pupils, others may be unreliable; some will subconsciously be seeking support for themselves and put additional burdens upon overpressed but sympathetic teachers.

It is obvious that diplomatic management and co-ordination skills are needed by any teachers wishing to embark on these suggestions and co-ordinate voluntary help. If such skills are available the effort may be amply rewarded.

d) Community and work experience

So far we have considered help coming into the school but the experiences pupils with special needs have outside school as they prepare to leave may be just as important. Teachers who arrange work experience placements or community projects may be able to foster contacts where they know that children with special needs will be supported and valued and able to gain some of the self-confidence that is often lacking in children who are apparently failures.

8.4. Special schools

In an age when any segregated provision is being closely scrutinised and questioned the special schools are trying to develop a new role in their educational communities. Very few have closed because the need for very special placements still seems to hold. Nevertheless, some are losing pupils to the ordinary schools and attempting to expand their client population indirectly by becoming an area resource. This changing role may bring several benefits to the secondary schools who are trying to make adequate provision for their pupils with special needs.

To revert to the question of work or community placements, secondary schools may well receive good advice from special schools who perforce are constantly in the business of trying to place hard-to-place youngsters.

There has always been an overlap of populations between special and ordinary schools and, where integration is popular, that overlap will have become greater. In some areas it is now becoming more common for teachers in ordinary schools to ask for advice on curriculum matters and management techniques from special school teachers whose efforts are totally geared to meeting special educational needs. In recent years special school staff have given a good deal of time and energy to rethinking and planning curricula, with particular attention to behavioural objectives and step by step learning.

Their efforts have been spurred on and supported by research reports and training schemes often initiated in higher education departments and research centres. These techniques certainly have relevance for a much wider population than the pupils in special schools – the general principles are relevant for all teachers. It is now possible for the special schools to offer a variety of services to colleagues in ordinary schools in the confidence that they have something worthwhile to say and give. This may be as practical as detailed curriculum materials or advice on the management of particular disabilities. It may be an offer of experience beneficial to both sides when teachers can exchange roles at times. Some special schools offer a direct service to some pupils through part-time participation in courses not available in the ordinary school. Some have intensive support classes for pupils from neighbouring schools.

When children are being integrated into ordinary schools the direct support of the special school before and during integration and the continued link afterwards may be one of the keys to success. More special schools now make this liaison work a post of special responsibility so that all parties can benefit from earlier mistakes and successes and develop guidelines for good practice rather than treating each candidate for integration in an ad hoc manner.

These collaborative links between ordinary and special schools are not necessarily well advanced in any area and even when there is enthusiasm and good will it can be thwarted by lack of time and resources. Nevertheless, it seems only sensible for any school considering how it may improve its special needs provision to look on any local special provision as a possible source of support and advice, even of inspiration. The freedom from conventional academic goals may enable special schools to be particularly imaginative and innovative.

8.5. External agents

Finally we must discuss the roles of external agents and the ways in which liaison between them and the schools may best assist children with special needs and their teachers. Some of these agents have educational qualifications – such as the educational psychologists and special needs advisers and peripatetic advisory teachers – in addition to a specialist training or experience. These should, therefore, be in a good position to understand the myriad pressures and demands placed upon teachers as well as the needs of the individual child. The other agents are less likely to have that educational bias and their work may well extend to other age groups than the school child. Their interest is primarily in managing and alleviating disability and disadvantage.

In some ways this distinction suggests different ways in which the groups might be approached. The para-medical and social services will usually only have time to concentrate on particular individuals with particular needs although they may be persuaded occasionally to talk in more general terms, e.g. at a staff meeting, about their work and how best they can be incorporated into a school's regime. The educational psychologists and advisers, however, may be able to enter a more general dialogue with schools which will give a forum for issues that go beyond the particular needs of a particular child and may lead to general changes and developments in schools to the benefit of many more children with special needs, and to the personal and professional development of many teachers.

There is a wide range of external agents who might have a part to play in helping to meet special needs. There are differences in the way they work

between different areas, even between individuals within the same area but the following section indicates some of the functions that might be expected or negotiated by schools.

a) Officers of the LEA

Issues of administration in the special needs area may centre upon one officer or be spread among several area officers. These issues may include: multi-professional assessment procedures and statements and any subsequent appeals by parents; the appointment of welfare or classroom assistants or other special staffing; the adaptation of buildings and the allocation of special equipment and arrangements for special transport.

b) Special needs advisers

Advisers may be closely involved in the issues above but will also have a more general advisory role for teachers managing children with special needs, such as giving careers advice to those teachers, and will have responsibilities for in-service provision. Under the new funding arrangements for in-service schools will have more influence in shaping in-service provision. The identification by individual schools or groups of schools of gaps or inadequacies in special needs expertise or awareness (as illustrated in earlier chapters) may well lead to fruitful negotiation with advisers over the development of relevant courses.

c) Educational psychologists

The old image of the psychologist as a person who tests children and announces IQ scores is becoming obsolete. There is still a need for testing – particularly for official documentation as in statements and in diagnosis but psychologists usually prefer to operate on a much wider base. Some try to help children through working closely with teachers, observing children in the class and advising teachers on a variety of teaching and behavioural techniques. Others make the family the focus for their work. Both hope to effect change in children through encouraging change in those who care for them both at home and at school. Although hard-pressed, with potential responsibility for thousands of children, some psychologists still manage to visit schools on a regular basis, regardless of particular clients, so that teachers become familiar with them and are able to discuss educational issues well before crisis point.

d) Social workers

Some generic social workers will be in contact with schools because pupils and their families are clients. Others may be able to maintain a regular link with local schools so that potential problems can be discussed at an early stage. Educational social workers have a very specific role to check on attendance and in consequence may be a very useful link between the schools and families of irregular attenders. Psychiatric social workers tend to work closely with psychiatrists or psychologists when children are diagnosed as having adjustment difficulties and in need of special provision either in the ordinary or special sectors. They too may be able to bridge the gap between parents and schools at times of considerable unhappiness and stress.

e) Psychiatrists

Psychiatrists who deal with children and adolescents need to consult closely with schools when children are referred for disturbance of behaviour. The information possessed by the schools on learning and behaviour may be very valuable in assessment and treatment. In the best of practices the school will in turn receive the kind of information that helps them to understand the child's difficulties and the ways in which that child may be helped in non-medical settings. The communication between the medical and educational professions is not always easy or effective, partly perhaps because it is not part of professional training to understand each other's perspectives or needs. When, however, that understanding is there the collaboration can be extremely helpful and there are psychiatrists who will take time to talk to teachers about their work and how teachers can be alerted early on to psychiatric difficulties and take appropriate action at an early and more remediable stage.

f) Paediatricians

Much the same issues could be raised with paediatricians as with the psychiatrists although school reports may not necessarily be any part of medical investigation. However, many paediatricians who deal with chronic medical conditions, such as diabetes or epilepsy, now realise the important educational implications of the disorders and are keen to disseminate helpful advice, and to receive feedback from schools on the circumstances surrounding episodes when the medical condition has had an adverse effect on the child's life in school.

g) Child health services

The child health services interact with schools at several points. The health screening tests are usually performed in schools and school medical officers and school nurses will keep an eye on children identified through tests as having actual or potential special needs. The service will also hold records centrally and in schools and usually co-ordinate any medical reports necessary for multi-professional assessments. The advice of school medical officers may also be useful when children with special needs leave school and are planning further or higher education or work applications. It is now becoming less popular to spend a good deal of time testing everyone for sight and hearing and general health but to concentrate time and efforts on identified need so that school referrals on new problems are an important element in a comprehensive service.

h) Para-medical services

There are many children with special needs who have particular physical or neurological conditions which respond to therapy and they may be visited in the schools by speech therapists, physio- or occupational therapists. These professionals are a scarce resource and may have a client population spanning all ages from birth to death, and may work in medical as well as community settings. Their time in schools is inevitably limited and there is particular concern when children integrate into ordinary schools and lose therapy time when it has to be spread rather than concentrated in special centres. In order

to make the most effective use of their time they may well work with teachers and welfare assistants so that special exercises or programmes may be pursued in the everyday timetable. More general advice may also be passed on at staff meetings on handling physically disabled pupils or on identifying and referring speech disorders which might respond to therapy. Schools might also seek the advice of para-medical professionals in decisions about aids and adaptations. Their wider clinical experience in medical settings is likely to introduce them to a considerable range of equipment not always known to advisory staff.

i) Peripatetic teaching staff

These too may be a scarce resource with responsibilities for whole authorities or a great number of schools. The most usual areas of expertise are in the education of the hearing impaired and the visually handicapped and in learning difficulties associated with low attainments in literacy skills. Teachers in the latter category are less likely to visit secondary schools than primary schools but some advisory teaching teams are now extending their work into secondary schools. Once more the amount of direct teaching of pupils may be strictly limited but the regular teachers may benefit considerably from advice on particular teaching strategies and on the use of particular equipment like radio microphones or low vision aids. Fitzherbert's book, *Child Care Services and the Teacher* (1977), is a useful source of more detailed description and discussion.

8.6. How can liaison be made to work?

The previous sections outline different groups of people who might support schools' efforts to cater for pupils with special needs. The total list is long and many of the individuals involved are not educators so that the task of enlisting and co-ordinating such support is not easy. If, however, schools recognise the value of such links the management of them has to be taken seriously and may be achieved in the following ways:

- Co-ordination should rest with someone of high status who can give it due priority.
- The channels of communication need to be clear and known to all concerned. Failures in communication and misunderstandings could undermine interactions which are often beyond the call of duty.
- Information has to be co-ordinated and available to all who have direct responsibility for the pupils. The issues of confidentiality and open records need to be understood and agreed.
- Records and referrals should be clear and specific, based on good observations, formal or informal tests as well as intuitive judgments and easily interpreted by other professionals.
- Where possible external agents should have some clear area responsibility so that they can get to know and be known by a group of schools so that trust and confidence can be developed between different professionals.
- Regular case conferences with good referral and review systems could help to prevent crisis management.
- Regular in-service sessions, perhaps with several disciplines participating could ease the difficulties of understanding the roles of different professionals and the most effective way of working together.

- If liaison work is to improve the lot of children with special needs all parties have to be prepared to negotiate and when necessary compromise. Conflicts in management techniques and advice are unlikely to be helpful.

At first sight it might seem that we are recommending that teachers should be all things to all people and lose their professional identity. Far from that we would wish them to recognise their particular contribution to a child's total welfare but also to acknowledge and exploit the skills and concerns of others. The school can become a natural focus for a multi-faceted support network because that is the one institution that all children have to attend. How well that network can function, however, rests largely with the teachers.

8.7. Some study suggestions

This chapter has been wide ranging in its discussion of support for special needs work which may come from outside the school. Since this aspect of school life is 'off-the-timetable' it may well be that many teachers have only a partial view and consequently may feel, unjustifiably, that they have little if any part to play in liaison. It is proposed, therefore, that each of the following topics could be a focus of discussion by a group of teachers, or preferably a whole staff so that the school's policy and practices could be identified and improvements suggested.

Primary-secondary transfer

1. What is the value of transfer documentation and other transfer procedures in the identification and support of children with special needs?
2. Which staff have access to the resulting information and how is that information used?
3. Is there any collaborative curriculum work across the sectors?

Parental involvement

1. What kind of links are made with parents, and by whom?
2. Where is contact made? always in school? in the parents' homes? on neutral ground?
3. What roles do parents play in interactions with school? clients? information givers? partners? co-educators? fund-raisers?
4. How much do parents of children with special needs feature in parental involvement schemes?

Community interest

1. List any member of the community who works in or out of the school with teachers and/or pupils on a voluntary basis. What do they bring to the work?
2. What advantages or disadvantages are there in community links?
3. How many links involve pupils with special needs?

Special schools

1. What links exist and for what purpose? integration? exchange educational visits by teachers and/or pupils? social events? community service?
2. How far do you regard a local special school or unit as a resource for advice or actual assistance in special needs provision?

External agents

1. List all those who have contacts with the school. Use the following list as a starting point:

   Special needs adviser   Paediatrician
   Educational psychologist   Child health staff
   Social workers   Para-medical therapists
   Psychiatrist   Peripatetic teachers

2. Who makes the contact? What is the referral procedure? What can and do the agents do? Are the contacts regular and ongoing or only at crisis points?
3. Do they ever address all the staff or are they available for staff consultation independent of individual casework?
4. What sort of advice and information do they want from teachers and can they give to teachers?

Overall school policy

1. Is there a teacher at senior level who can offer an overview and expertise on all these topics? Should there be? Can and should all staff share in this work?
2. How clear are lines of communication and responsibility for liaison work?
3. Is there a need for joint in-service sessions with representatives from primary, secondary, special schools, parents, community and external agents in order to understand the differing roles and responsibilities in any shared work?

Summary

The intention of this book is to provide some insights into the issues surrounding the organisation of formal special needs support systems in schools, and to discuss some ideas which might be useful in helping staff to develop such support systems in their own schools. To increase the practical value of the text, we have provided a number of activities which we hope will be useful to staff in applying these ideas in their own school contexts. These could be used by individual teachers, by groups coming together on in-service training courses, or by groups which form on an ad hoc basis within a school. A further aim of the book is to provide material which will help to raise awareness of general special needs issues amongst student teachers who are engaged in a period of initial teacher education. As such, this book complements the other volumes in this series which are both concerned with the skills which teachers need to develop in order that they can make appropriate provision for pupils with special needs in their own classes.

In this last chapter we will summarise, very briefly, some of the main points which we have developed in the text.

For example, we discuss the idea that the concept of pupils with special educational needs should be broad, encompassing, for example, pupils with general and specific learning difficulties, behavioural and emotional difficulties, physical handicaps, sensory handicaps and medical disorders, and pupils with particularly high ability. We also draw attention to the range which can exist in both the severity and persistence of any type of need, and to the fact that severity and persistence are not necessarily linked (e.g. one can have short-lived, but severe problems). We argue that a school should have a planned response to cover needs of all types, all severities and all levels of persistence (e.g. short-lived, severe behaviour problems; long-lived, moderate physical handicaps; short-lived, moderate learning problems etc.). However, at least for some kinds of need, this response may not necessarily be one which involves the 'special needs department' as currently defined.

We argue that, in planning this response, the school should recognise the interactive nature of special needs (i.e. that they arise out of characteristics of both the learner and the teaching situation).

We remind the reader of the Warnock Report's estimate that some 20 per cent of pupils should be regarded as having special needs, and draw attention to the fact that this estimate explicitly omitted pupils of very high ability. Much current activity in the 'gifted' field is focused on the top 10 per cent or so of pupils. The implication is that the special needs population is a substantial proportion – perhaps as much as a third – of a school's intake.

We point out that the Education Act 1981 encourages the integration of pupils with special needs from the special school sector into the mainstream sector, subject to various conditions being met. The implication is, of course, that some of this substantial number of pupils with special needs will have quite severe difficulties. We also point out that the Act imposes a duty on those responsible for making provision for any pupil with special needs in a mainstream school to ensure that 's/he engages in the activities of the school together with other children who do not have special needs' – though this duty, too, is subject to conditions.

In connection with the identification and assessment of special needs, we develop the argument that identification should be simple; should err on the side of over-inclusiveness; should cover the whole range of special needs and not just reading ability (say); should either be continuous or regularly repeated (so that changes in pupils can be monitored and pupils who were overlooked at one time can be identified at another). Similarly we argue that diagnosis should be a two stage process: the first stage being simple so that wrongly identified pupils can be sifted out, the second being more detailed so that an understanding of the pupil's problems in the context of the lesson s/he attends can be determined. At this second stage we regard teacher-based, criterion-referenced, subject-specific diagnostic assessment as an extremely valuable complement to any diagnostic testing, or assessment by other experts such as educational psychologists or doctors.

In discussing curriculum differentiation we make the point that for most pupils, the aims and objectives of the curriculum should be the same and that 'great attention should be paid to the development and trial of alternative teaching styles and special resources so that (this option) can be kept open for as many pupils as possible, for as long as possible'. However, we accept that for some pupils it may be necessary to devise an alternative (perhaps developmental) curriculum and suggest that this option should always be kept in mind – even though it may not often need to be brought into play.

We point out that special needs lie on a continuum, with no clear dividing lines between those pupils who have special needs and those who do not, and we emphasise that many aspects of special needs (notably behavioural, physical and medical difficulties, but also some specific cognitive problems) are not always (and in some cases, not usually) related to low general ability. Pupils with some kinds of special need can be average or even very able in other respects.

We make the case that the proportion of pupils having special needs, the concept of special needs lying on a continuum, the fact that many aspects of special need are unrelated to overall low ability, and the idea that some special needs may be short-lived, all serve to emphasise that every mainstream teacher will have pupils with special needs in his or her classes – perhaps even in every class s/he teaches. These points therefore imply that a school's planned system of provision for pupils with special needs must include ways of enabling mainstream teachers to make a response to these needs. This might be achieved through a general commitment to include consideration of such pupils in any piece of curriculum planning in any mainstream department; through a recognition of the value of special needs staff playing a consultancy role in the school; through the availability of in-class support from a classroom assistant which can give the mainstream teacher more options than when s/he has, alone, to deal with the whole class for the whole lesson.

The importance of mainstream teachers accepting a responsibility to consider their own response to pupils with special needs is further underlined by the notion that special needs arise out of an interaction between the characteristics of the learner and those of the school structure and the individual teacher's teaching style – for to focus attention only on the learner is inevitably to address only one side of the issue.

However, we also point out that the range of severity of need suggests that, vital though this response from mainstream teachers is, more specialist support will also be needed for some pupils. The necessary specialist support might be delivered by special needs teachers working in the mainstream classroom, by short-term or long-term withdrawal, or by enlisting the services of LEA staff such as educational psychologists or specialist teachers of the hearing impaired. This range of expert support itself implies that there must be clear lines of communication between different staff, and that the skills that are needed to refer pupils effectively must be learnt.

The three previous paragraphs summarise the point that a range of different support strategies might be needed. We discuss the need for these to be used as a co-ordinated system of provision. For example, we point out that in-class support prior to a period of withdrawal could help to ensure that the most appropriate things were tackled during the withdrawal sessions, and that further in-class support after withdrawal could ensure that the problems associated with re-entry were minimised. Linking some in-class activity to withdrawal could also reduce the limitations of withdrawal which arise from the fact that it tends, by focusing only on the pupil, to pay too little attention to the possibility that some of the problems for that pupil may arise out of the nature of the teaching style and resources offered by the mainstream teacher. The general point which we seek to develop is that the different support strategies should be used by a school, not simply as alternatives for different pupils, but in a co-ordinated way so that each school, in its own unique context, capitalises on what, for it, will be the strengths of each approach and reduces the impact of what, for it, will be the disadvantages.

We discuss the integration of pupils with more severe difficulties from special schools into mainstream schools and point out some of the advantages and disadvantages of integration from the points of view of the pupil with special needs, the other pupils, the staff, and others in the community.

We discuss the importance of planned liaison with parents and with professionals external to the school (e.g. the educational psychologist, speech therapist, teacher for the visually handicapped, primary school teacher). We argue for a member of the secondary school staff to have a co-ordinating role to facilitate such liaison; for channels of communication to be clear and procedures to be known by all staff; for information obtained to be made available in agreed ways to agreed staff; for issues of confidentiality to be considered and general guidelines to be established with each external professional; for records to be clear and specific; where possible for some regular system of liaison to operate so that problems are not shelved until some point of crisis.

This brief summary, and to an even greater extent the text itself, emphasises what we regard as an extremely important comment in the Warnock Report: namely that attending to the issue of pupils with special needs, and responding to such needs within one's own classroom, provides one of the most intellectually as well as personally demanding challenges which a teacher has to face. It also, perhaps, emphasises the centrality of the special needs issue. Attention given to the challenge of meeting special educational needs will, we feel, pay enormous dividends in improving education for all pupils in school.

Bibliography

Advisory Committee on the Supply and Education of Teachers, 1984, *Teacher Training and Special Educational Needs*, London, Department of Education and Science.

Ainscow, M. & Tweddle, D.A., 1979, *Preventing Classroom Failure*, Chichester, John Wiley.

Biklen, D., 1982, 'The Least Restrictive Environment: Its Application to Education', *Child and Youth Services*, 121–144.

Bines, H., 1986, *Redefining Remedial Education: Policies and Practices in Secondary Schools*, London, Croom Helm.

Booth, T., 1983, 'Integrating Special Education', in Booth, T. & Potts, P. (eds), *Integrating Special Education*, Oxford, Blackwell.

Booth, T. & Potts, P., 1983, *Integrating Special Education*, Oxford, Blackwell.

Brennan, W.K., 1979, *Curricular Needs of Slow Learners*, London, Evans/Methuen, for the Schools Council.

Burnham, M. & Robbins, G., 1980, 'Catching the 22', *Times Educational Supplement,* 12 December 1980.

Clunies-Ross, L. & Wimshurst, S., 1983, *The Right Balance*, Windsor, NFER-Nelson.

Cohen, L., 1976, *Educational Research in Classrooms and Schools*, London, Harper and Row.

Cox, B., 1985, *The Law of Special Educational Needs. A Guide to the Education Act 1981*, London, Croom Helm.

Cruickshank, W.M. (ed), 1980, *Psychology of Exceptional Children and Youth*, Englewood Cliffs, Prentice-Hall.

C.S.I.E. (Centre for Studies on Integration in Education), 1983, *Results of a local authority survey of policy and practices on integration*, from C.S.I.E., The Spastics Society, 16 Fitzroy Square, London.

C.S.I.E. (Centre for Studies on Integration in Education), undated, *The Marlborough/Ormerod Project: An Integration Initiative in a Rural Comprehensive School*, from C.S.I.E., The Spastics Society, 16 Fitzroy Square, London.

Cunningham, C. & Davis, H., 1985, *Working with Parents: a Framework for Collaboration*, Milton Keynes, Open University Press.

Dawson, R., 1985, *The Macmillan Teacher Information Pack, Teachers' Guide*, Basingstoke, Macmillan.

Deans, J.M., 1983, 'The management of provision for special educational needs including the needs of the more able child', Unpublished thesis submitted for the Special Diploma in Educational Studies, University of Oxford.

Denton, C. & Postlethwaite, K.C., 1985, *Able Children*, Windsor, NFER-Nelson.

DES, 1978, *Special Educational Needs, Report of the Committee of Enquiry into the Education of Handicapped Children and Young People (Warnock Report)*, London, HMSO.

DES, 1983, *Curriculum 11–16, Towards a statement of entitlement*, London, Department of Education and Science.

DES, 1984, *Slow Learning and Less Successful Pupils in Secondary Schools*, London, Department of Education and Science.

DES/WO, 1984a, *The Organisation and Content of the Curriculum: Special Schools*, London, Department of Education and Science and Welsh Office.

DES/WO, 1984b, *The Organisation and Content of the 5–16 Curriculum*, London, Department of Education and Science and Welsh Office.

DES/WO, 1984c, *Circular 3/84 Initial Teacher Training: Approval of Courses*, London, Department of Education and Science and Welsh Office.

Ferguson, N. & Adams, M., 1982, 'Assessing the advantages of team teaching in remedial education: the remedial teacher's role', *Remedial Education, 17, 1*, 24–30.

Fish, J., 1985, *Special Education: the way ahead*, Milton Keynes, Open University Press.

Fitzherbert, K., 1977, *Child Care Services and the Teacher*, Temple Smith.

Fransella, F. & Bannister, D., 1977, *A Manual for Repertory Grid Techniques*, London, Academic Press.

Gipps, C. & Goldstein, H., 1984, 'You can't trust a special', *Times Educational Supplement*, 27 July 1984.

Gray, J.R., Richer, J. & Howarth, R., (in press), 'Disruptive Behaviour in School', in Macfarlane, A. (ed), *Progress in Child Health Vol. 3*, London, Churchill Livingstone.

Hackney, A.C., 1985, 'Integration from Special to Ordinary Schools in Oxfordshire', *Educational and Child Psychology, 2,3*, 88–95.

Hackney, A.C., 1985a, 'Epilepsy', in *Teacher Information Pack*, Basingstoke, Macmillan.

Hegarty, S. & Pocklington, K. with Lucas, D., 1981, *Educating Pupils with Special Needs in the Ordinary School*, Windsor, NFER-Nelson.

Hodgson, A., 1984, 'Integrating Physically Handicapped Pupils', *Special Education: Forward Trends, 11,1*.

Hodgson, A., 1984, 'How to Integrate the Hearing Impaired', *Special Education: Forward Trends, 11,1*.

Hodgson, A., 1985, 'How to integrate the Visually Handicapped', *British Journal of Special Education, 12,1*.

Hodgson, A., Clunies-Ross, L. & Hegarty, S., 1984, *Learning Together*, Windsor, NFER-Nelson.

Hyde, T., 1984, 'Secondary Remedial Provision within one Metropolitan Authority', *Remedial Education, 19,2*, 85–91.

Jones, G.R., 1984, 'An investigation of liaison and transfer procedures between primary and secondary schools with particular reference to the special needs pupils', Unpublished dissertation submitted for the Special Diploma in Education Studies, University of Oxford.

Jones, N., 1983, 'The Management of Integration in the Oxfordshire Experience', in Booth, T. & Potts, P. (eds), *Integrating Special Education*, Oxford, Blackwell.

Kellmer-Pringle, M.L., 1970, *Able Misfits*, London, Longmans.

Kerry, T., 1978, 'Remedial Education in the Regular Classroom', *Remedial Education, 13,3*,117–121.

Malecka, M., 1985, 'Teaching French in a Special School', *NCSE Research Exchange, Vol 4*.

Mittler, P. (ed), 1970, *The Psychological Assessment of Mental and Physical Handicaps*, London, Methuen.

Mittler, P., 1985, 'Integration: the Shadow and the Substance', *Educational and Child Psychology, 2,3*, 8–22.

100

Mortimore, J. & Blackstone, T., 1982, *Disadvantage and Education*, Heinemann.

Newell, P., 1983, *ACE Special Education Handbook – the new law on children with special needs*, London, Advisory Centre for Education.

Newell, P., 1985, 'The Children's Legal Centre', *Educational and Child Psychology, 12,3*.

Open University Press, *Course 241: Special Needs in Education*.

Paton, I.D., 1984, 'The Role of the Head of the Special Needs Department in a Secondary School', Unpublished thesis submitted for the Special Diploma in Educational Studies, University of Oxford.

Postlethwaite, K.C., 1984, 'Teacher-based identification of pupils with high potential in physics and English', Unpublished D.Phil. thesis, Oxford.

Roaf, M.C., 1985, 'An inquiry into the way in which schools respond to whole-school policies with particular reference to policies for education for a multi-cultural society and the education of children with special educational needs', Unpublished dissertation submitted for the Special Diploma in Educational Studies, University of Oxford.

Rutter, M., Cox, A., Tupling, C., Berger, M. & Yule, W., 1975, 'Attainment and adjustment in two geographical areas', *British Journal of Psychiatry, 126*.

Rutter, M., Graham, P. & Whitmore, K. (1970), *Education, Health and Behaviour*, London, Longman.

Sarason, S. & Doris, J., 1979, *Educational Handicap, Public Policy and Social History*, The Free Press.

Sayer, J., 1983, 'A Comprehensive School for All', in Booth, T. & Potts, P. (eds), *Integrating Special Education*, Oxford, Blackwell.

Sayer, J., 1983, 'Assessments for All, Statements for None?', *Special Education: Forward Trends, 10,4*.

Sayer, J., 1985, *What Future for Secondary Schools?*, London, Falmer Press.

Sharron, H., 1985, 'Needs musts', *Times Educational Supplement,* 22 February 1985, 20.

Swann, W., 1985, 'Is the Integration of Children with Special Needs Happening?', *Oxford Review of Education, 11,1,* 3–18.

Tannenbaum, A.J., 1983, *Gifted Children: Psychological and Educational Perspectives*, Macmillan.

Vincent, D., Green, L., Francis, J. & Powney, J., 1983, *A Review of Reading Tests*, Windsor, NFER-Nelson.

Weber, K.J., 1978, *Yes, They Can!*, Milton Keynes, Open University Press.

Wilson, M. & Evans M., 1980, *Education of Disturbed Pupils,* London, Methuen for Schools Council.

Wilson, J. & Cowell, B., 1984, How should we define handicap? *Special Education: Forward Trends, 11,2*.

Wolfendale, S., 1984, *Parental Participation in Children's Development and Education*, Gordon and Breach.

Wrigley, J. (ed), 1983, *Guides to Assessment in Education,* Basingstoke, Macmillan Education.

Notes for tutors

Introduction

This book is intended to help students raise their awareness of the issues surrounding the design of special needs support systems in secondary schools. By 'students' in this context we mean a wide range of people:

a) they may be student teachers following a course of pre-service training who need to have some understanding of the issues in order that their work with special needs pupils in their own classroom can properly be related to the formal support structures existing in their school, and who also need such understanding so that they can make appropriate contributions to staff discussion on the special needs system of that school;

b) they may be practising mainstream teachers whose needs may be similar to those described above (though their level of engagement in the issues may well, of course, be different);

c) they may be special needs staff or members of school management teams who either work in the special needs system or have responsibility for organising it.

Such 'students' may use the book in different ways. They may work with it on an individual basis, or they may be able to join with colleagues to consider it as a group. Such groups may be set up as part of the structure of formal pre-service or in-service courses, or may arise because a number of colleagues in a given school or group of schools (e.g. secondary schools in one area of a county, or a secondary school with its partner primary schools) choose to come together on an informal basis.

We feel that group-based study has much to commend it, especially if such groups can be established with representatives from a range of subject backgrounds. This is important as the effects of some decisions about special needs arrangements can be very different for teachers in different subject areas. A good example is the issue of the integration of physically handicapped pupils which may have widely varied implications for teachers of, say, English, science, CDT and PE. Mixed subject groups have the opportunity to recognise such differences and seek resolutions of them. Students working alone, or only with colleagues from the same subject area, may not always be aware of the range of points of view.

We also feel that group study will be enhanced if groups can meet under the guidance of a tutor. Again the term can be interpreted in a broad way. The tutor may be a university or college lecturer, a special needs adviser, a head of special needs, or simply one of the group who has agreed to act in this role.

The notes presented in this section are intended to provide some support for such tutors.

Structure of the text

The first four chapters of the book present some broad principles which should be taken into account in discussing practice. Chapter 1 and 4 highlight some fundamental aspects of the notion of special needs. These chapters are based on theory, and on empirical evidence. Chapter 2 concentrates on legal constraints. We feel that the principles of equality and natural justice provide a further set of ideas against which practice should be considered. The most explicit way in which we have used these principles is, in Chapter 3, to structure our discussion of the curriculum for pupils with special needs. However, we would argue that the principles have application to the whole debate about special needs provision.

Chapters 5 and 6 develop some of the implications of the background ideas rehearsed in Chapters 1 to 4. They are particularly concerned with the implications for identification, assessment and provision.

Chapters 7 and 8 discuss two specific issues, integration of pupils from special schools into mainstream schools, and liaison between mainstream staff, specialist teachers and others.

Chapter 9 summarises the text and the relationship between broad principles and recommendations for practice.

Using the text*

1. Throughout the book we have provided activities which students might undertake to explore some of the ideas which have been presented. One important set of tasks for tutors is to encourage students to carry out these activities, to make any organisational arrangements necessary to enable them to do so, and to debrief students so that individual insights can be shared and extended through group discussion.

2. Another way in which a tutor can help students is to use the text to widen the range of practice, or of opinion, which is considered during the group's discussions. Students will, of course, bring to group sessions their own experience of how special needs provision is organised in their school, and of teachers' attitudes to different approaches. These will be important starting points for discussion, but they may be limited. For example, the students in the group may have experience of only one or two schools. (This could well be the case in a school-based in-service course, or if a group of pre-service student teachers are all doing their teaching practice in one or two schools.) Under such circumstances the tutor will find it necessary to use the text to point out that there are other ways of, say, organising provision, or to show that empirical evidence on teachers' opinions does not always match with the range of opinion to which the students have been exposed.

3. A third role for a group tutor is to encourage a critical, reflective attitude on the part of students. In many ways we would see this as the most important part of the tutor's role. Such critical reflection can be of various kinds.

* We are indebted to colleagues in Oxford for initiating many of these ideas.

One approach is to focus on current practice in a school. In this approach students attempt to match the school's current practice against the various theoretical and empirical foundations, against the legal requirements, and against the notions of equality and natural justice which we have presented in the book (especially in the first four chapters). Indeed, some of the activities which we have provided in the text are of precisely this kind (e.g. Activity 2.6a and Activity 6.1a). To facilitate such reflection, tutors might need to help students:

a) to identify the key ideas in the text (perhaps using an underlining exercise such as that suggested in Activity 6.3a),

b) to make explicit what actually goes on in their school (perhaps after a short period of investigation where individual students take responsibility for finding out exactly how particular bits of their system work),

c) to discuss this practice in relation to the key ideas (e.g. to consider how far total dependence on remedial class provision can be justified given the theoretical notions that special needs are not always related to low general ability, and that they can be quite short-lived),

d) to suggest some developments in practice that seem to be desirable.

Another sort of reflection is focused upon the particular implications for practice which *we* have drawn from the theoretical ideas in the text. In this approach students might be asked to question, for example, the implications for systems of identification which we have set out in Chapter 5, or the overall implications for special needs practice which we have summarised in Chapter 9. They might be asked to do this on the grounds of the acceptability of the ideas to teachers, to parents and/or to pupils. (Practical investigation of the acceptability of the ideas to these groups might profitably be required of students.) Alternatively, they might be asked to do it in terms of the practicality of the ideas. Having discussed *our* ideas in these terms, students should be invited to develop their own ideas for recommended practice *bearing in mind the basic principles from which our suggestions grew* (e.g. bearing in mind the legal position, the notion of pupils with special needs being present in all classes and so on).

With some groups it may be appropriate to go a stage further and examine the basic principles themselves. This might involve discussing such things as the empirical base for the 'Warnock figure' of 20 per cent, or the evidence for the view that some cognitive difficulties are not necessarily related to low general ability. It might also involve scrutiny of the Education Act 1981 and related legislation to explore the validity of our summary or to see what else might need to be taken into account. It might involve discussion of our view that general notions of equality and 'natural justice' should have a place in guiding decision-making in this area. If such a fundamental study of principles is undertaken there should still be a stage at which students work out practical implications of their newly developed framework, and then go back to test *their* ideas against criteria such as acceptability and practicality.

4. With some groups (e.g. experienced teachers on a long in-service course), it may be appropriate to encourage students, after recommendations for practice have been discussed through the kinds of activities suggested above, to try out some of the these recommendations (ours or theirs) in their own schools and to research the effects of the changes in an action research model.

The recommendations that could be explored in this way would depend on the role which the students normally played in school (or could reasonably assume in the school for the purposes of the action research study). Thus it might be appropriate for a head of special needs on a long course to decide on a desirable overall structure for special needs provision through the processes of critical reflection which we have described, to negotiate this structure with colleagues and to research the course of these negotiations and the outcome of acting upon them. It would be entirely innappropriate for an inexperienced mainstream teacher to attempt to do this. Such a teacher might, however, be able to investigate the effects of implementing some of our ideas for teacher-based identification and assessment because the changes to practice needed for such an investigation could be confined to the teacher's own classroom.

Even these very brief notes indicate that the text can be used in a variety of ways to help to achieve objectives which vary widely in their sophistication. Perhaps the greatest value of the notes will be that they will encourage tutors to be flexible in thinking of their own ways of using the book. If, through their ingenuity, tutors are able to use the text to support everything from awareness raising sessions for PGCE students to long-term action research studies by senior teachers working towards a substantial dissertation, we will be very well pleased.

Index

THE PILGRIM OF HATE

Pilgrims are gathering from far and wide to celebrate the fourth anniversary of the translation of Saint Winifred's bones to the Benedictine Abbey at Shrewsbury. In distant Winchester, a knight, supporter of the Empress Maud, has been murdered—not apparently an event of importance to those seeking miraculous cures at the saint's shrine. But among the throng some strange customers indeed begin to puzzle Brother Cadfael and as the story unfolds it becomes evident that the murder is a much less remote affair than it first seemed.

THE PILGRIM OF HATE

The Tenth Chronicle
of Brother Cadfael

Ellis Peters

CHIVERS PRESS
BATH

First published 1984
by
Macmillan London Limited
This Large Print edition published by
Chivers Press
by arrangement with
Little, Brown (UK) Ltd
1999

ISBN 0 7540 1310 3

British Library Cataloguing in Publication Data available

Printed in Great Britain by
Redwood Books, Trowbridge, Wiltshire.

CHAPTER ONE

They were together in Brother Cadfael's hut in the herbarium, in the afternoon of the twenty-fifth day of May, and the talk was of high matters of state, of kings and empresses, and the unbalanced fortunes that plagued the irreconcilable contenders for thrones.

'Well, the lady is not crowned yet!' said Hugh Beringar, almost as firmly as if he saw a way of preventing it.

'She is not even in London yet,' agreed Cadfael, stirring carefully round the pot embedded in the coals of his brazier, to keep the brew from boiling up against the sides and burning. 'She cannot well be crowned until they let her in to Westminster. Which it seems, from all I gather, they are in no hurry to do.'

'Where the sun shines,' said Hugh ruefully, 'there whoever's felt the cold will gather. My cause, old friend, is out of the sun. When Henry of Blois shifts, all men shift with him, like starvelings huddled in one bed. He heaves the coverlet, and they go with him, clinging by the hems.'

'Not all,' objected Cadfael, briefly smiling as he stirred. 'Not you. Do you think you are the only one?'

'God forbid!' said Hugh, and suddenly laughed, shaking off his gloom. He came back from the open doorway, where the pure light spread a soft golden sheen over the bushes and beds of the herb-garden and the moist noon air drew up a heady languor of spiced and drunken odours, and plumped his slender person down again on the bench against the timber wall, spreading his booted feet on the earth floor. A small man in one sense only, and even so trimly made. His modest stature and light weight had deceived many a man to his undoing. The sunshine from without, fretted by the breeze that swayed the bushes, was reflected from one of Cadfael's great glass flagons to illuminate by flashing glimpses a lean, tanned face, clean shaven, with a quirky mouth, and agile black eyebrows that could twist upward sceptically into cropped black hair. A face at once eloquent and inscrutable. Brother Cadfael was one of the few who knew how to read it. Doubtful if even Hugh's wife Aline understood him better. Cadfael was in his sixty-second year, and Hugh still a year or two short of thirty but, meeting thus in easy companionship in Cadfael's workshop among the herbs, they felt themselves contemporaries.

'No,' said Hugh, eyeing circumstances narrowly, and taking some cautious comfort, 'not all. There are a few of us yet, and not so badly placed to hold on to what we have. There's the queen in Kent with her army.

Robert of Gloucester is not going to turn his back to come hunting us here while she hangs on the southern fringes of London. And with the Welsh of Gwynedd keeping our backs against the earl of Chester, we can hold this shire for King Stephen and wait out the time. Luck that turned once can turn again. And the empress is not queen of England yet.'

But for all that, thought Cadfael, mutely stirring his brew for Brother Aylwin's scouring calves, it began to look as though she very soon would be. Three years of civil war between cousins fighting for the sovereignty of England had done nothing to reconcile the factions, but much to sicken the general populace with insecurity, rapine and killing. The craftsman in the town, the cottar in the village, the serf on the demesne, would be only too glad of any monarch who could guarantee him a quiet and orderly country in which to carry on his modest business. But to a man like Hugh it was no such indifferent matter. He was King Stephen's liege man, and now King Stephen's sheriff of Shropshire, sworn to hold the shire for his cause. And his king was a prisoner in Bristol castle since the lost battle of Lincoln. A single February day of this year had seen a total reversal of the fortunes of the two claimants to the throne. The Empress Maud was up in the clouds, and Stephen, crowned and anointed though he might be, was down in the midden, close-bound and close-guarded,

3

and his brother Henry of Blois, bishop of Winchester and papal legate, far the most influential of the magnates and hitherto his brother's supporter, had found himself in a dilemma. He could either be a hero, and adhere loudly and firmly to his allegiance, thus incurring the formidable animosity of a lady who was in the ascendant and could be dangerous, or trim his sails and accommodate himself to the reverses of fortune by coming over to her side. Discreetly, of course, and with well-prepared arguments to render his about-face respectable. It was just possible, thought Cadfael, willing to do justice even to bishops, that Henry also had the cause of order and peace genuinely at heart, and was willing to back whichever contender could restore them.

'What frets me,' said Hugh restlessly, 'is that I can get no reliable news. Rumours enough and more than enough, every new one laying the last one dead, but nothing a man can grasp and put his trust in. I shall be main glad when Abbot Radulfus comes home.'

'So will every brother in this house,' agreed Cadfael fervently. 'Barring Jerome, perhaps, he's in high feather when Prior Robert is left in charge, and a fine time he's had of it all these weeks since the abbot was summoned to Winchester. But Robert's rule is less favoured by the rest of us, I can tell you.'

'How long is it he's been away now?' pondered Hugh. 'Seven or eight weeks! The legate's keeping his court well stocked with mitres all this time. Maintaining his own state no doubt gives him some aid in confronting hers. Not a man to let his dignity bow to princes, Henry, and he needs all the weight he can get at his back.'

'He's letting some of his cloth disperse now, however,' said Cadfael. 'By that token, he may have got a kind of settlement. Or he may be deceived into thinking he has. Father Abbot sent word from Reading. In a week he should be here. You'll hardly find a better witness.'

Bishop Henry had taken good care to keep the direction of events in his own hands. Calling all the prelates and mitred abbots to Winchester early in April, and firmly declaring the gathering a legatine council, no mere church assembly, had ensured his supremacy at the subsequent discussions, giving him precedence over Archbishop Theobald of Canterbury, who in purely English church matters was his superior. Just as well, perhaps. Cadfael doubted if Theobald had greatly minded being outflanked. In the circumstances a quiet, timorous man might be only too glad to lurk peaceably in the shadows, and let the legate bear the heat of the sun.

'I know it. Once let me hear his account of what's gone forward, down there in the south, and I can make my own dispositions. We're remote enough here, and the queen, God keep her, has gathered a very fair array, now she has

5

the Flemings who escaped from Lincoln to add to her force. She'll move heaven and earth to get Stephen out of hold, by whatever means, fair or foul. She is,' said Hugh with conviction, 'a better soldier than her lord. Not a better fighter in the field—God knows you'd need to search Europe through to find such a one, I saw him at Lincoln—a marvel! But a better general, that she *is*. She holds to her purpose, where he tires and goes off after another quarry. They tell me, and I believe it, she's drawing her cordon closer and closer to London, south of the river. The nearer her rival comes to Westminster, the tighter that noose will be drawn.'

'And is it certain the Londoners have agreed to let the empress in? We hear they came late to the council, and made a faint plea for Stephen before they let themselves be tamed. It takes a very stout heart, I suppose, to stand up to Henry of Winchester face to face, and deny him,' allowed Cadfael, sighing.

'They've agreed to admit her, which is as good as acknowledging her. But they're arguing terms for her entry, as I heard it, and every delay is worth gold to me and to Stephen. If only,' said Hugh, the dancing light suddenly sharpening every line of his intent and eloquent face, 'if only I could get a good man into Bristol! There are ways into castles, even into the dungeons. Two or three good, secret men might do it. A fistful of gold to a

6

malcontent gaoler . . . Kings have been fetched off before now, even out of chains, and he's not chained. She has not gone so far, not yet. Cadfael, I dream! My work is here, and I am but barely equal to it. I have no means of carrying off Bristol, too.'

'Once loosed,' said Cadfael, 'your king is going to need this shire ready to his hand.'

He turned from the brazier, hoisting aside the pot and laying it to cool on a slab of stone he kept for the purpose. His back creaked a little as he straightened it. In small ways he was feeling his years, but once erect he was spry enough.

'I'm done here for this while,' he said, brushing his hands together to get rid of the hollow worn by the ladle. 'Come into the daylight, and see the flowers we're bringing on for the festival of Saint Winifred. Father Abbot will be home in good time to preside over her reception from Saint Giles. And we shall have a houseful of pilgrims to care for.'

*　　　*　　　*

They had brought the reliquary of the Welsh saint four years previously from Gwytherin, where she lay buried, and installed it on the altar of the church at the hospital of Saint Giles, at the very edge of Shrewsbury's Foregate suburb, where the sick, the infected, the deformed, the lepers, who might not venture within the walls, were housed and cared for. And thence they had borne her casket in splendour to her altar in the abbey church, to be an ornament and a wonder, a means of healing and blessing to all who came reverently and in need. This year they had undertaken to repeat that last journey, to bring her from Saint Giles in procession, and open her altar to all who came with prayers and offerings. Every year she had drawn many pilgrims. This year they would be legion.

'A man might wonder,' said Hugh, standing spread-footed among the flower beds just beginning to burn from the soft, shy colours of spring into the blaze of summer, 'whether you were not rather preparing for a bridal.'

Hedges of hazel and may-blossom shed silver petals and dangled pale, silver-green catkins round the enclosure where they stood, cowslips were rearing in the grass of the meadow beyond, and irises were in tight, thrusting bud. Even the roses showed a harvest of buds, erect and ready to break and display the first colour. In the walled shelter of Cadfael's herb-garden there were fat globes of peonies, too, just cracking their green sheaths. Cadfael had medicinal uses for the seeds, and Brother Petrus, the abbot's cook, used them as spices in the kitchen.

'A man might not be so far out, at that,' said Cadfael, viewing the fruits of his labours complacently. 'A perpetual and pure bridal.

8

This Welsh girl was virgin until the day of her death.'

'And you have married her off since?'

It was idly said, in revulsion from pondering matters of state. In such a garden a man could believe in peace, fruitfulness and amity. But it encountered suddenly so profound and pregnant a silence that Hugh pricked up his ears, and turned his head almost stealthily to study his friend, even before the unguarded answer came. Unguarded either from absence of mind, or of design, there was no telling.

'Not wedded,' said Cadfael, 'but certainly bedded. With a good man, too, and her honest champion. He deserved his reward.'

Hugh raised quizzical brows, and cast a glance over his shoulder towards the long roof of the great abbey church, where reputedly the lady in question slept in a sealed reliquary on her own altar. An elegant coffin just long enough to contain a small and holy Welshwoman, with the neat, compact bones of her race.

'Hardly room within there for two,' he said mildly.

'Not two of our gross make, no, not there. There was space enough where we put them.' He knew he was listened to, now, and heard with sharp intelligence, if not yet understood.

'Are you telling me,' wondered Hugh no less mildly, 'that she is *not* there in that elaborate shrine of yours, where everyone else *knows* she is?'

'Can I tell? Many a time I've wished it could be possible to be in two places at once. A thing too hard for me, but for a saint, perhaps, possible? Three nights and three days she was in there, that I do know. She may well have left a morsel of her holiness within—if only by way of thanks to us who took her out again, and put her back where I still, and always shall, believe she wished to be. But for all that,' owned Cadfael, shaking his head, 'there's a trailing fringe of doubt that nags at me. How if I read her wrong?'

'Then your only resort is confession and penance,' said Hugh lightly.

'Not until Brother Mark is full-fledged a priest!' Young Mark was gone from his mother-house and from his flock at Saint Giles, gone to the household of the bishop of Lichfield, with Leoric Aspley's endowment to see him through his studies, and the goal of all his longings shining distant and clear before him, the priesthood for which God had designed him. 'I'm saving for him,' said Cadfael, 'all those sins I feel, perhaps mistakenly, to be no sins. He was my right hand and a piece of my heart for three years, and knows me better than any man living. Barring, it may be, yourself?' he added, and slanted a guileless glance at his friend. 'He will know the truth of me, and by his judgement and for his absolution I'll embrace any

10

penance. You might deliver the judgement, Hugh, but you cannot deliver the absolution.'

'Nor the penance, neither,' said Hugh, and laughed freely. 'So tell it to me, and go free without penalty.'

The idea of confiding was unexpectedly pleasing and acceptable. 'It's a long story,' [See *A Morbid Taste for Bones*.] said Cadfael warningly.

'Then now's your time, for whatever I can do here is done, nothing is asked of me but watchfulness and patience, and why should I wait unentertained if there's a good story to be heard? And you are at leisure until Vespers. You may even get merit,' said Hugh, composing his face into priestly solemnity, 'by unburdening your soul to the secular arm. And I can be secret,' he said, 'as any confessional.'

'Wait, then,' said Cadfael, 'while I fetch a draught of that maturing wine, and come within to the bench under the north wall, where the afternoon sun falls. We may as well be at ease while I talk.'

*   *   *

'It was a year or so before I knew you,' said Cadfael, bracing his back comfortably against the warmed, stony roughness of the herb-garden wall. 'We were without a tame saint to our house, and somewhat envious of Wenlock, where the Cluny community had discovered

11

their Saxon foundress Milburga, and were making great play with her. And we had certain signs that sent off an ailing brother of ours into Wales, to bathe at Holywell, where this girl Winifred died her first death, and brought forth her healing spring. There was her own patron, Saint Beuno, ready and able to bring her back to life, but the spring remained, and did wonders. So it came to Prior Robert that the lady could be persuaded to leave Gwytherin, where she died her second death and was buried, and come and bring her glory to us here in Shrewsbury. I was one of the party he took with him to deal with the parish there, and bring them to give up the saint's bones.'

'All of which,' said Hugh, warmed and attentive beside him, 'I know very well, since all men here know it.'

'Surely! But you do not know to the end what followed. There was one Welsh lord in Gwytherin who would not suffer the girl to be disturbed, and would not be persuaded or bribed or threatened into letting her go. And he died, Hugh—murdered. By one of us, a brother who came from high rank, and had his eyes already set on a mitre. And when we came near to accusing him, it was his life or a better. There were certain young people of that place put in peril by him, the dead lord's daughter and her lover. The boy lashed out in anger, with good reason, seeing his girl wounded and bleeding. He was stronger than he knew. The murderer's neck was broken.'

'How many knew of this?' asked Hugh, his eyes narrowed thoughtfully upon the glossy-leaved rose-bushes.

'When it befell, only the lovers, the dead man and I. And Saint Winifred, who had been raised from her grave and laid in that casket of which you and all men know. *She* knew. She was there. From the moment I raised her,' said Cadfael, 'and by God, it was I who took her from the soil, and I who restored her—and still that makes me glad—from the moment I uncovered those slender bones, I felt in mine they wished only to be left in peace. It was so little and so wild and quiet a graveyard there, with the small church long out of use, meadow flowers growing over all, and the mounds so modest and green. And Welsh soil! The girl was Welsh, like me, her church was of the old persuasion, what did she know of this alien English shire? And I had those young things to keep. Who would have taken their word or mine against all the force of the church? They would have closed their ranks to bury the scandal, and bury the boy with it, and he guilty of nothing but defending his dear. So I took measures.'

Hugh's mobile lips twitched. 'Now indeed you amaze me! And what measures were those? With a dead brother to account for, and Prior Robert to keep sweet . . .'

13

'Ah, well, Robert is a simpler soul than he supposes, and then I had a good deal of help from the dead brother himself. He'd been busy building himself such a reputation for sanctity, delivering messages from the saint herself—it was he told us she was offering the grave she'd left to the murdered man—and going into trance-sleeps, and praying to leave this world and be taken into bliss living ... So we did him that small favour. He'd been keeping a solitary night-watch in the old church, and in the morning when it ended, there were his habit and sandals fallen together at his prayer-stool, and the body of him lifted clean out of them, in sweet odours and a shower of may-blossom. That was how he claimed the saint had already visited him, why should not Robert recall it and believe? Certainly he was gone. Why look for him? Would a modest brother of our house be running through the Welsh woods mother-naked?'

'Are you telling me,' asked Hugh cautiously, 'That what you have there in the reliquary is *not* ... Then the casket had not yet been sealed?' His eyebrows were tangling with his black forelock, but his voice was soft and unsurprised.

'Well ...' Cadfael twitched his blunt brown nose bashfully between finger and thumb. 'Sealed it was, but there are ways of dealing with seals that leave them unblemished. It's one of the more dubious of my remembered

14

skills, but for all that I was glad of it then.'

'And you put the lady back in the place that was hers, along with her champion?'

'He was a decent, good man, and had spoken up for her nobly. She would not grudge him house-room. I have always thought,' confided Cadfael, 'that she was not displeased with us. She has shown her power in Gwytherin since that time, by many miracles, so I cannot believe she is angry. But what a little troubles me is that she has not so far chosen to favour us with any great mark of her patronage here, to keep Robert happy, and set my mind at rest. Oh, a few little things, but nothing of unmistakable note. How if I have displeased her, after all? Well for me, who *know* what we have within there on the altar— and *mea culpa* if I did wrongly! But what of the innocents who do *not* know, and come in good faith, hoping for grace from her? What if I have been the means of their deprivation and loss?'

'I see,' said Hugh with sympathy, 'that Brother Mark had better make haste through the degrees of ordination, and come quickly to lift the load from you. Unless,' he added with a flashing sidelong smile, 'Saint Winifred takes pity on you first, and sends you a sign.'

'I still do not see,' mused Cadfael, 'what else I could have done. It was an ending that satisfied everyone, both here and there. The children were free to marry and be happy, the village still had its saint, and she had her own people round her. Robert had what he had gone to find—or thought he had, which is the same thing. And Shrewsbury abbey has its festival, with every hope of a full guest-hall, and glory and gain in good measure. If she would but just cast an indulgent look this way, and wink her eye, to let me know I understood her aright.'

'And you've never said word of this to anyone?'

'Never a word. But the whole village of Gwytherin knows it,' admitted Cadfael with a remembering grin. 'No one told, no one had to tell, but they knew. There wasn't a man missing when we took up the reliquary and set out for home. They helped to carry it, whipped together a little chariot to bear it. Robert thought he had them nicely tamed, even those who'd been most reluctant from the first. It was a great joy to him. A simple soul at bottom! It would be great pity to undo him now, when he's busy writing his book about the saint's life, and how he brought her to Shrewsbury.'

'I would not have the heart to put him to such distress,' said Hugh. 'Least said, best for all. Thanks be to God, I have nothing to do with canon law, the common law of a land almost without law costs me enough pains.' No need to say that Cadfael could be sure of his secrecy, that was taken for granted on both

16

sides. 'Well, you speak the lady's own tongue, no doubt she understood you well enough, with or without words. Who knows? When this festival of yours takes place—the twenty-second day of June, you say?—she may take pity on you, and send you a great miracle to set your mind at rest.'

*   *   *

And so she might, thought Cadfael an hour later, on his way to obey the summons of the Vesper bell. Not that he had deserved so signal an honour, but there surely must be one somewhere among the unceasing stream of pilgrims who did deserve it, and could not with justice be rejected. He would be perfectly and humbly and cheerfully content with that. What if she was eighty miles or so away, in what was left of her body? It had been a miraculous body in this life, once brutally dead and raised alive again, what limits of time or space could be set about such a being? If it so pleased her she could be both quiet and content in her grave with Rhisiart, lulled by bird-song in the hawthorn trees, and here attentive and incorporeal, a little flame of spirit in the coffin of unworthy Columbanus, who had killed not for her exaltation but for his own.

Brother Cadfael went to Vespers curiously relieved at having confided to his friend a secret from before the time when they had first

17

known each other, in the beginning as potential antagonists stepping subtly to outwit each other, then discovering how much they had in common, the old man—alone with himself Cadfael admitted to being somewhat over the peak of a man's prime—and the young one, just setting out, exceedingly well-equipped in shrewdness and wit, to build his fortune and win his wife. And both he had done, for he was now undisputed sheriff of Shropshire, if under a powerless and captive king, and up there in the town, near St Mary's church, his wife and his year-old son made a nest for his private happiness when he shut the door on his public burdens.

Cadfael thought of his godson, the sturdy imp who already clutched his way lustily round the rooms of Hugh's town house, climbed unaided into a godfather's lap, and began to utter human sounds of approval, enquiry, indignation and affection. Every man asks of heaven a son. Hugh had his, as promising a sprig as ever budded from the stem. So, by proxy, had Cadfael, a son in God.

There was, after all, a great deal of human happiness in the world, even a world so torn and mangled with conflict, cruelty and greed. So it had always been, and always would be. And so be it, provided the indomitable spark of joy never went out.

*   *   *

In the refectory, after supper and grace, in the grateful warmth and lingering light of the end of May, when they were shuffling their benches to rise from table, Prior Robert Pennant rose first in his place, levering erect his more than six feet of lean, austere prelate, silver-tonsured and ivory-featured.

'Brothers, I have received a further message from Father Abbot. He has reached Warwick on his way home to us, and hopes to be with us by the fourth day of June or earlier. He bids us be diligent in making proper preparation for the celebration of Saint Winifred's translation, our most gracious patroness.' Perhaps the abbot had so instructed, in duty bound, but it was Robert himself who laid such stress on it, viewing himself, as he did, as the patron of their patroness. His large patrician eye swept round the refectory tables, settling upon those heads most deeply committed. 'Brother Anselm, you have the music already in hand?'

Brother Anselm the precentor, whose mind seldom left its neums and instruments for many seconds together, looked up vaguely, awoke to the question, and stared, wide-eyed. 'The entire order of procession and office is ready,' he said, in amiable surprise that anyone should feel it necessary to ask.

'And Brother Denis, you have made all the preparations necessary for stocking your halls to feed great numbers? For we shall surely

19

need every cot and every dish we can muster.'

Brother Denis the hospitaller, accustomed to outer panics and secure ruler of his own domain, testified calmly that he had made the fullest provision he considered needful, and further, that he had reserves laid by to tap at need.

'There will also be many sick persons to be tended, for that reason they come.'

Brother Edmund the infirmarer, not waiting to be named, said crisply that he had taken into account the probable need, and was prepared for the demands that might be made on his beds and medicines. He mentioned also, being on his feet, that Brother Cadfael had already provided stocks of all the remedies most likely to be wanted, and stood ready to meet any other needs that should arise.

'That is well,' said Prior Robert. 'Now, Father Abbot has yet a special request to make until he comes. He asks that prayers be made at every High Mass for the repose of the soul of a good man, treacherously slain in Winchester as he strove to keep the peace and reconcile faction with faction, in Christian duty.'

For a moment it seemed to Brother Cadfael, and perhaps to most of the others present, that the death of one man, far away in the south, hardly rated so solemn a mention and so signal a mark of respect, in a country where deaths had been commonplace for so long, from the field of Lincoln strewn with bodies to the sack of Worcester with its streets running blood, from the widespread baronial slaughters by disaffected earls to the sordid village banditries where law had broken down. Then he looked at it again, and with the abbot's measuring eyes. Here was a good man cut down in the very city where prelates and barons were parleying over matters of peace and sovereignty, killed in trying to keep one faction from the throat of the other. At the very feet, as it were, of the bishop-legate. As black a sacrilege as if he had been butchered on the steps of the altar. It was not one man's death, it was a bitter symbol of the abandonment of law and the rejection of hope and reconciliation. So Radulfus had seen it, and so he recorded it in the offices of his house. There was a solemn acknowledgement due to the dead man, a memorial lodged in heaven.

'We are asked,' said Prior Robert, 'to offer thanks for the just endeavour and prayers for the soul of one Rainald Bossard, a knight in the service of the Empress Maud.'

*　　　*　　　*

'One of the enemy,' said a young novice doubtfully, talking it over in the cloisters afterwards. So used were they, in this shire, to thinking of the king's cause as their own, since it had been his writ which had run here now in orderly fashion for four years, and kept off the worst of the chaos that troubled so much of England elsewhere.

'Not so,' said Brother Paul, the master of the novices, gently chiding. 'No good and honourable man is an enemy, though he may take the opposing side in this dissension. The fealty of this world is not for us, but we must bear it ever in mind as a true value, as binding on those who owe it as our vows are on us. The claims of these two cousins are both in some sort valid. It is no reproach to have kept faith, whether with king or empress. And this was surely a worthy man, or Father Abbot would not thus have recommended him to our prayers.'

Brother Anselm, thoughtfully revolving the syllables of the name, and tapping the resultant rhythm on the stone of the bench on which he sat, repeated to himself softly: 'Rainald Bossard, Rainald Bossard . . .'

The repeated iambic stayed in Brother Cadfael's ear and wormed its way into his mind. A name that meant nothing yet to anyone here, had neither form nor face, no age, no character; nothing but a name, which is either a soul without a body or a body without a soul. It went with him into his cell in the dortoir, as he made his last prayers and shook off his sandals before lying down to sleep. It may even have kept a rhythm in his sleeping mind, without the need of a dream to house it, for the first he knew of the thunder-storm was a silent double-gleam of lightning that spelled out the same iambic, and caused him to start awake with eyes still closed, and listen for the answering thunder. It did not come for so long that he thought he had dreamed it, and then he heard it, very distant, very quiet, and yet curiously ominous. Beyond his closed eyelids the quiet lightnings flared and died, and the echoes answered so late and so softly, from so far away . . .

As far, perhaps, as that fabled city of Winchester, where momentous matters had been decided, a place Cadfael had never seen, and probably never would see. A threat from a town so distant could shake no foundations here, and no hearts, any more than such far-off thunders could bring down the walls of Shrewsbury. Yet the continuing murmur of disquiet was still in his ears as he fell asleep.

CHAPTER TWO

Abbot Radulfus rode back into his abbey of Saint Peter and Saint Paul on the third day of June, escorted by his chaplain and secretary, Brother Vitalis, and welcomed home by all the fifty-three brothers, seven novices and six schoolboys of his house, as well as all the lay stewards and servants.

The abbot was a long, lean, hard man in his fifties, with a gaunt, ascetic face and a shrewd, scholar's eye, so vigorous and able of body that he dismounted and went straight to preside at High Mass, before retiring to remove the stains of travel or take any refreshment after his long ride. Nor did he forget to offer the prayer he had enjoined upon his flock, for the repose of the soul of Rainald Bossard, slain in Winchester on the evening of Wednesday, the ninth day of April of this year of Our Lord 1141. Eight weeks dead, and half the length of England away, what meaning could Rainald Bossard have for this indifferent town of Shrewsbury, or the members of this far-distant Benedictine house?

Not until the next morning's chapter would the household hear its abbot's account of that momentous council held in the south to determine the future of England; but when Hugh Beringar waited upon Radulfus about mid-afternoon, and asked for audience, he was not kept waiting. Affairs demanded the close co-operation of the secular and the clerical powers, in defence of such order and law as survived in England.

The abbot's private parlour in his lodging was as austere as its presiding father, plainly furnished, but with sunlight spilled across its flagged floor from two open lattices at this hour of the sun's zenith, and a view of gracious greenery and glowing flowers in the small walled garden without. Quiverings of radiance flashed and vanished and recoiled and collided over the dark panelling within, from the new-budded life and fresh breeze and exuberant light outside. Hugh sat in shadow, and watched the abbot's trenchant profile, clear, craggy and dark against a ground of shifting brightness.

'My allegiance is well known to you, Father,' said Hugh, admiring the stillness of the noble mask thus framed, 'as yours is to me. But there is much that we share. Whatever you can tell me of what passed in Winchester, I do greatly need to know.'

'And I to understand,' said Radulfus, with a tight and rueful smile. 'I went as summoned, by him who has a right to summon me, and I went knowing how matters then stood, the king a prisoner, the empress mistress of much of the south, and in due position to claim sovereignty by right of conquest. We knew, you and I both, what would be in debate down there. I can only give you my own account as I saw it. The first day that we gathered there, a Monday it was, the seventh of April, there was nothing done by way of business but the ceremonial of welcoming us all, and reading out—there were many of these!—the letters sent by way of excuse from those who remained absent. The empress had a lodging in the town then, though she made several moves about the region, to Reading and other places, while we debated. She did not attend. She has a measure of discretion.' His tone was dry. It was not clear whether he considered her measure of that commodity to be adequate or somewhat lacking. 'The second day . . .' He fell silent, remembering what he had witnessed. Hugh waited attentively, not stirring.

'The second day, the eighth of April, the legate made his great speech . . .'

It was no effort to imagine him. Henry of Blois, bishop of Winchester, papal legate, younger brother and hitherto partisan of King Stephen, impregnably ensconced in the chapter house of his own cathedral, secure master of the political pulse of England, the cleverest manipulator in the kingdom, and on his own chosen ground—and yet hounded on to the defensive, in so far as that could ever happen to so expert a practitioner. Hugh had never seen the man, never been near the region where he ruled, had only heard him described, and yet could see him now, presiding with imperious composure over his half-unwilling assembly. A difficult part he had to play, to extricate himself from his known allegiance to his brother, and yet preserve his face and his status and influence with those who had shared it. And with a tough, experienced woman narrowly observing his every word, and holding in reserve her own new powers to destroy or preserve, according to how he managed his ill-disciplined team in

26

this heavy furrow.

'He spoke a tedious while,' said the abbot candidly, 'but he is a very able speaker. He put us in mind that we were met together to try to salvage England from chaos and ruin. He spoke of the late King Henry's time, when order and peace was kept throughout the land. And he reminded us how the old king, left without a son, commanded his barons to swear an oath of allegiance to his only remaining child, his daughter Maud the empress, now widowed, and wed again to the count of Anjou.'

And so those barons had done, almost all, not least this same Henry of Winchester. Hugh Beringar, who had never come to such a test until he was ready to choose for himself, curled a half-disdainful and half-commiserating lip, and nodded understanding. 'His lordship had somewhat to explain away.'

The abbot refrained from indicating, by word or look, agreement with the implied criticism of his brother cleric. 'He said that the long delay which might then have arisen from the empress's being in Normandy had given rise to natural concern for the well-being of the state. An interim of uncertainty was dangerous. And thus, he said, his brother Count Stephen was accepted when he offered himself, and became king by consent. His own part in this acceptance he admitted. For he it was who pledged his word to God and men that King Stephen would honour and revere the Holy Church, and maintain the good and just laws of the land. In which undertaking, said Henry, the king has shamefully failed. To his great chagrin and grief he declared it, having been his brother's guarantor to God.'

So that was the way round the humiliating change of course, thought Hugh. All was to be laid upon Stephen, who had so deceived his reverend brother and defaulted upon all his promises, that a man of God might well be driven to the end of his patience, and be brought to welcome a change of monarch with relief tempering his sorrow.

'In particular,' said Radulfus, 'he recalled how the king had hounded certain of his bishops to their ruin and death.'

There was more than a grain of truth in that, though the only death in question, of Robert of Salisbury, had resulted naturally from old age, bitterness and despair, because his power was gone.

'Therefore, *he said*,' continued the abbot with chill deliberation, 'the judgement of God had been manifested against the king, in delivering him up prisoner to his enemies. And he, devout in the service of the Holy Church, must choose between his devotion to his mortal brother and to his immortal father, and could not but bow to the edict of heaven. Therefore he had called us together, to ensure that a kingdom lopped of its head should not founder in utter ruin. And this very matter, he told the assembly, had been discussed most gravely on the day previous among the greater part of the clergy of England, who—*he said!*— had a prerogative surmounting others in the election and consecration of a king.'

There was something in the dry, measured voice that made Hugh prick up his ears. For this was a large and unprecedented claim, and by all the signs Abbot Radulfus found it more than suspect. The legate had his own face to save, and a well-oiled tongue with which to wind the protective mesh of words before it.

'Was there such a meeting? Were you present at such, Father?'

'There was a meeting,' said Radulfus, 'not prolonged, and by no means very clear in its course. The greater part of the talking was done by the legate. The empress had her partisans there.' He said it sedately and tolerantly, but clearly he had not been one. 'I do not recall that he then claimed this prerogative for us. Nor that there was ever a count taken.'

'Nor, as I guess, declared. It would not come to a numbering of heads or hands.' Too easy, then, to start a counter-count of one's own, and confound the reckoning.

'He continued,' said Radulfus coolly and drily, 'by saying that we had chosen as Lady of England the late king's daughter, the inheritor of his nobility and his will to peace. As the sire

29

was unequalled in merit in our times, so might his daughter flourish and bring peace, as he did, to this troubled country, where we now offer her—*he said*!—our whole-hearted fealty.'

So the legate had extricated himself as adroitly as possible from his predicament. But for all that, so resolute, courageous and vindictive a lady as the empress was going to look somewhat sidewise at a whole-hearted fealty which had already once been pledged to her, and turned its back nimbly under pressure, and might as nimbly do so again. If she was wise she would curb her resentment and take care to keep on the right side of the legate, as he was cautiously feeling his way to the right side of her; but she would not forget or forgive.

'And there was no man raised a word against it?' asked Hugh mildly.

'None. There was small opportunity, and even less inducement. And with that the bishop announced that he had invited a deputation from the city of London, and expected them to arrive that day, so that it was expedient we should adjourn our discussion until the morrow. Even so, the Londoners did not come until next day, and we met again somewhat later than on the days previous. Howbeit, they did come. With somewhat dour faces and stiff necks. They said that they represented the whole commune of London, into which many barons had also entered as members after Lincoln, and that they all, with no wish to challenge the legitimacy of our assembly, yet desired to put forward with one voice the request that the lord king should be set at liberty.'

'That was bold,' said Hugh with raised brows. 'How did his lordship counter it? Was he put out of countenance?'

'I think he was shaken, but not disastrously, not then. He made a long speech—it is a way of keeping others silent, at least for a time—reproving the city for taking into its membership men who had abandoned their king in war, after leading him astray by their evil advice, so grossly that he forsook God and right, and was brought to the judgement of defeat and captivity, from which the prayers of those same false friends could not now reprieve him. These men do but flatter and favour you now, he said, for their own advantage.'

'If he meant the Flemings who ran from Lincoln,' Hugh allowed, 'he told no more than truth there. But for what other end is the city ever flattered and wooed? What then? Had they the hardihood to stand their ground against him?'

'They were in some disarray as to what they should reply, and went apart to confer. And while there was quiet, a man suddenly stepped forward from among the clerks, and held out a parchment to Bishop Henry, asking him to

31

read it aloud, so confidently that I wonder still he did not at once comply. Instead, he opened and began to read it in silence, and in a moment more he was thundering in a great rage that the thing was an insult to the reverend company present, its matter disgraceful, its witnesses attainted enemies of Holy Church, and not a word of it would he read aloud to us in so sacred a place as his chapter house. Whereupon,' said the abbot grimly, 'the clerk snatched it back from him, and himself read it aloud in a great voice, riding above the bishop when he tried to silence him. It was a plea from Stephen's queen to all present, and to the legate in especial, own brother to the king, to return to fealty and restore the king to his own again from the base captivity into which traitors had betrayed him. And I, said the brave man who read, am a clerk in the service of Queen Matilda, and if any ask my name, it is Christian, and true Christian I am as any here, and true to my salt.'

'Brave, indeed!' said Hugh, and whistled softly. 'But I doubt it did him little good.'

'The legate replied to him in a tirade, much as he had spoken already to us the day before, but in a great passion, and so intimidated the men from London that they drew in their horns, and grudgingly agreed to report the council's election to their citizens, and support it as best they could. As for the man Christian,

32

who had so angered Bishop Henry, he was attacked that same evening in the street, as he set out to return to the queen empty-handed. Four or five ruffians set on him in the dark, no one knows who, for they fled when one of the empress's knights and his men came to the rescue and beat them off, crying shame to use murder as argument in any cause, and against an honest man who had done his part fearlessly in the open. The clerk got no worse than a few bruises. It was the knight who got the knife between his ribs from behind and into the heart. He died in the gutter of a Winchester street. A shame to us all, who claim to be making peace and bringing enemies into amity.'

By the shadowed anger of his face it had gone deep with him, the single wanton act that denied all pretences of good will and justice and conciliation. To strike at a man for being honestly of the opposite persuasion, and then to strike again at the fair-minded and chivalrous who sought to prevent the outrage—very ill omens, these, for the future of the legate's peace.

'And no man taken for the killing?' demanded Hugh, frowning.

'No. They fled in the dark. If any creature knows name or hiding-place, he has spoken no word. Death is so common a matter now, even by stealth and treachery in the darkness, this will be forgotten with the rest. And the next day our council closed with sentence of excommunication against a great number of Stephen's men, and the legate pronounced all men blessed who would bless the empress, and accursed those who cursed her. And so dismissed us,' said Radulfus. 'But that we monastics were not dismissed, but kept to attend on him some weeks longer.'

'And the empress?'

'Withdrew to Oxford, while these long negotiations with the city of London went on, how and when she should be admitted within the gates, on what terms, what numbers she might bring in with her to Westminster. On all which points they have wrangled every step of the way. But in nine or ten days now she will be installed there, and soon thereafter crowned.' He lifted a long, muscular hand, and again let it fall into the lap of his habit. 'So, at least, it seems. What more can I tell you of her?'

'I meant, rather,' said Hugh, 'how is she bearing this slow recognition? How is she dealing with her newly converted barons? And how do they rub, one with another? It's no easy matter to hold together the old and the new liegemen, and keep them from each other's throats. A manor in dispute here and there, a few fields taken from one and given to another ... I think you know the way of it, Father, as well as I.'

'I would not say she is a wise woman,' said

34

Radulfus carefully. 'She is all too well aware how many swore allegiance to her at her father's order, and then swung to King Stephen, and now as nimbly skip back to her because she is in the ascendant. I can well understand she might take pleasure in pricking into the quick where she can, among these. It is not wise, but it is human. But that she should become lofty and cold to those who never wavered—for there are some,' said the abbot with respectful wonder, 'who have been faithful throughout at their own great loss, and will not waver even now, whatever she may do. Great folly and great injustice to use them so high-handedly, who have been her right hand and her left all this while.'

You comfort me, thought Hugh, watching the lean, quiet face intently. The woman is out of her wits if she flouts even the like of Robert of Gloucester, now she feels herself so near the throne.

'She has greatly offended the bishop-legate,' said the abbot, 'by refusing to allow Stephen's son to receive the rights and titles of his father's honours of Boulogne and Mortain, now that his father is a prisoner. It would have been only justice. But no, she would not suffer it. Bishop Henry quit her court for some while, it took her considerable pains to lure him back again.'

Better and better, thought Hugh, assessing his position with care. If she is stubborn enough to drive away even Henry, she can undo everything he and others do for her. Put the crown in her hands and she may, not so much drop it, as hurl it at someone against whom she has a score to settle. He set himself to extract every detail of her subsequent behaviour, and was cautiously encouraged. She had taken land from some who held it and given it to others. She had received her naturally bashful new adherents with arrogance, and reminded them ominously of their past hostility. Some she had even repulsed with anger, recalling old injuries. Candidates for a disputed crown should be more accommodatingly forgetful. Let her alone, and pray! She, if anyone, could bring about her own ruin.

At the end of a long hour he rose to take his leave, with a very fair picture in his mind of the possibilities he had to face. Even empresses may learn, and she might yet inveigle herself safely into Westminster and assume the crown. It would not do to underestimate William of Normandy's grand-daughter and Henry the First's daughter. Yet that very stock might come to wreck on its own unforgiving strength.

He was never afterwards sure why he turned back at the last moment to ask: 'Father Abbot, this man Rainald Bossard, who died ... A knight of the empress, you said. In whose following?'

All that he had learned he confided to Brother Cadfael in the hut in the herb-garden, trying out upon his friend's unexcitable solidity his own impressions and doubts, like a man sharpening a scythe on a good memorial stone. Cadfael was fussing over a too-exuberant wine, and seemed not to be listening, but Hugh remained undeceived. His friend had a sharp ear cocked for every intonation, even turned a swift glance occasionally to confirm what his ear heard, and reckon up the double account.

'You'd best lean back, then,' said Cadfael finally, 'and watch what will follow. You might also, I suppose, have a good man take a look at Bristol? He is the only hostage she has. With the king loosed, or Robert, or Brian FitzCount, or some other of sufficient note made prisoner to match him, you'd be on secure ground. God forgive me, why am I advising you, who have no prince in this world!' But he was none too sure about the truth of that, having had brief, remembered dealings with Stephen himself, and liked the man, even at his ill-advised worst, when he had slaughtered the garrison of Shrewsbury castle, to regret it as long as his ebullient memory kept nudging him with the outrage. By now, in his dungeon in Bristol, he might well have forgotten the uncharacteristic savagery.

'And do you know,' asked Hugh with

deliberation, 'whose man was this knight Rainald Bossard, left bleeding to death in the lanes of Winchester? He for whom your prayers have been demanded?'

Cadfael turned from his boisterously bubbling jar to narrow his eyes on his friend's face. 'The empress's man is all we've been told. But I see you're about to tell me more.'

'He was in the following of Laurence d'Angers.'

Cadfael straightened up with incautious haste, and grunted at the jolt to his ageing back. It was the name of a man neither of them had ever set eyes on, yet it started vivid memories for them both.

'Yes, *that* Laurence! A baron of Gloucestershire, and liegeman to the empress. One of the few who has not once turned his coat yet in this to-ing and fro-ing, and uncle to those two children you helped away from Bromfield to join him, when they went astray after the sack of Worcester. Do you still remember the cold of that winter? And the wind that scoured away hills of snow overnight and laid them down in fresh places before morning? I still feel it, clean through flesh and bone . . .'

There was nothing about that winter journey that Cadfael would ever forget. [See *The Virgin in the Ice*.] It was hardly a year and a half past, the attack on the city of Worcester, the flight of brother and sister northwards

towards Shrewsbury, through the worst
weather for many a year. Laurence d'Angers
had been but a name in the business, as he was
now in this. An adherent of the Empress
Maud, he had been denied leave to enter King
Stephen's territory to search for his young kin,
but he had sent a squire in secret to find and
fetch them away. To have borne a hand in the
escape of those three was something to
remember lifelong. All three arose living
before Cadfael's mind's eye, the boy Yves,
thirteen years old then, ingenuous and gallant
and endearing, jutting a stubborn Norman
chin at danger, his elder sister Ermina, newly
shaken into womanhood and resolutely
shouldering the consequences of her own
follies. And the third . . .

'I have often wondered,' said Hugh
thoughtfully, 'how they fared afterwards. I
knew you would get them off safely, if I left it
to you, but it was still a perilous road before
them. I wonder if we shall ever get word. Some
day the world will surely hear of Yves
Hugonin.' At the thought of the boy he smiled
with affectionate amusement. 'And that dark
lad who fetched them away, he who dressed
like a woodsman and fought like a paladin . . .
I fancy you knew more of him than ever I got
to know.'

Cadfael smiled into the glow of the brazier
and did not deny it. 'So his lord is there in the
empress's train, is he? And this knight who was

killed was in d'Angers' service? That was a very ill thing, Hugh.'

'So Abbot Radulfus thinks,' said Hugh sombrely.

'In the dusk and in confusion—and all got clean away, even the one who used the knife. A foul thing, for surely that was no chance blow. The clerk Christian escaped out of their hands, yet one among them turned on the rescuer before he fled. It argues a deal of hate at being thwarted, to have ventured that last moment before running. And is it left so? And Winchester full of those who should most firmly stand for justice?'

'Why, some among them would surely have been well enough pleased if that bold clerk had spilled his blood in the gutter, as well as the knight. Some may well have set the hunt on him.'

'Well for the empress's good name,' said Cadfael, 'that there was one at least of her men stout enough to respect an honest opponent, and stand by him to the death. And shame if that death goes unpaid for.'

'Old friend,' said Hugh ruefully, rising to take his leave, 'England has had to swallow many such a shame these last years. It grows customary to sigh and shrug and forget. At which, as I know, you are a very poor hand. And I have seen you overturn custom more than once, and been glad of it. But not even you can do much now for Rainald Bossard, bar

40

praying for his soul. It is a very long way from here to Winchester.'

'It is not so far,' said Cadfael, as much to himself as to his friend, 'not by many a mile, as it was an hour since.'

*   *   *

He went to Vespers, and to supper in the refectory, and thereafter to Collations and Compline, and all with one remembered face before his mind's eye, so that he paid but fractured attention to the readings, and had difficulty in concentrating his thoughts on prayer. Though it might have been a kind of prayer he was offering throughout, in gratitude and praise and humility.

So suave, so young, so dark and vital a face, startling in its beauty when he had first seen it over the girl's shoulder, the face of the young squire sent to bring away the Hugonin children to their uncle and guardian. A long, spare, wide-browed face, with a fine scimitar of a nose and a supple bow of a mouth, and the fierce, fearless, golden eyes of a hawk. A head capped closely with curving, blue-black hair, coiling crisply at his temples and clasping his cheeks like folded wings. So young and yet so formed a face, east and west at home in it, shaven clean like a Norman, olive-skinned like a Syrian, all his memories of the Holy Land in one human countenance. The favourite squire

41

of Laurence d'Angers, come home with him from the Crusade. Olivier de Bretagne.

If his lord was there in the south with his following, in the empress's retinue, where else would Olivier be? The abbot might even have rubbed shoulders with him, unbeknown, or seen him ride past at his lord's elbow, and for one absent moment admired his beauty. Few such faces blaze out of the humble mass of our ordinariness, thought Cadfael, the finger of God cannot choose but mark them out for notice, and his officers here will be the first to recognise and own them.

And this Rainald Bossard who is dead, an honourable man doing right by an honourable opponent, was Olivier's comrade, owning the same lord and pledged to the same service. His death will be grief to Olivier. Grief to Olivier is grief to me, a wrong done to Olivier is a wrong done to me. As far away as Winchester may be, here am I left mourning in that dark street where a man died for a generous act, in which, by the same token, he did not fail, for the clerk Christian lived on to return to his lady, the queen, with his errand faithfully done.

The gentle rustlings and stirrings of the dortoir sighed into silence outside the frail partitions of Cadfael's cell long before he rose from his knees, and shook off his sandals. The little lamp by the night stairs cast only the faintest gleam across the beams of the roof, a ceiling of pearly grey above the darkness of his

42

cell, his home now for—was it eighteen years or nineteen?—he had difficulty in recalling. It was as if a part of him, heart, mind, soul, whatever that essence might be, had not so much retired as come home to take seisin of a heritage here, his from his birth. And yet he remembered and acknowledged with gratitude and joy the years of his sojourning in the world, the lusty childhood and venturous youth, the taking of the Cross and the passion of the Crusade, the women he had known and loved, the years of his sea-faring off the coast of the Holy Kingdom of Jerusalem, all that pilgrimage that had led him here at last to his chosen retreat. None of it wasted, however foolish and amiss, nothing lost, nothing vain, all of it somehow fitting him to the narrow niche where now he served and rested. God had given him a sign, he had no need to regret anything, only to lay all open and own it his. For God's viewing, not for man's.

He lay quiet in the darkness, straight and still like a man coffined, but easy, with his arms lax at his sides, and his half-closed eyes dreaming on the vault above him, where the faint light played among the beams.

There was no lightning that night, only a consort of steady rolls of thunder both before and after Matins and Lauds, so unalarming that many among the brothers failed to notice them. Cadfael heard them as he rose, and as he returned to his rest. They seemed to him a reminder and a reassurance that Winchester had indeed moved nearer to Shrewsbury, and consoled him that his grievance was not overlooked, but noted in heaven, and he might look to have his part yet in collecting the debt due to Rainald Bossard. Upon which warranty, he fell asleep.

CHAPTER THREE

On the seventeenth day of June Saint Winifred's elaborate oak coffin, silver-ornamented and lined with lead behind all its immaculate seals, was removed from its place of honour and carried with grave and subdued ceremony back to its temporary resting-place in the chapel of the hospital of Saint Giles, there to wait, as once before, for the auspicious day, the twenty-second of June. The weather was fair, sunny and still, barely a cloud in the sky, and yet cool enough for travelling, the best of weather for pilgrims. And by the eighteenth day the pilgrims began to arrive, a scattering of fore-runners before the full tide began to flow.

Brother Cadfael had watched the reliquary depart on its memorial journey with a slightly guilty mind, for all his honest declaration that he could hardly have done otherwise than he had done, there in the summer night in

Gwytherin. So strongly had he felt, above all, her Welshness, the feeling she must have for the familiar tongue about her, and the tranquil flow of the seasons in her solitude, where she had slept so long and so well in her beatitude, and worked so many small, sweet miracles for her own people. No, he could not believe he had made a wrong choice there. If only she would glance his way, and smile, and say, well done!

The very first of the pilgrims came probing into the walled herb-garden, with Brother Denis's directions to guide him, in search of a colleague in his own mystery. Cadfael was busy weeding the close-planted beds of mint and thyme and sage late in the afternoon, a tedious, meticulous labour in the ripeness of a favourable June, after spring sun and shower had been nicely balanced, and growth was a green battlefield. He backed out of a cleansed bed, and backed into a solid form, rising startled from his knees to turn and face a rusty black brother shaped very much like himself, though probably fifteen years younger. They stood at gaze, two solid, squarely built brethren of the Order, eyeing each other in instant recognition and acknowledgement.

'You must be Brother Cadfael,' said the stranger-brother in a broad, melodious bass voice. 'Brother Hospitaller told me where to find you. My name is Adam, a brother of Reading. I have the very charge there that you

45

bear here, and I have heard tell of you, even as far south as my house.'

His eye was roving, as he spoke, towards some of Cadfael's rarer treasures, the eastern poppies he had brought from the Holy Land and reared here with anxious care, the delicate fig that still contrived to thrive against the sheltering north wall, where the sun nursed it. Cadfael warmed to him for the quickening of his eye, and the mild greed that flushed the round, shaven face. A sturdy, stalwart man, who moved as if confident of his body, one who might prove a man of his hands if challenged. Well-weathered, too, a genuine outdoor man.

'You're more than welcome, brother,' said Cadfael heartily. 'You'll be here for the saint's feast? And have they found you a place in the dortoir? There are a few cells vacant, for any of our own who come, like you.'

'My abbot sent me from Reading with a mission to our daughter house of Leominster,' said Brother Adam, probing with an experimental toe into the rich, well-fed loam of Brother Cadfael's bed of mint, and raising an eyebrow respectfully at the quality he found. 'I asked if I might prolong the errand to attend on the translation of Saint Winifred, and I was given the needful permission. It's seldom I could hope to be sent so far north, and it would be pity to miss such an opportunity.'

'And they've found you a brother's bed?' Such a man, Benedictine, gardener and herbalist, could not be wasted on a bed in the guest-hall. Cadfael coveted him, marking the bright eye with which the newcomer singled out his best endeavours.

'Brother Hospitaller was so gracious. I am placed in a cell close to the novices.'

'We shall be near neighbours,' said Cadfael contentedly. 'Now come, I'll show you whatever we have here to show, for the main garden is on the far side of the Foregate, along the bank of the river. But here I keep my own herber. And if there should be anything here that can be safely carried to Reading, you may take cuttings most gladly before you leave us.'

They fell into a very pleasant and voluble discussion, perambulating all the walks of the closed garden, and comparing experiences in cultivation and use. Brother Adam of Reading had a sharp eye for rarities, and was likely to go home laden with spoils. He admired the neatness and order of Cadfael's workshop, the collection of rustling bunches of dried herbs hung from the roof-beams and under the eaves, and the array of bottles, jars and flagons along the shelves. He had hints and tips of his own to propound, too, and the amiable contest kept them happy all the afternoon. When they returned together to the great court before Vespers it was to a scene notably animated, as if the bustle of celebration was already beginning. There were horses being led down into the stableyard, and bundles being carried in at the guest-hall. A stout elderly man, well equipped for riding, paced across towards the church to pay his first respects on arrival, with a servant trotting at his heels.

Brother Paul's youngest charges, all eyes and curiosity, ringed the gatehouse to watch the early arrivals, and were shooed aside by Brother Jerome, very busy as usual with all the prior's errands. Though the boys did not go very far, and formed their ring again as soon as Jerome was out of sight. A few of the citizens of the Foregate had gathered in the street to watch, excited dogs running among their legs.

'Tomorrow,' said Cadfael, eyeing the scene, 'there will be many more. This is but the beginning. Now if the weather stays fair we shall have a very fine festival for our saint.'

And she will understand that all is in her honour, he thought privately, even if she does lie very far from here. And who knows whether she may not pay us a visit, out of the kindness of her heart? What is distance to a saint, who can be where she wills in the twinkling of an eye?

*   *   *

The guest-hall filled steadily on the morrow. All day long they came, some singly, some in groups as they had met and made comfortable

48

acquaintance on the road, some afoot, some on ponies, some whole and hearty and on holiday, some who had travelled only a few miles, some who came from far away, and among them a number who went on crutches, or were led along by better-sighted friends, or had grievous deformities or skin diseases, or debilitating illnesses; and all these hoping for relief.

Cadfael went about the regular duties of his day, divided between church and herbarium, but with an interested eye open for all there was to see whenever he crossed the great court, boiling now with activity. Every arriving figure, every face, engaged his notice, but as yet distantly, none being provided with a name, to make him individual. Such of them as needed his services for relief would be directed to him, such as came his way by chance would be entitled to his whole attention, freely offered.

It was the woman he noticed first, bustling across the court from the gatehouse to the guest-hall with a basket on her arm, fresh from the Foregate market with new-baked bread and little cakes, soon after Prime. A careful housewife, to be off marketing so early even on holiday, decided about what she wanted, and not content to rely on the abbey bakehouse to provide it. A sturdy, confident figure of a woman, perhaps fifty years of age but in full rosy bloom. Her dress was sober and

49

plain, but of good material and proudly kept, her wimple snow-white beneath her head-cloth of brown linen. She was not tall, but so erect that she could pass for tall, and her face was round, wide-eyed and broad-cheeked, with a determined chin to it.

She vanished briskly into the guest-hall, and he caught but a glimpse of her, but she was positive enough to stay with him through the offices and duties of the morning, and as the worshippers left the church after Mass he caught sight of her again, arms spread like a hen-wife driving her birds, marshalling two chicks, it seemed, before her, both largely concealed beyond her ample width and bountiful skirts. Indeed she had a general largeness about her, her head-dress surely taller and broader than need, her hips bolstered by petticoats, the aura of bustle and command she bore about with her equally generous and ebullient. He felt a wave of warmth go out to her for her energy and vigour, while he spared a morsel of sympathy for the chicks she mothered, stowed thus away beneath such ample, smothering wings.

In the afternoon, busy about his small kingdom and putting together the medicaments he must take along the Foregate to Saint Giles in the morning, to be sure they had provision enough over the feast, he was not thinking of her, nor of any of the inhabitants of the guest-hall, since none had as yet had occasion to call for his aid. He was packing lozenges into a small box, soothing tablets for scoured, dry throats, when a bulky shadow blocked the open door of his workshop, and a brisk, light voice said, 'Pray your pardon, brother, but Brother Denis advised me to come to you, and sent me here.'

And there she stood, filling the doorway, shoulders squared, hands folded at her waist, head braced and face full forward. Her eyes, wide and wide-set, were bright blue but meagrely supplied with pale lashes, yet very firm and fixed in their regard.

'It's my young nephew, you see, brother,' she went on confidently, 'my sister's son, that was fool enough to go off and marry a roving Welshman from Builth, and now her man's gone, and so is she, poor lass, and left her two children orphan, and nobody to care for them but me. And me with my own husband dead, and all his craft fallen to me to manage, and never a chick of my own to be my comfort. Not but what I can do very well with the work and the journeymen, for I've learned these twenty years what was what in the weaving trade, but still I could have done with a son of my own. But it was not to be, and a sister's son is dearly welcome, so he is, whether he has his health or no, for he's the dearest lad ever you saw. And it's the pain, you see, brother. I don't like to see him in pain, though he doesn't complain. So I'm come to you.'

51

Cadfael made haste to wedge a toe into this first chink in her volubility, and insert a few words of his own into the gap.

'Come within, mistress, and welcome. Tell me what's the nature of your lad's pain, and what I can do for you and him I'll do. But best I should see him and speak with him, for he best knows where he hurts. Sit down and be easy, and tell me about him.'

She came in confidently enough, and settled herself with a determined spreading of ample skirts on the bench against the wall. Her gaze went round the laden shelves, the stored herbs dangling, the brazier and the pots and flasks, interested and curious, but in no way awed by Cadfael or his mysteries.

'I'm from the cloth country down by Campden, brother, Weaver by name and by trade was my man, and his father and grandfather before him, and Alice Weaver is my name, and I keep up the work just as he did. But this young sister of mine, she went off with a Welshman, and the pair of them are dead now, and the children I sent for to live with me. The girl is eighteen years old now, a good, hard-working maid, and I daresay we shall contrive to find a decent match for her in the end, though I shall miss her help, for she's grown very handy, and is strong and healthy, not like the lad. Named for some outlandish Welsh saint, she is, Melangell, if ever you heard the like!'

'I'm Welsh myself,' said Cadfael cheerfully. 'Our Welsh names do come hard on your English tongues, I know.'

'Ah well, the boy brought a name with him that's short and simple enough. Rhun, they named him. Sixteen he is now, two years younger than his sister, but wants her heartiness, poor soul. He's well-grown enough, and very comely, but from a child something went wrong with his right leg, it's twisted and feebled so he can put but the very toe of it to the ground at all, and even that turned on one side, and can lay no weight on it, but barely touch. He goes on two crutches. And I've brought him here in the hope good Saint Winifred will do something for him. But it's cost him dear to make the walk, even though we started out three weeks ago, and have taken it by easy shifts.'

'He's walked the whole way?' asked Cadfael, dismayed.

'I'm not so prosperous I can afford a horse, more than the one they need for the business at home. Twice on the way a kind carter did give him a ride as far as he was bound, but the rest he's hobbled on his crutches. Many another at this feast, brother, will have done as much, in as bad case or worse. But he's here now, safe in the guest-hall, and if my prayers can do anything for him, he'll walk home again on two sound legs as ever held up a hale and hearty man. But now for these few days he suffers as bad as before.'

'You should have brought him here with you,' said Cadfael. 'What's the nature of his pain? Is it in moving or when he lies still? Is it the bones of the leg that ache?'

'It's worst in his bed at night. At home I've often heard him weeping for pain in the night, though he tries to keep it so silent we need not be disturbed. Often he gets little or no sleep. His bones do ache, that's truth, but also the sinews of his calf knot into such cramps it makes him groan.'

'There can be something done about that,' said Cadfael, considering. 'At least we may try. And there are draughts can dull the pain and help him to a night's sleep, at any rate.'

'It isn't that I don't trust to the saint,' explained Mistress Weaver anxiously. 'But while he waits for her, let him be at rest if he can, that's what I say. Why should not a suffering lad seek help from ordinary decent mortals, too, good men like you who have faith and knowledge both?'

'Why not, indeed!' agreed Cadfael. 'The least of us may be an instrument of grace, though not by his own deserving. Better let the boy come to me here, where we can be private together. The guest-hall will be busy and noisy, here we shall have quiet.'

She rose, satisfied, to take her leave, but she had plenty yet to say even in departing of the long, slow journey, the small kindnesses they had met with on the way, and the fellow pilgrims, some of whom had passed them and arrived here before them.

'There's more than one in there,' said she, wagging her head towards the lofty rear wall of the guest-hall, 'will be needing your help, besides my Rhun. There were two young fellows we came along with the last days, we could keep pace with them, for they were slowed much as we were. Oh, the one of them was hale and lusty enough, but would not stir a step ahead of his friend, and that poor soul had come barefoot more miles even than Rhun had come crippled, and his feet a sight for pity, but would he so much as bind them with rags? Not he! He said he was under vow to go unshod to his journey's end. And a great heavy cross on a string round his neck, too, and he rubbed raw with the chafing of it, but that was part of his vow, too. I see no reason why a fine young fellow should choose such a torment of his own will, but there, folk do strange things, I daresay he hopes to win some great mercy for himself with his austerities. Still, I should think he might at least get some balm for his feet, while he's here at rest? Shall I bid him come to you? I'd gladly do a small service for that pair. The other one, Matthew, the sturdy one, he hefted my girl safe out of the way of harm when some mad horsemen in a hurry all but rode us down into the ditch, and he carried our bundles for her after, for she

55

was well loaded, I being busy helping Rhun along. Truth to tell, I think the young man was taken with our Melangell, for he was very attentive to her once we joined company. More than to his friend, though indeed he never stirred a step away from him. A vow is a vow, I suppose, and if a man's taken all that suffering on himself of his own will, what can another do to prevent it? No more than bear him company, and that the lad is doing, faithfully, for he never leaves him.'

She was out of the door and spreading appreciative nostrils for the scent of the sunlit herbs, when she looked back to add: 'There's others among them may call themselves pilgrims as loud and often as they will, but I wouldn't trust one or two of them as far as I could throw them. I suppose rogues will make their way everywhere, even among the saints.'

'As long as the saints have money in their purses, or anything about them worth stealing,' agreed Cadfael wryly, 'rogues will never be far away.'

Whether Mistress Weaver did speak to her strange travelling companion or not, it was he who arrived at Cadfael's workshop within half an hour, before ever the boy Rhun showed his face. Cadfael was back at his weeding when he heard them come, or heard, rather, the slow, patient footsteps of the sturdy one stirring the gravel of his pathways. The other made no sound in walking, for he stepped tenderly and carefully in the grass border, which was cool and kind to his misused feet. If there was any sound to betray his coming it was the long, effortful sighing of his breath, the faint, indrawn hiss of pain. As soon as Cadfael straightened his back and turned his head, he knew who came.

They were much of an age, and even somewhat alike in build and colouring, above middle height but that the one stooped in his laboured progress, brown-haired and dark of eye, and perhaps twenty-five or twenty-six years old. Yet not so like that they could have been brothers or close kin. The hale one had the darker complexion, as though he had been more in the air and the sun, and broader bones of cheek and jaw, a stubborn, proud, secret face, disconcertingly still, confiding nothing. The sufferer's face was long, mobile and passionate, with high cheekbones and hollow cheeks beneath them, and a mouth tight-drawn, either with present pain or constant passion. Anger might be one of his customary companions, burning ardour another. The young man Matthew stalked at his heels mute and jealously watchful in attendance on him.

Mindful of Mistress Weaver's loquacious confidences, Cadfael looked from the scarred and swollen feet to the chafed neck. Within the collar of his plain dark coat the votary had wound a length of linen cloth, to alleviate the rubbing of the thin cord from which a heavy cross of iron, chaced in a leaf pattern with what looked like gold, hung down upon his breast. By the look of the seam of red that marked the linen, either this padding was new, or else it had not been effective. The cord was mercilessly thin, the cross certainly heavy. To what desperate end could a young man choose so to torture himself? And what pleasure did he think it could give to God or Saint Winifred to contemplate his discomfort?

Eyes feverishly bright scanned him. A low voice asked: 'You are Brother Cadfael? That is the name Brother Hospitaller gave me. He said you would have ointments and salves that could be of help to me. So far,' he added, eyeing Cadfael with glittering fixity, 'as there is any help anywhere for me.'

Cadfael gave him a considering look for that, but asked nothing until he had marshalled the pair of them into his workshop and sat the sufferer down to be inspected with due care. The young man Matthew took up his stand beside the open door, careful to avoid blocking the light, but would not come further within.

'You've come a fairish step unshod,' said Cadfael, on his knees to examine the damage. 'Was such cruelty needful?'

'It was. I do not hate myself so much as to bear this to no purpose.' The silent youth by the door stirred slightly, but said no word. 'I am under vow,' said his companion, 'and will

58

not break it.' It seemed that he felt a need to account for himself, forestalling questioning. 'My name is Ciaran, I am of a Welsh mother, and I am going back to where I was born, there to end my life as I began it. You see the wounds on my feet, brother, but what most ails me does not show anywhere upon me. I have a fell disease, no threat to any other, but it must shortly end me.'

And it could be true, thought Cadfael, busy with a cleansing oil on the swollen soles, and the toes cut by gravel and stones. The feverish fire of the deep-set eyes might well mean an even fiercer fire within. True, the young body, now eased in repose, was well-made and had not lost flesh, but that was no sure proof of health. Ciaran's voice remained low, level and firm. If he knew he had his death, he had come to terms with it.

'So I am returning in penitential pilgrimage, for my soul's health, which is of greater import. Barefoot and burdened I shall walk to the house of canons at Aberdaron, so that after my death I may be buried on the holy isle of Ynys Enlli, where the soil is made up of the bones and dust of thousands upon thousands of saints.'

'I should have thought,' said Cadfael mildly, 'that such a privilege could be earned by going there shod and tranquil and humble, like any other man.' But for all that, it was an understandable ambition for a devout man of

Welsh extraction, knowing his end near. Aberdaron, at the tip of the Lleyn peninsula, fronting the wild sea and the holiest island of the Welsh church, had been the last resting place of many, and the hospitality of the canons of the house was never refused to any man. 'I would not cast doubt on your sacrifice, but self-imposed suffering seems to me a kind of arrogance, and not humility.'

'It may be so,' said Ciaran remotely. 'No help for it now, I am bound.'

'That is true,' said Matthew from his corner by the door. A measured and yet an abrupt voice, deeper than his companion's. 'Fast bound! So are we both, I no less than he.'

'Hardly by the same vows,' said Cadfael drily. For Matthew wore good, solid shoes, a little down at heel, but proof against the stones of the road.

'No, not the same. But no less binding. And I do not forget mine, any more than he forgets his.'

Cadfael laid down the foot he had anointed, setting a folded cloth under it, and lifted its fellow into his lap. 'God forbid I should tempt any man to break his oath. You will both do as you must do. But at least you may rest your feet here until after the feast, which will give you three days for healing, and here within the pale the ground is not so harsh. And once healed, I have a rough spirit that will help to harden your soles for when you take to the road again. Why not, unless you have forsworn all help from men? And since you came to me, I take it you have not yet gone so far. There, sit a while longer, and let that dry.'

He rose from his knees, surveying his work critically, and turned his attention next to the linen wrapping about Ciaran's neck. He laid both hands gently on the cord by which the cross depended, and made to lift it over the young man's head.

'No, no, let be!' It was a soft, wild cry of alarm, and Ciaran clutched at cross and cord, one with either hand, and hugged his burden to him fiercely. 'Don't touch it! Let it be!'

'Surely,' said Cadfael, startled, 'you may lift it off while I dress the wound it's cost you? Hardly a moment's work, why not?'

'*No!*' Ciaran fastened both hands upon the cross and hugged it to his breast. 'No, never for a moment, night or day! No! Let it alone!'

'Lift it, then,' said Cadfael resignedly, 'and hold it while I dress this cut. No, never fear, I'll not cheat you. Only let me unwind this cloth, and see what damage you have there, hidden.'

'Yet he should doff it, and so I have prayed him constantly,' said Matthew softly. 'How else can he be truly rid of his pains?'

Cadfael unwound the linen, viewed the scored line of half-dried blood, still oozing, and went to work on it with a stinging lotion first to clean it of dust and fragments of frayed skin, and then with a healing ointment of

61

cleavers. He refolded the cloth, and wound it carefully under the cord. 'There, you have not broken faith. Settle your load again. If you hold up the weight in your hands as you go, and loosen it in your bed, you'll be rid of your gash before you depart.'

It seemed to him that they were both of them in haste to leave him, for the one set his feet tenderly to ground as soon as he was released, holding up the weight of his cross obediently with both hands, and the other stepped out through the doorway into the sunlit garden, and waited on guard for his friend to emerge. The one owed no special thanks, the other offered only the merest acknowledgement.

'But I would remind you both,' said Cadfael, and with a thoughtful eye on both, 'that you are now present at the feast of a saint who has worked many miracles, even to the defiance of death. One who may have life itself within her gift,' he said strongly, 'even for a man already condemned to death. Bear it in mind, for she may be listening now!'

They said never a word, neither did they look at each other. They stared back at him from the scented brightness of the garden with startled, wary eyes, and then they turned abruptly as one man, and limped and strode away.

CHAPTER FOUR

There was so short an interval, and so little weeding done, before the second pair appeared, that Cadfael could not choose but reason that the two couples must have met at the corner of his herber, and perhaps exchanged at least a friendly word or two, since they had travelled side by side the last miles of their road here.

The girl walked solicitously beside her brother, giving him the smoothest part of the path, and keeping a hand supportingly under his left elbow, ready to prop him at need, but barely touching. Her face was turned constantly towards him, eager and loving. If he was the tended darling, and she the healthy beast of burden, certainly she had no quarrel with the division. Though just once she did look back over her shoulder, with a different, a more tentative smile. She was neat and plain in her homespun country dress, her hair austerely braided, but her face was vivid and glowing as a rose, and her movements, even at her brother's pace, had a spring and grace to them that spoke of a high and ardent spirit. She was fair for a Welsh girl, her hair a coppery gold, her brows darker, arched hopefully above wide blue eyes. Mistress Weaver could not be far out in supposing that a young man who had hefted this neat little woman out of harm's way in his arms might well remember the experience with pleasure, and not be averse to repeating it. If he could take his eyes from his fellow-pilgrim long enough to attempt it!

The boy came leaning heavily on his crutches, his right leg dangling inertly, turned with the toe twisted inward, and barely brushing the ground. If he could have stood erect he would have been a hand's-breadth taller than his sister, but thus hunched he looked even shorter. Yet the young body was beautifully proportioned, Cadfael judged, watching his approach with a thoughtful eye, wide-shouldered, slim-flanked, the one good leg long, vigorous and shapely. He carried little flesh, indeed he could have done with more, but if he spent his days habitually in pain it was unlikely he had much appetite.

Cadfael's study of him had begun at the twisted foot, and travelling upward, came last to the boy's face. He was fairer than the girl, wheat-gold of hair and brows, his thin, smooth face like ivory, and the eyes that met Cadfael's were a light, brilliant grey-blue, clear as crystal between long, dark lashes. It was a very still and tranquil face, one that had learned patient endurance, and expected to have need of it lifelong. It was clear to Cadfael, in that first exchange of glances, that Rhun did not look for any miraculous deliverance, whatever Mistress Weaver's hopes might be.

'If you please,' said the girl shyly, 'I have brought my brother, as my aunt said I should. And his name is Rhun, and mine is Melangell.'

'She has told me about you,' said Cadfael, beckoning them with him towards his workshop. 'A long journey you've had of it. Come within, and let's make you as easy as we may, while I take a look at this leg of yours. Was there ever an injury brought this on? A fall, or a kick from a horse? Or a bout of the bone-fever?' He settled the boy on the long bench, took the crutches from him and laid them aside, and turned him so that he could stretch out his legs at rest.

The boy, with grave eyes steady on Cadfael's face, slowly shook his head. 'No such accident,' he said in a man's low, clear voice. 'It came, I think, slowly, but I don't remember a time before it. They say I began to falter and fall when I was three or four years old.'

Melangell, hesitant in the doorway—strangely like Ciaran's attendant shadow, thought Cadfael—had her chin on her shoulder now, and turned almost hastily to say: 'Rhun will tell you all his case. He'll be better private with you. I'll come back later, and wait on the seat outside there until you need me.'

Rhun's light, bright eyes, transparent as sunlit ice, smiled at her warmly over Cadfael's shoulder. 'Do go,' he said. 'So fine and sunny a day, you should make good use of it, without me dangling about you.'

She gave him a long, anxious glance, but half her mind was already away; and satisfied that he was in good hands, she made her hasty reverence, and fled. They were left looking at each other, strangers still, and yet in tentative touch.

'She goes to find Matthew,' said Rhun simply, confident of being understood. 'He was good to her. And to me, also—once he carried me the last piece of the way to our night's lodging on his back. She likes him, and he would like her, if he could truly see her, but he seldom sees anyone but Ciaran.'

This blunt simplicity might well get him the reputation of an innocent, though that would be the world's mistake. What he saw, he said—provided, Cadfael hoped, he had already taken the measure of the person to whom he spoke—and he saw more than most, having so much more need to observe and record, to fill up the hours of his day.

'They were here?' asked Rhun, shifting obediently to allow Cadfael to strip down the long hose from his hips and his maimed leg.

'They were here. Yes, I know.'

'I would like her to be happy.'

'She has it in her to be very happy,' said Cadfael, answering in kind, almost without his will. The boy had a quality of dazzle about him that made unstudied answers natural, almost inevitable. There had been, he thought, the slightest of stresses on 'her'. Rhun had little

66

enough expectation that he could ever be happy, but he wanted happiness for his sister. 'Now pay heed,' said Cadfael, bending to his own duties, 'for this is important. Close your eyes, and be at ease as far as you can, and tell me where I find a spot that gives pain. First, thus at rest, is there any pain now?'

Docilely Rhun closed his eyes and waited, breathing softly. 'No, I am quite easy now.'

Good, for all his sinews lay loose and trustful, and at least in that state he felt no pain. Cadfael began to finger his way, at first very gently and soothingly, all down the thigh and calf of the helpless leg, probing and manipulating. Thus stretched out at rest, the twisted limb partially regained its proper alignment, and showed fairly formed, though much wasted by comparison with the left, and marred by the inturned toe and certain tight, bunched knots of sinew in the calf. He sought out these, and let his fingers dig deep there, wrestling with hard tissue.

'There I feel it,' said Rhun, breathing deep. 'It doesn't feel like pain—yes, it hurts, but not for crying. A good hurt . . .'

Brother Cadfael oiled his hands, smoothed a palm over the shrunken calf, and went to work with firm fingertips, working tendons unexercised for years, beyond that tensed touch of toe upon ground. He was gentle and slow, feeling for the hard cores of resistance. There were unnatural tensions there, that would not melt to him yet. He let his fingers work softly, and his mind probe elsewhere.

'You were orphaned early. How long have you been with your Aunt Weaver?'

'Seven years now,' said Rhun almost drowsily, soothed by the circling fingers. 'I know we are a burden to her, but she never says it, nor she would never let any other say it. She has a good business, but small, it provides her needs and keeps two men at work, but she is not rich. Melangell works hard keeping the house and the kitchen, and earns her keep. I have learned to weave, but I am slow at it. I can neither stand for long nor sit for long, I am no profit to her. But she never speaks of it, for all she has an edge to her tongue when she pleases.'

'She would,' agreed Cadfael peacefully. 'A woman with many cares is liable to be short in her speech now and again, and no ill meant. She has brought you here for a miracle. You know that? Why else would you all three have walked all this way, measuring out the stages day by day at your pace? And yet I think you have no expectation of grace. Do you not believe Saint Winifred can do wonders?'

'I?' The boy was startled, he opened great eyes clearer than the clear waters Cadfael had navigated long ago, in the eastern fringes of the Midland Sea, over pale and glittering sand. 'Oh, you mistake me, I *do* believe. But why for me? In case like mine we come by our thousands, in worse case by the hundred. How dare I ask to be among the first? Besides, what I have I can bear. There are some who cannot bear what they have. The saint will know where to choose. There is no reason her choice should fall on me.'

'Then why did you consent to come?' Cadfael asked.

Rhun turned his head aside, and eyelids blue-veined like the petals of anemones veiled his eyes. 'They wished it, I did what they wanted. And there was Melangell . . .'

Yes, Melangell who was altogether comely and bright and a charm to the eye, thought Cadfael. Her brother knew her dowryless, and wished her a little of joy and a decent marriage, and there at home, working hard in house and kitchen, and known for a penniless niece, suitors there were none. A venture so far upon the roads, to mingle with so various a company, might bring forth who could tell what chances?

In moving Rhun had plucked at a nerve that gripped and twisted him, he eased himself back against the timber wall with aching care. Cadfael drew up the homespun hose over the boy's nakedness, knotted him decent, and gently drew down his feet, the sound and the crippled, to the beaten earth floor.

'Come again to me tomorrow, after High Mass, for I think I can help you, if only a little. Now sit until I see if that sister of yours is waiting, and if not, you may rest easy until she comes. And I'll give you a single draught to take this night when you go to your bed. It will ease your pain and help you to sleep.'

The girl was there, still and solitary against the sun-warmed wall, the brightness of her face clouded over, as though some eager expectation had turned into a grey disappointment; but at the sight of Rhun emerging she rose with a resolute smile for him, and her voice was as gay and heartening as ever as they moved slowly away.

*   *   *

He had an opportunity to study all of them next day at High Mass, when doubtless his mind should have been on higher things, but obstinately would not rise above the quivering crest of Mistress Weaver's head-cloth, and the curly dark crown of Matthew's thick crop of hair. Almost all the inhabitants of the guest-halls, the gentles who had separate apartments as well as the male and female pilgrims who shared the two common dortoirs, came in their best to this one office of the day, whatever they did with the rest of it. Mistress Weaver paid devout attention to every word of the office, and several times nudged Melangell sharply in the ribs to recall her to duty, for as often as not her head was turned sidewise, and her gaze directed rather at Matthew than at the altar. No question but her fancy, if not her whole heart, was deeply engaged there. As for Matthew, he stood at Ciaran's shoulder, always within touch. But twice at least he looked round, and his brooding eyes rested, with no change of countenance, upon Melangell. Yet on the one occasion when their glances met, it was Matthew who turned abruptly away.

That young man, thought Cadfael, aware of the broken encounter of eyes, has a thing to do which no girl must be allowed to hinder or spoil: to get his fellow safely to his journey's end at Aberdaron.

He was already a celebrated figure in the enclave, this Ciaran. There was nothing secret about him, he spoke freely and humbly of himself. He had been intended for ordination, but had not yet gone beyond the first step as sub-deacon, and had not reached, and now never would reach, the tonsure. Brother Jerome, always a man to insinuate himself as close as might be to any sign of superlative virtue and holiness, had cultivated and questioned him, and freely retailed what he had learned to any of the brothers who would listen. The story of Ciaran's mortal sickness and penitential pilgrimage home to Aberdaron was known to all. The austerities he practised upon himself made a great impression. Brother Jerome held that the house was honoured in receiving such a man. And indeed that lean, passionate face, burning-eyed beneath the uncropped brown hair, had a vehement force and fervour.

Rhun could not kneel, but stood steady and stoical on his crutches throughout the office, his eyes fixed, wide and bright, upon the altar. In this soft, dim light within, already reflecting from every stone surface the muted brightness of a cloudless day outside, Cadfael saw that the boy was beautiful, the planes of his face as suave and graceful as any girl's, the curving of his fair hair round ears and cheeks angelically pure and chaste. If the woman with no son of her own doted on him, and was willing to forsake her living for a matter of weeks on the off-chance of a miracle that would heal him, who could wonder at her?

Since both his attention and his eyes were straying, Cadfael gave up the struggle and let them stray at large over all those devout heads, gathered in a close assembly and filling the nave of the church. An important pilgrimage has much of the atmosphere of a public fair about it, and brings along with it all the hangers-on who frequent such occasions, the pickpockets, the plausible salesmen of relics, sweetmeats, remedies, the fortune-tellers, the gamblers, the swindlers and cheats of all kinds. And some of these cultivate the most respectable of appearances, and prefer to work from within the pale rather than set up in the Foregate as at a market. It was always worth

72

running an eye over the ranks within, as Hugh's sergeants were certainly doing along the ranks without, to mark down probable sources of trouble before ever the trouble began.

This congregation certainly looked precisely what it purported to be. Nevertheless, there were a few there worth a second glance. Three modest, unobtrusive tradesmen who had arrived closely one after another and rapidly and openly made acquaintance, to all appearances until then strangers: Walter Bagot, glover; John Shure, tailor; William Hales, farrier. Small craftsmen making this their' summer holiday, and modestly out to enjoy it. And why not? Except that Cadfael had noted the tailor's hands devoutly folded, and observed that he cultivated the long, well-tended nails of a fairground sharper, hardly suitable for a tailor's work. He made a mental note of their faces, the glover rounded and glossy, as if oiled with the same dressing he used on his leathers, the tailor lean-jowled and sedate, with lank hair curtaining a lugubrious face, the farrier square, brown and twinkling of eye, the picture of honest good-humour.

They might be what they claimed. They might not. Hugh would be on the watch, so would the careful tavern-keepers of the Foregate and the town, by no means eager to hold their doors open to the fleecers and skinners of their own neighbours and customers.

Cadfael went out from Mass with his brethren, very thoughtful, and found Rhun already waiting for him in the herbarium.

*   *   *

The boy sat passive and submitted himself to Cadfael's handling, saying no word beyond his respectful greeting. The rhythm of the questing fingers, patiently coaxing apart the rigid tissues that lamed him, had a soothing effect, even when they probed deeply enough to cause pain. He let his head lean back against the timbers of the wall, and his eyes gradually closed. The tension of his cheeks and lips showed that he was not sleeping, but Cadfael was able to study the boy's face closely as he worked on him, and note his pallor, and the dark rings round his eyes.

'Well, did you take the dose I gave you for the night?' asked Cadfael, guessing at the answer.

'No.' Rhun opened his eyes apprehensively, to see if he was to be reproved for it, but Cadfael's face showed neither surprise nor reproach.

'Why not?'

'I don't know. Suddenly I felt there was no need. I was happy,' said Rhun, his eyes again closed, the better to examine his own actions and motives. 'I had prayed. It's not that I doubt the saint's power. Suddenly it seemed to me that I need not even wish to be healed … that I ought to offer up my lameness and pain freely, not as a price for favour. People bring offerings, and I have nothing else to offer. Do you think it might be acceptable? I meant it humbly.'

There could hardly be, thought Cadfael, among all her devotees, a more costly oblation. He has gone far along a difficult road who has come to the point of seeing that deprivation, pain and disability are of no consequence at all, beside the inward conviction of grace, and the secret peace of the soul. An acceptance which can only be made for a man's own self, never for any other. Another's grief is not to be tolerated, if there can be anything done to alleviate it.

'And did you sleep well?'

'No. But it didn't matter. I lay quiet all night long. I tried to bear it gladly. And I was not the only one there wakeful.' He slept in the common dormitory for the men, and there must be several among his fellows there afflicted in one way or another, besides the sick and possibly contagious whom Brother Edmund had isolated in the infirmary. 'Ciaran was restless, too,' said Rhun reflectively. 'When it was all silent, after Lauds, he got up very quietly from his cot, trying not to disturb anyone, and started towards the door. I thought then how strange it was that he took his belt and scrip with him . . .'

Cadfael was listening intently enough by this time. Why, indeed, if a man merely needed relief for his body during the night, should he burden himself with carrying his possessions about with him? Though the habit of being wary of theft, in such shared accommodation, might persist even when half-asleep, and in monastic care into the bargain.

'Did he so, indeed? And what followed?'

'Matthew has his own pallet drawn close beside Ciaran's, even in the night he lies with a hand stretched out to touch. Besides, you know, he seems to know by instinct whatever ails Ciaran. He rose up in an instant, and reached out and took Ciaran by the arm. And Ciaran started and gasped, and blinked round at him, like a man startled awake suddenly, and whispered that he'd been asleep and dreaming, and had dreamed it was time to start out on the road again. So then Matthew took the scrip from him and laid it aside, and they both lay down in their beds again, and all was quiet as before. But I don't think Ciaran slept well, even after that, his dream had disturbed his mind too much, I heard him twisting and turning for a long time.'

'Did they know,' asked Cadfael, 'that you were also awake, and had heard what passed?'

'I can't tell. I made no pretence, and the pain was bad, I think they must have heard me shifting . . . I couldn't help it. But of course I

76

made no sign, it would have been discourteous.'

So it passed as a dream, perhaps for the benefit of Rhun, or any other who might be wakeful as he was. True enough, a sick man troubled by night might very well rise by stealth to leave his friend in peace, out of consideration. But then, if he needed ease, he would have been forced to explain himself and go, when his friend nevertheless started awake to restrain him. Instead, he had pleaded a deluding dream, and lain down again. And men rousing in dreams do move silently, almost as if by stealth. It could be, it must be, simply what it seemed.

'You travelled some miles of the way with those two, Rhun. How did you all fare together on the road? You must have got to know them as well as any here.'

'It was their being slow, like us, that kept us all together, after my sister was nearly ridden down, and Matthew ran and caught her up and leaped the ditch with her. They were just slowly overtaking us then, after that we went on all together for company. But I wouldn't say we got to know them—they are so rapt in each other. And then, Ciaran was in pain, and that kept him silent, though he did tell us where he was bound, and why. It's true Melangell and Matthew took to walking last, behind us, and he carried our few goods for her, having so little of his own to carry. I never

77

wondered at Ciaran being so silent,' said Rhun simply, 'seeing what he had to bear. And my Aunt Alice can talk for two,' he ended guilelessly.

So she could, and no doubt did, all the rest of the way into Shrewsbury.

'That pair, Ciaran and Matthew,' said Cadfael, still delicately probing, 'they never told you how they came together? Whether they were kin, or friends, or had simply met and kept company on the road? For they're much of an age, even of a kind, young men of some schooling, I fancy, bred to clerking or squiring, and yet not kin, or don't acknowledge it, and after their fashion very differently made. A man wonders how they ever came to be embarked together on this journey. It was south of Warwick when you met them? I wonder from how far south they came.'

'They never spoke of such things,' owned Rhun, himself considering them for the first time. 'It was good to have company on the way, one stout young man at least. The roads can be perilous for two women, with only a cripple like me. But now you speak of it, no, we did not learn much of where they came from, or what bound them together. Unless my sister knows more. There were days,' said Rhun, shifting to assist Brother Cadfael's probings into the sinews of his thigh, 'when she and Matthew grew quite easy and talkative behind us.'

Cadfael doubted whether the subject of their conversation then had been anything but

78

their two selves, brushing sleeves pleasurably along the summer highways, she in constant recall of the moment when she was snatched up bodily and swung across the ditch against Matthew's heart, he in constant contemplation of the delectable creature dancing at his elbow, and recollection of the feel of her slight, warm, frightened weight on his breast.

'But he'll hardly look at her now,' said Rhun regretfully. 'He's too intent on Ciaran, and Melangell will come between. But it costs him a dear effort to turn away from her, all the same.'

Cadfael stroked down the misshapen leg, and rose to scrub his oily hands. 'There, that's enough for today. But sit quiet a while and rest before you go. And will you take the draught tonight? At least keep it by you, and do what you feel to be right and best. But remember it's a kindness sometimes to accept help, a kindness to the giver. Would you wilfully inflict torment on yourself as Ciaran does? No, not you, you are too modest by far to set yourself up for braver and more to be worshipped than other men. So never think you do wrong by sparing yourself discomfort. Yet it's your choice, make it as you see fit.'

When the boy took up his crutches again and tapped his way out along the path towards the great court, Cadfael followed him at a distance, to watch his progress without embarrassing him. He could mark no change as yet. The stretched toe still barely dared touch ground, and still turned inward. And yet the sinews, cramped as they were, had some small force in them, instead of being withered and atrophied as he would have expected. If I had him here long enough, he thought, I could bring back some ease and use into that leg. But he'll go as he came. In three days now all will be over, the festival ended for this year, the guest-hall emptying. Ciaran and his guardian shadow will pass on northwards and westwards into Wales, and Dame Weaver will take her chicks back home to Campden. And those two, who might very well have made a fair match if things had been otherwise, will go their separate ways, and never see each other again. It's in the nature of things that those who gather in great numbers for the feasts of the church should also disperse again to their various duties afterwards. Still, they need not all go away unchanged.

CHAPTER FIVE

Brother Adam of Reading, being lodged in the dortoir with the monks of the house, had had leisure to observe his fellow pilgrims of the guest-hall only at the offices of the church, and in their casual comings and goings about the precinct; and it happened that he came from the garden towards mid-afternoon, with Cadfael beside him, just as Ciaran and Matthew were crossing the court towards the cloister garth, there to sit in the sun for an hour or two before Vespers. There were plenty of others, monks, lay servants and guests, busy on their various occasions, but Ciaran's striking figure and painfully slow and careful gait marked him out for notice.

'Those two,' said Brother Adam, halting, 'I have seen before. At Abingdon, where I spent the first night after leaving Reading. They were lodged there the same night.'

'At Abingdon!' Cadfael echoed thoughtfully. 'So they came from far south. You did not cross them again after Abingdon, on the way here?'

'It was not likely. I was mounted. And then, I had my abbot's mission to Leominster, which took me out of the direct way. No, I saw no more of them, never until now. But they can hardly be mistaken, once seen.'

'In what sort of case were they at Abingdon?' asked Cadfael, his eyes following the two inseparable figures until they vanished into the cloister. 'Would you say they had been long on the road before that night's halt? The man is pledged to go barefoot to Aberdaron, it would not take many miles to leave the mark on him.'

'He was going somewhat lamely, even then. They had both the dust of the roads on them.

It might have been their first day's walking that ended there, but I doubt it.'

'He came to me to have his feet tended, yesterday,' said Cadfael, 'and I must see him again before evening. Two or three days of rest will set him up for the next stage of his walk.' From more than a day's going south of Abingdon to the remotest tip of Wales, a long, long walk. 'A strange, even a mistaken, piety it seems to me, to take upon oneself ostentatious pains, when there are poor fellows enough in the world who are born to pain they have not chosen, and carry it with humility.'

'The simple believe it brings merit,' said Brother Adam tolerantly. 'It may be he has no other claim upon outstanding virtue, and clutches at this.'

'But he's no simple soul,' said Cadfael with conviction, 'whatever he may be. He has, he tells me, a mortal disease, and is going to end his days in blessedness and peace at Aberdaron, and have his bones laid in Ynys Enlli, which is a noble ambition in a man of Welsh blood. The voluntary assumption of pain beyond his doom may even be a pennon of defiance, a wag of the hand against death. That I could understand. But I would not approve it.'

'It's very natural you should frown on it,' agreed Adam, smiling indulgence upon his companion and himself alike, 'seeing you are schooled to the alleviation of pain, and feel it to be a violator and an enemy. By the very virtue of these plants we have learned to use.' He patted the leather scrip at his girdle, and the soft rustle of seeds within answered him. They had been sorting over Cadfael's day saucers of new seed from this freshly ripening year, and he had helped himself to two or three not native in his own herbarium. 'It is as good a dragon to fight as any in this world, pain.'

They had gone some yards more towards the stone steps that led up to the main door of the guest-hall, in no hurry, and taking pleasure in the contemplation of so much bustle and motion, when Brother Adam checked abruptly and stood at gaze.

'Well, well, I think you may have got some of our southern sinners, as well as our would-be saints!'

Cadfael, surprised, followed where Adam was gazing, and stood to hear what further he would have to say, for the individual in question was the least remarkable of men at first glance. He stood close to the gatehouse, one of a small group constantly on hand there to watch the new arrivals and the general commerce of the day. A big man, but so neatly and squarely built that his size was not wholly apparent, he stood with his thumbs in the belt of his plain but ample gown, which was nicely cut and fashioned to show him no nobleman, and no commoner, either, but a solid, respectable, comfortably provided fellow of the middle kind, merchant or tradesman. One of those who form the backbone of many a township in England, and can afford the occasional pilgrimage by way of a well-earned holiday. He gazed benignly upon the activity around him from a plump, shrewd, well-shaven face, favouring the whole creation with a broad, contented smile.

'That,' said Cadfael, eyeing his companion with bright enquiry, 'is, or so I am informed, one Simeon Poer, a merchant of Guildford, come on pilgrimage for his soul's sake, and because the summer chances to be very fine and inviting. And why not? Do you know of a reason?'

'Simeon Poer may well be his name,' said Brother Adam, 'or he may have half a dozen more ready to trot forward at need. I never knew a name for him, but his face and form I do know. Father Abbot uses me a good deal on his business outside the cloister and I have occasion to know most of the fairs and markets in our shire and beyond. I've seen that fellow—not gowned like a provost, as he is now, I grant you, but by the look of him he's been doing well lately—round every fairground, cultivating the company of those young, green roisterers who frequent every such gathering. For the contents of their pockets, surely. Most likely, dice. Even more likely, loaded dice. Though I wouldn't say he

84

might not pick a pocket here and there, if business was bad. A quicker means to the same end, if a riskier.'

So knowing and practical a brother Cadfael had not encountered for some years among the innocents. Plainly Brother Adam's frequent sallies out of the cloister on the abbot's business had broadened his horizons. Cadfael regarded him with respect and warmth, and turned to study the smiling, benevolent merchant more closely.

'You're sure of him?'

'Sure that he's the same man, yes. Sure enough of his practices to challenge him openly, no, hardly, since he has never yet been taken up but once, and then he proved so slippery he slithered through the bailiff's fingers. But keep a weather eye on him, and this may be where he'll make the slip every rogue makes in the end, and get his comeuppance.'

'If you're right,' said Cadfael, 'has he not strayed rather far from his own haunts? In my experience, from years back I own, his kind seldom left the region where they knew their way about better than the bailiffs. Has he made the south country so hot for him that he must run for a fresh territory? That argues something worse than cheating at dice.'

Brother Adam hoisted dubious shoulders. 'It could be. Some of our scum have found the disorders of faction very profitable, in their own way, just as their lords and masters have in theirs. Battles are not for them—far too dangerous to their own skins. But the brawls that blow up in towns where uneasy factions come together are meat and drink to them. Pockets to be picked, riots to be started—discreetly from the rear—unoffending elders who look prosperous to be knocked on the head or knifed from behind or have their purse-strings cut in the confusion . . . Safer and easier than taking to the woods and living wild for prey, as their kind do in the country.'

Just such gatherings, thought Cadfael, as that at Winchester, where at least one man was knifed in the back and left dying. Might not the law in the south be searching for this man, to drive him so far from his usual hunting-grounds? For some worse offence than cheating silly young men of their money at dice? Something as black as murder itself?

'There are two or three others in the common guest-hall,' he said, 'about whom I have my doubts, but this man has had no truck with them so far as I've seen. But I'll bear it in mind, and keep a watchful eye open, and have Brother Denis do the same. And I'll mention what you say to Hugh Beringar, too, before this evening's out. Both he and the town provost will be glad to have fair warning.'

*   *   *

86

Since Ciaran was sitting quietly in the cloister garth, it seemed a pity he should be made to walk through the gardens to the herbarium, when Cadfael's broad brown feet were in excellent condition, and sensibly equipped with stout sandals. So Cadfael fetched the salve he had used on Ciaran's wounds and bruises, and the spirit that would brace and toughen his tender soles, and brought them to the cloister. It was pleasant there in the afternoon sun, and the turf was thick and springy and cool to bare feet. The roses were coming into full bloom, and their scent hung in the warm air like a benediction. But two such closed and sunless faces! Was the one truly condemned to an early death, and the other to lose and mourn so close a friend?

Ciaran was speaking as Cadfael approached, and did not at first notice him, but even when he was aware of the visitor bearing down on them he continued steadily to the end, ' . . . you do but waste your time, for it will not happen. Nothing will be changed, don't look for it. Never! You might far better leave me and go home.'

Did the one of them believe in Saint Winifred's power, and pray and hope for a miracle? And was the other, the sick man, all too passionately of Rhun's mind, and set on offering his early death as an acceptable and willing sacrifice, rather than ask for healing?

Matthew had not yet noticed Cadfael's

approach. His deep voice, measured and resolute, said just audibly, 'Save your breath! For I will go with you, step for step, to the very end.'

Then Cadfael was close, and they were both aware of him, and stirred defensively out of their private anguish, heaving in breath and schooling their faces to confront the outer world decently. They drew a little apart on the stone bench, welcoming Cadfael with somewhat strained smiles.

'I saw no need to make you come to me,' said Cadfael, dropping to his knees and opening his scrip in the bright green turf, 'when I am better able to come to you. So sit and be easy, and let me see how much work is yet to be done before you can go forth in good heart.'

'This is kind, brother,' said Ciaran, rousing himself with a sigh. 'Be assured that I do go in good heart, for my pilgrimage is short and my arrival assured.'

At the other end of the bench Matthew's voice said softly, 'Amen!'

After that it was all silence as Cadfael anointed the swollen soles, kneading spirit vigorously into the misused skin, surely heretofore accustomed always to going well shod, and soothed the ointment of cleavers into the healing grazes.

'There! Keep off your feet through tomorrow, but for such offices as you feel you must attend. Here there's no need to go far.

And I'll come to you tomorrow and have you fit to stand somewhat longer the next day, when the saint is brought home.' When he spoke of her now, he hardly knew whether he was truly speaking of the mortal substance of Saint Winifred, which was generally believed to be in that silver-chaced reliquary, or of some hopeful distillation of her spirit which could fill with sanctity even an empty coffin, even a casket containing pitiful, faulty human bones, unworthy of her charity, but subject, like all mortality, to the capricious, smiling mercies of those above and beyond question. If you could reason by pure logic for the occurrence of miracles, they would not be miracles, would they?

He scrubbed his hands on a handful of wool, and rose from his knees. In some twenty minutes or so it would be time for Vespers.

He had taken his leave, and almost reached the archway into the great court, when he heard rapid steps at his heels, a hand reached deprecatingly for his sleeve, and Matthew's voice said in his ear, 'Brother Cadfael, you left this lying.'

It was his jar of ointment, of rough, greenish pottery, almost invisible in the grass. The young man held it out in the palm of a broad, strong, workmanlike hand, long-fingered and elegant. Dark eyes, reserved but earnestly curious, searched Cadfael's face.

Cadfael took the jar with thanks, and put it

away in his scrip. Ciaran sat where Matthew had left him, his face and burning gaze turned towards them; they stood at a distance, between him and the outer day, and he had, for one moment, the look of a soul abandoned to absolute solitude in a populous world.

Cadfael and Matthew stood gazing in speculation and uncertainty into each other's eyes. This was that able, ready young man who had leaped into action at need, upon whom Melangell had fixed her young, unpractised heart, and to whom Rhun had surely looked for a hopeful way out for his sister, whatever might become of himself. Good, cultivated stock, surely, bred of some small gentry and taught a little Latin as well as his schooling in arms. How, except by the compulsion of inordinate love, did this one come to be ranging the country like a penniless vagabond, without root or attachment but to a dying man?

'Tell me truth,' said Cadfael. 'Is it indeed true—is it *certain*—that Ciaran goes this way towards his death?'

There was a brief moment of silence, as Matthew's wide-set eyes grew larger and darker. Then he said very softly and deliberately, 'It is truth. He is already marked for death. Unless your saint has a miracle for us, there is nothing can save him. Or me!' he ended abruptly, and wrenched himself away to return to his devoted watch.

*   *   *

Cadfael turned his back on supper in the refectory, and set off instead along the Foregate towards the town. Over the bridge that spanned the Severn, in through the gate, and up the curving slope of the Wyle to Hugh Beringar's town house. There he sat and nursed his godson Giles, a large, comely, self-willed child, fair like his mother, and long of limb, some day to dwarf his small, dark, sardonic father. Aline brought food and wine for her husband and his friend, and then sat down to her needlework, favouring her menfolk from time to time with a smiling glance of serene contentment. When her son fell asleep in Cadfael's lap she rose and lifted the boy away gently. He was heavy for her, but she had learned how to carry him lightly balanced on arm and shoulder. Cadfael watched her fondly as she bore the child away into the next room to his bed, and closed the door between.

'How is it possible that that girl can grow every day more radiant and lovely? I've known marriage rub the fine bloom off many a handsome maid. Yet it suits her as a halo does a saint.'

'Oh, there's something to be said for marriage,' said Hugh idly. 'Do I look so poorly on it? Though it's an odd study for a man of your habit, after all these years of celibacy . . .

And all the stravagings about the world before that! You can't have thought too highly of the wedded state, or you'd have ventured on it yourself. You took no vows until past forty, and you a well-set-up young fellow crusading all about the east with the best of them. How do I know you have not an Aline of your own locked away somewhere, somewhere in your remembrance, as dear as mine is to me? Perhaps even a Giles of your own,' he added, whimsically smiling, 'a Giles God knows where, grown a man now...'

Cadfael's silence and stillness, though perfectly easy and complacent, nevertheless sounded a mute warning in Hugh's perceptive senses. On the edge of drowsiness among his cushions after a long day out of doors, he opened a black, considering eye to train upon his friend's musing face, and withdrew delicately into practical business.

'Well, so this Simeon Poer is known in the south. I'm grateful to you and to Brother Adam for the nudge, though so far the man has set no foot wrong here. But these others you've pictured for me ... At Wat's tavern in the Foregate they've had practice in marking down strangers who come with a fair or a feast, and spread themselves large about the town. Wat tells my people he has a group moving in, very merry, some of them strangers. They could well be these you name. Some of them, of course, the usual young fellows of the town and the Foregate with more pence than sense. They've been drinking a great deal, and throwing dice. Wat does not like the way the dice fall.'

'It's as I supposed,' said Cadfael, nodding. 'For every Mass of ours they'll be celebrating the Gamblers' Mass elsewhere. And by all means let the fools throw their money after their sense, so the odds be fair. But Wat knows a loaded throw when he sees one.'

'He knows how to rid his house of the plague, too. He has hissed in the ears of one of the strangers that his tavern is watched, and they'd be wise to take their school out of there. And for tonight he has a lad on the watch, to find out where they'll meet. Tomorrow night we'll have at them, and rid you of them in good time for the feast day, if all goes well.'

*　　　*　　　*

Which would be a very welcome cleansing, thought Cadfael, making his way back across the bridge in the first limpid dusk, with the river swirling its coiled currents beneath him in gleams of reflected light, low summer water leaving the islands outlined in swathes of drowned, browning weed. But as yet there was nothing to shed light, even by reflected, phantom gleams, upon that death so far away in the south country, whence the merchant Simeon Poer had set out. On pilgrimage for his respectable soul? Or in flight from a law aroused too fiercely for his safety, by something graver than the cozening of fools? Though Cadfael felt too close to folly himself to be loftily complacent even about that, however much it might be argued that gamblers deserved all they got.

The great gate of the abbey was closed, but the wicket in it stood open, shedding sunset light through from the west. In the mild dazzle Cadfael brushed shoulders and sleeves with another entering, and was a little surprised to be hoisted deferentially through the wicket by a firm hand at his elbow.

'Give you goodnight, brother!' sang a mellow voice in his ear, as the returning guest stepped within on his heels. And the solid, powerful, woollen-gowned form of Simeon Poer, self-styled merchant of Guildford, rolled vigorously past him, and crossed the great court to the stone steps of the guest-hall.

CHAPTER SIX

They were emerging from High Mass on the morning of the twenty-first day of June, the eve of Saint Winifred's translation, stepping out into a radiant morning, when the abbot's sedate progress towards his lodging was rudely disrupted by a sudden howl of dismay among the dispersing multitude of worshippers, a wild ripple of movement cleaving a path through their ranks, and the emergence of a frantic figure lurching forth on clumsy, naked feet to clutch at the abbot's robe, and appeal in a loud, indignant cry, 'Father Abbot, stand my friend and give me justice, for I am robbed! A thief, there is a thief among us!'

The abbot looked down in astonishment and concern into the face of Ciaran, convulsed and ablaze with resentment and distress.

'Father, I beg you, see justice done! I am helpless unless you help me!'

He awoke, somewhat late, to the unwarranted violence of his behaviour, and fell on his knees at the abbot's feet. 'Pardon, pardon! I am too loud and troublous, I hardly know what I say!'

The press of gossiping, festive worshippers just loosed from Mass had fallen quiet all in a moment, and instead of dispersing drew in about them to listen and stare, avidly curious. The monks of the house, hindered in their orderly departure, hovered in quiet deprecation. Cadfael looked beyond the kneeling, imploring figure of Ciaran for its inseparable twin, and found Matthew just shouldering his way forward out of the crowd, open-mouthed and wide-eyed in patent bewilderment, to stand at gaze a few paces apart, and frown helplessly from the abbot to Ciaran and back again, in search of the cause of this abrupt turmoil. Was it possible that something had happened to the one that the other of the matched pair did not know?

'Get up!' said Radulfus, erect and calm. 'No need to kneel. Speak out whatever you have to say, and you shall have right.'

The pervasive silence spread, grew, filled even the most distant reaches of the great court. Those who had already scattered to the far corners turned and crept unobtrusively back again, large-eyed and prick-eared, to hang upon the fringes of the crowd already assembled.

Ciaran clambered to his feet, voluble before he was erect. 'Father, I had a ring, the copy of one the lord bishop of Winchester keeps for his occasions, bearing his device and inscription. Such copies he uses to afford safe-conduct to those he sends forth on his business or with his blessing, to open doors to them and provide protection on the road. Father, the ring is gone!'

'This ring was given to you by Henry of Blois himself?' asked Radulfus.

'No, Father, not in person. I was in the service of the prior of Hyde Abbey, a lay clerk, when this mortal sickness came on me, and I took this vow of mine to spend my remaining days in the canonry of Aberdaron. My prior— you know that Hyde is without an abbot, and has been for some years—my prior asked the lord bishop, of his goodness, to give me what protection he could for my journey . . .'

So that had been the starting point of this barefoot journey, thought Cadfael, enlightened. Winchester itself, or as near as made no matter, for the New Minster of that city, always a jealous rival of the Old, where Bishop Henry presided, had been forced to abandon its old home in the city thirty years ago, and banished to Hyde Mead, on the north-western outskirts. There was no love lost between Henry and the community at Hyde, for it was the bishop who had been instrumental in keeping them deprived of an abbot for so long, in pursuit of his own ambition of turning them into an episcopal monastery. The struggle had been going on for some time, the bishop deploying various schemes to get the house into his own hands, and the prior using every means to resist these manipulations. It seemed Henry had still the grace to show compassion even on a servant of the hostile house, when he fell under the threat of disease and death. The traveller over whom the bishop-legate spread his protecting hand would pass unmolested wherever law retained its validity. Only those irreclaimably outlaw already would dare interfere with him.

'Father, the ring is gone, stolen from me this very morning. See here, the slashed threads that held it!' Ciaran heaved forward the drab linen scrip that rode at his belt, and showed two dangling ends of cord, very cleanly severed. 'A sharp knife—someone here has such a dagger. And my ring is gone!'

Prior Robert was at the abbot's elbow by then, agitated out of his silvery composure. 'Father, what this man says is true. He showed me the ring. Given to ensure him aid and hospitality on his journey, which is of most sad and solemn import. If now it is lost, should not the gate be closed while we enquire?'

'Let it be so,' said Radulfus, and stood silent to see Brother Jerome, ever ready and assiduous on the prior's heels, run to see the order carried out. 'Now, take breath and thought, for your loss cannot be lost far. You did not wear the ring, then, but carried it knotted securely by this cord, within your scrip?'

'Yes, Father. It was beyond words precious to me.'

'And when did you last ascertain that it was still there, and safe?'

'Father, this very morning I know I had it. Such few things as I possess, here they lie before you. Could I fail to see if this cord had been cut in the night while I slept? It is not so. This morning all was as I left it last night. I have been bidden to rest, by reason of my barefoot vow. Today I ventured out only for Mass. Here in the very church, in this great press of worshippers, some malevolent has broken every ban, and slashed loose my ring from me.'

And indeed, thought Cadfael, running a considering eye round all the curious, watching faces, it would not be difficult, in such a press, to find the strings that anchored the hidden ring, flick it out from its hiding-place, cut the strings and make away with it, discreetly between crowding bodies, and never be seen by a soul or felt by the victim. A neat thing, done so privately and expertly that even Matthew, who missed nothing that touched his friend, had missed this impudent assault. For Matthew stood there staring, obviously taken by surprise, and unsure as yet how to take this turn of events. His face was unreadable, closed and still, his eyes narrowed and bright, darting from face to face as Ciaran or abbot or prior spoke. Cadfael noted that Melangell had stolen forward close to him, and taken him hesitantly by the sleeve. He did not shake her off. By the slight lift of his head and widening of his eyes he knew who had touched him, and he let his hand feel for hers and clasp it, while his whole attention seemed to be fixed on Ciaran. Somewhere not far behind them Rhun leaned on his crutches, his fair face frowning in anxious dismay, Aunt Alice attendant at his shoulder, bright with curiosity. Here are we all, thought Cadfael, and not one of us knows what is in any other mind, or who has done what has been done, or what will come of it for any of those who look on and marvel.

'You cannot tell,' suggested Prior Robert,

agitated and grieved, 'who stood close to you during the service? If indeed some ill-conditioned person has so misused the holy office as to commit theft in the very sacredness of the Mass . . .'

'Father, I was intent only upon the altar.' Ciaran shook with fervour, holding the ravished scrip open before him with his sparse possessions bared to be seen. 'We were close pressed, so many people . . . as is only seemly, in such a shrine . . . Matthew was close at my back, but so he ever is. Who else there may have been by me, how can I say? There was no man nor woman among us who was not hemmed in every way.'

'It is truth,' said Prior Robert, who had been much gratified at the large attendance. 'Father, the gate is now closed, we are all here who were present at Mass. And surely we all have a desire to see this wrong righted.'

'All, as I suppose,' said Radulfus drily, 'but one. One, who brought in here a knife or dagger sharp enough to slice through these tough cords cleanly. What other intents he brought in with him, I bid him consider and tremble for his soul. Robert, this ring must be found. All men of goodwill here will offer their aid, and show freely what they have. So will every guest who has not theft and sacrilege to hide. And see to it also that enquiry be made, whether other articles of value have not been missed. For one theft means one thief, here within.'

'It shall be seen to, Father,' said Robert fervently. 'No honest, devout pilgrim will grudge to offer his aid. How could he wish to share his lodging here with a thief?'

There was a stir of agreement and support, perhaps slightly delayed, as every man and woman eyed a neighbour, and then in haste elected to speak first. They came from every direction, hitherto unknown to one another, mingling and forming friendships now with the abandon of holiday. But how did they know who was immaculate and who was suspect, now the world had probed a merciless finger within the fold?

'Father,' pleaded Ciaran, still sweating and shaking with distress, 'here I offer in this scrip all that I brought into this enclave. Examine it, show that I have indeed been robbed. Here I came without even shoes to my feet, my all is here in your hands. And my fellow Matthew will open to you his own scrip as freely, an example to all these others that they may deliver themselves pure of blame. What we offer, they will not refuse.'

Matthew had withdrawn his hand from Melangell's sharply at this word. He shifted the unbleached cloth scrip, very like Ciaran's, round upon his hip. Ciaran's meagre travelling equipment lay open in the prior's hands. Robert slid them back into the pouch from which they had come, and looked where

101

Ciaran's distressed gaze guided him.

'Into your hands, Father, and willingly,' said Matthew, and stripped the bag from its buckles and held it forth.

Robert acknowledged the offering with a grave bow, and opened and probed it with delicate consideration. Most of what was there within he did not display, though he handled it. A spare shirt and linen drawers, crumpled from being carried so, and laundered on the way, probably more than once. The means of a gentleman's sparse toilet, razor, morsel of lye soap, a leather-bound breviary, a lean purse, a folded trophy of embroidered ribbon. Robert drew forth the only item he felt he must show, a sheathed dagger, such as any gentleman might carry at his right hip, barely longer than a man's hand.

'Yes, that is mine,' said Matthew, looking Abbot Radulfus straightly in the eyes. 'It has not slashed through those cords. Nor has it left my scrip since I entered your enclave, Father Abbot.'

Radulfus looked from the dagger to its owner, and briefly nodded. 'I well understand that no young man would set forth on these highroads today without the means of defending himself. All the more if he had another to defend, who carried no weapons. As I understand is your condition, my son. Yet within these walls you should not bear arms.'

'What, then, should I have done?'

demanded Matthew, with a stiffening neck, and a note in his voice that just fell short of defiance.

'What you must do now,' said Radulfus firmly. 'Give it into the care of Brother Porter at the gatehouse, as others have done with their weapons. When you leave here you may reclaim it freely.'

There was nothing to be done but bow the head and give way gracefully, and Matthew managed it decently enough, but not gladly. 'I will do so, Father, and pray your pardon that I did not ask advice before.'

'But, Father,' Ciaran pleaded anxiously, 'my ring . . . How shall I survive the way if I have not that safe-conduct to show?'

'Your ring shall be sought throughout this enclave, and every man who bears no guilt for its loss,' said the abbot, raising his voice to carry to the distant fringes of the silent crowd, 'will freely offer his own possessions for inspection. See to it, Robert!'

With that he proceeded on his way, and the crowd, after some moments of stillness as they watched him out of sight, dispersed in a sudden murmur of excited speculation. Prior Robert took Ciaran under his wing, and swept away with him towards the guest-hall, to recruit help from Brother Denis in his enquiries after the bishop's ring; and Matthew, not without one hesitant glance at Melangell, turned on his heel and went hastily after them.

*　　　*　　　*

A more innocent and co-operative company than the guests at Shrewsbury abbey that day it would have been impossible to find. Every man opened his bundle or box almost eagerly, in haste to demonstrate his immaculate virtue. The quest, conducted as delicately as possible, went on all the afternoon, but they found no trace of the ring. Moreover, one or two of the better-off inhabitants of the common dormitory, who had had no occasion to penetrate to the bottom of their baggage so far, made grievous discoveries when they were obliged to do so. A yeoman from Lichfield found his reserve purse lighter by half than when he had tucked it away. Master Simeon Poer, one of the first to fling open his possessions, and the loudest in condemning so blasphemous a crime, claimed to have been robbed of a silver chain he had intended to present at the altar next day. A poor parish priest, making this pilgrimage the one fulfilled dream of his life, was left lamenting the loss of a small casket, made by his own hands over more than a year, and decorated with inlays of silver and glass, in which he had hoped to carry back with him some memento of his visit, a dried flower from the garden, even a thread or two drawn from the fringe of the altar-cloth under Saint Winifred's reliquary. A merchant from Worcester could not find his good leather belt to his best coat, saved up for the morrow. One or two others had a suspicion that their belongings had been fingered and scorned, which was worst of all.

It was all over, and fruitless, when Cadfael at last repaired to his workshop in time to await the coming of Rhun. The boy came prompt to his hour, great-eyed and thoughtful, and lay submissive and mute under Cadfael's ministrations, which probed every day a little deeper into his knotted and stubborn tissues.

'Brother,' he said at length, looking up, 'you did not find a dagger in any other man's pouch, did you?'

'No, no such thing.' Though there had been, understandably, a number of small, homely knives, the kind a man needs to hack his bread and meat in lodgings along the way, or meals under a hedge. Many of them were sharp enough for most everyday purposes, but not sharp enough to leave stout cords sheared through without a twitch to betray the assault. 'But men who go shaven carry razors, too, and a blunt razor would be an abomination. Once a thief comes into the pale, child, it's hard for honest men to be a match for him. He who has no scruple has always the advantage of those who keep to rule. But you need not trouble your heart, you've done no wrong to any man. Never let this ill thing spoil tomorrow for you.'

'No,' agreed the boy, still preoccupied. 'But,

brother, there *is* another dagger—one, at least. Sheath and all, a good length—I know, I was pressed close against him yesterday at Mass. You know I have to hold fast by my crutches to stand for long, and he had a big linen scrip on his belt, hard against my hand and arm, where we were crowded together. I felt the shape of it, cross-hilt and all. I know! But you did not find it.'

'And who was it,' asked Cadfael, still carefully working the tissues that resisted his fingers, 'who had this armoury about him at Mass?'

'It was that big merchant with the good gown—made from valley wool. I've learned to know cloth. They call him Simeon Poer. But you didn't find it. Perhaps he's handed it to Brother Porter, just as Matthew has had to do now.'

'Perhaps,' said Cadfael. 'When was it you discovered this? Yesterday? And what of today? Was he again close to you?'

'No, not today.'

No, today he had stood stolidly to watch the play, eyes and ears alert, ready to open his pouch there before all if need be, smiling complacently as the abbot directed the disarming of another man. He had certainly had no dagger on him then, however he had disposed of it in the meantime. There were hiding-places enough here within the walls, for a dagger and any amount of small, stolen

106

valuables. To search was itself only a pretence, unless authority was prepared to keep the gates closed and the guests prisoned within until every yard of the gardens had been dug up, and every bed and bench in dortoir and hall pulled to pieces. The sinners have always the start of the honest men.

'It was not fair that Matthew should be made to surrender his dagger,' said Rhun, 'when another man had one still about him. And Ciaran already so terribly afraid to stir, not having his ring. He won't even come out of the dortoir until tomorrow. He is sick for loss of it.'

Yes, that seemed to be true. And how strange, thought Cadfael, pricked into realisation, to see a man sweating for fear, who has already calmly declared himself as one condemned to death? Then why fear? Fear should be dead.

Yet men are strange, he thought in revulsion. And a blessed and quiet death in Aberdaron, well-prepared, and surrounded by the prayers and compassion of like-minded votaries, may well seem a very different matter from crude slaughter by strangers and footpads somewhere in the wilder stretches of the road.

But this Simeon Poer—say he had such a dagger yesterday, and therefore may well have had it on him today, in the crowded array of the Mass. Then what did he do with it so quickly, before Ciaran discovered his loss? And how did he know he must perforce dispose of it quickly? Who had such fair warning of the need, if not the thief?

'Trouble your head no more,' said Cadfael, looking down at the boy's beautiful, vulnerable face, 'for Matthew nor for Ciaran, but think only of the morrow, when you approach the saint. Both she and God see you all, and have no need to be told of what your needs are. All you have to do is wait in quiet for whatever will be. For whatever it may be, it will not be wanton. Did you take your dose last night?'

Rhun's pale, brilliant eyes were startled wide open, sunlight and ice, blindingly clear. 'No. It was a good day, I wanted to give thanks. It isn't that I don't value what you can do for me. Only I wished also to give something. And I did sleep, truly I slept well . . .'

'So do tonight also,' said Cadfael gently, and slid an arm round the boy's body to hoist him steadily upright. 'Say your prayers, think quietly what you should do, do it, and sleep. There is no man living, neither king nor emperor, can do more or better, or trust in a better harvest.'

*   *   *

Ciaran did not stir from within the guest-hall again that day. Matthew did, against all
108

precedent emerging from the arched doorway without his companion, and standing at the head of the stone staircase to the great court with hands spread to touch the courses of the deep doorway, and head drawn back to heave in great breaths of evening air. Supper was eaten, the milder evening stir of movement threaded the court, in the cool, grateful lull before Compline.

Brother Cadfael had left the chapter house before the end of the readings, having a few things to attend to in the herbarium, and was crossing towards the garden when he caught sight of the young man standing there at the top of the steps, breathing in deeply and with evident pleasure. For some reason Matthew looked taller for being alone, and younger, his face closed but tranquil in the soft evening light. When he moved forward and began to descend to the court, Cadfael looked instinctively for the other figure that should have been close behind him, if not in its usual place a step before him, but no Ciaran emerged. Well, he had been urged to rest, and presumably was glad to comply, but never before had Matthew left his side, by night or day, resting or stirring. Not even to follow Melangell, except broodingly with his eyes and against his will.

People, thought Cadfael, going on his way without haste, people are endlessly mysterious, and I am endlessly curious. A sin to be

109

confessed, no doubt, and well worth a penance. As long as man is curious about his fellowman, that appetite alone will keep him alive. Why do folk do the things they do? Why, if you know you are diseased and dying, and wish to reach a desired haven before the end, why do you condemn yourself to do the long journey barefoot, and burden yourself with a weight about your neck? How are you thus rendered more acceptable to God, when you might have lent a hand to someone on the road crippled not by perversity but from birth, like the boy Rhun? And why do you dedicate your youth and strength to following another man step by step the length of the land, and why does he suffer you to be his shadow, when he should be composing his mind to peace, and taking a decent leave of his friends, not laying his own load upon them?

There he checked, rounding the corner of the yew hedge into the rose garden. It was not his fellow-man he beheld, sitting in the turf on the far side of the flower beds, gazing across the slope of the pease-fields beyond and the low, stony, silvery summer waters of the Meole brook, but his fellow-woman, solitary and still, her knees drawn up under her chin and encircled closely by her folded arms. Aunt Alice Weaver, no doubt, was deep in talk with half a dozen worthy matrons of her own generation, and Rhun, surely, already in his bed. Melangell had stolen away alone to be quiet here in the garden and nurse her lame dreams and indomitable hopes. She was a small, dark shape, gold-haloed against the bright west. By the look of that sky tomorrow, Saint Winifred's day, would again be cloudless and beautiful.

The whole width of the rose garden was between them, and she did not hear him come and pass by on the grassy path to his final duties of the day in his workshop, seeing everything put away tidily, checking the stoppers of all his flagons and flasks, and making sure the brazier, which had been in service earlier, was safely quenched and cooled. Brother Oswin, young, enthusiastic and devoted, was nonetheless liable to overlook details, though he had now outlived his tendency to break things. Cadfael ran an eye over everything, and found it good. There was no hurry now, he had time before Compline to sit down here in the wood-scented dimness and think. Time for others to lose and find one another, and use or waste these closing moments of the day. For those three blameless tradesmen, Walter Bagot, glover; John Shure, tailor; William Hales, farrier; to betake themselves to wherever their dice school was to meet this night, and run their necks into Hugh's trap. Time for that more ambiguous character, Simeon Poer, to evade or trip into the same snare, or go the other way about some other nocturnal business of his own. Cadfael had seen two of the former three go out from the gatehouse, and the third follow some minutes later, and was sure in his own mind that the self-styled merchant of Guildford would not be long after them. Time, too, for that unaccountably solitary young man, somehow loosed off his chain, to range this whole territory suddenly opened to him, and happen upon the solitary girl.

Cadfael put up his feet on the wooden bench, and closed his eyes for a brief respite.

*　　*　　*

Matthew was there at her back before she knew it. The sudden rustle as he stepped into sun-dried long grass at the edge of the field startled her, and she swung round in alarm, scrambling to her knees and staring up into his face with dilated eyes, half-blinded by the blaze of the sunset into which she had been steadily staring. Her face was utterly open, vulnerable and childlike. She looked as she had looked when he had swept her up in his arms and leaped the ditch with her, clear of the galloping horses. Just so she had opened her eyes and looked up at him, still dazed and frightened, and just so had her fear melted away into wonder and pleasure, finding in him nothing but reassurance, kindness and admiration.

That pure, paired encounter of eyes did not last long. She blinked, and shook her head a little to clear her dazzled vision, and looked beyond him, searching, not believing he could be here alone.

'Ciaran . . .? Is there something you need for him?'

'No,' said Matthew shortly, and for a moment turned his head away. 'He's in his bed.'

'But you never leave his bed!' It was said in innocence, even in anxiety. Whatever she grudged to Ciaran, she still pitied and understood him.

'You see I have left it,' said Matthew harshly. 'I have needs, too . . . a breath of air. And he is very well where he is, and won't stir.'

'I was well sure,' she said with resigned bitterness, 'that you had not come out to look for me.' She made to rise, swiftly and gracefully enough, but he put out a hand, almost against his will, as it seemed, to take her under the wrist and lift her. It was withdrawn as abruptly when she evaded his touch, and rose to her feet unaided. 'But at least,' she said deliberately, 'you did not turn and run from me when you found me. I should be grateful even for that.'

'I am not free,' he protested, stung. 'You know it better than any.'

'Then neither were you free when we kept pace along the road,' said Melangell fiercely,

113

'when you carried my burden, and walked beside me, and let Ciaran hobble along before, where he could not see how you smiled on me then and were gallant and cherished me when the road was rough, and spoke softly, as if you took delight in being beside me. Why did you not give me warning then that you were not free? Or better, take him some other way, and leave us alone? Then I might have taken good heed in time, and in time forgotten you. As now I never shall! Never, to my life's end!'

All the flesh of his lips and cheeks shrank and tightened before her eyes, in a contortion of either rage or pain, she could not tell which. She was staring too close and too passionately to see very clearly. He turned his head sharply away, to evade her eyes.

'You charge me justly,' he said in a harsh whisper, 'I was at fault. I never should have believed there could be so clean and sweet a happiness for me. I should have left you, but I could not . . . Oh, God! You think I could have turned him? He clung to you, to your good aunt . . . Yet I should have been strong enough to hold off from you and let you alone . . .' As rapidly as he had swung away from her he swung back again, reaching a hand to take her by the chin and hold her face to face with him, so ungently that she felt the pressure of his fingers bruising her flesh. 'Do you know how hard a thing you are asking? No! This countenance you never saw, did you, never but

114

through someone else's eyes. Who would provide you a mirror to see yourself? Some pool, perhaps, if ever you had the leisure to lean over and look. How should you know what this face can do to a man already lost? And you marvel I took what I could get for water in a drought, when it walked beside me? I should rather have died than stay beside you, to trouble your peace. God forgive me!'

She was five years nearer childhood than he, even taking into account the two years or more a girl child has advantage over the boys of her own age. She stood entranced, a little frightened by his intensity, and inexpressibly moved by the anguish she felt emanating from him like a raw, drowning odour. The long-fingered hand that held her shook terribly, his whole body quivered. She put up her own hand gently and closed it over his, uplifted out of her own wretchedness by his greater and more inexplicable distress.

'I dare not speak for God,' she said steadily, 'but whatever there may be for me to forgive, that I dare. It is not your fault that I love you. All you ever did was be kinder to me than ever man was since I left Wales. And I did know, love, you did tell me, if I had heeded then, you did tell me you were a man under vow. What it was you never told me, but never grieve, oh, my own soul, never grieve so . . .'

While they stood rapt, the sunset light had deepened, blazed and burned silently into glowing ash, and the first feathery shade of twilight, like the passing of a swift's wings, fled across their faces and melted into sudden pearly, radiant light. Her wide eyes were brimming with tears, almost the match of his. When he stooped to her, there was no way of knowing which of them had begun the kiss.

* * *

The little bell for Compline sounded clearly through the gardens on so limpid an evening, and stirred Brother Cadfael out of his half-doze at once. He was accustomed, in this refuge of his maturity as surely as in the warfaring of his youth, to awake fresh and alert, as he fell asleep, making the most of the twin worlds of night and day. He rose and went out into the earliest glowing image of evening, and closed the door after him.

It was but a few moments back to church through the herbarium and the rose garden. He went briskly, happy with the beauty of the evening and the promise for the morrow, and never knew why he should look aside to westward in passing, unless it was that the whole expanse of the sky on that side was delicate, pure and warming, like a girl's blush. And there they were, two clear shadows clasped together in silhouette against the fire of the west, outlined on the crest above the slope to the invisible brook. Matthew and

Melangell, unmistakable, constrained still but in each other's arms, linked in a kiss that lasted while Brother Cadfael came, passed and slipped away to his different devotions, but with that image printed indelibly on his eyes, even in his prayers.

CHAPTER SEVEN

The outrider of the bishop-legate's envoy—or should he rather be considered the empress's envoy?—arrived within the town and was directed through to the gatehouse of the castle in mid-evening of that same twenty-first day of June, to be presented to Hugh Beringar just as he was marshalling a half-dozen men to go down to the bridge and take an unpredicted part in the plans of Master Simeon Poer and his associates. Who would almost certainly be armed, being so far from home and in hitherto unexplored territory. Hugh found the visitor an unwelcome hindrance, but was too well aware of the many perils hemming the king's party on every side to dismiss the herald without ceremony. Whatever this embassage might be, he needed to know it, and make due preparation to deal with it.

In the gatehouse guard-room he found himself facing a stolid middle-aged squire, who delivered his errand word perfect.

'My lord sheriff, the Lady of the English and the lord bishop of Winchester entreat you to receive in peace their envoy, who comes to you with offerings of peace and good order in their name, and in their name asks your aid in resolving the griefs of the kingdom. I come before to announce him.'

So the empress had assumed the traditional title of a queen-elect before her coronation! The matter began to look final.

'The lord bishop's envoy will be welcome,' said Hugh, 'and shall be received with all honour here in Shrewsbury. I will lend an attentive ear to whatever he may have to say to me. As at this moment I have an affair in hand which will not wait. How far ahead of your lord do you ride?'

'A matter of two hours, perhaps,' said the squire, considering.

'Good, then I can set forward all necessary preparations for his reception, and still have time to clear up a small thing I have in hand. With how many attendants does he come?'

'Two men-at-arms only, my lord, and myself.'

'Then I will leave you in the hands of my deputy, who will have lodgings made ready for you and your two men here in the castle. As for your lord, he shall come to my own house, and my wife shall make him welcome. Hold me excused if I make small ceremony now, for this business is a twilight matter, and will not wait. Later I will see amends made.'

The messenger was well content to have his horse stabled and tended, and be led away by Alan Herbard to a comfortable lodging where he could shed his boots and leather coat, and be at his ease, and take his time and his pleasure over the meat and wine that was presently set before him. Hugh's young deputy would play the host very graciously. He was still new in office, and did everything committed to him with a flourish. Hugh left them to it, and took his half-dozen men briskly out through the town.

It was past Compline then, neither light nor dark, but hesitant between. By the time they reached the High Cross and turned down the steep curve of the Wyle they had their twilight eyes. In full darkness their quarry might have a better chance of eluding them, by daylight they would themselves have been too easily observed from afar. If these gamesters were experts they would have a lookout posted to give fair warning.

The Wyle, uncoiling eastward, brought them down to the town wall and the English gate, and there a thin, leggy child, shaggy-haired and bright-eyed, started out of the shadows under the gate to catch at Hugh's sleeve. Wat's boy, a sharp urchin of the Foregate, bursting with the importance of his errand and his own wit in managing it, had pinned down his quarry, and waited to inform and advise.

'My lord, they're met—all the four from the abbey, and a dozen or more from these parts, mostly from the town.' His note of scorn implied that they were sharper in the Foregate. 'You'd best leave the horses and go afoot. Riders out at this hour—they'd break and run as soon as you set hooves on the bridge. The sound carries.'

Good sense, that, if the meeting-place was close by. 'Where are they, then?' asked Hugh, dismounting.

'Under the far arch of the bridge, my lord— dry as a bone it is, and snug.' So it would be, with this low summer water. Only in full spate did the river prevent passage beneath that arch. In this fine season it would be a nest of dried-out grasses.

'They have a light, then?'

'A dark lantern. There's not a glimmer you'll see from either side unless you go down to the water, it sheds light only on the flat stone where they're throwing.'

Easily quenched, then, at the first alarm, and they would scatter like startled birds, every way. The fleecers would be the first and fleetest. The fleeced might well be netted in some numbers, but their offence was no more than being foolish at their own expense, not theft nor malpractice on any other.

'We leave the horses here,' said Hugh, making up his mind. 'You heard the boy. They're under the bridge, they'll have used the path that goes down to the Gaye, along the riverside. The other side of the arch is thick bushes, but that's the way they'll break. Three men to either slope, and I'll bear with the western three. And let our own young fools by, if you can pick them out, but hold fast the strangers.'

In this fashion they went to their raiding. They crossed the bridge by ones and twos, above the Severn water green with weedy shallows and shimmering with reflected light, and took their places on either side, spaced among the fringing bushes of the bank. By the time they were in place the afterglow had dissolved and faded into the western horizon, and the night came down like a velvet hand. Hugh drew off to westward along the by-road until at length he caught the faint glimmer of light beneath the stone arch. They were there. If in such numbers, perhaps he should have held them in better respect and brought more men. But he did not want the townsmen. By all means let them sneak away to their beds and think better of their dreams of milking cows likely to prove drier than sand. It was the cheats he wanted. Let the provost of the town deal with his civic idiots.

He let the sky darken somewhat before he took them in. The summer night settled, soft wings folding, and no moon. Then, at his whistle, they moved down from either flank.

It was the close-set bushes on the bank,

rustling stealthily in a windless night, that betrayed their coming a moment too soon. Whoever was on watch, below there, had a sharp ear. There was a shrill whistle, suddenly muted. The lantern went out instantly, there was black dark under the solid stonework of the bridge. Down went Hugh and his men, abandoning stealth for speed. Bodies parted, collided, heaved and fled, with no sound but the panting and gasping of scared breath. Hugh's officers waded through bushes, closing down to seal the archway. Some of those thus penned beneath the bridge broke to left, some to right, not venturing to climb into waiting arms, but wading through the shallows and floundering even into deeper water. A few struck out for the opposite shore, local lads well acquainted with their river and its reaches, and water-borne, like its fish, almost from birth. Let them go, they were Shrewsbury born and bred. If they had lost money, more fools they, but let them get to their beds and repent in peace. If their wives would let them!

But there were those beneath the arch of the bridge who had not Severn water in their blood, and were less ready to wet more than their feet in even low water. And suddenly these had steel in their hands, and were weaving and slashing and stabbing their way through into the open as best they could, and without scruple. It did not last long. In the quaking dark, sprawled among the trampled grasses up the riverside, Hugh's six clung to such captives as they could grapple, and shook off trickles of blood from their own scratches and gashes. And diminishing in the darkness, the thresh and toss of bushes marked the flight of those who had got away. Unseen beneath the bridge, the deserted lantern and scattered dice, grave loss to a trickster who must now prepare a new set, lay waiting to be retrieved.

Hugh shook off a few drops of blood from a grazed arm, and went scrambling through the rough grass to the path leading up from the Gaye to the highroad and the bridge. Before him a shadowy body fled, cursing. Hugh launched a shout to reach the road ahead of them: 'Hold him! The law wants him!' Foregate and town might be on their way to bed, but there were always late strays, both lawful and unlawful, and some on both sides would joyfully take up such an invitation to mischief or justice, whichever way the mind happened to bend.

Above him, in the deep, soft summer night that now bore only a saffron thread along the west, an answering hail shrilled, startled and merry, and there were confused sounds of brief, breathless struggle. Hugh loped up to the highroad to see three shadowy horsemen halted at the approach to the bridge, two of them closed in to flank the first, and that first leaning slightly from his saddle to grip in one hand the collar of a panting figure that leaned against his mount heaving in breath, and with small energy to attempt anything besides.

'I think, sir,' said the captor, eyeing Hugh's approach, 'this may be what you wanted. It seemed to me that the law cried out for him? Am I then addressing the law in these parts?'

It was a fine, ringing voice, unaccustomed to subduing its tone. The soft dark did not disclose his face clearly, but showed a body erect in the saddle, supple, shapely, unquestionably young. He shifted his grip on the prisoner, as though to surrender him to a better claim. Thus all but released, the fugitive did not break free and run for it, but spread his feet and stood his ground, half-defiant, eyeing Hugh dubiously.

'I'm in your debt for a minnow, it seems,' said Hugh, grinning as he recognised the man he had been chasing. 'But I doubt I've let all the salmon get clear away up-river. We were about breaking up a parcel of cheating rogues come here looking for prey, but this young gentleman you have by the coat turns out to be merely one of the simpletons, our worthy goldsmith out of the town. Master Daniel, I doubt there's more gold and silver to be lost than gained, in the company you've been keeping.'

'It's no crime to make a match at dice,' muttered the young man, shuffling his feet sullenly in the dust of the road. 'My luck would have turned . . .'

'Not with the dice they brought with them. But true it's no crime to waste your evening and go home with empty pockets, and I've no charge to make against you, provided you go back now, and hand yourself over with the rest to my sergeant. Behave yourself prettily, and you'll be home by midnight.'

Master Daniel Aurifaber took his dismissal thankfully, and slouched back towards the bridge, to be gathered in among the captives. The sound of hooves crossing the bridge at a trot indicated that someone had run for the horses, and intended a hunt to westward, in the direction the birds of prey had taken. In less than a mile they would be safe in woodland, and it would take hounds to run them to earth. Small chance of hunting them down by night. On the morrow something might be attempted.

'This is hardly the welcome I intended for you,' said Hugh, peering up into the shadowy face above him. 'For you, I think, must be the envoy sent from the Empress Maud and the bishop of Winchester. Your herald arrived little more than an hour ago, I did not expect you quite so soon. I had thought I should be done with this matter by the time you came. My name is Hugh Beringar, I stand here as sheriff for King Stephen. Your men are provided for at the castle, I'll send a guide with them. You, sir, are my own guest, if you will do my house that honour.'

'You're very gracious,' said the empress's messenger blithely, 'and with all my heart I will. But had you not better first make up your accounts with these townsmen of yours, and let them creep away to their beds? My business can well wait a little longer.'

* * *

'Not the most successful action ever I planned,' Hugh owned later to Cadfael. 'I under-estimated both their hardihood and the amount of cold steel they'd have about them.'

There were four guests missing from Brother Denis's halls that night: Master Simeon Poer, merchant of Guildford; Walter Bagot, glover; John Shure, tailor; William Hales, farrier. Of these, William Hales lay that night in a stone cell in Shrewsbury castle, along with a travelling pedlar who had touted for them in the town, but the other three had all broken safely away, bar a few scratches and bruises, into the woods to westward, the most northerly outlying spinneys of the Long Forest, there to bed down in the warm night and count their injuries and their gains, which were considerable. They could not now return to the abbey or the town; the traffic would in any case have stood only one more night at a profit. Three nights are the most to be reckoned on, after that some aggrieved wretch is sure to grow suspicious. Nor could they yet venture south again. But the man who lives on his wits must keep them well honed and adaptable, and there are more ways than one of making a dishonest living.

As for the young rufflers and simple tradesmen who had come out with visions of rattling their winnings on the way home to their wives, they were herded into the gatehouse to be chided, warned, and sent home chapfallen, with very little in their pockets.

And there the night's work would have ended, if the flare of the torch under the gateway had not caught the metal gleam of a ring on Daniel Aurifaber's right hand, flat silver with an oval bezel, for one instant sharply defined. Hugh saw it, and laid a hand on the goldsmith's arm to detain him.

'That ring—let me see it closer!'

Daniel handed it over with a hint of reluctance, though it seemed to stem rather from bewilderment than from any feeling of guilt. It fitted closely, and passed over his knuckle with slight difficulty, but the finger bore no sign of having worn it regularly.

'Where did you get this?' asked Hugh, holding it under the flickering light to examine the device and inscription.

'I bought it honestly,' said Daniel defensively.

'That I need not doubt. But from whom? From one of those gamesters? Which one?'

'The merchant—Simeon Poer he called himself. He offered it, and it was a good piece of work. I paid well for it.'

'You have paid double for it, my friend,' said Hugh, 'for you bid fair to lose ring and money and all. Did it never enter your mind that it might be stolen?'

By the single nervous flutter of the goldsmith's eyelids the thought had certainly occurred to him, however hurriedly he had put it out of his mind again. 'No! Why should I think so? He seemed a stout, prosperous person, all he claimed to be . . .'

'This very morning,' said Hugh, 'just such a ring was taken during Mass from a pilgrim at the abbey. Abbot Radulfus sent word up to the provost, after they had searched thoroughly within the pale, in case it should be offered for sale in the market. I had the description of it in turn from the provost. This is the device and inscription of the bishop of Winchester, and it was given to the bearer to secure him safe-conduct on the road.'

'But I bought it in good faith,' protested Daniel, dismayed. 'I paid the man what he asked, the ring is mine, honestly come by.'

'From a thief. Your misfortune, lad, and it may teach you to be more wary of sudden kind acquaintances in the future who offer you rings to buy—wasn't it so?—at somewhat less than you know to be their value? Travelling men rattling dice give nothing for nothing, but take whatever they can get. If they've emptied your purse for you, take warning for the next time. This must go back to the lord abbot in the morning. Let him deal with the owner.' He saw the goldsmith draw angry breath to complain of his deprivation, and shook his head to ward off the effort, not unkindly. 'You have no remedy. Bite your tongue, Daniel, and go make your peace with your wife.'

* * *

The empress's envoy rode gently up the Wyle in the deepening dark, keeping pace with Hugh's smaller mount. His own was a fine, tall beast, and the young man in the saddle was long of body and limb. Afoot, thought Hugh, studying him sidelong, he will top me by a head. Very much of an age with me, I might give him a year or two, hardly more.

'Were you ever in Shrewsbury before?'

'Never. Once, perhaps, I was just within the shire, I am not sure how the border runs. I was near Ludlow once. This abbey of yours, I marked it as I came by, a very fine, large enclosure. They keep the Benedictine Rule?'

'They do.' Hugh expected further questions, but they did not come. 'You have kinsmen in the Order?'

Even in the dark he was aware of his companion's grave, musing smile. 'In a manner of speaking, yes, I have. I think he would give

129

me leave to call him so, though there is no blood-kinship. One who used me like a son. I keep a kindness for the habit, for his sake. And did I hear you say there are pilgrims here now? For some particular feast?'

'For the translation of Saint Winifred, who was brought here four years ago from Wales. Tomorrow is the day of her arrival.' Hugh had spoken by custom, quite forgetting what Cadfael had told him of that arrival, but the mention of it brought his friend's story back sharply to mind. 'I was not in Shrewsbury then,' he said, withholding judgement. 'I brought my manors to King Stephen's support the following year. My own country is the north of the shire.'

They had reached the top of the hill, and were turning towards Saint Mary's church. The great gate of Hugh's courtyard stood wide, with torches at the gateposts, waiting for them. His message had been faithfully delivered to Aline, and she was waiting for them with all due ceremony, the bedchamber prepared, the meal ready to come to table. All rules, all times, bow to the coming of a guest, the duty and privilege of hospitality.

She met them at the door, opening it wide to welcome them in. They stepped into the hall, and into a flood of light from torches at the walls and candles on the table, and instinctively they turned to face each other, taking the first long look. It grew ever longer as their intent eyes grew wider. It was a question which of them groped towards recognition first. Memory pricked and realisation awoke almost stealthily. Aline stood smiling and wondering, but mute, eyeing first one, then the other, until they should stir and shed a clearer light.

'But I know you!' said Hugh. 'Now I see you, I do know you.'

'I have seen you before,' agreed the guest. 'I was never in this shire but the once, and yet . . .'

'It needed light to see you by,' said Hugh, 'for I never heard your voice but the once, and then no more than a few words. I doubt if you even remember them, but I do. Six words only. "Now have ado with a man!" you said. And your name, your name I never heard but in a manner I take as it was meant. You are Robert, the forester's son who fetched Yves Hugonin out of that robber fortress up on Titterstone Clee. And took him home with you, I think, and his sister with him.'

'And you are that officer who laid the siege that gave me the cover I needed,' cried the guest, gleaming. 'Forgive me that I hid from you then, but I had no warranty there in your territory. How glad I am to meet you honestly now, with no need to take to flight.'

'And no need now to be Robert, the forester's son,' said Hugh, elated and smiling. 'My name I have given you, and the freedom

131

of this house I offer with it. Now may I know yours?'

'In Antioch, where I was born,' said the guest, 'I was called Daoud. But my father was an Englishman of Robert of Normandy's force, and among his comrades in arms I was baptised a Christian, and took the name of the priest who stood my godfather. Now I bear the name of Olivier de Bretagne.'

*   *   *

They sat late into the night together, savouring each other now face to face, after a year and a half of remembering and wondering. But first, as was due, they made short work of Olivier's errand here.

'I am sent,' he said seriously, 'to urge all sheriffs of shires to consider, whatever their previous fealty, whether they should not now accept the proffered peace under the Empress Maud, and take the oath of loyalty to her. This is the message of the bishop and the council: This land has all too long been torn between two factions, and suffered great damage and loss through their mutual enmity. And here *I* say that I lay no blame on that party which is not my own, for there are valid claims on both sides, and equally the blame falls on both for failing to come to some agreement to end these distresses. The fortune at Lincoln might just as well have fallen the opposing way, but it

132

fell as it did, and England is left with a king made captive, and a queen-elect free and in the ascendant. Is it not time to call a halt? For the sake of order and peace and the sound regulation of the realm, and to have a government in command which can and must put down the many injustices and tyrannies which you know, as well as I, have set themselves up outside all law. Surely any strong rule is better than no rule at all. For the sake of peace and order, will you not accept the empress, and hold your county in allegiance to her? She is already in Westminster now, the preparations for her coronation go forward. There is a far better prospect of success if all sheriffs come in to strengthen her rule.'

'You are asking me,' said Hugh gently, 'to go back on my sworn fealty to King Stephen.'

'Yes,' agreed Olivier honestly, 'I am. For weighty reasons, and in no treasonous mind. You need not love, only forbear from hating. Think of it rather as keeping your fealty to the people of this county of yours, and this land.'

'That I can do as well or better on the side where I began,' said Hugh, smiling. 'It is what I am doing now, as best I can. It is what I will continue to do while I have breath. I am King Stephen's man, and I will not desert him.'

'Ah, well!' said Olivier, smiling and sighing in the same breath. 'To tell you truth, now I've met you, I expected nothing less. I would not go from my oath, either. My lord is the empress's man, and I am my lord's man, and if our positions were changed round, my answer would be the same as yours. Yet there is truth in what I have pleaded. How much can a people bear? Your labourer in the fields, your little townsman with a bare living to be looted from him, these would be glad to settle for Stephen or for Maud, only to be rid of the other. And I do what I am sent out to do, as well as I can.'

'I have no fault to find with the matter or the manner,' said Hugh. 'Where next do you go? Though I hope you will not go for a day or two, I would know you better, and we have a great deal to talk over, you and I.'

'From here north-east to Stafford, Derby, Nottingham, and back by the eastern parts. Some will come to terms, as some lords have done already. Some will hold to their own king, like you. And some will do as they have done before, go back and forth like a weather-cock with the wind, and put up their price at every change. No matter, we have done with that now.'

He leaned forward over the table, setting his wine-cup aside. 'I had—I have—another errand of my own, and I should be glad to stay with you a few days, until I have found what I'm seeking, or made certain it is not here to be found. Your mention of this flood of pilgrims for the feast gives me a morsel of hope. A man who wills to be lost could find cover among so many, all strangers to one another. I am looking for a young man called Luc Meverel. He has not, to your knowledge, made his way here?'

'Not by that name,' said Hugh, interested and curious. 'But a man who willed to be lost might choose to doff his own name. What's your need of him?'

'Not mine. It's a lady who wants him back. You may not have got word, this far north,' said Olivier, 'of everything that happened in Winchester during the council. There was a death there that came all too near to me. Did you hear of it? King Stephen's queen sent her clerk there with a bold challenge to the legate's authority, and the man was attacked for his audacity in the street by night, and got off with his life only at the cost of another life.'

'We have indeed heard of it,' said Hugh with kindling interest. 'Abbot Radulfus was there at the council, and brought back a full report. A knight by the name of Rainald Bossard, who came to the clerk's aid when he was set upon. One of those in the service of Laurence d'Angers, so we heard.'

'Who is my lord, also.'

'By your good service to his kin at Bromfield that was plain enough. I thought of you when the abbot spoke of d'Angers, though I had no name for you then. Then this man Bossard was well known to you?'

'Through a year of service in Palestine, and the voyage home together. A good man he was, and a good friend to me, and struck down in defending his honest opponent. I was not with him that night, I wish I had been, he might yet be alive. But he had only one or two of his own people, not in arms. There were five or six set on the clerk, it was a wretched business, confused and in the dark. The murderer got clean away, and has never been traced. Rainald's wife . . . Juliana . . . I did not know her until we came with our lord to Winchester, Rainald's chief manor is nearby. I have learned,' said Olivier very gravely, 'to hold her in the highest regard. She was her lord's true match, and no one could say more or better of any lady.'

'There is an heir?' asked Hugh. 'A man grown, or still a child?'

'No, they never had children. Rainald was nearly fifty, she cannot be many years younger. And very beautiful,' said Olivier with solemn consideration, as one attempting not to praise, but to explain. 'Now she's widowed she'll have a hard fight on her hands to evade being married off again—for she'll want no other after Rainald. She has manors of her own to bestow. They had thought of the inheritance, the two of them together, that's why they took into their household this young man Luc Meverel, only a year ago. He is a distant cousin of Dame Juliana, twenty-four or twenty-five years old, I suppose, and landless. They meant to make him their heir.'

He fell silent for some minutes, frowning past the guttering candles, his chin in his palm. Hugh studied him, and waited. It was a face worth studying, clean-boned, olive-skinned, fiercely beautiful, even with the golden, falcon's eyes thus hooded. The blue-black hair that clustered thickly about his head, clasping like folded wings, shot sullen bluish lights back from the candle's waverings. Daoud, born in Antioch, son of an English crusading soldier in Robert of Normandy's following, somehow blown across the world in the service of an Angevin baron, to fetch up here almost more Norman than the Normans ... The world, thought Hugh, is not so great, after all, but a man born to venture may bestride it.

'I have been three times in that household,' said Olivier, 'but I never knowingly set eyes on this Luc Meverel. All I know of him is what others have said, but among the others I take my choice which voice to believe. There is no one, man or woman, in that manor but agrees he was utterly devoted to Dame Juliana. But as to the manner of his devotion ... There are many who say he loved her far too well, by no means after the fashion of a son. Again, some say he was equally loyal to Rainald, but their voices are growing fainter now. Luc was one of those with his lord when Rainald was stabbed to death in the street. And two days later he

137

vanished from his place, and has not been seen since.'

'Now I begin to see,' said Hugh, drawing in cautious breath. 'Have they gone so far as to say this man slew his lord in order to gain his lady?'

'It is being said now, since his flight. Who began the whisper there's no telling, but by this time it's grown into a bellow.'

'Then why should he run from the prize for which he had played? It makes poor sense. If he had stayed there need have been no such whispers.'

'Ah, but I think there would have been, whether he went or stayed. There were those who grudged him his fortune, and would have welcomed any means of damaging him. They are finding two good reasons, now, why he should break and run. The first, pure guilt and remorse, too late to save any one of the three of them. The second, fear—fear that someone had got wind of his act, and meant to fetch out the truth at all costs. Either way, a man might break and take to his heels. What you kill for may seem even less attainable,' said Olivier with rueful shrewdness, 'once you have killed.'

'But you have not yet told me,' said Hugh, 'what the lady says of him. Hers is surely a voice that should be heeded.'

'She says that such a vile suspicion is impossible. She did, she does, value her young cousin, but not in the way of love, nor will she

138

have it that he has ever entertained such thoughts of her. She says he would have died for his lord, and that it is his lord's death which has driven him away, sick with grief, a little mad—who knows how deluded and haunted? For he was there that night, he saw Rainald die. She is sure of him. She wants him found and brought back to her. She looks upon him as a son, and now more than ever she needs him.'

'And it's for her sake you're seeking him. But why look for him here, northwards? He may have gone south, west, across the sea by the Kentish ports. Why to the north?'

'Because we have just one word of him since he was lost from his place, and that was going north on the road to Newbury. I came by that same way, by Abingdon and Oxford, and I have enquired for him everywhere, a young man travelling alone. But I can only seek him by his own name, for I know no other for him. As you say, who knows what he may be calling himself now!'

'And you don't even know what he looks like—nothing but merely his age? You're hunting for a spectre!'

'What is lost can always be found, it needs only enough patience.' Olivier's hawk's face, beaked and passionate, did not suggest patience, but the set of his lips was stubborn and pure in absolute resolution.

'Well, at least,' said Hugh, considering, 'we

may go down to see Saint Winifred brought home to her altar, tomorrow, and Brother Denis can run through the roster of his pilgrims for us, and point out any who are of the right age and kind, solitary or not. As for strangers here in the town, I fancy Provost Corviser should be able to put his finger on most of them. Every man knows every man in Shrewsbury. But the abbey is the more likely refuge, if he's here at all.' He pondered, gnawing a thoughtful lip. 'I must send the ring down to the abbot at first light, and let him know what's happened to his truant guests, but before I may go down to the feast myself I must send out a dozen men and have them beat the near reaches of the woods to westward for our game birds. If they're over the border, so much the worse for Wales, and I can do no more, but I doubt if they intend to live wild any longer than they need. They may not go far. How if I should leave you with the provost, to pick his brains for your quarry here within the town, while I go hunting for mine? Then we'll go down together to see the brothers bring their saint home, and talk to Brother Denis concerning the list of his guests.'

'That would suit me well,' said Olivier gladly. 'I should like to pay my respects to the lord abbot, I do recall seeing him in Winchester, though he would not notice me. And there was a brother of that house, if you

140

recall,' he said, his golden eyes veiled within long black lashes that swept his fine cheekbones, 'who was with you at Bromfield and up on Clee, that time . . . You must know him well. He is still here at the abbey?'

'He is. He'll be back in his bed now after Lauds. And you and I had better be thinking of seeking ours, if we're to be busy tomorrow.'

'He was good to my lord's young kinsfolk,' said Olivier. 'I should like to see him again.'

No need to ask for a name, thought Hugh, eyeing him with a musing smile. And indeed, should he know the name? He had not mentioned any, when he spoke of one who was no blood-kin, but who had used him like a son, one for whose sake he kept a kindness for the Benedictine habit.

'You shall!' said Hugh, and rose in high content to marshal his guest to the bedchamber prepared for him.

CHAPTER EIGHT

Abbot Radulfus was up long before Prime on the festal morning, and so were his obedientiaries, all of whom had their important tasks in preparation for the procession. When Hugh's messenger presented himself at the abbot's lodging the dawn was still fresh, dewy and cool, the light lying brightly across the roofs while the great court lay in lilac-tinted shadow. In the gardens every tree and bush cast a long band of shade, striping the flower-beds like giant brush-strokes in some gilded illumination.

The abbot received the ring with astonished pleasure, relieved of one flaw that might have marred the splendour of the day. 'And you say these malefactors were guests in our halls, all four? We are well rid of them, but if they are armed, as you say, and have taken to the woods close by, we shall need to warn our travellers, when they leave us.'

'My lord Beringar has a company out beating the edges of the forest for them this moment,' said the messenger. 'There was nothing to gain by following them in the dark, once they were in cover. But by daylight we'll hope to trace them. One we have safe in hold, he may tell us more about them, where they're from, and what they have to answer for elsewhere. But at least now they can't hinder your festivities.'

'And for that I'm devoutly thankful. As this man Ciaran will certainly be for the recovery of his ring.' He added, with a glance aside at the breviary that lay on his desk, and a small frown for the load of ceremonial that lay before him for the next few hours: 'Shall we not see the lord sheriff here for Mass this morning?'

'Yes, Father, he does intend it, and he brings

142

a guest also. He had first to set this hunt in motion, but before Mass they will be here.'

'He has a guest?'

'An envoy from the empress's court came last night, Father. A man of Laurence d'Angers' household, Olivier de Bretagne.'

The name that had meant nothing to Hugh meant as little to Radulfus, though he nodded recollection and understanding at mention of the young man's overlord. 'Then will you say to Hugh Beringar that I beg he and his guest will remain after Mass, and dine with me here. I should be glad to make the acquaintance of Messire de Bretagne, and hear his news.'

'I will so tell him, Father,' said the messenger, and forthwith took his leave.

Left alone in his parlour, Abbot Radulfus stood for a moment looking down thoughtfully at the ring in his palm. The sheltering hand of the bishop-legate would certainly be a powerful protection to any traveller so signally favoured, wherever there existed any order or respect for law, whether in England or Wales. Only those already outside the pale of law, with lives or liberty already forfeit if taken, would defy so strong a sanction. After this crowning day many of the guests here would be leaving again for home. He must not forget to give due warning, before they dispersed, that malefactors might be lurking at large in the woods to westward, and that they were armed, and all too handy at using their daggers. Best that the pilgrims should make sure of leaving in companies stout enough to discourage assault.

Meantime, there was satisfaction in returning to one pilgrim, at least, his particular armour.

The abbot rang the little bell that lay upon his desk, and in a few moments Brother Vitalis came to answer the summons.

'Will you enquire at the guest-hall, brother, for the man called Ciaran, and bid him here to speak with me?'

*   *   *

Brother Cadfael had also risen well before Prime, and gone to open his workshop and kindle his brazier into cautious and restrained life, in case it should be needed later to prepare tisanes for some ecstatic souls carried away by emotional excitement, or warm applications for weaker vessels trampled in the crowd. He was used to the transports of simple souls caught up in far from simple raptures.

He had a few things to tend to, and was happy to deal with them alone. Young Oswin was entitled to his fill of sleep until the bell awoke him. Very soon now he would graduate to the hospital of Saint Giles, where the reliquary of Saint Winifred now lay, and the unfortunates who carried their contagion with them, and might not be admitted into the town, could find rest, care and shelter for as long as they needed it. Brother Mark, that dearly-missed disciple, was gone from there now, already ordained deacon, his eyes fixed ahead upon his steady goal of priesthood. If ever he cast a glance over his shoulder, he would find nothing but encouragement and affection, the proper harvest of the seed he had sown. Oswin might not be such another, but he was a good enough lad, and would do honestly by the unfortunates who drifted into his care.

Cadfael went down to the banks of the Meole brook, the westward boundary of the enclave, where the pease-fields declined to the sunken summer water. The rays from the east were just being launched like lances over the high roofs of the monastic buildings, and piercing the scattered copses beyond the brook, and the grassy banks on the further side. This same water, drawn off much higher in its course, supplied the monastery fishponds, the hatchery, and the mill and millpond beyond, and was fed back into the brook just before it entered the Severn. It lay low enough now, an archipelago of shoals, half sand, half grass and weed, spreading smooth islands across its breadth. After this spell, thought Cadfael, we shall need plenty of rain. But let that wait a day or two.

He turned back to climb the slope again. The earlier field of pease had already been

145

gleaned, the second would be about ready for harvesting after the festival. A couple of days, and all the excitement would be over, and the horarium of the house and the cycle of the seasons would resume their imperturbable progress, two enduring rhythms in the desperately variable fortunes of mankind. He turned along the path to his workshop, and there was Melangell hesitating before its closed door.

She heard his step in the gravel behind her, and looked round with a bright, expectant face. The pearly morning light became her, softened the coarseness of her linen gown, and smoothed cool lilac shadows round the childlike curves of her face. She had gone to great pains to prepare herself fittingly for the day's solemnities. Her skirts were spotless, crisped out with care, her dark-gold hair, burning with coppery lustre, braided and coiled on her head in a bright crown, its tight plaits drawing up the skin of her temples and cheeks so strongly that her brows were pulled aslant, and the dark-lashed blue eyes elongated and made mysterious. But the radiance that shone from her came not from the sun's caresses, but from within. The blue of those eyes burned as brilliantly as the blue of the gentians Cadfael had seen long ago in the mountains of southern France, on his way to the east. The ivory and rose of her cheeks glowed. Melangell was in the highest state of hope, happiness and expectation.

She made him a very pretty reverence, flushing and smiling, and held out to him the little vial of poppy-syrup he had given to Rhun three days ago. Still unopened!

'If you please, Brother Cadfael, I have brought this back to you. And Rhun prays that it may serve some other who needs it more, and with the more force because he has endured without it.'

He took it from her gently and held it in his cupped hand, a crude little vial stopped with a wooden stopper and a membrane of very thin parchment tied with a waxed thread to seal it. All intact. The boy's third night here, and he had submitted to handling and been mild and biddable in all, but when the means of oblivion was put into his hand and left to his private use, he had preserved it, and with it some core of his own secret integrity, at his own chosen cost. God forbid, thought Cadfael, that I should meddle there. Nothing short of a saint should knock on that door.

'You are not angry with him?' asked Melangell anxiously, but smiling still, unable to believe that any shadow should touch the day, now that her love had clasped and kissed her. 'Because he did not drink it? It was not that he ever doubted *you*. He said so to me. He said— I never quite understand him!—he said it was a time for offering, and he had his offering prepared.'

147

Cadfael asked: 'Did he sleep?' To have deliverance in hand, even unopened, might well bring peace. 'Hush, now, no, how could I be angry! But *did* he sleep?'

'He says that he did. I think it must be true, he looks so fresh and young. I prayed hard for him.' With all the force of her new happiness, loaded with bliss she felt the need to pour out upon all those near to her. In the conveyance of blessedness by affection Cadfael firmly believed.

'You prayed well,' said Cadfael. 'Never doubt he has gained by it. I'll keep this for some soul in worse need, as Rhun says. It will have the virtue of his faith to strengthen it. I shall see you both during the day.'

She went away from him with a light, springing step and a head reared to breathe in the very space and light of the sky. And Cadfael went in to make sure he had everything ready to provide for a long and exhausting day.

So Rhun had arrived at the last frontier of belief, and fallen, or emerged, or soared into the region where the soul realises that pain is of no account, that to be within the secret of God is more than well being, and past the power of the tongue to utter. To embrace the decree of pain is to translate it, to shed it like a rain of blessing on others who have not yet understood.

Who am I, thought Cadfael, alone in the

solitude of his workshop, that I should dare to ask for a sign? If he can endure and ask nothing, must not I be ashamed of doubting?

*   *   *

Melangell passed with a dancing step along the path from the herbarium. On her right hand the western sky soared, in such reflected if muted brightness that she could not forbear from turning to stare into it. A counter-tide of light flowed in here from the west, surging up the slope from the brook and spilling over the crest into the garden. Somewhere on the far side of the entire monastic enclave the two tides would meet, and the light of the west falter, pale and die before the onslaught from the east; but here the bulk of guest-hall and church cut off the newly-risen sun, and left the field to this hesitant and soft-treading antidawn.

There was someone labouring along the far border of the flower-garden, going delicately on still tender feet, watching where he trod. He was alone. No attendant shadow appeared at his back, yesterday's magic still held. She was staring at Ciaran, Ciaran without Matthew. That in itself was a minor miracle, to bring in this day made for miracles.

Melangell watched him begin to descend the slope towards the brook, and when he was no more than a head and shoulders black

149

against the brightness, she suddenly turned and went after him. The path down to the water skirted the growing pease, keeping close to a hedge of thick bushes above the mill-pool. Halfway down the slope she halted, uncertain whether to intrude on his solitude. Ciaran had reached the waterside, and stood surveying what looked like a safe green floor, dappled here and there with the bleached islands of sand, and studded with a few embedded rocks that stood dry from three weeks of fine weather. He looked upstream and down, even stepped into the shallow water that barely covered his naked feet, and surely soothed and refreshed them. Yet how strange, that he should be here alone! Never, until yesterday, had she seen either of these two without the other, yet now they went apart.

She was on the point of stealing away to leave him undisturbed when she saw what he was doing. He had some tiny thing in his hand, into which he was threading a thin cord, and knotting the cord to hold it fast. When he raised both hands to make fast the end of his cord to the tether that held the cross about his neck, the small talisman swung free into the light and glimmered for an instant in silver, before he tucked it away within the neck of his shirt, out of sight against his breast. Then she knew what it was, and stirred in pure pleasure for him, and uttered a small, breathless sound. For Ciaran had his ring again, the safe-conduct that was to ensure him passage to his journey's end.

He had heard her, and swung about, startled and wary. She stood shaken and disconcerted, and then, knowing herself discovered, ran down the last slope of grass to his side. 'They've found it for you!' she said breathlessly, in haste to fill the silence between them and dispel her own uneasiness at having seemed to spy upon him. 'Oh, I am glad! Is the thief taken, then?'

'Melangell!' he said. 'You're early abroad, too? Yes, you see I am blessed, after all, I have it again. The lord abbot restored it to me only some minutes ago. But no, the thief is not caught, he and some fellow-rogues are fled into the woods, it seems. But I can go forth again without fear now.'

His dark eyes, deep-set under thick brows, opened wide upon her, smiling, holding her charmed in the abrupt discovery that he was, despite his disease, a young and comely man, who should have been in the fulness of his powers. Either she was imagining it, or he stood a little straighter, a little taller, than she had ever yet seen him, and the burning intensity of his face had mellowed into a brighter, more human ardour, as if some foreglow of the day's spiritual radiance had given him new hope.

'Melangell,' he said in a soft, vehement rush of words, 'you can't guess how glad I am of this

151

meeting, it was God sent you here to me. I've long wanted to speak to you alone. Never think that because I myself am doomed, I can't see what's before my eyes concerning others who are dear to me. I have something to ask of you, to beg of you, most earnestly. Don't tell Matthew that I have my ring again!'

'Does he not know?' she asked, astray.

'No, he was not by when the abbot sent for me. He must not know! Keep my secret, if you love him—if you have some pity, at least for me. I have told no one, and you must not. The lord abbot is not likely to speak of it to any other, why should he? That he would leave to me. If you and I keep silent, there's no need for anyone else to find out.'

Melangell was lost. She saw him through a rainbow of starting tears, for very pity of his long face hollowed in shade, his eyes glowing like the quiet, living heart of a banked fire.

'But why? Why do you want to keep it from him?'

'For his sake and yours—yes, and mine! Do you think I have not understood long ago that he loves you?—that you feel as much also for him? Only I stand in the way! It's bitter to know it, and I would have it changed. My one wish now is that you and he should be happy together. If he loves me so faithfully, may not I also love him? You know him! He will sacrifice himself, and you, and all things beside, to finish what he has undertaken, and see me safe into Aberdaron. I don't accept his sacrifice, I won't endure it! Why should you both be wretched, when my one wish is to go to my rest in peace of mind and leave my friend happy? Now, while he feels secure that I dare not set out without the ring, for God's sake, girl, leave him in innocence. *And I will go*, and leave you both my blessing.'

Melangell stood quivering, like a leaf shaken by the soft, vehement wind of his words, uncertain even of her own heart. 'Then what must I do? What is it you want of me?'

'Keep my secret,' said Ciaran, 'and go with Matthew in this holy procession. Oh, he'll go with you, and be glad. He won't wonder that I should stay behind and wait the saint's coming here within the pale. And while you're gone, I'll go on my way. My feet are almost healed, I have my ring again, I shall reach my haven. You need not be afraid for me. Only keep him happy as long as you may, and even when my going is known, then use your arts, keep him, hold him fast. That's all I shall ever ask of you.'

'But he'll know,' she said, alert to dangers. 'The porter will tell him you're gone, as soon as he looks for you and asks.'

'No, for I shall go by this way, across the brook and out to the west, for Wales. The porter will not see me go. See, it's barely ankle-deep in this season. I have kinsmen in Wales, the first miles are nothing. And among so great a throng, if he does look for me, he'll

153

hardly wonder at not finding me. Not for hours need he so much as think of me, if you do your part. You take care of Matthew, I will absolve both you and him of all care of me, for I shall do well enough. All the better for knowing I leave him safe with you. For you do love him,' said Ciaran softly.

'Yes,' said Melangell in a long sigh.

'Then take and hold him, and my blessing on you both. You may tell him—but well afterwards!—that it is what I designed and intended,' he said, and suddenly and briefly smiled at some unspoken thought he did not wish to share with her.

'You will really do this for him and for me? You mean it? You would go on alone for his sake ... Oh, you are good!' she said passionately, and caught at his hand and pressed it to her heart for an instant, for he was giving her the whole world at his own sorrowful cost, and for selfless love of his friend, and there might never be any time but this one moment even to thank him. 'I'll never forget your goodness. All my life long I shall pray for you.'

'No,' said Ciaran, the same dark smile plucking at his lips as she released his hand, 'forget me, and help him to forget me. That is the best gift you can make me. And better you should not speak to me again. Go and find him. That's your part, and I depend on you.'

She drew back from him a few paces, her

eyes still fixed on him in gratitude and worship, made him a strange little reverence with head and hands, and turned obediently to climb the field into the garden. By the time she reached level ground and began to thread the beds of the rose garden she was breaking into a joyous run.

*   *   *

They gathered in the great court as soon as everyone, monk, lay servant, guest and townsman, had broken his fast. Seldom had the court seen such a crowd, and outside the walls the Foregate was loud with voices, as the guildsmen of Shrewsbury, provost, elders and all, assembled to join the solemn procession that would set out for Saint Giles. Half of the choir monks, led by Prior Robert, were to go in procession to fetch home the reliquary, while the abbot and the remaining brothers waited to greet them with music and candles and flowers on their return. As for the devout of town and Foregate, and the pilgrims within the walls, they might form and follow Prior Robert, such of them as were able-bodied and eager, while the lame and feeble might wait with the abbot, and prove their devotion by labouring out at least a little way to welcome the saint on her return.

'I should so much like to go with them all the way,' said Melangell, flushed and excited

155

among the chattering, elbowing crowd in the court. 'It is not far. But too far for Rhun—he could not keep pace.'

He was there beside her, very silent, very white, very fair, as though even his flaxen hair had turned paler at the immensity of this experience. He leaned on his crutches between his sister and Dame Alice, and his crystal eyes were very wide, and looked very far, as though he was not even aware of their solicitude hemming him in on either side. Yet he answered simply enough, 'I should like to go a little way, at least, until they leave me behind. But you need not wait for me.'

'As though I would leave you!' said Mistress Weaver, comfortably clucking. 'You and I will keep together and see the pilgrimage out to the best we can, and heaven will be content with that. But the girl has her legs, she may go all the way, and put up a few prayers for you going and returning, and we'll none of us be the worse for it.'

She leaned to twitch the neck of his shirt and the collar of his coat into immaculate neatness, and to fuss over his extreme pallor, afraid he was coming down with illness from over-excitement, though he seemed tranquil as ivory, and serenely absent in spirit, gone somewhere she could not follow. Her hand, rough-fingered from weaving, smoothed his well-brushed hair, teasing every tendril back from his tall forehead.

'Run off, then, child,' she said to Melangell, without turning from the boy. 'But find someone we know. There'll be riffraff running alongside, I dare say—no escaping them. Stay by Mistress Glover, or the apothecary's widow . . .'

'Matthew is going with them,' said Melangell, flushing and smiling at his very name. 'He told me so. I met him when we came from Prime.'

It was only half-true. She had rather confided boldly to him that she wished to tread every step of the way, and at every step remember and intercede for the souls she most loved on earth. No need to name them. He, no doubt, thought with reflected tenderness of her brother; but she was thinking no less of this anguished pair whose fortunes she now carried delicately and fearfully in her hands. She had even said, greatly venturing, 'Ciaran cannot keep pace, poor soul, he must wait here, like Rhun. But can't we make our steps count for them?'

But for all that, Matthew had looked over his shoulder, and hesitated a sharp instant before he turned his face fully to her, and said abruptly: 'Yes, we'll go, you and I. Yes, let's go that short way together, surely I have the right, this once . . . I'll make my prayers for Rhun every step of the way.'

'Trot and find him, then, girl,' said Dame Alice, satisfied. 'Matthew will take good care

157

of you. See, they're forming up, you'd best hurry. We'll be here to watch you come in.'

Melangell fled, elated. Prior Robert had drawn up his choir, with Brother Anselm the precentor at their head, facing the gate. The shifting, murmuring, excited column of pilgrims formed up at his rear, twitching like a dragon's tail, a long, brightly-coloured, volatile train, brave with flowers, lighted tapers, offerings, crosses and banners. Matthew was waiting to reach out an eager hand to her and draw her in beside him. 'You have leave? She trusts you to me . . . ?'

'You're not troubled about Ciaran?' she could not forbear asking anxiously. 'He's right to stay here, he couldn't manage the walk.'

The choir monks before them began their processional psalm, Prior Robert led the way through the open gate, and after him went the brothers in their ordered pairs, and after them the notabilities of the town, and after them the long retinue of pilgrims, crowding forward eagerly, picking up the chant where they had knowledge of it or a sensitive ear, pouring out past the gatehouse and turning right towards Saint Giles.

*   *   *

Brother Cadfael went with Prior Robert's party, with Brother Adam of Reading walking beside him. Along the broad road by the

158

enclave wall, past the great triangle of trodden grass at the horse-fair ground, and again bearing right with the road, between scattered houses and sun-bleached pastures and fields to the very edge of the suburb, where the squat tower of the hospital church, the roof of the hospice, and the long wattle fence of its garden showed dark against the bright eastern sky, slightly raised from the road on a gentle green mound. And all the way the long train of followers grew longer and more gaily-coloured, as the people of the Foregate in their best holiday clothes came out from their dwellings and joined the procession.

There was no room in the small, dark church for more than the brothers and the civic dignitaries of the town. The rest gathered all about the doorway, craning to get a glimpse of the proceedings within. With his lips moving almost soundlessly on the psalms and prayers, Cadfael watched the play of candle-light on the silver tracery that ornamented Saint Winifred's elegant oak coffin, elevated there on the altar as when they had first brought it from Gwytherin, four years earlier. He wondered whether his motive in securing for himself a place among the eight brothers who would bear her back to the abbey had been as pure as he had hoped. Had he been staking a proprietory claim on her, as one who had been at her first coming? Or had he meant it as a humble and penitential gesture? He was, after all, past sixty, and as he recalled, the oak casket was heavy, its edges sharp on a creaky shoulder, and the way back long enough to bring out all the potential discomforts. She might yet find a way of showing him whether she approved his proceedings or no, by striking him helpless with rheumatic pains!

The office ended. The eight chosen brothers, matched in height and pace, lifted the reliquary and settled it upon their shoulders. The prior stooped his lofty head through the low doorway into the mid-morning radiance, and the crowd clustered about the church opened to make way for the saint to ride to her triumph. The procession reformed, Prior Robert before with the brothers, the coffin with its bearers, flanked by crosses and banners and candles, and eager women bringing garlands of flowers. With measured pace, with music and solemn joy, Saint Winifred—or whatever represented her there in the sealed and secret place—was borne back to her own altar in the abbey church.

Curious, thought Cadfael, carefully keeping the step by numbers, it seems lighter than I remember. Is that possible? In only four years? He was familiar with the curious propensities of the body, dead or alive, he had once been led into a gallery of caverns in the desert where ancient Christians had lived and died, he knew what dry air can do to flesh, preserving the light and shrivelled shell while the juice of life was drawn off into spirit. Whatever was there in the reliquary, it rode tranquilly upon his shoulder, like a light hand guiding him. It was not heavy at all!

CHAPTER NINE

Something wonderful happened along the way to Matthew and Melangell, hemmed in among the jostling, singing, jubilant train. Somewhere along that half-mile of road they were caught up in the fever and joy of the day, borne along on the tide of music and devotion, forgetting all others, forgetting even themselves, drawn into one without any word or motion of theirs. When they turned their heads to look at each other, they saw only mated eyes and a halo of sunshine. They did not speak at all, not once along the way. They had no need of speech. But when they had turned the corner of the precinct wall by the horse-fair, and drew near to the gatehouse, and heard and saw the abbot leading his own party out to meet them, splendidly vested and immensely tall under his mitre; when the two chants found their measure while yet some way apart, and met and married in a triumphant, soaring cry of worship, and all the ardent followers drew gasping breaths of exultation, Melangell heard

161

beside her a broken breath drawn, like a soft sob, that turned as suddenly into a peal of laughter, out of pure, possessed joy. Not a loud sound, muted and short of breath because the throat that uttered it was clenched by emotion, and the mind and heart from which it came quite unaware of what it shed upon the world. It was a beautiful sound, or so Melangell thought, as she raised her head to stare at him with wide eyes and parted lips, in dazzled and dazzling delight. Matthew's wry and rare smile she had seen sometimes, and wondered and grieved at its brevity, but never before had she heard him laugh.

The two processions merged. The cross-bearers walked before, Abbot Radulfus, prior and choir monks came after, and Cadfael and his peers with their sacred burden followed, hemmed in on both sides by worshippers who reached and leaned to touch even the sleeve of a bearer's habit, or the polished oak of the reliquary as it passed. Brother Anselm, in secure command of his choir, raised his own fine voice in the lead as they turned in at the gatehouse, bringing Saint Winifred home.

Brother Cadfael, by then, was moving like a man in a dual dream, his body keeping pace and time with his fellows, in one confident rhythm, while his mind soared in another, carried aloft on the cushioned cloud of sounds, compounded of the eager footsteps, exalted murmurs and shrill acclamations of hundreds of people, with the chant borne above it, and the voice of Brother Anselm soaring over all. The great court was crowded with people to watch them enter, the way into the cloister, and so into the church, had to be cleared by slow, shuffling paces, the ranks pressing back to give them passage, Cadfael came to himself with some mild annoyance when the reliquary was halted in the court, to wait for a clear path ahead. He braced both feet almost aggressively into the familiar soil, and for the first time looked about him. He saw, beyond the throng already gathered, the saint's own retinue melting and flowing to find a place where eye might see all, and ear hear all. In this brief halt he saw Melangell and Matthew, hand in hand, hunt round the fringes of the crowd, and find a place to gaze.

They looked to Cadfael a little tipsy, like unaccustomed drinkers after strong wine. And why not? After long abstention he had felt the intoxication possessing his own feet, as they held the hypnotic rhythm, and his own mind, as it floated on the cadences of song. Those ecstasies were at once native and alien to him, he could both embrace and stand clear of them, feet firmly planted, gripping the homely earth, to keep his balance and stand erect.

They moved forward again into the nave of the church, and then to the right, towards the bared and waiting altar. The vast, dreaming, sun-warmed bulk of the church enclosed them, dim, silent and empty, since no other could enter until they had discharged their duty, lodged their patroness and retired to their own insignificant places. Then they came, led by abbot and prior, first the brothers to fill up their stalls in the choir, then the provost and guildsmen of the town and the notables of the shire, and then all that great concourse of people, flooding in from hot mid-morning sunlight to the cool dimness of stone, and from the excited clamour of festival to the great silence of worship, until all the space of the nave was filled with the colour and warmth and breath of humanity, and all as still as the candle-flames on the altar. Even the reflected gleams in the silver chacings of the casket were fixed and motionless as jewels.

Abbot Radulfus stood forth. The sobering solemnity of the Mass began.

For the very intensity of all that mortal emotion gathered thus between confining walls and beneath one roof, it was impossible to withdraw the eyes for an instant from the act of worship on which it was centred, or the mind from the words of the office. There had been times, through the years of his vocation, when Cadfael's thoughts had strayed during Mass to worrying at other problems, and working out other intents. It was not so now. Throughout, he was unaware of a single face in all that throng, only of the presence of humankind, in whom his own identity was lost;

or, perhaps, into whom his own identity expanded like air, to fill every part of the whole. He forgot Melangell and Matthew, he forgot Ciaran and Rhun, he never looked round to see if Hugh had come. If there was a face before his mind's eye at all it was one he had never seen, though he well remembered the slight and fragile bones he had lifted with such care and awe out of the earth, and with so much better heart again laid beneath the same soil, there to resume her hawthorn-scented sleep under the sheltering trees. For some reason, though she had lived to a good old age, he could not imagine her older than seventeen or eighteen, as she had been when the king's son Cradoc pursued her. The slender little bones had cried out of youth, and the shadowy face he had imagined for her was fresh and eager and open, and very beautiful. But he saw it always half turned away from him. Now, if ever, she might at last look round, and show him fully that reassuring countenance.

At the end of Mass the abbot withdrew to his own stall, to the right of the entrance from nave to choir, round the parish altar, and with lifted voice and open arms bade the pilgrims advance to the saint's altar, where everyone who had a petition to make might make it on his knees, and touch the reliquary with hand and lip. And in orderly and reverent silence they came. Prior Robert took his stand at the foot of the three steps that led up to the altar, ready to offer a hand to those who needed help to mount or kneel. Those who were in health and had no pressing requirements to advance came through from the nave on the other side, and found corners where they might stand and watch, and miss nothing of this memorable day. They had faces again, they spoke in whispers, they were as various as an hour since they had been one.

On his knees in his stall, Brother Cadfael looked on, knowing them one from another now as they came, kneeled and touched. The long file of petitioners was drawing near its end when he saw Rhun approaching. Dame Alice had a hand solicitously under his left elbow, Melangell nursed him along on his right, Matthew followed close, no less anxious than they. The boy advanced with his usual laborious gait, his dragging toe just scraping the tiles of the floor. His face was intensely pale, but with a brilliant pallor that almost dazzled the watching eyes, and the wide gaze he fixed steadily upon the reliquary shone translucent, like ice with a bright bluish light behind it. Dame Alice was whispering low, encouraging entreaties into one ear, Melangell into the other, but he was aware of nothing but the altar towards which he moved. When his turn came, he shook off his supporters, and for a moment seemed to hesitate before venturing to advance alone.

Prior Robert observed his condition, and

held out a hand. 'You need not be abashed, my son, because you cannot kneel. God and the saint will know your goodwill.'

The softest whisper of a voice, though clearly audible in the waiting silence, said tremulously: 'But, Father, I can! I will!'

Rhun straightened up, taking his hands from his crutches, which slid from under his armpits and fell. That on the left crashed with an unnerving clatter upon the tiles, on the right Melangell started forward and dropped to her knees, catching the falling prop in her arms with a faint cry. And there she crouched, embracing the discarded thing desperately, while Rhun set his twisted foot to the ground and stood upright. He had but two or three paces to go to the foot of the altar steps. He took them slowly and steadily, his eyes fixed upon the reliquary. Once he lurched slightly, and Dame Alice made a trembling move to run after him, only to halt again in wonder and fear, while Prior Robert again extended his hand to offer aid. Rhun paid no attention to them or to anyone else, he did not seem to see or hear anything but his goal, and whatever voice it might be that called him forward. For he went with held breath, as a child learning to walk ventures across perilous distances to reach its mother's open arms and coaxing, praising blandishments that wooed it to the deed.

It was the twisted foot he set first on the

lowest step, and now the twisted foot, though a little awkward and unpractised, was twisted no longer, and did not fail him, and the wasted leg, as he put his weight on it, seemed to have smoothed out into shapeliness, and bore him up bravely.

Only then did Cadfael become aware of the stillness and the silence, as if every soul present held his breath with the boy, spellbound, not yet ready, not yet permitted to acknowledge what they saw before their eyes. Even Prior Robert stood charmed into a tall, austere statue, frozen at gaze. Even Melangell, crouching with the crutch hugged to her breast, could not stir a finger to help or break the spell, but hung upon every deliberate step with agonised eyes, as though she were laying her heart under his feet as a voluntary sacrifice to buy off fate.

He had reached the third step, he sank to his knees with only the gentlest of manipulations, holding by the fringes of the altar frontal, and the cloth of gold that was draped under the reliquary. He lifted his joined hands and starry face, white and bright even with eyes now closed, and though there was hardly any sound they saw his lips moving upon whatever prayers he had made ready for her. Certainly they contained no request for his own healing. He had put himself simply in her hands, submissively and joyfully, and what had been done to him and for him surely she had done, of her own perfect will.

He had to hold by her draperies to rise, as babes hold by their mothers' skirts. No doubt but she had him under the arms to raise him. He bent his fair head and kissed the hem of her garment, rose erect and kissed the silver rim of the reliquary, in which, whether she lay or not, she alone commanded and had sovereignty. Then he withdrew from her, feeling his way backward down the three steps. Twisted foot and shrunken leg carried him securely. At the foot he made obeisance gravely, and then turned and went briskly, like any other healthy lad of sixteen, to smile reassurance on his trembling womenfolk, take up gently the crutches for which he had no further use, and carry them back to lay them tidily under the altar.

The spell broke, for the marvellous thing was done, and its absolute nature made manifest. A great, shuddering sigh went round nave, choir, transepts and all, wherever there were human creatures watching and listening. And after the sigh the quivering murmur of a gathering storm, whether of tears or laughter there was no telling, but the air shook with its passion. And then the outcry, the loosing of both tears and laughter, in a gale of wonder and praise. From stone walls and lofty, arched roof, from rood-loft and transept arcades, the echoes flew and rebounded, and the candles that had stood so still and tall shook and guttered in the gale. Melangell hung weak with weeping and joy in Matthew's arms, Dame Alice whirled from friend to friend, spouting tears like a fountain, and smiling like the most blessed of women. Prior Robert lifted his hands in vindicated stewardship, and his voice in the opening of a thanksgiving psalm, and Brother Anselm took up the chant.

A miracle, a miracle, a miracle . . .

And in the midst Rhun stood erect and still, even a little bewildered, braced sturdily on his two long, shapely legs, looking all about him at the shouting, weeping, exulting faces, letting the meaningless sounds wash over him in waves, wanting the quiet he had known when there had been no one here in this holy place but himself and his saint, who had told him, in how sweet and private conference, all that he had to do.

*   *   *

Brother Cadfael rose with his brothers, after the church was cleared of all others, after all that jubilant, bubbling, boiling throng had gone forth to spill its feverish excitement in open summer air, to cry the miracle aloud, carry it out into the Foregate, beyond into the town, buffet it back and forth across the tables at dinner in the guest-hall, and return to extol it at Vespers with what breath was left. When they dispersed the word would go with them wherever they went, sounding Saint Winifred's praises, inspiring other souls to take to the roads and bring their troubles to Shrewsbury. Where healing was proven, and attested by hundreds of voices.

The brothers went to their modest, accustomed dinner in the refectory, and observed, whatever their own feelings were, the discipline of silence. They were very tired, which made silence welcome. They had risen early, worked hard, been through fire and flood body and soul, no wonder they ate humbly, thankfully, in silence.

CHAPTER TEN

It was not until dinner was almost over in the guest-hall that Matthew, seated at Melangell's side and still flushed and exalted from the morning's heady wonders, suddenly bethought him of sterner matters, and began to look back with a thoughtful frown which as yet only faintly dimmed the unaccustomed brightness of his face. Being in attendance on Mistress Weaver and her young people had made him a part, for a while, of their unshadowed joy, and caused him to forget everything else. But it could not last, though Rhun sat there half-lost in wonder still, with hardly a word to say, and felt no need of food or drink, and his womenfolk fawned on him unregarded. So far away had he been that the return took time.

'I haven't seen Ciaran,' said Matthew quietly in Melangell's ear, and he rose a little in his place to look round the crowded room. 'Did you catch ever a glimpse of him in the church?'

She, too, had forgotten until then, but at sight of his face she remembered all too sharply, with a sickening lurch of her heart. But she kept her countenance, and laid a persuasive hand on his arm to draw him down again beside her. 'Among so many? But he surely would be there. He must have been among the first, he stayed here, he would find a good place. We didn't see all those who went to the altar—we all stayed with Rhun, and his place was far back.' Such a mingling of truth and lies, but she kept her voice confident, and clung to her shaken hope.

'But where is he now? I don't see him within here.' Though there was so much excitement, so much moving about from table to table to talk with friends, that one man might easily avoid detection. 'I must find him,' said Matthew, not yet greatly troubled but wanting reassurance, and rose.

'No, sit down! You know he must be here somewhere. Let him alone, and he'll appear when he chooses. He may be resting on his bed, if he has to go forth again barefoot tomorrow. Why look for him now? Can you

172

not do without him even one day? And such a day?'

Matthew looked down at her with a face from which all the openness and joy had faded, and freed his sleeve from her grasp gently enough, but decidedly. 'Still, I must find him. Stay here with Rhun, I'll come back. All I want is to see him, to be sure . . .'

He was away, slipping quietly out between the festive tables, looking sharply about him as he went. She was in two minds about following him, but then she thought better of it, for while he hunted time would be slipping softly away, and Ciaran would be dwindling into distance, as later she prayed he could fade even out of mind, and be forgotten. So she remained with the happy company, but not of it, and with every passing moment hesitated whether to grow more reassured or more uneasy. At last she could not bear the waiting any longer. She rose quietly and slipped away. Dame Alice was in full spate, torn between tears and smiles, sitting proudly by her prodigy, and surrounded by neighbours as happy and voluble as herself, and Rhun, still somehow apart though he was the centre of the group, sat withdrawn into his revelation, even as he answered eager questions, lamely enough but as well as he could. They had no need of Melangell, they would not miss her for a little while.

When she came out into the great court, into the brilliance of the noonday sun, it was

173

the quietest hour, the pause after meat. There never was a time of day when there was no traffic about the court, no going and coming at the gatehouse, but now it moved at its gentlest and quietest. She went down almost fearfully into the cloister, and found no one there but a single copyist busy reviewing what he had done the previous day, and Brother Anselm in his workshop going over the music for Vespers; into the stable-yard, though there was no reason in the world why Matthew should be there, having no mount, and no expectation that his companion would or possibly could acquire one; into the gardens, where a couple of novices were clipping back the too exuberant shoots of a box hedge; even into the grange court, where the barns and storehouses were, and a few lay servants were taking their ease, and harrowing over the morning's marvel, like everyone else within the enclave, and most of Shrewsbury and the Foregate into the bargain. The abbot's garden was empty, neat, glowing with carefully-tended roses, his lodging showed an open door, and some ordered bustle of guests within.

She turned back towards the garden, now in deep anxiety. She was not good at lying, she had no practice, even for a good end she could not but botch the effort. And for all the to and fro of customary commerce within the pale, never without work to be done, she had seen nothing of Matthew. But he could not be gone, no, the porter could tell him nothing, Ciaran had not passed there; and she would not, never until she must, never until Matthew's too fond heart was reconciled to loss, and open and receptive to a better gain.

She turned back, rounding the box hedge and out of sight of the busy novices, and walked breast to breast into Matthew.

They met between the thick hedges, in a terrible privacy. She started back from him in a brief revulsion of guilt, for he looked more distant and alien than ever before, even as he recognised her, and acknowledged with a contortion of his troubled face her right to come out in search of him, and almost in the same instant frowned her off as irrelevant.

'He's gone!' he said in a chill and grating voice, and looked through her and far beyond. 'God keep you, Melangell, you must fend for yourself now, sorry as I am. He's gone—fled while my back was turned. I've looked for him everywhere, and never a trace of him. Nor has the porter seen him pass the gate, I've asked there. But he's gone! Alone! And I must go after him. God keep you, girl, as I cannot, and fare you well!'

And he was going so, with so few words and so cold and wild a face! He had turned on his heel and taken two long steps before she flung herself after him, caught him by the arms in both hands, and dragged him to a halt.

'No, no, *why*? What need has he of you, to

match with my need? He's gone? Let him go! Do you think your life belongs to him? He doesn't want it! He wants you free, he wants you to live your own life, not die his death with him. He knows, he knows you love me! Dare you deny it? He knows I love you. He wants you happy! Why should not a friend want his friend to be happy? Who are you to deny him his last wish?'

She knew by then that she had said too much, but never knew at what point the error had become mortal. He had turned fully to her again, and frozen where he stood, and his face was like chiselled marble. He tugged his sleeve out of her grasp this time with no gentleness at all.

'*He wants!*' hissed a voice she had never heard before, driven through narrowed lips. 'You've spoken with him! You speak *for* him! *You knew!* You knew he meant to go, and leave me here bewitched, damned, false to my oath. *You knew!* When? When did you speak with him?'

He had her by the wrists, he shook her mercilessly, and she cried out and fell to her knees.

'You knew he meant to go?' persisted Matthew, stooping over her in a cold frenzy.

'Yes—yes! This morning he told me . . . he wished it . . .'

'*He wished it!* How dared he wish it? How could he dare, robbed of his bishop's ring as he

176

was? He dared not stir without it, he was terrified to set foot outside the pale . . .'

'He has the ring,' she cried, abandoning all deceit. 'The lord abbot gave it back to him this morning, you need not fret for him, he's safe enough, he has his protection . . . He doesn't need you!'

Matthew had fallen into a deadly stillness, stooping above her. *'He has the ring?* And you knew it, and never said word! If you know so much, how much more do you know. Speak! *Where is he?'*

'Gone,' she said in a trembling whisper, 'and wished you well, wished us both well . . . wished us to be happy . . . Oh, let him go, let him go, he sets you free!'

Something that was certainly a laugh convulsed Matthew, she heard it with her ears and felt it shiver through her flesh, but it was like no other laughter she had ever heard, it chilled her blood. *'He* sets *me* free! And you must be his confederate! Oh, God! He never passed the gate. If you know all, then tell all— how did he go?'

She faltered, weeping: 'He loved you, he willed you to live and forget him, and be happy . . .'

'How did he go?' repeated Matthew, in a voice so ill-supplied with breath it seemed he might strangle on the words.

'Across the brook,' she said in a broken whisper, 'making the quickest way for Wales.

177

He said . . . he has kin there . . .'

He drew in hissing breath and took his hands from her, leaving her drooping forward on her face as he let go of her wrists. He had turned his back and flung away from her, all they had shared forgotten, his obsession plucking him away. She did not understand, there was no way she could come to terms so rapidly with all that had happened, but she knew she had loosed her hold of her love, and he was in merciless flight from her in pursuit of some incomprehensible duty in which she had no part and no right. She sprang up and ran after him, caught him by the arm, wound her own arms about him, lifted her imploring face to his stony, frantic stare, and prayed him passionately: 'Let him go! Oh, let him go! He wants to go alone and leave you to me . . .'

Almost silently above her the terrible laughter, so opposed to that lovely sound as he followed the reliquary with her, boiled like some thick, choking syrup in his throat. He struggled to shake off her clinging hands, and when she fell to her knees again and hung upon him with all her despairing weight he tore loose his right hand, and struck her heavily in the face, sobbing, and so wrenched himself loose and fled, leaving her face-down on the ground.

*　　　*　　　*

In the abbot's lodging Radulfus and his guests sat long over their meal, for they had much to discuss. The topic which was on everyone's lips naturally came first.

'It would seem,' said the abbot, 'that we have been singularly favoured this morning. Certain motions of grace we have seen before, but never yet one so public and so persuasive, with so many witnesses. How do you say? I grow old in experience of wonders, some of which turn out to fall somewhat short of their promise. I know of human deception, not always deliberate, for sometimes the deceiver is himself deceived. If saints have power, so have demons. Yet this boy seems to me as crystal. I cannot think he either cheats or is cheated.'

'I have heard,' said Hugh, 'of cripples who discarded their crutches and walked without them, only to relapse when the fervour of the occasion was over. Time will prove whether this one takes to his crutches again.'

'I shall speak with him later,' said the abbot, 'after the excitement has cooled. I hear from Brother Edmund that Brother Cadfael has been treating the boy these three days he has been here. That may have eased his condition, but it can scarcely have brought about so sudden a cure. No, I must say it, I truly believe our house has been the happy scene of divine grace. I will speak also with Cadfael, who must know the boy's condition.'

Olivier sat quiet and deferential in the presence of so reverend a churchman as the abbot, but Hugh observed that his arched lids lifted and his eyes kindled at Cadfael's name. So he knew who it was he sought, and something more than a distant salute in action had passed between that strangely assorted pair.

'And now I should be glad,' said the abbot, 'to hear what news you bring from the south. Have you been in Westminster with the empress's court? For I hear she is now installed there.'

Olivier gave his account of affairs in London readily, and answered questions with goodwill. 'My lord has remained in Oxford, it was at his wish I undertook this errand. I was not in London, I set out from Winchester. But the empress is in the palace of Westminster, and the plans for her coronation go forward— admittedly very slowly. The city of London is well aware of its power, and means to exact due recognition of it, or so it seems to me.' He would go no nearer than that to voicing whatever qualms he felt about his liege lady's wisdom or want of it, but he jutted a dubious underlip, and momentarily frowned. 'Father, you were there at the council, you know all that happened. My lord lost a good knight there, and I a valued friend, struck down in the street.'

'Rainald Bossard,' said Radulfus sombrely.

'I have not forgotten.'

'Father, I have been telling the lord sheriff here what I should like to tell also to you. For I have a second errand to pursue, wherever I go on the business of the empress, an errand for Rainald's widow. Rainald had a young kinsman in his household, who was with him when he was killed, and after that death this young man left the lady's service without a word, secretly. She says he had grown closed and silent even before he vanished, and the only trace of him afterwards was on the road to Newbury, going north. Since then, nothing. So knowing I was bound north, she begged me to enquire for him wherever I came, for she values and trusts him, and needs him at her side. I may not deceive you, Father, there are those who say he has fled because he is guilty of Rainald's death. They claim he was besotted with Dame Juliana, and may have seized his chance in this brawl to widow her, and get her for himself, and then taken fright because these things were so soon being said. But *I* think they were not being said at all until after he had vanished. And Juliana, who surely knows him better than any, and looks upon him as a son, for want of children of her own, she is quite sure of him. She wants him home and vindicated, for whatever reason he left her as he did. And I have been asking at every lodging and monastery along the road for word of such a young man. May I also ask here? Brother Hospitaller will know the names of all his guests. Though a name,' he added ruefully, 'is almost all I have, for if ever I saw the man it was without knowing it was he. And the name he may have left behind him.'

'It is not much to go on,' said Abbot Radulfus with a smile, 'but certainly you may enquire. If he has done no wrong, I should be glad to help you to find him and bring him off without reproach. What is his name?'

'Luc Meverel. Twenty-four years old, they tell me, middling tall and well made, dark of hair and eye.'

'It could fit many hundreds of young men,' said the abbot, shaking his head, 'and the name I doubt he will have put off if he has anything to hide, or even if he fears it may be unfairly besmirched. Yet try. I grant you in such a gathering as we have here now a young man who wished to be lost might bury himself very thoroughly. Denis will know which of his guests is of the right age and quality. For clearly your Luc Meverel is well-born, and most likely tutored and lettered.'

'Certainly so,' said Olivier.

'Then by all means, and with my blessing, go freely to Brother Denis, and see what he can do to help you. He has an excellent memory, he will be able to tell you which, among the men here, is of suitable years, and gentle. You can but try.'

On leaving the lodging they went first, however, to look for Brother Cadfael. And Brother Cadfael was not so easily found. Hugh's first resort was the workshop in the herbarium, where they habitually compounded their affairs. But there was no Cadfael there. Nor was he with Brother Anselm in the cloister, where he well might have been debating some nice point in the evening's music. Nor checking the medicine cupboard in the infirmary, which must surely have been depleted during these last few days, but had clearly been restocked in the early hours of this day of glory. Brother Edmund said mildly: 'He was here. I had a poor soul who bled from the mouth—too gorged, I think, with devotion. But he's quiet and sleeping now, the flux has stopped. Cadfael went away some while since.'

Brother Oswin, vigorously fighting weeds in the kitchen garden, had not seen his superior since dinner. 'But I think,' he said, blinking thoughtfully into the sun in the zenith, 'he may be in the church.'

* * *

Cadfael was on his knees at the foot of Saint Winifred's three-tread stairway to grace, his hands not lifted in prayer but folded in the lap of his habit, his eyes not closed in entreaty but

183

wide open to absolution. He had been kneeling there for some time, he who was usually only too glad to rise from knees now perceptibly stiffening. He felt no pains, no griefs of any kind, nothing but an immense thankfulness in which he floated like a fish in an ocean. An ocean as pure and blue and drowningly deep and clear as that well-remembered eastern sea, the furthest extreme of the tideless midland sea of legend, at the end of which lay the holy city of Jerusalem, Our Lord's burial-place and hard-won kingdom. The saint who presided here, whether she lay here or no, had launched him into a shining infinity of hope. Her mercies might be whimsical, they were certainly magisterial. She had reached her hand to an innocent, well deserving her kindness. What had she intended towards this less innocent but no less needy being?

Behind him, approaching quietly from the nave, a known voice said softly: 'And are you demanding yet a second miracle?'

He withdrew his eyes reluctantly from the reflected gleams of silver along the reliquary, and turned to look towards the parish altar. He saw the expected shape of Hugh Beringar, the thin dark face smiling at him. But over Hugh's shoulder he saw a taller head and shoulders loom, emerging from dimness in suave, resplendent planes, the bright, jutting cheekbones, the olive cheeks smoothly hollowed below, the falcon's amber eyes beneath high-arched black brows, the long, supple lips tentatively smiling upon him.

It was not possible. Yet he beheld it. Olivier de Bretagne came out of the shadows and stepped unmistakable into the light of the altar candles. And that was the moment when Saint Winifred turned her head, looked fully into the face of her fallible but faithful servant, and also smiled.

A second miracle! Why not? When she gave she gave prodigally, with both hands.

CHAPTER ELEVEN

They went out into the cloister all three together, and that in itself was memorable and good, for they had never been together before. Those trusting intimacies which had once passed between Cadfael and Olivier, on a winter night in Bromfield priory, were unknown still to Hugh, and there was a mysterious constraint still that prevented Olivier from openly recalling them. The greetings they exchanged were warm but brief, only the reticence behind them was eloquent, and no doubt Hugh understood that well enough, and was willing to wait for enlightenment, or courteously to make do without it. For that there was no haste, but for

Luc Meverel there might be.

'Our friend has a quest,' said Hugh, 'in which we mean to enlist Brother Denis's help, but we shall also be very glad of yours. He is looking for a young man by the name of Luc Meverel, strayed from his place and known to be travelling north. Tell him the way of it, Olivier.'

Olivier told the story over again, and was listened to with close attention. 'Very gladly,' said Cadfael then, 'would I do whatever man can do not only to bring off an innocent man from such a charge, but also to bring the charge home to the guilty. We know of this murder, and it sticks in every gullet that a decent man, protecting his honourable opponent, should be cut down by one of his own faction . . .'

'Is that certain?' wondered Hugh sharply.

'As good as certain. Who else would so take exception to the man standing up for his lady and doing his errand without fear? All who still held to Stephen in their hearts would approve, even if they dared not applaud him. And as for a chance attack by sneak-thieves— why choose to prey on a mere clerk, with nothing of value on him but the simple needs of his journey, when the town was full of nobles, clerics and merchants far better worth robbing? Rainald died only because he came to the clerk's aid. No, an adherent of the empress, like Rainald himself but most unlike, committed that infamy.'

'That's good sense,' agreed Olivier. 'But my chief concern now is to find Luc, and send him home again if I can.'

'There must be twenty or more young fellows in that age here today,' said Cadfael, scrubbing thoughtfully at his blunt brown nose, 'but I dare wager most of them can be pricked out of the list as well known to some of their companions by their own right names, or by reason of their calling or condition. Solitaries may come, but they're few and far between. Pilgrims are like starlings, they thrive on company. We'd best go and talk to Brother Denis. He'll have sorted out most of them by now.'

Brother Denis had a retentive memory and an appetite for news and rumours that usually kept him the best-informed person in the enclave. The fuller his halls, the more pleasure he took in knowing everything that went on there, and the name and vocation of every guest. He also kept meticulous books to record the visitations.

They found him in the narrow cell where he kept his accounts and estimated his future needs, thoughtfully reckoning up what provisions he still had, and how rapidly the demands on them were likely to dwindle from the morrow. He took his mind from his store-book courteously in order to listen to what Brother Cadfael and the sheriff required of

187

him, and produced answers with exemplary promptitude when asked to sieve out from his swollen household males of about twenty-five years, bred gentle or within modest reach of gentility, lettered, of dark colouring and medium tall build, answering to the very bare description of Luc Meverel. As his forefinger flew down the roster of his guests the numbers shrank remarkably. It seemed to be true that considerably more than half of those who went on pilgrimage were women, and that among the men the greater part were in their forties or fifties, and of those remaining, many would be in minor orders, either monastics or secular priests or would-be priests. And Luc Meverel was none of these.

'Are there any here,' asked Hugh, viewing the final list, which was short enough, 'who came solitary?'

Brother Denis cocked his round, rosy, tonsured head aside and ran a sharp brown eye, very reminiscent of a robin's, down the list. 'Not one. Young squires of that age seldom go as pilgrims, unless with an exigent lord—or an equally exigent lady. In such a summer feast as this we might have young friends coming together, to take the fill of the time before they settle down to sterner disciplines. But alone . . . Where would be the pastime in that?'

'Here are two, at any rate,' said Cadfael, 'who came together, but surely not for pastime. They have puzzled me, I own. Both are of the proper age, and such word as we have of the man we're looking for would fit either. You know them, Denis—that youngster who's on his way to Aberdaron, and his friend who bears him company. Both lettered, both bred to the manor. And certainly they came from the south, beyond Abingdon, according to Brother Adam of Reading, who lodged there the same night.'

'Ah, the barefoot traveller,' said Denis, and laid a finger on Ciaran in the shrunken toll of young men, 'and his keeper and worshipper. Yes, I would not put half a year between them, and they have the build and colouring, but you needed only one.'

'We could at least look at two,' said Cadfael. 'If neither of them is what we're seeking, yet coming from that region they may have encountered such a single traveller somewhere on the road. If we have not the authority to question them closely about who they are and whence they come, and how and why thus linked, then Father Abbot has. And if they have no reason to court concealment, then they'll willingly declare to him what they might not as readily utter to us.'

'We may try it,' said Hugh, kindling. 'At least it's worth the asking, and if they have nothing to do with the man we are looking for, neither they nor we have lost more than half an hour of time, and surely they won't grudge us that.'

'Granted what is so far related of these two hardly fits the case,' Cadfael acknowledged doubtfully, 'for the one is said to be mortally ill and going to Aberdaron to die, and the other is resolute to keep him company to the end. But a young man who wishes to disappear may provide himself with a circumstantial story as easily as with a new name. And at all events, between Abingdon and Shrewsbury it's possible they may have encountered Luc Meverel alone and under his own name.'

'But if one of these two, either of these two, should truly be the man I want,' said Olivier doubtfully, 'then who, in the name of God, is the other?'

'We ask each other questions,' said Hugh practically, 'which either of these two could answer in a moment. Come, let's leave Abbot Radulfus to call them in, and see what comes of it.'

*   *   *

It was not difficult to induce the abbot to have the two young men sent for. It was not so easy to find them and bring them to speak for themselves. The messenger, sent forth in expectation of prompt obedience, came back after a much longer time than had been expected, and reported ruefully that neither of the pair could be found within the abbey walls. True, the porter had not actually seen either of

190

them pass the gatehouse. But what had satisfied him that the two were leaving was that the young man Matthew had come, no long time after dinner, to reclaim his dagger, and had left behind him a generous gift of money to the house, saying that he and his friend were already bound away on their journey, and desired to offer thanks for their lodging. And had he seemed—it was Cadfael who asked it, himself hardly knowing why— had he seemed as he always was, or in any way disturbed or alarmed or out of countenance and temper, when he came for his weapon and paid his and his friend's score?

The messenger shook his head, having asked no such question at the gate. Brother Porter, when enquiry was made direct by Cadfael himself, said positively: 'He was like a man on fire. Oh, as soft as ever in voice, and courteous, but pale and alight, you'd have said his hair stood on end. But what with every soul within here wandering in a dream, since this wonder, I never thought but here were some going forth with the news while the furnace was still white-hot.'

'Gone?' said Olivier, dismayed, when this word was brought back to the abbot's parlour. 'Now I begin to see better cause why one of these two, for all they come so strangely paired, and so strangely account for themselves, may be the man I'm seeking. For if I do not know Luc Meverel by sight, I have been two or three times his lord's guest recently, and he may well have taken note of me. How if he saw me come, today, and is gone hence thus in haste because he does not wish to be found? He could hardly know I am sent to look for him, but he might, for all that, prefer to put himself clean out of sight. And an ailing companion on the way would be good cover for a man wanting a reason for his wanderings. I wish I might yet speak with these two. How long have they been gone?'

'It cannot have been more than an hour and a half after noon,' said Cadfael, 'according to when Matthew reclaimed his dagger.'

'And afoot!' Olivier kindled hopefully. 'And even unshod, the one of them! It should be no great labour to overtake them, if it's known what road they will have taken.'

'By far their best way is by the Oswestry road, and so across the dyke into Wales. According to Brother Denis, that was Ciaran's declared intent.'

'Then, Father Abbot,' said Olivier eagerly, 'with your leave I'll mount and ride after them, for they cannot have got far. It would be a pity to miss the chance, and even if they are not what I'm seeking, neither they nor I will have lost anything. But with or without my man, I shall return here.'

'I'll ride through the town with you,' said Hugh, 'and set you on your way, for this will be new country to you. But then I must be about my own business, and see if we've gathered any harvest from this morning's hunt. I doubt they've gone deeper into the forest, or I should have had word by now. We shall look for you back before night, Olivier. One more night at the least we mean to keep you and longer if we can.'

Olivier took his leave hastily but gracefully, made a dutiful reverence to the abbot, and turned upon Brother Cadfael a brief, radiant smile that shattered his preoccupation for an instant like a sunburst through clouds. 'I will not leave here,' he said in simple reassurance, 'without having quiet conference with you. But this I must see finished, if I can.'

They were gone away briskly to the stables, where they had left their horses before Mass. Abbot Radulfus looked after them with a very thoughtful face.

'Do you find it surprising, Cadfael, that these two young pilgrims should leave so soon, and so abruptly? Is it possible the coming of Messire de Bretagne can have driven them away?'

Cadfael considered, and shook his head. 'No, I think not. In the great press this morning, and the excitement, why should one man among the many be noticed, and one not looked for at all in these parts? But, yes, their going does greatly surprise me. For the one, he should surely be only too glad of an extra day or two of rest before taking barefoot to the roads again. And for the other—Father, there is a girl he certainly admires and covets, whether he yet knows it to the full or no, and with her he spent this morning, following Saint Winifred home, and I am certain there was then no other thought in his mind but of her and her kin, and the greatness of this day. For she is sister to the boy Rhun, who came by so great a mercy and blessing before our eyes. It would take some very strong compulsion to drag him away suddenly like this.'

'The boy's sister, you say?' Abbot Radulfus recalled an intent which had been shelved in favour of Olivier's quest. 'There is still an hour or more before Vespers. I should like to talk with this youth. You have been treating his condition, Cadfael. Do you think your handling has had anything to do with what we witnessed today? Or could he—though I would not willingly attribute falsity to one so young—could he have made more of his distress than it was, in order to produce a prodigy?'

'No,' said Cadfael very decidedly. 'There is no deceit at all in him. And as for my poor skills, they might in a long time of perseverance have softened the tight cords that hampered the use of his limb, and made it possible to set a little weight on it—but straighten that foot and fill out the sinews of the leg—never! The greatest doctor in the world could not have done it. Father, on the day he came I gave him a draught that should have eased his pain and brought him sleep.

194

After three nights he sent it back to me untouched. He saw no reason why he should expect to be singled out for healing, but he said that he offered his pain freely, who had nothing else to give. Not to buy grace, but of his goodwill to give and want nothing in return. And further, it seems that thus having accepted his pain out of love, his pain left him. After Mass we saw that deliverance completed.'

'Then it was well deserved,' said Radulfus, pleased and moved. 'I must indeed talk with this boy. Will you find him for me, Cadfael, and bring him here to me now?'

'Very gladly, Father,' said Cadfael, and departed on his errand. Dame Alice was sitting in the sunshine of the cloister garth, the centre of a voluble circle of other matrons, her face so bright with the joy of the day that it warmed the very air; but Rhun was not with them. Melangell had withdrawn into the shadow of the arcade, as though the light was too bright for her eyes, and kept her face averted over the mending of a frayed seam in a linen shirt which must belong to her brother. Even when Cadfael addressed her she looked up only very swiftly and timidly, and again stooped into shadow, but even in that glimpse he saw that the joy which had made her shine like a new rose in the morning was dimmed and pale now in the lengthening afternoon. And was he merely imagining that her left cheek showed the faint bluish tint of a bruise? But at the mention of Rhun's name she smiled, as though at the recollection of happiness rather than its presence.

'He said he was tired, and went away into the dortoir to rest. Aunt Weaver thinks he is lying down on his bed, but I think he wanted only to be left alone, to be quiet and not have to talk. He is tired by having to answer things he seems not to understand himself.'

'He speaks another tongue today from the rest of mankind,' said Cadfael. 'It may well be we who don't understand, and ask things that have no meaning for him.' He took her gently by the chin and turned her face up to the light, but she twisted nervously out of his hold. 'You have hurt yourself?' Certainly it was a bruise beginning there.

'It's nothing,' she said. 'My own fault. I was in the garden, I ran too fast and I fell. I know it's unsightly, but it doesn't hurt now.'

Her eyes were very calm, not reddened, only a little swollen as to the lids. Well, Matthew had gone, abandoned her to go with his friend, letting her fall only too disastrously after the heady running together of the morning hours. That could account for tears now past. But should it account for a bruised cheek? He hesitated whether to question further, but clearly she did not wish it. She had gone back doggedly to her work, and would not look up again.

Cadfael sighed, and went out across the

great court to the guest-hall. Even a glorious day like this one must have its vein of bitter sadness.

In the men's dortoir Rhun sat alone on his bed, very still and content in his blissfully restored body. He was deep in his own rapt thoughts, but readily aware when Cadfael entered. He looked round and smiled.

'Brother, I was wishing to see you. You were there, you know. Perhaps you even heard . . . See, how I'm changed!' The leg once maimed stretched out perfect before him, he bent and stamped the boards of the floor. He flexed ankle and toes, drew up his knee to his chin, and everything moved as smoothly and painlessly as his ready tongue. 'I am whole! I never asked it, how dared I? Even then, I was praying not for this, and yet this was given . . .' He went away again for a moment into his tranced dream.

Cadfael sat down beside him, noting the exquisite fluency of those joints hitherto flawed and intransigent. The boy's beauty was perfected now.

'You were praying,' said Cadfael gently, 'for Melangell.'

'Yes. And Matthew, too. I truly thought . . . But you see he is gone. They are both gone, gone together. Why could I not bring my sister into bliss? I would have gone on crutches all my life for that, but I couldn't prevail.'

'That is not yet determined,' said Cadfael

197

firmly. 'Who goes may also return. And I think your prayers should have strong virtue, if you do not fall into doubt now, because heaven has need of a little time. Even miracles have their times. Half our lives in this world are spent in waiting. It is needful to wait with faith.'

Rhun sat listening with an absent smile, and at the end of it he said: 'Yes, surely, and I will wait. For see, one of them left this behind in his haste when he went away.'

He reached down between the close-set cots, and lifted to the bed between them a bulky but lightweight scrip of unbleached linen, with stout leather straps for the owner's belt. 'I found it dropped between the two beds they had, drawn close together. I don't know which of them owned this one, the two they carried were much alike. But one of them doesn't expect or want ever to come back, does he? Perhaps Matthew does, and has forgotten this, whether he meant it or no, as a pledge.'

Cadfael stared and wondered, but this was a heavy matter, and not for him. He said seriously: 'I think you should bring this with you, and give it into the keeping of Father Abbot. For he sent me to bring you to him. He wants to speak with you.'

'With me?' wavered Rhun, stricken into a wild and rustic child again. 'The lord abbot himself?'

'Surely, and why not? You are Christian soul as he is, and may speak with him as equal.'

The boy faltered: 'I should be afraid . . .'

'No, you would not. You are not afraid of anything, nor need you ever be.'

Rhun sat for a moment with fists doubled into the blanket of his bed; then he lifted his clear, ice-blue gaze and blanched, angelic face and smiled blindingly into Cadfael's eyes. 'No, I need not. I'll come.' And he hoisted the linen scrip and stood up stately on his two long, youthful legs, and led the way to the door.

*   *   *

'Stay with us,' said Abbot Radulfus, when Cadfael would have presented his charge and left the two of them together. 'I think he might be glad of you.' Also, said his eloquent, austere glance, your presence may be of value to me as witness. 'Rhun knows you. Me he does not yet know, but I trust he shall, hereafter.' He had the drab, brownish scrip on the desk before him, offered on entry with a word to account for it, until the time came to explore its possibilities further.

'Willingly, Father,' said Cadfael heartily, and took his seat apart on a stool withdrawn into a corner, out of the way of those two pairs of formidable eyes that met, and wondered, and probed with equal intensity across the small space of the parlour. Outside the windows the garden blossomed with drunken exuberance, in the burning colours of summer,

199

and the blanched blue sky, at its loftiest in the late afternoon, showed the colour of Rhun's eyes, but without their crystal blaze. The day of wonders was drawing very slowly and radiantly towards its evening.

'Son,' said Radulfus at his gentlest, 'you have been the vessel for a great mercy poured out here. I know, as all know who were there, what we saw, what we felt. But I would know also what you passed through. I know you have lived long with pain, and have not complained. I dare guess in what mind you approached the saint's altar. Tell me, what was it happened to you then?'

Rhun sat with his empty hands clasped quietly in his lap, and his face at once remote and easy, looking beyond the walls of the room. All his timidity was lost.

'I was troubled,' he said carefully, 'because my sister and my Aunt Alice wanted so much for me, and I knew I needed nothing. I would have come, and prayed, and passed, and been content. But then I heard her call.'

'Saint Winifred spoke to you?' asked Radulfus softly.

'She called me to her,' said Rhun positively.

'In what words?'

'No words. What need had she of words? She called me to go to her, and I went. She told me, here is a step, and here, and here, come, you know you can. And I knew I could, so I went. When she told me, kneel, for so you

200

can, then I kneeled, and I could. Whatever she told me, that I did. And so I will still,' said Rhun, smiling into the opposing wall with eyes that paled the sun.

'Child,' said the abbot, watching him in solemn wonder and respect, 'I do believe it. What skills you have, what gifts to stead you in your future life, I scarcely know. I rejoice that you have to the full the blessing of your body, and the purity of your mind and spirit. I wish you whatever calling you may choose, and the virtue of your resolve to guide you in it. If there is anything you can ask of this house, to aid you after you go forth from here, it is yours.'

'Father,' said Rhun earnestly, withdrawing his blinding gaze into shadow and mortality, and becoming the child he was, 'need I go forth? She called me to her, how tenderly I have no words to tell. I desire to remain with her to my life's end. She called me to her, and I will never willingly leave her.'

CHAPTER TWELVE

'And will you keep him?' asked Cadfael, when the boy had been dismissed, made his deep reverence, and departed in his rapt, unwitting perfection.

'If his intent holds, yes, surely. He is the living proof of grace. But I will not let him take vows in haste, to regret them later. Now he is transported with joy and wonder, and would embrace celibacy and seclusion with delight. If his will is still the same in a month, then I will believe in it, and welcome him gladly. But he shall serve his full novitiate, even so. I will not let him close the door upon himself until he is sure. And now,' said the abbot, frowning down thoughtfully at the linen scrip that lay upon his desk, 'what is to be done with this? You say it was fallen between the two beds, and might have belonged to either?'

'So the boy said. But, Father, if you remember, when the bishop's ring was stolen, both those young men gave up their scrips to be examined. What each of them carried, apart from the dagger that was duly delivered over at the gatehouse, I cannot say with certainty, but Father Prior, who handled them, will know.'

'True, so he will. But for the present,' said Radulfus, 'I cannot think we have any right to probe into either man's possessions, nor is it of any great importance to discover to which of them this belongs. If Messire de Bretagne overtakes them, as he surely must, we shall learn more, he may even persuade them to return. We'll wait for his word first. In the meantime, leave it here with me. When we know more we'll take whatever steps we can to restore it.'

The day of wonders drew in to its evening as

graciously as it had dawned, with a clear sky and soft, sweet air. Every soul within the enclave came dutifully to Vespers, and supper in the guest-hall as in the refectory was a devout and tranquil feast. The voices hasty and shrill with excitement at dinner had softened and eased into the grateful languor of fulfilment.

Brother Cadfael absented himself from Collations in the chapter house, and went out into the garden. On the gentle ridge where the gradual slope of the pease-fields began he stood for a long while watching the sky. The declining sun had still an hour or more of its course to run before its rim dipped into the feathery tops of the copses across the brook. The west which had reflected the dawn as this day began triumphed now in pale gold, with no wisp of cloud to dye it deeper or mark its purity. The scent of the herbs within the walled garden rose in a heady cloud of sweetness and spice. A good place, a resplendent day—why should any man slip away and run from it?

A useless question. Why should any man do the things he does? Why should Ciaran submit himself to such hardship? Why should he profess such piety and devotion, and yet depart without leave-taking and without thanks in the middle of so auspicious a day? It was Matthew who had left a gift of money on departure. Why could not Matthew persuade his friend to stay and see out the day? And why should he, who had glowed with excited joy in the morning, and run hand in hand with Melangell, abandon her without remorse in the afternoon, and resume his harsh pilgrimage with Ciaran as if nothing had happened?

Were they two men or three? Ciaran, Matthew and Luc Meverel? What did he know of them, all three, if three they were? Luc Meverel had been seen for the last time south of Newbury, walking north towards that town, and alone. Ciaran and Matthew were first reported, by Brother Adam of Reading, coming from the south into Abingdon for their night's lodging, two together. If one of them was Luc Meverel, then where and why had he picked up his companion, and above all, *who was his companion*?

By this time, surely Olivier should have overhauled his quarry, and found the answers to some of these questions. And he had said he would return, that he would not leave Shrewsbury without having some converse with a man remembered as a good friend. Cadfael took that assurance to his heart, and was warmed.

It was not the need to tend any of his herbal potions or bubbling wines that drew him to walk on to his workshop, for Brother Oswin, now in the chapter house with his fellows, had tidied everything for the night, and seen the brazier safely out. There was flint and tinder

204

there in a box, in case it should be necessary to light it again in the night or early in the morning. It was rather that Cadfael had grown accustomed to withdrawing to his own special solitude to do his best thinking, and this day had given him more than enough cause for thought, as for gratitude. For where were his qualms now? Miracles may be spent as frequently on the undeserving as on the deserving. What marvel that a saint should take the boy Rhun to her heart, and reach out her sustaining hand to him? But the second miracle was doubly miraculous, far beyond her sorry servant's asking, stunning in its generosity. To bring him back Olivier, whom he had resigned to God and the great world, and made himself content never to see again! And then Hugh's voice, unwitting herald of wonders, said out of the dim choir, 'And are you demanding yet a second miracle?' He had rather been humbling himself in wonder and thanks for one, demanding nothing more; but he had turned his head, and beheld Olivier.

The western sky was still limpid and bright, liquid gold, the sun still clear of the treetops, when he opened the door of his workshop and stepped within, into the timber-warm, herb-scented dimness. He thought and said afterwards that it was at that moment he saw the inseparable relationship between Ciaran and Matthew suddenly overturned, twisted into its opposite, and began, in some enclosed and detached part of his intelligence, to make sense of the whole matter, however dubious and flawed the revelation. But he had no time to catch and pin down the vision, for as his foot crossed the threshold there was a soft gasp somewhere in the shadowy corner of the hut, and a rustle of movement, as if some wild creature had been disturbed in its lair, and shrunk into the last fastness to defend itself.

He halted, and set the door wide open behind him for reassurance that there was a possibility of escape. 'Be easy!' he said mildly. 'May I not come into my own workshop without leave? And should I be entering here to threaten any soul with harm?'

His eyes, growing accustomed rapidly to the dimness, which seemed dark only by contrast with the radiance outside, scanned the shelves, the bubbling jars of wine in a fat row, the swinging, rustling swathes of herbs dangling from the beams of the low roof. Everything took shape and emerged into view. Stretched along the broad wooden bench against the opposite wall, a huddle of tumbled skirts stirred slowly and reared itself upright, to show him the spilled ripe-corn gold of a girl's hair, and the tear-stained, swollen-lidded countenance of Melangell.

She said no word, but she did not drop blindly into her sheltering arms again. She was long past that, and past being afraid to show herself so to one secret, quiet creature whom she trusted. She set down her feet in their scuffed leather shoes to the floor, and sat back against the timbers of the wall, bracing slight shoulders to the solid contact. She heaved one enormous, draining sigh that was dragged up from her very heels, and left her weak and docile. When he crossed the beaten earth floor and sat down beside her, she did not flinch away.

'Now,' said Cadfael, settling himself with deliberation, to give her time to compose at least her voice. The soft light would spare her face. 'Now, child dear, there is no one here who can either save you or trouble you, and therefore you can speak freely, for everything you say is between us two only. But we two together need to take careful counsel. So what is it you know that I do not know?'

'Why should we take counsel?' she said in a small, drear voice from below his solid shoulder. 'He is gone.'

'What is gone may return. The roads lead always two ways, hither as well as yonder. What are you doing out here alone, when your brother walks erect on two sound feet, and has all he wants in this world, but for your absence?'

He did not look directly at her, but felt the stir of warmth and softness through her body, which must have been a smile, however flawed. 'I came away,' she said, very low, 'not to spoil his joy. I've borne most of the day. I think no one has noticed half my heart was gone out of me. Unless it was you,' she said, without blame, rather in resignation.

'I saw you when we came from Saint Giles,' said Cadfael, 'you and Matthew. Your heart was whole then, so was his. If yours is torn in two now, do you suppose his is preserved without wound? No! So what passed, afterwards? What was this sword that shore through your heart and his? You know! You may tell it now. They are gone, there is nothing left to spoil. There may yet be something to save.'

She turned her forehead into his shoulder and wept in silence for a little while. The light within the hut grew rather than dimming, now that his eyes were accustomed. She forgot to hide her forlorn and bloated face, he saw the bruise on her cheek darkening into purple. He laid an arm about her and drew her close for the comfort of the flesh. That of the spirit would need more of time and thought.

'He struck you?'

'I held him,' she said, quick in his defence. 'He could not get free.'

'And he was so frantic? He *must* go?'

'Yes, whatever it cost him or me. Oh, Brother Cadfael, why? I thought, I believed he loved me, as I do him. But see how he used me in his anger!'

'Anger?' said Cadfael sharply, and turned her by the shoulders to study her more intently. 'Whatever the compulsion on him to go with his friend, why should he be angry with you? The loss was yours, but surely no blame.'

'He blamed me for not telling him,' she said drearily. 'But I did only what Ciaran asked of me. For his sake and yours, he said, yes, and for mine, too, let me go, but hold him fast. Don't tell him I have the ring again, he said, and I will go. Forget me, he said, and help him to forget me. He wanted us to remain together and be happy . . .'

'Are you telling me,' demanded Cadfael sharply, 'that *they did not go together*? That Ciaran made off without him?'

'It was not like that,' sighed Melangell. 'He meant well by us, that's why he stole away alone . . .'

'When was this? When? When did you have speech with him? *When* did he go?'

'I was here at dawn, you'll remember. I met Ciaran by the brook . . .' She drew a deep, desolate breath and loosed the whole flood of it, every word she could recall of that meeting in the early morning, while Cadfael gazed appalled, and the vague glimpse he had had of enlightenment awoke and stirred again in his mind, far clearer now.

'Go on! Tell me what followed between you and Matthew. You did as you were bidden, I know, you drew him with you, I doubt he ever gave a thought to Ciaran all those morning hours, believing him still penned within doors, afraid to stir. When was it he found out?'

'After dinner it came into his mind that he had not seen him. He was very uneasy. He went to look for him everywhere . . . He came to me here in the garden. "God keep you, Melangell," he said, "you must fend for yourself now, sorry as I am . . ." ' Almost every word of that encounter she had by heart, she repeated them like a tired child repeating a lesson. 'I said too much, he knew I had spoken with Ciaran . . . he knew that I knew he'd meant to go secretly . . .'

'And then, after you had owned as much?'

'He laughed,' she said, and her very voice froze into a despairing whisper. 'I never heard him laugh until this morning, and then it was such a sweet sound. But this laughter was not so! Bitter and raging.' She stumbled through the rest of it, every word another fine line added to the reversed image that grew in Cadfael's mind, mocking his memory. 'He sets *me* free!' And '*You* must be his confederate!' The words were so burned on her mind that she even reproduced the savagery of their utterance. And how few words it took, in the end, to transform everything, to turn devoted attendance into remorseless pursuit, selfless love into dedicated hatred, noble self-sacrifice into calculated flight, and the voluntary mortification of the flesh into body armour which must never be doffed.

He heard again, abruptly and piercingly,

Ciaran's wild cry of alarm as he clutched his cross to him, and Matthew's voice saying softly: 'Yet he should doff it. How else can he truly be rid of his pains?'

How else, indeed! Cadfael recalled, too, how he had reminded them both that they were here to attend the feast of a saint who might have life itself within her gift—'even for a man already condemned to death!' Oh, Saint Winifred, stand by me now, stand by us all, with a third miracle to better the other two!

He took Melangell brusquely by the chin, and lifted her face to him. 'Girl, look to yourself now for a while, for I must leave you. Do up your hair and keep a brave face, and go back to your kin as soon as you can bear their eyes on you. Go into the church for a time, it will be quiet there now, and who will wonder if you give a longer time to your prayers? They will not even wonder at past tears, if you can smile now. Do as well as you can, for I have a thing I must do.'

There was nothing he could promise her, no sure hope he could leave with her. He turned from her without another word, leaving her staring after him between dread and reassurance, and went striding in haste through the gardens and out across the court, to the abbot's lodging.

*   *   *

If Radulfus was surprised to have Cadfael ask audience again so soon, he gave no sign of it, but had him admitted at once, and put aside his book to give his full attention to whatever this fresh business might be. Plainly it was something very much to the current purpose and urgent.

'Father,' said Cadfael, making short work of explanations, 'there's a new twist here. Messire de Bretagne has gone off on a false trail. Those two young men did not leave by the Oswestry road, but crossed the Meole brook and set off due west to reach Wales the nearest way. Nor did they leave together. Ciaran slipped away during the morning, while his fellow was with us in the procession, and Matthew has followed him by the same way as soon as he learned of his going. And, Father, there's good cause to think that the sooner they're overtaken and halted, the better surely for one, and I believe for both. I beg you, let me take a horse and follow. And send word of this to Hugh Beringar in the town, to come after us on the same trail.'

Radulfus received all this with a grave but calm face, and asked no less shortly: 'How did you come by this word?'

'From the girl who spoke with Ciaran before he departed. No need to doubt it is all true. And, Father, one more thing before you bid me go. Open, I beg you, that scrip they left behind, let me see if it has anything more to tell us of this pair—at the least, of one of them.'

Without a word or an instant of hesitation, Radulfus dragged the linen scrip into the light of his candles, and unbuckled the fastening. The contents he drew out fully upon the desk, sparse enough, what the poor pilgrim would carry, having few possessions and desiring to travel light.

'You know, I think,' said the abbot, looking up sharply, 'to which of the two this belonged?'

'I do not know, but I guess. In my mind I am sure, but I am also fallible. Give me leave!'

With a sweep of his hand he spread the meagre belongings over the desk. The purse, thin enough when Prior Robert had handled it before, lay flat and empty now. The leather-bound breviary, well-used, worn but treasured, had been rolled into the folds of the shirt, and when Cadfael reached for it the shirt slid from the desk and fell to the floor. He let it lie as he opened the book. Within the cover was written, in a clerk's careful hand, the name of its owner: 'Juliana Bossard.' And below, in newer ink and a less practised hand: *Given to me, Luc Meverel, this Christmastide, 1140. God be with us all!*

'So I pray, too,' said Cadfael, and stooped to pick up the fallen shirt. He held it up to the light, and his eye caught the thread-like outline of a stain that rimmed the left shoulder. His eye followed the line over the shoulder, and found it continued down and round the left side of the breast. The linen, otherwise, was clean enough, bleached by several launderings from its original brownish natural colouring. He spread it open, breast up, on the desk. The thin brown line, sharp on its outer edge, slightly blurred within, hemmed a great space spanning the whole left part of the chest and the upper part of the left sleeve. The space within the outline had been washed clear of any stain, even the rim was pale, but it stood clear to be seen, and the scattered shadowings of colour within it preserved a faint hint of what had been there.

Radulfus, if he had not ventured as far afield in the world as Cadfael, had nevertheless stored up some experience of it. He viewed the extended evidence and said composedly, 'This was blood.'

'So it was,' said Cadfael, and rolled up the shirt.

'And whoever owned this scrip came from where a certain Juliana Bossard was chatelaine.' His deep eyes were steady and sombre on Cadfael's face. 'Have we entertained a murderer in our house?'

'I think we have,' said Cadfael, restoring the scattered fragments of a life to their modest lodging. A man's life, shorn of all expectation of continuance, even the last coin gone from the purse. 'But I think we may have time yet to prevent another killing—if you give me leave to go.'

'Take the best of what may be in the stable,' said the abbot simply, 'and I will send word to Hugh Beringar, and have him follow you, and not alone.'

CHAPTER THIRTEEN

Several miles north on the Oswestry road, Olivier drew rein by the roadside where a wiry, bright-eyed boy was grazing goats on the broad verge, lush in summer growth and coming into seed. The child twitched one of his long leads on his charges, to bring him along gently where the early evening light lay warm on the tall grass. He looked up at the rider without awe, half-Welsh and immune from servility. He smiled and gave an easy good evening.

The boy was handsome, bold, unafraid; so was the man. They looked at each other and liked what they saw.

'God be with you!' said Olivier. 'How long have you been pasturing your beasts along here? And have you in all that time seen a lame man and a well man go by, the pair of them much of my age, but afoot?'

'God be with you, master,' said the boy cheerfully. 'Here along this verge ever since noon, for I brought my bit of dinner with me. But I've seen none such pass. And I've had a word by the road with every soul that did go by, unless he were galloping.'

'Then I waste my hurrying,' said Olivier, and idled a while, his horse stooping to the tips of the grasses. 'They cannot be ahead of me, not by this road. See, now, supposing they wished to go earlier into Wales, how may I bear round to pick them up on the way? They went from Shrewsbury town ahead of me, and I have word to bring to them. Where can I turn west and fetch a circle about the town?'

The young herdsman accepted with open arms every exchange that refreshed his day's labour. He gave his mind to the best road offering, and delivered judgement: 'Turn back but a mile or more, back across the bridge at Montford, and then you'll find a well-used cart-track that bears off west, to your right hand it will be. Bear a piece west again where the paths first branch, it's no direct way, but it does go on. It skirts Shrewsbury a matter of above four miles outside the town, and threads the edges of the forest, but it cuts across every path out of Shrewsbury. You may catch your men yet. And I wish you may!'

'My thanks for that,' said Olivier, 'and for your advice also.' He stooped to the hand the boy had raised, not for alms but to caress the horse's chestnut shoulder with admiration and pleasure, and slipped a coin into the smooth palm. 'God be with you!' he said, and wheeled his mount and set off back along the road he had travelled.

'And go with you, master!' the boy called after him, and watched until a curve of the road took horse and rider out of sight beyond a stand of trees. The goats gathered closer; evening was near, and they were ready to turn homeward, knowing the hour by the sun as well as did their herd. The boy drew in their tethers, whistled to them cheerily, and moved on along the road to his homeward path through the fields.

Olivier came for the second time to the bridge over the Severn, one bank a steep, tree-clad escarpment, the other open, level meadow. Beyond the first plane of fields a winding track turned off to the right, between scattered stands of trees, bearing at this point rather south than west, but after a mile or more it brought him on to a better road that crossed his track left and right. He bore right into the sun, as he had been instructed, and at the next place where two dwindling paths divided he turned left, and keeping his course by the sinking sun on his right hand, now just resting upon the rim of the world and glimmering through the trees in sudden blinding glimpses, began to work his way gradually round the town of Shrewsbury. The tracks wound in and out of copses, the fringe woods of the northern tip of the Long Forest, sometimes in twilight among dense trees, sometimes in open heath and scrub,

217

sometimes past islets of cultivated fields and glimpses of hamlets. He rode with ears pricked for any promising sound, pausing wherever his labyrinthine path crossed a track bearing westward out of Shrewsbury, and wherever he met with cottage or assart he asked after his two travellers. No one had seen such a pair pass by. Olivier took heart. They had had some hours start of him, but if they had not passed westward by any of the roads he had yet crossed, they might still be within the circle he was drawing about the town. The barefoot one would not find these ways easy going, and might have been forced to take frequent rests. At the worst, even if he missed them in the end, this meandering route must bring him round at last to the highroad by which he had first approached Shrewsbury from the south-east, and he could ride back into the town to Hugh Beringar's welcome, none the worse for a little exercise in a fine evening.

*　　　*　　　*

Brother Cadfael had wasted no time in clambering into his boots, kilting his habit, and taking and saddling the best horse he could find in the stables. It was not often he had the chance to indulge himself with such half-forgotten delights, but he was not thinking of that now. He had left considered word with the messenger who was already hurrying across the bridge and into the town, to alert Hugh; and Hugh would ask no questions, as the abbot had asked none, recognising the grim urgency there was no leisure now to explain.

'Say to Hugh Beringar,' the order ran, 'that Ciaran will make for the Welsh border the nearest way, but avoiding the too open roads. I think he'll bear south a small way to the old road the Romans made, that we've been fools enough to let run wild, for it keeps a steady level and makes straight for the border north of Caus.'

That was drawing a bow at a venture, and he knew it, none better. Ciaran was not of these parts, though he might well have some knowledge of the borderland if he had kin on the Welsh side. But more than that, he had been here these three days past, and if he had been planning some such escape all that time, he could have picked the brains of brothers and guests, on easily plausible ground. Time pressed, and sound guessing was needed. Cadfael chose his way, and set about pursuing it.

He did not waste time in going decorously out at the gatehouse and round by the road to take up the chase westward, but led his horse at a trot through the gardens, to the blank astonishment of Brother Jerome, who happened to be crossing to the cloisters a good ten minutes early for Compline. No doubt he would report, with a sense of outrage, to Prior Robert. Cadfael as promptly forgot him, leading the horse round the unharvested pease-field and down to the quiet green stretches of the brook, and across to the narrow meadow, where he mounted. The sun was dipping its rim beyond the crowns of the trees to westward. Into that half-shine, half-shadow Cadfael spurred, and made good speed while the tracks were familiar to him as his own palm. Due west until he hit the road, a half-mile on the road at a canter, until it turned too far to the south, and then westward again for the setting sun. Ciaran had a long start, even of Matthew, let alone of all those who followed now. But Ciaran was lame, burdened and afraid. Almost he was to be pitied.

Half a mile further on, at an inconspicuous track which he knew, Cadfael again turned to bear south-west, and burrowed into deepest shade, and into the northernmost woodlands of the Long Forest. No more than a narrow forest ride, this, between sweeping branches, a fragment of ancient wood not worth clearing for an assart, being bedded on rock that broke surface here and there. This was not yet border country, but close kin to it, heaving into fretful outcrops that broke the thin soil, bearing heather and coarse upland grasses, scrub bushes and sparsity trees, then bringing forth prodigal life roofed by very old trees in

220

every wet hollow. A little further on this course, and the close, dark woods began, tall top cover, heavy interweaving of middle growth, and a tangle of bush and bramble and ground-cover below. Undisturbed forest, though there were rare islands of tillage bright and open within it, every one an astonishment.

Then he came to the old, old road, that sliced like a knife across his path, heading due east, due west. He wondered about the men who had made it. It was shrunken now from a soldiers' road to a narrow ride, mostly under thin turf, but it ran as it had always run since it was made, true and straight as a lance, perfectly levelled where a level was possible, relentlessly climbing and descending where some hummock barred the way. Cadfael turned west into it, and rode straight for the golden upper arc of sun that still glowed between the branches.

*   *   *

In the parcel of old forest north and west of the hamlet of Hanwood there were groves where stray outlaws could find ample cover, provided they stayed clear of the few settlements within reach. Local people tended to fence their holdings and band together to protect their own small ground. The forest was for plundering, poaching, pasturing of swine, all with secure precautions. Travellers, though

221

they might call on hospitality and aid where needed, must fend for themselves in the thicker coverts, if they cared to venture through them. By and large, safety here in Shropshire under Hugh Beringar was as good as anywhere in England, and encroachment by vagabonds could not survive long, but for brief occupation the cover was there, and unwanted tenants might take up occupation if pressed.

Several of the lesser manors in these border regions had declined by reason of their perilous location, and some were half-deserted, leaving their fields untilled. Until April of this year the border castle of Caus had been in Welsh hands, an added threat to peaceful occupation, and there had not yet been time since Hugh's reclamation of the castle for the depleted hamlets to re-establish themselves. Moreover, in this high summer it was no hardship to live wild, and skilful poaching and a little profitable thievery could keep two or three good fellows in meat while they allowed time for their exploits in the south to be forgotten, and made up their minds where best to pass the time until a return home seemed possible.

Master Simeon Poer, self-styled merchant of Guildford, was not at all ill-content with the pickings made in Shrewsbury. In three nights, which was the longest they dared reckon on operating unsuspected, they had taken a fair amount of money from the hopeful gamblers of the town and Foregate, besides the price Daniel Aurifaber had paid for the stolen ring, the various odds and ends William Hales had abstracted from market stalls, and the coins John Shure had used his long, smooth, waxed finger-nails to extract from pocket and purse in the crowds. It was a pity they had had to leave William Hales to his fate during the raid, but all in all they had done well to get out of it with no more than a bruise or two, and one man short. Bad luck for William, but it was the way the lot had fallen. Every man knew it could happen to him.

They had avoided the used tracks, refraining from meddling with any of the local people going about their business, and done their plundering by night and stealthily, after first making sure where there were dogs to be reckoned with. They even had a roof of sorts, for in the deepest thickets below the old road, overgrown and well-concealed, they had found the remains of a hut, relic of a failed assart abandoned long ago. After a few days more of this easy living, or if the weather should change, they would set off to make their way somewhat south, to be well clear of Shrewsbury before moving across to the east, to shires where they were not yet known.

When the rare traveller came past on the road, it was almost always a local man, and they let him alone, for he would be missed all too soon, and the hunt would be up in a day.

But they would not have been averse to waylaying any solitary who was clearly a stranger and on his way to more distant places, since he was unlikely to be missed at once, and further, he was likely to be better worth robbing, having on him the means to finance his journey, however modestly. In these woods and thickets, a man could vanish very neatly, and for ever.

They had made themselves comfortable that night outside their hut, with the embers of their fire safe in the clay-lined hollow they had made for it, and the grease of the stolen chicken still on their fingers. The sunset of the outer world was already twilight here, but they had their night eyes, and were wide awake and full of restless energy after an idle day. Walter Bagot was charged with keeping such watch as they thought needful, and had made his way in cover some distance along the narrow track towards the town. He came sliding back in haste, but shining with anticipation instead of alarm.

'Here's one coming we may safely pick off. The barefoot fellow from the abbey . . . well back as yet, and lame as ever, he's been among the stones, surely. Not a soul will know where he went to.'

'He?' said Simeon Poer, surprised. 'Fool, he has always his shadow breathing down his neck. It would mean both—if one got away he'd raise the hunt on us.'

'He has not his shadow now,' said Bagot gleefully. 'Alone, I tell you, he's shaken him off, or else they've parted by consent. Who else cares a groat what becomes of him?'

'And a groat's his worth,' said Shure scornfully. 'Let him go. It's never worth it for his hose and shirt, and what else can he have on him?'

'Ah, but he has! Money, my friend!' said Bagot, glittering. 'Make no mistake, that one goes very well provided, if he takes good care not to let it be known. I know! I've felt my way about him every time I could get crowded against him in church, he has a solid, heavy purse belted about him inside coat, hose, shirt and all, but I never could get my fingers into it without using the knife, and that was too risky. He can pay his way wherever he goes. Come, rouse, he'll be an easy mark now.'

He was certain, and they were heartily willing to pick up an extra purse. They rose merrily, hands on daggers, worming their way quietly through the underbrush towards the thin thread of the track, above which the ribbon of clear sky showed pale and bright still. Shure and Bagot lurking invisible on the near side of the path, Simeon Poer across it, behind the lush screen of bushes that took advantage of the open light to grow leafy and tall. There were very old trees in their tract of forest, enormous beeches with trunks so gnarled and thick three men with arms outspread could hardly clip them. Old woodland was being cleared, assarted and turned into hunting-grounds in many places, but the Long Forest still preserved large tracts of virgin growth untouched. In the green dimness the three masterless men stood still as the trees, and waited.

Then they heard him. Dogged, steady, laborious steps that stirred the coarse grasses. In the turfed verge of a highroad he could have gone with less pain and covered twice the miles he had accomplished on these rough ways. They heard his heavy breathing while he was still twenty yards away from them, and saw his tall, dark figure stir the dimness, leaning forward on a long, knotty staff he had picked up somewhere from among the debris of the trees. It seemed that he favoured the right foot, though both trod with wincing tenderness, as though he had trodden askew on a sharp-edged stone, and either cut his sole or twisted his ankle-joint. He was piteous, if there had been anyone to pity him.

He went with ears pricked, and the very hairs of his skin erected, in as intense wariness as any of the small nocturnal creatures that crept and quaked in the underbrush around him. He had walked in fear every step of the miles he had gone in company, but now, cast loose to his own dreadful company, he was even more afraid. Escape was no escape at all.

It was the extremity of his fear that saved

him. They had let him pass slowly by the first covert, so that Bagot might be behind him, and Poer and Shure one on either side before him. It was not so much his straining ears as the prickly sensitivity of his skin that sensed the sudden rushing presence at his back, the shifting of the cool evening air, and the weight of body and arm launched at him almost silently. He gave a muted shriek and whirled about, sweeping the staff around him, and the knife that should have impaled him struck the branch and sliced a ribbon of bark and wood from it. Bagot reached with his left hand for a grip on sleeve or coat, and struck again as nimbly as a snake, but missed his hold as Ciaran leaped wildly back out of reach, and driven beyond himself by terror, turned and plunged away on his lacerated feet, aside from the path and into the deepest and thickest shadows among the tangled trees. He hissed and moaned with pain as he went, but he ran like a startled hare.

Who would have thought he could still move so fast, once pushed to extremes? But he could not keep it up long, the spur would not carry him far. The three of them went after, spreading out a little to hem him from three sides when he fell exhausted. They were giggling as they went, and in no special haste. The mingled sounds of his crashing passage through the bushes and his uncontrollable whining with the pain of it, rang unbelievably

227

strangely in the twilit woods.

Branches and brambles lashed Ciaran's face. He ran blindly, sweeping the long staff before him, cutting a noisy swathe through the bushes and stumbling painfully in the thick ground-debris of dead branches and soft, treacherous pits of the leaves of many years. They followed at leisure, aware that he was slowing. The lean, agile tailor had drawn level with him, somewhat aside, and was bearing round to cut him off, still with breath enough to whistle to his fellows as they closed unhurriedly, like dogs herding a stray sheep. Ciaran fell out into a more open glade, where a huge old beech had preserved its own clearing, and with what was left of his failing breath he made a last dash to cross the open and vanish again into the thickets beyond. The dry silt of leaves among the roots betrayed him. His footing slid from under him, and fetched him down heavily against the bole of the tree. He had just time to drag himself up and set his back to the broad trunk before they were on him.

He flailed about him with the staff, screaming for aid, and never even knew on what name he was calling in his extremity.

'Help! Murder! Matthew, Matthew, help me!'

There was no answering shout, but there was an abrupt thrashing of branches, and something hurtled out of cover and across the grass, so suddenly that Bagot was shouldered aside and stumbled to his knees. A long arm swept Ciaran back hard against the solid bole of the tree, and Matthew stood braced beside him, his dagger naked in his hand. What remained of the western light showed his face roused and formidable, and gleamed along the blade.

'Oh, no!' he challenged loud and clear, lips drawn back from bared teeth. 'Keep your hands off! This man is mine!'

CHAPTER FOURTEEN

The three attackers had drawn off instinctively, before they realised that this was but one man erupting in their midst, but they were quick to grasp it, and had not gone far. They stood, wary as beasts of prey but undeterred, weaving a little in a slow circle out of reach, but with no thought of withdrawing. They watched and considered, weighing up coldly these altered odds. Two men and a knife to reckon with now, and this second one they knew as well as the first. They had been some days frequenting the same enclave, using the same dortoir and refectory. They reasoned without dismay that they must be known as well as they knew their prey. The twilight made faces shadowy, but a man is recognised by more things than his face.

'I said it, did I not?' said Simeon Poer, exchanging glances with his henchmen, glances which were understood even in the dim light. 'I said he would not be far. No matter, two can lie as snug as one.'

Once having declared his claim and his rights, Matthew said nothing. The tree against which they braced themselves was so grown that they could not be attacked from close behind. He circled it steadily when Bagot edged round to the far side, keeping his face to the enemy. There were three to watch, and Ciaran was shaken and lame, and in no case to match any of the three if it came to action, though he kept his side of the trunk with his staff gripped and ready, and would fight if he must, tooth and claw, for his forfeit life. Matthew curled his lips in a bitter smile at the thought that he might be grateful yet for that strong appetite for living.

Round the bole of the tree, with his cheek against the bark, Ciaran said, low-voiced: 'You'd have done better not to follow me.'

'Did I not swear to go with you to the very end?' said Matthew as softly. 'I keep my vows. This one above all.'

'Yet you could still have crept away safely. Now we are two dead men.'

'Not yet! If you did not want me, why did you call me?'

There was a bewildered silence. Ciaran did

not know he had uttered a name.

'We are grown used to each other,' said Matthew grimly. 'You claimed me, as I claim you. Do you think I'll let any other man have you?'

The three watchers had gathered in a shadowy group, conferring with heads together, and faces still turned towards their prey.

'Now they'll come,' said Ciaran in the dead voice of despair.

'No, they'll wait for darkness.'

They were in no hurry. They made no loose, threatening moves, wasted no breath on words. They bided their time as patiently as hunting animals. Silently they separated, spacing themselves round the clearing, and backing just far enough into cover to be barely visible, yet visible all the same, for their presence and stillness were meant to unnerve. Just so, motionless, relentless and alert, would a cat sit for hours outside a mousehole.

'This I cannot bear,' said Ciaran in a faint whisper, and drew sobbing breath.

'It is easily cured,' said Matthew through his teeth. 'You have only to lift off that cross from your neck, and you can be loosed from all your troubles.'

The light faded still. Their eyes, raking the smoky darkness of the bushes, were beginning to see movement where there was none, and strain in vain after it where it lurked and shifted to baffle them more. This waiting would not be long. The attackers circled in cover, watching for the unguarded moment when one or other of their victims would be caught unawares, staring in the wrong direction. Past all question they would expect that failure first from Ciaran, half-foundering as he already was. Soon now, very soon.

*   *   *

Brother Cadfael was some half-mile back along the ride when he heard the cry, ahead and to the right of the path, loud, wild and desperate. The words were indistinguishable, but the panic in the sound there was no mistaking. In this woodland silence, without even a wind to stir the branches or flutter the leaves, every sound carried clearly. Cadfael spurred ahead in haste, with all too dire a conviction of what he might find when he reached the source of that lamentable cry. All those miles of pursuit, patient and remorseless, half the length of England, might well be ending now, barely a quarter of an hour too soon for him to do anything to prevent. Matthew had overtaken, surely, a Ciaran grown weary of his penitential austerities, now there was no one by to see. He had said truly enough that he did not hate himself so much as to bear his hardships to no purpose. Now that he was alone, had he felt

232

safe in discarding his heavy cross, and would he next have been in search of shoes for his feet? If Matthew had not come upon him thus recreant and disarmed.

The second sound to break the stillness almost passed unnoticed because of the sound of his own progress, but he caught some quiver of the forest's unease, and reined in to listen intently. The rush and crash of something or someone hurtling through thick bushes, fast and arrow-straight, and then, very briefly, a confusion of cries, not loud but sharp and wary, and a man's voice loud and commanding over all. Matthew's voice, not in triumph or terror, rather in short and resolute defiance. There were more than the two of them, there ahead, and not so far ahead now.

He dismounted, and led his horse at an anxious trot as far as he dared along the path, towards the spot from which the sounds had come. Hugh could move very fast when he saw reason, and in Cadfael's bare message he would have found reason enough. He would have left the town by the most direct way, over the western bridge and so by a good road south west, to strike this old path barely two miles back. At this moment he might be little more than a mile behind. Cadfael tethered his horse at the side of the track, for a plain sign that he had found cause to halt here and was somewhere close by.

All was quiet about him now. He quested

along the fringe of bushes for a place where he might penetrate without any betraying noise, and began to work his way by instinct and touch towards the place whence the cries had come, and where now all was almost unnaturally silent. In a little while he was aware of the last faint pallor of the afterglow glimmering between the branches. There was a more open glade ahead of him.

He froze and stood motionless, as a shadow passed silently between him and this lingering glimpse of light. Someone tall and lean, slithering snake-like through the bushes. Cadfael waited until the faint pattern of light was restored, and then edged carefully forward until he could see into the clearing.

The great bole of a beech-tree showed in the centre, a solid mass beneath its spread of branches. There was movement there in the dimness. Not one man, but two, stood pressed against the bole. A brief flash of steel caught just light enough to show what it was, a dagger naked and ready. Two at bay here, and surely more than one pinning them thus helpless until they could be safely pulled down. Cadfael stood still to survey the whole of the darkening clearing, and found, as he had expected, another quiver of leaves that hid a man, and then, on the opposite side, yet another. Three, probably all armed, certainly up to no good, thus furtively prowling the woods by night, going nowhere, waiting to make the kill. Three had vanished from the dice school under the bridge at Shrewsbury, and fled in this direction. Three reappeared here in the forest, still doing after their disreputable kind.

Cadfael stood hesitant, pondering how best to deal, whether to steal back to the path and wait and hope for Hugh's coming, or attempt something alone, at least to distract and dismay, to bring about a delay that might afford time for help to come. He had made up his mind to return to his horse, mount, and ride in here with as much noise and turmoil as he could muster, trying to sound like six mounted men instead of one, when with shattering suddenness the decision was taken out of his hands.

One of the three besiegers sprang out of cover with a startling shout, and rushed at the tree on the side where the momentary flash of steel had shown one of the victims, at least, to be armed. A dark figure leaned out from the darkness under the branches to meet the onslaught, and Cadfael knew him then for Matthew. The attacker swerved aside, still out of reach, in a calculated feint, and at the same moment both the other lurking shadows burst out of cover and bore down upon the other side of the tree, falling as one upon the weaker opponent. There was a confusion of violence, and a wild, tormented scream, and Matthew whirled about, slashing round him and stretching a long arm across his companion, pinning him back against the tree. Ciaran hung half-fainting, slipping down between the great, smooth bastions of the bole, and Matthew bestrode him, his dagger sweeping great swathes before them both.

Cadfael saw it, and was held mute and motionless, beholding this devoted enemy. He got his breath only as all three of the predators closed upon their prey together, slashing, mauling, by sheer weight bearing them down under them.

Cadfael filled his lungs full, and bellowed to the shaken night: 'Hold, there! On them, hold them all three. These are our felons!' He was making so much noise that he did not notice or marvel that the echoes, which in his fury he heard but did not heed, came from two directions at once, from the path he had left, and from the opposite point, from the north. Some corner of his mind knew he had roused echoes, but for his part he felt himself quite alone as he kept up his roaring, spread his sleeves like the wings of a bat, and surged headlong into the mêlée about the tree.

Long, long ago he had forsworn arms, but what of it? Barring his two stout fists, still active but somewhat rheumatic now, he was unarmed. He flung himself into the tangle of men and weapons under the beech, laid hands on the back of a dangling capuchon, hauled its wearer bodily backwards, and twisted the cloth to choke the throat that howled rage and venom at him. But his voice had done more than his martial progress. The black huddle of humanity burst into its separate beings. Two sprang clear and looked wildly about them for the source of the alarm, and Cadfael's opponent reached round, gasping, with a long arm and a vicious dagger, and sliced a dangling streamer out of a rusty black sleeve. Cadfael lay on him with all his weight, held him by the hair, and ground his face into the earth, shamelessly exulting. He would do penance for it some day soon, but now he rejoiced, all his crusader blood singing in his veins.

Distantly he was aware that something else was happening, more than he had reckoned on. He heard and felt the unmistakable quiver and thud of the earth reacting to hooves, and heard a peremptory voice shouting orders, the purport of which he did not release his grip to decipher or attend to. The glade was filled with motion as it filled with darkness. The creature under him gathered itself and heaved mightily, rolling him aside. His hold on the folds of the hood relaxed, and Simeon Poer tore himself free and scrambled clear. There was running every way, but none of the fugitives got far.

Last of the three to roll breathless out of hold, Simeon groped about him vengefully in the roots of the tree, touched a cowering body, found the cord of some dangling relic, possibly precious, in his hand, and hauled with all his

237

strength before he gathered himself up and ran for cover. There was a wild scream of pain, and the cord broke, and the thing, whatever it was, came loose in his hand. He got his feet under him, and charged head-down for the nearest bushes, hurtled into them and ran, barely a yard clear of hands that stooped from horse-back to claw at him.

Cadfael opened his eyes and hauled in breath. The whole clearing was boiling with movement, the darkness heaved and trembled, and the violence had ordered itself into purpose and meaning. He sat up, and took his time to look about him. He was sprawled under the great beech, and somewhere before him, towards the path where he had left his horse, someone with flint and dagger and tinder, was striking sparks for a torch, very calmly. The sparks caught, glowed, and were gently blown into flame. The torch, well primed with oil and resin, sucked in the flame and gave birth to a small, shapely flame of its own, that grew and reared, and was used to kindle a second and a third. The clearing took on a small, confined, rounded shape, walled with close growth, roofed with the tree.

Hugh came out of the dark, smiling, and reached a hand to haul him to his feet. Someone else came running light-footed from the other side, and stooped to him a wonderful, torch-lit face, high-boned, lean-cheeked, with eager golden eyes, and blue-black raven wings of hair curving to cup his cheeks.

'Olivier?' said Cadfael, marvelling. 'I thought you were astray on the road to Oswestry. How did you ever find us here?'

'By grace of God and a goat-herd,' said the warm, gay, remembered voice, 'and your bull's bellowing. Come, look round! You have won your field.'

They were gone, Simeon Poer, merchant of Guildford, Walter Bagot, glover, John Shure, tailor, all fled, but with half a dozen of Hugh's men hard on their heels, all to be brought in captive, to answer for more, this time, than a little cheating in the marketplace. Night stooped to enfold a closed arena of torchlight, very quiet now and almost still. Cadfael rose, his torn sleeve dangling awkwardly. The three of them stood in a half-circle about the beech-tree.

The torchlight was stark, plucking light and shadow into sharp relief. Matthew stirred out of his colloquy between life and death very slowly as they watched him, heaved his wide shoulders clear of the tree, and stood forth like a sleeper roused before his time, looking about him as if for something by which he might hold, and take his bearings. Between his feet, as he emerged, the coiled, crumpled form of Ciaran came into view, faintly stirring, his head huddled into his close-folded arms.

'Get up!' said Matthew. He drew back a
239

little from the tree, his naked dagger in his hand, a slow drop gathering at its tip, more drops falling steadily from the hand that held it. His knuckles were sliced raw. 'Get up!' he said. 'You are not harmed.'

Ciaran gathered himself very slowly, and clambered to his knees, lifting to the light a face soiled and leaden, gone beyond exhaustion, beyond fear. He looked neither at Cadfael nor at Hugh, but stared up into Matthew's face with the helpless intensity of despair. Hugh felt the clash of eyes, and stirred to make some decisive movement and break the tension, but Cadfael laid a hand on his arm and held him still. Hugh gave him a sharp sidelong glance, and accepted the caution. Cadfael had his reasons.

There was blood on the torn collar of Ciaran's shirt, a stain that grew sluggishly before their eyes. He put up hands that seemed heavy as lead, and fumbled aside the linen from throat and breast. All round the left side of his neck ran a raw, bleeding slash, thin as a knife-cut. Simeon Poer's last blind clutch for plunder had torn loose the cross to which Ciaran had clung so desperately. He kneeled in the last wretched extreme of submission, baring a throat already symbolically slit.

'Here am I,' he said in a toneless whisper. 'I can run no further, I am forfeit. Now take me!'

Matthew stood motionless, staring at that savage cut the cord had left before it broke.

The silence grew too heavy to be bearable, and still he had no word to say, and his face was a blank mask in the flickering light of the torches.

'He says right,' said Cadfael, very softly and reasonably. 'He is yours fairly. The terms of his penance are broken, and his life is forfeit. Take him!'

There was no sign that Matthew so much as heard him, but for the spasmodic tightening of his lips, as if in pain. He never took his eyes from the wretch kneeling humbly before him.

'You have followed him faithfully, and kept the terms laid down,' Cadfael urged gently. 'You are under vow. Now finish the work!'

He was on safe enough ground, and sure of it now. The act of submission had already finished the work, there was no more to be done. With his enemy at his mercy, and every justification for the act of vengeance, the avenger was helpless, the prisoner of his own nature. There was nothing left in him but a drear sadness, a sick revulsion of disgust and self-disgust. How could he kill a wretched, broken man, kneeling here unresisting, waiting for his death? Death was no longer relevant.

'It is over, Luc,' said Cadfael softly. 'Do what you must.'

Matthew stood mute a moment longer, and if he had heard his true name spoken, he gave no sign, it was of no importance. After the abandonment of all purpose came the awful sense of loss and emptiness. He opened his blood-stained hand and let the dagger slip from his fingers into the grass. He turned away like a blind man, feeling with a stretched foot for every step, groped his way through the curtain of bushes, and vanished into the darkness.

Olivier drew in breath sharply, and started out of his tranced stillness to catch eagerly at Cadfael's arm. 'Is it true? You have found him out? *He* is Luc Meverel?' He accepted the truth of it without another word said, and sprang ardently towards the place where the bushes still stirred after Luc's passing, and he would have been off in pursuit at a run if Hugh had not caught at his arm to detain him.

'Wait but one moment! You also have a cause here, if Cadfael is right. This is surely the man who murdered your friend. He owes you a death. He is yours if you want him.'

'That is truth,' said Cadfael. 'Ask him! He will tell you.'

Ciaran crouched in the grass, drooping now, bewildered and lost, no longer looking any man in the face, only waiting without hope or understanding for someone to determine whether he was to live or die, and on what abject terms. Olivier cast one wondering glance at him, shook his head in emphatic rejection, and reached for his horse's bridle. 'Who am I,' he said, 'to exact what Luc Meverel has remitted? Let this one go on his

242

way with his own burden. My business is with the other.'

He was away at a run, leading the horse briskly through the screen of bushes, and the rustling of their passage gradually stilled again into silence. Cadfael and Hugh were left regarding each other mutely across the lamentable figure crouched upon the ground.

Gradually the rest of the world flowed back into Cadfael's ken. Three of Hugh's officers stood aloof with the horses and the torches, looking on in silence; and somewhere not far distant sounded a brief scuffle and outcry, as one of the fugitives was overpowered and made prisoner. Simeon Poer had been pulled down barely fifty yards in cover, and stood sullenly under guard now, with his wrists secured to a sergeant's stirrup-leather. The third would not be a free man long. This night's ventures were over. This piece of woodland would be safe even for barefoot and unarmed pilgrims to traverse.

'What is to be done with him?' demanded Hugh openly, looking down upon the wreckage of a man with some distaste.

'Since Luc has waived his claim,' said Cadfael, 'I would not dare meddle. And there is something at least to be said for him, he did not cheat or break his terms voluntarily, even when there was no one by to accuse him. It is a small virtue to have to advance for the defence of a life, but it is something. Who else has the right to foreclose on what Luc has spared?'

Ciaran raised his head, peering doubtfully from one face to the other, still confounded at being so spared, but beginning to believe that he still lived. He was weeping, whether with pain, or relief, or something more durable than either, there was no telling. The blood was blackening into a dark line about his throat.

'Speak up and tell truth,' said Hugh with chill gentleness. 'Was it you who stabbed Bossard?'

Out of the pallid disintegration of Ciaran's face a wavering voice said: 'Yes.'

'Why did you so? Why attack the queen's clerk, who did nothing but deliver his errand faithfully?'

Ciaran's eyes burned for an instant, and a fleeting spark of past pride, intolerance and rage showed like the last glow of a dying fire. 'He came high-handed, shouting down the lord bishop, defying the council. My master was angry and affronted . . .'

'Your master,' said Cadfael, 'was the prior of Hyde Mead. Or so you claimed.'

'How could I any longer claim service with one who had discarded me? I lied! The lord bishop himself—I served Bishop Henry, had his favour. Lost, lost now! I could not brook the man Christian's insolence to him . . . he stood against everything my lord planned and willed. I hated him! I thought then that I hated

244

him,' said Ciaran, drearily wondering at the recollection. 'And I thought to please my lord!'

'A calculation that went awry,' said Cadfael, 'for whatever he may be, Henry of Blois is no murderer. And Rainald Bossard prevented your mischief, a man of your own party, held in esteem. Did that make him a traitor in your eyes—that he should respect an honest opponent? Or did you strike out at random, and kill without intent?'

'No,' said the level, lame voice, bereft of its brief spark. 'He thwarted me, I was enraged. I knew what I did. I was glad ... *then!*' he said, and drew bitter breath.

'And who laid upon you this penitential journey?' asked Cadfael, 'and to what end? Your life was granted you, upon terms. What terms? Someone in the highest authority laid that load upon you.'

'My lord the bishop-legate,' said Ciaran, and wrung wordlessly for a moment at the pain of an old devotion, rejected and banished now for ever. 'There was no other soul knew of it, only to him I told it. He would not give me up to law, he wanted this thing put by, for fear it should threaten his plans for the empress's peace. But he would not condone. I am from the Danish kingdom of Dublin, my other half Welsh. He offered me passage under his protection to Bangor, to the bishop there, who would see me to Caergybi in Anglesey, and have me put aboard a ship for Dublin. But I must go barefoot all that way, and wear the cross round my neck, and if ever I broke those terms, even for a moment, my life was his who cared to take it, without blame or penalty. And I could never return.' Another fire, of banished love, ruined ambition, rejected service, flamed through the broken accents for a moment, and died of despair.

'Yet if this sentence was never made public,' said Hugh, seizing upon one thing still unexplained, 'how did Luc Meverel ever come to know of it and follow you?'

'Do I know?' The voice was flat and drear, worn out with exhaustion. 'All I know is that I set out from Winchester, and where the roads joined, near Newbury, this man stood and waited for me, and fell in beside me, and every step of my way on this journey he has gone on my heels like a demon, and waited for me to play false to my sentence—for there was no point of it he did not know!—to take my life without guilt, without a qualm, as so he might. He trod after me wherever I trod, he never let me from his sight, he made no secret of his wants, he tempted me to go aside, to put on shoes, to lay by the cross—and sirs, it was deathly heavy! Matthew, he called himself . . . Luc, you say he is? You know him? I never knew . . . He said I had killed his lord, whom he loved, and he would follow me to Bangor, to Caergybi, even to Dublin if ever I got aboard ship without putting off the cross or

246

putting on shoes. But he would have me in the end. He had what he lusted for—why did he turn away and spare?' The last words ached with his uncomprehending wonder.

'He did not find you worth the killing,' said Cadfael, as gently and mercifully as he could, but honestly. 'Now he goes in anguish and shame because he spent so much time on you that might have been better spent. It is a matter of values. Study to learn what is worth and what is not, and you may come to understand him.'

'I am a dead man while I live,' said Ciaran, writhing, 'without master, without friends, without a cause . . .'

'All three you may find, if you seek. Go where you were sent, bear what you were condemned to bear, and look for the meaning,' said Cadfael. 'For so must we all.'

He turned away with a sigh. No way of knowing how much good words might do, or the lessons of life, no telling whether any trace of compunction moved in Ciaran's bludgeoned mind, or whether all his feeling was still for himself. Cadfael felt himself suddenly very tired. He looked at Hugh with a somewhat lopsided smile. 'I wish I were home. What now, Hugh? Can we go?'

Hugh stood looking down with a frown at the confessed murderer, sunken in the grass like a broken-backed serpent, submissive, tear-stained, nursing minor injuries. A piteous spectacle, though pity might be misplaced. Yet he was, after all, no more than twenty-five or so years old, able-bodied, well-clothed, strong, his continued journey might be painful and arduous, but it was not beyond his powers, and he had his bishop's ring still, effective wherever law held. These three footpads now tethered fast and under guard would trouble his going no more. Ciaran would surely reach his journey's end safely, however long it might take him. Not the journey's end of his false story, a blessed death in Aberdaron and burial among the saints of Ynys Ennli, but a return to his native place, and a life beginning afresh. He might even be changed. He might well adhere to his hard terms all the way to Caergybi, where Irish ships plied, even as far as Dublin, even to his ransomed life's end. How can you tell?

'Make your own way from here,' said Hugh, 'as well as you may. You need fear nothing now from footpads here, and the border is not far. What you have to fear from God, take up with God.'

He turned his back, with so decisive a movement that his men recognised the sign that all was over, and stirred willingly about the captives and the horses.

'And those two?' asked Hugh. 'Had I not better leave a man behind on the track there, with a spare horse for Luc? He followed his quarry afoot, but no need for him to foot it back. Or ought I to send men after them?'

'No need for that,' said Cadfael with certainty. 'Olivier will manage all. They'll come home together.'

He had no qualms at all, he was beginning to relax into the warmth of content. The evil he had dreaded had been averted, however narrowly, at whatever cost. Olivier would find his stray, bear with him, follow if he tried to avoid, wrung and ravaged as he was, with the sole obsessive purpose of his life for so long ripped away from him, and within him only the aching emptiness where that consuming passion had been. Into that barren void Olivier would win his way, and warm the ravished heart to make it habitable for another love. There was the most comforting of messages to bring from Juliana Bossard, the promise regained of a home and a welcome. There was a future. How had Matthew-Luc seen his future when he emptied his purse of the last coin at the abbey, before taking up the pursuit of his enemy? Surely he had been contemplating the end of the person he had hitherto been, a total ending, beyond which he could not see. Now he was young again, there was a life before him, it needed only a little time to make him whole again.

Olivier would bring him back to the abbey, when the worst desolation was over. For Olivier had promised that he would not leave without spending some time leisurely with

Cadfael, and upon Olivier's promise the heart could rest secure.

As for the other ... Cadfael looked back from the saddle, after they had mounted, and saw the last of Ciaran, still on his knees under the tree, where they had left him. His face was turned to them, but his eyes seemed to be closed, and his hands were wrung tightly together before his breast. He might have been praying, he might have been simply experiencing with every particle of his flesh the life that had been left to him. When we are all gone, thought Cadfael, he will fall asleep there where he lies, he can do no other, for he is far gone in something beyond exhaustion. Where he falls asleep, there he will have died. But when he awakes, I trust he may understand that he has been born again.

The slower cortège that would bring the prisoners into the town began to assemble, making the tethering thongs secure, and the torch-bearers crossed the clearing to mount, withdrawing their yellow light from the kneeling figure, so that Ciaran vanished gradually, as though he had been absorbed into the bole of the beech-tree.

Hugh led the way out to the track, and turned homeward. 'Oh, Hugh, I grow old!' said Cadfael, hugely yawning. 'I want my bed.'

CHAPTER FIFTEEN

It was past midnight when they rode in at the gatehouse, into a great court awash with moonlight, and heard the chanting of Matins within the church. They had made no haste on the way home, and said very little, content to ride companionably together as sometimes before, through summer night or winter day. It would be another hour or more yet before Hugh's officers got their prisoners back to Shrewsbury Castle, since they must keep a foot-pace, but before morning Simeon Poer and his henchmen would be safe in hold, under lock and key.

'I'll wait with you until Lauds is over,' said Hugh, as they dismounted at the gatehouse. 'Father Abbot will want to know how we've sped. Though I hope he won't require the whole tale from us tonight.'

'Come down with me to the stables, then,' said Cadfael, 'and I'll see this fellow unsaddled and tended, while they're still within. I was always taught to care for my beast before seeking my own rest. You never lose the habit.'

In the stable-yard the moonlight was all the light they needed. The quietness of midnight and the stillness of the air carried every note of the office to them softly and clearly. Cadfael unsaddled his horse and saw him settled and

251

provided in his stall, with a light rug against any possible chill, rites he seldom had occasion to perform now. They brought back memories of other mounts and other journeys, and battlefields less happily resolved than the small but desperate skirmish just lost and won.

Hugh stood watching with his back turned to the great court, but his head tilted to follow the chant. Yet it was not any sound of an approaching step that made him look round suddenly, but the slender shadow that stole along the moonlit cobbles beside his feet. And there hesitant in the gateway of the yard stood Melangell, startled and startling, haloed in that pallid sheen.

'Child,' said Cadfael, concerned, 'what are you doing out of your bed at this hour?'

'How could I rest?' she said, but not as one complaining. 'No one misses me, they are all sleeping.' She stood very still and straight, as if she had spent all the hours since he had left her in earnest endeavour to put away for ever any memories he might have of the tear-stained, despairing girl who had sought solitude in his workshop. The great sheaf of her hair was braided and pinned up on her head, her gown was trim, and her face resolutely calm as she asked, 'Did you find him?'

A girl he had left her, a woman he came back to her. 'Yes,' said Cadfael, 'we found them both. There has nothing ill happened to

252

either. The two of them have parted. Ciaran goes on his way alone.'

'And Matthew?' she asked steadily.

'Matthew is with a good friend, and will come to no harm. We two have outridden them, but they will come.' She would have to learn to call him by another name now, but let the man himself tell her that. Nor would the future be altogether easy, for her or for Luc Meverel, two human creatures who might never have been brought within hail of each other but for freakish circumstance. Unless Saint Winifred had had a hand in that, too? On this night Cadfael could believe it, and trust her to bring all to a good end. 'He will come back,' said Cadfael, meeting her candid eyes, that bore no trace of tears now. 'You need not fear. But he has suffered a great turmoil of the mind, and he'll need all your patience and wisdom. Ask him nothing. When the time is right he will tell you everything. Reproach him with nothing—'

'God forbid,' she said, 'that I should ever reproach him. It was I who failed him.'

'No, how could you know? But when he comes, wonder at nothing. Be like one who is thirsty and drinks. And so will he.'

She had turned a little towards him, and the moonlight blanched wonderfully over her face, as if a lamp within her had been newly lighted. 'I will wait,' she said.

'Better go to your bed and sleep, the waiting

may be longer than you think, he has been wrung. But he will come.'

But at that she shook her head. 'I'll watch till he comes,' she said, and suddenly smiled at them, pale and lustrous as pearl, and turned and went away swiftly and silently towards the cloister.

'That is the girl you spoke of?' asked Hugh, looking after her with somewhat frowning interest. 'The lame boy's sister? The girl that young man fancies?'

'That is she,' said Cadfael, and closed the half-door of the stall.

'The weaver-woman's niece?'

'That, too. Dowerless and from common stock,' said Cadfael, understanding but untroubled. 'Yes, true! I'm from common stock myself. I doubt if a young fellow who has been torn apart and remade as Luc has tonight will care much about such little things. Though I grant you others may! I hope the lady Juliana has no plans yet for marrying him off to some heiress from a neighbour manor, for I fancy things have gone so far now with these two that she'll be forced to abandon her plans. A manor or a craft—if you take pride in them, and run them well, where's the difference?'

'Your common stock,' said Hugh heartily, 'gave growth to a most uncommon shoot! And I wouldn't say but that young thing would grace a hall better than many a highbred dame I've seen. But listen, they're ending. We'd best

254

present ourselves.'

*   *   *

Abbot Radulfus came from Matins and Lauds with his usual imperturbable stride, and found them waiting for him as he left the cloister. This day of miracles had produced a fittingly glorious night, incredibly lofty and deep, coruscating with stars, washed white with moonlight. Coming from the dimness within, this exuberance of light showed him clearly both the serenity and the weariness on the two faces that confronted him.

'You are back!' he said, and looked beyond them. 'But not all! Messire de Bretagne—you said he had gone by a wrong way. He has not returned here. You have not encountered him?'

'Yes, Father, we have,' said Hugh. 'All is well with him, and he has found the young man he was seeking. They will return here, all in good time.'

'And the evil you feared, Brother Cadfael? You spoke of another death ...'

'Father,' said Cadfael, 'no harm has come tonight to any but the masterless men who escaped into the forest there. They are now safe in hold, and on their way under guard to the castle. The death I dreaded has been averted, no threat remains in that quarter to any man. I said, if the two young men could be

255

overtaken, the better surely for one, and perhaps for both. Father, they were overtaken in time, and better for both it surely must be.'

'Yet there remains,' said Radulfus, pondering, 'the print of blood, which both you and I have seen. You said—you will recall—that, yes, we have entertained a murderer among us. Do you still say so?'

'Yes, Father. Yet not as you suppose. When Olivier de Bretagne and Luc Meverel return, then all can be made plain, for as yet,' said Cadfael, 'there are still certain things we do not know. But we do know,' he said firmly, 'that what has passed this night is the best for which we could have prayed, and we have good need to give thanks for it.'

'So all is well?'

'All is very well, Father.'

'Then the rest may wait for morning. You need rest. But will you not come in with me and take some food and wine, before you sleep?'

'My wife,' said Hugh, gracefully evading, 'will be in some anxiety for me. You are kind, Father, but I would not have her fret longer than she need.'

The abbot eyed them both, and did not press them.

'And God bless you for that!' sighed Cadfael, toiling up the slight slope of the court towards the dortoir stair and the gatehouse where Hugh had hitched his horse. 'For I'm asleep on my feet, and even a good wine could not revive me.'

*   *   *

The moonlight was gone, and there was as yet no sunlight, when Olivier de Bretagne and Luc Meverel rode slowly in at the abbey gatehouse. How far they had wandered in the deep night neither of them knew very clearly, for this was strange country to both. Even when overtaken, and addressed with careful gentleness, Luc had still gone forward blindly, hands hanging slack at his sides or vaguely parting the bushes, saying nothing, hearing nothing, unless some core of feeling within him was aware of this calm, relentless pursuit by a tolerant, incurious kindness, and distantly wondered at it. When he had dropped at last and lain down in the lush grass of a meadow at the edge of the forest, Olivier had tethered his horse a little apart and lain down beside him, not too close, yet so close that the mute man knew he was there, waiting without impatience. Past midnight Luc had fallen asleep. It was his greatest need. He was a man ravished and emptied of every impulse that had held him alive for the past two months, a dead man still walking and unable quite to die. Sleep was his ransom. Then he could truly die to this waste of loss and bitterness, the awful need that had driven him, the corrosive grief that had eaten his heart out for his lord, who had died in his arms, on his shoulder, on his heart. The bloodstain that would not wash out, no matter how he laboured over it, was his witness. He had kept it to keep the fire of his hatred white-hot. Now in sleep he was delivered from all.

And he had awakened in the first mysterious pre-dawn stirring of the earliest summer birds, beginning to call tentatively into the silence, to open his eyes upon a face bending over him, a face he did not know, but remotely desired to know, for it was vivid, friendly and calm, waiting courteously on his will.

'Did I kill him?' Luc had asked, somehow aware that the man who bore this face would know the answer.

'No,' said a voice clear, serene and low. 'There was no need. But he's dead to you. You can forget him.'

He did not understand that, but he accepted it. He sat up in the cool, ripe grass, and his senses began to stir again, and record distantly that the earth smelled sweet, and there were paling stars in the sky over him, caught like stray sparks in the branches of the trees. He stared intently into Olivier's face, and Olivier looked back at him with a slight, serene smile, and was silent.

'Do I know you?' asked Luc wonderingly.

'No. But you will. My name is Olivier de Bretagne, and I serve Laurence d'Angers, just as your lord did. I knew Rainald Bossard well, he was my friend, we came from the Holy Land together in Laurence's train. And I am sent with a message to Luc Meverel, and that, I am sure, is your name.'

'A message to me?' Luc shook his head.

'From your cousin and lady, Juliana Bossard. And the message is that she begs you to come home, for she needs you, and there is no one who can take your place.'

He was slow to believe, still numbed and hollow within; but there was no impulsion for him to go anywhere or do anything now of his own will, and he yielded indifferently to Olivier's promptings. 'Now we should be getting back to the abbey,' said Olivier practically, and rose, and Luc responded, and rose with him. 'You take the horse, and I'll walk,' said Olivier, and Luc did as he was bidden. It was like nursing a simpleton gently along the way he must go, and holding him by the hand at every step.

They found their way back at last to the old track, and there were the two horses Hugh had left behind for them, and the groom fast asleep in the grass beside them. Olivier took back his own horse, and Luc mounted the fresh one, with the lightness and ease of custom, his body's instincts at least reawakening. The yawning groom led the way, knowing the path well. Not until they were halfway back towards the Meole brook and the narrow bridge to the highroad did Luc say a word of his own volition.

'You say she wants me to come back,' he said abruptly, with quickening pain and hope in his voice. 'Is it true? I left her without a word, but what else could I do? What can she think of me now?'

'Why, that you had your reasons for leaving her, as she has hers for wanting you back. Half the length of England I have been asking after you, at her entreaty. What more do you need?'

'I never thought to return,' said Luc, staring back down that long, long road in wonder and doubt.

No, not even to Shrewsbury, much less to his home in the south. Yet here he was, in the cool, soft morning twilight well before Prime, riding beside this young stranger over the wooden bridge that crossed the Meole brook, instead of wading through the shrunken stream to the pease-fields, the way by which he had left the enclave. Round to the highroad, past the mill and the pond, and in at the gatehouse to the great court. There they lighted down, and the groom took himself and his two horses briskly away again towards the town.

Luc stood gazing about him dully, still clouded by the unfamiliarity of everything he beheld, as if his senses were still dazed and clumsy with the effort of coming back to life. At this hour the court was empty. No, not quite empty. There was someone sitting on the stone steps that climbed to the door of the guest-hall, sitting there alone and quite composedly, with her face turned towards the gate, and as he watched she rose and came down the wide steps, and walked towards him with a swift, light step. Then he knew her for Melangell.

In her at least there was nothing unfamiliar. The sight of her brought back colour and form and reality into the very stones of the wall at her back, and the cobbles under her feet. The elusive grey between-light could not blur the outlines of head and hand, or dim the brightness of her hair. Life came flooding back into Luc with a shock of pain, as feeling returns after a numbing wound. She came towards him with hands a little extended and face raised, and the faintest and most anxious of smiles on her lips and in her eyes. Then, as she hesitated for the first time, a few paces from him, he saw the dark stain of the bruise that marred her cheek.

It was the bruise that shattered him. He shook from head to heels in a great convulsion of shame and grief, and blundered forward blindly into her arms, which reached gladly to receive him. On his knees, with his arms wound about her and his face buried in her breast, he burst into a storm of tears, as spontaneous and as healing as Saint Winifred's own miraculous spring.

He was in perfect command of voice and face when they met after chapter in the abbot's parlour, abbot, prior, Brother Cadfael, Hugh Beringar, Olivier and Luc, to set right in all its details the account of Rainald Bossard's death, and all that had followed from it.

'Unwittingly I deceived you, Father,' said Cadfael, harking back to the interview which had sent him forth in such haste. 'When you asked if we had entertained a murderer unawares, I answered truly that I did think so, but that we might yet have time to prevent a second death. I never realised until afterwards how you might interpret that, seeing we had just found the blood-stained shirt. But, see, the man who struck the blow might be spattered as to sleeve or collar, but he would not be marked by this great blot that covered breast and shoulder over the heart. No, that was rather the sign of one who had held a wounded man, a man wounded to death, in his arms as he died. Nor would the slayer, if his clothing was blood-stained, have kept and carried it with him, but burned or buried it, or somehow rid himself of it. But this shirt, though washed most carefully, still bore the outline of the stain clear to be seen, and it was carried as a sacred relic is carried, perhaps as a pledge to exact vengeance. So I knew that this same Luc whom we knew as Matthew, and in whose scrip the talisman was found, was not the murderer. But when I recalled all the words I had heard those two young men speak, and all the evidence of devoted attendance, the one on the other, then suddenly I saw that pairing in the utterly opposed way, as a pursuit. And I feared it must be to the death.'

The abbot looked at Luc, and asked simply: 'Is that a true reading?'

'Father, it is.' Luc set forth with deliberation the progress of his own obsession, as though he discovered it and understood it only in speaking. 'I was with my lord that night, close to the Old Minster it was, when four or five set on the clerk, and my lord ran, and we with him, to beat them off. And then they fled, but one turned back and struck. I saw it done, and it was done of intent! I had my lord in my arms—he had been good to me, and I loved him,' said Luc with grimly measured moderation and burning eyes as he remembered. 'He was dead in a mere moment, in the twinkling of an eye . . . And I had seen where the murderer fled, into the passage by the chapter house. I went after him, and I heard their voices in the sacristy—Bishop Henry had come from the chapter house after the council ended for the night, and there Ciaran had found him and fell on his knees to him, blurting out all. I lay in hiding, and heard every word. I think he even hoped for praise,'

263

said Luc with bitter deliberation.

'Is it possible?' wondered Prior Robert, shocked to the heart. 'Bishop Henry could not for one moment connive at or condone an act so evil.'

'No, he did not condone. But neither would he deliver over one of his own intimate servants as a murderer. To do him justice,' said Luc, but with plain distaste, 'his concern was not to cause further anger and quarrelling, but to put away and smooth over everything that threatened the empress's fortunes and the peace he was trying to make. But condone murder—no, that he would not. Therefore I overheard the sentence he laid upon Ciaran—though then I did not know who he was, nor that Ciaran was his name. He banished him back to his Dublin home, for ever, and condemned him to go every step of the way to Bangor and to the ship at Caergybi barefoot, and carrying that heavy cross. And if ever he put on shoes or laid by the cross from round his neck, then his forfeit life was no longer spared, but might be taken by whoever willed, without sin or penalty. But see,' said Luc, merciless in judgement, 'how he cheated! For not only did he give his creature the ring that would ensure him the protection of the church to Bangor, but also, mark, not one word was ever made public of this guilt or this sentence, so how was that forfeit life in danger? No one was to know of it but they two, if God had not prevented and brought there a witness to hear the sentence and take upon himself the vengeance due.'

'As you did,' said the abbot, and his voice was even and calm, avoiding judgement.

'As I did, Father. For as Ciaran swore to keep the terms laid down on pain of death, so did I swear an oath as solemn to follow him the length of the land, and if ever he broke his terms for a moment, to have his life as payment for my lord.'

'And how,' asked Radulfus in the same mild tone, 'did you know what man you were thus to hunt to his death? For you say you did not see his face clearly or know his name then.'

'I knew the way he was bound to go, and the day of his setting out. I waited by the roadside for one walking north, barefoot—and one not used to going barefoot, but very well shod,' said Luc with a brief, wry smile. 'I saw the cross at his neck. I fell in at his side, and I told him, not who I was, but what. I took another name, so that no failure nor shame of mine should ever cast a shadow on my lady or her house. One Evangelist in exchange for another! Step for step with him I went all this way, here to this place, and never let him from my sight and reach, night or day, and never let him forget that I meant to be his death. He could not ask help to rid himself of me, since I could then as easily strip him of his pilgrim holiness and show what he really was. And I could not denounce him—partly for fear of Bishop Henry, partly because neither did I want more feuding between factions—my feud was between two men!—but chiefly because he was mine, mine, and I would not let any other vengeance or danger reach him. So we kept together, he trying to elude me—but he was court-bred and tender and crippled by the miles—and I holding fast to him, and waiting.'

He looked up suddenly and caught the abbot's compassionate but calm eyes upon him, and his own eyes were wide, dark and clear. 'It is not beautiful, I know. Neither was murder beautiful. And this blotch was only mine—my lord went to his grave immaculate, defending one opposed to him.'

It was Olivier, silent until now, who said softly: *And so did you!'*

*   *   *

The grave, thought Cadfael at the height of the Mass, had closed firmly to deny Luc entrance, but that arm outstretched between his enemy and the knives of three assailants must never be forgotten. Hell had also shut its mouth and refused to devour him. He was young, clean, alive again after a kind of death. Yes, Olivier had uttered truth. His own life ventured, his enemy's life defended, what was there between Luc and his lord but the accident, the vain and random accident, of the death itself?

He recalled also, when he was most diligent in prayer, that these few days while Saint Winifred was manifesting her virtue in disentangling the troubled lives of some half-dozen people in Shrewsbury, were also the vital days when the fates of Englishmen in general were being determined, perhaps with less compassion and wisdom. For by this time the date of the empress's coronation might well be settled, the crown even now placed upon her head. No doubt God and the saints had that consideration in mind, too.

*   *   *

Matthew-Luc came once again to ask audience of the abbot, a little before Vespers. Radulfus had him admitted without question, and sat with him alone, divining his present need.

'Father, will you hear me my confession? For I need absolution from the vow I could not keep. And I do earnestly desire to be clean of the past before I undertake the future.'

'It is a right and a wise desire,' said Radulfus. 'One thing tell me—are you asking absolution for failing to fulfil the oath you swore?'

Luc, already on his knees, raised his head for a moment from the abbot's knee, and showed a face open and clear. 'No, Father, but for ever swearing such an oath. Even grief has its arrogance.'

'Then you have learned, my son, that vengeance belongs only to God?'

'More than that, Father,' said Luc. 'I have learned that in God's hands vengeance is safe. However long delayed, however strangely manifested, the reckoning is sure.'

When it was done, when he had raked out of his heart, with measured voice and long pauses for thought, every drifted grain of rancour and bitterness and impatience that fretted him, and received absolution, he rose with a great sigh, and raised a bright and resolute face.

'Now, Father, if I may pray of you one more grace, let me have one of your priests to join me to a wife before I go from here. Here, where I am made clean and new, I would have love and life begin together.'

CHAPTER SIXTEEN

On the next morning, which was the twenty-fourth day of June, the general bustle of departure began. There was packing of belongings, buying and parcelling of food and drink for the journey, and much leave-taking from friends newly made, and arranging of company for the road. No doubt the saint would have due regard for her own reputation, and keep the June sun shining until all her devotees were safely home, and with a wonderful tale to tell. Most of them knew only half the wonder, but even that was wonder enough.

Among the early departures went Brother Adam of Reading, in no great hurry along the way, for today he would go no farther than Reading's daughter-house of Leominster, where there would be letters waiting for him to carry home to his abbot. He set out with a pouch well filled with seeds of species his garden did not yet possess, and a scholarly mind still pondering the miraculous healing he had witnessed from every theological angle, in order to be able to expound its full significance when he reached his own monastery. It had been a most instructive and enlightening festival.

'I'd meant to start for home today, too,' said Mistress Weaver to her cronies Mistress Glover and the apothecary's widow, with whom she had formed a strong matronly alliance during these memorable days, 'but now there's such work doing, I hardly know whether I'm waking or sleeping, and I must stay over yet a night or two. Who'd ever have thought what would come of it, when I told my lad we ought to come and make our prayers here to the good saint, and have faith that she'd be listening? Now it seems I'm to lose the both of them, my poor sister's chicks; for

Rhun, God bless him, is set on staying here and taking the cowl, for he says he won't ever leave the blessed girl who healed him. And truly I don't wonder at it, and won't stand in his way, for he's too good for this wicked world outside, so he is! And now comes young Matthew—no, but it seems we must call him Luc, now, and he's well-born, if from a poor landless branch, and will come in for a manor or two in time, by his good kinswoman's taking him in . . .'

'Well, and so did you take the boy and girl in,' pointed out the apothecary's widow warmly, 'and gave them a roof and a living. There's good sound justice there.'

'Well, so Matthew, I mean Luc, he comes to me and asks for my girl for his wife, last night it was, and when I answered honestly, for honest I am and always will be, that my Melangell has but a meagre dowry, though the best I can give her I will, what says he? That as at this moment he himself has not one penny to his name in this world, but must go debtor to the young lord's charity that came to find him, and as for the future, if fortune favours him he'll be thankful, and if not, he has hands and a will, and can make a way for two to live. Provided the other is my girl, he says, for there's none other for him. So what can I say but God bless them both, and stay to see them wedded?'

'It's a woman's duty,' said Mistress Glover

heartily, 'to make sure all's done properly, when she hands over a young girl to a husband. But sure, you'll miss the two of them.'

'So I will,' agreed Dame Alice, shedding a few tears rather of pride and joy than of grief, at the advancement to semi-sainthood and promising matrimony of the charges who had cost her dear enough, and could now be blessed and sped on their respective and respectable ways with a quiet mind. 'So I will! But to see them both set up where they would be ... And good children both, that will take pains for me when I come to need, as I have for them.'

'And they're to marry here, tomorrow?' asked the apothecary's widow, visibly considering putting off her own departure for another day.

'They are indeed, before Mass in the morning. So it seems I'll have none to take home but my sole self,' said Dame Alice, dropping another proud tear or two, and wearing her reflected glory with admirable grace, 'when I take to the road again. But the day after tomorrow there's a sturdy company leaving southward, and with them I'll go.'

'And duty well done, my dear soul,' said Mistress Glover, embracing her friend in a massive arm, 'duty very well done!'

* * *

They were married in the privacy of the Lady Chapel, by Brother Paul, who was not only master of the novices, but the chief of their confessors, too, and already had Rhun under his care and instruction, and felt a fatherly interest in him, which the boy's affection very readily extended to embrace the sister. No one else was present but the family and their witnesses, and the bridal pair wore no festal garments, for they had none. Luc was in the serviceable brown cotte and hose he had slept in, out in the fields, and the same crumpled shirt, though newly washed and smoothed. Melangell was neat and modest in her homespun, proudly balancing her coronal of braided, deep-gold hair. They were pale as lilies, bright as stars, and solemn as the grave.

*   *   *

After high and moving events, daily life must still go on. Cadfael went to his work that afternoon well content. With the meadow grasses in ripe seed and the harvest imminent he had preparations to make for two seasonal ailments which could be relied upon to recur every year. There were some who suffered with eruptions on their hands when working in the harvest, and others who took to sneezing and wheezing, with running eyes, and needed lotions to help them.

272

He was busy bruising fresh leaves of dock and mandrake in a mortar for a soothing ointment, when he heard light, long-striding steps approaching along the gravel of the path, and then half of the sunlight from the wide-open door was cut off, as someone hesitated in the doorway. He turned with the mortar hugged to his chest, and the green-stained wooden pestle arrested in his hand, and there stood Olivier, dipping his tall head to evade the hanging bunches of herbs, and asking, in the mellow, confident voice of one assured of the answer, 'May I come in?'

He was in already, smiling, staring about him with a boy's candid curiosity, for he had never been here before. 'I've been a truant, I know, but with two days to wait before Luc's marriage I thought best to get on with my errand to the sheriff of Stafford, being so close, and then come back here. I was back, as I said I'd be, in time to see them wedded. I thought you would have been there.'

'So I would, but I was called out to Saint Giles. Some poor soul of a beggar stumbled in there overnight covered with sores, they were afraid of a contagion, but it's no such matter. If he'd had treatment earlier it would have been an easy matter to cure him, but a week or so resting in the hospital will do him no harm. Our pair of youngsters here had no need of me. I'm a part of what's over and done with for them, you're a part of what's beginning.'

273

'Melangell told me where I should find you, however, you were missed. And here I am.'

'And as welcome as the day,' said Cadfael, laying his mortar aside. Long, shapely hands gripped both his hands heartily, and Olivier stooped his olive cheek for the greeting kiss, as simply as for the parting kiss when they had separated at Bromfield. 'Come, sit, let me offer you wine—my own making. You knew, then, that those two would marry?'

'I saw them meet, when I brought him back here. Small doubt how it would end. Afterwards he told me his intent. When two are agreed, and know their own minds,' said Olivier blithely, 'everything else will give way. I shall see them both properly provided for the journey home, since I must go by a more roundabout way.'

When two are agreed, and know their own minds! Cadfael remembered confidences now a year and a half past. He poured wine carefully, his hand being a shade less steady than usual, and sat down beside his visitor, the young, wide shoulder firm and vital against his elderly and stiff one, the clear, elegant profile close, and a pleasure to his eyes. 'Tell me,' he said, 'about Ermina,' and was sure of the answer even before Olivier turned on him his sudden blinding smile.

'If I had known my travels would bring me to you, I should have had so many messages to bring you, from both of them. From Yves—

and from my wife!'

'Aaaah!' breathed Cadfael, on a deep, delighted sigh. 'So, as I thought, as I hoped! You have made good, then, what you told me, that they would acknowledge your worth and give her to you.' Two, there, who had indeed known their own minds, and been invincibly agreed! 'When was this match made?'

'This Christmas past, in Gloucester. She is there now, so is the boy. He is Laurence's heir—just fifteen now. He wanted to come to Winchester with us, but Laurence wouldn't let him be put in peril. They are safe, I thank God. If ever this chaos is ended,' said Olivier very solemnly, 'I will bring her to you, or you to her. She does not forget you.'

'Nor I her, nor I her! Nor the boy. He rode with me twice, asleep in my arms, I still recall the warmth and the shape and the weight of him. A good boy as ever stepped!'

'He'd be a load for you now,' said Olivier, laughing. 'This year past, he's shot up like a weed, he'll be taller than you.'

'Ah, well; I'm beginning to shrink like a spent weed. And you are happy?' asked Cadfael, thirsting for more blessedness even than he already had. 'You and she both?'

'Beyond what I know how to express,' said Olivier no less gravely. 'How glad I am to have seen you again, and been able to tell you so! Do you remember the last time? When I waited with you in Bromfield to take Ermina

275

and Yves home? And you drew me maps on the floor to show me the ways?'

There is a point at which joy is only just bearable. Cadfael got up to refill the wine-cups, and turn his face away for a moment from a brightness almost too bright. 'Ah, now, if this is to be a contest in "do-you-remembers" we shall be at it until Vespers, for not one detail of that time have I forgotten. So let's have this flask here within reach, and settle down to it in comfort.'

*   *   *

But there was an hour and more left before Vespers when Hugh put an abrupt end to remembering. He came in haste, with a face blazingly alert, and full of news. Even so he was slow to speak, not wishing to exult openly in what must be only shock and dismay to Olivier.

'There's news. A courier rode in from Warwick just now, they're passing the word north by stages as fast as horse can go.' They were both on their feet by then, intent upon his face, and waiting for good or evil, for he contained it well. A good face for keeping secrets, and under strong control now out of courteous consideration. 'I fear,' he said, 'it will not come as gratefully to you, Olivier, as I own it does to me.'

'From the south . . .' said Olivier, braced

and still. 'From London? The empress?'

'Yes, from London. All is overturned in a day. There'll be no coronation. Yesterday as they sat at dinner in Westminster, the Londoners suddenly rang the tocsin—all the city bells. The entire town came out in arms, and marched on Westminster. They're fled, Olivier, she and all her court, fled in the clothes they wore and with very little else, and the city men have plundered the palace and driven out even the last hangers-on. She never made move to win them, nothing but threats and reproaches and demands for money ever since she entered. She's let the crown slip through her fingers for want of a few soft words and a queen's courtesy. For your part,' said Hugh, with real compunction, 'I'm sorry! For mine, I find it a great deliverance.'

'With that I find no fault,' said Olivier simply. 'Why should you not be glad? But she . . . she's safe? They have not taken her?'

'No, according to the messenger she's safely away, with Robert of Gloucester and a few others as loyal, but the rest, it seems, scattered and made off for their own lands, where they'd feel safe. That's the word as he brought it, barely a day old. The city of London was being pressed hard from the south,' said Hugh, somewhat softening the load of folly that lay upon the empress's own shoulders, 'with King Stephen's queen harrying their borders. To get relief their only way was to drive the empress

277

out and let the queen in, and their hearts were on her side, no question, of the two they'd liefer have her.'

'I knew,' said Olivier, 'she was not wise—the Empress Maud. I knew she could not forget grudges, no matter how sorely she needed to close her eyes to them. I have seen her strip a man's dignity from him when he came submissive, offering support ... Better at making enemies than friends. All the more she needs,' he said, 'the few she has. Where is she gone? Did your messenger know?'

'Westward for Oxford. And they'll reach it safely. The Londoners won't follow so far, their part was only to drive her out.'

'And the bishop? Is he gone with her?' The entire enterprise had rested upon the efforts of Henry of Blois, and he had done his best for her, not entirely creditably but understandably and at considerable cost, and his best she herself had undone. Stephen was a prisoner in Bristol, but Stephen was still crowned and anointed king of England. No wonder Hugh's eyes shone.

'Of the bishop I know nothing as yet. But he'll surely join her in Oxford. Unless ...'

'Unless he changes sides again,' Olivier ended for him, and laughed. 'It seems I shall have to leave you in more haste than I expected,' he said with regret. 'One fortune rises, another falls. No sense in quarrelling with the lot.'

278

'What will you do?' asked Hugh, watching him steadily. 'You know, I think, that whatever you may ask of us here, is yours, and the choice is yours. Your horses are fresh. Your men will not yet have heard the news, they'll be waiting on your word. If you need stores for a journey, take whatever you will. Or if you choose to stay . . .'

Olivier shook his blue-black head, and the clasping curves of glossy hair danced on his cheeks. 'I must go. Not north, where I was sent. What use in that, now? South for Oxford. Whatever she may be else, she is my liege lord's liege lady, where she is he will be, and where he is, I go.'

They eyed each other silently for a moment, and Hugh said softly, quoting remembered words: 'To tell you truth, now I've met you I expected nothing less.'

'I'll go and rouse my men, and we'll get to horse. You'll follow to your house, before I go? I must take leave of Lady Beringar.'

'I'll follow you,' said Hugh.

Olivier turned to Brother Cadfael without a word but with the brief golden flash of a smile breaking through his roused gravity for an instant, and again vanishing. 'Brother . . . remember me in your prayers!' He stooped his smooth cheek yet again in farewell, and as the elder's kiss was given he embraced Cadfael vehemently, with impulsive grace. 'Until a better time!'

'God go with you!' said Cadfael.

And he was gone, striding rapidly along the gravel path, breaking into a light run, in no way disheartened or down, a match for disaster or for triumph. At the corner of the box hedge he turned in flight to look back, and waved a hand before he vanished.

'I wish to God,' said Hugh, gazing after him, 'he was of our party! There's an odd thing, Cadfael! Will you believe, just then, when he looked round, I thought I saw something of you about him. The set of the head, something . . .'

Cadfael, too, was gazing out from the open doorway to where the last sheen of blue had flashed from the burnished hair, and the last echo of the light foot on the gravel died into silence. 'Oh, no,' he said absently, 'he is altogether the image of his mother.'

An unguarded utterance. Unguarded from absence of mind, or design?

The following silence did not trouble him, he continued to gaze, shaking his head gently over the lingering vision, which would stay with him through all his remaining years, and might even, by the grace of God and the saints, be made flesh for him yet a third time. Far beyond his deserts, but miracles are neither weighed nor measured, but as uncalculated as the lightnings.

'I recall,' said Hugh with careful deliberation, perceiving that he was permitted to speculate, and had heard only what he was meant to hear, 'I do recall that he spoke of one for whose sake he held the Benedictine order in reverence . . . one who had used him like a son . . .'

Cadfael stirred, and looked round at him, smiling as he met his friend's fixed and thoughtful eyes. 'I always meant to tell you, some day,' he said tranquilly, 'what he does not know, and never will from me. He *is* my son.'

CONTENTS

WHO WAS CHARLES RENNIE MACKINTOSH ?

L ook for a book about Charles Rennie Mackintosh in a library and it will probably be shelved under '**architecture**'. But Mackintosh thought of himself as an artist. Many people nowadays think of him as an interior decorator and designer. In his short working life he designed over 400 pieces of furniture but completed only about a dozen buildings. Much of his time and talent was spent on alterations to buildings which already existed, or on preparing designs for projects which never happened. For the last ten years of his life he devoted himself to painting **watercolours**, and only just managed to earn a living by designing **textiles**.

A ROLLER-COASTER REPUTATION

Mackintosh's career began in obscurity and ended in failure. But for a brief period of little more than a decade he was hailed as one of the most exciting talents in Europe. Almost all of Mackintosh's work was

HEINEMANN Profiles

Charles Rennie Mackintosh

Richard Tames

First published in Great Britain by Heinemann
Library, Halley Court, Jordan Hill, Oxford
OX2 8EJ, a division of Reed Educational and
Professional Publishing Ltd.
Heinemann is a registered trademark of Reed
Educational & Professional Publishing Limited.

OXFORD MELBOURNE AUCKLAND
JOHANNESBURG BLANTYRE
GABORONE IBADAN PORTSMOUTH
NH (USA) CHICAGO

Designed by Visual Image
Originated by Dot Gradations
Printed and bound in Hong Kong/China

05 04 03 02 01
10 9 8 7 6 5 4 3 2 1

ISBN 0 431 08640 0
This title is also available in a hardback library
edition (ISBN 0 431 08633 8)

**British Library Cataloguing
in Publication Data**

Tames, Richard, 1946-
Charles Rennie Mackintosh. –
  (Heinemann Profiles)
1. Mackintosh, Charles Rennie, 1868–1928
  – Juvenile literature 2. Artists – Scotland
  – Biography – Juvenile literature
I. Title
709.2
ISBN 0431086400

Acknowledgements
The Publishers would like to thank the following
for permission to reproduce photographs: T & R
Annan & Sons Ltd: pp5, 18, 19, 33; Glasgow
Museums: pp36, 39; Glasgow School of Art
Collection: pp11, 15, 22, 23, 32, 40, 42, 43, 47;
Hunterian Art Gallery, University of Glasgow:
pp8, 10, 12, 24, 35, 38; Manchester Central
Libraries: p26; Popperfoto: p7; Scotland in Focus:
D Corrance pp4, 16, 44, 49, A G Firth pp9, 27,
29, I McLean p20, R Schofield pp17, 31, 51.

Cover photograph reproduced with permission of
T & R Annan & Sons Ltd.

Every effort has been made to contact copyright
holders of any material reproduced in this book.
Any omissions will be rectified in subsequent
printings if notice is given to the Publisher.

For more information about Heinemann Library
books, or to order, please phone ++44 (0)1865
888066, or send a fax to ++44 (0)1865 314091.
You can visit our website at
www.heinemann.co.uk.

Any words appearing in the text in bold, **like
this**, are explained in the Glossary.

donc in or around his native city of Glasgow, in
Scotland, but his designs were applauded and
imitated from Belgium to Hungary – though in
England he remained virtually unknown.

The last fifteen years of Mackintosh's life should
have seen him at the height of success. But, by the
time Mackintosh died at the age of 60, he had been
all but forgotten. The furniture, drawings and
paintings he left behind were officially valued as
virtually worthless. Had Mackintosh lived another
60 years, however, he would have seen a desk he
designed fetch the highest-ever price paid at auction
for an item of twentieth-century furniture.

BACKGROUND AND BOYHOOD

Charles Rennie Mackintosh, the fourth of eleven children, was born into an ordinary, respectable family in 1868. His father was a policeman and a keen gardener. The Mackintosh home, a three-roomed **tenement** flat in the oldest part of Glasgow, was always full of flowers.

When Mackintosh was six years old the family moved into a five-room house, in the **suburbs**. The house overlooked a vast cemetery, filled with

Glasgow – no mean city

Mackintosh was born, educated and found fame in one of the boom cities of the nineteenth century. By 1901 Glasgow was not only by far the largest city in Scotland but also the 'second city of the **British Empire**'. Its expansion was based on modern industries such as cotton, chemicals, engineering and, above all, shipbuilding. Glaswegians were rightly proud of their city and used their prosperity to support **civic** projects such as laying out Kelvingrove Park and constructing magnificent new **Gothic** buildings for the ancient university. In such a thriving city ambitious architects, artists and designers could see opportunities for work all around them.

elaborately carved tombs and monuments.
Mackintosh passed it every day on his way to school
and played there afterwards. As a schoolboy he had
great problems with reading and spelling but showed
an early talent for drawing. Mackintosh also
developed a limp, caused by a **contracted sinew** in
one foot. This disability made an office job desirable,
rather than one which involved physical work, and
at sixteen he started work with the architect John
Hutchison.

Much of Glasgow's prosperity was built on the shipbuilding industry.

A STAR STUDENT

After his day in the office Mackintosh went to evening classes at Glasgow School of Art. He worked hard at drawing, passed examinations and won prizes. He also studied **architecture** and was encouraged to enter designs for the annual National Competition of the Department of Science and Art. Francis Newbery, the School's new head, recognized Mackintosh as an outstanding student.

Mackintosh's design for an art school diploma uses the stretched, curving shapes he later applied to furniture and buildings.

In 1888, at the age of 20, Mackintosh was awarded a prize by the Glasgow Institute of Fine Arts for a design for a terraced house. In the same year he was paid for his first piece of professional work as a designer – a gravestone for Chief Constable Andrew McCall. Having a policeman for a father and a graveyard for a view had unexpected advantages.

Glasgow's architecture included both Gothic and Classical styles.

THE ARCHITECT AS ARTIST

In 1889 Mackintosh completed his **pupilage** and left John Hutchison to join Glasgow's fourth largest architectural **practice**, Honeyman and Keppie. Honeyman was 58, cultured and experienced. Keppie was only 27, a better organizer than designer, but brought much-needed cash into the business. Four-fifths of all the firm's projects were alterations or extensions, rather than **commissions** for brand-new buildings. This meant that there were few opportunities for Mackintosh to reveal his very individual talent.

Compare this sketch with the staircase towers shown on page 27.

CRM
1891.

MAKING A NAME

In 1890 Mackintosh's design for a public meeting hall won him a travelling studentship, offered in memory of Glasgow architect Alexander Thomson. The £60 prize paid for three months sketching in Italy. The following year Mackintosh lectured on Scottish **baronial architecture**, arguing that it was Scotland's national style, based on the **fortified** houses of the turbulent sixteenth and seventeenth centuries.

Outside office hours Mackintosh continued to enter design competitions. He also gave more public lectures and began to dress like an artist, wearing a floppy bow-tie and sporting a dashing, pointed moustache.

NEW FRIENDS, NEW INTERESTS

In 1891 Mackintosh and his best friend, fellow **draughtsman** Herbert McNair, met a group of women students who called themselves 'The **Immortals**'. The group included two sisters, Frances and Margaret Macdonald, who soon joined Mackintosh and McNair to become 'The Four'. Inspired by **Celtic myths** they produced paintings of willowy women and contorted trees in eerie twilight settings. Critics thought their work clever but weird, and called them 'The Spook School'.

PROFESSIONAL LANDMARKS, PRIVATE PASTIMES

This design combines circles and flowing curves in a balanced geometry.

As a junior **draughtsman** Mackintosh worked on projects controlled by senior colleagues, providing decorative details at Craigie Hall and Glasgow Art Club. He got his first big job, designing a rear extension for the *Glasgow Herald* building, in 1893. Its angular corner water-tower (a precaution against printing-room fires) is a clear echo of the Scottish baronial style, which featured overhanging turrets called bartizans. In 1895 he helped design Martyrs' Public School, to be built on the very street where he was born. Its unusual roof-timbers look distinctly Japanese – a new influence on art and design at that time.

In his spare time Mackintosh began to design wooden furniture and, as one of 'The Four', helped design **controversial** posters. Gleeson White, editor of *The Studio*, defended his work on the grounds that, although 'Mr Mackintosh's posters may be somewhat trying to the average person', they were wonderfully decorative – and did grab the attention of the passer-by, which is just what a poster is supposed to do.

The Glasgow Herald building – like a Scottish fortress in brick.

FAME AT LAST

1896 marked the turning-point in Mackintosh's life. He was invited to exhibit at the Arts and Crafts Exhibition Society's annual London show. He met Hermann Muthesius, a German architect and diplomat who was to be his greatest **champion**. He was introduced to Miss Kate Cranston, his best **patron**. And he won a competition to design a new home for the Glasgow School of Art, where he had so recently been a student.

MISS CRANSTON

Kate Cranston, sister of a Glasgow tea-merchant, was a firm believer that alcohol – the 'demon drink' – was a curse on Scotland. As an alternative to Glasgow's hundreds of public houses, she built up a chain of tea rooms, offering light meals, excellent service and elegant surroundings, where people could meet, chat, refresh themselves, read newspapers or play chess, dominoes or billiards. Miss Cranston realized that daring **decor** could be a talking-point for her customers and in 1896 **commissioned** the **controversial** Mackintosh to decorate the walls of the lunch room at her Buchanan Street premises. Two years later she asked him to design furniture as part of the make-over of her first branch, on Argyle Street.

THE SCHOOL OF ART

Francis ('Fra') Newbery was determined that Glasgow's School of Art should have a new home to match those of Birmingham or Manchester, its nearest rivals. In 1896 Honeyman and Keppie were invited to enter the design competition. What they submitted was Mackintosh's work but the formal credit went to Keppie, because he was the supervising **partner**.

Elongated female figures framed in drapery were a characteristic Mackintosh motif.

Mackintosh's masterpiece was built on a steeply sloping site, which meant that it had three storeys on one side and five on the other. It incorporated two dozen different types of studio and classroom, plus offices, meeting rooms, lecture theatres, common rooms, store areas, etc. At first glance a bold, bare building, it is in fact full of decorative detail. Light and spacious inside, it also meets the practical needs of teachers and students alike. The delicately curved iron window-brackets ingeniously double as supports for window-cleaners' planks. But many features were just for effect. The tower beside the entrance is higher than the staircase inside it. And the balcony over the entrance is useless for seeing the fine view – which is on the other side.

The Glasgow School of Art.

Bold straight lines are offset with delicate curving details.

OTHER TRIUMPHS

By the time the School of Art opened in 1899, Mackintosh had also completed Queen's Cross Church and hall at Springbank and the Free Church Halls at Ruchill Street. In 1897 Mackintosh and the Macdonald sisters were profiled in *The Studio* and mentioned in the first issue of a German art magazine, *Dekorative Kunst* (Decorative Art), whose publisher **commissioned** Mackintosh to design dining-room furniture. A Glasgow publisher, Robert Maclehose, ordered a bedroom.

In 1898 Mackintosh's partners set him to produce the firm's entries for competitions for a National Bank of Scotland headquarters and for the **pavilions** of a Glasgow International Exhibition to be held in 1901. Neither of these designs won but they showed that his seniors at last recognized his professionalism and talent.

MARRIAGE AND MARGARET

'The Four' ended as two twos. In 1899 Herbert McNair married Frances Macdonald and moved to Liverpool to teach decorative design. Mackintosh married Margaret Macdonald in 1900, and they settled in Glasgow.

Margaret Macdonald – a partner in art as well as marriage.

A HOME OF THEIR OWN

The Mackintoshes' first home was a flat. Only photographs survive to show how it set the basic pattern for their later work as decorators. The spacious rooms were kept uncluttered, except for a carefully positioned flower arrangement or a small group of pots. Even their Persian cats had their own cushions, either side of the fireplace. Walls, floors and ceilings were kept plain, as a backdrop to the few pieces of furniture which, like the light-fittings, were individually designed. The materials used for decorating were often unusual: coarse brown wrapping-paper on the dining-room walls; hard-wearing sailcloth, **stencilled** with a chequerboard pattern, on the stairs. Small panels of cheap **enamel** and coloured glass were used to catch the light with jewel-like gleams. The Mackintoshes' home was not

**The drawing-
room of the
Mackintoshes'
first home at 120
Mains Street.**

meant to display wealth but art and taste. The overall
effect was both striking and restful.

INDEPENDENT PROJECTS

Mackintosh's first independent architectural work
was a home for Glasgow provisions merchant,
William Davidson. The site, at Kilmacolm, gave the
house its name – Windyhill. Mackintosh's design was
suitably rugged, like a rambling Scottish **fortified**
manor–house, built of rubble and faced with
roughcast, called harling in Scotland. L-shaped in
plan, the living rooms were ranged along the long
arm of the L, the kitchen, laundry, etc. in the short
arm. Davidson's neighbours thought Windyhill
looked like a prison but the Davidsons remained
warm admirers of Mackintosh's work.

Hill House, Helensburgh, built for the Glasgow publisher Walter Blackie between 1902 and 1904, was a luxurious version of Windyhill, costing over twice as much. Based on the same L-shaped plan and also surfaced with harling, the house had over two dozen rooms and 58 windows of 40 different shapes, sizes or materials.

Hill House seen from the south-east.

Mackintosh's approach was to understand the family's way of life and design from the inside out, arranging the plan and then clothing it with the walls and roof, rather than deciding on the overall shape and adjusting the interior to fit. The library, where Blackie worked or had business meetings, was thoughtfully placed nearest the main door and as far

as possible from the nursery. The drawing-room had a **recess** to hold a piano or serve as a stage for family theatricals.

No detail was too small for Mackintosh's attention – the cupboard for table-linen was heated by a hot-water cylinder to keep it dry and the drawing-room window-seat had built-in magazine racks and a radiator concealed underneath. When he handed it over to its owner Mackintosh proudly declared: 'Here is the house. It is not an Italian villa, an English mansion house, a Swiss chalet or a Scottish castle. It is a dwelling house.'

EXHIBITIONS, COMPETITIONS AND PUBLICATIONS

Architects and designers accept that every completed project requires many **draft** designs as it **evolves**, and many schemes never get beyond the drawing board. But even plans that never happen can influence other artists when seen in exhibitions or magazines. This was certainly true of the Mackintoshes' work.

VIENNA

In 1897 a group of young Viennese artists formed a breakaway organization to promote modern art. Known as 'the **Secession**', they invited the Mackintoshes to contribute to their winter exhibition of 1900. The room-setting the

The Mackintoshes' exhibit at the 1900 Vienna Secession exhibition.

Mackintoshes put together included decorative panels, made of hessian, string and beads, which Margaret had made for one of Miss Cranston's tea rooms, and furniture they had designed for their own flat. Looking back on this first instance of recognition abroad, Mackintosh called it the high point of his life.

NO PRIZES

In 1901 Mackintosh entered a competition to design an Art-Lover's House. The competition was organized by Alexander Koch of Darmstadt, Germany, a publisher and manufacturer of wallpaper. There were 36 entries but no first prize was awarded. It would almost certainly have gone to Mackintosh if he had not broken the competition rules by failing to send three **perspective** views of his proposed interior designs. Koch did, however, award him a special prize and published Mackintosh's entry in one of his magazines.

Mackintosh's House for an Art-Lover. The symmetrical centre section contrasts with asymmetrical sections either side.

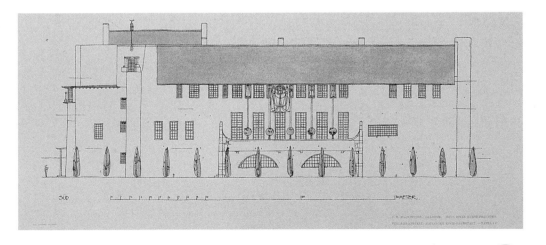

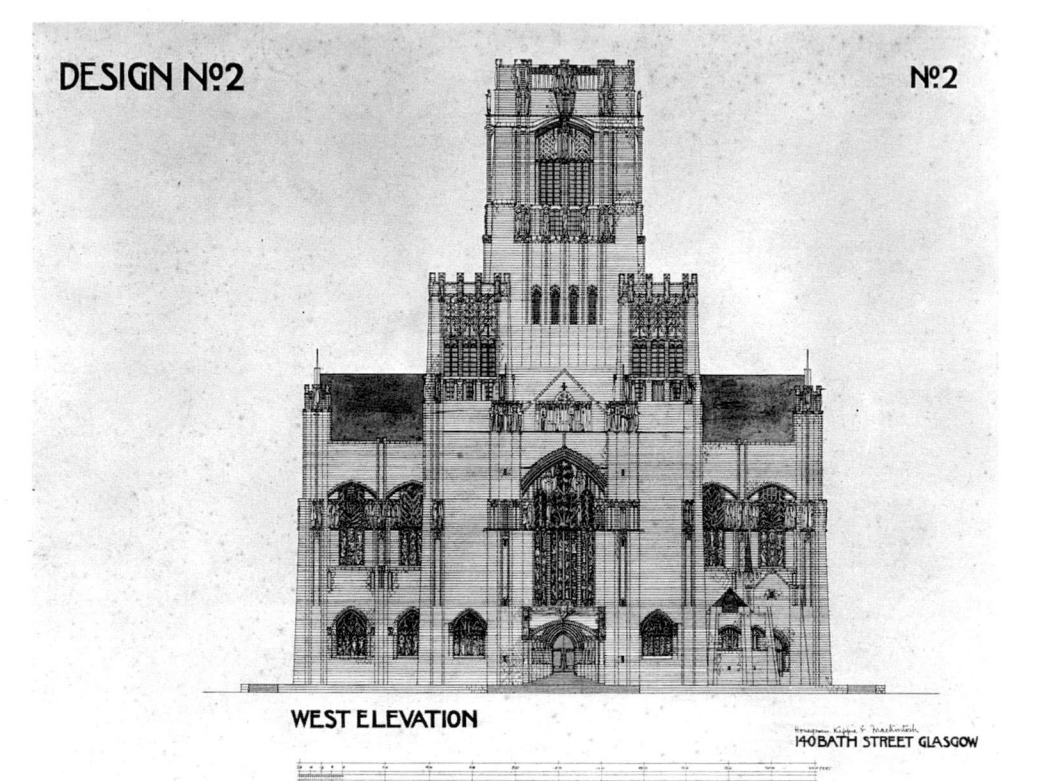

WEST ELEVATION

Honeyman Keppie & Mackintosh
140 BATH STREET GLASGOW

From drawing-board to dustbin – Mackintosh's rejected design for Liverpool Cathedral.

In the same year Mackintosh entered the competition to design a new Anglican Cathedral for Liverpool, basing his plan on the great medieval cathedral at Durham. Mackintosh's entry never even got to the second round. Mackintosh, probably wrongly, blamed the professional jealousy of one of the judges.

SUPPORT FROM FRIENDS

In 1902 the Mackintoshes' old teacher 'Fra' Newbery was put in charge of organizing the Scottish section of an International Exhibition of Modern Decorative Art, staged by the Italian government in Turin. At Newbery's invitation the Mackintoshes contributed a room-setting in white, pink, silver and green featuring roses everywhere and called 'The Rose Boudoir'. Pictures of their exhibit were published in *Deutsche Kunst und Dekoration* (German Art and Decoration), which later featured their work at Hill House.

Over the next decade the work of the Mackintoshes was to appear in other international exhibitions organized in Moscow, Dresden, Berlin, Budapest and Venice. But in Britain practical appreciation of their talent – outside the pages of **avant-garde** art magazines – remained confined to a circle of faithful supporters in and around Glasgow.

German support

In March 1902 *Dekorative Kunst* carried an article by Hermann Muthesius on the work of the Mackintoshes. It was the longest piece to appear about them in their lifetime. Concentrating on their joint work as interior decorators, rather than on Mackintosh's work as an architect, Muthesius stressed their unique talent to create rooms not just to contain works of art but to be works of art themselves. He also emphasized their ability to successfully combine opposing but **complementary** elements in Scottish tradition – from the dreamy, mystical world of **Celtic myth** and the dour harshness of the **Puritanical Calvinists** and **border chieftains**. Muthesius also devoted an entire chapter to the work of the Mackintoshes, particularly their Glasgow apartment, in his highly influential book *Das Englische Haus* (The English House), published in 1904.

THE PARTNER

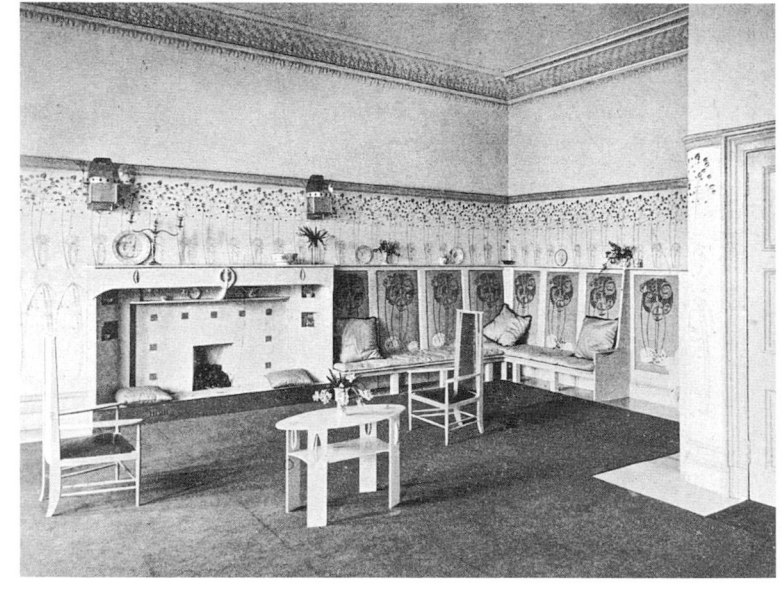

I n 1901 Mr Honeyman retired and Mackintosh
became a **partner** in the firm of Honeyman,
Keppie and Mackintosh. He was, however, very
much a junior partner. As a young married man
with no family fortune behind him he had to buy
his share of the business in stages over a number of
years. Fortunately Mackintosh's growing reputation
brought him an increasing number of
commissions, including church decorations,
furniture and fittings, and a music salon in Vienna.

SCOTLAND STREET SCHOOL
In 1903 Mackintosh was appointed by the School
Board of Glasgow to build a new school in Scotland
Street. Its design showed the same attention to

practical detail as Mackintosh had shown at Hill House. The games hall and domestic science room faced north so that they could be as cool as possible. In the cloakrooms hot-water pipes ran behind the coat hooks so that wet clothing could be dried out and warmed before the children put it on again. The grand staircase towers over the entrances have walls of glass to flood the interior with light. Infants were given their own little entrance so that they would not be jostled by the older children.

THE WILLOW TEA ROOMS

Glasgow's main street, Sauchiehall Street, means 'alley of the willows' and this gave Mackintosh his theme for decorating Miss Cranston's Willow Tea Rooms.

Scotland Street School.

Part of the pleasure of going to one of these tea rooms was to see other people and be seen by them. Mackintosh played on this by using screens and balconies to create three connected but separate apartments. Sitting in one of his high-backed chairs gave a sense of privacy, like being protected by a wall which wasn't actually there at all, seeing other people quite clearly but feeling somehow that they were not seeing you. The colour scheme **harmonized** rich purple upholstery with silver mirrors and soft grey carpets, offset by tiny touches of pink or mauve on doors or windows. The walls were covered with panels of white plaster and leaded glass. A local newspaper praised the overall effect as 'simply a marvel of the art of the upholsterer and decorator'.

In 1906 Mackintosh added a 'Dutch kitchen' to Miss Cranston's Argyle street premises. Apart from the tiles in the fireplace there was little that was Dutch about it. The main **motif** was a black–and-white chequer pattern, appearing in varying sizes. The only splashes of colour were the bright green Windsor-style chairs and a touch of pink in the one window. The overall effect was dark and cosy, quite unlike his previous schemes which played with light and relied on bold, swirling shapes and patterns.

Whereas Mackintosh's other projects were intended for particular groups of people – students or schoolchildren, a congregation of worshippers or the residents of a house – the tea rooms were open to anyone who cared to come in, giving thousands of people the chance to look at and experience 'the Mackintosh style'.

The Salon de Luxe at the Willow Tea Rooms.

THE BEGINNING OF THE END

By 1906 the Mackintoshes could afford to buy, rather than rent, a home. They chose a three-storey end of terrace house, built in the 1850s. Almost six months was spent altering and decorating it to their taste. The ground-floor dining-room was dark, reflecting their belief that a candle-lit table, sparkling with silver and glass, should be the main focus. The first-floor drawing-room, by contrast, was an explosion of light, thanks to the long, south-facing window they had put in.

LOSING HIS WAY

In 1906 Mackintosh was elected a Fellow of the Royal Institute of British Architects, recognizing his position as a leading member of the profession. But, just when he might be expected to have gone from strength to strength, his career began to falter.

In one of his public lectures Mackintosh had argued that any real artist must be prepared to struggle for his or her art and if necessary to put up with misunderstanding and even ridicule. In 'Fra' Newbery, Miss Cranston, William Davidson and Walter Blackie, Mackintosh had found supporters who believed in his talent. But such **patrons** were not easy to find. In 1906 Mackintosh agreed to build a house at Killearn, Stirlingshire, in whatever style the client wanted, which turned out to be a Cotswold stone manor-house. Mackintosh's design was perfectly competent but obviously the work was of little interest to him. Every time he visited the site he spent most of his time drinking in the local public house. In the end another architect was appointed to finish off the project.

Only the door hints at the unusual interior of the Mackintoshes' house.

THE SCHOOL OF ART EXTENDED

Mackintosh's powers of invention were, however, by no means dead. In 1907 he submitted plans – late – for an extension to the Glasgow School of Art. Its central core was a library whose complex woodwork and furniture show just how much Mackintosh had absorbed from the craft techniques of Japan. Three massive windows, 25 feet high, flood the interior with light. Mackintosh also designed special box-like light-fittings which directed light downwards onto individual study-spaces. Nowadays the Glasgow School of Art is regarded as Mackintosh's masterpiece and a work of genius. But when it was completed in 1909 many Glasgow folk thought it looked very odd indeed.

Mackintosh's library at the Glasgow School of Art.

The firm in crisis

The amount of business coming into the **practice** halved in 1910 and halved again in 1911. Mackintosh's only major **commissions** were **refurbishments** for Miss Cranston's tea rooms. According to people who worked with him at the time, Mackintosh would often go to lunch at one and drink the afternoon away, not returning until just before the office closed at five. He needed the routine and discipline of coming to work – but could no longer find work to do.

Strong natural lighting contrasts dark wood and light textiles.

THE TURNING-POINT

Mackintosh's only architectural work in 1912 was a ladies' hairdressers and minor alterations to some houses. But, even though he could scarcely plead pressure of work, when a competition was announced to design a huge new teacher training college, Mackintosh failed to go beyond producing a few vague sketches. As the deadline drew nearer the responsibility for designing the firm's entry was simply passed over to someone else.

RESIGNATION

In June 1913 Mackintosh resigned his partnership. His relations with Keppie had never been particularly good. Keppie may well have resented Mackintosh's clearly superior talent as a designer. As the firm's main organizer he was doubtless irritated by Mackintosh's **perfectionism** which often led to delays, cost over-runs and arguments with clients. And Keppie's sister, Jessie, had a longstanding **grievance** against Mackintosh. She had once hoped she might marry him, and believed he had dropped her in favour of Margaret.

FRUSTRATION

After leaving the partnership Mackintosh made a half-hearted attempt to go it alone. He missed the

A simple square motif in varying sizes makes a complex effect.

routine of the office but made no effort to set one up, preferring to work at home. Walter Blackie called round – 'I found Mackintosh sitting at his desk, evidently in a deeply depressed frame of mind. To my enquiry as to how he was keeping and what he was doing he made no response. But presently he began to talk slowly and **dolefully**. He said how hard he found it to receive no general recognition; only a very few saw merit in his work and the many passed him by ... He was leaving Glasgow, he told me ... I never saw Mackintosh again.'

The Hall at 78 Derngate, Northampton.

GOING SOUTH

In 1914 the Mackintoshes settled in Walberswick, on the Suffolk coast. Mackintosh painted **watercolours** of flowers for a book to be published in Germany. When war broke out with Germany and Austria in August 1914, the planned book had to be shelved. War also cut Mackintosh off from his greatest admirers, in central Europe, who might have saved his career.

Unfortunately war also brought spy scares, even to sleepy Suffolk. Mackintosh's solitary life and strange accent made local people suspicious. In May 1915 soldiers raided his lodgings and found letters to artists in Vienna. Mackintosh was ordered to leave the east coast, where a German invasion was thought most likely.

LONDON

In August 1915 the Mackintoshes settled in neighbouring studios in Chelsea, London. Drawings surviving from this period show Mackintosh's designs for a block of shops and offices, a warehouse, a fountain, lamp **standards** and a war memorial. None came to anything. Thanks to the war, big architectural projects were impossible. But the war was good for engineering firms. In 1916 the engineer Wenman J. Bassett–Lowke asked Mackintosh to alter, redecorate and furnish a narrow, terraced house he had bought in Northampton. Mackintosh was inspired and transformed 78 Derngate into a stunning residence.

Transformation

Mackintosh's transformation of 78 Derngate in Northampton was a minor miracle. He put a bay window on the dull street front. He turned the staircase sideways, changing a tiny front parlour into a hall doubling as a lounge and making space for a pantry and bathroom. Adding a three-storey bay to the back enlarged the basement kitchen and dining-room and gave balconies to two bedrooms. The ingenious alterations were matched by dramatic decorations, contrasting black walls, screens and **lacquered** furniture with bright **stencilled** panels of bold, triangular patterns.

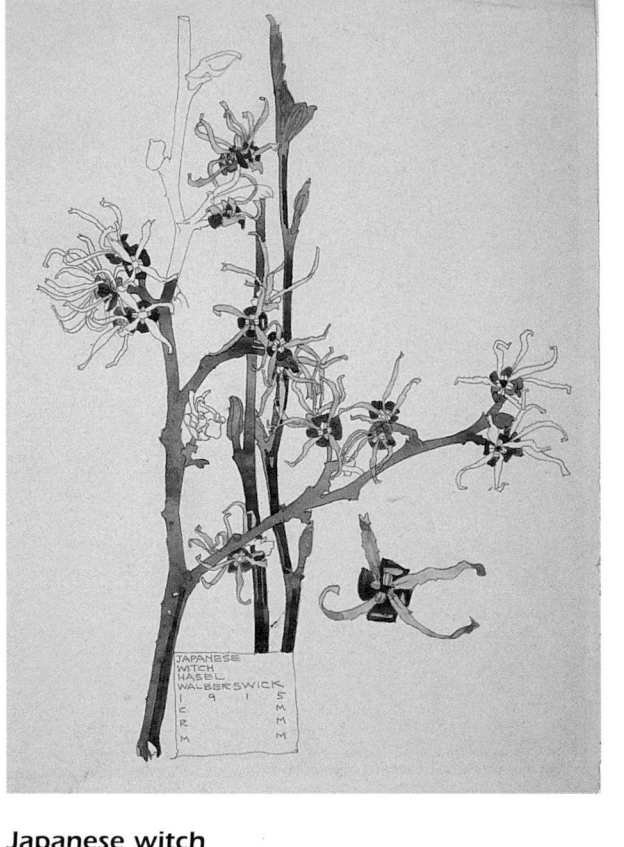

Mackintosh's only other war-time project was the Dug-Out, a basement addition to Miss Cranston's Willow Tea Rooms. Back in Chelsea both he and Margaret designed **textiles** to bring in cash they badly needed. Apart from that Mackintosh spent his time on **watercolours** of flowers and designing sets and costumes for The Plough, a local theatre group.

Japanese witch hazel painted in a Japanese style.

DESIGNS FOR DISAPPOINTMENT

By the war's end Mackintosh was reduced to begging William Davidson of Kilmacolm to buy a picture so that he could pay his outstanding rent and taxes. In 1920 things finally seemed to look up when a large building-plot became available in Glebe Place, where Mackintosh lived. Within the year artistic friends asked him to design three neighbouring studio houses, a block of apartments and a small theatre. But money and planning problems meant that only one was ever built – painter Harold Squire's studio house at No. 49. And he moved out two years later after seeing a ghostly rider. (A horse, buried on the site, was found during building.)

Designing textiles still brought in a trickle of money. Publisher Walter Blackie **commissioned** some designs for leaflets and book covers. But, frustrated by the failure of his Chelsea projects, Mackintosh became increasingly depressed. The last entry in his office diary, 13th January 1921, recorded the purchase of three pencils and two bottles of ink – but no project to use them on. Perhaps it was time to move again.

Hours on this clock are marked by 1 to 12 tiny holes.

RETIREMENT AND REMEMBRANCE

With no major project to work on Mackintosh became frustrated and depressed. J. D. Fergusson suggested a long holiday in the sunshine. In 1923 the Mackintoshes left London for southern France where they could live cheaply. What began as a long holiday stretched into a four-year stay. Mackintosh at last accepted that his career as an architect was over and chose to devote himself to an old and constant passion – **watercolour** painting.

In France Mackintosh painted both flower studies and dramatic landscapes.

After moving from one modest hotel to another the Mackintoshes finally settled in the winters at the Hotel du Commerce at Port Vendres. In the summers they retreated inland to the mountains, where it was cooler and even cheaper to live. Money was a real problem. When Margaret went to London for medical treatment in 1927, Mackintosh was wretchedly lonely without her. To save on postage he would wait until he had filled five sheets – the most that could be sent for the cheapest stamp – before sending off each letter. Margaret, meanwhile, tried to sell some of her husband's flower paintings to *Homes and Gardens* magazine.

FLOWERS AND LANDSCAPES

Mackintosh, who painted outdoors most of the time, appreciated the fine climate and also enjoyed the good French food and wine. The bright colours and harsh, rocky landscape of the region fascinated him but he felt no need to paint it exactly as it was. When picturing the village of Palalda, for example, he left out buildings he disliked and changed the colour of the roofs. Mackintosh was less interested in recording a view than in re-designing it to his taste. He worked slowly at his watercolours, finishing only about 40 in all. Both his flower pictures and his landscapes were painted in fine detail. A picture could take up to three weeks and when the weather was bad nothing got done.

No happy ending

Mackintosh intended to do enough watercolours for a show in London. But it was not to be. After complaining that French tobacco blistered his mouth he returned to Britain for treatment and was diagnosed as having cancer of the throat and tongue. In 1928 he went into hospital for painful **radium** treatment. For a few months he was well enough to sit out under a tree in the garden of a rented house in Hampstead. He died, aged sixty, on 19 December 1928 and was cremated at Golders Green Cemetery in north London. Margaret went back to France each year for the summer and died five years later.

Mackintosh at 52 – and looking even older.

CHARLES RENNIE WHO ... ?

In 1929 a group of Austrian architects, after tracking down an address for Mackintosh, invited him to Vienna so that they could honour his influence on the art and architecture of their country. They did not even know that their hero had died.

After Margaret's death the entire contents of their Chelsea studio were valued at £88. A large collection of Mackintosh's drawings and 31 of his paintings were listed as being 'practically of no value'. Four of the remarkable chairs Mackintosh designed were valued at £1. Just over 40 years later a single Mackintosh chair would be sold at auction for £9,300!

A meeting room at the Glasgow School of Art.

STILL STANDING

A lthough some of Mackintosh's buildings have been demolished most are still standing, some have been restored and a number are open to visitors. Hill House in Helensburgh is now owned by the National Trust for Scotland and open to visitors, who can see an audio-visual programme about the architect's life. The gardens are being restored to Mackintosh's original design.

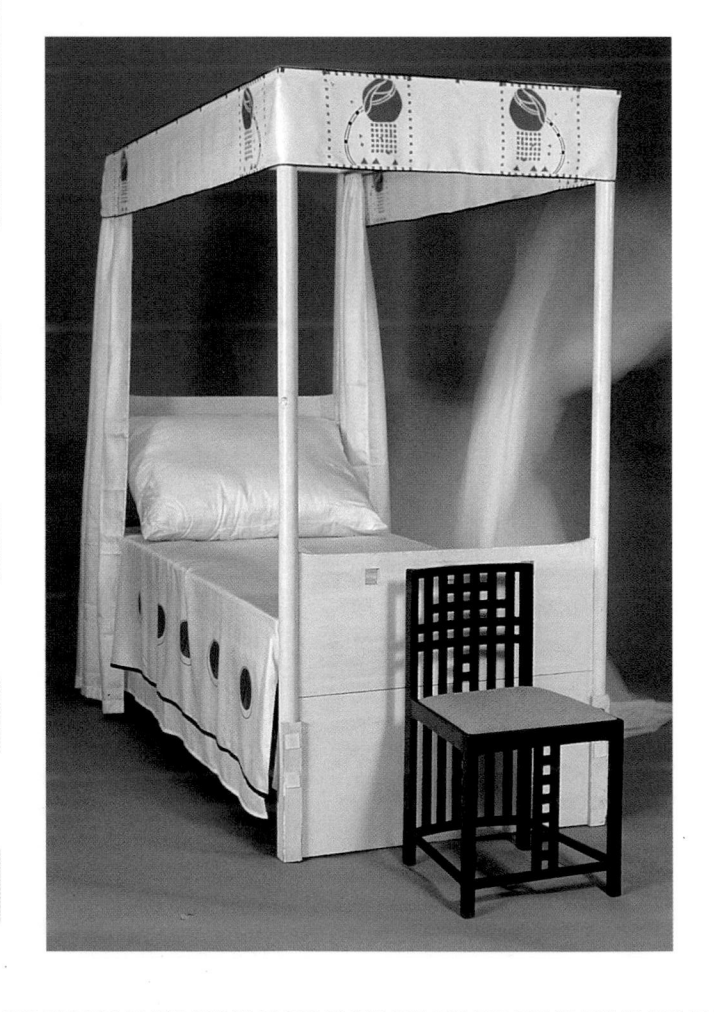

Chair and bed from Hous'hill, Glasgow, home of Miss Cranston.

Public buildings in Glasgow

○ The Glasgow School of Art, now recognized as one of Mackintosh's greatest works, is still an art school.

○ The Willow Tea Room at 217 Sauchiehall Street has been partly restored to his original design but most of it is now a jeweller's.

○ Queen's Cross Church at 870 Garscube Road is now the headquarters of the Charles Rennie Mackintosh Society, with its
○ own information centre, reference library and bookstall.

○ Scotland Street School is now a Museum of Education, illustrating the changes in school furniture and equipment since Mackintosh's day.

○ Craigie Hall at 6 Rowan Road contains a music room and library incorporating Mackintosh designs.

○ The premises of the *Glasgow Herald* are at 68-76 Mitchell Street and those of the *The Daily Record* are at 20-28 Renfield
○ Lane.

○ Other surviving Mackintosh exteriors include Martyr's Public School, Ruchill Church Hall and the Ladies' Art Club.

FURNITURE AND INTERIOR DESIGN

Mackintosh furniture can be seen in the main Glasgow Museum and Art Gallery in Kelvingrove Park and in the Hunterian Art Gallery in Hillhead Street. The Hunterian collection includes a reconstruction of three floors of the now demolished home at 6 Florentine Terrace where the Mackintoshes lived between 1906 and 1914. The rooms show all the alterations and improvements they made to the original house, together with some from their flat at 120 Mains Street.

The Glasgow School of Art has furniture from Windyhill and several of Miss Cranston's Tea Rooms. Other public collections containing work by Mackintosh include the British Museum, Tate Gallery and Victoria and Albert Museum in London, the Scottish National Gallery of Modern Art in Edinburgh, Northampton Museum, Brighton Museum and Graves Art Gallery in Sheffield. Overseas Mackintosh is represented in collections in Paris, Vienna, Trondheim, New York and Richmond, Virginia.

MACKINTOSH REBORN

Since 1973, when the University of Glasgow granted them the legal right, the Italian firm Cassina has reproduced furniture in Mackintosh designs. They began with four chairs and expanded the list to twenty different items, all faithfully reproduced to his **specifications**. The Mackintosh **copyright** expired 50 years after his death, so since 1978 the 'Mackintosh' style has been borrowed in the design of clocks and cutlery, tiles and **textiles**, light-fittings and lampshades. Many of these items are packaged and marketed with 'Mackintosh' lettering, despite the fact that he never designed a whole alphabet.

Mackintosh is unlikely to have approved the greedy abuse of his ideas but he would surely have been flattered by the construction in 1992 of an Artist's

Cottage at Farr, near Inverness, based on a design of his, prepared in 1900 but never built. Even more pleasing would be the knowledge that the Art-Lover's House he submitted for the 1901 Darmstadt competition has now been built at Bellahouston Park, Glasgow, as an international study centre for **architecture** and the visual arts.

A Mackintosh chair manufactured by Cassina of Milan.

CHARLES RENNIE MACKINTOSH – OPINIONS

'… if one were to go through the list of truly original artists, the creative minds of the modern movement, the name of Charles Mackintosh would certainly be included even amongst the few that one can count on the fingers of a single hand.'   Hermann Muthesius, German architect, diplomat and personal friend, 1902

'No artist owes less to tradition than Charles Rennie Mackintosh: as an **originator** he is supreme.'
J.Taylor, art critic, 1906

'The whole **modernist movement** in European **architecture** looks to him as one of its chief originators.'
Obituary of Charles Rennie Mackintosh, *The Times*, 1928.

… the European counterpart of Frank Lloyd Wright and one of the few true forerunners of the most ingenious juggler with space now alive: Le Corbusier. Le Corbusier once confessed that his desire in building is to create poetry. Mackintosh's attitude is very similar. Building in his hands becomes an **abstract** art, both musical and mathematical.'
Professor Nikolaus Pevsner, architectural historian, 1936

The Willow
Tea Rooms
exterior
today.

'During the planning and building of the Hill House I necessarily saw much of Mackintosh and could not but recognize, with wonder, his inexhaustible fertility in design and his astonishing powers of work ... he was a man of much practical competence, satisfactory to deal with in every way, and of a most likeable nature.'

Walter Blackie, publisher and **patron**, 1943

'Employing only the finest obtainable craftsmen, accepting only the finest materials and workmanship, never hurrying, he lost money on every job he undertook, was the despair of his **partners**, and lived and died a gloriously poor man. But he **revolutionized** world architecture.'

Desmond Chapman-Huston, friend, 1947

'... no English craft furniture had the daring of that designed by Charles Rennie Mackintosh for his Glasgow buildings ...'

Marigold Coleman,
Deputy Director of the Crafts Council, 1983

'Although Mackintosh is now one of the world's most famous architects, his work was not always highly rated. He died in 1928 a neglected figure and the postwar period saw some of his most famous buildings threatened with demolition. It was not until the 1960s that his work was reassessed, and his importance as a key **transitional** figure from the **historicism** of the nineteenth century to the **abstraction** of the twentieth century acknowledged. '

Catherine McDermott,
university lecturer in design history, 1997

Mackintosh – no longer forgotten.

CHARLES RENNIE MACKINTOSH – TIMELINE

1865	Margaret Macdonald born
1868	Charles Rennie Mackintosh born
1884	Begins training under John Hutchison, architect
1888	Enters first design competition, for a mountain chapel
1889	Joins architectural partnership of Honeyman and Keppie
1890	Wins the Alexander Thomson Travelling Studentship
1891	Lectures on 'Scottish Baronial Architecture' and tours Italy Meets Margaret Macdonald
1893	Designs an extension to the *Glasgow Herald* building
1895	Assists in designs for Martyrs' Public School
1896	Introduced to Hermann Muthesius by Francis Newbery Catherine Cranston commissions decorations for her Buchanan Street Tea Rooms
1897	Profiled with the Macdonald sisters in *The Studio* magazine
1897–1899	Queen's Cross Church built First phase of the Glasgow School of Art built
1898	Exhibits in Munich
1899–1901	Windyhill, Kilmacolm built
1900	Marries Margaret Macdonald Exhibits with the Vienna Secession
1901	Enters the Darmstadt competition for design of An Art-Lover's House Designs the *Daily Record* office, Glasgow Becomes a partner in Honeyman and Keppie
1902	Designs Scottish section of the Exhibition of Modern Decorative Art, Turin Muthesius profiles the decorative work of the Mackintoshes in *Dekorative Kunst*

1902–1903 Hill House, Helensburgh built

1903 Designs decorations and furniture for Miss Cranston's Willow Tea Rooms

Exhibits in Moscow

1906 Scotland Street School built

Elected a Fellow of the Royal Institute of British Architects

Moves from 120 Mains Street to 6 Florentine Terrace

1907–1909 Glasgow School of Art extended

1909 Paints flower studies at Withyam, Kent

1910 Disastrous decline in business for Mackintosh's architectural practice

1911 Designs a Cloister Room and Chinese Room at the Ingram Street Tea Room

1913 Resigns from his architectural partnership with Honeyman and Keppie

1914 Outbreak of the First World War

Moves to Walberswick, Suffolk

1915 Settles in Chelsea, London

1916 Designs decorations and furniture for 78 Derngate, Northampton

Designs fabrics for Liberty's and Foxton and Sefton of London

1920 Prepares designs for studios, flats and a theatre in Chelsea

1923 Moves to France

1927 Diagnosed with cancer of the tongue and returns to London

1928 Death of Charles Rennie Mackintosh

1933 Death of Margaret Mackintosh

Mackintosh Memorial exhibition held at McLellan Galleries, Glasgow

1952 Thomas Howarth's biography of Mackintosh published

1963 Mackintoshes' home at 6 Florentine Terrace demolished

1973 Cassina of Milan begin to reproduce Mackintosh furniture

1977 Queen's Cross Church becomes headquarters of Charles Rennie Mackintosh Society

1978 Copyright of Mackintosh's designs expires

1992 Artist's Cottage built at Farr to Mackintosh designs

GLOSSARY

abstract not intended to look like a particular thing

architecture the art of designing buildings

asymmetrical when the two halves of something are not symmetrical

avant-garde new or experimental movement in art

baronial in the style of a lord or chieftain

border chieftain head of clan of warriors who raided the border lands between Scotland and England

British Empire overseas areas ruled or settled by Britain

Celtic myth ancient legends about gods and heroes of the non-English speaking peoples of the British Isles – the Scots, Welsh and Irish

champion strong supporter of a person or idea

civic of or to do with a city

cloister open-sided, covered passageway

commission order for a job or project

complementary going well together

contracted sinew part of a muscle which fails to flex properly

controversial causing an argument

copyright legal right to produce copies and control an original artistic work

decor decoration of a room or house

draft first or early sketch

dolefully sadly

draughtsman person skilled at technical drawing

enamel coloured, glasslike decorative coating on metal

evolve take shape gradually through stages

Fellow full member of a professional association

fortified strengthened for defence

Gothic architectural style of the Middle Ages, featuring pointed arches

grievance cause for complaint or resentment

harmonized blended in a pleasing way

historicism tradition relying on the ideas and examples of the past

immortal living for ever

Impressionist style of painting which aims to convey the effects of light

lacquered painted with lacquer as a decoration or protection

modernist movement group of artists who favoured new or experimental styles

motif decorative shape

originator inventor or pioneer

partner senior member of a firm entitled to a share in the profits

patron person who uses their money to support an art or artist

pavilion temporary building to house an exhibition

perfectionism demanding the highest standards

practice architect's business and network of clients

pupilage period of training as the pupil of a master

Puritanical Calvinists followers of religious teacher John Calvin who held very strict views

radium radioactive substance used to treat cancer

recess part of a room set back from the wall

refurbishment renewal of decoration or fittings

Renaissance style based on the 'Classical' models of ancient Greece and Rome

revolutionized changed completely

roughcast surfacing made of tiny stones

secession breakaway movement

specifications particular requirements

standard frame to hold up a lamp

stencilled pattern painted on using a cut-out

suburbs areas where people live, on the edges of town

symmetrical where the two halves of something are identical reflections of each other on opposite sides of a central line

tenement large block of flats

textiles woven cloth

transitional linking one period or style with the next

watercolours paintings done on paper with water-based paints

Whistler (John Abbot MacNeill) nineteenth-century American painter who settled in London, and is famous for his portraits of people and views of the Thames

INDEX

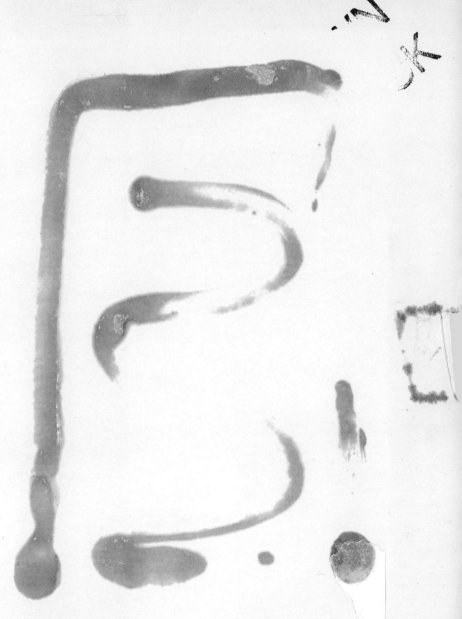

FILM ESSAYS
with a lecture

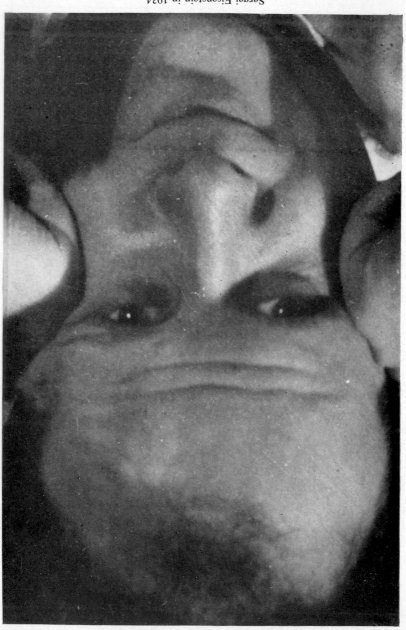

Sergei Eisenstein in 1934.
Photograph by Jay Leyda

FILM ESSAYS

with a Lecture

by

SERGEI EISENSTEIN

edited by

JAY LEYDA

Foreword by Grigori Kozintsev

London

DENNIS DOBSON

This collection of translations

is dedicated to

PERA ATASHEVA

First published in 1968 by

Dobson Books Ltd.

80 Kensington Church Street, London W.8

Made and printed in Great Britain by

The Garden City Press Limited

Letchworth, Hertfordshire

SBN 234 77822 9

CONTENTS

ILLUSTRATIONS

Eisenstein in 1934   *Frontispiece*

Foreword

by

GRIGORI KOZINTSEV

An Eisenstein is born but once in a century. Human nature reaches a zenith of spiritual development. An instrument of astonishing responsiveness is formed, unique and never to be duplicated: a genius has been added to mankind. If that man is an artist, his imaginative world leaves a mark on the real world of his time and conquers time itself: some part of his epoch will live on in his art. He does not function as a mirror: the quality of his image of the epoch stirs more than a reflecting surface.

The art of Eisenstein was inseparable from his temperament, and his taste. Temperament and taste could be observed in everything about him—in the nature of his creative work, in the appearance of his rooms, in his way of speaking. Wherever he lived, you could walk in and know at once who lived there. All bore the imprint of this occupant. From the door-sill, heaps of books; doubled rows of them on the shelves; on tables, chairs, anywhere: philosophy, painting, psychology, theory of humour, history of photography, dictionaries of slang and argot, circus, caricature ... even to name their subjects would consume too much space here. Erudition and imagination combined to produce inventions of fun all around the room. He treated objects like pieces of a joke: a strange bas-relief on the wall turned out to be a globe of the earth sawn in half set in a magnificent renaissance frame; a silver candelabrum served as a necktie-hanger. A corner of one book-shelf was filled with a gallery of astonishing faces, autographed— from the inventor of the safety razor, Gillette, to Yvette Guilbert. On top of the wardrobe personages from the Chinese theatre gestured among wooden Russian angels. In

7

the place of honour—a rubber glove inscribed to him by Harpo Marx (who had employed it in a "number" as an udder). Any room of his reminded one of a theatre warehouse, inundated with objects from some recent carnival. No resemblance to a collector of precious antiques. No ordinary order, no hint of recognizable unity. His juxtapositions had a single governing power: contrasts. And over it all he thumbed his nose at aesthetics.

But books were his passion. His library was in ceaseless motion, here books were allowed no rest: the volumes of a work were rarely in the right order; you could see bookmarks (made of anything that was handy!) sticking out everywhere, margins were thick with annotations, even sketches, many lines were marked and underlined, often with coloured pencils. Everything in the room was sucked into this whirlpool. But the appearance of the room often changed. And all this apparatus of treatises, reproductions, curiosities—from research into primitive thought to a nineteenth-century rebus—was treated like some sort of clay: the sculptor remoulds it, converts it all into pliable material for his next work. Without comprehending this fusion and flexibility its nourishment of Eisenstein's art can be either under-estimated or over-estimated.

When Eisenstein entered films he decided: It's time to plan the miracle of art. If only we apply more strength, we'll find the philosopher's stone, and straightway *any* material can be changed to gold. And this pure gold—composition to shake the souls of people—would have nothing in common with what we knew as artistic cinema. A new art would be shaped somewhere where the sciences must intersect all those monumental forms of art—the fresco, the symphony, the tragic rituals of ancient theatre—there, where the structure of pathos lived and waited to be used.

In order to understand the art of Eisenstein, one must find the unfinished research in his films, and find in his research—the films he never made. Perhaps of all that he achieved *Potemkin* was the only completed work, and that because there was no time to spare, no time to reconsider the problems.

* * *

Nowadays there is little respect for aesthetic manifestoes: who in art today attaches any value to words? But our generation felt differently about this. Without having accomplished very much, people would immediately launch theoretical structures, and attract disciples. All young film directors were to this degree also "researchers". No limits to their production plans, but the projects rarely found room in the actual films they made. Such research usually came to an end in montage-lists, diaries, stenographic records of feelings. Substance consisted not so much in analysis as in prospects. It is not easy to read such old pages. Even their language belongs to other times.

Eisenstein's first essays had an individuality peculiar to him. One was struck by an oddness of juxtaposition: the wildest artistic ideas with an academically impassive tone, and scientific phraseology:

> The basic materials of the theatre arise from the spectator himself—and from our guidance of the spectator into the desired direction (or desired mood), which is the main task of every functional theatre (agitational, poster, health education, etc.). The weapons for this purpose are to be found in all the left-over apparatus of theatre (the "chatter" of Ostuzhev no more than the pink tights of the prima-donna, a roll on the kettledrums as much as Romeo's soliloquy, the cricket on the hearth no less than the cannon fired over the heads of the audience). For all, in their individual ways, bring us to a single ideal— from their individual laws to their common quality of an *attraction*.

This was written in 1923, and we fought academicism with lowly genres (circus and vaudeville, for instance), shocking juxtapositions and a cult of tricks—how this smells of the past! Note, however, that young people then did not resort to scientific terminology, they neither sought nor used a calm voice. And no one had yet referred to the pink tights of the prima-donna as an "ideal" or "weapon". Eisenstein seems to have made use of LEF theories: functionalism, directness, social demand. But the term "attrac-

tion" itself, with its brisk circus associations and objective
(Ostrovsky adapted to the music-hall) had little in common
with constructivism. The same issue of LEF that published
Eisenstein's essay included a photograph, LEF in practice:
two armchairs arranged in a bed. No, the "ideal" of Sergei
Mikhailovich was the sum of other elements.

To understand the essays of Eisenstein one can recall his
definition of a scenario. Meyerhold's pupil saw a scenario
in the same way that his teacher saw a play. Only one
author—the director. Mise-en-scène and gesture are the real
language of the production (a literary scenario is merely a
departure point for associations), and the film is made with
movement and montage. The scenario—in Eisenstein's
definition (at the end of the '20s)—sets down the emotional
perception of an event; the director interprets it in images.

In many ways the essays of Sergei Mikhailovich bear the
same relation to his films that his ideal scenario bore to his
ideal film. His thoughts or, more exactly, his feelings,
usually outran the reality of film. And he would feverishly
hurry to fix on paper the countless clusters of associations:
his concept would be embodied in something new, not yet
realised in art.

He wanted to express the scene of the separator in *Old
and New* with a structure built entirely on pathos. Explaining why the leading role in this scene was not taken by the
farmers (their shy behaviour gives them a secondary role),
but by "pure cinema", revealing the inner pathos of the
event through montage, the director made this retreat:

Imagine a scene of Moses smiting a rock in the desert
with his rod, causing a stream of water to burst forth,
and thousands who are dying of thirst throw themselves
towards it,
or the frenzied dance of the godless around the golden
calf,
or the Shakhsei-Vakhsei with its frenzied hundreds
throwing themselves on the sabres of the fanatics,
or even the zeal of the flagellants,
—then you could reverse the picture of the crowd in my

10

scene, absorbing into the pathetic structure the ecstasy of their action!*

(Notice that modest "even"—and one finds the word "frenzied" rather often in his essays.)

It would be meaningless now to dispute old concepts of the scenario, to explain to a great artist that he should have directed our attention to the people in the scene, etc., etc. His world now leaves us nothing to quarrel with. And we don't know the cinema he might have achieved. Too often, and through no fault of his own, his films were not finished and his researches were cut short.

* From the chapter on "Pathos" in an unfinished book (written in 1946–47), published in Vol. III (1964) of Eisenstein's selected works.

A Personal Statement

written for a Berlin newspaper, 1926

I am twenty-eight years old. Before 1918 I was a student for three years. At first I wanted to become an engineer and architect. During the civil war I was a sapper in the Soviet Army. While doing that work I spent any free time in studying questions of art and theatre: in particular theatre history and theory. In 1921 I entered the Proletcult organization as a theatre designer. The Proletcult Theatre busily sought new art forms that would correspond to the ideology of the new Russian state structure. Our troupe was composed of young workers who wished to create genuine art; they brought to this aim a quite new kind of temperament and a new viewpoint on the world and on art. At that time their artistic ideas and demands fully concurred with mine, though I, belonging to another class, had arrived at their deductions only through a process of speculation. The next years were a fierce struggle. In 1922 I became director of the First Moscow Workers' Theatre and completely broke with the views of the Proletcult administration. The Proletcult staff adhered to Lunacharsky's position: to maintain old traditions and to compromise on the question of pre-revolutionary artistic efficiency. I was one of the most unbending supporters of LEF (Left Front), where we wanted *the new*, meaning works that would correspond to the new social conditions of art. We had on our side at that time all the young people and innovators, including the futurists Meyerhold and Mayakovsky; in the most rigid opposition to us were the traditionalist Stanislavsky* and the opportunist Tairov.

* I have always been amused when the German press identified my anonymous actors, my "simple people", as artists of the Moscow Art Theatre, my "deadly enemy"!

13

In 1922–23 I staged three dramas at the Workers' Theatre: in principle their staging was a mathematical calculation of the elements of affect, which at that time I called "actions". In the first production, *The Sage*, I tried to dissect cubistically a classical play into separately affective "attractions". The action took place in a circus. In the second production, *Do You Hear, Moscow?*, I used fundamentally technical means in trying to realize theatrical illusions with mathematical calculations. This was the first success of the new theatrical affects. The third production, *Gas Masks*, was staged in a gas factory, during working hours. The machines worked and the "actors" worked; for the first time this represented the success of an absolutely *real*, highly objective art.

Such an understanding of theatre led in a straight path to cinema; only the most inexorable objectivity could be the sphere of cinema. My first film was begun in 1924; it was produced with members of Proletcult and was entitled *Strike*. The film had no story in the generally accepted sense: there were the progressive stages of a strike, there was a "montage of attractions". According to my artistic principle, we did not depend on intuitive creativeness but on a rational construction of affective elements; each affect must be subjected previously to a thorough analysis and calculation: this is the most important thing. Whether there are individual elements of affect within the story (in the generally accepted sense of the term) or whether they are strung along the "story carcass", as in my *Potemkin*, I cannot perceive any substantial distinction here. I myself am neither sentimental, nor bloodthirsty, nor at heart lyrical, as I have been occasionally in Germany accused of being. Yet all these elements are, of course, familiar to me, and I am quite aware that temptation is all that is needed to combine these with whatever is at hand to arouse the required reaction and to achieve the greatest tension. I am sure that this is a purely mathematical matter and that "sincerely creative genius" has no place here. No more readiness of wit is needed here than in the design of the most utilitarian building of reinforced concrete.

As for my view on cinema in general, I must confess that

I understand it as bias and only bias. In my opinion, without a clear presentation of the "why" one cannot begin work on a film. It is impossible to create without acknowledging on what latent feelings and passions you wish to speculate—excuse the expression, I know that it is not "nice", but it is professionally and by definition exact. We goad the passions of the spectators, but we also employ a safety valve, a lightning-rod, and this is—bias. To ignore bias and to waste energy I consider the greatest crime of our generation. For me and in itself bias is a great artistic potential, though it need not always be as political, as consciously political, as in *Potemkin*. When it is completely absent, when the film is regarded as a simple time-killer, as a sedative or hypnotic, then such an absence of bias can be interpreted as quite biased in the maintaining of tranquillity and keeping the audience satisfied with conditions as they are. Just as if the cinema "community", similar to the church community, had to train the good, the well-balanced, the stripped-away wishes of the citizens. Isn't this the philosophy of the American "happy ending"?

It has been alleged against me that the German adaptation of *Potemkin* weakens the power of its political tension, makes it too pathetic. But, after all, aren't we people with temperament, with passions? Is it possible for us to be unaware of duties or aims? The success of the film in Berlin and in post-war Europe, sinking in the twilight of a shaky *status quo*, must have been heard as a summons to whatever of dignified humanity that has survived. For this, isn't pathos justified? The bias of this film demands that one lifts one's head and feels oneself a person—a human, becoming human.

Battleship Potemkin was made for the twentieth anniversary of the 1905 Revolution, and had to be ready by December 1925: three months for production—even in Germany this might be considered a record production schedule. Two-and-a-half weeks were left to me for the montage of the film, for the editing of 15,000 metres of film.

Even if all roads lead to Rome—even if all genuine works of art come, in the long run, to the same intellectual level—I must emphasize that neither Stanislavsky and the

Art Theatre, nor Proletcult, for that matter, can create anything at present. I have not worked in Proletcult for a long time. I have completely moved into cinema, while the Proletcult people stay in the theatre. It's my opinion that an artist must make his choice between theatre and cinema; he cannot be "possessed" by both at the same time if he wants to really create.

There are no actors in *Battleship Potemkin*,* there are only real people in this film and the director's task was to find the right people; instead of looking for creative revelations of talent, he sought the correct physical appearances. Such a filming method is possible in Russia, where each and every matter is a government matter. The slogan of "All for one—one for all!" is more than a sub-title on the screen. If we are making a naval film, the whole fleet is at our service; if a battle film, the whole Red Army; when we make an agricultural subject, various Commissariats give us assistance. The point is that we film not just for ourselves, nor just for you, not for this or that person, but for all.

I am positive that the cinema collaboration of Germany and Russia could have great results. The fusion of German technical potentialities and Russian creative fire could produce something extraordinary. But for me personally to work in Germany is extremely doubtful. I could not forsake my native soil, which gives me the strength to create. Perhaps I can make myself understood more easily by reminding you of the myth of Antaeus rather than giving a Marxist explanation of the links between artistic creation and the social economic base. Furthermore, there is in the German film industry a tendency to follow stereotypes and to aim at profits that could create for me quite impossible working conditions. There have been, of course, German films that one must respect, but now I can see that a *Faust* or a *Metropolis* had to fight its way through distracting triviali-

* It was only at the time of *Potemkin*'s introduction to European and American screens that E. insisted on this half-truth, though a justification for it may be that the functions of the several actor-assistants were not, strictly, *acting* functions. It was probably the fabricated publicity story that *Potemkin* was acted by "members of the Moscow Art Theatre" that made him swing to this extreme statement.—J. L.

16

ties; pornography on the one hand and sentimentality on the other. German films are not audacious. We Russians either break our necks or win the day, and more often than not we win.

And so, for the present, I'll stay at home. I am at the moment making a film on the economic struggle in the countryside, an intense struggle for a new agricultural policy.

The appealingly brash tone of this statement (written during a brief visit to Berlin at the time of Potemkin's *triumph there) is characteristic of Eisenstein's youthful writings. He knew that his revolutionary ideals for the theatre and cinema would excite opposition, and he made each of his public declarations as challenging as a performance. His earliest manifesto, "Montage of Attractions", appeared in 1923, just before his theatre work led him to apply the same method of "a montage of attractions" to films. Two years later another important declaration grew from his first film,* Strike.

The Method of Making Workers' Films

There is one *method* for making *any* film: montage of attractions. To know what this is and why, see the book, *Cinema Today*,[1] where, rather dishevelled and illegible, my approach to the construction of film works is described.

Our class approach introduces:

1. A *specific purpose for the work*—a socially useful emotional and psychological affect on the audience; this to be composed of a chain of suitably directed stimulants. This *socially useful affect* I call the *content of the work*.

17

It is thus possible, for example, to define the *content* of a production. *Do You Hear, Moscow?* : the maximum tension of aggressive reflexes in social protest. *Strike*: an accumulation of reflexes without intervals (satisfaction), that is, a focusing of reflexes on struggle (and a lifting of potential class tone).

2. A *choice of the stimulants*. In two directions. In making a correct appraisal of the class inevitability of their nature, certain stimulants are capable of evoking a certain reaction (affect) only among spectators of a certain class. For a more precise affect the audience must be even more unified, if possible along professional lines: any director of "living newspaper" performances in clubs knows how different audiences, say metal workers or textile workers, react completely differently and at different places to the same work.

Such class "inevitability" in matters of action can be easily illustrated by the amusing failure of one attraction that was strongly affected by the circumstances of one audience: I refer to the slaughter-house sequence in *Strike*. Its concentratedly associative affect of bloodiness among certain strata of the public is well known. The Crimean censor even cut it, along with—the latrine scene. (That certain sharp affects are inadmissible was indicated by an American after seeing *Strike*: he declared that this scene would surely have to be removed before the film was sent abroad.) It was the same kind of simple reason that prevented the usual "bloody" affect of the slaughter-house sequence from shocking certain worker-audiences: among these workers the blood of oxen is first of all associated with the by-product factories near the slaughter-house! And for peasants who are accustomed to the slaughter of cattle this affect would also be cancelled out.

The other direction in the choice of stimulants appears to be the class accessibility of this or that stimulant.

Negative examples: the variety of sexual attractions that are fundamental to the majority of bourgeois works placed on the market; methods that lead one away from concrete reality, such as the sort of expressionism used in *Caligari*; or the sweet middle-class poison of Mary Pickford, the ex-

18

ploited and systematically trained stimulation of all middle-class inclinations, even in our healthy and advanced audiences.

The bourgeois cinema is no less aware than we are of class taboos. In New York City's censorship regulations[2] we find a list of thematic attractions undesirable for film use: "relations between labour and capital" appears alongside "sexual perversion", "excessive brutality", "physical deformity" . . .

The study of stimulants and their montage for a particular purpose provides us with exhaustive materials on the question of *form*. As I understand it, content is the *summary of all that is subjected to the series of shocks* to which in a particular order the audience is to be exposed. (Or more crudely: so much per cent of material to fix the attention, so much to rouse bitterness, etc.). But this material must be organized in accordance with a principle that leads to the desired effect.

Form is the *realization of these intentions* in a particular material, as precisely those stimulants which are able to summon this indispensable per cent are created and assembled—in the concrete expression of the factual side of the work.

One should, moreover, keep in mind the "attractions of the moment", that is, those reactions that flame forth temporarily in connection with certain courses or events of social life.

In contrast to these there are a series of "eternal" attraction phenomena and methods.

Some of these have a class usefulness. For example, a healthy and integrated audience always reacts to an epic of class struggle.

Equal with these are the "neutrally" affective attractions, such as death-defying stunts, *double entendres*, and the like.

To use these independently leads to *l'art pour l'art* so as to reveal their counter-revolutionary essence.

As with the attraction moments, one ought to remember that neutral or accidental attractions cannot, ideologically, be taken for granted, but should be used only as a method of exciting those unconditioned reflexes that are necessary to us not in themselves but in the training of socially useful conditioned reflexes that we wish to combine with certain objectives of our social aims.

When this manifesto appeared in Kino, *on 11 August 1925, the Eisenstein group had put aside the planned sequels to* Strike *and were shooting a film to celebrate the twentieth anniversary of the 1905 Revolution. Out of the broad scope of* The Year 1905 *came the concentrated drama of* Battleship Potemkin, *the first world-wide triumph of the Soviet cinema.*

The subject to follow Potemkin *was not an easy choice. There was a plan for* First Cavalry Army, *with the help of Isaac Babel, and a plan for* Zhunguo, *a Chinese epic with a script by Sergei Tretiakov; the group finally went to work on a dramatization of the new agricultural policy. This film,* The General Line *(eventually released as* Old and New*), was interrupted in 1927 to make* October, *to celebrate the tenth anniversary of the October Revolution.*

In 1928, during the final cutting of October *and before returning to the revised agricultural film, Eisenstein enjoyed an interval of writing and teaching. Joseph Freeman invited him to contribute a cinema chapter to a volume on Soviet arts that was published two years later in the United States as* Voices of October. *Following is the article as it appeared there, with a few passages restored from Eisenstein's manuscript.*

Soviet Cinema

In a militant and active culture, the subject of this book, bookkeeping and statistics cannot occupy the central place. In this matter one must be intolerant, implacable, fundamental. Nor is this a question yet to be shelved in archives.

We must be prepared daily for quarrels, mistakes, corrections and fresh mistakes.

I shall use the section of the book that has been allotted to me for an analysis, according to my principles, of that section of Soviet culture where I have worked for seven out of its ten years of existence (three years in the theatre and four years in the cinema).

Thus you have before you, not a mere report, but a militant programme.

Imagine a cinema which is not dominated by the dollar; a cinema industry where one man's pocket is not filled at other people's expense; which is not for the pockets of two or three people, but for the heads and hearts of 150 million people. Every motion picture affects heads and hearts, but as a rule motion pictures are not produced especially for heads and hearts. Most motion pictures are turned out for the benefit of two or three pockets; only incidentally do they affect the heads and hearts of millions.

Suddenly a new system arises. A cinema is created, based not on private profit but on popular needs. Such a cinema may be hard to imagine; it may even be considered impossible; but one has merely to study the Soviet cinema, and one will see that it is not only possible, but has already been achieved.

To achieve such a cinema, however, certain prerequisites are necessary. Commercial competition must be eliminated. Big pockets must not devour little pockets; big fish must not be swallowed up by still bigger fish. The simplest way to arrive at such a state of affairs would be to destroy the big fish and deprive the bigger fish of their food, and to unite the little fish in innumerable shoals with common interests.

In 1917, something like that took place in Russia. The fat individual whales were terrified by a vast collective whale composed of little fish. The fat individual whales fled through all the seas and oceans; while the herd, 150 million strong, which for centuries had been oppressed by a small body of masters, suddenly became master of itself: the immense collective master of an immense collective enterprise. Everyone protected and continues to protect his own personal interest; but the amusing part of it all is that these interests need not collide with the interests of one's neighbour, for the simple reason that all these personal interests are directed towards one goal. There is no longer a mutual destruction of energy and power; instead, there is a tremendous accumulation of collective energy for the benefit of all these interests.

These interests are class interests, the interests of that young proletarian class which took power into its hands in 1917. This class is a single organism based on solidarity, collectivism and collaboration. It realizes that, if all are to be fed, there is no worse way of attaining it than by throttling one's fellow worker. Hence, this class abolished the system of throttling one's neighbour and established a system of healthy collaboration.

This class realizes that when the general interests of all are satisfied, the individual interests of each are satisfied. In the place of individual competition there has been substituted planned collective construction. This was the intention of the victorious working class, and its highest expression was achieved in social centralization and monopoly. These form part of the indestructible basis of the first Soviet state; they were attained by concentrating productive forces and implements in one organizing centre. There can be no regularity of supply without system; there can be no system without centralization and monopoly. Rationalization is unthinkable without the participation of the masses in every aspect of work and construction whose goal is the satisfaction of the interests of the working masses.

"EVERY COOK SHOULD BE ABLE TO GOVERN"

A Soviet poster, showing the figure of a woman in a red shawl, carries this phrase by the "Utopian" Lenin. This is the teaching of the leader Lenin; and every cook in the Soviet Union realizes that she must know how to govern. What is more, she does govern. As a delegate to the Congress of Soviets, the Women's Congress, the Party Congress, the trade union, she rules, improves and corrects the policies of her government. These corrections are necessary, for where can there be more errors and unexpected situations than in this new and unprecedented social structure?

In the workers' and peasants' State, which is one organism, there must be on the part of the people the most vigilant attention, control and concentration of the State's creative energies. For if there are errors and inaccuracies in one section, if a single part is defective, the whole apparatus suffers. If in one region of the country the grain harvest fails, this calamity does not enrich some speculator in a more fortunate region; the crop failure is rather a tragedy for every worker and every peasant homestead, whose interests all merge in the general interests of the state.

But the country of the Soviets is not yet a paradise; it is surrounded on every hand by more or less unfriendly neighbours. The fat whales driven away in 1917 anxiously await an opportunity to strike a blow at the new social structure. This state of affairs gives our art, like our politics, a peculiar character. Centralization and monopoly determine the organizational method of the cinema in the Soviet Union, and the dictatorship of the proletariat determines the militant and "aggressive" character which differentiates our culture generally from other cultures, but more especially our cinema from the cinema of other countries.

Lenin said: "The cinema is the most important of all the arts." We firmly believe this. The innovations of our cinema in form, organization, and technique have been possible only as a result of our social innovations, as a result of our social order and the new modes of thought it has stimulated. In art innovations are not produced at will; they are dictated by new social forms. The apprehension of the social order is the high goal towards which artists proceed slowly and mathematically, attaining it only after great effort. An art corresponding to the social order develops according to the laws of natural selection; an art which is unsuited to the social order in which it seeks to function suffers greatly; on the other hand, a social system which is unsuited to our highest conception of art should be swept away.

Nowhere except in the Soviet Union does the cinema benefit by a unification of three forms of centralization. These are: the centralization of economic production, the centralization of ideology, and the centralization of method.

As in other countries, the Soviet cinema is one of our leading industries, and organizationally it is conducted like other
branches of our socialized industry. Both the production
and the sale of Soviet motion pictures have been centralized.
At present, for example, Sovkino controls all foreign sales
through its representatives in those countries which have
trade relations with the Soviet Union, as well as all business
connected with the purchase of motion picture equipment
and machinery. It also controls the entire purchase and sale
of foreign films in the Soviet Union. It controls 60 per cent
of the domestic market in the Soviet Union, monopolizing
the entire production and sale of Soviet films with the exception of the autonomous republics, such as the Ukrainian
and Georgian films. Sovkino also controls a large number of
motion picture theatres throughout the Soviet Union and
handles 25 per cent of the sales to those theatres which it
does not control. The cinema organizations of the autonomous republics, while acting independently and exercising a
monopoly within their own national boundaries, have close
business relations with Sovkino. It is to be hoped that in the
future there will be a still further concentration of the
cinema industry, which will unify the various cinema organizations into one state monopoly. Such a unification will
make the cinema one of the strongest of Soviet industries,
and will eventually lead to a change in economic control. At
present the cinema is under the control of educational and
political institutions; when completely unified, its economic
administration should logically be handed over to the
Supreme Economic Council.

Centralization of production is the first stage towards a
highly unified cinema. At present we are also developing the
second stage: the centralization of ideology. We are convinced that the cinema is intended not for mere entertainment, but for general cultural and social aims. These aims
should be pursued without any element of private interest
or private gain. The cinema is partly an industrial undertaking, and partly an art. The commercial and economic
aspects of this art must be completely subordinated to the
social and cultural tasks set by the Revolution of 1917. The
plan for completely unifying the industrial side of the Soviet

cinema makes it possible to establish not only the economic but primarily the ideological dictatorship of those organs established by the workers for the protection and propagation of those ideas for which they fought.

The Soviet cinema aims primarily to educate the masses. It seeks to give them a general education and a political education; it conducts an extensive campaign of propaganda for the Soviet State and its ideology among the people. These aims are pursued by all the arts in the Soviet Union, guided by the agitational-propaganda section of the Central Committee of the Communist Party. The Soviet cinema, specifically, works under the direction of the People's Commissariat of Education and the Supreme Council of Political Education. With us "art" is not a mere word. We look upon it as only one of many instruments used on the battle-fronts of the class struggle and the struggle for socialist construction. Art is in the same class as the metallurgical industry, for example.

In the Soviet Union art is responsive to social aims and demands. One day, for example, all attention is centred on the village; it is imperative to raise the village from the slough of ancient custom and bring it into line with the Soviet system as a whole; the peasant must learn to see the difference between private ownership and individualistic survivals on the one hand, and co-operation and collective economy on the other.

S O S !

The seismograph of the Party apparatus notes a vacillation in this section of Soviet life. At once, all social thought is directed towards it. Throughout the country the press, literature, the fine arts are mobilized to ward off danger. The slogan is: "Face the Village!" The *smichka*, the union of proletarian and poor peasant is established. Opponents of Soviet aims are ousted. The strongest propaganda guns are put in action; there begins a bombardment on behalf of socialist economy. Here the cinema plays a big role.

Again, attention may be concentrated in another direction. There has been a break with a foreign country. War seems imminent. Defend the Soviet Union! Every form of art co-operates with the country in clarifying the situation.

What shall we defend? Our achievements, our all—not the private wealth of a few individuals or financial concessions in the colonies or recently seized markets.

The Soviet cinema and theatre can hardly keep pace with the new social orders issued every day by the people carrying out tremendous social tasks. There is no time to reflect, to present the situation "objectively" through art. It is a neck and neck race between the cinema and the newspaper. For instance, the campaign for grain sowing begins. Motion pictures dealing with the most suitable kinds of grain must be rushed to various parts of the country. Motion pictures impressing the necessity for sowing selected seeds must be exhibited in the villages again and again. The peasant must be shown that crops cannot improve as a result of religious processions and prayers for rain.

The twentieth anniversary of the 1905 revolution arrives. The Soviet cinema must reproduce that stirring year. The workers must know the history of their past, when the proletariat of St Petersburg and Odessa sacrificed their lives for freedom. Or the tenth anniversary of the 1917 revolution comes. The great fighters who participated in the "ten days that shook the world" are passing away; the towns which were the centres of the Revolution of 7 November are changing. The events of those days must be accurately recorded by the cinema while there are still living eyewitnesses. Posterity must have a photographic reproduction of the great Revolution, a living textbook for the inspiration of other generations.

As for history "in general", that is a sweet idealization of bourgeois historians. The "great" and "illustrious" personages of the past ruled the fate of millions according to their limited views. They were "gods" invented out of whole cloth. It is time to reveal the truth about these paid romantic heroes. The concealed traps of official history must be exposed. We want to know the social basis of these fabulous figures, glorified by hired scholars in the interests of their class and their descendants. Ivan the Terrible as a personality in the manner of Edgar Allan Poe will hardly interest the young Soviet worker; but as the creator of the linen trade, the Czar who enriched and strengthened Russia's economic position, he becomes a more interesting figure. The story of Ivan the Terrible should go on to tell how he became absolute monarch, head of a dominant aristocratic class; it should tell of the struggle among the higher classes of society, how they became weakened. On this basis the story would be nearer reality and of more importance than a fantasy about a mephistophelian figure, a Czar who was a wild beast. The merchant-Czar, what could be more concrete! Recall our recent "first landlord", Nicholas II. In a motion picture lasting an hour and a half all the years of tinsel, falsehood and deception are dispersed.

The Soviet cinema, then, is a cultural instrument serving the cultural aims of the Soviet state. In our country the leaders of the cinema do not sit around discussing whether or not the public wants sea films; or that movie fans are crazy about costume films dealing with the eighteenth century; or that it is too soon to change the programme to a new wild west film; or that it has been a long time since there have been jungle films and they would now be a great novelty; or that *The Big Parade* continues to hold the interest of the public and there must therefore be an increased production of war movies. In the Soviet Union a discussion of proposed films is not carried on with both eyes on the box office. If it is planned to produce a photoplay dealing with the life of Soviet youth, the cinema directors talk the matter over with the Young Communist League, which is the leader of Soviet youth. The object of the film is to clarify various problems in such a way that it will arouse discussion and thought among the young people of the Soviet Union. Love films are not produced for the mere purpose of exciting the audience, but to throw some light on sexual relations, on the new moral code which has taken the place of the old.

The cinema handles other living problems in the same way. There are themes on every hand. The government is carrying on a campaign for the reduction of prices by lowering the cost of production through efficient methods. We call this "rationalization"; but we do not wish to impose rationalization by force. It must come through understanding. The situation must be made clear; the masses must be made enthusiastic about it. A fascinating theme for a movie. Again, the local and central economic institutions are too rigid. Bureaucracy interferes with socialist construction. This weakness must be attacked either by treatment in satire or in tragedy or in both. The cinema must show how the tragedy of the small man is caused by the inflexibility of the credit apparatus. The cinema finds another theme in nepotism. Some responsible workers have an over-developed family feeling; they introduce relatives and friends into the institutions where they work. Such preferences are forbidden by Soviet law. The wife may live with her husband, but she cannot serve under him in public office. Regulations for obtaining positions are established by the trade unions and labour exchanges; and the cinema assists in impressing the evils of nepotism on millions of spectators. In this way the Soviet film is an integral part of the entire cultural apparatus of the country, which is directed towards a better life for all.

Occasionally, someone makes the mistake of trying to improve the commercial aspects of a film to the detriment of its educational aspects. Organized Soviet society meets such attempts with the most merciless criticism and the fiercest attacks. Dispute follows dispute. Conferences are held. The matter is discussed at provincial and national congresses, and finally the Communist Party institutes an official discussion on the cinema which results in definitely laying down a correct policy. We realize that every ideological or tactical institution is primarily based on organized society, and, as in the nervous system, every part affects the whole.

The internal organization of our cinema industry is like that of other Soviet industries. All workers connected with the cinema industry, in whatever capacity, belong to a trade union, to the Photo-Cinema Section of the Union of Art Workers. Every cinema unit, like every Soviet factory, has its factory committee, elected by the workers of the unit. The factory committee is the vigilant defender of the workers' rights, especially of those rights which they secured through the October revolution. The factory committee is the centre of social life in the factory. One of its jobs is to conduct regular discussions on film production. These discussions are attended by every kind of worker in the industry, and everything is considered which in any way pertains to the enterprise. Nobody is omitted, from the director to the janitor, from the costume-maker to the "star". Before such meetings of all the workers in his unit the director reports on the plan of work for the coming year. At the end of a year, the workers make a strict examination of his report and of the actual work accomplished. The manager of the laboratory reports on possible innovations. The director of the cinema is called to order for exceeding the financial estimates of a film or for the misdeeds of its hero. All the workers participate in the appraisal of a new film, each on the basis of his speciality.

I should like to see how Von Stroheim would reply to the attacks of the youngest critics on excessive expenditures for *The Wedding March*; or Griffith listening to the tailors pointing out that *America* does not sufficiently establish the economic basis of the War of Independence;[1] or Carl Laemmle explaining his balance sheet to carpenters, painters. In our country that is what every movie director must do; and under our conditions I cannot imagine a healthier or more useful system. These tailors, assistants, carpenters and painters represent those countless tailors, assistants, carpenters and painters in whose interests, and in whose interests alone, the film is made and released. Every penny wasted is the workers' penny; it is a loss which his enterprise and his factory sustains. In addition to serious criticism from the members of the factory committee, the movie director has to submit to criticism in caricature and satire in the factory's wall newspaper.

On a small scale, the factory committee reflects the structure of the cinema industry as a whole, from the chief regulating committee and the estimating department of the Commissariat of Education, which controls the ideological and economic plans of the cinema industry as a whole, to the Workers and Peasants Inspection, that strict ultimate censor which controls the ideological and economic aspects of all Soviet enterprises.

One solution we have arrived at already: the Soviet film serves the mass of people, their interests, their organizations; it is the expression of the collective strivings of various organized units. Specialists, directors, cameramen and scenario writers realize that they are the voice of this collective mass demand. Hence the Soviet film has real life; hence it expresses the true spirit of the people and the essence of the epoch. Soviet films are based on Soviet life; whether they deal with the new moral code, the workers' family or films celebrating historical events and requiring the collaboration of thousands of people, they are true to life. They must be true to life. This was impressed on me in the making of my own films, beginning with *Strike* and ranging through *Potemkin*, *Old and New* and *October*. The Soviet scenario writer and film producer must draw his material from living sources. If the scenario deals with family problems, they must get in touch with the Women's Section, that department of the Communist Party which specializes in work among women, which knows most about what is being done for mothers and children. If a film is to deal with historical subjects, the director gets in touch with local and central historical associations which specialize in collecting material about the Revolution, with the Association of Old Bolsheviks, with the Association of Ex-Political Prisoners, with the Communist Academy and so on. If the theme deals with village life, the director obtains invaluable material from the Commissariat of Agriculture, from the trade union of agricultural workers and similar bodies. Through these organizations, and under their leadership, the movie director obtains the co-operation of every organized body which knows anything about the theme of his film. He has at his disposal as advisers and actors those who personally participated in historical events; organisations of specialists; newspapers and magazines specializing in the subject of the film. All these collaborators in the making of the film meet and express opinions; material is collected; the most important facts about the theme of the film are placed at the director's disposal. Throughout the making of the film the director works in the closest co-operation with these organizations. This contact with the life of the Soviet Union is carried even further. The scenario is taken directly to the people. A scenario dealing with the new relations in the worker's family is discussed at factory meetings and out of their own experience the workers make extensive alterations. A scenario dealing with farm problems is submitted to agricultural experts; biologists revise scenarios where cattle-breeding is described.

This system pervades the whole Soviet cinema. We are opposed to "constructing" sets. Our system is different from Hollywood's. If we need a factory for a film, we do not have to "construct" one; we go to an actual factory; we believe that a faked factory can never reproduce the atmosphere of a real one. When we made *October*, I needed the Winter Palace in Leningrad; I preferred to transplant the production of the film to this dead palace, rather than make it in the comfortable atmosphere of a studio. The damp cellars and the rats of the real palace helped us in our work, so that on the screen we were able to reproduce with complete accuracy the milieu necessary for our film. Furthermore, in making this film three or four thousand organized workers participate in it as actors depicting the mass shooting in the streets of Petrograd in July 1917. No rehearsals were necessary; the workers know too well just how it was done. Thus the film was the product of an immense collective effort, in which thousands of experts and workers participated, and whose contributions were shaped according to the individuality of the director. This is one of our methods of work; and developing it, we are moving to the third and last centralization necessary for the cinema: the centralization of method.

translation by Joseph Freeman

Nineteen twenty nine was a critical year in the development of Eisenstein's theories as well as in his career. During the completion of the final version of the agricultural policy film, released as Old and New, *Eisenstein glimpsed a new, startling direction that the Soviet film could take—towards the filming of abstract ideas. In the hasty production of* October *there had been opportunities to test this discovery*

31

in several passages (notably in the "gods" sequence) and, despite official interference in Old and New, *that film remains the only finished work by Eisenstein to convey what he intended by the term, "intellectual cinema". However, his statements and interviews and lectures of this year positively bubble with the excitement of his discovery, into which his ideas about sound-film were also poured.*

An important untitled manuscript, written in German, and dated "Moscow April 1929", was later published abroad in two variants: "The Principles of Film Form" and "A Dialectic Approach to Film Form". Written at the same time were two additions to Russian books on film subjects quite remote from Eisenstein's chief concerns: the more familiar of these is his afterword to N. Kaufmann's brochure on the Japanese cinema; the other is his foreword to the translation by Vladimir Nilsen (supervised by Tisse) of Der Trickfilm, *by the German cameraman, Guido Seeber.*

The New Language of Cinema

Soviet cinema has now arrived at the most curious stage of its development.

More than this.

I believe that only now can we begin to hazard a guess concerning the ways in which a genuine Soviet cinema will be formed, i.e. a cinema which not only will be opposed to bourgeois cinema in respect of its class attributes, but will also categorically *excel* it by virtue of *its methods*. Not long ago I expressed the view that cinematography began its career by making use of popular literature (of the detective-story genre), through the system of highly sophisticated theatrical art (the system of the "star" and "vedette"), German pictorial films (from impressionism to *Caligari*), of

32

films without any definite aim, etc.—and is now returning to that condition, which I named, to distinguish it from the first, the *second literary period*.

But if, in the first literary period, cinematography had recourse to the fabulous subjects and the dramatic and epic experience of literature, i.e. borrowed from literature the elements of construction as a whole; the second literary period, on the contrary, makes use of literature along a different line—along the line of its experience in the technology of the materials with which literature is concerned.

Here cinema is for the first time availing itself of the experience of literature for the purpose of working out *its own language, its own speech, its own vocabulary, its own imagery*. The period is ending when the most brilliant productions—from a dramaturgical point of view—were pronounced, from the point of view of genuine cinematography, in a childish lisp. As an example we might instance Chaplin's *A Woman of Paris*, perhaps the most remarkable production of the past epoch of cinematography.*

The new period of cinema attacks the question *from within*—along the line of the methodology of purely cinematographic *expressiveness*.

It is not surprising that at first the construction should be somewhat halting. The truth is that the new cinema language which is being formed is only beginning to grope its way towards a perception of that for which it is suitable and intended. The attempts to say what is unsuitable and ill-

---

* This remarkable picture, which has very striking merits, is quite incorrectly judged by us as regards the nature of its significance. According to my point of view, its significance is in no sense practical, but of a purely stimulative character. *A Woman of Paris* is for us significant in a purely abstract sense, as a stage of accomplishment possible of attainment in any domain whatsoever. In this respect its significance for the cinema is of exactly the same order as the Doric temple, a well-executed somersault, or the Brooklyn bridge.

In our country it was received as a phenomenon of practical advantage to us: in fact, as an object for imitation and even plagiarism. Examples of such an attitude are among the sad pages of our cinema history: elements of reaction and retrogression along the line of the general development of the ideology of the forms of the Soviet cinema.

33

adapted lead to confusion. The sphere of work of the new cinematographic possibilities seems to be the *direct screening of class-useful conceptions*, methods, tactics and practical watchwords, not having recourse for this purpose to the aid of the suspect trappings of the dramatic and psychological past. The social aim of cinematography is being essentially transposed. The cinematography of the first period was primarily confronted with the task of straining to the utmost the aggressive emotions in a definite direction, with a direct (and, as far as possible, deafening) temperamental volley in that direction, whereas the task of cinematography at the present day is very much more complicated: its task is the deep and slow drilling in of new conceptions or the transplanting of generally accepted notions into the consciousness of the audience. Whereas in the first case we were striving for a quick emotional *discharge*, the new cinema must *include deep reflective processes*, the result of which will find expression neither immediately nor directly.

Such a task was, of course, beyond the scope of the old halting cinematography. The new cinematography, by which conceptions are conveyed, is still at its initial stage of formal construction.

And, just as examination, from the new point of view, of the first guide to cinema's infancy—literature—did immeasurably much to strengthen the actual formal ideology of the new cinema, so examination (also from the new point of view) of the technical alphabet of its possibilities, doubly popular in its youthful period, should give a great multitude of data for the new formal methods.

The technical cinema trick *yesterday*—was a playing to the gallery (trick in the true sense) or an employment of the overloaded baroque style of the letters of eloquent stage-managers (the picture postcard effects repeatedly on exhibition, or purely stylistic mannerism, for instance—meaningless dissolves in and out). *Today* it has a new significance. "The technical possibility", foolishly called a "trick", is undoubtedly just as important a factor in the construction of the new cinematography as is the new conception of film-making from which it is sprung.

translation by Winifred Ray

34

One of Eisenstein's most important essays was published shortly before the release of Old and New *and his departure in August 1929, with Alexandrov and Tisse, to study sound-film techniques abroad. "Perspectives" is his fullest formulation in the Soviet press of the "intellectual cinema" theory; it was then and since used as evidence by his critics of "decadent" or "formalist" tendencies. The severe reaction to this essay may even have contributed to the early death of the journal* Iskusstvo (Art), *sponsored by Lunacharsky, in which the essay appeared. It may be helpful for the reader of this key piece of Eisenstein's writing to keep in mind that the first subject to which he planned to apply his new theory was the filming of Marx's* Capital—*hence the emphasis here on the clarification and definition of terms. In his mind the journey abroad was as related to the wish to film* Capital *as it was to the study of sound-film in European and American studios.*

Perspectives

In the hurly-burly of crises, imagined and real,

in the chaos of discussions, serious or worthless (example: "to work with or without actors?"),

there is a need—with scissors clenched in fist—to move film culture forward, together with the need to make it immediately accessible to all.

In the jostlings and contradictions between the urgency to find forms equal in height with the post-capitalist forms of our socialist construction and the cultural capacity of the class that is creating this construction,

in the steady fundamental direction towards an immediacy of communication to masses and the understanding by millions,

we have no right to establish limits of theoretical

solutions to this problem or this basic condition alone.

Parallel with this must come solutions in the daily tactical course of research on cinema form, to work out problems and general principles on how to advance our cinema's perspectives.

But if we put on one side all the clever practical approaches to the social consumer's narrowly day-to-day instruction, we must think out all the more sharply a programme for a theoretical Five-Year-Plan for the future.

And find the new functional perspectives for a genuinely Communist cinema—as distinguished from all past and present cinematography.

It is in such a context that the following considerations are offered.

*   *   *

In general it is pleasant and useful to understand Marxism. But to Mr Gorky this understanding brings more of that irreplaceable benefit of making clear how unsuitable is the role of preacher, that is, of the man who prefers to speak in the *language of logic*, rather than the role of the artist, that is, of the man who prefers to speak in the *language of images*. When Mr Gorky realizes that this is so, he will be saved . . .[1]

Thus wrote Plekhanov—fifteen years ago.

Since then Gorky has, fortunately, been "saved". Apparently he mastered Marxism.

Since those times the role of the preacher has merged with that of the artist. There has arisen the *propagandist*.

Yet the dispute continues between the language of images and the language of logic. Nor can they "come to terms" in the language of dialectics.

Indeed on the arts front the centre of attention has shifted from the Plekhanov antithesis to a quite different pair of antagonists.

Let us deal with them first so that later we can indicate the possibility of a synthesis as a way out of their initial opposition.

And so: contemporary art-understanding ranges itself

36

from pole to pole, starting from the formula: "art is the perception of life" to the formula: "art is the building of life." Such a polar opposition is, in my view, deeply mistaken: not in its functional definition of art, but in its incorrect understanding of what lies hidden behind the term, "perception".

Colliding with the definition of a concept, it would be wrong for us to disregard the method of purely linguistic analysis of its significance. Sometimes the words we pronounce are often "more clever" than we.

We are often quite irrationally reluctant to investigate a definition in the purified and contracted formula of its verbal significance, as opposed to its concept. To analyse this formula means freeing it of its extraneous "marketable" trappings of associative material: chiefly superficial associations, distorting its essence.

The dominant associations are, of course, those responding to the class that dominates in the era in which this or that term was formulated or had its maximum use. We have received all our "rational" verbal and terminological baggage from the hands of the bourgeoisie. Along with the dominant bourgeois understanding of a term come whole bundles of associations that correspond to bourgeois ideology and convenience.

Meanwhile each term, as with any phenomenon, has a "duality" of reading—I might even say, an "ideological reading". Static and dynamic. Social and individual.

The traditionalism of such an associative "encirclement", responding to the previous class hegemony, invariably baffles us.

And instead of effecting an internal verbal "class stratification", the word-concept is written, understood and used by us in its traditional form, in no way corresponding to our class-outlook.

This fact of a word's significance, analysed for the meaning of its concept, is a matter noted by Berkeley:

It cannot be deny'd that words are of excellent use, in that by their means all that stock of knowledge which has been purchas'd by the joint labours of inquisitive men in

37

all ages and nations, may be drawn into the view and made the possession of one single person.[2]

He also notes what we indicated above: the distortion of a concept's perception by applying a one-sided or incorrect use of a term:

> But at the same time it must be owned that most parts of knowledge, whose fruit is excellent, and within the reach by the abuse of words, and general ways of speech wherein they are deliver'd, that it may almost be made a question whether language, has contributed more to the hindrance or advancement of the sciences.

Berkeley's proposed escape from this situation is that of an idealist, not in making a cleansing, based on class analysis, of a term from the viewpoint of its social comprehension, but in aiming at "pure idea".

> It were, therefore, to be wish'd that every one wou'd use his utmost endeavors, to obtain a clear view of the ideas he'd consider, separating from them all that dress and incumbrance of words which so much contribute to blind the judgment and divide the attention ... we need only draw the curtain of words, to behold the fairest tree of knowledge, whose fruit is excellent, and within the reach of our hand.

It is in a quite different way that Plekhanov approaches the similar problem of "word usage". He studies the word in an inseparable social-productive connection, restoring it for analysis from the sphere of the superstructure to the sphere of productive base and its practical connections and origins. His approach seems a convincing materialist argument, as much as the other research materials that we use. Thus basing "the inevitability of a materialist explanation of history on the most studied part of primitive society's ideology, its art" he brings in as evidence the linguistic considerations of von den Steinen:

> Von den Steinen considers that "Zeichnen" [drawing] developed from "Zeichen" [making signs], adopted with a practical aim in order to point out objects.[3]

38

Our habitual acceptance of words makes us reluctant to listen to them carefully, and our ignoring of this sphere of research leads to much distress and to a sea of irrational wastage of diverse polemical temperaments!

For example, see how many broken bayonets lie around the question of "form and content"!

All because the dynamic, active and real act of "content" (with-keeping, as "keeping to ourselves") changed to an amorphous and static, passive understanding of content—as *capacity*.

Though it occurs to no one to speak of the "capacity" of the play, *The Rails Are Humming*, or the novel, *The Iron Flood*.

And how much inky blood has been spilt because of the persistent wish to understand *form* only as deriving from the Greek *phormos* (wicker basket) with all the consequent "organizational deductions" from that.

A wicker basket in which, quivering under the inky flood of polemics, rests that same unhappy "capacity".

Meanwhile, just turn from the Greek dictionary to a Russian dictionary of 'foreign words', where you will see that in Russian *form* is *obraz* (image). *Obraz* itself is a crossbreeding of the meanings of *obrez* (edge) and *obnaruzheniye* (disclosure)—according to Preobrazhensky's *Etymological Dictionary of the Russian Language*. Each of these points of view gives a brilliant characterization of form: from an individually static (*an und für sich*) viewpoint, as "edge"— the cutting off of a given phenomenon from attendant circumstances (for example, an un-Marxist definition of form, such as Leonid Andreyev's, which confines it *strictly* to this definition).

"Disclosure" characterizes *obraz* from another viewpoint —the socially active function of "disclosure", i.e., determining the social connection between a given phenomenon and its environment.

"Content"—an act of restraint—is a *principle of organization*, to express it in a contemporary way. The principle of organized thinking is the factual "content" of a work. This principle, the materializing combination of socio-physiological stimulants, by means of *disclosure*, appears as form.

39

No one assumes that the *content* of a newspaper is: news about the Kellogg Pact, a scandal at the *Gazette de France*, or such a daily incident as that of a drunken husband murdering his wife with a hammer.

When we speak of the *content* of a newspaper we mean the principle of organization and cultivation of the newspaper's *capacities*—aimed at the class-cultivation of the reader.

And in this is the production-based inseparability of combined content and form that makes an *ideology*.

Though proletarian newspapers and bourgeois newspapers may have equal factual capacities, this is what sets them poles apart in *content*.

As for the term "perception", where is our error here?

Its roots are linked to the ancient North German "Kna"* (I can) and with another word, the ancient Saxon "biknegon" (I take part)—which is forced out of existence by the one-sided contemplative *understanding* of "perception" as an abstractly contemplative function, the "pure perception of an idea", i.e., a deeply bourgeois understanding of this term.

By now it seems impossible to make any replacement in the term *perception* of the act of "perception" as an act with immediately operative consequences.

Though in reflexology it has been sufficiently determined that the process of perception is to increase the number of conditioned stimulants, conducive to the operative reflex reaction of the given subject—i.e. even in the most mechanical process is an actively operative but not passive manifestation—yet *practically*, when we get down to reasoning about perception, we tend to go even further in this perverted formula of separation from activity and labour, similar to the aim of "pure perception" that Plekhanov found expressed by Renan:

> ... Ernest Renan, in his essay on *Intellectual and Moral Reform*, called for a strong government, "which would compel the sturdy country folk to do our work for us, while we give ourselves up to reflections".[4]

* From this came directly into the German language "Können" (power) and "kennen" (to perceive).

40

Perceptional abstraction outside immediately active effectiveness is, for us, inadmissible. The dissociation of the perceptional process from the productive can have no place with us.

It is worth our attention that in Renan's original text this citation ends: "tandis que nous spéculons". "Spéculons" could be translated "give ourselves up to speculations". It is also noteworthy that we link such a term, inseparably, to a quite different chain of associations.

In abstract science scientific thinking is outside all links with immediate operation—"science for the sake of science", "perception for perception's sake"—attitudes that we are ready to brand as 'speculation', no matter in which branches of science they may rise.

Speculative philosophy has as little place in conditions of socialist construction as does speculation in products of prime necessity.

For us, to know is to participate.

For this we value the biblical term—"and Abraham *knew* his wife Sarah"—by no means meaning that he became acquainted with her!

Perceiving is building. The perceiving of life—indissolubly—is the construction of life—the *rebuilding* of it.

In the epoch of construction an opposition to such an understanding cannot be! Not even in the form of research dissection. The very fact of the existence of our epoch of socialist reconstruction and of our social order refutes this.

The forward movement of our epoch in art must blow up the Chinese Wall that stands between the primary antithesis of the "language of logic" and the "language of images".

We demand from the coming epoch of art a rejection of such opposition.

Qualitatively: we desire to return the differentiated and insulated concepts to the *quantitatively* correlated. We do not wish any further to oppose science and art *qualitatively*.

We want to compare them quantitatively, in order to introduce them into a *unified new view of socially-active factors*.

Is there a basis for foreseeing such a synthetic path? I say *synthetic*, for we expect this solution to be infinitely remote

41

from any departmental formula, such as that "instructional work must not be devoid of entertainment, and entertainment must not be without didactics".

Is there a basis? In their sphere of influence what have these domains, for the moment mutually antagonistic, in common?

There is no art outside conflict. Art as a process.

As in the collision of the arrow-like flight of Gothic vaults with the inexorable law of gravity.

In the clash of the hero with the turns of fate in a tragedy.

In the functional purpose of a building with the conditions of soil and building materials.

In the conquering rhythms of verse over the dead metrics of the canons of versification.

Everywhere—struggle. A stabilization born from the clash of opposites.

The fulfilment of this increases in intensity, drawing in ever new spheres of perceptional sense-responses. Meanwhile, at the apogee, it is not altogether involved. Not units, individuals, but a collective, an audience. Moreover, this audience meanwhile does not enter into creative play. Here is the split.

Collective from collective. Split by little walls. Even in sport-play, walls attempt to divide one collective from another. Sport-play viewed as art, completely involving both spectator and creator. Into participation. Into a contemporary aspect of returning through sport to the cycle that began with the pre-tragedy play of the ancients.

There is, of course, such a "formal" correlation, in certain communities, between modern communism and primitive communism.

Nevertheless—what about *science*?

Book. Printed word. Eyes. Eyes—to brain. Bad!

Book. Word. Eyes. *Moving* from corner to corner. Better! . . .

Who hasn't crammed, pacing from corner to corner of a four-walled space, book in hand?

Who hasn't drummed rhythmically with his fist as he committed to memory, "surplus value is . . ."! i.e. who has not

42

helped his optical stimulation by including some sort of motor rhythm in fixing an abstraction in his memory?

Better. Audience. Lecturer. Of course, not some emasculated bureaucrat from Education. But one of those flaming old fanatics (fewer around now) like the late Professor Sokhotzki,* who could by the hour and with the same fire of enthusiasm, discourse on integral calculus and analyse in infinite detail how Camille Desmoulins, Danton, Gambetta or Volodarsky thundered against the enemies of the people and the revolution.

The temperament of the lecturer absorbs you completely. And all those around you. In this steely embrace the breathing of the entire electrified audience suddenly becomes rhythmic.

The audience suddenly becomes one—as at a circus, a hippodrome, or a meeting. In this arena there is a single collective impulse. A single pulsating interest.

And suddenly the mathematical abstraction has become flesh and blood.

The most difficult formula is committed to memory—in the rhythm of your breathing—

A dry integral is recalled in the feverish glow of eyes. In the mnemonics of a *collectively* experienced *perception*.

To go further. To the theory of music. A rattling one-horse carriage exhaustingly strives to climb the dusty hills in a scale of intervals—*do-re, re-mi, mi-fa, sol* ... The piano overstrains itself. In the end strings as well as nerves are jangling ... No, it doesn't work out. You can't turn back to the organic dissociation process that links voice and hearing. And then suddenly a chorus of all the individual "pipes". And a "miracle" takes place. Rapping out distinctly interval by interval, in *collective action*, the weak little voices are expanded, built up. It sounds—it works out—it's accomplished.

Suddenly it slips away. And a strangely measured dance moves through the room. What is this? Dionysian ecstasy? No—this is Jaques-Dalcroze who had the idea of perfecting

---

* In his German text for this part of the essay E. mentions that Sokhotzki was his mathematics professor at the engineering academy.—J. L.

43

the rhythmic memory of his students in solfeggio, by intro-
ducing a rhythmic movement of the *entire body* instead of
merely clapping hands. He found that this helped to conquer
the most delicate nuances of tempo.

And yet further. And the collective is torn in two. Two
desks. Two opponents. Two "catapults". In the fires of
dialectics, in discussion, the objective data, the values of
phenomena, of facts, are tempered and forged—"from wall
to wall".

The authoritarian-teleological "Thus it is so" flies to the
devil. Axioms taken on faith—crash. "In the beginning was
the Word . . ." But, *perhaps*, not "was"? A theorem in contradictions, requiring demonstration, includes *dialectical*
conflict.

Includes a dialectic comprehension of contradictions to
grasp the essence of a phenomenon. Irrefutably.

With *limited intensity*. Resolved in an internal struggle,
the opposing viewpoints must comprehend elements of personal logic and temperament. A complex deepened by the
experience of conditioned reflexes and the immediate
flaming of unconditioned reflexes.

In the test of dialectical fires is smelted the new factor of
construction. A new social reflex is wrought.

Where is the difference? Where is the abyss between
tragedy and essay? Isn't the reason for both *to awaken
inner conflicts and through their dialectical resolution to
provide a fresh stimulus for creativity in the perceptive
masses?*

Where is the difference between a perfected method of
oratory and a perfected method of gaining knowledge?

The duality in the spheres of "feeling" and "reasoning"
must have new limits by the new art:

To restore sensuality to science.

To restore to the intellectual process its fire and passion.

To plunge the abstract reflective process into the fervour
of practical action.

To give back to emasculated theoretical *formulas* the
rich exuberance of life-felt *forms*.

To give to formal *arbitrariness* the clarity of ideological
formulation.

44

Those are the challenges. Those are the demands that we make on the period of art that we are now entering.

To which art will this not be too much to demand?

Wholly and only to the cinema.

Wholly and only to the *intellectual cinema.* A synthesis of the emotional, the documentary, and the absolute film.

Only an *intellectual* cinema can resolve the discord between the "language of logic" and the "language of images". Based on a language of film-dialectics.*

An *intellectual* cinema unprecedented in form and social function. A cinema with new boundaries of perception and sensuality, mastering the whole arsenal of affective stimulants—visual, aural, bio-mechanical.

But on the road to it someone will have to be sacrificed.

Someone lying across the road.

Who is this? This is the so-called "living man".

He is being asked for in literature. In theatre he is already half-abandoned at the stage door of the Moscow Art Theatre.

Now he is knocking at the door of cinema.

Comrade "Living Man"! As to literature I am not qualified to say. Nor as to theatre. But your place is not in

* For his German text E. provided at this point a new conclusion for the essay (quoted here in Christel Gang's translation for *The Left*, Autumn 1931):

Only through such a cinema, which alone is capable of uniting immediate dialectical conflicts in the development of conceptions, does it become possible to penetrate the mind of the great masses with new ideas and new perceptions. Such a cinema alone will dominate, by its form, the summit of modern industrial technique. Such a cinema alone will have a right to exist among the wonders of radio, the telescope and the theory of relativity. The old type of primitive cinema as well as the type of abstract-aloof film will disappear before the new intellectual, *concrete* film. Nor will the former be saved by its combination with the sound film. In the intellectual film sound will receive its humble necessary place among the other means of effect! The revolution of the cinema will not come from the sound-film. The revolution of the cinema will be along the lines of the intellectualization of the film.

This is the genuine contribution which Soviet art brings to the universal history of the arts. This will be the contribution of our whole epoch to art. To art, which has ceased to be art, on its way to the goal, which is Life.

cinema. In cinema you are a "right deviation". The demand
for you is not on the highest level of technical means and
potentialities, nor could you fulfil the duty of expressing
that—for the level of industrial growth dictates ideological
form. You have been dictated by what, in the field of art,
corresponds to the lowest stage of industrial development.
Thematically you are too plough-like for a highly industrialized form of art, such as cinema in general, and the intellectual cinema in particular. To adapt such cinema to you,
or you to it, would be like using the hand of a stop-watch
to gut a whitefish!

The "living man" is exhaustingly appropriate within the
cultural limits and the cultural limitations of the theatre
medium. And then not of theatre of the Left, but the Moscow Art Theatre in particular: The Moscow Art Theatre
and its tendencies; and this is quite logical and consistent at
this moment, pompously celebrating its "second youth"
around these demands.

The Left theatre, owing to inadaptability, factually hasn't
survived. It split up in its last stage of growth—either into
the cinema or else returned to its former stage of the
AKhRR* type. Between these two stages remains only
Meyerhold, not as a theatre but as a master.

In the conditions of *Realpolitik* the cinema does not
reject certain Moscow Art Theatre influences, but nevertheless must stubbornly hold its course in the direction of
intellectual cinema as the highest possible form of cinema.
To have the "living man" capture the screen would be precisely "unsuitable progress" on the way to the industrializa-
tion of film-culture.

The cinema is capable of, and consequently must achieve,
a concrete sensual translation to the screen of the essential
dialectics in our ideological debates. Without recourse to
story, plot, or the living man.

The intellectual cinema can and must resolve the thema-
tics of such matters as "right deviation", "left deviation",
"dialectic method", "tactics of Bolshevism". Not only in
characteristic "little scenes and episodes", but in the
arrangement of whole *systems* and *systems of reasoning*.

* Association of Artists of Revolutionary Russia.

Specifically "Tactics of Bolshevism" and now "The October Revolution" or "The Year 1905" for example. Schemes, more primitive both in its themes—psychological and psycho-representative—and in its method of exposition "via intermediary protagonists", remain the share of less highly industrialized means of expression. And the very method and system, undoubtedly, must use concrete material, but in a totally different setting and from another point of view.

Theatre and cinema of the old play-acting type.

To the share of the new cinema, the only one capable of including dialectical conflict in the promotion of understanding, falls the task of inculcating Communist ideology in the millions.

This comes as the last link in the chain of means employed in the cultural revolution, linking up everything in a single monistic system, from collective training and complex methods of instruction to the newest form of art, as it ceases to be an art and moves on to the next stage of its development.

Only with such a solution of its problems can the cinema truly deserve the designation, "the most important of the arts".

Only as such will it be distinguished fundamentally from bourgeois cinema.

Only as such will it become a part of the future epoch of Communism.

The Capital *project and the "intellectual cinema" theory went with the Eisenstein group to the United States in 1930 when the Paramount studio signed a contract with Eisenstein. But the project and the theory remained as unrealized in Hollywood as did the dozen other film projects proposed to them and by them. Just before leaving for Mexico to make a film financed by Mr and Mrs Upton Sinclair, Eisenstein attended a special meeting, on 17 September 1930, organized by the Academy of Motion Picture Arts and Sciences, to discuss new screen dimensions suggested by the wide films recently introduced. He was not satisfied that his contribution had clarified his position, so, soon after getting*

47

to Mexico, he set out his ideas in an article which he sent to Kenneth Macpherson for publication in Close Up. *Macpherson introduced the article with a portion of Eisenstein's accompanying letter.*

The Dynamic Square

It is possible that, at first glance, this article may seem too detailed or its subject not of sufficiently "profound" value, but it is my wish to point out the basic importance of this problem for every creative art director, director, and cameraman. And I appeal to them to take this problem as seriously as possible. For a shudder takes me when I think that, by not devoting enough attention to this problem, and permitting the standardization of a new screen shape without the thorough weighing of all the pros and cons of the question, we risk paralysing once more, for years and years to come, our compositional efforts in new shapes as unfortunately chosen as those from which the practical realization of the Wide Film and Wide Screen now seems to give us the opportunity of freeing ourselves.

S. M. E.

Rio Papagayo
Guerrero
Mexico

Mr Chairman, Gentlemen of the Academy,
 I think this actual moment is one of the great historical moments in the pictorial development of the screen. At the moment when incorrect handling of sound is at the point of ruining the *pictorial* achievements of the screen—and we all know only too many examples where this actually has been done!—the arrival of the wide screen with its opportunities for a new screen shape throws us once more headlong into

questions of purely spatial composition. And much more—
it affords us the possibility of reviewing and re-analysing
the whole aesthetic of pictorial composition in the cinema
which for thirty years has been rendered inflexible by the
inflexibility of the once and for all inflexible frame proportions of the screen.

Gee, it is a great day!

And the more tragic therefore appears the terrible en-
slavement of mind by traditionalization and tradition that
manifests itself on this happy occasion.

The card of invitation to this meeting bears the representation of three differently proportioned horizontal rectangles: 3—4: 3 × 5: 3—6, as suggestions for the proportions of the screen for wide film projection. They also
represent the limits within which revolves the creative
imagination of the screen reformers and the authors of the
coming era of a new frame shape.

I do not desire to be exaggeratedly symbolic, or rude, or
to compare the creeping rectangles of these proposed shapes
to the creeping mentality of the film reduced thereto by the
weight upon it of the commercial pressure of dollars,
pounds, francs, or marks according to the locality in which
the cinema happens to be suffering!

But I must point out that, in proposing these proportions
for discussion, we only underline the fact that for thirty
years we have been content to see excluded 50 per cent of
composition possibilities, in consequence of the *horizontal
shape* of the frame.

By the word "excluded" I refer to all the possibilities of
vertical, upright composition. And instead of using the
opportunity afforded by the advent of wide film to break
that loathsome upper part of the frame, which for thirty
years—me personally for six years—has bent and bound us
to a passive horizontalism, we are on the point of emphasizing this horizontalism still more.

It is my purpose to defend the cause of this 50 per cent of
compositional possibilities which have been banished from
the light of the screen. It is my desire to chant the hymn of
the male, the strong, the virile, active, *vertical* composition!

I am not anxious to enter into the dark phallic and sexual

ancestry of the vertical shape as symbol of growth, strength, or power. It would be too easy, and possibly too offensive for many a sensitive hearer!

But I do want to point out that the movement towards a vertical perception led our savage ancestors on their way to a higher level. This vertical tendency can be traced in their biological, cultural, intellectual and industrial efforts and manifestations.

We started as worms creeping on our stomach. Then for hundreds of years we ran horizontally on our four legs. But we became something like human only from the moment when we hoisted ourselves on to our hind legs and assumed the vertical position.

Repeating the same process locally in the verticalization of our facial angle too.

I cannot, nor need I, enter in detail into an outline of the whole influence of the biological and psychological revolution and shock which followed from that paramount change of attitude. Enough if we mention man's activities. For long years man was herded in tribes on an endless expanse of fields, bound to the earth in an age-long bondage by the nature of the primitive plough. But he marked in vertical milestones each achievement of his progress to a higher level of social, cultural, or intellectual development. The upright lingam of the mystical Indian knowledge of the olden time, the obelisks of the Egyptian astrologers, Trajan's column incarnating the political power of Imperial Rome, the cross of the new spirit brought in by Christianity. The high point of medieval mystical knowledge bursting upright in the Gothic ogive arch and spire. Just as the era of exact mathematical knowledge shouts its paean to the sky with the Eiffel Tower! And introduces the huge skylines assailing the vault of amazed heaven with armies of skyscrapers and infinite rows of the smoking chimneys or trellised oilpumps of our great industries. The endless trails of wandering wagons have heaped themselves upon one another to form the tower of a Times or Chrysler building. And the camp fire, once the homely centre of the travellers' camp, has now paused to vomit its smoke from the unending heights of factory chimneys. . . .

50

By now, surely, you will suppose that my suggestion for
the optical frame of the supreme and most synthetic of all
arts—the possibilities of all of which are included in the
cinema notwithstanding the fact that it doesn't use them!—
is that it must be vertical.

Not at all.

For in the heart of the super-industrialized American, or
the busily self-industrializing Russian, there still remains a
nostalgia of infinite horizons, of fields, of plains and deserts.
Individual or nation attaining the height of mechanization
and yet marrying it to our peasant and farmer yesterday.

The nostalgia of "big trails", "fighting caravans", "covered wagons" and the endless breadth of "old man
rivers" . . .

This nostalgia cries out for horizontal space.

And on the other hand industrial culture too sometimes
brings tribute to this "despised form". She throws the interminable Brooklyn Bridge to the left of Manhattan and
attempts to surpass it by Hudson Bridge to the right. She
expands without end the length of the body of poor *Puffing
Billy* to that of the Southern Pacific locomotives of today.
She lines up endless outspread chains of human bodies (as
a matter of fact—legs) in the innumerable rows of musical-
hall girls, and indeed what limit is there to the other horizontal victories of the age of electricity and steel!

Just as, in contrast to her pantheistic horizontal tendencies, mother nature provides us at the edge of Death Valley
or Mojave Desert with the huge 300-foot height of the
General Sherman and General Grant trees, and the other
giant Sequoias, created (if we may believe the geography
school books of every country) to serve as tunnels for
coaches or motor cars to pass through their pierced feet;
just as, opposed to the infinite horizontal contredanse of the
waves, at the edge of the ocean, we encounter the same
element shot upright to the sky as geysers; just as the croco-
dile stretched out basking in the sun is flanked by upright
standing giraffe in the company of the ostrich and flamingo
—all three clamouring for a decent screen frame appropriate to their upright shape!

51

So neither the horizontal nor the vertical proportion of the screen *alone* is ideal for it.

Actually, as we saw, in the forms of nature as in the forms of industry, and in the mutual encounters of these forms, we have the struggle, the conflict of both tendencies. And the screen, as a faithful mirror, not only of conflicts emotional and tragic, but equally of conflicts psychological and optically spatial, must be an appropriate battleground for the skirmishes of both these optical-by-view, but profoundly psychological-by-meaning, space tendencies of the spectator.

What is it that, by readjustment, can in equal degree be made the figure of both vertical and horizontal tendencies of a picture?

The battlefield for such a fight is easily found—*it is the square*—the rectangular space form exemplifying the quality of equal length of its dominant axes.

The one and only form equally fit by alternate suppression of right and left, or of up and down, to embrace all the multitude of expressive rectangles of the world. Or used as a whole to engrave itself by the "cosmic" imperturbability of its *squareness* in the psychology of the audience.

And this specially in a *dynamic* succession of *dimensions* from a tiny square in the centre to the all-embracing of a full sized square of the whole screen!

The "dynamic" square screen, that is to say one providing in its dimensions the opportunity of impressing, in projection, with absolute grandeur every geometrically conceivable form of the picture limit.

(Note here 1 : This means that dynamism of changeable proportion of the projected picture is accomplished by masking a part of the shape of the film square—the frame.

And note here 2 : This has nothing to do with the suggestion that the proportions 1:2 (3:6) give a "vertical possibility" in masking the right and the left to such an extent that the remaining area has the form of an upright standing strip. The *vertical spirit* can never thus be attained: 1st, because the occupied space comparative to the horizontal masked space will never be interpreted as something *axially opposed to it*, but always *as a part* of the latter, and

52

2nd, because, *never surpassing the height* that is bound to the horizontal dominant, it will never impress as an opposite space axis—the one of uprightness. That is why my suggestion of squareness puts the question in quite a new field, notwithstanding the fact that vari-typed masking has been used even in the dull proportions of the present standard film size, and even by myself—in the opening shot of the Odessa steps in *Potemkin*.)

No matter what the theoretic premises, only the square will afford us the real opportunity at last to give decent shots of so many things banished from the screen until today. Glimpses through winding medieval streets or huge Gothic cathedrals overwhelming them. Or these replaced by minarets if the town portrayed should happen to be oriental. Decent shots of totem poles. The Paramount building in New York, Primo Carnera, or the profound and abysmal canyons of Wall Street in all their expressiveness—shots available to the cheapest magazine—yet debarred for thirty years from the screen.

So far for my form.

And I believe profoundly in the rightness of my statement because of the synthetic approach upon which its conclusions are based. Further, the warm reception of my statement encourages me to a certainty in the theoretic soundness of my argument.

But the lying form of the screen (so appropriate to its lying spirit!) has a host of refined and sophisticated defenders. There exists even a special and peculiar literature on these questions and we should leave our case incomplete did we not pass in critical review the arguments therein contained for the form it prefers.

II

The memorandum distributed to us before this meeting (attached to this discourse as appendix[1]) and brilliantly compiled by Mr Lester Cowan, assistant secretary of the Academy) provides a brief and objective survey of all that has been written regarding the proportions of the screen. Most of these writings show a preference for the horizontal frame.

Let us examine the arguments that have brought different authors from different sides and special fields, to the same, unanimously acclaimed, —— wrong suggestion.

The principal arguments are four:

Two from the dominion of aesthetics.

One physiological.

And one commercial.

Let us demolish them in that order.

The two aesthetic arguments in favour of the horizontal shape of the screen are based on deductions deriving from traditions in the art forms of painting and stage practice. As such, they should be eliminated from discussion even without being taken into consideration, for the greatest errors invariably arise from the attempt to transplant practical results based upon the resemblance of the superficial appearances of one branch of art to those of another. (An entirely different practice is the discovery of similarity in the *methods* and *principles* of different arts corresponding to the psychological phenomena identical and basic to all art perceptions—but the present superficially exposed *analogies,* as we shall see, are far from this!)

Indeed, from the methodological similiarity of different arts it is our task to seek out the strictest differentiation in adapting and handling them according to the organic specifics typical for each. To enforce adoption of the laws organic to one art upon another is profoundly wrong. This practice has something of adultery in it. Like sleeping in another person's wife's bed . . .

But in this case the arguments in themselves bring so mistaken a suggestion from their own proper dominion that it is worth while considering them to demonstrate their falsity.

1. Loyd A. Jones (No. 9 on the list) discusses the various rectangular proportions employed in artistic composition and gives the result of a statistical study of the proportions of paintings. The results of his research seem to favour a ratio of base to altitude considerably larger than 1, and probably over 1·5.

A statement startling in itself. I don't repudiate the enormous bundle of statistics that was doubtless at the disposal of Mr Jones in enabling him to make so decisive a statement.

But as I set about summoning up my pictorial recollections gathered through all the museums that I have so lately visited during my rush through Europe and America, and recalling the heaps of graphic works and compositions studied during my work, it seems to me that there are exactly as many upright standing pictures as pictures disposed in horizontal line.

And everyone will agree with me.

The statistical paradox of Mr Jones derives probably from an undue weight placed upon compositional proportions of the nineteenth century pre-impressionistic period—the worst period of painting—the "narrative" type of picture. Those second- and third-rate paintings, right off the progressive highroad of painting development, and even today far surpassing in volume the new schools of painting, abundant even in the neighbourhood of Picasso and Léger as petty-bourgeois oleographs in most concierge offices of the world!

In this "narrative" group of painting the $1 : 1 \cdot 5$ proportion is certainly predominant, but this fact is absolutely unreliable if considered from the point of view of pictorial composition. These proportions in themselves are "borrowed goods"—entirely unconnected with pictorial space organization, which is a painting problem. These proportions are barefacedly borrowed—not to say stolen!—from—the stage.

The *stage composition* each of these pictures intentionally or unintentionally reproduces, a process in itself quite logical, since the pictures of this school are occupied not with pictorial problems but with "representing scenes"—a painting purpose even formulated in *stage* terms!

I mention the nineteenth century as especially prolific in this type of picture, but I do not wish to convey the impression that other periods are entirely lacking in them! Consider, for example, Hogarth's series *Marriage à la Mode*—satirically and scenically in their "represented" anecdotes a most thrilling series of pictures . . .

It is remarkable that in another case, where the author of

55

the painting was, practically and professionally, at the same time a stage composer (or "art director" as we would say in Hollywood), this phenomenon has no place. I mean the case of the medieval miniature. Authors of the tiniest filigree brushwork in the world, on the leaves of gilded bibles, or *livres d'heures* (do not confound with *hors d'oeuvres*!), they were at the same time architects of the various settings of the mysteries and miracles. (Thus Fouquet and an innumerable quantity of artists whose names have been lost to posterity.) Here, where, owing to subject, we ought to have the closest reproduction of the aperture of the stage—we miss it. And find a freedom entirely void of such bounds. And why? Because at that time *the stage aperture did not exist*. The stage was then limited far off to right and left by Hell and Heaven, covered with frontally disposed parts of settings (the so-called mansions) with blue unlimited sky overshining them—as in many Passion Plays of today.

Thus we prove that the supposedly "predominant" and characteristic form of the painting by itself belongs properly to another branch of art.

And from the moment in which painting liberates itself by an impressionistic movement, turning to purely pictorial problems, it abolishes every form of aperture and establishes, as an example and an ideal, the framelessness of a Japanese impressionistic drawing. And, symbolic as it may be, it is the moment for the dawn of—photography. Which, extraordinary to remark, conserves in its later metempsychosis, the moving picture, certain (*vital* this time) traditions of this period of the maturity of one art (painting) and the infantilism of its successor (photography). Notice the relationship between Hokusai's *Hundred Views of Fuji* and so many camera shots made with so pronounced a tendency towards shooting two planes of depth—one through another (especially *Fuji seen through a cobweb* and *Fuji seen through the legs*, or Edgar Degas, whose startling series of compositions of women in the bath, *modistes* and *blanchisseuses*, is the best school in which to acquire training in ideas about space composition within the limits of a frame —and about frame composition too, which, in this series, restlessly jumps from $1:2$ over $1:1$ to $2:1$.

56

This is, I think, the right point at which to quote one of Miles's (1) arguments much more closely concerned with the pictorial element here discussed than with the psychological where it was intended to be placed. For Miles, "the whole thing (the inclination towards horizontal perception) is perhaps typified in the opening through which the human eye looks; this is characteristically much wider than it is high".

Let us suppose for a moment this argument to be true in itself, and we can even provide him with a brilliant example for his statement, one even "plus royaliste que le roi".—Still it won't help him!—But, by the way, the example is the typical shape of a typical Japanese landscape woodcut. This is the only type of standardized (not occasional) composition known, compositionally not limited at the sides by the bounds of any frame, and typified in its vertical limit by a shaded narrow strip from lowest white to, at its topmost, darkest blue, rushing in this limited space through all the shades of this celestial colour.

This last phenomenon is explained as the impression of the shadow falling on the eye from the upper eyelid, caught by the supersensitive observation of the Japanese.

It might be presumed that we have here, in this configuration, the fullest pictorial testimony to the above view of Miles. But once more we must disappoint: inasmuch as the idea of a framed picture derives not from the limits of the view field of our eyes but from the fact of the usual framedness of the glimpse of nature we catch through the frame of the window or the door—or stage aperture as shown above —equally the composition of the Japanese derives from his lack of door frames, doors being replaced by the sliding panels of the walls of a typical Japanese house opening on to an infinite horizon.

But, even supposing that this shape represents the proportions of the view field, we must consider yet another remarkable phenomenon of Japanese art: the materialization on paper of the above-mentioned absence of side boundaries in the form of the horizontal *roll picture*, born only in Japan and China, and not prevalent elsewhere. I would call it *unroll picture*, because, unwound horizontally from one roll to another, it shows interminable episodes of

57

battles, festivals, processions: for example, the pride of the Boston Museum: the many-foot-long *Burning of the Sanjo Palace*; or the immortal *Killing of the Bear in the Emperor's Garden* at the British Museum. Having created this unique type of horizontal picture out of the supposed horizontal tendency of perception, the Japanese, with their supersensitive artistic feeling, then created, illogical as it may be according to the view of Mr Miles, *the opposite form*—as a matter of purely aesthetic need for counter-balance, for Japan (with China) is also the birthplace of the *vertical roll picture*. The tallest of all vertical compositions (if we disregard the Gothic vertical window compositions). Roll pictures are also found to take the form of curiously shaped coloured woodcuts of upright composition, with the most amazing compositional disposition of faces, dresses, background elements and stage attributes.

This, I hold, shows pretty clearly that even if the diagnosis of perception as horizontal should be correct (which should by no means be regarded as proved), vertical composition also is needed as harmonic counter-balance to it.

This tendency towards harmony, and perceptive equilibrium, is of a nature quite other than a different "harmonic" and "aesthetic" argument introduced by another group of defendants of the horizontal screen.

To quote Mr Cowan's summary:

> Howell and Dubray (10), Lane (7), Westerberg (11), and Dieterich (8) agree that the most desirable proportions are those approximating 1·618 : 1, which correspond to those of the so-called "whirling square" rectangle (also known as the "golden cut"), based on the principles of dynamic symmetry which have predominated in the arts for centuries. For simplicity the ratio 5 : 3 (which equals 1·667 : 1), or 8 : 5 (equalling 1·6 : 1) are generally advocated instead of 1·618 : 1. . . .

"Predominance in the arts for centuries" should in itself be a cause for the profoundest suspicion when the idea is applied to an entirely and basically new form of art, such as the youngest art, the art of cinema.

Cinema is the first and only art based entirely on dynamic

and speed phenomena, and yet *everlasting* as a cathedral or a temple; having, with the latter, the characteristics of the static arts—i.e. the possibility of intrinsic existence by itself freed from the creative effort giving it birth (the theatre, the dance, music*—the only dynamic arts before the cinema, lacked this possibility, the quality of everlastingness independent of the artistic act that created it, and by this means were characteristically distinguished from the contrasting group of static arts).

Why should a holy veneration for this mistaken "golden cut" persist if all the basic elements of this newcomer in art —the cinema—are entirely different, its premises being entirely different from those of all that has gone before?

Consider the two other denominations of the "golden cut", denominations expressive for the tendency of these proportions: the "whirling square", the principle of "dynamic symmetry".

They are the *cry* of the static hopelessly longing towards dynamism. These proportions are probably those most fitted to give the maximum tension to the eye in causing it to follow one direction and then throw itself afterwards to follow the other.

But—have we not attained, by projection of our film on the screen, a "whirling" square that exists in actuality?

And have we not discovered in the principle of the rhythmical cutting of the strip a "dynamic symmetry" that exists in actuality?

A tendency practically attained and triumphantly materialized by the *cinema as a whole*. And which therefore does not need to be advanced by the *screen shape*.

And why the hell should we drag behind us in these days of triumph the melancholy memory of the unfulfilled desire of the static rectangle striving to become dynamic?

Just as the moving picture is the tombstone of the futuristic effort of dynamism in the static painting.

There is no logical basis for preserving this mystical worship of the "golden cut". We are far enough away from

* The gramophone record, also a dynamic form made everlasting, has to be considered now as a part of the film.

the Greeks who, in exaggeration of their extraordinary feeling for harmonic proportion, used a proportion for their irrigation channels based upon some sacred harmonic formula, dictated by no practical consideration. (Or was that case one of war trenches? I don't remember exactly but I do remember that it was some practical enchannelling process determined by considerations purely abstract, aesthetic and unpractical.)

The imposition of these century-old proportions upon the month-young wide screen by force would be as illogical as this Greek business was. And, to finish with all this painting tradition, *if* it be desired to establish the relationship of the screen frame to *something else*, why on earth not use for comparison the intermediary between painting and the moving picture—the postcard or amateur photography?

Well, here we can insist that, at least in this field, justice be equally done to both tendencies!

By the mere fact that our pocket Kodak snaps with equal facility and accuracy either vertical or horizontal shots of our kid, pa, ma or grandma, according to whether they are lying in the sunshine on the beach, or posing hand in hand in their wedding, silver wedding or golden wedding dress!

The second aesthetic argument emerges from the domain of the theatre and musical show, and, as reproduced by Mr Cowan, runs as follows: "... another argument for wide film rests on the possibilities inherent in sound pictures which were lacking [were they really lacking???—S.E.] in the silent pictures of presenting entertainment more of the nature of the spoken drama of the stage." (Rayton (3)).

Preserving my usual politeness, I shall not say outright that this is the most terrific plague hanging over the talkie. I won't say it, I shall only think it, and shall confine myself to an observation with which every one must agree, viz., that the aesthetics and laws of composition of the sound film and talkie are far from being established. And to consider the present misuse of the talking screen as the basis for a suggestion that will bind us for the next thirty years to a proportion fitting that thirty months' misuse of the screen, is, to say at least, presumptuous.

Instead of approximating the cinema to the stage, the

wide screen, in my opinion, should drag the cinema still further away from it, opening up for the magic power of montage, an entirely new era of constructive possibilities.

But more of that later—as dessert.

The third distinctly formulated argument for horizontal proportion derives from the domain of physiology. It does not prevent it from being as mistaken as its predecessors. Dieterich (8) and Miles (1) have pointed out that the wider picture shows itself more accessible to the eye by virtue of the physiological properties of the latter. As Miles says,

> The eyes have one pair of muscles for moving them in the horizontal but two pairs for moving them in the vertical. Vertical movements are harder to make over a wide visual angle. As man has lived in his natural environment, he has usually been forced to perceive more objects arranged in the horizontal than in the vertical [!!!—S.E.]. This has apparently established a very deep seated habit which operates throughout his visual perception. . . .

This argument sounds very plausible. But its plausibility largely disappears the moment our research glides from the surface of the face, provided with its horizontally disposed perceptive eyes, towards . . . the neck. Here we could paraphrase exactly the same quotation in the directly opposite sense. For here the mechanism of bending and lifting the head as opposed to its turning movement from right to left provides for exactly the opposite conditions of muscular effort. The lifting and bending of the head (vertical perception) is carried out just as easily as eye movement from left to right (horizontal perception). We see that also in this case, in the purely physiological means of perception, the Wisdom of Nature has provided us with compensatory movements tending to the same all-embracing square harmony. But that is not all.

My example, as well as my counter-example, has established another phenomenon of the perceptive auditor: the phenomenon of *dynamism in perception*. In horizontal dimensions of the eyes and vertical of the head.

And this by itself overthrows another of Dieterich's (8) arguments:

On physiological grounds that the total field covered by the vision of both eyes (for fixed head position), and also the field comfortably covered by the vision of both eyes, both approximate, a 5×8 rectangular form, although the actual boundaries of these fields are somewhat irregular curves . . .

For fixed head position . . . but the *unfixed* head position has just been established and that argument thereby loses its force.

(By the way, the only really insuperably bound and fixed position of the head in a movie theatre is when it is at rest . . . on one's sweetheart's shoulder. But we cannot pause for the consideration of such facts, notwithstanding that they concern at the very least 50 per cent of the audience.)

III

There remains the last argument—the economic.

The horizontally extended form corresponds most closely to the shape left for the eye by the balcony overhanging the back of the parterre, and by the series of balconies each overhanging the other. The absolute possible limit of screen height in these conditions is estimated by Sponable (2) as 23 feet to every 46 of horizontal possibilities.

If we are to remain governed by strictly economic considerations—we might well allow that by using vertical compositions we should oblige the public to move to the more expensive forward seats free of overhanging balconies. . . .

But another fact comes to our rescue—and this is the inappropriateness of the present shape and proportions of the present-day cinema theatre for *sound purposes.*

Acoustics help optics!

I have not the time to examine references in looking up the ideal proportions for a sound theatre.

I faintly recall from my dim and distant past study of architecture that, in theatre and concert buildings, the vertical cut should, for optimum acoustics, be parabolic.

What I do remember clearly is the shape and the typical proportions of two ideal buildings. One ideal for optical display:

Let us take the Roxy (New York).

And one for auditive display:

The Salle Pleyel in Paris—the peak acoustic perfection hitherto attained in a concert hall.

They are *exactly* opposed in proportions to each other. If the Salle Pleyel were to lie down upon its side it would become a Roxy. If the Roxy were to stand upright it would become a Salle Pleyel. Every proportion of the Roxy split horizontally into parterres and balconies opposes itself directly to the strictly vertical, deeply receding, corridor-like Salle Pleyel.

The sound film—the intersection of optic and auditive display, will have to synthesize, in the shape of its display hall, both tendencies with equal force.

In the days to come the sound theatre will have to be reconstructed. And its new shape—in intersecting the horizontal and vertical tendencies of "ye olden Roxy" and "ye olden Pleyel" for these new coming days conditioned by a mingling of an optic and acoustic perception—will be the one most perfectly appropriate to the dynamic square screen and its display of vertical and horizontal affective impulses.*

* The actual reconstruction and readjustment of the now existing theatres, to adapt them to new forms of screen, would cost (considered entirely independently of the artistic value consquent upon any given kind of adaption), on the estimate of the experts of the Motion Picture Academy, about $40,000,000. But mechanical genius has found a way out: by the method of first taking the picture on 65 mm. Grandeur negative; reducing it so as to confine it where desired to the limits of a 35 mm. positive (not covering the whole field provided in the smaller-sized celluloid, owing to its different proportion); and finally throwing it on to the screen by magnifying lenses, enlarging it in dimension and transforming its proportion in accordance with the facing wall of the cinema theatre. This same proceeding would equally well be used for vertical composition which, as shown by the drawing, could, by a very slight alteration of horizontal line, provide for the equally vertical, and then (when reduced) would equally not surpass the dimension of the ordinary screen. It remains to bewail the partial and very slight loss of the limits of the vertically composed pictures, and that wail only for the worst balcony and parterre seats, and even there only a very small loss.

And now, last but not least, I must emphatically challenge one more creeping tendency that has partly triumphed over the talkies and is now stretching out its unclean hands towards the Grandeur film, hastening to force it into still more abject subservience to its base desires. This is the tendency to entirely smother the principles of montage, already weakened by the 100 per cent talkies, which are none the less awaiting the first powerful example of the perfectly cut and constructed sound film that will establish anew the montage principle as the basic, everlasting, and vital principle of cinematographic expression and creation.

I refer to innumerable quotations, quotations partially accepted even by such great masters of the screen as my friend Vidor and the Grand Old Man of all of us—D. W. Griffith. For example: "Dance scenes need no longer be 'followed' as there is ample room in a normal long shot for all the lateral movement used in most dances. . . ." [The "moving camera" is a means of producing in the spectator a specific dynamic feeling, and not a means of investigation or of following a dancing girl's feet! See the rocking movement of the camera in the reaping scene of *Old and New* and the same with the machine gun in *All Quiet on the Western Front.*—S.E.] ". . . Close-ups can be made on the wide film. Of course, it is not necessary to get as close as you do with the 35 mm. camera, but, comparatively speaking, you can make the same size of close-up. . . ."! [The impressive value of a close-up lies not at all in its absolute size, but entirely in its size relation to the optical affective impulse produced by the dimension of the previous and following shots.—S.E.] "However, with the wide film very few close-ups are needed. After all, the main reason for close-ups is to get over thought [! ! !—S.E.] and with the wide film you can get all the detail and expression in a full-sized figure that you would get in a six foot close-up with the 35 mm. film. . . ." [Although preferring, as far as my personal tastes are concerned in *screen* acting, the nearly imperceptible movement of the eyebrow, I none the less acclaim the possibility of a whole body expressing something. Still, however, we cannot admit the expulsion of the close-up—the fixing of attention by the isolation of a desired

During the filming of *Battleship Potemkin*, 1925. Eisenstein in cap and grey jacket; three assistants are seen: Alexandrov at the right of the camera, Levshin in striped shirt, and Antonov at the far right.

Eisenstein has written of illustrations seen in his childhood, at the time of the 1905 Revolution, that may have influenced the images of *Potemkin*. For a recent analysis of *Potemkin* (Moscow 1962), I Rostovtsev found this image of the Odessa mutiny in an Italian illustrated magazine, *Via Nuovo*, to compare with the opening of the sequence on the steps.

Photograph from the Paul Rotha collection, British Film Institute

fact or detail, an effect by no means achieved by merely
providing the body with disproportionate increase in absolute size.—S.E.]

Close-ups, moving camera shots, absolute dimensional
variation of figures and objects on the screen, and the other
elements concerned with montage, are far more fundamentally bound up with the expressive means of cinema
and cinema perception than is involved in the task of merely
facilitating the view of a face, or the "getting over of a
thought" on it.

As we have proclaimed (and as Alexandrov tried to show
in humble essay form in that piece of irony, *Romance
Sentimentale*, so grievously misunderstood in its intentions),
with the coming of sound montage does not die but
develops, amplifying and multiplying its possibilities and
its methods.

In the same way the advent of the wide screen marks one
further stage of enormous progress in the development of
montage, which once more will have to undergo a critical
review of its laws; laws mightily affected by the change of
absolute screen dimension, making impossible or unsuitable
quite a number of the montage processes of the days of the
olden screen, but on the other hand providing us with such
a gigantic new agent of impression as the rhythmic assem-
blage of varied screen shapes, the attack upon our perceptive field of the affective impulses associated with the
geometric and dimensional variation of the successive
various possible dimensions, proportions and designs.

And, accordingly, if to many of the qualities of Normal
Screen montage laws we must proclaim: "le roi est mort!"
yet with much greater strength we must cry "vive le roi!"
in welcome to the newcoming of the montage possibilities
of Grandeur Film, never hitherto envisaged or imaginable.

Santa Maria Tonantzintla, Cholula, Mexico

*In 1928, before Eisenstein left for Europe and America,
he had experienced his first attempt at teaching the principles of film-making. After he returned to the Soviet Union*

In December 1929, during his stay in London, Eisenstein visited the film-making class
conducted by Hans Richter in a studio over Foyle's, in Manette Street, where Richter
directed a short improvisation about a London policeman, acted by Eisenstein. Some of
the group shown in this photograph have been identified: Eisenstein (in policeman's
helmet) is communicating (by cane) with Richter, in the left-hand corner; Mark Segal
is playing the warming-pan; Lionel Britton (leaning on the helmet) is feverishly telephoning;
Jimmy Rogers (Cavalcanti's cameraman) is smiling at his Debrie; Len Lye is in hat, and
the trio behind him, from right to left, are Michael Hankinson, Basil Wright, and Towndrow.

Photograph from British Film Institute

in 1932 a series of frustrated efforts to resume film production made him turn again to the profession of teaching. The combining of this with more continuous theoretical work than had previously been possible made his work at GIK, the State Cinema Institute, an experience as rewarding to himself as to his students. The classroom of the Direction Course became his studio, his workshop, his laboratory, his stage and his screen. At the end of 1934, partly owing to his intense application to its problems, the Institute was raised to the status of a Higher Institute, VGIK, and Eisenstein celebrated the occasion with a declaration of purpose.

GTK—GIK—VGIK
Past—Present—Future*

The anniversary of the Cinema Institute has a special importance, for nowhere else in the world is there a film school on such a scale. There's nothing like our Institute, neither in the film-Babylon of Hollywood nor in the countless other Babylons of the world's film industries.

The reason for this strange circumstance should be obvious. It is not for lack of means in America, nor of raw film in Germany, nor of the wish to learn in England. Such an institute could be born and could function only in the Land of the Soviets. Only here were swept away those basic barriers that preclude the possibility of a similar institution in the West. Only here, in a country of socialist competition, has an end been put to the chaos of capitalist competition. Only here can that reflection of traditional relationships in bourgeois society, the traditional concept of success, with

* Written for the fifteenth jubilee of the Cinema Institute; this essay, however, does not pretend to deal with the whole history of the Institute, but only with that period when I was associated with it—that is, from 1928 to the present [the essay was written at the end of 1934].

the successful triumphing over the unsuccessful, be regarded with a new understanding.

Two contestants. One beats the other. X is less good, while Y is better. Hurrah for Y. But with us the unprecedented paradox (if examined from the same viewpoint). Two contestants. One is defeated. The other wins. So the other is better. But is the first bad? Nothing of the sort! Both are good. And this is because they are not competing against each other. It is because both of their interests reside in the general good. It is this general good that takes first place. And the loser in a contest can be just as proud as the winner.

For us this has become a—b—c. For us this is now flesh and blood.

But you should see the incredulity, amazement and consternation of European and American film directors when they are told that our master film-makers take their "professional secrets" to the rising young generation. When you begin to tell them about the Institute, you can see their eyes open wide in astonishment; you can see what they're thinking: "They'll snatch the bread out of your mouths. Why do you do it?"

Yet we do it—and we draw others into doing it as well.

There's enough bread in our country for all. Property relationships long ago departed from our psyche. Moreover, through many years of practice and experience, new material or spiritual values have arisen. And there is only one anxiety: will there be enough hands, enough heads, enough creative temperaments to fill the ranks of production in all the increasing scope of our growing cinematography?

In any country engineers instruct engineers. Technicians instruct technicians. The arts also can achieve such a level of personalization. Yet nowhere else can a creative worker teach a younger creative worker in an organized, socialized arrangement.

Elsewhere a "creative talent" is a ticket of admission into the privileged caste of supermen. A creative person does not even "mystically" comprehend his own activity. In the interest of this activity it pays to keep the caste as sparse as possible. A bourgeois collector who finds a duplicate of an object in his collection which is thought to be unique will spend any amount of money to destroy the duplicate and remain the possessor of the "unique" object.

A big artist does everything he can to "lose" the young beginner. All because the demand for creative work is limited. Because theatres and cinemas are not opening, but closing.

Because the demand for skillls does not expand, but contracts. Because beyond the talents of two or three stars the demands do not exceed the narrow channel of petty-bourgeois taste.

We, on the contrary, aim at a broad range and numerous applications for creative activity and creative energy. Theatre and cinema grow wider in subject and in quantity. And basically, there is an increase in demands and requirements for quality, for cultural quality, and for the qualifications of achievement.

And this situation produces a new necessity—to explore scientifically, with research and experiment, the questions of creation, of creative instruction and creative training. To strip away the veils of caste mystique that prevent the study of creative problems, and the theories and practice of creative work.

Only we have made this possible socially. Methodically as well.

No other social structure than ours can establish the social and psychological premises for such activity. Our social system alone possesses the desire and the means of removing all the wrappings of secrecy and mystique from the way things happen. In the matter of perceiving creative problems and processes we can claim to have advanced one step from infancy; we are at least of primary school age.

Already our method of research into certain areas of phenomena has revealed enormous horizons of understanding matters which have always been regarded as some kind of sacred mystery. Having brought such clarity into the field of the analysis and knowledge of art, this method could be applied with even more remarkable success to "practical aesthetics"—constructive creative practice. On the first level, every day adds to the volume of research that enriches the fund of Marxist classics on this question; on the second level, we have taken only the first steps.

It must be frankly acknowledged: the Institute wears me out. I'm worn out by the furious enthusiasm of the research work being done: by the revelation of fundamental laws and proportions in the construction of works, and by the process of their creation. And all this is along a line in the area of film craft that is least known and least investigated: the activity of the director as a composer of the audio-visual complex of a film. This may be terribly harmful for a creative worker. Perhaps this may explain the disappearance of his own creative career. Creative muteness may be the reward of those who allow themselves to introduce the scalpel of analysis into areas where entrance has always been forbidden.

Some even spitefully say: "He who can—creates; he who can't—teaches." Yet this does not take one thing into account. Study has not yet reached the level of automatic teaching. "To teach" in the present stage still means really "to create", for this is almost a bare place where one must form one's system and method for creatively apprehending the art of film direction. And work in this constructive sense is no less and no more than one's own creative tasks.

But on the other hand, what can compare with the feeling of an explorer, a pioneer, who gathers and links the experience of predecessors and contemporaries in the building of a synthetic constructive methodology, absorbing into itself all the highest achievements in the arts!

Only in close contact with those who grow, aspire, extend, achieve, miscarry or fail alongside the creative strivings of the younger generation, is it possible to see into this active application of the principles of the great heritage of scientific Marxism to the creative constructive process.

The old Proletcult view of the spontaneous birth of great artists solely from the ranks of the working class has long since been discarded. A thirst for study in a creative worker, for the study of direction, is obvious to everyone who speaks of creative longings. To meet this creative desire in the younger generation of the victorious working class, to meet the developing of his own experience and the summed-up experience of the older generation of film-makers, to meet it not with stories and anecdotes of production, but with experiment, with the intelligence of precise methods—those are the aims that must stand before those film-makers who can imagine their creative participation in the building of the Soviet cinema as extending beyond the frame of their own films.

For us an anniversary is not an occasion for banquets. To us an anniversary has something of the effect of that poster of the civil war period, with a finger pointing directly at the passer-by: "And what were YOU doing then?" The approach of a jubilee makes everyone accountable to the segment of history just past. And this accounting must always start from a recognition that what has been done is too little. This isn't modesty. This is a natural feeling when comparing either the little or much that has been done with the immense perspectives of what is left to be done in the future.

The Institute has a double account: of people and of the things they have done. Many of our people have been absorbed into film production. In addition to the great masters—Pudovkin (of whom Kuleshov's workshop can be proud), the Vasilievs (of whom my workshop is proud), Golovnya and Volchok (who do honour to the cameramen's course), GTK* and GIK can list many, many workers of various calibres and specialities, who have harmoniously joined the production family.

Nor is the service and task of the Institute confined to this. Its duty extends beyond urgent training of new film-makers. No less important a task is the setting in motion of the very understanding of the method and science of cinematography. The organizing of this work of scientific calculation, within the faculties, seminars, officers, or in special scientific bodies is the work of NIS.† Their job is to provide research forces and proposals reflecting all the immediate themes and problems of current cinematographic practice. They are also responsible for the general methodo-

* The first stage of GIK was as a State Technicum of Cinema: GTK.
† NIS: the Scientific-Research Department of GIK.

logical lines of two of GIK's faculties in particular: direction and photography.

Here we should note the decisive turn taken by the Institute since 1928. Developing from a technicum towards an eventual academy, the direction course has shown two prominent tendencies that were absent from the activity of GIK in its earliest stages.

First, in its adopting a higher educational level than an "artistic" studio, which is often the only ultimate aim of an instructional administration linked with art.

Second, in its relating cinema to the other arts, as distinct from the former tendency to seek cinema specified as "self-born," based on the suspect term of "photogenic" and the special aesthetics of keeping cinema separated from its parentage of other arts.

It is only on the basis of the closest contact with the culture of literature, theatre, painting and music, only in the most serious examination of the newest scientific disclosures in reflexes and psychology and related sciences, that the study of cinema specifics can be co-ordinated in some constructive and workable system of instruction and perception.

The direction course in the academic year of 1932/33 undertook the large task of organizing these conditions into the first detailed programme on the subject of the theory and practice of direction to be issued by the Institute.[1] This document, exhaustive or not, is the first formulation of a "codex" on what a film director must study and know in order to fulfil the great tasks that await him.

This programme also includes the core of the training method which, as the school work has shown us, is the one best adapted for creative education. This "socratic" method is called "directorial practice".

But our work doesn't stop at this. The present programme develops along two further lines. The Institute is directing the formation of a normal college plan of teaching, attached to any given basic discipline. Our work is also proceeding towards the "synchronization" of the whole complex of taught subjects and spheres of knowledge that are necessary to a director for the many facets of his activity. This will be a substitute for the unsystematic accumulation of subjects

71

that is typical of the worst specialized institutions on the college level.

The work projected by the direction course inevitably touches other faculties also. We are at present conducting a basic reconstruction of the cameramen's faculty, based fundamentally on those principles which we have been checking and elaborating in recent years. For the first time in the existence of the Institute friendship and co-operation have been established between the two faculties on the base of a unified theoretical understanding of the subjects taught and a unified method of research and instruction. For the first time, with the combined strengths of both faculties, the question of the cameraman's craft has been raised to the position of highly qualified creative work, as distinct from the attitude, which we can remember all too easily and which remains almost unchanged in the West, of treating the cameraman as a "technical" worker, deprived of creative independence and personality.

The initial difficulty encountered with almost the entire student body was the low general cultural level of students at their admission. Nor has this defect been remedied. It is this general culture and cultural basis in the arts that is, perhaps more than in any other artistic field, required in film direction. Its many sides require a many-sided background. And this is one of the most serious problems facing our young people.

Looking through the lives of artists, we may notice particularly those who have achieved something in the field of cinema arts. The first note struck is almost inevitably, "In childhood his parents' home was often visited by actors, writers, artists . . ."—"The child grew up amidst the lively surroundings of art interests and problems that concerned his parents . . ."—"He moved to the home of his uncle who was a great lover of antiquities and the arts . . ."—"From his earliest conscious years he was accustomed to drawing and music . . .", etc.

But our young creative worker had no such childhood. His mother did not grace a literary salon. His father did not patronize the Muses. During the hardest years his mother worked heroically in a factory. As he grew up his involvement was in the work of liquidating disorder. The young fellow was soon immersed in an atmosphere of feverish construction, liquidation of deficiencies, liquidation of the class enemy. He is filled with the most valuable first-hand experience of participation in forming the most remarkable Socialist actuality. No time for any profound study of Tolstoy or Dickens, like the future poets of a previous generation, whose biographies record their gulping down mountains of "forbidden writers" in their grandfathers' libraries.

Beginning with the warm caresses of the Muses, obligingly bending over their cradles, the lives of the great artists go on to record a feverish ill-digested diet, mad nights, racing through books by the light of a tallow candle—fantastically grabbing at knowledge and culture in maturity, while regretting the lack of opportunity for nurture in their childhood.

Yet there is no way round this. The sleepless nights and long hours of obsessive study cannot be dispensed with. The more knowledge one gains in childhood, the less expenditure of strength later. One way or another the knowledge must be acquired. An elementary accumulation of knowledge is unavoidable and necessary for every single person who wishes by means of self-education to express actuality by this or that path. Without such a cultural basis he will be doomed to pitiable babbling that might be sufficient for primitive circumstances, but shows up miserably when surrounded by those demands that are made by a growing Socialist country.

What should be done? How to start? Such primary conditions of nurture do not exist. You cannot reconstruct them. Besides, in those traditional forms they are quite unserviceable today. One meets many students—or, rather, one used to meet students who grew up amidst Bach and Beethoven, Bryusov and Blok, from their earliest years. All the better —it would seem. But those little pigeons tend to take first place and to forget those who came from factory or farm without ever having read Balzac or Mark Twain. Nevertheless, it's remarkable how "truth" almost always takes sides with the latter. They show creative power, energy, original research, even though there may be less "first-class apprenticeship" or "swift progress". These creative youngsters, representatives of the young class that has taken power into its own hands, can also seize and keep the fortress of knowledge. Their creation can be deeper, more full of sap, more original and powerful than those who, in spite of all the trappings they have picked up, lack these basic conditions of vitality. I say this as the result of several years of work with Soviet youth.

Yet the cultural defect remains painful for both student and instructor. It blocks the course of training. It delays the possibility of associative consolidation of materials in the consciousness and in the senses. No, we can't reproduce the cultural nursery of an "intellectual" or "aristocratic" family. But there is another means. Our genuine family has become our Socialist society. Through the system of social organizations it can link up and fill in this layer of nourishing surroundings, needed both by the growing seed and the forming senses, to shape the consciousness of the future builder of cultural and artistic values.

Obviously we are speaking of linking the first steps of training with a tendency towards the arts. And of creating ties between the lower and middle school links, where alongside a general cultural education a person with a predisposition to art could obtain the necessary complex of information and knowledge.

It would be better in a consistently planned arrangement to re-initiate that type of specialized school for artistically gifted youngsters of middle and senior years who, though perhaps inconsistent and sporadic, nevertheless sprang from the first years of the revolution.

Such schools—the first links of artistic training—would turn out young people at a level approximating to that aimed at by technical colleges, but with a programme heading them in the direction of specialization that is primarily creative. If the technical students at the end of their schooling are well up in the subtle prerequisite knowledge of all types of engineering, then the students predisposed to art would possess an accumulation of those particular perceptions in the area of the humanities and a mastery of basic qualifications in graphic art, music, movement, etc., that would be useful to follow through towards any art. In such schools there need not and cannot be specialization, but their students must be culturally prepared for that which would be suitable for a college of art, architecture, literature, music or cinema.

In his subsequent cinema training the student could expect a normal four-year course at college. At the time of his admittance there would be expected of him no specialized knowledge of the photo-chemical process or of optics. These would be dealt with later in either the director's or the cameraman's course.

But in the second year of the Institute it could suddenly become clear that he had read neither *Dead Souls* nor *Le Père Goriot* (and I know such instances in our Institute). Even so there would be no necessity for such a shameful spectacle as that of a student rattling off in faultless phrases a history of literature with Marxist appraisals of this or that literary-social phenomenon, only to find out later that he had never actually read—or even seen—the works he had talked so fluently about. Such cases also are too familiar to us at the Institute. If our higher authorities were to decree the reorganization of the teaching of geography and history, and the extension of that principle to areas not already covered by decrees, students would not have to stoop to such evasions.

A four-year course, according to the revised and broadened programme of the practical work of our Institute on similar principles, should be more than enough for the education of genuinely qualified trainees in the specialized skills of film direction. Only a few additional practical production tests would be required before the final "ordination" to the status of director.

There is a third level, not yet absolutely necessary, but included for those who want to achieve the highest standards of qualification by specializing in scientific work on film problems: the Academy level.

Here there would be more than the acquisition of knowledge; this would be a place for actively creative, educationally experimental and experimentally scientific work. Practical experience, hitherto accidentally acquired, could be transmuted, in conditions of collective scientific research with laboratory equipment, to methodological generalization. Here such data could emerge from and carry forward the knowledge and style of the Soviet cinema. Two years of such work in an experimental studio, with growing acquaintance with the newest data of creative and theoretical ideas, technical discoveries and accomplishments, would make an excellent preparation for workers of the highest qualifications and could well lift our cinema culture to unprecedented heights.

Here would be realized the slogan on the indivisibility of practice and theory that is needed in such a creative base, relating the Academy to the factory that produces the films. Such an Academy would make it possible for those whose years of practical work had shown them the need for theoretical intelligence and summing up, to take part in further scientific planning of perspectives that evolve from immediate film problems.

Three such links for the cultural formation of cinematographers would, I think, answer the problem of creating basic cadres of film-makers. Child prodigies and naturally talented persons could always find a footing in one of these three links, according to their development and talents, and help in the gleaning of knowledge for their future work.

Such are the outlines of the future. Such, approximately, are the forms and directions developed by our Institute in the years of its most recent formation and maturity. This gives us an approximate outline of those perspectives towards which it is aiming its further growth.

Eisenstein's teaching arrangements at VGIK provided leave of absence for any production project he might begin. At the time of this essay's publication, just when circumstances and his own desires seemed to have committed him to a professorial rather than a production career, Eisenstein announced that he was preparing a new film, Bezhin Lug, *and requested leave from the Institute. The leave was to be temporary and short, the production was to be rapid and efficient, but it was two-and-a-half years later that the production of* Bezhin Lug *was stopped by the film administration. Soon afterwards the film administration itself was totally overhauled and Eisenstein's next project,* Alexander Nevsky, *was as efficiently made as he promised.*

During the preparation of Nevsky *and the next project,* Ferghana Canal, *he continued to superintend the progress of the directors' course at VGIK, and to plan a book.* Pushkin and Cinema. *It was during a trip to Uzbekistan for* Ferghana Canal *that Eisenstein drafted the foreword to his Pushkin book.*

Lessons from Literature

The heritage of all mankind is ours to master and apply.—Lenin

It is our responsibility to put into practice Lenin's great directive on our cultural heritage. We must learn how to do it—for too many of us do not know. In our profession it is especially complicated, for the cinema has no *direct* ancestors.

To write "in imitation of Tolstoi" or "in imitation of Hemingway" is, comparatively, easy. Nor is this so silly as it may sound. For everything begins with imitation. We know instances of writers transcribing entire masterworks. This is not a naïve undertaking. This is a way of finding the *movement* of another, perhaps a classical, writer, and of learning by this means the ideas and feelings embedded in this or that system of visual and aural images, in his word-combinations and so forth.

In ascending to the factors that emerge from movement —from this primary gesture of the writer—there is, on the one hand, complexity, for it is always easier to "skin" than to learn. On the other hand, literature can be treated not only directly, as by literary heirs, but in the interests of its *indirect* heirs; for example, the cinema.

77

And here there is another peculiarity, one to which comparatively little attention has been given.

The epoch of victorious Socialism is the only epoch that makes it possible to create a comprehensively perfected work in all its manifold aspects.

It is by this standard that we examine and will continue to examine our classics. The reflection of this standard in literature is and will be as manifold as in the perfection of social conditions, and works will be achieved with a full harmony of all their elements such as has not been and could not be attained in previous epochs.

The accomplishment of this in past epochs was extremely rare and accessible exclusively to creative geniuses (their possession of this feature was one of the conditions that determined their genius). But even in those conditions, each of them, even the greatest of writers, bore elements within himself that stood in the way of perfection, elements that did not reach his highest level. Balzac is accused of slovenly literary language, Shakespeare of negligence in the composition and uneven qualities of *Hamlet*,* Goethe's *Hermann und Dorothea*: "positively impossible to read"; and his *Iphigenie auf Tauris*: "cannot be staged". In the works of Kleist has been discovered side by side with his genius a triviality worthy of Klopstock (Stefan Zweig has written very perceptibly about this), and so on.

The task of the historical-literary critic includes the selection and appraisal of these phenomena. As with Wagner's Beckmesser in *Die Meistersinger*, his duties also include the establishment of categories, as well as critical recommendations of this or that author. It is here that any disproportions in the desired perfection are branded for all to observe. The premises and conditions of similarly emerging phenomena are analysed. Here also there is an especially severe emphasis on any inadequacy in the social reflection of his epoch, resulting from an undue subservience of the writer's conscience in observing the social limitations of his times, and his difficulties in overcoming these pressures.

* Theoretical conjectures (Aksyonov's for example) have been advanced about the imperfections of the tragedy as it has been handed down to us.

Lenin's comments on Tolstoi and Engels's strictures on Zola are especially prominent examples of such criticism.

But to *learn* from the classics is an altogether different matter. Here the exaggeration of separate features of a work is by no means an invariably negative phenomenon. In this function it can even be thought of as positively useful, for it holds up, as it were, an enlarging mirror to features which in conditions of ideal harmony are so "soldered" into the structural whole that to isolate them for study is an extremely laborious task.

To be brief, one must know what, in each writer, is to be studied. Particularly outside literary study—in study for the purposes of the cinema.

In this connection all arguments about who is the best writer, or about which writer one must attach oneself to, are irrelevant.

What concerns us here is not this or that writer's work as a whole, but the particular features in his creative work that provide illumination on a particular problem—composition or viewpoint, for example. Obviously, "minor" writers will have less to contribute, and the genius of Shakespeare or Tolstoi will have much to teach us in almost every problem with which we have to deal.

I conducted, in 1928-29, a seminar at GIK on Emile Zola. We accomplished a great deal in the examination of several purely cinematic elements in the plastic side of his creative work, drawing attention to a series of compositional peculiarities which in literature are found almost exclusively in this writer, and which are very close in their nature to cinema. Thereupon, without considering why we had chosen the creative work of Zola for study, several comrades, armed with Engels's well-known quotation on Balzac's superiority to Zola, announced a campaign against our project, declaring that we ought to be studying Balzac and that an "orientation" to Zola was "perverse".

In the first place the matter is not one of "orientation", for we were not making an acceptance of the whole canon of Zola's work as a unit; we were studying a series of specific features, illustrated especially instructively in Zola's work. In the second place, Engels's directive on the superiority of Balzac is centred on one specific element: the socioeconomic documentation that interested Engels was less conspicuous in Zola—as with many other writers.

On the other hand we can find in Zola a huge quantity of elements, extremely important to film-makers, that are quite absent from Balzac's writings. Open Zola at any page. It is so plastic, so *visually* written that according to it a whole "scene" could be prepared, starting with the director's indications (the emotional characteristics of the scene), exact directions to the designer, the lighting cameraman, the setdresser, the actors, everyone. Here is the kind of scene you can find on every page of Zola; it is the opening of Chapter II of *La Terre*:

> Maître Baillehache, notary of Cloyes, lived on the lefthand side of the Rue Grouaise, on the way to Châteaudun, in a small white one-storey house; from a corner hung the solitary street-lamp that lit up the wide paved street, deserted during the week but loud and lively on Saturdays with the influx of peasants on their way to market. The two professional plates were visible from afar, shining against the chalky surface of the low buildings; behind the house, a narrow garden ran right down to the bank of the Loir.
>
> On this particular Saturday, in the room to the right of the entrance hall, overlooking the street, the underclerk, a pale puny lad of fifteen, had lifted one of the muslin curtains to watch the people passing. The other two clerks, an old man, pot-bellied and dirty, and a younger man, emaciated, ravaged with liver-trouble, were busy writing at a double desk of ebonized deal, the only piece of furniture in the room except for seven or eight chairs and a cast-iron stove which was never lighted until December, even if snow fell on All Saints' Day. The pigeon-holes covering the walls, the greenish cardboard boxes, broken at the corners and bursting with yellowed papers, fouled the atmosphere of the room with a smell of sour ink and dust-eaten papers.[1]

Compare this with any of the most brilliant pages of Balzac: its visual embodiment seems so grandiose, so literary, that it is not *directly* transferable to a system of visual images. Read this opening of *La Peau de Chagrin*:

> Towards the close of October, 1829, a young man entered the Palais Royal at the hour when the gaming houses opened their doors in compliance with the law which protects an essentially taxable passion. Without undue hesitation, he went up the stairway leading to a gambling den known as number thirty-six.
>
> "Your hat, please sir," a little old man called to him curtly and querulously. His face was cadaverous and he crouched in the shadows behind a railing. Suddenly, he rose, exhibiting a degraded countenance.[2]

That's all very well, I'm told—this is not merely a matter of plasticity; what's basic is the images and characters of people, and in this Balzac is superior to Zola.

Exactly! In seeking characters we turn to Balzac, but for the plastic of film style, to Zola—and first of all to Zola.

But there is another element, closely connected with character, that we can seek in Zola: this is the ability to link man plastically with his environment.

We hear too often of the "incompleteness" of a person as outlined by Zola—compared with the "deep relief" of a Balzac character.

A personage in Balzac, thanks to his manner of exposition, always reminds me of the fat señor painted by Velásquez (perhaps because of a resemblance to Balzac himself!). Old Goriot, and Vautrin, and father Grandet, and Cousin Bette, and Cousin Pons, and Cesare Birotteau all resemble the Velásquez personage—three-dimensional, seen at full height on a pedestal, in boots and sword, characterized to the last ringlet or whisker, mitten or glove.

Zola's characters, as we call them to mind, can invariably be imagined in styles dear to him—expressed by Degas or Manet. Particularly Manet. And, if I may say so, most of all in the manner of his "Bar at the Moulin Rouge".* Their

---

* Writing from memory, and far from his Moscow library, E. has unwittingly synthesized *two* Manet paintings, the "Bar at the Moulin Rouge", and the "Bar at the Folies-Bergère".—J. L.

incompleteness seems the same as the incompleteness of the painted girl behind the bar. She seems cut in half by the counter. It is also an incomplete figure who looks at her friend, the waitress, from another part of the painting, where the legs are cut short by the picture frame, and the left breast is covered by the round head of a drinking guest.

It would never occur to anyone to think of this girl as, anatomically, a half-girl. Nor do we think of the engulfing shadow on the face of a Rembrandt sitter as being an absence of part of the jaw, the temple, the forehead, or the eye deep in the eye-socket—all this being particularly notable in the etchings.

Obviously, what Manet gives us are "clots" of real detail —the personage in "close-up"—for it is no accident that the painting of Zola's time is linked with those masters of the close-up, the Japanese artists of the wood-block. Though Manet's image may not be fully drawn, it cannot be said to be undetermined. It is rounded off with the counter of the bar, the reflection in the mirror behind the girl, the tankard of beer, and the guest's head, so craftily concealing the girl's breast. Even the image of a subsidiary figure is drawn with the same customary complex of elements that is inseparable from the central personage.

Balzac is no less accurate in defining the elements connected with the habits and actions of a person. But Balzac only *names* these, as if describing the supplying firm, their method of ordering, often with attached prices—you almost expect catalogue numbers. So that Balzac gives you the person and all pertaining to him—objects, habits, setting—all gathered by him into a picture, the legs of his personage hidden by the edge of the table, the personage himself hidden in a detailed description of the wall's upholstery, the objects arranged in methodical order. For our art Balzac's method does not give us much help.

On the other hand Zola takes you *into* the image; for example, Nana at the race meeting—though the race is just as much a race as she is Nana, they cannot be taken apart. And Zola cuts his way into your visual memory with an unforgettable "shot", as when the black figure of Eugène Rougon casts its shadow across the white sculptures in the

Chambre, or when the carnally red tonality flows into Nôtre Dame in the scene of the christening of Napoleon III's son. Les Rougon-Macquart are not merely providing a commentary on a full socio-economic picture of Napoleon III's epoch; they encourage each of us, as we read—especially with such a purpose as ours—to do our own creative work. This gives us more than the full personality of Nucingen writing to a Sachar.

So we return to our premises: to ask of each writer that quality that makes him a master. And to leave to the literary critic those matters of academic calculation—such as assigning to each writer his place "in the ranks", or defining his degree of greatness.

No, please: don't confuse the addresses. Don't demand of Flaubert the virtues of Gogol—don't seek in Dostoevski lessons in the art of Tolstoi—and vice versa! That's as unreasonable as to want apples in the spring, or snow in the summer.

What we need is a "cinematographer's guide" to the classics of literature. And to painting, too. And to theatre. And music. How fascinating, for example, to define in detail what can be learned in Repin's work as distinct from Serov's work. What can be learned from Bach as distinct from Wagner. From Ben Jonson as distinct from Shakespeare.

We must learn in the way that Busygin writes with such modesty in his autobiography: "At the Industrial Academy the chief thing I'm learning is—how to learn."

We must study how to read.

This is essential in order to write:

for a writer—the pages of a literary scenario (or treatment).

for a director—the sheets of a shooting-script, or the shots in preliminary sketch, or completed images on the canvas of the screen.

Literature *per se* has as many means and circuitous expositions as there are ways of perception. But without our premises these mingled forms remain closed to us.

For film-writing the responsibility is of immeasurable extent.

83

The greatness of Pushkin is not for films—but how filmic!

That is why we begin with Pushkin.

Kokand, Uzbekistan
13 October 1939

Ferghana Canal *was left among the unrealized films, and the planned* Pushkin and Cinema *was left among the unrealized books. This winter several other films were planned before Eisenstein finally returned to production: among them a film about Pushkin, using an untried colour idea—selected, single, essential colours. While Eisenstein was deep in the problems of fusing the elements of drama, colour, music, movement and space, the Bolshoi Opera Theatre invited him to stage a new production of Wagner's* Die Walküre, *and he at once accepted this opportunity to practise the theories of greatest concern to him at that moment.*

The Embodiment of a Myth

My latest work has been on the production of the opera *The Valkyrie* in the Bolshoi Theatre in Moscow, the largest and finest opera house in the Soviet Union. As a cinema director I was quite surprised when one day the Art Director of the Bolshoi Theatre rang me up and invited me to produce *The Valkyrie*. I had never worked in a musical theatre before, although over twenty years ago I had experimented in the legitimate theatre. Nevertheless, I accepted the offer. Now that, after eight months of work on this production, the date of the première of the opera is approaching, I feel as though I had long been striving precisely towards this work. Wagner proved to be quite a natural step in my creative path.

In Wagnerian opera I particularly appreciate the epic quality of the theme, the romanticism of the subject, and the surprising pictorial nature of the music, which calls for plastic and visual embodiment. But what most attracted me in Wagner were his opinions on synthetic spectacle which are to be found scattered throughout the great composer's theoretical works. And the very nature of Wagner's music dramas confronts producers with the task of creating internal unity of sound and sight in the production.

The problem of the synthesis of the arts is of vital concern to cinematography, the field in which I am principally engaged. Men, music, light, landscape, colour, and motion brought into one integral whole by a single piercing emotion, by a single theme and idea—this is the aim of modern cinematography. Although as yet there are all too few examples of the true cinematography of sound-and-sight consonance (only a few scenes, for instance in Disney's wonderful *Snow White* or individual scenes from *Alexander Nevsky*, such as the "Attack of the Knights"), advanced cinema directors are engrossed in the problem of spectacle synthesis, experimenting in this field and accumulating a certain amount of experience.

Wagner's unusually descriptive music raises particularly keenly the question of seeking and finding the adequate visual image. The solution of the sound-and-sight problems involved in the production of Wagnerian music dramas is of tremendous interest and is capable of enriching the sound cinema, especially at a time when the latter is beginning to become not merely sound-and-sight cinema but colour and stereoscopic cinema as well.

Early cinematography was engendered by the theatre. Subsequently it came into sharp conflict with the theatre, relentlessly discarding everything faintly suggestive of the stage—even going to the point of dispensing with unified dramas and with the persons playing, the actors. But now, after the intensified "rehistrionization" of cinematography and the attempts to "cinematographize" the theatre that may be observed lately, there is again coming to the fore a mutually creative enrichment of both cinematography and the theatre—without the suppression of the spontaneity of either of them—that is leading both to the resolution of new artistic problems.

It is not for me to judge the measure in which success has been achieved in practice by a film director staging a music drama in the theatre.

Wagner's *Ring of the Nibelung* is wholly based on folk epic material. The material from which Wagner shaped his tetralogy holds a place in the epic lore of the German peoples equal to that held by the *Iliad* and the *Odyssey* in antiquity, *The Song of Roland* among the French, *The Knight in the Tiger Skin* among the Georgians, or *Djangar* in Kalmuck folk poetry.

In the splendid and majestic figures of the heroes of ancient folk lore, resurrected by Wagner, and in the very subjects and themes of the myth of *The Ring of the Nibelung*, the composer was able to express in poetic form ideas that are near and dear to us, ideas by which he was himself inspired in the period of the Revolution of 1848, in which Wagner himself took part. This revolution failed to bring liberation to the people, but although its outcome brought disappointment to Wagner, it was here that the composer found the inspiration for his tetralogy on the curse of gold, in which he envisaged not only the conflict of gods, men, dragons, and dwarfs for the possession of treasure, but primarily that curse which property brings down on men, property which inevitably urges men against each other, property which gives rise to all the misdeeds of "mythology and history", as Wagner himself writes.

The last part of the tetralogy, *The Twilight of the Gods*, symbolizes the death of the whole "world of murder and plunder, legalized by falsehood, deceit and hypocrisy", the world that the young Wagner abhorred. As is well known, Wagner subsequently abandoned these sentiments of his youth, but *The Ring of the Nibelung* preserves in the impassioned emotional quality of its music the tragedy of the great conflict between the human feelings of love and self-abnegation and the curse of property; the greatest of all his works, it expresses Wagner's purest and noblest feelings.

Significant in concept, Wagner's work is not a bare scheme based on a preconceived thesis. The heroes of the *Ring* are not abstractions; nor are they megaphones proclaiming the propaganda maxims of the author. The innermost meaning of the events is as much contained in the depths of Wagner's poetry as the very treasure that gives rise to the play of human passions which become so intertwined and grow so involved that we are wholly engrossed in the human side of the destinies of the characters he depicted. And within the limits of *The Valkyrie* their fate is profoundly tragic and human. Allow me to recall the subject of this opera.

In his childhood Siegmund lost his twin sister Sieglinde. He searches for her in vain. And finally, one day, pursued by enemies from whom he had desired to protect a girl as defenceless as his sister, he finds himself in the hut of Hunding. There he finds a beautiful woman languishing in bondage to an unloved husband. They fall in love with each other at first sight. Siegmund wishes to rescue her from her husband. When it turns out that Hunding, who has returned, is Siegmund's sworn enemy and that on the morrow he means to challenge the unarmed Siegmund to battle and to kill him, Hunding's wife administers a sleeping draught to her husband and flees with Siegmund. In an ecstasy of love, in passionate words of endearment, they tell each other the stories of their lives, from which it appears that Hunding's wife is actually Siegmund's long-lost sister Sieglinde for whom he has been searching so long.

In primitive society marriage between brother and sister was a normal and natural thing. But the tragedy of Siegmund and Sieglinde lies in the fact that they live in a transition period, when such love has already come under the ban. Thus their behaviour evokes the wrath of the gods.

Three moral and ethical points of view clash with each other in judgment on the behaviour of Siegmund and Sieglinde. The representative of one of them is Wotan, the ancient German personification of the forces of nature. He takes Siegmund, who, moreover, proves to be his son, under his protection. But he has to yield to the representative of another point of view—to his wife Fricka, the goddess who

87

protects the sanctity of the domestic hearth. He therefore orders the Valkyrie Brünnhilde, the executress of his will, to give Hunding, the injured husband, the victory in his duel with Siegmund.

But here the third point of view comes in: the point of view of Brünnhilde. Touched by the great love felt for Sieglinde by Siegmund, who is ready to give up all blessings hereafter in order to save his beloved, Brünnhilde rebels against the orders of her father, Wotan, and tries to give the victory to Siegmund.

Wotan's interference prevents her from carrying out her intention. Wotan punishes Brünnhilde: he deprives her of her godhead because she allowed human feelings to sway her so powerfully. Brünnhilde only manages to save Sieglinde and her future son, and is herself doomed to slumber on a solitary rock and to become the wife of the first man who wakes her. The only thing to which the wrathful father consents is to surround the rock with flames so that Brünnhilde shall not be won by a coward. Flames thereupon burst from the ground and surround the sleeping Brünnhilde. This concludes the first day of the *Ring*.

In the following musical drama, *Siegfried*, it falls to Siegfried, the youthful son of Siegmund and Sieglinde, the favourite hero of northern folk lore, to awaken Brünnhilde from her long slumber and to become her husband. But this, as well as the subsequent vicissitudes of the drama, falls outside the scope of *The Valkyrie*.

The humanity of the themes, the epic nature of the subject, the dramatic quality of the situations, and the poetical nature of the myth upon which the Wagnerian drama is based cannot but enchant the artist.

"It is harmonious, and let this fact become evident to you on the stage . . ." These words of Wagner's about music are the key to the scenic interpretation of his works.

The main task of the producer lies in the direct perception of the music and in its answering embodiment on the stage, for in no other music but Wagner's do thought and concept so utterly colour the element of music. Listening to *The Valkyrie*, or, rather, immersing oneself in its musical element, one may not only grasp the dramatic structure of the work but also sense the form in which it should be unfolded on the stage. Thus, the sensing of the music dictates the form of the production. Wagner's music calls for visual embodiment, and its visual embodiment must be incisively clear-cut, impalpable, frequently shifting, material.

Everything in *The Valkyrie* is activity and passion, which, even though it may be chained, is not directed inward; passion that strains outward and breaks out; passion that turns into action, into insubordination, into a conflict of wills, into a duel and the thunderous interference of higher powers, into a saturnalia of elemental forces and passions.

That is what Wagner himself wrote to Franz Liszt. *The Valkyrie*, this first day of the *Ring*, dictates the scenic solution of visibility, objectivity, activity, the mobility of men and scenery, the play of light and fire.

The music of *The Valkyrie* is impregnated with the sense of some ancient past—a past that never, it seems, existed. It has no archaisms, no stylization, and yet this atmosphere of the ancient past of mankind which suddenly makes itself felt before us is suggested by a number of miracle-working nuances. And, working on a new interpretation of the Wagnerian drama, we tried to convey this atmosphere of the past not by ethnographically transferring pictures of Nordic life to the boards of the opera theatre, but by delving deep not only into the characters of the personages of the drama, but also into the historical consciousness that gave birth to their system of thinking. Primitive man envisaged nature as an independent living being, now gracious, now austere, at times echoing his own feelings, at others opposing them, sometimes friendly, sometimes hostile to him.

In our production the lives of the heroes of the opera are echoed by the phenomena of nature—by a tree that seems just about to speak, by the mountains that rise up during the duel between Siegmund and Hunding, by the elemental force of the flames that range around Brünnhilde, and in the heavens by the thunder cloud that bears Wotan. That is how ancient man, the author of myths, folk lore, and epics, pictured nature's participation in his personal life.

It was this idea that prompted us to introduce one other element in our production—original pantomime choruses. Our aim was to convey through them the feeling that is typical of the period of epics, legends, and myths. That is the feeling that man is not yet cognizant of himself as an independent unit set apart from nature, as an individual that has already acquired independence within the collective body.

For this reason, in our production many of the characters are at certain moments enfolded, as it were, by these choruses, from which they seem inseparable, which vibrate with one emotion, one and the same feeling with them. Thus Hunding, the representative of the crudest, atavistic stage of the trible—when the tribe is still nothing more than a horde close to the flock, the herd, or the pack—appears surrounded by the myriopod, shaggy body of his pack, a body which on falling to the earth appears to be the hunting pack of a leader, and which on rising to its feet apears to be Hunding's encirclement—kinsfolk, armour-bearers, servants.

In just the same manner Fricka, his patroness and defender, comes upon the stage surrounded by a chorus of golden-fleeced half-sheep, half-men—partly like domesticated animals, partly like men who have abjured their own passions and have voluntarily put on the yoke of the tamed instead. Fricka exercises sole sway over them. Fawning in servile fashion, bent to the ground, whipped on by her, they swiftly pull her wraithlike and victorious chariot from the stage.

And whereas the first two mimic choruses, upon falling to the ground, spread along its surface, the third—the chorus of the Valkyries, indomitable and headstrong as their father Wotan—flies upward into the unclouded distance.

From the purely plastic angle these choruses have still another special task. They serve as something like a group connecting link between the individual human beings and the environment, that is, between the soloist and the substantial arrangement of the scenic space—the decorations. It was our idea that the decorations in this production should serve not merely for the ornamentation or artistic arrangement of the stage, not merely as laconic data on the place of the action, but as the support of the plastic action, just as that inimitable music which calls the performance as a whole into life serves as the sound support for it. In our production the decorations would be that part of the single dynamic whirlwind that engendered the music to whose lot it fell to congeal fast in the scenic space as machines and colours, steps and precipices, surfaces and planes, so as to serve as a support for the actions and deeds of the actors.

There is much I should like to say about the ideas that came from this absorbing work on the production of a Wagnerian opera, but I must not, by my "interpretations" as a theatrical producer, transfer into the sphere of reason that which sprang directly from the emotions.

Let us follow Wagner's behest: "... I believe that a totally true instinct saved me from striving too excessively to be clear: I see distinctly, by feeling, that too open a revelation of the author's concepts only hampers comprehension. . . ."

condensed and translated by Bernard Koten

Eisenstein's great project, a book on direction to absorb the materials and ideas of his teaching programme, was continually going forward. The theme of the book was more than technical: this was to channel all his excitement and research in the creative process, in nature and in art—towards the new art of synthesis. In 1939 a fragment of his book was published as On Structure; *a year later another fragment,* Once More on Structure, *appeared. It is revealing to read these within the period of Eisenstein's publication, to listen to him using his powers of persuasion and logic to propose methods and viewpoints that were not then popular nor even acceptable.*

More Thoughts on Structure

In writing my book on direction I have noticed, among other questions, a curious fact. Namely, that in the realm of composition a dialectical position usually, somehow, finds its unity in opposition.

It finds its reflection in this circumstance, that *for any given composition using a direct solution there are also equally correct and impressive solutions that are in direct opposition.*

This phenomenon can also be found in the richest expressive manifestations of mankind—in nature itself.

Thus, for example, in a moment of terror a man not only retreats from the cause of his terror, but just as often, as if bewitched, he is drawn to the very thing that inspires his terror. The edge of a cliff "draws" us to it. The criminal is "drawn" to the scene of his crime, rather than fleeing from it. And so on.

And in composition, that draws its sustenance from the experience of actuality, this circumstance may be swiftly discovered in even the most trifling instances.

If, for example, it is decided that a certain moment in a rôle must lead to a delirious scream, we can say with conviction that that moment will be served just as powerfully—by a scarcely heard whisper. If rage is expressed by maximum movement, then an absolutely stony immobility will be no less impressive.

If Lear is strong in the tempest that envelopes his madness, then no less powerful will be the effect of a directly opposite solution: madness surrounded by the calm of "indifferent nature".*

Of two opposites one is usually more "saleable" and cus-

* This phrase of Pushkin's stimulated one of Eisenstein's most important essays, unpublished in his lifetime. See No. 296 in the Bibliography.—J. L.

tomary. And therefore it comes first to mind. The second acts more unexpectedly and more sharply, bringing with it an unaccustomed freshness. We can recall the stunning effect of Negro syncopated jazz, where the rhythmic principle was usually in contrast to what the European ear had been taught.

In his autobiography[1] Paul Whiteman writes:

> ... jazz is a method of saying the old things with a twist, with a bang, with a rhythm that makes them seem new ... The first beat in any bar, which normally is accented, is passed over, and the second, third or even fourth beats are accented.

This can be roughly illustrated with a familiar bar of music. Suppose we take "Home, Sweet Home". Here it is in its original form:

Now let us jazz it up:

Jazz quickly won popularity, but often the intrusion of similar "unusual" opposites is not smooth.

See what happened to Dumas *père* at the Théâtre-Français at a period when this theatre was still ignorant of *la poésie de l'immobilité*.

And Dumas shows us a vivid example in action of direct and opposite solutions in the composition of an actor's performance. It is described in his memoirs.

The famous Mlle Mars was to play in Dumas's new play, *Antony*. They could agree on nothing, nor could Dumas agree with the theatre, neither in the understanding of his drama, nor in the handling of its rehearsals. So he took the play to another theatre, where the rôle of Adèle was to be played by another leading actress, the young Dorval. The memoirs tell of the final rehearsals and performance of *Antony*:

> Madame Dorval had made the very utmost out of the part of Adèle. She enunciated her words with admirable precision, all the striking points were brought out, except one which she had not yet discovered. "Then I am lost!" ('Mais je suis perdue moi!') she had to exclaim, when she heard of her husband's arrival. Well, she did not know how to render those few words. And yet she realised that, if said properly, they would produce a splendid effect. All at once an illumination flashed across her mind.
>
> "Are you here, author?" she asked, coming to the edge of the footlights to scan the seats.
>
> "Yes . . . what is it?" I replied.
>
> "How did Mlle Mars say: 'Then I am lost!'?"
>
> "She was sitting down, and got up."
>
> "Good!" replied Dorval, returning to her place, "I will be standing, and will sit down."[2]

In the excitement of the successful première (3 May 1831) the actor Bocage forgot to move the armchair ready to receive Adèle, when she is overwhelmed at the news of her husband's arrival.

But Dorval was too much carried away by passion to be put out by such a trifle. Instead of falling on the cushion, she fell on to the arm of the chair, and uttered a cry of despair, with such a piercing grief of soul wounded, torn, broken, that the whole audience rose to its feet.

The "opposite" solution justified itself no less powerfully than the "direct" one.

Of course, a purely mechanical opposition, not growing from *a genuine feeling of opposition within the phenomenon itself, or*—to be more exact—not growing from the possible

94

contradictions *within the phenomenon's relationships,* can never be sufficiently convincing.

This would remain a superficial *game of contrasts* in relation to current acceptance, and could not possibly be lifted to the embodiment of a unified theme, if merely presented in the less usual of two equally possible and basic opposites.

Yet the "formal" aspect of our first glance at the "opposite" structure in what Mme Dorval did—is only apparently "formal".

In actuality we can find in this little example of two treatments of one and the same movement an opportunity to examine the whole warring contradiction of two styles of acting, a struggle between the classicism of the champions of romanticism, a struggle that reflects the complex social processes of the beginning of the nineteenth century. The opposing solution in our example only reflects the opposing of a tradition, with which the "classical" actress Mars was departing from theatre history just as the "romantic" actress Dorval was arriving.

It is easy "arithmetically" to calculate a third solution that, regardless of its unexpectedness, could seem in opposition at the same time to *both* earlier solutions: to play this scene without a *sweep of movement* upwards or downwards—but, ignoring both, to use restrained movement and rely on intonation. But below the "arithmetic" of this lies a most complicated social process, reflected in that style of acting about which some of the first practitioners of this new theatre wrote to each other:

> Suffering ought to be expressed as it is in life—that is, not by the arms and legs, but by the tone and expression; not by gesticulation, but by grace.[3]

Perhaps it is not astonishing that what now appears to us as a possibly personal variation on a single scenic solution was once a type, the only possible stylistic solution. Actors came to other solutions only through a difficult struggle that was accompanied by the mastery of a new artistic ideology.

Quite unastonishing.

We are the heirs of the whole incredible fund of past human culture.

In its hues, in its stylistic peculiarities, in its genres, and simply in certain of its features, our art embraces all the experience which for the pre-synthetic stage of the history of arts appeared as leading banners for whole epochs, for whole styles, for whole stages of art ideology.

And art ideas that were once shaped on the battlefield of changing styles now appear as the means for variations and hues *within the unity of our style* of Socialist realism. Apart from all that is new and unprecedented in it, its particular works can catch fire from those *hues* that once were obligatory and then were doomed to be the sole possible and exhausted *colours*.

Naturally the conditions for an inner-based choice of this or that hue or this or that opposition within it depend now on what strength is applied and on which particular day. Similarly there can be exchanges with each other. That is what makes the example of Mlle Mars and Mme Dorval so apposite, not only in its circumstances of historic upheaval and changing styles.

Many other cases could be brought in evidence. To find analogies one does not have to stretch so far. In fact the most pertinent cases, available in quantity, are to be found on Soviet screens.

Both *Strike* and *Battleship Potemkin* are instances of stylistic particularity.

I can remember when the cycle *Toward Dictatorship,* though only one film was realized, was worked out stylistically. I can even remember where we discussed this. It was by the curved wall of the now demolished Strastnoi Monastery. Along it ran a path that led to "Kino Malaya Dmitrovka 6", noted for its showings of the most triumphantly successful American films. Here we saw *Robin Hood* and *The Thief of Bagdad, The Gray Ghost* and *The House of Hate.**

How to beat these "giants" of the American cinema—and just as we were taking our first timid steps in film-making?

* *The Gray Ghost* (1917, with Priscilla Dean and Eddie Polo) was the first U.S. serial to reach Russian audiences ; *The House of Hate* (1918) was also a serial, directed by George Seitz, with Pearl White.—J. L.

96

How could our young cinema be heard with a voice of its own, against the noisy roar of the American-European film industry that controlled all the channels of trade and production? Where could we find stories that would be just as sharp, if not sharper, than the plots of these American successes?

Where should we find native "stars" whose radiance could compete with whole "constellations" from America and Europe? And heroes whose originality would displace the accepted heroes of the bourgeois cinema?

The task was not one merely of making good films. The area of our task was much broader—the whole area of culture: to make an impact on bourgeois culture *by showing a contrasting culture and art*. To compel it to listen to and respect what was coming from the young Land of the Soviets, so enigmatic and so little known in those years to Europe and America.

An impetuous twenty-six-year-old thus sketched a promethean task for himself.

And the solution came—almost "mathematically".

A story sharper than the American ones? What could be sharper than to reject "story" altogether?

"Stars" superior to the American-European ones? How about doing the unthinkable for that time—making films without "stars"?

Individualities more significant than the current film-heroes? What if we should turn our backs on all that and build with quite different materials?

And in "countering" all—abolishing story, discarding stars—to push into the dramatic centre the mass as the basic *dramatis persona*, that same mass that heretofore had provided a background for the solo performance of actors.*

Thus by an almost formally "opposite" direction was formulated that stylistic peculiarity of our cinema which for many years served as its determining image.

Of course it would be naïve to suppose that "mathematics"

---

* In this connection let's not forget the reaction to the completed *Strike* of one of the oldest actors of the Russian cinema, the late Saltykov, whose approving comment after a screening was: "If only, against that background, there could be—me."

alone could give birth to that which was so characteristic and expressive of its time.

The liberation of the consciousness from all that representational structure linked to the bourgeoisie; a new world revealed in the entrance of a new class upon the arena of world history; October—and the rising ideology of the victorious proletariat: these are the premises from which arose the possibilities of a new language in culture and the arts.

And from this came the opposition and interchange of those two class ideologies. Such oppositions always reveal those stylistic peculiarities in which the art of these classes speak at their moment of sharpest impact.

It is quite impossible to find and reveal simply "formal" opposing solutions to these deep inner roots.

This is a far broader phenomenon than is assumed by those who love to draw imaginary pictures of how works of art are created, a fact they could prove for themselves by observing this creation. Many such writers try to expound the history of the creation of a work by fitting it into some rigid formula. Too little is written honestly and frankly about how this or that work was conceived and realized.

Anecdotal details, surprises or apparent accidents need remove nothing from the recognized basic principles of a developing work of art. Such genuine details of creative biographies convey a sense of life in the description of the process of creation. This cannot be an abstract schema, certainly not with such a full-blooded process as creation.

Here is another instance of such a frank page of creative autobiography — Vladimir Nemirovich-Danchenko's — one that is quite near to that which was discussed above:

> During the same season as that of Chekhov's *Sea-Gull* I produced *The Price of Life*—in Moscow in the *benefice* of Lensky, in St Petersburg in that of Savina. In Moscow the success of the play was foreshadowed from the first act, and developed into an ovation.
>
> ... The price of life, the question of suicide, naturally presupposes that the author is consumed with this tremendous moral problem, that he has been seized with the

phenomenon of suicide epidemics, and so forth. Actually, such was not the case. The author, during the summer, sat in his house in the village and said to himself that it was now absolutely necessary to write a play—necessary according to various earthly considerations. What play he himself did not yet know. It was necessary to find a theme. And one day he put before himself the question: "Contemporary plays usually end in suicide, but suppose I take a theme and *begin* with a suicide? A play that begins with a suicide; is it not an engaging idea?"

And then, somehow, I put before myself this problem: "Playwrights always write so that the third act shall be the act of conflict, the most effective act—a big ensemble scene . . . But suppose the most important act should be built on a duet? Yes, so that the entire act might be played, say by Yermolova and Lensky, and yet be thoroughly absorbing . . ."

And when the plot of the play had already been told, suicide still remained the spur for dramatic situations. It must be remembered that two acts had already taken place, yet the author had not yet begun to reflect upon the moral essence of the "price of life"; this problem must of itself rise above the images, the scenes, the fragments of observation, even as the mist rises above the bogs, the hillocks, and the shrubs . . .

The Griboyedov prize—for the season's best play—was awarded to *The Price of Life* . . .[4]

In conclusion I'd like to submit one more example of opposite structure, as a means of simply producing something "original". Here the matter is one of terminology, which often takes a thing to the opposite extreme. The term here is "an opposite generality".

Somehow our conversation moved on to Dostoyevsky. As we know, Turgenev did not like Dostoyevsky. To the best of my recollection this is how he spoke about him:

"Do you know what an opposite generality is? When a man is in love, his heart beats faster; when he's angry, his face reddens, etc. But in Dostoyevsky everything is made deliberately contrary. For instance a man is about to

shoot a lion. What does he do? In actuality he grows
pale and tries to run away or hide himself. In any simple
tale, say by Jules Verne, for example, that's the way it
would be told. But Dostoyevsky tells it the other way.
The hunter blushes and stands still. That's an opposite
generality. This is a cheap way to pass for an original
writer."[5]

I'll neither quarrel nor agree with Turgenev. But I know
that some film-makers, in order "to pass for an original",
resort to this same method. Thus, for example, most of
Marlene Dietrich's "mystery" was built by Sternberg exactly
on this principle. In such films as *Morocco*, all the mystery
of her personality was based on the simple device of having
her pronounce all her affirmative remarks . . . in a questioning tone. "You've already dined?" is answered by Marlene's
attenuated "Yes-s-s" in which one can hear the question-
mark. And the audience at once supposes Heaven knows
what secret relationships and a whole multitude of mysterious motives. And this too is only—"an opposite generality".

To penetrate to all the strata that lie beneath this phenomenon is not within the scope of this essay, but I want to
pursue it into one relevant area. For this rule on the correct-
ness of an opposite solution, as observed in the conditions
noted above, is true for more than particular solutions. It
can be justified in whole systems of principles that are connected with certain compositional structures.

The pathos construction as sketched in my previous
essay* would not be complete without presenting an example of an opposite type of structure—leading, however, to
an effect of pathos that is equally strong.

The pathos of a theme can also be resolved through the
two oppositions that are always at the disposal of the
compositional structure.

* This essay, *On Structure,* was translated as "The Structure of
the Film" in *Film Form.* The quotations that follow are from that
translation.

Russian uses of the terms *pathos* and *pathetic* are closer to their
original Greek roots—to suffer, to go through passion—than to
modern English usage.—J. L.

In the example from *Potemkin* I showed the *direct method* in the construction of pathos.

The basic indication of a pathetic composition is that for each element of the work there must be maintained the condition of "going out of oneself" and passing into a new quality. I drew attention to the behaviour of a man in this state:

Seated—he stands. Standing—he collapses. Motionless—he moves. Silent—he cries out. Dull—he shines. Dry—he is moistened by tears ... etc.

Of his speech I wrote:

The unorganized customary flow of speech, made pathetic, immediately invents the pattern of clearly behaviouristic rhythm; prose that is also prosaic in its form, begins to scintillate at once with forms and turns of speech that are poetic in nature ... etc.

And, finally, the sequence of the "Odessa steps" was analysed in detail to show these conditions applied to composition. All this demonstrated the "direct method" in constructing pathos.

For an "opposite" structure, producing a similar effect, we can take a quite different example: also a film, one of high socialist pathos—*Chapayev*.

However, if anyone, after reading my previous essay, should try to apply that research on *Potemkin* directly to *Chapayev*, he would place himself in an extremely embarrassing position. A formula doesn't fit. In this case he would find that either the formula would have to be put "under suspicion"—or deny the fact that *Chapayev* is pathetic. Both one and the other would be a mistake.

For the secret lies in the fact that *Chapayev* is built on the *second opposition*, through which can be seen that a unity for both bases is the principle of a pathetic construction.

For such accomplished works as *Chapayev* we are right to expect to find within the work itself a "key" scene, where one of the decisive inner technical and stylistic conditions invariably "bursts through" to the action itself, or to the dialogue or in the dramatic situation. Such a scene or phrase must be one of the most memorable, one of the most "characteristic" for the film.

In such a scene the key must open the base of the theme itself. This should also function as a key to the correct understanding of composition as an embodiment of this particular theme.

This was the justification of the "Odessa steps" in *Potemkin*: the cumulative point of the film's drama, it seemed also the sharpening point for the compositional movements, advancing towards a disclosure of their "secret" and leading to a revelation of the method itself.

I believe that *Chapayev*, notwithstanding all the rich drama of the work, will show its "method" most characteristically in one of its *least* dramatic episodes.

In the episode of *"Where should the commander be?"*

It is precisely in this episode that we see introduced into the practice of our Soviet cinema something new—in principle, in style and in quality.

It is characteristic of the *pathos* of *Chapayev* that its hero is not put on a pedestal. That the hero is shown as not separated from the humans around him, as not standing over other people, not leaping ahead of other people. Here the hero is shown as flesh of his class's flesh; within it; with it; not only *leading* it, but also *listening* to it—a genuine people's hero.

This could be the "ecstatic" image of an ordinary soldier who *from his place in the ranks* breaks *forward*: a hero. In such a hero we can feel that he is—us; that he is each one of us, ordinary soldiers, too. Along with this feeling there is no lowering of the hero, no levelling. The hero remains aware of his relationship to the ranks—and his relationships to all people.

There is a remarkable scene in Abel Gance's *Napoleon*.

Napoleon, still as General Bonaparte, is reviewing the troops after some victory in Italy.

In the front rank there is a rank-and-file former friend (excellently played by Kolin) of Napoleon. He boasts to the soldiers beside him of his intimacy with Napoleon.

He will prove it: he will break discipline by taking a step forward from his rank, and nothing will happen to him.

102

He takes this step forward.

Bonaparte approaches on a galloping horse.

Bonaparte sees the transgressor.

The horse is drawn up short.

Bonaparte recognizes the transgressor.

A dead pause.

A brief, harsh command.

And . . . the whole rank of soldiers takes a step forward.

The horse turns sharply. Napoleon gallops off.

Kolin faints in the arms of his mates . . .

And a film treatment that forces Chapayev to step back, to stand in the same rank with the rest, is essentially a step by which he forces all to sound in key equally with him as heroes. For in Chapayev there is no distinction between the general-Bonaparte and the soldier-Kolin.

We found the key scene of the drama not in a dramatic scene.

This in itself is significant from the viewpoint of those speculations that I presented on the "opposite" solution of pathos in this film. Let us look into that circumstance more intently.

In the episode the argument is about where the commander should be. The argument develops from the group's general agreement that the commander's place is *ahead*, with drawn sabre. Only Chapayev, out of his military wisdom, says that this is *not always so*, that there are times when the commander ought to be *behind*, in order to confront the pursuing enemy—and then once more be ahead.

What a lesson in dialectic struggle!

And the researchers into pathos who wish to propagate a mechanical view on pathos as identical in *Potemkin* and *Chapayev* could learn a lesson in the dialectics of composition from the film of *Chapayev* itself.

In the developing circumstances of the film's battles we see that the commander who should be *ahead* must also be *behind*. And these two opposites of his locations, penetrating each other through the film's action, are finally, to an equal degree, summed up in unity—in the commander's behaviour in battle.

Thus through the inner content of the theme the structure

103

of pathos must be "tearing along with drawn sabre before him", and also "disposed behind", i.e., developed not through contrasts, as in *Potemkin*, but through contrasting oppositions.

Both, penetrating each other, merge in a unity of that general method of pathetic composition that I described in the previous essay and which remains true, independently of the fact that it is on one of two possible oppositions that the pathetic structure of this or that work can move.

In the previous essay I produced the example of the behaviour of a man in ecstasy, a man consumed by pathos.

I spoke about eyes suddenly full of tears. I spoke about silence bursting into shouts. I spoke of immobility suddenly transformed into applause.

I spoke of *prosaic* prose, unexpectedly changing into the structure of poetry.

But would not a *reversal* of these phenomena also correspond to that formula of "going out of oneself"?

Shining eyes, suddenly dry. A paroxysm of cries, suddenly hushed. Applause, abruptly ceased.

Fully and appropriately elevated poetic speech, suddenly sounding like ... ordinary prosaic conversational speech.

Doesn't this remind us of the time when Russian names unexpectedly appeared in the pages of novels, hitherto peopled by Héloïse, Clarissa, Aline, Pauline and Céline?

... Tatyana was her sister's name:
For the first time in any novel
It humbly asks romantic fame ...[6]

There is, of course, no analogy here in content. We are speaking of a completely different historical matter.

As for the high images in pathetic films of the first type one cannot say that our cinema behaved like Tatyana's mother:

She used a sing-song voice; and, posing,
Praskovya she would call "Pauline" ...

It would be just as untrue and offensive for our cinema to say that with the arrival of *Chapayev* our cinematography

... called "Akulka" the former Céline ...

104

Yet if we wish, however ironically, to equate the poetic speech of our cinema with "Céline", and its high prose, humbly, with "Akulka", then we may have found *Chapayev's* place.

Actually *Chapayev* speaks of things that we are used to hear only with the structures of a hymn, of elevated speech, of verse—but says them in simple conversational speech.

The heroics of its story might have sounded the drum; but composition forced its exposition from the "elevated writing" that would have been natural and appropriate for it —into an everyday prosaic structure.

Engels popularized the memory of M. Jourdain who was quite astonished to realize that he had always spoken prose.

It could be said of *Chapayev*'s story that, though it does not pursue that aim, its essence is poetic.

Poetry for such an inner-excited subject is just as obvious and usual as a prosaic structure of speech for an unexcited person.

And the shift from a naturally anticipated elevated style to a deliberately prosaic quality—this is the same sort of jump from quality to quality as in the more customary reverse order, a leap from spoken prose into the dimension of oratory.

Here are examples of two orators:

One of them snatches a certain phenomenon from life. In itself this would be quite normal. It seems natural and requires no extra thought. It seems contemporary and commonly prosaic. And then he discloses the power of pathos in fiery speech as he plucks all coverings from the phenomenon, sublimating this particular thing, this solitary instance on to the plane of a universal generalization, revealing all the significance concealed at its core.

We can't imagine this first orator without pathos—even with so "natural" a phenomenon as the exploitation of one class by another—or even with such a decisive moment as: to take or not to take power in one's hands. This is the fiery pathetic style of the speeches and editorials of Lenin.

Then let us take an opposite case. The revolution is now victorious. Socialism is being constructed. We are making the transition to Communism. The fulfilled thousand-year dream of generations of oppressed peoples is written into the unforgettable articles of the Stalin Constitution.

These very lines blaze, resound, glow with enthusiasm. And their high pathos is achieved when they are uttered . . . in a low voice, with even intonation, almost devoid of gesture.

This is the pathos style of a conquering October.

This is the pathos style of a victorious October.

This is the pathos style in the report of the Central Committee preceding a congress.

The pathos style of a conquering October is reflected in the compositional structure of *Potemkin*.

The pathos style of a victorious October is reflected in the compositional structure of *Chapayev*.

Just as the victories of Bolshevism before October and after are united in method, so the pathos structures of *Potemkin* and *Chapayev* are equally united in method.

Once more let us recall that the opposite is *not chosen arbitrarily by the author*. It is always historically dictated by the epoch, by the moment.

There was a time when I was much abused because I divided the first fifteen years of Soviet cinema into three five-year periods, each with its specific traits and sharply distinguished in physiognomy from the others.*

Regardless of whether I was right or wrong, it is now established that there must be a detailed new treatment of the history of our cinema.

But the unity of stylistic principles in whole groups of films, "leading" the specific periods—that is now beyond question. So this matter makes some progress, especially in regard to those indications of pathetic style that I've now outlined in these two essays.

Strike, Potemkin, Mother, Arsenal are films of the first type of pathos.

Chapayev, the *Maxim* trilogy, *Baltic Deputy* are vivid examples of another, *opposite* pathetic composition.

In considering this it is interesting to note with what

* In his essays, "The Middle of Three" and "At Last!" (Nos. 116 and 114 in the Bibliography).—J. L.

degree of firmness this or that film is attached to this or that stylistic method.

In the fine *Baltic Deputy*, for example, one observes that when it departs from the characteristics defined by its manner of pathetic style, it becomes compositionally helpless. For this reason the film's finale—the departure for the front —insoluble by the "second method", seems incomparably below the rest of the film.

Something similar can be detected in *We From Kronstadt*. In the scenario the scene of the landing was splendidly conceived, but in execution it was unable to rise to the necessary pathetic power of a composition of the "first order". Incidentally, of this film as a whole it can be said, paradoxically, that its scenario attaches it to the first method, but through its director's sympathies and tendency it leans to the second.

In the fourth five-year period that is now closing (1935–1940) it is interesting to note that alongside high examples of the second type of pathetic style—in *Lenin in October* and *Lenin in 1918*—it also returned to enrich the first type of pathetic composition. Both *Alexander Nevsky* (1938) and *Shchors* (1939) provide new aspects for the tradition of pathetic style in the pre-*Chapayev* era of *Potemkin* and *Arsenal*.

We can detect in this that some historical "principle" must have "powered" this change. And the historical determination of the stylistic peculiarity of both these films is now clear. The climactic creative period of their production coincided with a tremendous patriotic surge of our whole country—with that flaming patriotism that is bound in our memories to the heroic battle at Lake Hassan. This militant pathos, touching all the people of the U.S.S.R., determined the methodological direction that embodied the pathetic style of both films.

Built by the patriotic enthusiasm of millions of people, these two films—*Nevsky* and *Shchors*—stand as the pylons of a gate through which, in the next five-year period, will newly surge towards us films of a great unfolding of the first type of pathos.

* * *

Many films of this type are mentioned by title in the thematic plans of the studios. Many are already in the scenario stage—and some in production. They do not interfere with films of the second type—they don't even engage in polemics with them. They compete with them, and successfully, in attracting the interest of the spectator.

And they immeasurably broaden the diapason of our cinema's stylistic possibilities.

The next four years were years of war. In the autumn of 1941 the Mosfilm studio was evacuated to Alma-Ata, in Soviet Asia, and with it went Eisenstein with his preparations for an historical tragedy, Ivan the Terrible. *In the difficult circumstances of the temporary studio, work went very slowly and the film was unfinished when the studio returned to Moscow in 1944. Moreover, the plan for the film had grown larger; begun as a two-part film, it was now to be in three parts. Part One was released on 30 December 1944 with success. While Part Two was being completed, Eisenstein contributed essays to two volumes on* The History of World Film Art: *these were his estimates of the work of Griffith and of Chaplin.*

Charlie the Kid

The Kid. The name of this most popular of Chaplin's films is worthy to stand beside his own name; it helps to reveal his character just as the names, "The Conqueror", "The Lion Heart", or the "Terrible", themselves designate the spirit of William who conquered the Great Britain of the future, the legendary courage of Richard of the Crusades, or the cunning Moscovite Tsar, Ivan IV Vasilievich.

Neither Direction; nor Method; nor Tricks; nor Comic

Technique: none of these things move me. I do not wish to probe these things.

In considering Chaplin, one's main aim must be to fathom that structure of thought which sees phenomena in so strange a fashion and responds to them with images of equal strangeness. And within that structure to discern that part which exists as a perception of the outside world, before it becomes a concept of life.

In short, we shall not concern ourselves with Chaplin's world outlook but with that perception of life which gives birth to the unique and inimitable conceptions of what is called Chaplinesque humour.

The fields of vision in a rabbit's eyes overlap behind the back of his head. He sees behind him. His lot being to run away rather than track down, he doesn't complain about that. But these fields of vision do not overlap each other in front. In front of the rabbit is a piece of space it does not see: a rabbit running forward may bump into an obstacle right in front of it.

The rabbit's outlook on the world is different from ours. The sheep's eyes are placed in such a way that its fields of vision do not overlap at all. The sheep sees two worlds—the right and the left, which do not merge into a visual whole.

Thus, a different kind of vision produces a different kind of picture-image.

Not to speak of the higher transformation of *vision* into a *perception* and then to a *point of view* which comes about the moment we rise from the sheep and rabbit to Man, with all his accompanying social factors. Till finally all this is synthesized into a world-outlook, a philosophy of life.

How those eyes see.

Extraordinary eyes.

The eyes of Chaplin.

Eyes able to see in the forms of careless merriment an Inferno as fierce as Dante's or the *Caprichos* that we were shown in *Modern Times*.

That is what excites me.

That is what interests me.

That is what I wish to find out.

With what eyes does Charlie Chaplin look on life?

The peculiarity of Chaplin consists in the fact that, despite his grey hairs, he has preserved a "child's outlook" and a spontaneous perception of events.

Hence his freedom from the "manacles of morals" and his ability to see in a comic spectacle that which causes others' flesh to creep.

Such a trait in an adult is called "infantilism".

Hence, the comedy of Chaplin's situations is based mainly on their infantile treatment.

To this point, however, there are two reservations:

This is not the only mode of treatment Chaplin uses.

And he is not the only one who uses it.

True, we were not trying so much to find his modes of treatment as to find out "the secret of his eyes", the secret of his outlook, the embryo from which any type of treatment can grow.

But first let us discuss the reason why, out of all the means available to him, Chaplin chooses this particular method of achieving a comic effect, and by this choice becomes the most representative figure of American humour.

Particularly because, through this trait of infantile humour, he becomes the most American of all American humorists. And I don't mean by this that, as is often said, the mentality of the average American is no higher than that of a 14-year-old!

In his *Dictionnaire des idées reçues* Flaubert did not include the word "infantilism".

Otherwise he would have written, as he did of Diderot: "Diderot—always followed by d'Alembert."

Infantilism is always followed by "escape" from reality.

In this case it is particularly to the point, for the same impulse to run away, driving Rimbaud from Paris to Abyssinia or Gauguin to Tahiti is, of course, able to drive one from the New York of today, only much further.

The fetters of "civilization" are now spread over such a wide area that one meets with exactly similar Ritz Hotels (and not only hotels) in all the great centres of Europe and the United States, and even in the most secluded corners of the island of Bali, in Addis Ababa, in the tropics, and amidst the eternal snows.

The wings of "geographical" escapism have been cut by the busy air-routes. Only "evolutionary" escapism is left: a downward course in one's own development. All that is left is a return into the circle of ideas and feelings of "golden childhood", a regress into infantilism, an escape into personal childishness.

In a strictly regulated society with strictly defined canons this urge to escape to freedom from the fetters of "the-once-and-for-all strictly laid down and established" must be especially strong.

Remembering America, two things come to my mind: the test for a driving licence; and a story from a students' magazine. In both cases: an examination.

In the first you are given a questionnaire.

The questions are to be answered simply "Yes" or "No".

The questions are put not like this: "What is the maximum speed at which you should drive past a school?" but like this: "Should one drive past a school at a higher speed than 30 miles an hour?"

The answer expected is "No".

"Should one approach a main road from a secondary road and cross it without waiting at the crossing?"

The answer expected is "No".

Similar questions are also given demanding "Yes" for an answer.

But nowhere will you find a question: "On approaching a main road from a side road, what do you do?"

The examinee is nowhere expected to think independently or to arrive at an independent conclusion.

Everything is reduced to automatic memorizing, to a reply of "Yes" or "No".

No less interesting is the automatic way the exam papers are checked.

Over the questionnaire a graph paper is placed with a perforated square matching wherever the answer "yes" should be placed.

Then a second perforated graph paper, punched to match the answer "No".

Just two glances by the examiner are enough:

Do the punched-out squares of the first graph show only the positive answers? And the second, negative answers?

A wonderful invention, one would think, for standardizing the issue of driver's licences.

But ...

Here in a students' magazine is a funny story about how a class is examined at a University.

Everyone holds his breath and listens.

They listen to the sound of a typewriter ... being typed by a blind student.

There are two taps. Then—three.

The whole room writes furiously.

In the first case the two letters mean "No".

In the second case the three letters mean "Yes".

Here is the same driver's test system. The same graphic grid. The same play on "Yes" and "No".

The mechanical grid and the blind student—the guide to the seeing ones—combine into one symbol.

The symbol of a whole mechanical and automatically intellectual system.

A kind of intellectual conveyor-belt system.

It is only natural to long to escape from it.

If Chaplin's physical exit from the single-track of machinism reaches its leaping representation in *Modern Times,* he achieves an intellectual and emotional exit by means of the *infantilism* method, with a similar liberating leap from the confines of intellectual machinism.

And in doing this Chaplin is a hundred per cent American. A general system of philosophy and its applied interpretation always reflects the basic nostalgia hidden in the heart of a people or a nation, existing in a definite social system.

"By their theories shall ye know them" might be said just as truthfully as "by their deeds".

Let us look at the typical American interpretation of the secret of comedy. And let us make clear that all theories and explanations of the comic are local and relative.

But here we are not interested in how much objective truth there is in his interpretation of the "secret of comedy".

We are interested in the specific American attitude to the problem of the comic, just as we are interested in the interpretations of Kant and Bergson primarily as personal and social "documents of the epoch", and not as universal truths and theories of the comic, objectively embracing absurdly tiny spheres of interpretation.

Our aim therefore will be to find out the most typically American *source* of the basic theory of the comic.

In searching for the "German" attitude to the comic we would turn to metaphysics. In search of the "English" attitude we would turn to the essayists who, through the mouth of George Meredith, consider humour to be the privilege of select minds, etc., etc.

In searching for the "American" approach and the most typical "American" understanding of humour, we shall not turn to metaphysicians or satirists, nor to philosophers or essayists.

We shall turn to—practice.

American pragmatism in philosophy reflects this avid search for what is, above all, *useful and applicable*—in everything that interests an American.

Hence countless books on methods of "conditioning people by means of humour".

I have read pages upon pages on the use of wit to arouse interest in a lecture or sermon, to increase the church collection; or the countless jokes with which a good salesman can inveigle a customer into buying a vacuum cleaner or a washing machine he doesn't need.

The recipe is strong, infallible and successful.

It all comes down to flattery, in one form or another, if not to pure bribery!

Often the recipe is supplied with a short theoretical introduction.

I will quote from a typical American book giving the perfect "American" approach to the basic appeal of humour.

We shall see that the method of the typical "American" comedian (despite his international fame) comes completely within this interpretation.

I shall not be sparing of quotations. Apart from their content, the very publication of such books is the clearest evidence of "Americanism", reaction to which gives birth to a particular form of comic treatment: that of escape from this kind of "Americanism".

There is a book written in 1925 by Professor H. A. Overstreet, Head of the Department of Philosophy, College of the City of New York. It is called *Influencing Human Behaviour* and is a symposium of lectures delivered at the request of a group of students.

As the author points out in his foreword, this request in itself was "unusual" and "significant".

And, indeed, the request was intelligent and businesslike and meant listening to a "course [of lectures] indicating how human behaviour can actually be changed in the light of the new knowledge gained through psychology". The authors of the request

> ... have in common an interest in understanding and improving social conditions. Besides this, and perhaps first of all, we desire to utilize as a part of our everyday technique of action such knowledge as modern psychology can furnish us. Our interest is not academic. We wish actually to function with such knowledge as we may gain.

In his preface the practical psychologist gives an answer in keeping with the technical nature of the request:

> The object of these chapters is to discover how far the data of modern psychology can be put to use by each of us in furthering what is really the central concern of our lives. That central concern is the same whether we be teachers, writers, parents, merchants, statesmen, preachers, or any other of the thousand and one types into which civilization has divided us. In each case the same essential problem confronts us. If we cannot solve it, we are failures; if we can, we are—in so far, at least— successes. What is this central problem? Obviously, it is to be, in some worthwhile manner, effective within our human environment.
>
> We are writers? Then there is the world of publishers, some of whom we must convince as to our ability. If we succeed in doing that, then there is, further, the reading

114

public. It is a bit of sentimental nonsense to say that it makes no difference at all if a writer convinces not even a single soul of his pertinence and value, so be it only that he "express" himself. We have a way of being over-generous with so-called misunderstood geniuses. True, this is a barbarian world; and the fine soul has its hard innings. . . . At any rate, as his manuscripts come back, he might well cease putting the blame on philistine pub-lishers and public long enough to ask himself whether, indeed, he is not deficient in the very elementary art of making the good things he has to say really understand-able.

We are businessmen? Then there are the thousands of potential customers whom we must induce to buy our product. If they refuse, then bankruptcy. . . .

We are parents? It may seem somewhat far fetched to say that the chief concern of a parent is to be accepted by his children. "What!" we cry, "aren't they *our* chil-dren; and aren't children required to respect their parents?" That, of course, is all old philosophy; old ethics; old psychology as well, coming from the day when children, like wives, were our property. Nowadays chil-dren are persons; and the task of parents is to be real persons themselves to such an extent that their children accept them as of convincing power in their lives. . . .

We need not specify further. As individuals, our chief task in life is to make our personality, and what our per-sonality has to offer, effective in our particular environ-ment of human beings. . . .

Life is many things; it is food-getting, shelter-getting, playing, fighting, aspiring, hoping, sorrowing. But at the centre of it all is this: it is the process of getting ourselves believed in and accepted. . . .

How are we to become intelligent about this? . . . Not by talking vaguely about goals and ideals; but by finding out quite specifically what methods are to be employed if the individual is to "get across" to his human fellows, is to capture their attention and win their regard, is to induce them to think and act along with him—whether his

115

human fellows be customers or clients or pupils or children or wife; and whether the regard which he wishes to win is for his goods, or ideas, or artistry, or a great human cause. . . .

To become skilled artists in the enterprise of life—there is hardly anything more basically needful than this. It is to this problem that we address ourselves.[1]

Only by a great effort I restrained myself from placing numerous exclamation marks after each pearl of this hymn to pragmatism, bringing together a writer, a businessman and a parent in one category, and uniting a customer with a wife, or goods with ideas!

However, let us peruse further Professor Overstreet's guide, which at times reads like some of the best pages of Labiche or Scribe.

For example, the section on the "Yes-Response Technique":

The canvasser rings the door-bell. The door is opened by a suspicious lady-of-the-house. The canvasser lifts his hat. "Would you like to buy an illustrated History of the World?" he asks. "No!" And the door slams.

. . . in the above there is a psychological lesson. A "No" response is a most difficult handicap to overcome. When a person has said "No", all his pride of personality demands that he remain consistent with himself. He may later feel that the "No" was ill-advised; nevertheless, there is his precious pride to consider! Once having said a thing, he must stick to it.

Hence it is of the very greatest imporance that we start a person in the affirmative direction. A wiser canvasser rings the door-bell. An equally suspicious lady-of-the-house opens. The canvasser lifts his hat. "This is Mrs. Armstrong?"

Scowlingly—"Yes."

"I understand, Mrs. Armstrong, that you have several children in school.

Suspiciously—"Yes."

"And of course they have much home work to do?"

Almost with a sigh—"Yes."

116

"That always requires a good deal of work with reference books, doesn't it—hunting things up, and so on? And of course we don't want our children running out to the library every night... better for them to have all these materials at home." Etc., etc.

We do not guarantee the sale. But that second agent is destined to go far! He has captured the secret of getting, at the outset, a number of "yes-responses". He has thereby set the psychological processes of his listener moving in the affirmative direction. . . .[2]

On page 259 of this "guide" is a businesslike presentation of the key, not to an abstract understanding of the principles of humour in general, but to an American understanding of the secret of humour, or rather, to that understanding of the nature of humour which is most effective in its application to an American.

Professor Overstreet starts with a correct observation:

. . . it is almost the greatest reproach to tell a person flatly that he has no sense of humour whatever. Tell him that he is disorderly, or lackadaisical, or homely, or awkward, he will bear up under these. But tell him that he has no sense of humour: it is a blow from which even the best of us find it difficult to recover.

People have a most curious sensitiveness in this regard.

I can confirm the truth of this observation by the most perfect example in the sphere of humour—Chaplin himself.

I am least of all interested in writing a theoretical treatise, and that is why I take any opportunity to leap to the sphere of personal reminiscences.

An evening in Beverly Hills. In Hollywood.

Chaplin is our guest.

We are playing a popular Hollywood game.

A cruel one.

This game is characteristic of Hollywood, where, in the small area of a few square miles, there is concentrated so much self-esteem, self-love and self-infatuation—deserved and undeserved, well-founded and unfounded, over-estimated and under-estimated, and all morbidly over-strained— enough to suffice for at least three-quarters of the globe.

This game is a variation of the popular game "Opinions".

With this difference, that here the opinion is expressed in answers to a questionnaire, which give "marks", i.e. "cleverness": 5; "wit": 3; "charm": 4, etc.

The one who is chosen as the subject for such a questionnaire, must fill up his own, giving himself marks accordingly.

"A game of Self-Criticism" we would call it in Moscow.

The more so, as the whole point of the game is not the guessing, but simply the degree of divergence of marks between the general opinion and the subject's own opinion of himself.

A cruel game!

Especially, as the column "Sense of Humour" occupies an important place in it.

"The King of Humour" goes quietly to the kitchen, and putting on his glasses, somewhere near the refrigerator, fills up his questionnaire.

Meanwhile a surprise is being prepared for him.

Public opinion has rated his sense of humour as low as 4.

Does he see the humour of the situation?

He doesn't.

The guest is offended.

The distinguished visitor lacked a sense of humour when it touched himself; so the mark of 4 was well-deserved! ...

Why is it, asks Professor Overstreet, that people are so sensitive when their sense of humour is in question?

Why is there this all but universal wish to be possessed of humour?

Apparently, the possession of humour implies the possession of a number of typical habit-systems. The first is an emotional one: the habit of playfulness. Why should one be proud of being playful? For a double reason. First, playfulness connotes childhood and youth. If one can be playful, one still possesses something of the vigour and the joy of young life. If one has ceased to be playful, one writes oneself down as rigidly old. And who wishes to confess to himself that, rheumatic as are his joints, his mind and spirit are really aged? So the old man is proud of the playful joke which assures him that he is still friskily young.

But there is a deeper implication. To be playful is, in a sense, to be free. When a person is playful, he momentarily disregards the binding necessities which compel him, in business, morals, domestic and community life. . . . Life is largely compulsion. But in play we are free! We do what we please. . . .

Apparently there is no dearer human wish than to be free.

But this is not simply a wish to be free *from*; it is also, and more deeply, a wish to be free *to*. What galls us is that the binding necessities do not permit us to shape our world as we please. They hand out the conditions to us. We must take them or leave them. What we most deeply desire, however, is to create our world for ourselves. Whenever we can do that, even in the slightest degree, we are happy. Now in play we create our own world. . . .

To imply, therefore, that a person has a fine sense of humour is to imply that he has still in him the spirit of play, which implies even more deeply the spirit of freedom and of creative spontaneity.[3]

All subsequent practical recipes stem wholly from these premises.

As regards the specifically American notion of humour, the observations of Professor Overstreet are very apt and very correctly derived from the basis of specifically American psychology.

Legions of American comedians fit into the limits of the framework laid down for them.

And the most perfect of them fits it to absolute perfection, for he carries out these principles not only through infantilism, gags and tricks as such, but through the subtlety of his method, by offering an infantile pattern for imitation, psychologically infecting the spectator with infantilism and drawing him into the infantile paradise of the golden age of childhood.

The leap into infantilism also serves Chaplin as a means of psychological escape from the limits of the regulated, ordained and calculated world around him. It is insufficient.

Merely a palliative. But it is the utmost he can do with the possibilities available to him. In his longing for freedom, Chaplin has defined the only means for the complete escape of an artist from all limitations through his art, in his comments on—animated cartoons.

> ... in my opinion the cartoon is the only real art of today, because in it and only in it the artist is absolutely free to use his fantasy and to do whatever he likes to do with the picture.[4]

This, of course, is a cry: a cry of longing for the most perfect form of escape from the inhibiting fetters of just such conventions and necessities of reality as Professor Overstreet has so obligingly enumerated above.

Chaplin finds a partial satisfaction of his nostalgia for freedom by plunging psychologically into the golden age of infantilism.

Similarly, satisfaction is found by the audience whom he takes with him on his magic journey into the world of fiction, light-heartedness and tranquillity, which hitherto they knew only in the cradle.

The businesslike formality of America is in many ways a younger brother of the primness of Dickens's Mr. Dombey. And it is not surprising that England too, in its own style, had the inevitable "infantile" reaction. On the one hand it is expressed by the entry of the child into subject and plot: for it was in England that the child was first introduced into the sphere of literature, and whole novels or large parts of them are dedicated to representing the psychology of little children. Passing into the pages of a novel, Mr Dombey becomes "Dombey & Son", and many pages are dedicated to little Paul, David Copperfield, Little Dorrit, Nicholas Nickleby, to name but a few characters from this most popular British author alone.

England was also fertile soil for the profuse growth of infantilism in what is known as *nonsense* literature. In the immortal *Alice* of Lewis Carroll and in Edward Lear's *Book of Nonsense* are preserved the finest examples of that style, although it is well known that Swinburne, Dante

Gabriel Rossetti, and even Ruskin have left amusing examples of poetic nonsense in the form of limericks.

"Flight from reality . . ."

"Return to childhood . . ."

"Infantilism . . ."

In the Soviet Union we don't like these words. We don't like these concepts. We don't sympathize with the fact of their existence.

Why?

Because in the very practice of the Soviet State we have approached the problem of the liberation of man and the human spirit from a completely different angle.

At the other end of the earth people have only one alternative: to flee, psychologically, fictitiously, back to the carefree abandon of childhood.

At our end of the world we do not flee from reality into fairy-tales; we make fairy-tales real.

Our task is not as grown-ups to plunge into childhood, but to make the children's paradise of the past accessible to every grown-up, to every citizen of the Soviet Union.

For no matter what paragraph of the Constitution we take, we are struck by the fact that here, systematically presented and state-legalized, are actually the very things which constitute the ideals of the golden age.

"The right to work."

What an unexpected conception was brought by this apparently paradoxical formula to those in whose minds work was inevitably linked with the idea of a heavy burden and an unpleasant necessity!

How new and unexpected the word "work" sounded in the company of words like "right", "glory", and "heroism"!

And yet this thesis, reflecting the real state of things in our country, the complete absence of unemployment and the ensuring of work for every citizen, is psychologically a wonderful resurrection, on a newly perfected—the most perfect—phase of human evolution, of just that premise, which at the very dawn, the Childhood of Mankind, in the past Golden Age seemed to man in his primeval, natural, and simple condition to be the natural conception of work and the rights and obligations involved therein.

We are the first to have completely cleared the road, so that all creative strivings can move along the path which the spirit of every individual thirsts for.

One does not need aristocratic connections to take up a diplomatic career.

To become a Civil Servant one doesn't have to be signed up at birth to a privileged public school, outside which such a political career is inevitably closed to him.

To achieve a high position in the Army one doesn't need membership of a caste or social position, and so forth.

Nowhere in the world hitherto has this happened, either in this fashion or on this scale.

And this is why from time immemorial man has had this dream, cast in the form of longings, myths, legends and songs, of the possibility of becoming whatever he wished.

Even more has been done in our country: the wise measures for the security of old age lifts from the backs of our citizens one more terrible burden—the burden of eternal fear of the future, feelings unknown to beasts, birds, flowers, or little children, who are completely free from care—the burden of worry about this much-vaunted "security" which weighs down every American, no matter what his material position or place in the social scale.

And that is why the genius of Chaplin could only be born at the *other* end of the earth, and not in the country where everything is done so that the golden paradise of childhood can become reality.

That is why his genius had to shine there, where the method and type of his comedy was a necessity, where the realization of the child's dream inevitably ends for the grown-up in nothing but disappointment.

"The Secret of his Eyes" is undoubtedly revealed in *Modern Times*. As long as he was concerned with the pleiad of the most beautiful of his comedies, of the clash of good and evil, of big and little, his eyes, as if accidentally and simultaneously lighting on the poor and the rich, laughed and cried in unison with his theme. But they apparently went contrary to their own theme when in the most modern times of American depression the good and evil "Uncles" turned out to be the real representatives of uncompromising social groups, at which the eyes of Chaplin first blinked, and then narrowed; but continued obstinately to look at modern times and phenomena in the old way. This led to a break in the style of things: in thematic treatment, to the monstrous and distorted: in the inner aspect of Chaplin himself, to a complete revelation of the secret of his eyes.

In the following discussion I do not wish by any means to say that Chaplin is indifferent to what is happening around him or that Chaplin does not (even though partly) understand it.

I am not interested in *what* he understands.

I am interested in how he perceives; how he looks and sees, when he is lost "in inspiration"; when he comes across a series of images of phenomena, which he is laughing at, and when laughter at what he perceives is remoulded into the forms of comic situations and tricks; and with what eyes one must look at the world, in order to see it as Chaplin sees it.

A group of delightful Chinese children are laughing.
One shot. Another. Close up. Mid shot. Again close up.
What are they laughing at?
Apparently at a scene taking place in the depths of the room.
What is taking place there?
A man sinks back on a bed. He is apparently drunk.
And a tiny woman—a Chinese—slaps him on the face furiously.
The children are overcome with uncontrollable laughter.
Although the man is their father. And the little Chinese woman their mother. And the big man is not drunk. And it is not for drunkenness the little wife is hitting him on the face.
The man is dead. . . .
And she is slapping the deceased on the face precisely because he has died and left to a hungry death her and the two little children who laugh so merrily.

That, of course, is not from one of Chaplin's films. These

are passing strokes from that wonderful novel by André Malraux, *La Condition Humaine.**

In thinking of Chaplin, I always see him in the image of the Chinese children, laughing merrily to see how comically the slaps of the little woman make the head of the big man wobble from side to side. It is not important that the Chinese woman is—the mother. That the man is—the father. And it is not at all important that in general he is dead.

In that is the secret of Chaplin.

In that is the secret of his eyes.

In that is his inimitability.

In that is his greatness.

To see things most terrible, most pitiful, most tragic through the eyes of a laughing child.

To see the images of these things spontaneously and suddenly—outside their moral-ethical significance, outside valuation, and outside judgement and condemnation—to see them as a child sees them through a burst of laughter.

In that Chaplin is outstanding, inimitable and unique.

The sudden immediacy of his look gives birth to a comic perception. This perception becomes transformed into a conception. Conceptions are of three kinds:

A phenomenon genuinely inoffensive. And Chaplin's perception clothes it with his inimitable Chaplinesque buffoonery.

* The difference between this "quotation" and Malraux's text may have an interesting explanation. Here is the passage, as translated by Alastair Macdonald in the Penguin edition:

> Like the starving Russian, living almost next door to him, who one day found life as a factory-hand a little more intolerable than he could bear, and committed suicide; and whose wife, mad with anger, had slapped the corpse which was leaving her to her fate; with four children crouching in the corners of the room, and one of them saying: 'Why are you fighting?'
>
> (*Man's Estate*, p. 168)

As Eisenstein began this essay on Chaplin soon after Malraux visited him to discuss their collaboration on a film to be based on *La Condition humaine,* E's free quotation may be the only surviving fragment of the lost script prepared at that time. On the other hand, and equally revealing, E's quotation may represent the way he recalled the passage.—J. L.

A phenomenon personally dramatic. And Chaplin's perception gives birth to the humorous melodrama of the finest images of his individual style—the fusion of laughter with tears.

The blind girl will call forth a smile when, blindly, she douses Charlie with water.

The girl with her sight restored might appear melodramatic when, in touching him with her hand, she does not fully realize that before her is the one who loves her and gave her back her sight. And then within that very incident the melodrama may be comically stood on its head—the blind girl repeats the episodes with the *bon vivant*, saved by Charlie from suicide: in which the *bon vivant* only recognizes his saviour and friend when he is "blind" drunk.

Finally, *socially tragic phenomena*—no longer a childish amusement, not a problem for a mind, not a child's plaything—the comical-childish vision gives birth to a series of terrible shots in *Modern Times*.

The ability to *see as a child*—is inimitably, irrepeatably inherent in Chaplin personally. Only Chaplin sees this way. What is astonishing is this very power of Chaplin's sight to see piercingly and immutably through all the workings of professional cunning.

Always and in everything: from the trifle, *A Night at the Show*, to the tragedy of contemporary society in *Modern Times*.

To see the world thus and have the courage to show it thus on the screen is the attribute of Genius alone.

Though, incidentally, he doesn't even need courage.

He can *only* see it that way, and no other.

Maybe I stress that point too much?

Possibly!

We are people with a "conscious purpose", "conscious tasks".

And inevitably "grown-ups".

We are grown-ups and may have lost the ability to laugh at the comic without taking into consideration its tragic significance and content.

We are grown-ups who have lost the lawless age of childhood, when there were as yet no ethics, morals, higher standards of judgements, etc., etc.

*   *   *

Chaplin plays up to actuality itself.

It is the bloody idiocy of war in the film *Shoulder Arms*. The modern era of the most modern times in *Modern Times*. Chaplin's partner is by no means the big, terrible, powerful and ruthless fat man, who, when not filming, runs a restaurant in Hollywood.

Chaplin's partner, throughout his repertoire, is another. Still bigger, still more terrible, powerful and ruthless. Chaplin and actuality itself, partners together, a pair in harness, play before us an endless string of circus acts. Actuality is like a serious "white" clown.

He seems clever and logical. Observant and foresighted. But it is he finally who remains the fool and is laughed at. His simple, childlike partner Charlie comes out on top. Laughing carelessly, without being aware that his laughter kills his partner.

And like a young chemist who for his first analysis is unsuspectingly given a glass of pure water, and finds in it all kinds of conceivable and inconceivable ingredients, so in this pure water of infantilism, of spontaneous comic perception, everyone sees what he wishes.

As a child I saw a magician. He moved across the darkened stage like a faintly visible phosphorescent ghost.

"Just think of someone you want to see," cried this circus Cagliostro from the stage, "and you will see him!"

And in this merry little fellow, who is himself a magician and a wizard, they also "see". See what he had never put there at all.

An evening in Hollywood. Charlie and I are going to Santa Monica, to the local Lido Venice festival by the sea. Presently we are taking pot-shots at mechanical pigs. Taking cock-shies at coconuts and bottles. Chaplin, putting his glasses on in a businesslike fashion, will add up the score, so that he can take one big prize instead of a lot of small ones, an alarm clock instead of say, plaster casts of Felix the Cat.

126

And the boys will slap him on the back with a familiar "Hello, Charlie!"

Later, as we are sitting in the car, he pushes over a book to me. It's in German. "Tell me what it's all about," he says. For he doesn't know German. But he knows the book says something about him.

"Please explain."

It is a German expressionist booklet[5] and at the end is a play, dealing, of course, with a cosmic cataclysm: Charlie Chaplin pierces through the revived chaos with his stick, and points the way of escape beyond the world's end, politely touching his bowler as he does so.

I had to admit I got stuck in interpreting this post-war delirium.

"Please tell me what it's all about" is what he might have said about much that is said about him.

It is extraordinary how much metaphysical nonsense sticks to Charlie Chaplin.

I remember one more anecdote.

It belongs to the late Elie Faure, who wrote of Chaplin:

> As he hops from one of these feet to the other—these feet so sad and yet so absurd—he represents the two extremes of the mind; one is named knowledge and the other desire. Leaping from one to the other he seeks the centre of gravity of the soul which he finds only to lose it again immediately.[6]

However, irrespective of the will of the artist, the social fate of his environment brings forth an unerringly true interpretation.

And so, one way or the other, Truth in the West chooses this little fellow with his comic outlook in order to replace what is comic for him with something that is by itself often beyond the category of the comic.

Yes, Chaplin's partner is reality.

What a satirist must introduce into his works on two planes, Chaplin the comedian presents on one plane. He laughs spontaneously. Satirical interpretation is achieved by the fade-in of Chaplin's grimace on the conditions that gave rise to it.

*　　　*　　　*

"You remember the scene in *Easy Street* where I scatter food from a box to poor children as if they were chickens?"

This conversation took place aboard Chaplin's yacht when we spent three days off Catalina Island, in the company of sea lions and flying fish, with underwater gardens that you could watch through glass-bottomed boats.

"You see, I did this because I despised them. I don't like children."

The author of *The Kid*, which made five-sixths of the globe shed tears over the fate of a neglected child, did not like children. Was he—a monster?

But who *normally* does not like children?

Why, children themselves.

The yacht plunges on its way. Its movements remind Chaplin of the rolling gait of an elephant.

"I despise elephants. To have such strength and to be so meekly submissive."

"Which animal do you like?"

"The wolf" came the unhesitating answer. And his grey eyes and the grey eyebrows and hair seemed wolf-like. His eyes peer into the sunny flickering of the Pacific Ocean sunset. Over the flickering ocean glides a destroyer of the U.S. Navy.

A wolf.

Obliged to live with the pack. But always to be alone. How like Chaplin that was! Always at war with his own pack. Each an enemy to the other and to all.

Maybe Chaplin doesn't really mean what he says. Maybe it's a bit of a "pose".

But if it is a pose, then, no doubt, it's that pose by which Chaplin with his inimitable and unique perception illuminates the world.

Six months later, on the day I was leaving for Mexico, Chaplin showed me the rough cutting copy, as yet without sound, of *City Lights*.

I was sitting on Chaplin's own black oilcloth chair. Charlie himself was busy: at the piano and with his lips, he was filling in the missing sound of the picture. Charlie (in the film) saves the life of a drunken millionaire who is trying

128

to drown himself. The saved one only recognizes his saviour when he is drunk.

Funny?—tragic.

That is Saltykov-Shchedrin. That is Dostoievski.

The big one beats the little one. He is beaten up.

At first—man by man. Then more—man by society.

Once, long ago, there was a widely popular photograph in either the London *Sketch* or the *Graphic*.

"His Majesty the Baby," was the title under it.

The photograph depicted a surging flood of street traffic, in Bond Street, the Strand or Piccadilly Circus, suddenly freezing at the lift of a "Bobby's" hand.

Across the street goes the child, and the flood of traffic humbly waits, until His Majesty the Baby has crossed from pavement to pavement.

"Stop for His Majesty the Baby!" one wants to shout to oneself, when attempting to approach Chaplin from a social-ethical and moral position in the widest and deepest sense of these words.

"Stop."

Let's take His Majesty as he is!

*   *   *

Chaplin's situations, after all, are just the same as those children read about in fairy stories, where an array of tortures, killings, fears and terrors are inevitable accompaniments.

Their favourite heroes—the terrible Barmaley ("He eats little children"), the Jabberwocky of Lewis Carroll, Baba Yaga and Kashei the Immortal.*

Stories take time to read. And their quintessence, for lighter reading, is distilled from verses.

Thus in the nurseries of England and America persists through the ages a merry obituary of "Ten Little Nigger Boys", who one after the other, in verse after verse, die all kinds of deaths.

* Russian folk-tale characters: Barmaley is the equivalent of the "Wicked Ogre", Baba Yaga to the "Horrid Witch" and Kashei the Immortal to the "Superman Hero".—H.M.

129

And, what is more, without any guilt at all and without any reason whatsoever.

a bumble bee stung one, and then there were five.

five little nigger boys going in for law:
one got in chancery, and then there were four.

four little nigger boys going out to sea;
a red herring swallowed one, and then there were three.

three little nigger boys walking in the zoo;
the big bear hugged one, and then there were two.

two little nigger boys sitting in the sun;
one got frizzled up, and then there was one.

one little nigger boy living all alone;
he got married, and then there was none.

Incidentally, it may be that this last line contains the "significance" of the whole nursery rhyme; Marriage is the end of childish infantile existence—the last little boy dies and an adult emerges!

However, the tendency we are discussing is still more clearly seen in the collection of Harry Graham's *Ruthless Rhymes for Heartless Homes* (the last London edition was the nineteenth!).

This dedication serves it as a foreword:

> With guilty, conscience-stricken tears,
>   I offer up these rhymes of mine,

To children of maturer years
(From seventeen to ninety-nine)
A special solace may they be
In days of second infancy.

The verses, addressed to those who have fallen into their
second childhood, are made according to all the canons dear
to—first childhood.

The Stern Parents
Father heard his Children scream,
So he threw them in the stream,
Saying, as he drowned the third,
"Children should be seen, *not* heard!"

Mr Jones
"There's been an accident!" they said,
"Your servant's cut in half; he's dead!"
"Indeed!" said Mr Jones, "and please
Send me the half that's got my keys."

One could write a whole dissertation on Anglo-Saxon
humour as compared to the "Slavonic Soul", if, in connection with the last example, one remembers the dramatic
treatment of Chekhov's short story "Sleepy". There a girl-
nurse—herself only a child—chokes a child given her to
look after, because the child cries at night and won't let her
sleep. And all this under the warm peaceful reflections of
the green-shaded oil lamp. . . .

But one way or another—in the dramatic description of
the adolescent girl, in the fantastic structure of the Grimms'
Fairy Tales or in the careless amusement of *Ruthless
Rhymes*—all have grasped the most important thing in child
psychology and the child soul, that which Leo Tolstoi long
ago pointed out.

Maxim Gorky recorded Tolstoi's words:

. . . [Hans] Andersen was very lonely. Very. I don't
know his life. It seems to me he lived, travelled a lot, but
this only confirms my feelings—that he was lonely. And
for that very reason he turned to children, although mistakenly, as if children would feel sorry for a person more

131

grown up. Children don't feel sorry for anything, they are incapable of feeling sorry . . .

And all specialists in the child soul say the same.

And it is interesting to note that it is this particularly which lies at the bottom of children's jokes and stories. Yelena Kononenko writes of Moscow children: 'Grandad, will you see the New Moscow? What do you think, will you still live to see it?' . . . Vladilev asked cruelly. 'And I see that presently he is confused, understanding a little that he should not have asked the old man that question. Obviously he is a little ashamed and sorry for Grandad. But speaking generally he is not sorry for old men and, when kids in the yard said that old people would be made into glue, he laughed till the tears ran and asked me slyly how much glue could be made out of Grandad. . . .'

Kimmins writes about English and American children. His conclusions are based on a colossal quantity of statistic material. In the section of his work dealing with "What Young Children Laugh At" we read:

The misfortunes of others as a cause of laughter are frequently referred to by young children, and form the basis of many funny stories. With children of 7 years of age, about twenty-five per cent of the boys' stories, and sixteen per cent of the girls' are of this nature. At 9 years of age there is a decrease to about eighteen and ten per cent respectively.[7]

But this concerns only *stories*. A description of similar *facts* continues to retain their mirth-invoking effect: they are "in special favour during the period of rapid growth from 12 to 14 years of age".

In another work Kimmins, in dealing with "The Child's Attitude to Life" on the basis of an analysis of children's stories, quotes this typical story, attributed to the medium-aged groups:

"A man was shaving, when a sudden knock was heard at the door; this startled him, and he had the misfortune to cut off his nose. In his excitement he dropped his razor, which cut off one of his toes. A doctor was called

132

in and bound up the wounds. After some days the bandages were removed, when it was found that the nose had been fixed on to the foot and the toe on to the face. The man made a complete recovery, but it was very awkward, because every time he wanted to blow his nose he had to take his boot off."[8]

This situation is exactly in the spirit of the English pantomime Pierrot (so typically English), which so amazed Baudelaire, accustomed to the French Debureau.

Here is what he wrote:

These were the dizzy heights of exaggeration.

Pierrot passes a woman who is washing her door-step: after rifling her pockets, he tries to bag the sponge, broom, bucket and even the water. . . .

For some misdeed Pierrot finally had to be guillotined. As it is England, why not a hanging rather than the guillotine? I do not know—the choice was doubtless determined by what was to follow. . . . After struggling and bellowing like a bullock that scents the slaughter-house Pierrot met his destiny at last. The head was detached from the neck, a big red and white head that rolled noisily to the edge of the executioner's pit, showing the bloody disc of the neck, the severed vertebrae and all the details of a butcher's joint just carved up for display. And suddenly the shortened trunk, moved by its irresistible mania for robbery, stood up, triumphantly snatched up its own head like a ham or a bottle of wine, and, more wisely than the great St Denis, stuffed it into its pocket![9]

To complete the "bouquet" one might call to mind a "fable" by Ambrose Bierce. The ruthless "humoresque" of this author is very apt, for the Anglo-American type of humour, which we are discussing here, arises completely from this same general source!

A Man was plucking a live Goose, when the bird addressed him thus:

"Suppose that you were a goose, do you think that you would relish this sort of thing?"

"Suppose that I were," said the Man; "do you think that you would like to pluck me?"

"Indeed I should!" was the natural, emphatic, but injudicious reply.

"Just so," concluded her tormentor, pulling out another handful of feathers; "that is the way *I* feel about it."[10]

The gags in *Modern Times* are completely in this spirit!

"Only children are happy, and that not for long," says wise Vassa Zheleznova in Gorky's play of the same name.

And not for long; because the stern "You mustn't" of tutors, and future standards of behaviour, begin to lay their interdiction on children's unrestricted desires from their very first steps.

He who is unable in time to subordinate these bonds and force their limitations to serve himself; he who, having become a man, continues to remain a child—will inevitably be unable to adapt himself to life, will always be placed in a ridiculous situation, will be funny and provoke laughter.

If the method of the child eyes of Chaplin determines the choice of his theme and the treatment of his comedies, then in the way of plot—it is nearly always the comedy of situations, the childish naïve approach to life clashing with its stern grown-up reprimands.

The genuine and touching "Simple Soul in Christ", over whose image dreamed the ageing Wagner, turns out to be not the Wagnerite *Parsifal*, surrounded by Bayreuth pomp and confronted by the Holy Grail, but none other than Charlie Chaplin, amidst the gutters and alleys of Kennington!

The amoral ruthlessness of the child's approach to phenomena in Chaplin's outlook appears, with all the other accompanying disarming traits of childhood, within the very characters of the personages of his comedies.

From this arises the genuine touchingness of Chaplin, almost always able to hold back from pre-conceived sentimentality.

Often this touchingness is able to achieve genuine pathos.

The finale of *The Pilgrim* has an effect of catharsis, when the Sheriff, losing his patience, kicks Charlie in the behind

—only after Charlie has not understood the good intentions of the Sheriff—to give him, the escaped convict, the possibility of escaping over the frontier into Mexico.

Realizing the goodness of the child-soul of the escaped convict Charlie, who passes himself as a parson and thereby saves the money of the little village church, the Sheriff does not wish to be out done in good deeds.

Taking Charlie along the frontier of Mexico, on the other side of which lies freedom, the Sheriff does all he can to make Charlie understand that he should take advantage of this proximity to escape.

But Charlie just cannot understand it.

Losing his patience, the Sheriff sends him to gather flowers on the other side of the frontier. Charlie obediently passes over the ditch dividing slavery from freedom.

Satisfied, the Sheriff goes off.

But then the childishly honest Charlie overtakes him with the flowers he has gathered.

A kick in the behind unties the dramatic knot.

Charlie is freed.

And the most brilliant finale of all his pictures—a work of genius—Charlie running from the camera with his hop, skip and jump as the iris closes.*

Along the line of the frontier—one foot in the United States, the other in Mexico.

As always, the most wonderful details or episodes in the films are those which, apart from everything else, serve as an image or symbol of the author's method, arising from the peculiarities of the author's make-up.

So here.

One foot on the territory of the Sheriff, the law, shackled feet; the other foot on the territory of freedom from law, responsibility, court and police.

The last shot of *The Pilgrim* is almost a blueprint of the inner character of the hero.

The blueprint of every conflict in all his films: a graph of the method by which he achieves his extraordinary effects.

---

* The diaphragm in front of the camera lens produces the effect of the picture being slowly encircled, smaller and smaller till it is totally obscured. Also known as the Iris out.—H. M.

The running away into the Iris Out is almost a symbol of perpetuity for a grown-up half-child in the environment and society of the full grown-up.

Let's dwell on this! Though the shade of Elie Faure stands in our path, a threatening warning against the insertion of superfluous metaphysics into the Tap-dance of Chaplin's boots!

Particularly because we interpret that drama more broadly, as the drama of the "Little Man" in the conditions of contemporary society.

Fallada's *Little Man, What Now?* is, as it were, a bridge linking these two interpretations.

However, Chaplin himself interprets his own finale; for the little man in contemporary society there is no way out.

Exactly the same as for the little child, who cannot remain as such for ever.

It is sad, but step by step it is necessary to cast off all attractive traits. . . .

— There goes naïveté. . . .

— There goes trustfulness. . . .

— There goes lightheartedness. . . .

. . . and similar traits out of place in cultured society. . . .

There goes unwillingness to consider the interests of a neighbour. . . .

There goes unwillingness to abide by the generally accepted rules. . . .

There goes a curb on the immediacy of a childish egoism. . . .

"Laughing, we part with our past",[11] and so here.

Laughing and sorrowing. . . .

But now let us for a moment imagine that a man has grown up and has, at the same time, retained unrestrained infantile traits in their fullest.

The first and most important of them—complete egoism and a complete lack of moral restraints.

Then before us is a shameless aggressor, a conqueror, an Attila. Chaplin, who has since branded the contemporary Attila could not help in the past wanting to play—Napoleon.

For long he has considered this thought and this plan.

In this scenario Napoleon does not die on St Helena. He

turns pacifist, succeeds in escaping from the island and secretly returns to France. There he gradually succumbs to temptation and prepares a *coup d'état*.

"However, when the revolution has to start, news comes from St Helena that Napoleon died. It was his double, you know, but all and everybody believe that the real one died. All his plans are ruined and Napoleon dies of sorrow. His last words will be: It is the news of my death that has killed me."[12]

This line surpasses the immortal telegram of Mark Twain: "The news of my death is somewhat exaggerated."

Chaplin himself describes the film as tragic. The film was conceived but not made.

Napoleon would have stood in the gallery of other Chaplin characters, an image of the broken ideal of infantilism.

* * *

Corresponding to the "Modern" times of fascism, taking the place of the epoch of Chaplin's *Modern Times,* a significant move takes place in Chaplin's art.

The method of comic effects of Chaplin, unerringly triumphant over the means of his infantile approach to phenomena, suddenly makes a basic change in the character of the persons portrayed, in *The Great Dictator*.

No longer broken as before, but now triumphant, unrestricted and impulsive.

The author's method becomes a graph of the characteristics of his hero.

And at the same time a hero whom the author himself brings to life on the screen by his own acting.

There he is—the "infantile" hero at the height of his power.

Hynkel examines inventions submitted to him by successful inventors.

Here is the "bullet-proof" jacket.

Hynkel's bullet pierces it without hindrance.

The inventor is killed instantaneously and falls like useless lumber.

137

Here is the man with an intriguing parachute-hat who jumps from the top of the palace.

The dictator listens.

Looks down.

The inventor has crashed.

His remark is superb.

"Again you palm off bad quality rubbish on me!"

Isn't that a scene in childhood?

Children's freedom from morals is what is so astonishing in Chaplin's vision.

Formerly Chaplin always played the side of the suffering only, the little barber from the ghetto, which he plays as a second role in *The Great Dictator*.

The Hynkels of his other films were first of all policemen; then the giant partner who wants to eat him under the guise of a chicken in *The Gold Rush*, then many, many policemen; the conveyor in *Modern Times*, and the image of the terrible environment of terrible actuality in that film.

In *The Great Dictator* he plays both.

He plays the two diametrically opposite poles of infantilism; the triumphant and the defeated.

And therefore, no doubt, the effect of this particular film is astonishing.

And no doubt particularly because in this film Chaplin speaks with his own voice.

For the first time it is not he who is in the power of his own method and vision, but method and consciously willed, purposeful presentation are in his adult hands. All this is because here from first to last speaks civil courage, clearly, ringingly and distinctly, the courage not just of a grown-up, but of a Great Man with capital letters.

And thereby Chaplin stands equally and firmly in the ranks of the greatest masters of the age-long struggle of Satire with Darkness, alongside Aristophanes of Athens, Erasmus of Rotterdam, François Rabelais from Meudon, Jonathan Swift from Dublin, François Marie Aroues de Voltaire of Ferney.

And even, maybe, in front of the others, if one bears in mind the scale of the Goliath of Fascist Baseness, Villainy and Obscurantism who is crushed by the sling of laughter from the tiniest of Davids—Charles Spencer Chaplin from Hollywood.

Hereinafter named:

Charlie, the Grown-Up.

translated by Herbert Marshall

"Charlie the Kid" appeared in the World Film Art volume on Chaplin and "Dickens, Griffith and the Film Today" appeared in the Griffith volume, but a change in cultural policy stopped the series. Among the cancelled volumes was one on John Ford, for which Eisenstein wrote the following tribute, published posthumously.

Mr Lincoln by Mr Ford

Suppose some truant Good Fairy were to ask me, "As I'm not employed just now, perhaps there's some small magic job I could do for you, Sergei Mikhailovich? Is there some American film that you'd like me to make you the author of—with a wave of my wand?"

I would not hesitate to accept the offer, and I would at once name the film that I wish I had made. It would be *Young Mr Lincoln*, directed by John Ford.*

There are films that are richer and more effective. There are films that are presented with more entertainment and more charm. Ford himself has made more extraordinary

* *Young Mr Lincoln* was released in the United States by 20th Century-Fox on 9 June 1939; *producer*, Darryl F. Zanuck; *associate producer*, Kenneth Macgowan; *scenario*, Lamar Trotti; *direction*, John Ford; *photography*, Bert Glennon; *design*, Richard Day and Mark-Lee Kirk; *costumes*, Royer; *music*, Alfred Newman; *editor*, Walter Thompson. With Henry Fonda, Alice Brady, Marjorie Weaver, Arleen Whelan, Eddie Collins, Richard Cromwell, Eddie Quillan, Donald Meek.

films than this one. Connoisseurs might well prefer *The Informer*. Audiences would probably vote for *Stagecoach*—and sociologists for *The Grapes of Wrath. Young Mr Lincoln* didn't even get one of those bronze Oscars.

Nevertheless, of all American films made up to now this is the film that I would wish, most of all, to have made. What is there in it that makes me love it so?

It has a quality, a wonderful quality, a quality that every work of art must have—an astonishing harmony of all its component parts, a really amazing harmony as a whole.

I believe that our age yearns for harmony. We look back on the past with envy, and we've made the sunny harmony of the Greeks into an ideal. And our yearning already has brought us some result. Especially in one-sixth of the earth our century has shaped positive ideals. And more: this is a century in which we have realized ideals.

Yet as a whole our globe is experiencing a century of lost harmonies. And a world war that has crushed our gardens and monuments of culture is a most germane phenomenon of this age.

That is why a word of harmony is especially attractive to our epoch. Through such a creation can be expressed active opposition to our discordant times, a force to help people hope for peace, to send representatives to conferences, to form national bodies and to unite nations together.

Among those few works of our time that possess a nearly classical harmony *Mr Lincoln* by Mr Ford occupies a place of honour.

This film is distinguished by something more than its marvellous craftsmanship, where the rhythm of the montage corresponds to the timbre of the photography, and where the cries of the waxwings echo over the turbid flow of muddy water and through the steady gait of the little mule that lanky Abe rides along the Sangamon River. And there is something here more than the skill of filming in a stylized daguerreotype manner that is in unison with the moral character of Lincoln's sentences, or the eccentricity of Henry Fonda's performance that keeps the genuinely moving situation from sliding into sentimentality, and instead reaches a rare degree of pathos, as in the stunning departure of Lincoln into the landscape at the end of the film.

There is a deeper thing here—in those fundamentals and premises from which craftsmanship and harmony grow. Its source is a womb of popular and national spirit—this could account for its unity, its artistry, its genuine beauty.

Historically Lincoln came from the depths of his people, absorbing into himself its most typical and fascinating features. And the film also seems to grow wholly from the fascinating image of this man who embodied the best and highest progressive traditions of America. The harmony of the work of art could be a reflection in images of those great principles that are common to all mankind, and this reflection shows us one of the loveliest aspects of mankind's creativity.

Thus through the image of his historical protagonist John Ford touches the principles whose bearer was the historical Lincoln, not only through the sentences spoken by his Lincoln character, but in the very structure of his film.

Here before us is a miracle—daguerreotypes come to life. Here are those dresses of "unspeakable" checks, tight in the waist and immense below, those ringlets peeping out from dainty caps, those earrings that vie in their perfect forms with the ringlets, those frock-coats and beaver hats, walking-sticks and waistcoats, beards and moustaches and various tufts of hair, fanciful military uniforms—no longer frozen on the metal daguerreotypes, but now with the vital breath brought to life. These gods of antiquity (though not in plaster casts) are suddenly not only living, but running through a gay country fair.

Here's a tug-of-war, with a rope stretched across a well-prepared mud puddle, into which the group at each end of the rope is trying to pull the other. At the last minute, joining the group that seems about to lose, comes one more to help pull—a gaunt and gawky youngster, just stepped from a gallery of daguerreotype portraits of American country youths.

With his long arms he comes very close to cheating: at a critical moment he catches hold of the wheel of a wagon

141

standing nearby. Yet his absolutely innocent look bespeaks only resourcefulness in a moment of decision. And the cluster of opponents at the other end of the rope are swept into the mud puddle with the enthusiastic shouts of the bettors and bystanders.

Our tall rustic is already well into a home-made pie, baked by one of the town's ladies for an eating contest—an indispensable feature of American country fairs.

Image after image of the daguerreotype era is thus brought magically to life in the reality of its great-grandchild —the cinema era. These are the living screen images of the first reels of film about Abraham Lincoln, filled with a feeling for the epoch, atmosphere and national character, and thrown on to the surface of the screen by the sure hand of John Ford.

Through all this moves a giant child, the young Lincoln. There he is involved in a tug-of-war, pulling as if his life depended on it. Here he is devouring pies in an eating contest. And there he is outstripping all the others in the art of rail-splitting. He looks awkward and even lazy, but he always seems to be where he is needed, with a resourceful gesture at the right moment. You sense in him the most practical skill in all sorts of work, the greatest endurance, with the greatest awareness and alertness in struggle.

From the beginning of the film he stands before us as an ideal warrior. He's as clumsy as the young Ilya Murometz, with his deliberate, drawling speech and slow gestures—all in order to gain time for a keen glance to seek a gap in the defences of the opponent, a careless movement of a rival, a weakness in the enemy forces. He reminds me of the anecdote of the stammering bargainer who employed his stammer as a business method, a persuasive tactic in a quarrel or a duel of wits.

The events of the film do not go as far as Lincoln's nation-wide struggle for the unity of the country—we don't even see the violent election campaign in which Lincoln's slogan of freedom was ranged against the slogans of reaction. Yet from the very first glimpse of young Abe's horseplay in the contests at the fair, you sense the fighter in him, a man of insatiable will and energy. Here is a simple and deep lad of the people, an embodiment of Karl Marx's favourite quotation from Terence: "Nothing that is human is alien to me,"—for only one to whom everything human is not alien can to the end maintain his intimacy with all that can be judged human.

Even if Ford did not intend this as a prelude to a later part of his film showing Lincoln's political struggles on the way to the presidency, or to a later indication of President Lincoln's articulation of the ideals of democracy within the nineteenth-century horizons of America, there is no doubt that Ford, always a clever master of his medium, wanted to make us conscious of all these scenes and details of a sketch necessary to any future film about Lincoln.

His informal plot, almost plotless or anecdotal, little more than a chapter in the biography of a man with a great future, looks on closer inspection like a thoroughly composed image synthesizing all those qualities that shone in the historical-political role played by this American giant.

Yet, strictly speaking, what do I know about Mr Lincoln historically? Very likely, nothing more than any more or less educated person knows about him.

We all know of some crafty figures of foreign history: Catherine de' Medici, Mazarin, Fouché...; some sly diplomats: Talleyrand, Metternich...; some downright villains: Cardinal de Retz, Cesare Borgia, Marquis de Sade...; some great conquerors: Attila, Caesar, Napoleon.

The great humanists whom we know are notably fewer. Among these and in one of the first places is the Illinois lawyer who became President of the United States—Abraham Lincoln.

We attach to his name the emancipation of the Negro slaves, and the fortunate conclusion of the fratricidal war between the North and South. Reading history in closer detail, we learn that in these matters Lincoln conducted himself somewhat less decisively and courageously than we might have wished, and considerably more slowly and cautiously than now—looking back—would seem necessary. And we learn that the leadership of the Northern cause was not ultimately disinterested. We also know that after the

143

war many of these liberators took their revenge by enslaving and exploiting not only Negroes but white slaves as well.

Despite these contrary factors in his history we are right to think of Lincoln as not only a bearer but a living embodiment of the positive ideals of freedom and justice for future generations of America. It is this that leaves with us a powerful image of a tireless fighter for freedom, justice, unity and democracy—and we know that he was murdered at Ford's Theatre in Washington on 14 April 1865.

There is an almost faultless criterion in establishing the historical relation of the people with their governments and leaders. By what nicknames do the latter go down in history?

The Carolingian dynasty ended in the tenth century with the characteristic figure of Louis V—"the Sluggard." The last Duke of Burgundy goes into history as "the Bold." With a reflection of evil and cruelty the popular memory of Henry VIII's first daughter is preserved as "Bloody Mary".

One of the wisest of names was that given by the people to the Moscow Tsar, Ivan Vasilyevich. The feudal forces destroyed by him howled about his bloodthirstiness, cruelty, mercilessness. The people dubbed him Grozny—"the Terrible".

The image of Lincoln, from the surface of his historic role, to its depths, is caught by the American nicknames for him that have come down to us. Here is the way he was painted by his contemporaries: The Great Emancipator, The Martyr Chief, The Sage of Springfield, Man of the People, The Great Heart, Honest Old Abe, Father Abraham, Uncle Abe, The Smart Lawyer, The Rail-Splitter. And there were the hostile names given him by the South: The Tyrant, Spindleshanks, The Crow. These last two remain on the surface. But what was there on the surface?

American film directors show a wonderful ability in choosing the people to whom they entrust the characters of literature or their own fantasies.

John Ford especially has this gift in abundance; he can bring to life so many and such unexpectedly varied aspects —look at the actors who play the roles of the passenger in the white hat (in *Stagecoach*), of Casey, the itinerant preacher (in *The Grapes of Wrath*), or the prison governor (in *The Prisoner of Shark Island*). And Victor McLaglen in *The Informer,* or Thomas Mitchell who played the drunken doctor in *Stagecoach* and in *Hurricane.*

All of these actors—and Ford himself, of course—could be students of American history, for in embodying their imagination with such striking and artistic flair they chose the particular image and figure of Lincoln!

When the world press reported Papanin's expedition, someone wrote that it would be impossible to invent a more suitable image of a man who could place an administrative foot on the North Pole.

But give any master of "personifying" historical monuments the task of inventing an appropriate figure, devoid of false pathos, for a bearer of the ideals of American democracy, and he would never think of creating such an extravagant figure—an exterior reminding one simultaneously of an old-fashioned semaphore telegraph, a well-worn windmill, and a scarecrow, clothed in a long, full-skirted frockcoat, and crowned with a shaggy top-hat in the shape of a stovepipe.

In all probability it is precisely through these external features that this historical figure can be shown as heroic and full of pathos, for he is so obviously free from all pose, free even from the slightest concern with himself. The business of this life was the most disinterested service in the interests of his people.

Outside films I know the image of Lincoln through the dozens of photographs gathered in one volume[1] by the conscientious hand of an emigrant from fascist Hungary who was received hospitably in America. Stefan Lorant did this in answer to his ten-year-old son's question, "What was Lincoln like?" From every page of the album this fanatic looks at us, changed and stooped by the years.

You are surprised to observe what accurate intuition and skill were shown by the pleasant-looking young Henry Fonda in transforming himself into this Don Quixote, whose armour was the U.S. Constitution, whose helmet was the traditional top-hat of a small-town lawyer, and whose Rosinante was a placid little mule that he straddled, his long legs almost touching the ground. This is a portrait finished with strength, pathos and life. The man has been reconstructed and passes alive before us on the screen.

The truthfulness of this image and figure in the film could be verified by the millions of pages that have been written in America about Lincoln—and there must be several hundred plays about him.

But it was enough for me to check it against three vivid glimpses of him, preserved in my memory, to be satisfied that before us moved a miraculous reincarnation of an image of the past in a living film-image of today.

The first is a first impression of the arrival in New York of the new President, elected by a provincial majority despite the antipathy to him in this already powerful city.

The second is an anecdote from the time when this man already held the reins of power with an iron hand.

And the third is a fragment of reminiscence, attached to life in the White House while the fate of the American nation, state and people was being decided in the Civil War.*

... I shall not easily forget the first time I ever saw Abraham Lincoln. It must have been about the 18th or 19th of February 1861. It was rather a pleasant afternoon, in New York city, as he arrived there from the West, to remain a few hours, and then pass on to Washington, to prepare for his inauguration. I saw him in Broadway, near the site of the present Post-office. He came down, I think from Canal street, to stop at the Astor House. The broad spaces, sidewalks, and streets in the neighborhood, and for some distance, were crowded with solid masses of people, many thousands. The omnibuses and other vehicles had all been turn'd off, leaving an unusual hush in that busy part of the city. Presently two or three shabby hack barouches made their way with some difficulty through the crowd, and drew up at the Astor House entrance. A tall figure stepp'd out of the centre of these barouches, paus'd leisurely on the sidewalk, look'd up at the granite walls and looming archi-

* The printed text of this essay must have been condensed, for only two of the three promised glimpses follow.—J. L.

tecture of the grand old hotel—then, after a relieving stretch of arms and legs, turn'd round for over a minute to slowly and good-humoredly scan the appearance of the vast and silent crowds. There were no speeches—no compliments—no welcome—as far as I could hear, not a word was said. Still much anxiety was conceal'd in that quiet. Cautious persons had fear'd some mark'd insult or indignity to the President-elect—for he possess'd no personal popularity at all in New York city, and very little political. But it was evidently tacitly agreed that if the few political supporters of Mr Lincoln present would entirely abstain from any demonstration on their side, the immense majority, who were anything but supporters, would abstain on their side also. The result was a sulky, unbroken silence, such as certainly never before characterized so great a New York crowd.

Almost in the same neighborhood I distinctly remember'd seeing Lafayette on his visit to America in 1825. I had also personally seen and heard, various years afterward, how Andrew Jackson, Clay, Webster, Hungarian Kossuth, Filibuster Walker, the Prince of Wales on his visit, and other célèbres, native and foreign, had been welcom'd there—all that indescribable human roar and magnetism, unlike any other sound in the universe—the glad exulting thunder-shouts of countless unloos'd throats of men! But on this occasion, not a voice—not a sound. From the top of an omnibus (driven up one side, close by, and block'd by the curbstone and the crowds), I had, I say, a capital view of it all, and especially of Mr Lincoln, his look and gait—his perfect composure and coolness—his unusual and uncouth height, his dress of complete black, stovepipe hat push'd back on the head, dark-brown complexion, seam'd and wrinkled, yet canny-looking face, black, bushy head of hair, disproportionately long neck, and his hands held behind as he stood observing the people. He look'd with curiosity upon that immense sea of faces, and the sea of faces return'd the look with similar curiosity. In both there was a dash of comedy, almost farce, such as Shakspere puts in his blackest tragedies. The crowd that hemm'd around consisted I should think of thirty to forty thousand men, not a single one his personal friend—while I have no doubt (so frenzied were the ferments of the time), many an assassin's knife and pistol lurk'd in hip or breast-pocket there, ready, soon as break and riot came.

But no break or riot came. The tall figure gave another relieving stretch or two of arms and legs; then with moderate pace, and accompanied by a few unknown-looking persons, ascended the portico-steps of the Astor House, disappear'd through its broad entrance—and the dumb-show ended.

I saw Abraham Lincoln often the four years following that date. He changed rapidly and much during his Presidency—but this scene, and him in it, are indelibly stamp'd upon my recollection. As I sat on the top of my omnibus, and had a good view of him, the thought, dim and inchoate then, has since come out clear enough, that four sorts of genius, four mighty and primal hands, will be needed to the complete limning of this man's future portrait—the eyes and brains and finger-touch of Plutarch and Eschylus and Michel Angelo, assisted by Rabelais ...

This vivid account is by a man whom we know and love for his extraordinary poems and poesy. It is from a lecture about a man whom he loved and saluted. Himself an enthusiast for the Coming Century of Democracy he could not but salute, he could not but love Lincoln.

Walt Whitman wrote this. It is a lecture[2] that he delivered in New York on 14 April 1879, the fourteenth anniversary of the president's assassination.

My earliest recollected encounter with the image of Lincoln was in a book whose title I've forgotten, an old collection of stories about the American Civil War.

The President was supremely simple and modest in his personal habits. He even cleaned his own boots—about which someone sarcastically remarked to him:

"A perfect gentleman never cleans his own boots!"

So Lincoln asked him, "And for whom does the perfect gentleman clean them?"

You can see the calm, unblinking, wise eyes raised to the sarcastic gentleman—and you can imagine that poor fellow fidgeting and wishing that the floor would open up and swallow him.

Here in the film, with wonderful imagery, is seized this exact gaze, a gaze of cosmic reproaches to worldly vanities, a gaze that does not miss the least trifle, a gaze that does not permit the least trifle to obscure the great meaning of all that stands beyond life's trifles, errors, blunders, sins, crimes—the evils of conditions and habits, all the accepted evils that must be changed for the sake of Man.

The film's story is limited to the youth of Lincoln. But Henry Fonda manages to convey much more than this fragmentary (on the surface) episode from the legal practice of Lincoln. Behind these visible events can be sensed the universal pathos with which Lincoln burned—as head and leader of the American people, elected President at the most critical moment of United States history. . . .

I first saw this film on the eve of the world war. It immediately enthralled me with the perfection of its harmony and the rare skill with which it employed all the expressive means at its disposal.

And most of all for the solution of Lincoln's image.

My love for this film has neither cooled nor been forgotten. It grows stronger and the film itself grows more and more dear to me.

By October 1945 most of the evacuated film industry had moved back from its temporary Asian bases to the former film centres, and in Moscow the important journal of film theory and criticism, Iskusstvo Kino *(Art of the Cinema), was revived. Its first post-war number contained several brief statements by film leaders; Eisenstein's contribution, "In Close Up", on the defects and ideals of film criticism, was regarded as so offensive that the entire editorial board was reprimanded and thereafter this journal remained closed to Eisenstein until his death.*

A Close-Up View

Everyone knows—though many forget—that cinema offers various camera positions, known as:

long shot, medium shot, and *close-up*

And we know that these shot-dimensions express varying viewpoints on phenomena.

The long shot conveys the general scope of the phenomenon.

The medium shot places the spectator in an intimate relationship to the players on the screen: he feels in the same room with them, on the same divan beside them, around the same tea-table.

And finally, with the help of the close-up (the enlarged detail), the spectator plunges into the most intimate matters on the screen: a flinching eye-lash, a trembling hand, finger-tips touching the lace at a wrist . . . All these at the required moment point to the person through those details in which he ultimately conceals or reveals himself.

If one can look at the phenomena within a film in these three different ways, then it is exactly thus—in three ways—that one can look at a film as a whole. Or I should say, it must be looked at in this way.

In this way, "in long shot" can stand for the view on the film as a whole: on its thematic necessity, on its contemporary quality, on its correspondence to the needs of the day, on the ideologically correct presentation of the questions it touches, on its accessibility to the masses, on its usefulness, on its fighting significance, on its evaluation in relation to the high reputation of Soviet film work.

Such is a broadly social appraisal of our film productions. And, basically, it is the reflection of this viewpoint that one finds in the central organs of our press.

The normal spectator, whether a member of the Young

Communist League, seamstress, general, student at the Suvorov school, metro-builder, academician, cashier, electrical technician, deep-sea diver, chemist, pilot, typesetter, or shepherd, looks at a film "in medium shot".

Before all other considerations this spectator is moved by the living play of emotions: his human nearness to the images on the screen; whether he is agitated by a concept or by feelings close to him, by the circumstances of a man's fate in his milieu, in the phases of struggle, in the joys of success and the sorrows of adversity. Man, filmed in medium shot, would appear to symbolize in himself this intimacy and the nearness of the spectator to the screen image.

The general characteristics of the theme enter the spectator's consciousness *en passant*. The generalized concept of the event is embedded in the spectator's feelings.

Merged with the hero through his experiences witnessed on the screen, the spectator gives second place to the important and indispensable general idea presented by the film.

Thus the spectator is, before all else, in the grip of the story, the event and the circumstances.

It's quite unimportant to him who wrote the scenario.

He sees the setting of the sun, not the skill of the cameraman.

He weeps with the heroine of the film, not with an actress who plays her role well or poorly.

He is immersed in the emotions of the music, and is often unaware that he is listening to music going on in the "background" of the dialogue that is engrossing him.

From the spectator's viewpoint there can be no higher appreciation than this.

This can happen in fullest measure only with films of perfect truth and artistic persuasiveness.

In the press it is the review-article that corresponds with this point of view. It is that type of synopsis-article, in which the screen images are not spoken of as actors in certain roles, but the behaviour and fates of their film images are appraised as if they were the actions of living beings, living completely real lives that have been somehow accidentally thrown on to a screen along with whatever else may be flowing past in the vicinity of the film theatre.

151

In this type of synopsis-article we are moved by the correct or incorrect behaviour of the characters—we take sides with one character against another, we seek a revelation of their inner motives, we really wish to read about the characters on the screen as people moving in genuine actuality. If such an article does not slide into being simply a synopsis, it can reflect the stimulated thoughts of a spectator under the immediate impression of the work.

And there is a third way to examine a film.

Not only can there be a third way—there *must* be this third way.

This is an examination of the film itself *in close-up*: through a prism of firm analysis the article "breaks down" the film into its parts, resolves its elements, to study the whole just as a new model of construction is studied by engineers and specialists in their own field of technique.

This must be the view of the film from the standpoint of a professional journal.

There must be an appraisal of the film from the positions of both "long shot" and "medium shot"—but firstly it must be an examination "in close-up"—a close-up view of all its component links.

Though in "long shot" view we can form a sharply accurate, even merciless social judgement of a film, and we can be occasionally lifted above the simple, uninvolved synopsis-article by a stimulated and thoughtful selection of a film's events and images, we are also obliged to give a firmly professional, *critical* look at the values and shortcomings of what is done. We must make the highest demands upon the production before us—and in this we are far from perfection.

Without this "third criticism" neither development nor progress nor a persistent heightening of our working level is possible.

A high social appraisal must not serve as a shield, behind which with impunity can be concealed poor editing or a low quality of enunciating those words which, in any final accounting of a film, also determine its value.

The spectator's interest in the story must not serve in mitigation of poor photography, nor should a record box office for a film divest us of responsibility for a poor musical accompaniment, a poorly recorded sound-track, or (so often!) bad laboratory work, especially in the release prints.

I recall those days long past of screenings in the early years of ARRK,* when, shaking and trembling, a director would bring his production before a professional gathering. His trembling was not for fear that after the screening he would be called ugly names by this or that colleague. He was trembling for the same reason that a singer trembles before an audience of singers, or a boxer before other boxers, or a matador before *aficionados* of bull-fighting— knowing that an untrue note, a false modulation, an incorrectly aimed blow or faulty timing *would be noticed by all*. The smallest fault against inner truth, the smallest slip in an editing join, the smallest defect of exposition, the slightest flaw in rhythm: any of these would instantly arouse a sharp reaction of disapproval from the professional audience.

This was because, to render the film as a whole its due, to participate in its events with ideas and feelings, the spectator-professional could not forget that he was not only a spectator—he was also a professional. He knew that the success of the film as a whole does not invariably mean the perfection of all its connected parts: the theme thrills or the acting satisfies, and this takes precedence over the plastic imperfections of the work. Yet this did not prevent him, pleased as he was by the truth of the work, from being harsh and demanding towards those parts that came short of perfection.

Then came a strange period.

The acceptance of a film as a whole began to be regarded as making up for all its particular sins and defects.

I recall a different era, during a decadent period of ARRK, when, in discussing a film that had turned out well, it was forbidden to say, for example, that its photography was pale or that graphically it was not sufficiently inventive. If you dared to go as far as that, all the blame and discredit of Soviet film errors would be heaped on you. Bugaboos

* Association of Workers in Revolutionary Cinema.

would be waved frighteningly before you—especially that you were denying "the unity of form and content"!

This may sound now no more than a story, but it is a bad story.

This dulled the sharpness of demand for film quality. It cooled the passion for more exacting standards of art. It undermined the sense of responsibility in the film-makers themselves. In many ways it bred indifference to the values of the separate components. The brilliant clarity and ideals of cinematic style grew dim and tarnished.

But now we have peace again.

The perfection of professional quality in what we are called to do, regardless of time, place and conditions—that is our sacred duty. And the struggle for conditions under which the desired quality may be achieved—is no less our duty.

The facilities to perfect the production conditions of our work, the capacities to secure this necessary quality for our productions—this is our fighting task, as well as the supreme service to the ideal, the struggle for artistic form and quality in our works. It is to this that we here summon all on the threshold of our new peace.

To show "in close-up" what we are called to do, to perceive, to criticize and to press forward—this must become the fighting line of the newly re-born journal, *Iskusstvo Kino*.

Bowing (where necessary) before certain films "in long shot", thrilled (where possible) like the rank-and-file spectator "in medium shot"—we, "in close-up", will be professionally relentless in our demands on all the components of a film.

Acting thus, we will not be frightened by the shouts of the weak-sighted uncritical folk, trying to scare us with the ghost of "a divided unity of form and content": and we will continue to point out qualitative divergences between a theme and its visualization.

Because a genuine unity of form and content also demands *a unity in the qualitative perfection of both*.

Only perfected art deserves to flash from the screens of our victorious era of post-war constructive creation.

154

Notwithstanding the success and honours achieved by Part I of Ivan the Terrible, the continuation of Eisenstein's last film was so abruptly halted as to bring his film-making career to an end. When Part II was condemned and shelved, and the completed portions of Part III were destroyed, Eisenstein, now in very poor health, returned to theory and teaching for his last years. In this respect 1946 and 1947 were productive years. After his first heart attack he tried to hurry books and ideas to completion that had long waited for this attention. He worked on the memoirs that he planned only for posthumous publication and resumed his lectures to the direction course at VGIK. The following lecture (preserved in a stenographic record) was delivered to his class of student-directors on Christmas Day 1946.

Problems of Composition

In this semester we have touched the most varied questions of composition. We have spoken about the general significance of composition, about the rôle of imagery in composition, and we have studied it in passages from Pushkin's works, where we tried to translate his poetry into montage-lists or into detailed plans for action. What should be our next problem?

Scenario material as received by directors often has a certain compositional fragmentation that tends to reduce its expressiveness. How can we take scenario material of such compositional friability and give it a firm structure and a compositional style?

I want to show you this process in an extract from V. Nekrasov's novel, *Stalingrad*.*

* E. refers to the first version of this novel, as published in *Znamya* (Nos. 8–9, 1946); its later publication was entitled *In the Trenches of Stalingrad*, a title that the author had used in his first sketches. The published English translation by David Floyd is entitled *Front-Line Stalingrad* (Harvill Press, London 1962).

But let us first agree on our viewpoint in examining the compositional question in relation to this extract. We can approach the question in its most narrow, one might even say, its most "operative" sense, that is, how to treat the material, how to arrange it and how to juxtapose its several elements.

We should not forget that the literal meaning of the term "composition" is, firstly, "to compare", and "to arrange". It is in that narrow sense that we shall examine this chosen material, in order to learn how to establish its proportions and the links between the separate parts of the work, its separate episodes and the separate elements within the episodes.

There are several methods and approaches by which one can determine the constructional firmness and wholeness of a work.

One of the simplest methods of establishing compositional ties and links between the separate parts is in finding *repetition*, the use of which we have repeatedly noticed in examples from the works of Pushkin.

The factor of repetition plays an important part in music. In music you will always find certain thematic material which penetrates the whole work at regular intervals of time and is subjected to various treatments.

Similarly, we find in poetry the repetition, with or without alteration, of a certain image, a certain rhythmical pattern, a certain element of subject or melodic arrangement.

Such repetition helps, more than anything else, to create a sense of the unity of the work.

The use of repetition can sometimes be found in the subtle outer structure of the work, for example, where the distance and intensity of separated accents can be discovered in familiar and strictly defined mathematical relationships—within the total rhythm.

It seems obvious that such elements of compositional connectives belong to a category of the simplest means for establishing the unity of a work, along with the usual proportional correlations of its parts.

Now we must speak of the simplest features of composition and show how it is achieved in the actual treatment of specific material. Such constructions can be of various kinds. One kind of construction can be completely arbitrary and unrelated to the real proportions of life. What elements will you find in such a construction?

Such a work, in so far as it employs a certain proportion, can to some degree affect the spectator. But, its "laws" of construction, in so far as they are accidental, cannot penetrate to the depths, nor in the right way; they cannot take possession of the spectator, nor will they convey to him a sense of reality, or the realization of the theme.

These works are inevitably formalistic, for they are not based on an aspiration to reflect in its totality the phenomenon of actuality and its inherent natural laws. And thus arises an artist's arbitrariness, completely without foundation.

A man who does not know how to find the exact rhythmic proportion that expresses the flow of the inner content of the theme will turn to some other solution: if he is an editor he might say, "Let's cut this sequence according to a waltz pattern", that is, in a rhythmic figure made of three beats.

Why? Based on what? For what reason?

It's just this sort of approach that can be found in the graphic arts when, for example, a young painter will suddenly, for no reason at all, decide to compose his painting in the form of a triangle. Now we know very well that the compositional base of many classical paintings is a triangle —but we also know that the authors of those works "arrived" at such compositional forms from the inner necessities of graphically expressing their themes.

Even without such an inner necessity it is possible for a picture to give an impression of proportional harmony, but even at its best it can only entertain the spectator as a play of formal abstractions.

It is an entirely different matter when the compositional structure emerges from the content and imagery of the work.

The classical structure of musical works, of dramas, of films or paintings is almost invariably derived from a struggle of opposites, linked by the unity of conflict.

Normally in drama there are two contending factors from

the beginning, where the emergent progressive element struggles with surviving elements of reaction.

Music ordinarily employs the collision of two themes, or one theme that divides into two. In development these themes interpenetrate each other, move alongside each other comparatively, or intertwine their lines of movement.

It is difficult to find examples of dramatic art having any genuine impact in which this basic condition for an overall compositional structure is not observed.

It is important for you to comprehend the need for making the composition strictly depend on the content and the aim of the work. Only then can veracity of the story and the whole work be achieved.

If the work follows a pattern that does not flow from the general pattern of the action, determined by its content, then it will always be perceived as contrived, stylized, formalist. I want to emphasize that such elements as the repetition of theme and the composition of its development will never seem contrived if every nuance of such composition comes, not from formal demands, but from concepts that express the theme and the author's relationship to the theme.

For this let's take an example from the classics. When we speak of Pushkin's tragedy, *Boris Godunov*, it is impossible not to recall its famous conclusion: "The people are silent."

Literary history tells us that this conclusion appears only in the printed copy of 1831, and that in the two authentic manuscripts of Pushkin, one in the Lenin Library and the other in the Public Library of Leningrad,* the play ends with the people shouting: "Long live Tsar Dimitri Ivanovich!"

Now which of these two conclusions genuinely responds to the wishes of Pushkin?

Literary research workers have offered many conjectures on this matter. It can be argued that the ending, "The people are silent", was inserted in the text under the pressure of the censorship that could not permit the people being shown taking the side of a Pretender instead of the rightful successor, "God's Anointed". From the censor's

* At present all Pushkin manuscripts are housed in the Pushkin House, Leningrad.

158

viewpoint any ending, other than that of the people in silence, would undermine the authority of Tsarism.

Nevertheless it is also granted that Pushkin is never known to have expressed dissatisfaction with this revision of the ending. And it is easy to believe that the ending in the printed copy of the tragedy gives a more menacing tone to the final moment than if the people had shouted, "Long live Tsar Dimitri Ivanovich!" In "The people are silent" one can sense not only a smouldering, threatening judgement on events, but even more noticeably, the ominous alertness of the people that takes its own time to say a weighty, decisive, historical word.

In citing this ending I want to show that an apparently outer compositional shift from one variant to another produces a totally different understanding of the work.

In examining the behaviour of the people through scene after scene of the tragedy we can discover that, without showing any initiative of their own, they somehow express their relation to events.

At the beginning the people quite apathetically go to beg Boris to assume the throne; their apathy is emphasized by the rubbing of onions in their eyes to bring tears, and in answer to someone's question, why they appeal to Boris particularly, they say, "The Boyars will manage him".

In this way Pushkin clears the enthusiastic summons of Boris to the throne of any suspicion of genuine feeling, alleged by Karamzin in his description of the scene. A comparison of Karamzin's description with Pushkin's text provides an excellent example of the reworking of material that is required when the author's attitude diverges from the ideological attitude of his source.

Later in the course of the tragedy, when the Pretender calls to the people to come to his side, they open the city gates to him and tie up the voyevod (Shuisky informs Boris of this).

And later—at the Place of Execution—Grigori Pushkin comes to deliver greetings and a summons to the people from the Pretender. The people respond to this ("Long live Dimitri, our father") and following a shout from a peasant in the pulpit ("Take Boris's pup") rush into the apartments of the Godunovs.

In the finale of the tragedy Mosalsky, after informing the people that "Maria Godunova and her son Fyodor have taken poison," turns on them with the question, "What makes you silent?"—and demands, "Shout! Long live Tsar Dimitri Ivanovich!" It is here that we have the two variant endings: according to the printed edition—*The people are silent*; according to the manuscripts—*The people: "Long live Tsar Dimitri Ivanovich!"*

If you bring together these separated scenes and the manuscript finale, it is possible to read the picture they present thus: the people are apathetic; the people don't want Boris Godunov, but they ask him to take power; at the call of the Pretender the people open the gates for him; the people run to "take Boris's pup"; when they learn from Mosalsky's word that Fyodor is dead, the people, according to Pushkin's direction, "are silenced by horror", and after this they obediently shout: "Long live Tsar Dimitri Ivanovich!"

With such a conclusion the whole action of the people, it would seem, corresponds to the words of Shuisky, that "the rabble . . . instantly obeys any suggestion . . ."

A quite different picture is gained from the second ending: the direction, "The people are silent." Now it would appear that the people, who throughout the tragedy have submissively followed orders, at the last moment do not do what they are told.

But can this "reverse repetition" of the end be regarded as simply a formal compositional twist? No, because if you read through the whole action of the people with the new ending, you find that it permits a total re-understanding of the characteristics of the rôle and meaning of the people in the tragedy.

Throughout the tragedy we see the people as witnesses of the struggle between Godunov and the Pretender, with its own viewpoint on this struggle, and even taking part in the struggle on that side that seems necessary at each moment— but what is most important is that after watching these events, the people, in the course of the tragedy, develop an

160

Eisenstein at Chichen-Itza.

Photograph by Alexandrov

During the making of *Que Viva Mexico!* Eisenstein and Tisse experimented with the use of extreme depth of focus. These two photographs by Alexandrov show a familiar "deep" composition and how it was made.

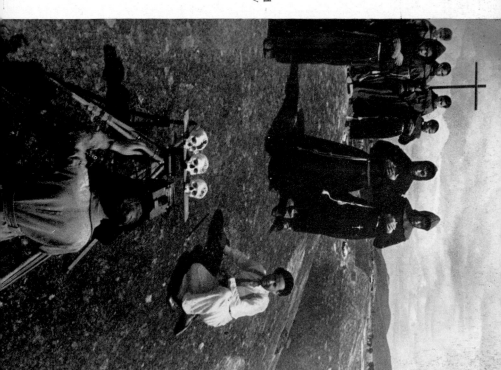

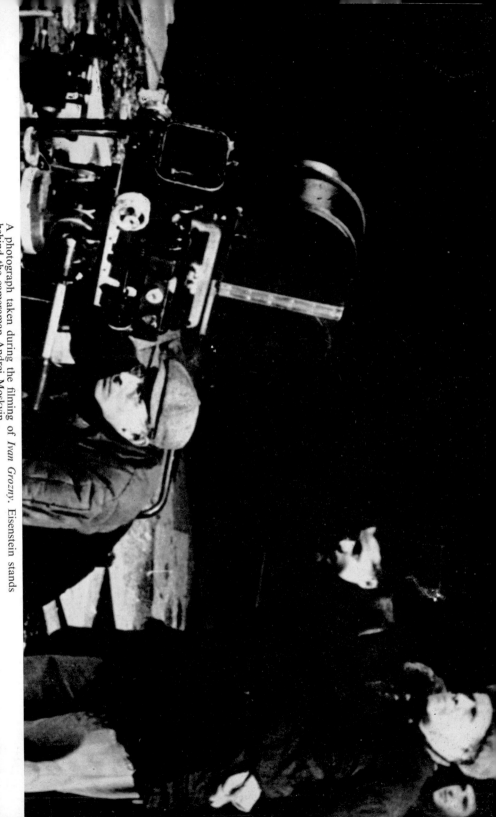

A photograph taken during the filming of *Ivan Grozny*. Eisenstein stands behind the cameraman Andrei Moskvin.

awful power. They have grown, and by the last moment they adopt by their silence an active judgement on the events before them.

We can see that the compositional turn of one element gives us evidence for a re-orientation of the treatment of a whole line of action within the tragedy.

It is curious to note that another type of solution has been proposed, not by Pushkin and not by a director staging the tragedy, but by an historian. The commentaries in one edition of *Boris Godunov* contain the suggestion that for a scenic interpretation the most correct choice would follow neither the first nor the second variant, but would give an "individualized" crowd—that is a broken mass, in which one would shout "Yes", another, "No", and a third would say nothing. According to the author of the commentaries, this would be the most correct and plausible solution for the end of the tragedy.

What would be the result of his solution? Under the banner of an "individualized" *crowd* this professor of history de-individualizes the *people*. Any real and active rôle of the people would be altogether lost in such an interpretation. The result would be what Gogol loved to define in the formula: neither this nor that. Here the rôle of the people as one of the leading characters of the tragedy is brought to naught.

A treatment of the people as "instantly obedient to a suggestion" is for us inadmissible. Therefore that ending in which the people hail Dimitri is also questionable.

The alternative treatment is determined by the ending: "The people are silent." Here the people's character is drawn as growing and beginning to feel its mission, its historic rôle.*

---

* At the end of Meyerhold's life he was rehearsing a production of Pushkin's *Boris Godunov*. Here is his comment at a rehearsal on the final stage direction: "When he complied with the censor's demand and substituted for the people's cheers of "Long live Tsar Dimitri Ivanovich!" the famous direction, "The people are silent," he outwitted the censor because instead of reducing the theme of the People he strengthened it. After all, between a people shouting long live this or that tsar and a people expressing its opinion by silence there is a world of difference. What is more, Pushkin gave

The "treatment" proposed by the aforementioned commentaries tells us nothing and as motivation for the behaviour of the whole people it only says, "thus it came to pass."

Such "reasons"—"it is always thus" and "anything is possible"—these make up that dreadful swamp of inexpressibles in which you sink when you have no clear aim or when your purpose is not cast in a firm compositional form, expressing one basic idea.

And thus we come to the conclusion that every apparently abstract compositional movement and method itself expresses an ideological and political purpose in relation to the formation of the subject.

There are various paths to the exposure and formation of the basic idea in the compositional structure of a work. There can be instances when, before determining the treatment of a work, it is mechanically divided into specific theses, and on the basis of those theses a solution is "worked out". Such a bookish way almost always leads to an abstract solution.

Organically and genuinely a different path offers itself, when in the process of work an understanding and a vital perception of the idea gradually begin to enter the material and determine the work's own compositional proportions. With such an approach all that we have said about the compositional growth of a work, about the establishment of its inner links and proportions, will organically flow from the ideational conception with which you approach any theme, any material.

These are the preliminary considerations on composition which are important to keep in mind before examining the task in hand.

---

the Russian theatre of the future a fascinating and extremely difficult task: how to act silence so that it sounds louder than shouting. I have found a solution to this problem and I thank the foolish censorship for spurring Pushkin to make his wonderful find." Meyerhold also had an explanation for the direction: "Obviously this is not merely a pause but a musical indication for the director. In Pushkin's time the art of theatre direction did not yet exist, but he had the genius to foresee it." (Alexander Gladkov, "Meyerhold on Theatrical Art", *Soviet Literature*, No. 1, 1962).—J. L.

Victor Nekrasov's novel *Stalingrad* received extremely favourable notices from the critics. At the same time there was noted, as an essential flaw in the novel, the circumstance that the author writes of the defence of Stalingrad from the viewpoint of a man who finds himself in the thick of events, but unable to comprehend events beyond those matters in which he directly participates; the author does not always generalize the separate facts that fall within his vision, and this prevents him from giving a full picture of the heroic action at Stalingrad.

The author might, of course, object that it was the editors of *Znamya* who gave his work the title, *Stalingrad*, though Nekrasov had called his work "sketches" and had entitled it *In the Trenches of Stalingrad*. Nevertheless his work has come to the critics and to us as a "novel" called *Stalingrad*.

It is curious to note that the same charge that was brought against the novel can be with equal consistency also levelled at its composition as a whole, and in its separate parts. If the historical-thematic plan of the novel is limited to a scrutiny of individual facts, outside the scope of the whole, then this very feature also distinguishes its compositional structure.

Perhaps the task of the author did not cover more than making sketches of separate passing events, in which he figured as witness or participant. If that is the case then it is necessary for us to estimate how, with the use of parallel cases, an impressionistic sketching of material can raise the combined elements of an artistic work to a certain level of thought.

The content of the novel is the activity of a young lieutenant—the author—in the conditions and surroundings of the Stalingrad struggle, and it is the story of how he, on receiving his assignment, comes to Stalingrad, takes part in its defence and in the defeat of the Germans.

We are to work on one fragment of the novel—the first bombing of Stalingrad by German planes. In our discussion of it I shall try to show not only how the composition in general is built, but also, to a certain degree, to look into what work must always be done in developing a shooting-script—for a shooting-script must have, besides all the

163

usual things, a film work's definite compositional structure.

Some consider that the writing of a shooting-script consists in breaking up the treatment (or literary scenario) into separate lines. On the left-hand side of the page we put the numbers of the shots, and at the right we list the usually fantastic figures for the footage. Nor do I imply that one can take the question of footage either irresponsibly or frivolously. Everyone must train himself to sense the length and time of sequences in order to be conscious of establishing clearly the future film in its footage-time factor.

But the basic and chief task of the shooting-script is in forming that compositional spine along which must move the development of the action, the composition of the episodes and the arrangement of their elements. In our example from *Boris Godunov* I tried to show that this compositional spine is simultaneously one of the sharpest of expressive forms in relation to a fact and also what is usually called the treatment of a work.

In the novel our fragment is preceded by a description of the weary days when the city, now virtually under siege, maintains an atmosphere of expectation and alarmed inactivity. Two young lieutenants—the author and his friend Igor—find themselves in this city and in this atmosphere; with them are Valega, the author's orderly (one of the most successful images in the novel) and the other lieutenant's orderly, Sedykh. Both young lieutenants kill time as best they can. In the local library one reads old numbers of *Apollo*, the other is enthralled by *Peruvian Tales*. But the library is closing. It is working only one shift—not enough staff. In saying good-bye, the librarian tells them that she has some more volumes of *Apollo*, for 1912 and 1917—and she asks them to come back tomorrow.

And then the passage[1] that we are to work on:

> We say goodbye and go. Valega is probably grumbling already—the dinner would be cold.
>
> Near the entrance to the station a square black loudspeaker wheezes hoarsely:
>
> "Citizens, an air-raid warning has been sounded in the city. Attention, citizens, an air-raid warning . . ."

In the last few days air-raid warnings have been sounded three or four times a day. Nobody pays attention to them any longer. There's some shooting—you can't see the aeroplane anyway—and then they give the all-clear.

Valega meets us with a sullen scowl.

"You know very well we've got no oven. I've warmed it up twice already. The potatoes have gone all soft and the borshch is quite . . ." He waves his hand in a hopeless gesture and uncovers the borshch which is wrapped in a greatcoat. Somewhere on the other side of the station the anti-aircraft guns begin to bang away.

The borshch is really good. With meat and sour cream. And plates—rather pretty ones, with little pink flowers—have appeared from somewhere.

"Just like in a restaurant," Igor laughs. "It only wants knife-rests and triangular napkins in the glasses."

And suddenly the whole lot goes flying—plates, spoons, windows and radio-receiver on the wall.

What the devil!

From behind the station the planes come in a steady stream, just as they do in a fly-past. I never saw so many of them. There are so many it is difficult to make out from where they are flying. The whole sky is studded with puffs of anti-aircraft fire.

We stand on the balcony gazing into the sky. Igor, Valega, Sedykh and I. We can't tear ourselves away.

The Germans fly straight at us. They fly in triangular formation, like migrating geese. They fly so low you can see the yellow tips of their wings, the white-bordered crosses and under-carriages exactly like claws . . . Ten . . . twelve . . . fifteen . . . eighteen . . . They draw themselves up in a line right opposite us. The leading one turns upside down, with his wheels in the air and goes into a dive. I can't take my eyes off him. He has red wheels and red cylinder heads. He switches on his siren. Little black spots begin to fall from beneath the wings. One, two, three, four, ten, twelve . . . The last one is white and big. Instinctively I shut my eyes and clutch at the rail. No earth in which to take cover. But you have to do something. A

165

singing sound seems to come from the diving plane. Then it is no longer possible to distinguish anything at all.

An uninterrupted roar. Everything shakes with a horrible tremor. I open my eyes for a second. Nothing to be seen. You can't tell whether it is smoke or dust. Everything is covered in something continuous and thick . . . Again more bombs shriek and more noise. I hang on to the rail. Somebody pinches my arm as if with pincers— above the elbow . . . Valega's face—caught motionless as if by a flash of lightning . . . white, with big round eyes and open mouth . . . Then it vanishes . . .

How long can it go on? An hour, or two hours, or fifteen minutes? There is neither time nor space. Only the thickness and the cold, rough rail. Nothing else.

The rail disappears. I lie on something soft, warm and uncomfortable. It moves under me. I clutch at it. It crawls away.

No thoughts. The brain has been switched off. There remains only instinct—the animal desire to live, and expectation. Not even expectation, but something like— Get it over, get it over quick. . . Whatever it is—only get it over!

Then we are sitting on the bed and smoking. How that happened I don't quite know. Dust all around—just like a fog. And the smell of pitch. In our teeth, in our ears and down the backs of our necks—sand everywhere. On the floor are pieces of plates, puddles of borshch, cabbage leaves and a hunk of meat. In the middle of the room sits a lump of asphalt. Every single window smashed. My neck aches as though somebody had struck it a blow with a stick.

We sit and smoke. I see Valega's fingers shaking. Mine doing the same probably. Sedykh is wiping his leg. Igor has an enormous bruise on his forehead. He tries to smile.

I go out on to the balcony. The station is burning. The little house to the right of the station is also on fire. That's where some sort of editorial office was or a political department—I can't remember. To the left, towards the grain elevator, a continuous glow. The square is empty. There are a few craters in the torn up asphalt.

166

Somebody is lying behind the fountain. An abandoned ramshackle cart looks as though it had sat down on its hindquarters. The horse is still struggling. Its belly has been ripped open and its intestines are scattered in a pink jelly over the asphalt. The smoke gets thicker and darker. It spreads over the square in a solid cloud.

"Will you want to eat?" Valega asks. His voice is quiet, not his own, rather shaky.

I don't know whether I want to eat, but I say Yes. We eat the cold potato straight from the frying-pan. Igor sits opposite me. His face is grey from dust, like a statue. The evil-looking purple bruise has spread over his whole forehead.

"Oh, to hell with the potato—it just won't go down my throat . . ." He goes out on to the balcony.

As you see, the situation is typical of the circumstances of war. Many have experienced such a situation and can recall it from their own personal point of view. Regardless of this fact, the fragment does not evoke the feeling that it should. The reason for this failing is that the purely compositional expressiveness has been left unfulfilled.

Here we have, rather poorly presented, a description of an aerial attack, stage by stage, with quite well observed individual details. Yet this account is given without "prodding" the means of literary possibilities. The description does not spring dramatically forward, but is content to be a narrative. Such accounts are occasionally found in literary texts as well as in scenarios.

Compare the account of this event, for example, with the representation by Pushkin of the Battle of Poltava. You will see to how large an extent dynamic, rhythmic and structural elements are employed to achieve that compositional relentlessness (remember that word—a composition must be *relentless*) that unswervingly expresses Pushkin's intention, gives three dimensions to the exposition of the subject matter and the author's attitude to it.

From our point of view the defect in the passage chosen from the novel is that the necessary emphases are not made in the material, nor are the high points of tension brought into relief by correspondingly expressive means. Notice the skill with which Pushkin, echoing the varying action of the Battle of Poltava, alters the compositional and rhythmic outlines. The smooth, long phrases of the opening change in rhythm with interjected scenes, which in turn, at the culminating points of the battle, are swiftly transformed into "chopped" lines; "Swede and Russ—stabbing, mangling, slashing". Furthermore, these lines that portray action and behaviour are emphasized with sound images: "Drumbeats, cries, gnashings". Here is not only a choice of characteristic sounds of battle and characteristic action; here, no less, is an inexorable staccato rhythm, a wisely calculated correlation of visual and aural impressions.

We are not demanding that Nekrasov should be a Pushkin. We wish to emphasize the need for choice and a conscious mastery of the medium of expression being used—and we note that the account in the fragment is diffuse, which derives from the almost uniform level of the description, both of the air-raid and of the characters after the attack and the landscape of the blazing city.

Nor is there any variation, either in compositional approach or in inner rhythmic treatment, of the individual parts of the narrative (before the air-raid, the planes, the bombing, after the raid, the burning city, end of scene). This weakens the impression of the fragment which, essentially, has an extremely powerful scene to convey.

As an event entered in a diary, purely for information, we might be satisfied with it, but from the point of view of emotional excitement this treatment of the scene doesn't come up to our demands.

Our task is to translate this material into cinematically striking form and to judge how to arrange it for compositional efficiency.

There is something more to be said about the choice of this fragment.

It is very likely that given a free range of choice of material for this purpose you might not have selected this. Quite understandably, for as treated by the author this fragment draws no attention to itself—the account is not dramatic enough, nor is it particularly thrilling, nor does it seize the imagination.

As for its position in the novel, it is one of the decisive points—for it is from here, from this moment that the epic of Stalingrad begins: this is the first air attack, the first bombing, and here begins the basic thematic line of the novel.

What must be done in order to translate the material of this fragment into a genuinely effective form? That is our present task. How do you think it is necessary to begin?

VOICE FROM THE CLASS: *Divide it into montage pieces!*

To divide it into montage pieces is not difficult. But what will control this division? What is to emerge from a breakdown into a montage list?

VOICE: *The montage pieces are clearly visible in the description of the scene.*

I am in complete agreement with you: the details here are described fully—the phrase is "well seen". However, what we need is to be not only well seen, but also "exposed", *revealed* in such a way that it will act upon our feelings and thoughts.

From this viewpoint what is lacking in this account? What is lacking here is a clearly accented aim or direction which would govern the grouping of its separate elements. The material now is set down in a rather crumbly way. Despite this, are there sequences that convey something deep and substantial which, according to their own nature, could serve as an organized starting-point for shaping the comprehension of the scene as a whole?

VOICES (simultaneously): *Of course, there are!*

When the planes appear — "Ten — twelve — fifteen — eighteen—"

You consider this place the strongest in depth of impression? You really do? But I am asking you to choose a place on which a compositional comprehension of the whole episode can be based. Such conception not to be a "piling up" of details, but primarily the expression of some idea, that continues through the whole sequence.

Could such a purely descriptive picture of an air-raid serve as the means of an inner comprehension of the whole scene? Of course not. This could be an effective scene, but in it there is no key to the compositional solution of the whole.

More suggestions, please.

VOICES: *"We sit and smoke..."*

I consider it to be the beginning of the bombardment—
"Instinctively I shut my eyes..."

"No earth in which to take cover. But you have to do something..."

Why? Why? And again— Why?

In the material of the episode isn't there even one detail that could be ranked beside such "details" as the famous "The people are silent", to which we gave so much attention at the beginning of this lecture? Pushkin's phrase is good, not merely as a stage direction (soundless), or a remark, but above all for the deep idea it contains.

And, as you approach composition, you must seize not only "effective material", but you must find details that touch you deeply, that "touch you to the quick".

Or perhaps the question could be put more clearly: In our material is there something, even a hint of something, through which the idea of the whole scene could be revealed?

VOICE: *It seems to me that the strongest place is when the siren is switched on—the culmination is here...*

I'm not against the blare, but is that really capable of revealing the idea of the scene?

VOICE: *But I think such a capacity is in the moment when the blare produces a blow.*

Isn't there a heavier blow to be seized for the comprehension of the episode?

VOICES: *"Somebody pinches my arm as if with pincers— above the elbow..."*

"From behind the station the planes come in a steady stream, just as they do in a fly-past."

None of this goes beyond the frame of the purely visual, the impression of pure action. In the next stages of the work these could, with a larger or smaller effect, fill out the separate pieces, but they give us nothing for the definition of the "spine", from which the episode as a whole unfolds.

But perhaps what I'm aiming at is not yet completely clear? Let me explain.

The way to "kindle" the creative fantasy of the artist confronted by an episode cannot be by exterior impressions, but by those containing the most broadly generalized idea of the work. It is that kind of detail that I ask you to find, within this material that has been offered to you.

You say: "The planes fly." Where do they fly? We know they are flying towards Stalingrad. But what is the significance of their flight within our composition? Is there some indication how they should be filmed? Is there some line of treatment for the imagery of their action? Can one really draw from this one fact—that they are flying to the city—an understanding of how they are to be represented in this particular episode?

VOICE: *Airplanes with swastikas, hostile to us, are flying over our city. The city is against them, they are against the city—here you have a collision or interaction of opposites.*

How is the city acting against them?

VOICE: *With anti-aircraft guns.*

Is that so? And is that the most significant characteristic in the defence of Stalingrad? And this information of the defence of Stalingrad as an interaction of attacking planes and sharp-shooting anti-aircraft guns—wouldn't this lower the struggle from the level of great pathos to an almost documentary-technical description of separate though very important facts? That's how it seems to me.

So as not to worry you any longer, I'll point to the place that moved me and which meets the conditions in choosing this extract for our work. You may not agree with me, but here is the place:

The smoke gets thicker and darker. It spreads over the square in a solid cloud.

"Will you eat now?" Valega asks. His voice is quiet, not his own, rather shaky.

That is the impressive phrase that caught my attention amidst the general material of the passage.

171

Why did it catch my attention? And are there grounds for being carried away by such a phrase?

VOICE: *In my opinion, perhaps it was because we see here the first man who did not lose himself in the circumstances of attack.*

Are there possibilities for our work that can grow from this piece?

VOICE: *Certainly, because it shows that a Human Being is always a Human Being and will always remain one.*

Any other considerations in favour of this piece?

VOICE: *I like the transition: after the terrible explosions, when everything flies apart, everything is broken, all is in ruins, comes the question: "Will you eat now?" I don't see here just a man asking a question. And this is because his question, as it were, brings to naught all the efforts of the Germans: the Germans smashed everything, even shattering the very asphalt, but through that question shines one idea: no matter how much the Germans hammer away, they can't beat us.*

Absolutely correct. This piece focuses attention on a magnificent clash: the spreading flames of the ruined city, with hell all around, and suddenly, in the face of all that, the orderly asks in a quiet voice: "Will you eat now?"

This question really has the sound of something "cosmic" overcoming the enemy. Though not yet conscious or deep there is already, as you correctly noted, a sense of elemental invincibility in those the enemy is advancing against. This is more than anti-aircraft guns shooting at bombers. Here is the conflict on a completely different scale and range.

From one side comes the enemy, moving with all the thundering and bursting of cannonades, planes, guns and bombs—and placed in opposition to all this is the intonation of an Altai orderly, speaking in a quiet, frustrating voice: "Will you eat now?" This question, in effect, already "negates", by means of its inner conceptual line, all the horror of the impending.

But is this as definite as we wished? Is there enough in this image of a conscious, purposeful opposition to the enemy, and a conscious will to overcome him?

No. For the present this is elemental inertia, an inertia

172

"common to all mankind": no matter how many will be killed, no matter how many of us will die, life will look after itself. Is such a motif adequate for us? Is this how we understand the defence of Stalingrad? Of course not.

And here we should ask ourselves whether there is also material in our episode that can reveal the defence of Stalingrad not only as an image of the inertia of life that overcomes death, but above all as a victory of conscious, purposeful Soviet people.

For this let us examine another aspect:

"I don't know whether I want to eat, but I say 'I will'."

What can be sensed in this line? Here is the first sound of a new motif—the incredible obstinacy and tenacity that characterized both the defence of Stalingrad and the defence of Leningrad, and all our other cities that were surrounded but never lost their resolution to defend themselves. Beneath these lines one may easily place another, which expresses its profound, innermost idea: "I don't yet know how we'll manage to defend the city, but I know that we will defend it."

As soon as you add to Valega's words the unspoken thought of the lieutenant, you gain a completed image of the invincibility of our people, possessing indestructible vitality as well as invincible purposefulness. The elemental sound of the orderly's question acquires its final definition in the conscious stubbornness of the officer's words. And both, put together, give a genuine meaningful culmination to the conflicting turns of the episode.

Where is the author's mistake? He is at fault in that he doesn't carve out compositionally these two decisive lines from the general narrative tone; instead, he lets them sound so indistinctly that a whole class of young people didn't catch their particular significance, and "missed" altogether this piece in the whole. It is possible, of course, that the fault lies with the class, but I believe that it is the author's presentation that is to blame. If a film should present these remarks as Nekrasov does, I believe they would never catch the attention of the spectator.

Here we have a typical example of insufficient sculptural

relief in the compositional presentation of the most significant element in the episode.

VOICE: *I like it that this remark is given in a quiet, frustrating voice, and not as a declamation.*

Do you believe that the emphasizing of this remark can be done only through declamatory underlining? Our discussion is not on intonation, but on finding that the most important element of an episode is allowed to be swamped in the general course of the narrative, and that the author by means of compositional structure did not single it out as the most meaningful and significant.

The solution does not lie in making an "exhaustive" treatment of the element itself, but in making a reasoned calculation of the resulting impression. We have seen how the mere extraction, no more, of the remark itself, without the slightest addition of declamation, makes it sound convincing and expressive against the background of the flaming and ruined city.

What causes this most important material to be so submerged that it drowns in the chaos of secondary material?

First of all, because these important remarks are given in exactly the same way as insignificant details of a purely genre order. See what the author writes immediately afterwards:

We eat cold potatoes straight from the frying pan. Igor sits opposite to me. His face is grey with dust just like a statue. A blue bruise spreads all over his brow, evilly-violet. "To hell with it," he waved his hand. "It sticks in my throat." He goes out on to the balcony.

Are these details necessary? I believe they are completely unnecessary. To add such elements, and to present them in such a matter-of-fact descriptive detail, seems to me simply like the inability to halt the episode at a vital point and place a full stop just where you have the maximum impressive strength.

The art of placing a period where it must be—that is a great art.*

* E. often quoted Babel's remark (in his 'Maupassant') that "there is no iron that can enter the human heart with such stupefying effect as a period, placed at the right moment".—J. L.

174

It's clear enough that the life of the characters is not broken off at this point. Dinner will go on, someone will get up, go out on the balcony, and do all sorts of things. But why do we need all this? It begins to resemble one of the commentator's proposals for the interpretation of the finale of *Boris Godunov*, with an aimless "individualization" of the crowd.

After making a remark about food play a role of great conceptual significance, it is tossed back once more, drowned in a chaos of genre details about food sticking in someone's throat but not in another's, while a third doesn't wish to think about food at all, etc. From this arrangement of the materials we must extract the theme of the birth of stubbornness in the future defenders of Stalingrad—and let nothing throw into shadow the distinctness of its expression.

If you want genre details they can be added *ad infinitum*. One could tell how Valega stands at attention by the table, and Sedykh rubs his leg, and make a string of observations on the fate of the evil-looking purple bruise on Igor's forehead—all is possible. But such a swamping of the essentials with a host of unnecessary, incidental particulars, contributes to the burial of the main thought, and the vital piece itself loses so much of its impressiveness that it seems uninteresting material even for a compositional étude!

I think we have now determined, though with considerable difficulty, the starting point which will permit us to organize the material harmoniously from a definite point of view. Let this serve as an example that the so-called "Breaking down into Units" and the "distribution of acting objectives" (terms used in the Stanislavsky method of Analysis), need not be reckoned from the beginning of an episode but are determined by the point of its maximum significance.

The compositional solution of any scene must be launched from that unit which more than any other impresses one with its content and originality. It must also be kept in mind that ordinarily the unit that strikes with greatest force is not only the most immediately effective, but also the one that contains the inner dynamic expression of the theme.

In the analysed scene with Valega we are moved and struck by the collision of two elements, two rhythms. When you begin to take apart the actual content of these impressions, you'll detect that such a clash of two elements is not accidental; through it is revealed, or can be revealed, a deep inner idea. In this clash, under the most acute conditions, are presented those elements of the conflict in the composition of which would be the dramatic working out of the whole episode.

Here we move on to the second chief method of extracting the essential compositional elements that we need. (As we have just said, the first method is to sift out the significant from the incidental.)

The method that I wish to present is the timely preparation for the extraction of the essential. The most effective means of doing this is to lead to the culmination point through a fixed line of recurrences, uncovered from somewhere near the beginning, and conducted through a series of distinctly memorable points.

We have already said that our chosen scene is very important for Nekrasov's book as a whole. We grow more convinced of this when we look into it intently. And not only because we see beginning here the theme of stubbornness, resistance, contempt for danger, and obstinacy. But also because in this episode's situation we are given, as it were, a vivid anticipation of one of the most serious motives within the general theme of the whole work.

The theme touched on in our chosen episode is resumed three chapters later:

Not long ago some soldiers had marched by. I was on duty at the telephone and went out to have a smoke. As they marched they sang, quietly, in low voices. I didn't even see them—I only heard their steps on the asphalt and the quiet, rather sad song about the Dnieper and the cranes. I went across to them. The men were resting along the roadside on the trampled-down grass under the acacias. The half-concealed lights of the cigarettes twinkled. And a young, quiet voice reached me from somewhere under the trees:

"No, Vasya ... don't say that. You'll never find any better than ours. Honestly, the soil's like butter, rich and

176

good." He even smacked his lips in a special way. "The corn will come up, it'll be over your head . . ."

Meanwhile the town was burning, and the red reflection of the flames flickered over the walls of the factory, and, somewhere quite near, machine-guns rattled—sometimes more and sometimes less frequently—and Very lights went up, and ahead was uncertainty and an almost inescapable death . . .

I never saw who said that. Someone shouted: "Get ready to move!" There was a clatter of mess-tins and they were off. They went off slowly with the heavy gait of the soldier.[2]

The same theme and almost the same circumstances: the burning city and here a conversation about growing corn:

And in that song and in those simple words about the soil as rich as butter, about the grain growing higher than your head, there was also *some*thing . . . I don't even know what to call it. Tolstoy called it the secret warmth of patriotism. Maybe that was the most accurate definition. Maybe that is the miracle that Georgi Akimovich is waiting for . . .

Even that intonation of Valega's ("his voice is quiet") continues in the speaking of the words or the twinkling of cigarettes:

As they marched they sang, quietly, in low voices. . . .
The half-concealed lights of the cigarettes twinkled. . . .
. . . a young, quiet voice . . .

There also continues what is for us the essential motif of convinced tenacity, as in: "I don't know whether I want to eat, but I say 'I will'." In answer to Georgi Akimovich's harsh words Igor says:

"They will go no further. I know they won't." And he walks off. It can't be . . . That is all we can say for the moment.

And this motif appeared even earlier—thirty pages before our episode:

"So long, Ma, we'll see you again, believe me, we shall meet again . . ."

And I have that faith . . . That is all we have now—faith.

Thus individual themes or leitmotifs run endlessly through scene after scene, developing, intertwining, intersecting, each carrying its own deposit in creating the image required by the whole work.

In what respect doesn't this equal the "classics"?

It is true that all these facts are actually present—but present within the material and as material, not in a conscious measure of juxtaposition, not in construction, not in compositional calculation, ensuring their faultless, clear-cut influence.

Individual links do not react to one another nor are sensed as a whole. Nor are the separate lines combined one with the other. Indeed the very lines themselves, in essence, do not exist. The author does not give them any significant form.

Instead we have a scattering of points; admittedly they are brilliant, but they do not fuse into a line. There are sometimes huge gaps. There is sometimes so much material between the thematic lines that we get a "disrupting" effect. Sometimes the reciprocal arrangement is simply chaotic.

In the novel the hero and Georgi Akimovich walk at length, seemingly endlessly, to check the cables linking the charges placed for the demolition of the power station. But the author does not do as much in relation to the thematic lines that run through his novel. Here the lines are torn apart. And the final explosion can't come off. The charges seem to be individually correct, but are not placed properly. The circuit is interrupted and the explosions misfire.

Only when we extract the chief points from the general flood of narrative, and stand them side by side, only then are these lines drawn together and seen as the main line of action in clearly traced contours. But in the novel they are so arranged that unity and connectives between the separate links cannot be perceived; motifs are lost in the flow of genre details that should be attached to the work itself as stubbornly as the resolution of the heroes of the novel.

In one place the author sets forth an idea that is neither new nor unexpected:

There are some little things that you remember all your life. And more than remember. Small and seemingly insignificant, they somehow eat into you, grow into something big and significant, absorbing into themselves the whole essence of events, and become a sort of symbol.[3]

Yet the author's own details remain only memorable particularities, only seeds, unconverted into sprouts that might bring the particularities to a generalized image.

Nor should one lapse into the other extreme—a naked schematic framework in which alone consists the unity of the work. This is just as shocking as the scanning of verses by "beating out" their metres, instead of the living pulsation of the rhythm gliding along the dead bones of the metre.

That is a skeleton in place of a living body!

You have no right to count on the "inexorability" of the influence of your work, if its beautiful elements, its construction materials, are not fused into an architectural entity, an engineered, worked out juxtaposition of all its parts. Your separate "bricks" may occasionally be very good, but their only hope of life is in a unity, arranged in a clear architectural form, as we have tried to show—and beyond the limits of "our" episode.

Involuntarily the questions arise: Are all these individual details consistently and consciously finished according to the mould of the chosen thematic lines?

What part does intuition play in making one's theme advance along all its graphic and perceived elements to complete the work?

Isn't the play of the living, perceptible, full-blooded musculature of a sportsman, under the integument of the living body, equally unlike the lymphatic, brittle non-muscularity of an untrained body, as it is to the over-developed system of muscles often transforming a living gymnast into the resemblance of an exhibit in a theatre of anatomy?

Nekrasov's work does not achieve that indispensable degree of inner graphic proportions. Here good "building materials" have not yet been brought together in a convincing architectural whole. In many places the material has been left in stacks. And our job is to sweep away the litter stuffed between the structurally related elements.

Our present task, of making a montage-list or shooting-script from the material of Nekrasov's novel, consists in doing just the opposite of what happened, for example, to the stage adaptation of *Anna Karenina*.

Though Tolstoy's novel with inimitable brilliance and finish images the ever tightening ring of the implacability of society which finally pushed Anna beneath the train, such an inexorably tragic course is absent from its theatrical adaptation. Instead we are given a chain of individual, independent genre episodes in the fate of Anna Karenina, which, though they have connections in them and subject, with those which pushed her to suicide, nevertheless lack the general sense of unrelenting pressure, of ever-diminishing encirclement, so strongly and irresistibly depicted in the novel.

Not only in our episode from Nekrasov's novel but throughout the entire novel there seems to be a single "mood" of the author, a scattering of separate genre and war episodes. But this mood is nowhere raised to a clean-cut purposeful conception that fuses separate elements into a unified, inviolable, interlocked organism, such as we have tried to indicate for the composition of our chosen episode, attempting to shape it into a unity of a strict musical style.

I find myself coming back to music again and again— though I must remind you that I am no musician.

A composer's creative work has long interested me. Not so much what is taught in the Conservatoire, that is, the subtleties of "treatment" of the composer's idea—nor the categories of musical form and general laws of musical construction taught there.

I have always been intrigued by the "mystery" of the birth of a musical image, the emergence of melodies and appearance of that captivating harmony and unity which arise from the chaos of the temporary correlations and disconnected sounds that fill the world around the composer.

I have always wondered how Prokofiev, knowing only

the number of seconds allotted to him and having seen the edited material twice (or thrice, at the most), can have the music ready on the very next day, music which corresponds unerringly and precisely in all its caesuras and accents not only with the general rhythm of the entire episode, but with all the subtlest nuances of the montage development.

Correspondence here is not a "matching of accents"—that primitive method of establishing a correspondence between pictures and music, but the astonishing contrapuntal development of music which fuses organically and sensually with the visual images.

Any composer setting out to write music for the screen, as well as any director with an ambition to work in the sound film, to say nothing of the chromophone film (that is, working with both music and colour), must possess this ability, although not necessarily so highly developed as in the case of Prokofiev.

I shall confine myself at present to analysing the methods by which Prokofiev finds structural and rhythmical equivalents for the edited piece of film that has been brought to him.

The projection-room is darkened . . .

The picture runs on the screen . . .

And on the arm of the chair, nervously drumming, exactly like a Morse telegrapher, tap the relentlessly precise, long fingers of Prokofiev.

Is Prokofiev beating time?

No. He is "beating" something more than that.

He is detecting the structural laws governing the lengths and tempo in the edited pieces, harmonizing these with the actions and intonations of the characters.

On the following day he will send me the music which will permeate my montage structure, the structural laws of which he will carry into the rhythmic figure that his fingers tapped out.

The situation is somewhat different when the composer has to work with unedited material. Then he has to discover the potentialities of structural laws inherent in it.

What should not be lost sight of is the circumstance that

the structure of the separate pieces shot for any scene is not accidental.

If it is really a "montage" piece, that is, not disconnected but meant to produce an image together with other pieces, it will, at the very moment it is shot, be infused with elements which characterize its inner content and at the same time contain the embryo of the structure most suited for the fullest possible revelation of this content in the finished compositional form.

And if the composer is faced with (for the time being) a chaotic agglomeration of pieces with such structural potentialities, his task will not be to discover the finished structure of the whole but to find in the individual elements the embryos of the future structure and, proceeding from these, to set down the compositional form into which the pieces will fit organically.[4]

Our apparent digression, directly related to the work of Prokofiev, closes with what we are doing in our fragment of the *Stalingrad* novel.

When we worked on a Pushkin poem, endeavouring to transpose its lines into adequate rhythmic and visual pictorial elements, we started with *discovering* the basic rules on which Pushkin had constructed them, so that we could transpose those rules into a base for our audio-visual structure.

Nekrasov's material, on the other hand, approximates to the second type of film composer's work that we described above. It bears more resemblance to the selection of pieces that are not yet organized into a final montage composition.

Our task in converting this material is to "listen" to the individual structural potentialities of each of the pieces, to extract them, to define their structure for ourselves, and, according to the compositional demands, to understand, treat, arrange, and group the separate pieces and details.

To be fair to Nekrasov, we must note that the weak montage combination of elements make up an authentically impressive whole and contain separate pieces that are not only excellent, but are also correctly perceived. Correctly in the sense that they are subordinated to a basic mood, corresponding to the author's basic conception and answering to that intonation in which the author senses its fullest expression.

At the same time one cannot help noticing a certain monotony in this intonation, which in my opinion results not so much from an inability to master a diversity of rhythmic styles as from the personal emotional colouring that his own memories and impressions have for the author and which in the novel he shares with his readers.

It is very curious that despite all the objective heroism described by the author the tonality of his exposition is unexpectedly in a minor key. "Musically" it goes contrary to the author's intention, adding to the whole novel a certain extra coating of "intellectualism", and "smoothing out" the expressiveness of the theme's rhythmic turns and the expressiveness of the whole composition.

So, when you take up this existing composition with all its defects and merits, you must do all in your power to make it effective.

Daumier said that "one must belong to one's own time". We can interpret this more profoundly by keeping in mind that we belong not only to our own time, but above all to the great ideas that our people are bringing to life. Therefore both our thoughts and our creative intentions and the concrete embodiments of our thoughts must be determined by our ideological direction.

In order to express organically our ideas in images, we must take care to master the practical skill of craftsmanship, so as to bring out the images inherent in the material.

And this is the most correct path by which to approach composition. It protects the "builder" against formal arbitrariness, as well as abstract preconceptions, and gives him each time the possibility of approaching the living material of the work afresh, and avoiding routine, stereotypes and clichés.

Sources and Notes

A Personal Statement
  see Bibliography, No. 14

The Method of Making Workers' Films
  see Bibliography, No. 8
  1. Alexander Belenson, *Cinema Today* (Moscow 1925).
  2. E. cites these censorship laws as from a New York book of 1911, "The Art of the Motion Picture", but I cannot identify this reference.

The Soviet Cinema
  see Bibliography, No. 68
  1. Though E.'s manuscript refers to Griffith's film *America*, the editors of *Voices of October* revised this to refer to *The Birth of a Nation*, a film that E. may not have known at that time; it is for this reason I have restored the original reference.

The New Language of Cinema
  see Bibliography, No. 52

Perspectives
  see Bibliography, No. 61
  1. G. V. Plekhanov, Foreword to the third edition (Moscow 1914) of *For Twenty Years*.
  2. George Berkeley, Bishop of Cloyne, *A Treatise Concerning the Principles of Human Knowledge;* cited here from a reproduction of the 1710 and 1734 editions (London 1937). These passages from Berkeley's Introduction were translated into Russian by E. from a German text cited by E. Cassirer in *Philosophie der symbolischen Formen*, Vol. I (Berlin 1923).
  3. G. V. Plekhanov, *Fundamental Problems of Marxism*, translated by Eden and Cedar Paul (London 1929),

184

quoting von den Steinen, *Unter den Naturvölkern Zentral-Brasiliens* (Berlin 1894).

4. The citation of Renan's *La Réforme intellectuelle et morale* was found in Plekhanov, *Art and Social Life*, translated by Eleanor Fox (London 1953), p. 190.

The Dynamic Square

see Bibliography, No. 74

1. This memorandum was compiled by Lester Cowan in preparation for the discussion on 17 Sept. 1930; all of E.'s quotations are from this memorandum, which can be consulted at the Academy of Motion Picture Arts and Sciences, Hollywood. Loyd A. Jones's paper, "Rectangle Proportions in Pictorial Composition", was published in *Journal of the Society of Motion Picture Engineers*, Jan. 1930; this issue contains other relevant papers.

GTK—GIK—VGIK

see Bibliography, No. 119

1. This reference is to E.'s first version of his teaching programme, published in *Sovietskoye kino*, Nos. 5–6, 1933, as "The Granite of Film Science". This programme, tested and enlarged, was later published in *Iskusstvo kino*, No. 4, 1936. For translations of this "second" programme, see Bibliography, No. 145.

Lessons from Literature

see Bibliography, No. 267

1. *Earth*, translated by Ann Lindsay (Elek Books, London 1954).
2. *The Fatal Skin*, translated by Cedar Paul (Hamish Hamilton, London 1949).

The Embodiment of a Myth

see Bibliography, No. 202.

More Thoughts on Structure

see Bibliography, No. 200

1. Paul Whiteman and Mary Margaret McBride, *Jazz* (New York 1926), p. 119.
2. Alexandre Dumas, *My Memoirs*, trans. by E. M. Waller (London 1908), vol. V., pp. 235, 245.
3. *The Letters of Anton Pavlovitch Tchehov to Olga Leonardovna Knipper*, translated by Constance Garnett (Chatto & Windus, London 1926), p. 33.
4. Vladimir Nemirovich-Danchenko, *My Life in the Russian Theatre*, translated by John Cournos (Geoffrey Bles, London 1937), pp. 67–71.
5. S. Tolstoy, "Turgenev at Yasnaya Polyana", in *Golos minuvshevo*, 1919, Nos. 1–14, p. 233.
6. Pushkin, *Eugene Onegin*, in translation by Babette Deutsch (*The Works of Pushkin*, Random House 1936).

Charlie the Kid
see Bibliography, No. 250

1. H. A. Overstreet, *Influencing Human Behaviour* (Jonathan Cape, London 1926), pp. 11–15.
2. Ibid, pp. 26–27.   3. Ibid, pp. 260–62.
4. Chaplin's interview with A. J. Urban, "I Talked with Charlie Chaplin", *Intercine* (Rome), October 1935.
5. Possibly Ywan Goll's *Die Chaplinade* (Dresden 1920), or *Das Chaplin-Drama*, by Melchior Bischer (Berlin 1924).
6. Elie Faure, "The Art of Charlie Chaplin", in *The Art of Cineplastics*, translated by Walter Pach (Boston 1923), pp. 62–63.
7. C. W. Kimmins, *The Springs of Laughter* (Methuen, London 1928), p. 95.
8. C. W. Kimmins, *The Child's Attitude to Life* (Methuen, London 1926), p. 60.
9. Charles Baudelaire, "De l'Essence du Rire," in *Curiosités esthétiques* (Editions de la Nouvelle Revue Française, Paris 1925).
10. *Fables from "Fun"* (these Bierce fables appeared in the London *Fun* in 1872–73); reprinted in *The Monk and the Hangman's Daughter* (New York 1926); E.

found "The Man and the Goose" in *Mark Twain's Library of Humour*.
11. Karl Marx, *Towards a Critique of Hegel's Philosophy*.
12. Urban's interview in *Intercine*.

Mr Lincoln by Mr Ford
see Bibliography, No. 283
1. *Lincoln, His Life in Photographs* (New York 1941).
2. "Death of Abraham Lincoln", in Walt Whitman, *Complete Poetry and Selected Prose and Letters*, ed. by Emory Holloway (The Nonesuch Press, London 1938), pp. 752–62.

A Close-Up View
see Bibliography, No. 249

Problems of Composition
see Bibliography, No. 266
1. Victor Nekrasov, *Front-Line Stalingrad*, translated by David Floyd (Harvill Press, London 1962), pp. 81–84. I have tampered with Mr Floyd's vigorous translation to bring it closer to the *Znamya* text used by Eisenstein; my chief alteration, here and in subsequent citations, is the restoration of the present tense of the original.
2. Ibid; Chap. XVI.   3. Ibid.
4. E. quotes his essay on Prokofiev, at that time not yet published in the Soviet Union (see Bibliography, No. 251).

The Published Writings (1922-1964) of Sergei Eisenstein
with notes on their English translations

This list is based on the bibliography (prepared by Venyamin Vishnevsky and Pera Atasheva) published in *Izbranniye stat'i*, edited by R. Yurenev; interviews, both in Russian and in English, have been omitted.—J. L.

If no place of publication is given, Moscow is to be understood.

1922

1 Letters to the Editors of *Zrelishcha*, 1922, No. 6, p. 26. The letter, commenting on an article by I. Aksyonov on Tairov, is signed by N. Foregger, V. Mass, S. Yutkevich, S. Eisenstein.

1923

2 MONTAGE OF ATTRACTIONS, in *Lef*, 1923, No. 3, pp. 70–75. Translated excerpt in *The Film Sense*, pp. 230–233.

1924

3 ABOUT WEST, in *Zrelishcha*, 1924, No. 83–84. On Kuleshov's new film, *Adventures of Mr West in the Land of the Bolsheviks*.

1925

4 Letter to the Editors of *Kino-nedelya*, 1925, No. 2. A polemic with V. Pletnyov on E.'s departure from Proletcult.

5 Letter to the Editors of *Kino-nedelya*, 1925, No. 10. Continuing the polemic.

188

6 ARE CRITICS NECESSARY?, in *Novyi zritel*, 1925, No. 13, p. 6. Reply to a questionnaire.

7 ON THE QUESTION OF A MATERIALIST APPROACH TO FORM, in *Kino-zhurnal ARK*, 1925, No. 4–5, pp. 5–8. On the experience of *Strike*, and the theories of Dziga Vertov.

8 THE METHOD OF MAKING WORKERS' FILMS, in *Kino*, 11 August 1925. Translation in *Film Essays*, pp. 17–20.

1926

9 WHAT THEY SAY ABOUT "BATTLESHIP POTEMKIN", in *Sovietskii ekran*, 1926, No. 2, p. 10. A reply to a questionnaire.

10 WHAT WAS SAID ABOUT "BATTLESHIP POTEMKIN", in *Vechernaya Moskva*, 1 February 1926. A brief reply to a questionnaire.

11 "POTEMKIN" THROUGH THE GERMAN CENSORSHIP, in *Sovietskoye kino*, 1926, No. 3, pp. 14–15. E.'s and Tisse's account of their visit to Berlin.

12 NOT AT ALL ODD, ABOUT KHOKHLOVA, in *Kino*, 30 March 1926, reprinted in the brochure, *A. Khokhlova*, 1926, pp. 5–9.

13 GERMAN CINEMA, in *Vestnik rabotnikov iskusstv*, 1926, No. 10, pp. 8–9.

14 S. EISENSTEIN ABOUT S. EISENSTEIN, in *Berliner Tageblatt*, Berlin, 7 June 1926. An autobiographical statement written for this newspaper. Translation in *Film Essays*, pp. 13–17.

15 FIVE EPOCHS, in *Pravda*, 6 July 1926. On the project for *The General Line*.

16 ON THE ROAD OF SOVIET FILMS, in *Rabochaya Moskva*, 15 July 1926. Reply to a questionnaire.

17 ON THE POSITION OF BELA BALAZS, in *Kino*, 20 July 1926. An answer to Balázs's article, "on the future of the film".

18 BELA FORGETS THE SCISSORS, in *Kino*, 10 August 1926. Continuing the discussion with Balázs.

19 THE TWO SKULLS OF ALEXANDER THE GREAT, in *Novyi zritel*, 1926, No. 35, p. 10. A reply to a questionnaire on "Theatre or Cinema?".

20 Letter to the Editor of *Molot*, Rostov-na-Don, 26 November 1926. Thanks to those who took part in the filming of *The General Line*.

1927

21 Letter to the Editors of *Novyi zritel*, 1927, No. 2. Protesting against their editorial commentary on E.'s letter to *Molot*.

22 WHAT THE DIRECTORS SAY, in *Komsomolskaya pravda*, 21 September 1927. A reply to a questionnaire on the libretto contest organized by this paper.

23 THE FUTURE OF SOVIET CINEMA, in *Krasnaya panorama*, Leningrad, 1927, No. 40, pp. 7–8.

24 FILM AND THE DEFENCE OF THE COUNTRY, in *Sovietskoye kino*, Leningrad, 1927, No. 7, p. 6. A reply to an anniversary questionnaire.

25 TO EACH HIS OWN, in *Krasnaya gazeta*, Leningrad, 20 October 1927. About the party conference on film questions.

26 WHY "OCTOBER" IS LATE, in *Kino*, 20 December 1927. Translated excerpt in *Kino* (London 1960), pp. 238–239.

27 S. M. EISENSTEIN ON "OCTOBER". In the brochure, *October*, 1927, pp. 7–8; reprinted in the brochure, *October* (Vladivostok 1928).

28 GIVE US A STATE PLAN, in *Kino-front*, 1927, No. 13–14, pp. 6–8. Reprinted in *Izbranniye stat'i* (1956).

1928

29 WHAT WE EXPECT FROM THE PARTY CONFERENCE ON FILM QUESTIONS, in *Sovietskii ekran*, 1928, No. 1, p. 6.

30 LITERATURE AND CINEMA, in *Na literaturnom postu*, 1928, No. 1, pp. 71–73. A reply to a questionnaire on the interrelations between the two arts.

31 FOR A SPECIAL SECTION, in *Kino-front*, 1928, No. 1, pp. 2–5. An argument for the formation of a special section for film affairs.

32 IN THE BATTLES FOR "OCTOBER", in *Komsomolskaya pravda*, 7 March 1928.

33 HOW WE MADE "OCTOBER", in *Vechernaya Moskva*, 8 March 1928. Signed by E. and Alexandrov.

34 FOR WORKERS' FILMS, in *Revolutzia i kultura*, 1928, No. 3–4, pp. 52–56.

35 OCTOBER, in *Kino*, 13 March 1928. Extracts from the scenario, signed by E. and Alexandrov. Translated in the *Daily Worker* (New York), 3 November 1928.

36 OUR "OCTOBER", ACTED AND NON-ACTED, in *Kino*, 13 and 20 March 1928. The second instalment signed by E. and Alexandrov.

37 FOR A SOVIET CINEMA, in *Na literaturnom postu*, 1928, No. 4, pp. 15–18.

38 WE'RE WAITING, in *Komsomolskaya pravda*, 1 April 1928. On the forthcoming release of *October*; signed by E. and Alexandrov.

39 "GENERAL LINE", in *Komsomolskaya pravda*, 30 April 1928. Signed by E. and Alexandrov.

40 THE FUTURE OF SOUND FILMS, A STATEMENT, in *Zhizn iskusstva*, Leningrad, 1928, No. 32, pp. 4–5, and *Sovietskii ekran*, 1928, No. 32, p. 5. Signed by E., Pudovkin, and Alexandrov. Translations in New York *Herald Tribune*, 21 September 1928; in New York *Times*, 7 October 1928; in *Close Up* (Territet), October 1928; in New York *Sun*, 5 June 1930; and in *Film Form*, pp. 257–259.

41 THEATRICAL TRASH AND NEW WEAPONS OF CULTURE. QUESTIONNAIRE: HOW CAN WE USE THE SOUND FILM, in *Sovietskii ekran*, 1928, No. 34, p. 6.

42 THE UNEXPECTED JUNCTION, in *Zhizn iskusstva*, Leningrad, 1928, No. 34, pp. 6–9. Translation in *Film Form*, pp. 18–27.

43 HOW WE ARE MAKING "GENERAL LINE", in *Vechernaya Moskva*, 5 October 1928.

44 TWELFTH, in *Sovietskii ekran*, 1928, No. 45, pp. 4–5. Signed by E. and Alexandrov.

45 LE CORBUSIER VISITS S. M. EISENSTEIN, in *Sovietskii ekran*, 1928, No. 46, p. 5. Signed with pseudonym, "R—k".

46 Open Letter, in *Izvestia*, 11 November 1928, p. 5. On the note in the foreign press that E. was "escaping" abroad.

47 "GENERAL LINE", in *Gudok*, 21 November 1928.

48 ONE, TWO, THREE—PANICKERS ARE WE, in *Kino*, Leningrad, 27 November 1928. Signed by E. and Alexandrov.

49 "GENERAL LINE", in *Izvestia*, 6 December 1928. Signed by E. and Alexandrov.

50 MY FIRST FILM, in *Sovietskii ekran*, 1928, No. 50, p. 10. On the film interlude ("Glumov's Diary") made for the Proletcult production of Ostrovsky's *Enough Simplicity in Every Wise Man*.

1929

51 OUTSIDE THE FRAME. Afterword to Nikolai Kaufman's *Japanese Cinema*, 1929, pp. 72–92. Translation (as "The Cinematograph Principle and Japanese Culture") in *Transition* (Paris), June 1930; reprinted in *Experimental Cinema*, No. 3, 1932; in *Film Form*, pp. 28–44; in *Film: an Anthology* (New York 1959).

52 FOREWORD, to the Russian translation of Guido Seeber's *Der Trickfilm*, 1929, pp. 3–8. Translation (as "The New Language of Cinematography") in *Close Up*, in May 1929; reprinted in *Film Essays*, pp. 32–34.

53 "GENERAL LINE", in *Komsomolskaya pravda*, 3 February 1929. Signed by E. and Alexandrov.

54 AN EXPERIMENT UNDERSTOOD BY MILLIONS, in *Sovietskii ekran*, 1929, No. 6, pp. 6–7. Signed by E. and Alexandrov. Reprinted in *Izbranniye stat'i* (1956).

55 FATHER MATVEI, in *Sovietskii ekran*, 1929, No. 7. A reminiscence from the filming of *General Line*.

56 ENTHUSIASTIC WORKDAYS, in *Rabochaya Moskva*, 22 February 1929. On the approaching release of *General Line*; signed by E. and Alexandrov.

57 WITHOUT ACTORS, in *Ogonyok*, 1929, No. 10, pp. 10–11. Signed by E. and Alexandrov. Translation in *Cinema* (New York), June 1930.

58 GTK—VUZ, in *Kino*, 12 March 1929. A proposal to reorganize the film technicum on a higher educational level.

59 THREE YEARS, in *Literaturnaya gazeta*, 1 July 1929. On the making of *General Line*; signed by E. and Alexandrov.

60 ABOUT THE FILM-SCHOOL, in *Rabis*, 1929, No. 32, pp. 6–7.

61 PERSPECTIVES, in *Iskusstvo*, 1929, No. 1–2, pp. 116–122. First translated from a condensed German text (prepared by E. for *Der Querschnitt*, January 1930) in *The Left* (Davenport), Autumn 1931; complete essay translated in *Film Essays*, pp. 35–47.

62 THE FILMIC FOURTH DIMENSION, in *Kino*, 27 August 1929. Translations in *Close Up*, March 1930, and *Film Form*, pp. 64–71.

63 THE SOUND FILM HERE, in *Rabis*, 1929, No. 38, p. 4.

On 19 August 1929 E., Alexandrov and Tisse leave the Soviet Union for a work-visit to Europe and America.

64 ON THE FORM OF THE SCENARIO, in *Bulletin kinokontori Torgpredstva SSSR v Germanii*, Berlin, 1929, No. 1–2, pp. 29–32, and in *Literaturnaya gazeta*, 9 December 1929.

65 DER FILM DER ZUKUNFT, in *Vossische Zeitung*, Berlin, 15 September 1929. Another section of "Perspectives", revised to announce project for filming *Capital*. Translated excerpt in New York *Herald Tribune*, 22 December 1929.

66 DER KAMPF UM DIE ERDE (Berlin 1929). Translation, by Erwin Honig, of the *Old and New* scenario, by E. and Alexandrov. Translation in *Film Writing Forms*, ed. by Lewis Jacobs (New York 1934); E.'s preface ("Drehbuch? Nein: Kinonovelle!"), partially translated in New York *Times*, 30 March 1930, is a German translation of No. 64.

67 Letter to the Editors of *Film Kurier*, 17 October 1929. A denial that he had directed scenes for Dubson's *Giftgas*.

1930

68 [Soviet Cinema], in *Voices of October* (New York 1930), pp. 225–239. Written in 1928, for incorporation into Joseph Freeman's essay on Soviet cinema in this volume. Reprinted in *Film Essays*, pp. 20–31.

69 GENDARMES IN THE SORBONNE, in *Kino*, 10 March 1930. Signed with pseudonym, "R.O.Rik".

70 LES PRINCIPES DU NOUVEAU CINEMA RUSSE, in *La Revue*

du Cinéma (Paris), April 1930. Transcription of E.'s lecture at the Sorbonne University, 17 February 1930.

71 [Methods of Montage], published as "The Fourth Dimension in the Kino: II", *Close Up*, April 1930, pp. 253–268. Written in London (dated Autumn 1929), to supplement the essay translated in *Close Up*, March 1930. Reprinted in *Film Form*, pp. 72–83.

72 OUR FILMS MUST SOUND AND SPEAK, in *Za kommunisticheskoye prosveshcheniye*, 18 September 1930.

73 Letter to Léon Moussinac (from Hollywood), published in *Cinémonde* (Paris), 9 October 1930.

1931

74 THE DYNAMIC SQUARE, in *Close Up*, March, June 1931. Based on the Hollywood speech made by E. during a discussion on the wide film, 17 September 1930; written in Mexico. Reprinted, in shortened version, in *Hound and Horn*, April 1931; reprinted in full in *Film Essays*, pp. 48–65.

75 THE PRINCIPLES OF FILM FORM, in *Close Up*, September 1931, pp. 167–181. Translation by Ivor Montagu from a German MS. (dated Zürich, 2 November 1929); also in *Experimental Cinema*, No. 4, 1932; expanded translation (as "A Dialectic Approach to Film Form") from an untitled German MS. (dated Moscow, April 1929) in *Film Form*, pp. 45–62.

76 Letter to GIK (from Guadalajara), published in *Kino*, 1 September 1931.

77 AMERICAN TRAGEDY, in *Proletarskoye kino*, 1931, No. 9, p. 59. Signed with pseudonym, "R.O.Rik".

78 Letter to the Editors of *The Nation*, published 9 December 1931. A reply to Edmund Wilson's article of 4 November 1931, "Eisenstein in Hollywood".

On 9 May 1932 E. and Tisse return to Moscow.

1932

79 INVESTMENT IN THE BUSINESS OF SOCIALISM, in *Za bolshevistskii film* (the Mosfilm newspaper), 16 May 1932.

80 THE MOST AMUSING, in *Sovietskoye iskusstvo*, 9 August 1932. On the staging of comedy.

81 OVERTAKE AND SURPASS, in *Proletarskoye kino*, 1932, No. 15–16, pp. 20–32. Translation (as "The Cinema in America: impressions of Hollywood, its life and values") in *International Literature*, July 1933.

82 OCTOBER AND ART, in *Soviet Culture Review*, 1932, No. 7–9. Russian text (as "Through Revolution to Art— Through Art to Revolution") in *Sovietskoye kino*, 1933, No. 1–2, pp. 34–36; and in *Izbranniye stat'i*. English translation reprinted in *International Literature*, October 1933; in the *Daily Worker* (New York), 29 January 1934; and in Marie Seton, *Sergei M. Eisenstein* (London 1952), pp. 479–481.

83 MUCH OBLIGED!, in *Proletarskoye kino*, 1932, No. 17–18, p. 19–29. Translation (as "Detective Work in the GIK", "Cinematography *with* Tears" and "An American Tragedy") in *Close Up*, December 1932, March and June 1933; E. added material from another article to the first translation; original text translated (as "A Course in Treatment") in *Film Form*, pp. 84–107.

84 IN THE FIRST RANK, in *Kino*, 6 September 1932. A salute to the anti-war congress in Amsterdam.

85 DIE ERSTE KOLONNE MARSCHIERT . . ., in *Kino*, 18 September 1932. On the film industry's thematic plan.

86 TO A FOUNDER OF CULTURE, in *Kino*, 24 September 1932. Greetings on the 40th anniversary of Gorky's literary career.

87 ON DETECTIVE WORK, in *Kino*, 18 October 1932. Translation incorporated into "Detective Work in the GIK", *Close Up*, December 1932.

88 "THE PEOPLE ARE SILENT . . .", in *Kino*, 24 October 1932. On the need to strengthen the social organizations connected with the film industry.

89 ON THAT SIDE, in *Vechernaya krasnaya gazeta*, Leningrad, 26 October 1932.

90 IN THE INTERESTS OF FORM, in *Kino*, 12 November 1932.

1933

91 PANTAGRUEL IS BORN, in *Kino*, 4 February 1933. On creative method.

92 "KINO" HAS A PROUD SOUND, in *Kino*, 16 February 1933. A reply to a questionnaire on administration.

93 IN PLACE!, in *Kino*, 10 March 1933. On the relations between director and scenarist.

94 DEATH TO BLYAMBAM!, in *Kino*, 28 March 1933. Comment on the unsatisfactory photo-reproductions in *Kino*.

95 THE MISTAKE OF GEORGES MELIES, in *Sovietskoye kino*, 1933, No. 3–4, pp. 63–64. The preface to *Technique of Process Filming* (1933), by Vladimir Nilsen.

96 INTRODUCTION, in *Za bolshevistskii film*, 15 April 1933. On the theme of rebirth.

96 SORTIE BY CLASS FRIENDS, in *Kino*, 22 and 28 June 1933. A reply to an article by S. Bartenev and M. Kalatozov, "Image and dramatic structure in Eisenstein's work", in *Kino*, 16 June 1933.

98 GRANITE OF FILM-SCIENCE, ON THE METHOD OF TEACHING THE SUBJECT OF DIRECTION, in *Sovietskoye kino*, 1933, No. 5–6, pp. 58–67; No. 7, pp. 66–74; No. 9, pp. 61–73. A programme for the film-direction course at GIK.

99 A FASTIDIOUS BRIDE, in *Literaturnaya gazeta*, 29 June 1933. Translation (as "The Difficult Bride") in *Film Art* (London), Spring 1934.

100 MOSCOW THROUGH THE AGES, in *Literaturnaya gazeta*, 11 July 1933. Idea and plan for a new film.

101 MOSCOW, in *Sovietskoye iskusstvo*, 20 July 1933. On the new film project.

102 FILM AND CLASSICS, in *Literaturnaya gazeta*, 23 December 1933. A reply to a questionnaire on the All-Union Thematic Conference on Cinema.

1934

103 FOR HIGH IDEALS, FOR FILM CULTURE!, in *Kino*, 22 January 1934. A report to the 17th Party Congress on the plan for *Moscow*, and on the work of GIK.

104 I OWE ALL TO THE PARTY, in *Rabis*, 1934, No. 1, p. 22.

105 THE AMERICAN WORKERS' FILM AND PHOTO LEAGUE, in *Kino*, 10 February 1934. Signed jointly with Pera Atasheva and Edward Tisse.

106 QUE VIVA MEXICO!, in *Experimental Cinema*, New York, No. 5, 1934, pp. 5–13, 52. The outline for the

Mexican film written in 1931 by E. and Alexandrov. Reprinted in Eisenstein, *Que Viva Mexico!* (London 1951).

107 ON FASCISM, GERMAN FILM ART AND REAL LIFE, An Open Letter to the German Minister of Propaganda, Dr Goebbels, in *Literaturnaya gazeta*, 22 March 1934. A reply to the propaganda minister's address to German film producers in February 1934. Translations in *International Theatre*, October 1934; *Film Art*, London, Winter 1934; and in the New York *Times*, 30 December 1934.

108 "E!" ON THE CLARITY OF FILM LANGUAGE, in *Sovietskoye kino*, 1934, No. 5, pp. 25–31. Translation (as "Film Language") in *Film Form*, pp. 108–121.

109 INCOMPARABLE, in *Literaturnaya gazeta*, 18 June 1934. On the *Chelyuskin* exploit.

110 SIKO, in *Kino*, 28 June 1934. Obituary of the director Siko Palavandishvili.

111 METRO, MOSCOW, LITERATURE, in *Pravda*, 17 August 1934.

112 END OF THE MANSARD ROOF, in *Izvestia*, 19 August 1934. On problems of the scenario, addressed to the First Congress of Soviet Writers; reprinted in *Izbranniye stat'i*.

113 WITH THE WEAPON OF CINEMA, in *Komsomolskaya pravda*, 7 November 1934. On the role of film in defence.

114 AT LAST!, in *Literaturnaya gazeta*, 18 November 1934. On the three stages of the Soviet cinema's development, and on *Chapayev* as a synthesis of the three. Translation (as "The New Soviet Cinema; entering the fourth period") in *New Theatre*, New York, January 1935.

115 FINISH OFF THE ENEMY, in *Komsomolskaya pravda*, 4 December 1934. On Kirov's assassination.

116 THE MIDDLE OF THREE (1924–1929), in *Sovietskoye kino*, 1934, No. 11–12, pp. 54–83. Translation (as "Through Theatre to Cinema") in *Theatre Arts Monthly*, New York, September 1936, and in *Film Form*, pp. 3–17.

117 KOMSOMOLS IN CINEMA, in *Kommunist,* Odessa, 5 December 1934. On the work of the Odessa studio.

118 PAUL ROBESON, in *Pravda,* 23 December 1934.

1935

119 GTK—GIK—VGIK, PAST—PRESENT—FUTURE, in *Sovietskoye kino,* 1935, No. 1, pp. 54–60. On the 15th birthday of the Cinema Institute. Reprinted (as edited by E. in 1947) in *Izbranniye stat'i.* Translation in *Film Essays,* pp. 66–76.

120 THE MOST IMPORTANT OF THE ARTS, in *Izvestia,* 6 January 1935. On the 15th anniversary of the Soviet film industry; revised by E. as "Le plus important", for *Quinze ans de cinématographie soviétique* (1935), pp. 53–58; expanded version printed in *Izbranniye stat'i.*

121 IN THE DAYS OF THE FIFTEENTH . . . , in *Za kommunisticheskoye prosveshcheniye,* 15 January 1935.

122 IN THE SIXTEENTH YEAR, in *Komsomolskaya pravda,* 11 January 1935.

123 THE TRUTH OF OUR EPOCH, in *Pravda,* 12 January 1935. E.'s speech at the Bolshoi Theatre ceremony of the 15th anniversary.

124 CONCLUDING SPEECH AT THE FIRST ALL-UNION MEETING OF CREATIVE WORKERS, in *Kino,* 17 January 1935; also in *Literaturnaya gazeta,* 15 January 1935. Translated excerpts in Seton, *Eisenstein,* pp. 331–335.

125 [Opening address], in *Za bolshoye kinoiskusstvo* (1935), pp. 22–49, 160–165. Translation (as edited by E.) in *Life and Letters To-day* (London), September–December 1935; in *New Theatre and Film* (New York), April, May, June 1936; and in *Film Form.*

126 WE KNOW WHAT WE MUST DO, in *Kino,* 15 January 1935.

127 BEZHIN MEADOW, in *Komsomolskaya pravda,* 5 February 1935. On a new film project.

128 PEASANTS, in *Izvestia,* 11 February 1935. Review of Ermler's new film.

129 CINEMA—A MIGHTY WEAPON, in *Radioprogramma,* 18 February 1935.

130 THE THEATRE OF MEI LAN-FANG, in *Komsomolskaya pravda*, 11 March 1935; expanded by E., as "The Enchanter of the Pear Garden", for the brochure published by VOKS on the occasion of Mei Lan-fang's performances in the Soviet Union (1935). Translation in *Theatre Arts Monthly* (New York), October 1935; a condensed translation in *International Literature*, No. 5, 1935.

131 LETTER TO PIONEERS, in *Znamya Tryokhgorki*, 8 April 1935.

132 THE APRIL DECREE OF THE PARTY—A BASE FOR CREATIVE GROWTH, in *Kino*, 22 April 1935.

133 FROM THE SCREEN INTO LIFE, in *Komsomolskaya pravda*, 27 June 1935. The history of the making of *Potemkin*, as told by E. at the 30th anniversary of the mutiny.

134 OURS, in *Kino*, 5 September 1935. An obituary of Henri Barbusse.

135 I CHALLENGE TO SOCIALIST COMPETITION, in *Za bolshevistskii film*, 9 September 1935.

136 WE CAN, in *Za bolshevistskii film*, 9 September 1935. A reply to those workers at Mosfilm who protested against working conditions there. Reprinted in *Izbranniye stat'i*.

137 A SENSIBLE MEASURE, in *Kino*, 17 November 1935. On the choice of new talents for Mosfilm.

138 WE'LL KEEP OUR PROMISE, in *Kino*, 23 November 1935.

139 THE YEAR IN ART, in *Sovietskoye iskusstvo*, 29 December 1935. A reply to a questionnaire on which art experiences had made the strongest impression during the past year; E.'s response provoked some angry comments in *Kino* and at Mosfilm.

1936

140 IN 1936, in *Izvestia*, 1 January 1936. Reply to questionnaire.

141 [Foreword], to Vladimir Nilsen's *The Cinema as a Graphic Art* (when translated in London, 1936); reprinted in *Theatre Arts Monthly* (New York), May 1938.

142 IN PLACE OF A SPEECH, in *Kino*, 11 March 1936. On

the questions of formalism and naturalism in the arts raised by recent articles in *Pravda*.

143 THIS WILL BE A FILM ABOUT HEROIC CHILDREN, in *Za kollektivizatziyu*, 18 March 1936.

144 "BEZHIN MEADOW", in *Krestyanskaya gazeta*, 31 March 1936.

145 PROGRAMME FOR TEACHING THE THEORY AND PRACTICE OF DIRECTION, in *Iskusstvo kino*, 1936, No. 4, pp. 51–58. Translation in *Life and Letters To-day* (London), June, July 1936; and in *Lessons with Eisenstein* (London 1962).

146 ABOUT MYSELF—ALOUD, in *Kino*, 6 May 1936. An analysis of his work in connection with the current discussion on formalism and naturalism in the arts.

147 A SCENARIO OF GENIUS FOR THE FUTURE, in *Kino*, 17 June 1936. On the proposed constitution for the USSR.

148 THE GREATEST CREATIVE HONESTY, in *Kino*, 22 June 1936. On the death of Gorky. Translation in *Notes of a Film Director*, pp. 138–140.

149 Letter to the Editors of *Kino*, 17 August 1936.

150 PUNISH THE MURDERER, in *Sovietskoye iskusstvo*, 23 August 1936.

151 PAUL ROBESON, in *Rabochaya Moskva*, 20 December 1936. On Robeson's Moscow concerts.

1937

152 Letter to the Editors of *Izvestia*, 8 February 1937. Contradicting rumour in foreign press about E.'s arrest.

153 THE MISTAKES OF "BEZHIN MEADOW", in *Sovietskoye iskusstvo*, 17 April 1937; reprinted in the brochure, *About the* Bezhin Lug *Film* (1937); and in *Izbranniye stat'i*. Translation in *International Literature*, No. 8, 1937; reprinted in Seton, *Eisenstein*, pp. 372–377.

154 WHY DID "BEZHIN MEADOW" FAIL?, in *Vechernaya Moskva*, 25 April 1937. E.'s speech at the Mosfilm discussion on the film.

155 THE EPIC IN SOVIET FILM, in *International Literature*, No. 10–11, 1937. An introduction to Vsevolod Vishnevsky's scenario, *We, the Russian People*, as trans-

lated from *Roman-gazeta* (1938); E.'s Russian text published in *Izbranniye stat'i*; reprinted in *Voprosi kino-dramaturgii* III (1959).

156 RUSS, in *Znamya*, 1937, No. 12. The scenario (later produced as *Alexander Nevsky*) by E. and Pyotr Pavlenko.

157 IMAGE OF ENORMOUS HISTORICAL TRUTH AND REALITY, in *Za bolshevistskii film*, 27 December 1937. On *Lenin in October*.

1938

158 LAND OF THE SOVIETS, in *Kino*, 17 February 1938. On the new film by Schub and Tisse.

159 THE FILM OF ALEXANDER NEVSKY, in *Krasnyi Oktyabr*, Syzran, 28 June 1938. Article on the filming in Pereyas-lavl-Zalesski, signed by E., and D. Vasiliev.

160 Letter to the Editors of *Teatr*, 1938, No. 7, pp. 156–158. On the necessity for establishing a people's theatre in the Park of Culture and Rest.

161 ALEXANDER NEVSKY AND THE DEFEAT OF THE GERMANS, in *Izvestia*, 12 July 1938. The historical events at the base of the film.

162 WHAT FILM-DIRECTORS ARE MAKING, in *Proletarskaya pravda*, Kalinin, 26 August 1938. Reply to question-naire.

163 PATRIOTISM IS OUR THEME, in *Kino*, 11 November 1938. Reprinted in *Izbranniye stat'i*. Translation in *International Literature*, No. 2, 1939, and in the *Daily Worker* (New York), 1 April 1939.

164 WE ARE READY FOR ANY TASK, in *Za bolshevistskii film*, 11 November 1938. On the crew filming *Alexander Nevsky*.

165 ALEXANDER NEVSKY, in *Gudok*, 14 November 1938.

166 A FILM ON THE GREAT PATRIOTISM OF THE RUSSIAN PEOPLE, in *Krasnaya gazeta*, Leningrad, 29 November 1938.

167 NOTES OF A DIRECTOR, in *Ogonyok*, 1938, No. 22, pp. 20–21. Characteristics of Alexander Nevsky and an account of the film about him.

168 WE AND THEY, in *Kino*, 5 December 1938. On meetings with Griffith, Chaplin, Flaherty.

169 HIS LIFE WAS A VICTORY, in *Sovietskoye iskusstvo*, 16 December 1938. On the death of Chkalov.

170 ENTHUSIASM IS THE BASIS OF CREATIVE WORK, in a collection, *Young Masters of Art* (1938), pp. 56–57. Reprinted in *Izbranniye stat'i*.

171 ALEXANDER NEVSKY (1938), pp. 76. The scenario (third and final version) by E. and Pyotr Pavlenko; reprinted in *Historical Scenarios* (1946), in *Selected Scenarios of Soviet Cinema* (1950), vol. IV; (1951), vol. III; in Pavlenko, *Film Scenarios* (1952); in Pavlenko, *Plays and Film Scenarios* (1954).

1939

172 MONTAGE IN 1938 in *Iskusstvo kino*, 1939, No. 1, pp. 37–49. Reprinted in Lev Kuleshov's *Fundamentals of Film Direction* (1941), and in *Izbranniye stat'i*. Translation in *Life and Letters To-day*, June–November 1939; and as Chap. I ("Word and Image") of *The Film Sense*; and in *Notes of a Film Director*.

173 BOOM YEAR FOR SOVIET CINEMA, in *Rabochii krai*, Ivanovo, 1 January 1939.

174 CORRECT PRINCIPLE, in *Kino*, 5 January 1939.

175 TO THE GLORY OF THE COUNTRY, in *Sovietskoye iskusstvo*, 4 February 1939. On creative responsibilities.

176 WITH HONOUR WE RECEIVE THE HIGH AWARD, in *Za bolshevistskii film*, 8 February 1939. On the Order of Lenin awarded to Mosfilm.

177 WE SERVE THE PEOPLE, in *Izvestia*, 11 February 1939. On the recent awards to film-makers. Reprinted in *Izbranniye stat'i*.

178 BEFORE MAKING A FILM ON FRUNZE, in *Kino*, 23 February 1939. On the planned film, *Perekop*, and on meetings with Frunze at Proletcult.

179 PROUD JOY, in *Za bolshevistskii film*, 23 March 1939. On Mosfilm's honours.

180 LENIN IN OUR HEARTS, in *Izvestia*, 6 April 1939. On *Lenin in 1918*.

181 HELLO, CHARLIE!, in *Kino*, 17 April 1939. On Chaplin's

fiftieth birthday. Reprinted in *Izbranniye stat'i*. Translation in *Notes of a Film Director*, pp. 197–198.

182 SPEECH AT THE MEETING OF INTELLECTUALS FROM MOSCOW'S STUDIOS, in *Kino*, 23 April 1939. An edited stenographic report.

183 THE SOVIET SCREEN (1939), pp. 39. A pamphlet (in English) issued for the Soviet pavilion's exhibit at the New York World's Fair.

184 FOREWORD to *Soviet Films 1938–1939* (1939). E.'s foreword (in English) is dated April 1939.

185 GRANDEUR OF SOVIET AVIATION, in *Vechernaya Moskva*, 1 May 1939.

186 25 AND 15, in *Kino*, 23 May 1939. On the 25th anniversary of Tisse's film career, and on his 15 years of work with E. Reprinted in *Izbranniye stat'i*. Translation in *Notes of a Film Director*, pp. 145–149.

187 ON STRUCTURE, in *Iskusstvo kino*, 1939, No. 6, pp. 7–20. Previously published, in shortened version, in *Anthology on Film Direction* (1939), and reprinted in *Izbranniye stat'i*. Translation (as "The Structure of the Film") in *Film Form*, pp. 150–178; in shortened version in *Notes of a Film Director*, pp. 53–62.

188 FILM ABOUT THE FERGHANA CANAL, in *Pravda*, 13 August 1939, and in *Iskusstvo kino*, 1939, No. 9, pp. 6–7.

189 FERGHANA CANAL, in *Iskusstvo kino*, 1939, No. 9, pp. 8–20. A shooting-script based on a treatment by Pyotr Pavlenko and E. (dated August 1–2–3, 1939); reprinted in *Voprosi kinodramaturgii III* (1959). Translated excerpt in *The Film Sense*, pp. 256–268.

190 A REGION BECOMES UNRECOGNIZABLE, in *Pravda*, 2 September 1939. On the builders' enthusiasm at the Ferghana Canal.

191 ALEXANDER NEVSKY, in the collection, *The Soviet Historical Film* (1939), pp. 14–25. Reprinted (as enlarged by E.) in *Izbranniye stat'i*. Translation in *Notes of a Film Director*, pp. 32–43.

1940

192 PRIDE, in *Iskusstvo kino*, 1940, No. 1–2, pp. 17–25. Translation in *International Literature*, April–May

1940, in the *Anglo–Soviet Journal*, April 1941, and in *Film Form* (as "Achievement"), pp. 179–194.

193 BIRTH OF A MASTER, in *Iskusstvo kino*, 1940, No. 1–2, pp. 94–95. On E.'s introduction to Dovzhenko and his work. Reprinted (as expanded by E. in 1946) in *Izbranniye stat'i*. Translation in *Notes of a Film Director*, pp. 140–145.

194 RAGING ARTISTS, in *Sovietskoye foto*, 1940, No. 1.

195 THE MOTHERLAND EMBRACES ITS WORTHY SONS, in *Literaturnaya gazeta*, 30 January 1940. Greetings to the returned ice-breaker *Sedov*.

196 THE SOVIET HISTORICAL FILM, in *Pravda*, 8 February 1940. Reprinted in *Izbranniye stat'i*; expanded as "The Problem of the Soviet Historical Film", and published in *Theses of the Addresses* ... (1940), pp. 3–15. The full text of E.'s speech (delivered 8 January 1940) published in *Iz istorii kino*, No. 4 (1961), pp. 7–27.

197 TWENTY, in the collection, *20 Years of Soviet Cinematography* (1940), pp. 18–31. Reprinted in *Izbranniye stat'i*.

198 WE ARE TWENTY YEARS OLD, foreword (dated 15 February 1940) to the anniversary album, *Soviet Film Art 1919–1939* (1940), pp. 5–7. Reprinted in *Izbranniye stat'i*.

199 NOT COLOURED, BUT OF COLOUR, in *Kino*, 29 May 1940. Reprinted in *Izbranniye stat'i*. Translation in *Notes of a Film Director*, pp. 114–119.

200 AGAIN ON STRUCTURE, in *Iskusstvo kino*, 1940, No. 6, pp. 27–32. Translation in *Film Essays*, pp. 92–108.

201 VERTICAL MONTAGE (First Essay), in *Iskusstvo kino*, 1940, No. 9, pp. 16–25. Translation as Chap. II ("Synchronization of Senses") of *The Film Sense*.

202 THE EMBODIMENT OF A MYTH, in *Teatr*, 1940, No. 10, pp. 13–38. The principles of E.'s staging of *Die Walküre* at the Bolshoi Theatre. Condensed translation in *Film Essays*, pp. 184–191.

203 THE EMBODIMENT OF A MYTH, in the brochure, *Walküre* (1940). Another treatment of the same subject.

204 CREATIVE ENCOUNTER WITH WAGNER, in *Ogonyok*, 1940,

No. 29, pp. 18. Translation in *Sunday Worker* (New York), 20 April 1940.

205 GREAT HAPPINESS, in *Trudovaya gazeta*, Riga, 24 August 1940.

206 BEFORE THE PREMIER OF WALKURE, in *Vechernaya Moskva*, 21 September 1940.

207 GREETINGS TO ARMENIA ON THE VICTORY OF SOCIALISM!, in *Kommunist*, Yerevan, 26 November 1940.

208 WHAT THE STUDIOS ARE WORKING ON, in *Izvestia*, 27 November 1940. A reply to a questionnaire; E. answers for Mosfilm.

209 FOREWORD to Lev Kuleshov's *Fundamentals of Film Direction* (1941), first published in *Sovietskii ekran*, 1940, No. 23, p. 12.

210 VERTICAL MONTAGE (Second Essay), in *Iskusstvo kino*, 1940, No. 12, pp. 27–35. Translation as Chap. III ("Colour and Meaning") of *The Film Sense*.

211 Letter to the Editors of *International Literature*, November–December 1940. On *The Birth of a Nation*. Russian text published in Russian edition, No. 5, 1941.

1941

212 VERTICAL MONTAGE (Third Essay), in *Iskusstvo kino*, 1941, No. 1, pp. 29–38. Translation as Chap. IV ("Form and Content: Practice") of *The Film Sense*.

213 FOR FRUITFUL WORK, in *Za bolshevistskii film*, 1 January 1941.

214 OUR CREATIVE TASKS, in *Za bolshevistskii film*, 12 February 1941.

215 ON THE "SECRETS" OF FILM TECHNIQUE, in *Illustrirovannaya gazeta*, 2 March 1941.

216 MEMORABLE DAYS, in *Izvestia*, 18 March 1941.

217 FORWARD!, in *Za bolshevistiskii film*, 21 March 1941. Announcement of the film about Ivan Grozny.

218 JUSTIFICATION FOR CONFIDENCE, in *Kino*, 21 March 1941.

219 FILM ABOUT IVAN GROZNY, in *Izvestia*, 30 April 1941. On the historical role of Ivan IV.

220 HEIRS AND BUILDERS OF WORLD CULTURE, in *Pravda*,

30 April 1941. On the responsibilities of Soviet film-makers.

221 THREE DIRECTORS. 1. A man and his film [Mikhail Romm]; 2. An original master [Friedrich Ermler]; 3. Artist-bolshevik [Alexander Dovzhenko]; in *Iskusstvo kino*, 1941, No. 5, pp. 32–37.

222 IVAN GROZNY, in *Vechernaya Moskva*, June 1941. A news item including portions of E.'s speech at a party-production conference at Mosfilm.

223 LET US MAKE EVEN STRONGER THE MILITARY MIGHT OF OUR COUNTRY, in *Za bolshevistskii film*, 3 June 1941. On the State Loan for the third five-year plan.

224 COMMENTS ON YOUNG CINEMATOGRAPHERS, in *Pravda*, 16 June 1941. Reprinted in *Izbranniye stat'i*.

225 "THE DICTATOR", CHARLIE CHAPLIN'S FILM, in *Kino*, 27 June 1941. Reproduced, in different variants, in several newspapers during June and July 1941; reprinted in *Izbranniye stat'i*. Translation in *Notes of a Film Director*, pp. 199–202.

226 A JUST MATTER, in *Kino*, 27 June 1941.

227 ORGANISATION AND DISCIPLINE, in *Za bolshevistskii film*, 1 July 1941. Mosfilm's adaptation to war-time conditions.

228 FASCIST BEASTLINESS ON THE SCREEN, in *Krasnyi voin*, 11 July 1941.

229 DESTROY, SMASH THE VILE INVADERS, in *Krasnyi flot*, 18 July 1941.

230 HITLER SQUEEZED IN THE PINCERS, in *Kino*, 18 July 1941. On the agreement between the USSR and England to unite their efforts against Germany.

231 CINEMA AGAINST FASCISM, in *Pravda*, 8 October 1941. On foreign anti-fascist films.

232 FASCISM MUST AND SHALL BE DESTROYED, in the collection (in English), *In Defence of Civilization Against Fascist Barbarism* (1941).

233 Speech, in brochure, *To Brother Jews of All the World* (1941), pp. 25–26. Transcription of a filmed speech.

1942

234 FOREWORD to *The Film Sense* (New York 1942). Translation reprinted in *Soviet Russia Today*, August 1942.

235 TEN YEARS AGO, in *Literatura i iskusstvo*, 1 May 1942. Memories of the last pre-Hitler May Day in Berlin.

236 IVAN GROZNY, in *Literatura i iskusstvo*, 4 July 1942. Translation in *VOKS Bulletin*, 1942, No. 7–8.

237 FRIENDS OVER THE OCEAN, in *Literatura i iskusstvo*, 15 August 1942. In preparation for a conference on American and British cinema.

238 AMERICAN FILMS REFLECT FIGHTING QUALITIES OF AMERICAN PEOPLE, in *Information Bulletin*, Embassy of the USSR (Washington), 1942 (Special Supplement). Partial text of a speech delivered at the Conference on American and British Cinema, Moscow, 21–22 August 1942.

239 "AN AMERICAN TRAGEDY", Reel 10, and "SUTTER'S GOLD", Reel 4, in *The Film Sense* (New York 1942), pp. 236–250. Excerpts from two scripts, written in Hollywood, 1930, by E., Alexandrov and Ivor Montagu.

240 ROUGH OUTLINE OF THE MEXICAN PICTURE, as drafted for Upton Sinclair, in *The Film Sense* (New York 1942), pp. 251–254.

1944

241 DICKENS, GRIFFITH AND WE, in the collection, *Amerikanskaya kinematografiya: D. U. Griffit* (1944), pp. 39–88. Reprinted (as revised by E. in 1946 for his proposed *Three Masters*) in *Izbranniye stat'i*. Translated in *Film Form*, pp. 195–255.

242 THE PERFORMANCE STIRS AND TOUCHES, in *Kazakhstanskaya pravda*, Alma-Ata, 6 August 1944. On an Alma-Ata production of Puccini's *Madama Butterfly*.

243 IVAN GROZNY (1944), pp. 189. The script, in treatment form. Translation in *Life and Letters*, November, December 1945; January–July 1946; a variant translation published 1963, New York and London.

1945

244 OUR WORK ON THE FILM, in *Izvestia*, 4 February 1945. On *Ivan Grozny*, Part I. Translation in *Film Chronicle*, February 1945.

245 IN A REGISSEUR'S LABORATORY, in *Film Chronicle*, February 1945. Revised translation in *Film Form*, pp.

261–265. Russian text published in *Iskusstvo kino*, No. 2, 1957.

246 THE GREATEST OF STATESMEN, in *Ogonyok*, 1945, No. 9–10, p. 14. On the image of Ivan IV in *Ivan Grozny*, Part I.

247 THE LIBERATION OF FRANCE, in *Sovietskoye iskusstvo*, 19 April 1945. On the new film compilation by Yutkevich. Reprinted in *Izbranniye stat'i*. Translated excerpt in *Films Beget Films* (London 1964), p. 70.

248 REBIRTH, in *Literaturnaya gazeta*, 23 June 1945. On Leningrad's reconstruction. Reprinted in *Izbranniye stat'i*.

249 IN CLOSE UP, in *Iskusstvo kino*, 1945, No. 1, pp. 6–8. Translation in *Film Essays*, pp. 150–154.

250 CHARLIE THE KID, in the collection, *Charles Spencer Chaplin* (1945), pp. 137–158. Reprinted (as expanded by E. in 1946 for his proposed *Three Masters*) in *Izbranniye stat'i*. Translation in *Sight and Sound*, Spring, Summer 1946; reprinted in *Film Essays*, pp. 108–139; another translation in *Notes of a Film Director*, pp. 167–197.

1946

251 PRKFV, an introduction to *Sergei Prokofiev: His Musical Life*, by Israel Nestyev (New York 1946); an expanded Russian text is published in *Izbranniye stat'i*. Translation (of the expanded version) in *Notes of a Film Director*, pp. 149–167.

252 ABOUT THE FILM "IVAN GROZNY", in *Kultura i zhizn*, 20 October 1946. An analysis of the mistakes in *Ivan Grozny*, Part II. Translation in Seton, *Eisenstein*, pp. 460–463.

253 HOW I BECAME A DIRECTOR, in the collection, *Kak ya stal rezhisserom* (1946), pp. 276–292. His experiences as a theatre-goer that led to his work in theatre and film. Reprinted in *Izbranniye stat'i*. Translation in *Notes of a Film Director*, pp. 9–18.

1947

254 PURVEYORS OF SPIRITUAL POISON, in *Kultura i zhizn*, 31 July 1947. Translation in *Sight and Sound*, Autumn 1947.

255 TO THE SOVIET MILITIAMAN, in *Na boyevom postu*, 12 November 1947.

1948

256 ABOUT STEREOSCOPIC CINEMA, in *Iskusstvo kino*, 1948, No. 2, pp. 5–7. Reprinted in *Izbranniye stat'i*. Translation in *Penguin Film Review*, No. 8 (London 1949) and in *Notes of a Film Director*, pp. 129–137.

On 11 February 1948 Sergei Mikhailovich Eisenstein died at the age of 50.

257 SPECTATOR-CREATOR, in *Ogonyok*, 1948, No. 26 [from a manuscript dated 7 November 1947]. Reprinted in *Izbranniye stat'i*.

1949

258 THIRTY YEARS OF SOVIET CINEMA AND THE TRADITION OF RUSSIAN CULTURE, in *Iskusstvo kino*, 1949, No. 5, pp. 7–11 [written in 1947 for the 30th anniversary of the October Revolution]. Translation in *The Anglo-Soviet Journal*, Summer 1950; reprinted (slightly abridged) in *Masses and Mainstream*, November 1950, as "The Soviet Cinema".

1950

259 BIRTH OF A FILM, in *Iskusstvo kino*, 1950, No. 4, pp. 13–16 [written in 1945 for an unpublished collection of essays on *Potemkin*]; reprinted in *Izbranniye stat'i*. Translation (as "The Twelve Apostles") in *VOKS Bulletin*, 1950, No. 63; in *The Cinema 1952* (London 1952), pp. 158–173; other translations in *The Hudson Review* (New York), Summer 1951; and in *Notes of a Film Director*, pp. 18–31.

260 IVAN GROZNY, in the collection, *Selected Scenarios of Soviet Cinema* (1950), vol. IV, pp. 483–524. Part One,

as filmed; reprinted in *Selected Scenarios* ... (1951), vol. IV.

1951

261 SIQUEIROS, a speech delivered at a 1931 exhibition of the paintings of David Siqueiros, in *Siqueiros* . . . (Mexico 1951).

1952

262 EVER FORWARD!, in *Iskusstvo kino*, 1952, No. 1, pp. 107–109. Written in 1947 as an "afterword" to a proposed collection of E.'s essays. Reprinted in *Izbranniye stat'i*. Translation in *Notes of a Film Director*, pp. 203–208.

263 AFTERWORD to the Libretto of *Que Viva Mexico!* [written in 1947], translated in Seton, *Eisenstein*, pp. 504–512. Russian text published in *Iskusstvo kino*, 1957, No. 5, pp. 113–117.

264 [Letters to various correspondents], published in Seton, *Sergei M. Eisenstein* (London 1952).

265 UNITED (IDEAS ON THE HISTORY OF SOVIET CINEMA), in *Iskusstvo kino*, 1952, No. 11, pp. 10–14. Written in November 1947, for the 30th anniversary of the October Revolution. Reprinted in *Izbranniye stat'i*.

1954

266 PROBLEMS OF COMPOSITION, in the collection, *Voprosi kinodramaturgii* I (1954), pp. 116–140. Stenographic record of a lecture given to the direction class at VGIK, 25 December 1946. Reprinted in *Izbranniye stat'i*, in *On Film Scenarios* (1956), and in Nizhny's *Lessons with Eisenstein*. Translation in *Film Essays*, pp. 155–183.

1955

267 [Three manuscripts relating to a book planned by E.: *Pushkin and Cinema*], in *Iskusstvo kino*, 1955, No. 4, pp. 75–96: (1) Foreword, dated Kokand, 13 October 1939; (2) Examples for the Study of Montage Style (a lecture given at VGIK, 13 October 1937); (3) Pushkin, Montageur (a chapter from the unfinished book). Translation of the Foreword (as "Lessons from Litera-

ture") in *Film Essays*, pp. 77–84, this translation previously published in *The Anglo-Soviet Journal* (London), Summer 1963.

1956

268 MONTAGE LISTS OF THE FILM, "BATTLESHIP POTEMKIN", in the collection, *Voprosi kino iskusstva* (1956), pp. 213–231, with facsimiles; prepared for publication by G. Chakhiryan.
[Previously unpublished manuscripts], in *Izbranniye stat'i* (1956), edited by R. Yurenev.

269 FOREWORD to a proposed collection of E.'s essays, dated Moscow-Kratovo, August 1946. Translations in *Film Form and The Film Sense* (combined Meridian edition, 1957), pp. ix–xi, and in *Notes of a Film Director*, pp. 5–8.

270 PEOPLE ON A FILM, fragment of a proposed book (in 1947) about the people who worked on *Ivan Grozny*; this fragment is about Lydia Lomova, dresser, and Goryunov, make-up man.

271 BOLSHEVIKS LAUGH (Thoughts about Soviet Comedy), written in 1937, for a proposed extensive work on comedy. Translation in *Notes of a Film Director*, pp. 106–112.

272 WOLVES AND SHEEP (Director and Actor), written in 1935, in reply to criticism that some directors crush the actor's will. Translation in *Notes of a Film Director*, pp. 112–114.

273 COLOUR FILM, the last unfinished essay by E., written in the form of an open letter to Lev Kuleshov, for use in a proposed second edition of Kuleshov's *Fundamentals of Film Direction*. Translation in *Notes of a Film Director*, pp. 119–128.

274 TRUE WAYS OF INVENTION, on sources of Alexander Nevsky, written 14 October 1946. Translation in *Notes of a Film Director*, p. 43–52.

1957

275 HOW I LEARNED TO DRAW, in *Kultura i zhizn*, 1957, No. 6. Fragment of E.'s memoirs. Translation in English

edition (*Culture and Life*), reprinted in S. Eisenstein, *Drawings* (1961), pp. 15–19.

276 ["OCTOBER"], in *Iskusstvo kino*, 1957, No. 10, pp. 104–129. Outlines for the script (dated 26 February 1927) and shooting-script for unrealized reels (dated 12 October 1927), introduced by co-author, G. Alexandrov.

276a LECTURES ON DIRECTION, edited by Vladimir Nizhny from stenographic notes, VGIK, 1957. Revised and enlarged in 1958, as *Lessons with Eisenstein*. English translation, London 1962.

1958

277 NOTES ON V. V. MAYAKOVSKY, in *Iskusstvo kino*, 1958, No. 1, pp. 73–75. Manuscript dated 5 April 1940. Translation in *The Anglo-Soviet Journal*, London, Summer 1958.

278 [Notes and drawings for unrealized films, including *Ferghana Canal* and *A Poet's Love* (*Pushkin*)], in I. Weisfeld, "Birth of an Idea", *Iskusstvo kino*, 1958, No. 1, pp. 86–94.

279 AUTOBIOGRAPHICAL NOTES, in *Kultura i zhizn*, 1958, No. 5, pp. 40–43. Written in 1939 for the 20th anniversary of Soviet cinema. Translation in English edition (*Culture and Life*).

280 [Shooting-script] (dated 17 December 1930) for the Epilogue of *Que Viva Mexico!*, and letter to Salka Viertel, 27 January 1932], in *Sight and Sound*, Autumn 1958, pp. 305–307. (E.'s original German text of the letter printed in *Sergei Eisenstein, Künstler der Revolution*, Berlin 1960, pp. 196–201.)

1959

281 [Scene from Pushkin's *Boris Godunov*, for the planned film on Pushkin], in *Iskusstvo kino*, 1959, No. 3, pp. 111–130. E.'s drawings and notes for a shooting-script, reproduced in facsimile* introduced by L. Pogozheva.

* Omitted from the facsimile is the original heading in English (complete with pun), dated 4 March 1940:

> If Godounoff
> and if not—a good
> exercise for the use of
> colour, word and sound.

282 MY DRAWINGS, in the collection, *Mosfilm: Articles*, etc, No. 1 (1959), pp. 207–212. On the sketches for *Ivan Grozny*, dated Alma-Ata, October 1943. Reprinted (as "A Few Words about My Drawings") in S. Eisenstein, *Drawings* (1961). Translation in S. Eisenstein, *Drawings* (1961), pp. 194–196.

1960

283 MISTER LINCOLN BY MISTER FORD, in *Iskusstvo kino*, 1960, No. 4, pp. 135–140. An essay (dated 1945) on John Ford and *Young Mr Lincoln*, written for a proposed volume on John Ford, in the series, "Materials on world cinema history" (volumes published on Griffith and Chaplin). Translation in *Film Essays*, pp. 139–149.

284 COLOUR—CLEAN, SHARP, RESONANT, in *Literaturnaya gazeta*, 9 July 1960. Translated (as "One Path to Colour") in *Sight and Sound*, Spring 1961.

285 PAGES OF A LIFE, in *Znamya*, 1960, No. 10 (pp. 147–176), No. 11 (pp. 146–190). Extracts from E.'s memoirs, written in 1946. Translated selections in *Soviet Literature*, 1961, No. 2, 3; two sections ("People, Events, Life . . ." and "Intellectual Cinema") revised and reprinted in *Atlas* (New York), May 1961.

286 BATTLESHIP "POTEMKIN", in *Sovietskii ekran*, 1960, No. 21, pp. 18–19. An extract from E.'s memoirs.

1961

287 QUESTIONS OF THE HISTORICAL FILM, in the collection, *Iz istorii kino*, No. 4 (1961), pp. 7–27. Stenographic record of a speech delivered 8 January 1940.

288 TO LIVE THUS WOULD BE UNTHINKABLE, in *With Their Own Weapons* (1961), pp. 279–286.

289 FROM THE CORRESPONDENCE OF S. PROKOFIEV AND S. EISENSTEIN, in *Sovietskaya muzika*, 1961, No. 4, pp. 105–113. Letters, 1939–1946.

290 ABOUT ART AND MYSELF, in *Nedelya*, 29 April 1961. Extract (subtitled "Inexhaustible topic") from E.'s memoirs. Translation in *Soviet Weekly*, London, 31 August 1961.

291 "POTEMKIN" IN AMERICA, in *Soviet Weekly,* 7 September 1961. From E.'s memoirs.

292 COLOUR AND MUSIC, The Colour Genealogy of "Moscow 800", in the collection, *Mosfilm: Articles,* etc. (1961), pp. 239–245. Printed from a manuscript dated 30 September and 29 November 1946, incorporating notes for portions of E.'s memoirs, especially for the section translated as "One Path to Colour".

293 [*A Poet's Love*], in Ilya Weisfeld, *The Craft of Film-Writing* (1961), pp. 214–224. A treatment for this colour-film project on Pushkin's life.

1962

294 AUTOBIOGRAPHICAL NOTES, in *Iskusstvo kino,* 1962, No. 1, pp. 127–146. Further autobiographical fragments; prepared for publication by Yuri Krasovsky.

295 [Documents on the preparation of "Ivan Grozny"], in *Voprosi kino-dramaturgii* IV (1962), pp. 343–390. Notebook entries dated from 21 September 1941 to 8 May 1943; prepared for publication by Naum Kleiman.

296 NATURE IS NOT INDIFFERENT, in *Iskusstvo kino,* 1962, No. 11, pp. 99–122. Fragments of a theoretical essay written in 1945; prepared for publication by Leonid Kozlov.

The above list, prepared in 1963, does not refer to reprints and new variants that have appeared in the following numbers.

1964

297 Volume I of *Selected Works in Six Volumes* (1964), pp. 691, compiled by Pera Atasheva, Yuri Krasovsky and V. Mikhailov. This volume contains all previously published fragments of E.'s memoirs, plus unpublished fragments, and essays relating to autobiography and his own films (both realized and unfinished).

298 WHAT LENIN GAVE ME, in *Iskusstvo kino,* 1964, No. 4, pp. 2–7. A 1932 manuscript (an unpublished response to a questionnaire from *Kino*), prepared for publication by Naum Kleiman.

299 Volume II of *Selected Works* (1964), pp. 564, compiled by Pera Atasheva, Naum Kleiman, Yuri Krasovsky and V. Mikhailov. This volume contains theoretical essays, including the first publication of the unfinished book, *Montage* [1937].

300 Volume III of *Selected Works* (1964), pp. 669, compiled by Pera Atasheva, Naum Kleiman and Leonid Kozlov. This volume reprints manuscripts recently published (see 296) and new documents on colour.

301 [Letters to Léon Moussinac], in Moussinac, *Serge Eisenstein* (Paris 1964).

1965

302 PEACE AND THE ATOM BOMB, in *Iskusstvo kino*, 1965, No. 12. Written in autumn 1945.

1966

303 Volume IV of *Selected Works* (1966), pp. 789, compiled by Pera Atasheva and Naum Kleiman. Contains the unfinished draft of *Direction, Art of Mise-en-scène*.

COLLECTIONS OF EISENSTEIN'S WRITINGS IN ENGLISH

The Film Sense (1942)
  contains Nos. 234, 172, 201, 210, 212, 2, 239, 240, 189.

Film Form (1949)
  contains Nos. 116, 42, 51, 75, 62, 71, 83, 108, 125, 187,
    192, 241, 40, 245.
[When these two collections were combined in a paperback
edition by Meridian Books in 1957, No. 269 was translated
as an introduction.]

Notes of a Film Director (1958)
  contains Nos. 269, 253, 259, 191, 108, 172, 83, 271, 270,
    199, 273, 148, 193, 186, 250, 181, 225, 262.

Film Essays (1968)
  contains Nos. 14, 8, 68, 52, 61, 74, 119, 267, 202, 200,
    250, 283, 249, 266.
[Grigori Kozintsev's introduction was written for his Eisenstein chapter in *The Deep Screen*.]

An English edition of the new materials published in
Eisenstein's *Selected Works* (1964–1966) is in preparation.

Index

217